Strategic Management in Information Technology

Strategic Management in Information Technology

David B. Yoffie

Harvard Business School

Prentice Hall, Englewood Cliffs, New Jersey 07632

Library of Congress Cataloging-in-Publication Data

YOFFIE, DAVID B.
    Strategic management in information technology / DAVID B. YOFFIE.
        p.   cm.
    Includes bibliographical references
    ISBN 0-13-098559-7
    1. Computer industry—Management.   I. Title.
HD9696.C62Y63   1994
338.4'7004—dc20   93-5827

Acquisitions editor *P.J. Boardman / David Shea*
Editorial/production supervision *Edie Riker*
Cover design Tommy Boy
Production coordinator *Patrice Fraccio*

 © 1994 by Prentice-Hall, Inc.
A Paramount Communications Company
Englewood Cliffs, NJ 07632

Printed in the United States of America

10   9   8   7   6   5   4   3   2   1

ISBN 0-13-098559-7

Prentice-Hall International (UK) Limited, *London*
Prentice-Hall of Australia Pty. Limited, *Sydney*
Prentice-Hall Canada Inc., *Toronto*
Prentice-Hall Hispanoamericana, S.A., *Mexico*
Prentice-Hall of India Private Limited, *New Delhi*
Prentice-Hall of Japan, Inc., *Tokyo*
Simon & Schuster Asia Pte. Ltd., *Singapore*
Editora Prentice-Hall do Brasil, Ltda., *Rio de Janeiro*

For my daughter, **Ariel**

who will live with the future
of INFORMATION TECHNOLOGY

Contents

Acknowledgments

An entire casebook dedicated to the information technology industry might seem odd; after all, how many casebooks are focused on the automobile or steel industries? Yet information technology seems so pervasive and so important in the 1990s and beyond that many companies and schools have found studying information technology central to management education.

I have to thank my colleague, Richard Vietor, for first proposing the idea for this casebook. Over the last five years I have written several loosely related cases on information technology companies that were sold separately or included in others' textbooks. It was Richard who suggested that the timely nature of these cases should have a strong market if they were packaged together. I also need to thank Robert Burgleman of Stanford University and Andy Grove, the CEO of Intel Corporation. In 1992, Burgleman and Grove offered a course at Stanford Business School on information technology that utilized virtually all of the cases in this collection.

Numerous colleagues also contributed cases to this book. While the core of the volume revolves around the series of cases I prepared on Intel, Apple,

IBM, and Microsoft, the book would have been impossible without the willingness of several Harvard and Stanford professors to allow me to include their case materials. Specifically, I want to express my gratitude to Carlise Baldwin, Robert Burgleman, Benjamin Gomes-Casseres, David Collis, Anirudh Dhebar, Ken Froot, Bob Hayes, Marco Iansiti, Phil Rozensweig, Elizabeth Teisberg, and Steve Wheelright.

I would also like to acknowledge that Harvard Business School Division of Research and Dean John McArthur, who funded virtually all of the cases. In addition, none of the writing would have been possible without the cooperation of senior management in virtually every major firm in the information technology industry. While it is impossible for me to estimate precisely, I would guess that more than 300 managers from at least 25 firms were interviewed over the last five years in the process of preparing these cases. Finally, I want to thank my wife, Terry, who put up with my Saturdays and Sundays and seemingly endless travels to put the book together, and my secretary, Cathyjean, who is absolutely necessary for quality control and making things happen.

DAVID B. YOFFIE
The Max and Doris Starr Professor of International Business Administration
Harvard Business School

Professor David B. Yoffie is the Max and Doris Starr Professor of International Business Administration. A member of the faculty of the Harvard Business School since 1981, Professor Yoffie received his Bachelor's degree summa cum laude and Phi Beta Kappa from Brandeis University and his Masters and Ph.D. degrees from Stanford University, where he was a lecturer for two years. Professor Yoffie is currently head of the required MBA course on Competition and Strategy, and faculty chair for the executive program, Managing Global Opportunities.

Professor Yoffie's research and consulting have focused on competitive strategy and international competition. From 1988 through 1992, he directed the Harvard Business School research project on global competition. In collaboration with twelve colleagues form American and European universities, the project studied how multinational firms and government policies influence the pattern of international trade and the competitive structure of global industries. Outside of the Harvard Business School, Professor Yoffie's activities include being a Director of Intel Corporation, serving on the Executive Committee for Harvard's Center for International Affairs and the Board of Overseers of Brandeis' Lemberg Program in International Economics and Finance, and consulting with several Fortune 500 industrial firms as well as large service (health care, hotel and consulting) companies. When appointed to Intel's board in 1989, he was the youngest outside director of America's largest 150 industrial corporations; he is currently the youngest chaired professor at the Harvard Business School.

Professor Yoffie's writings on international business and competitive strategy have been widely published. Professor Yoffie is the author or editor of five books, including most recently, ***Beyond Free Trade: Firms, Governments and Global Competition*** (Harvard Business School Press, 1993). In addition, Professor Yoffie has written several pieces for *The New York Times* and *The Wall Street Journal* and numerous scholarly and managerial articles on international trade, firm strategy, and global competition in high technology industries. Professor Yoffie has also published more than 50 case studies on business strategy and international management issues, that have sold more than a half million copies.

Strategic Management in Information Technology

Introduction

1992 was a nightmare for firms competing in the information processing industry. Until the mid-1980s, competitors in this quintessential high-growth business had been accustomed to high profits, booming revenues, and the stabilizing influence of IBM's leadership. While the industry had been changing for some time, prices and profits collapsed in 1992. The huge losses suffered by some of the biggest, most powerful competitors, like IBM and DEC, coupled with the impressive earnings registered by such newcomers to the industry, like Microsoft and Intel, signaled a sea change in competitive dynamics. For the first time in 30 years since IBM introduced its famous System/360, it was becoming apparent that new leaders would emerge to control the destiny of a trillion dollar business.

This casebook is designed to explore the strategy and management issues at the heart of this transition. The importance of this transition reaches far beyond the participants in the industry. Virtually all firms have a stake in the evolution of the industry as customers of information technology (IT). In addition, the successes and failures of players in IT give us clues about strategy and management in the twenty-first century. The competitive struggle of IT businesses is undoubtedly more intense than most. Nonetheless, exploring competition and management in IT gives us a way to look at common problems faced by managers around the globe. The most obvious issues found in this casebook, including intense price competition, declining opportunities for differentiation, shorter product life cycles, achieving superior quality, focusing an organization on new, emerging growth businesses, motivating and empowering employees, are common themes in the study of management. And while managers in relatively mature industries often have more time to tackle these problems, examining competition in information technology gives managers a window for exploring their own future.

Organization of the Book

The book is divided into three sections: industry dynamics, competitive and functional strategies, and general management. This introduction will describe the major themes which cut across the various sections. The reader should remember that while it is convenient to divide the book into distinct pieces, the reality of strategic management in information technology is that all three areas quickly become blurred. Strategies cannot be made in the absence of a deep understanding of the industry segments and technologies, and an assessment of management practices is difficult or impossible without a clear view of a firm's strategy.

The first section of the book provides the essential background required to discuss the economics and technology of IT industries. The industry notes explore the dynamics of semiconductors, personal computers, workstations, minicomputers, mainframes, [networking] software, and telecommunications equipment. Set at different points in time since 1987, the notes provide an in-depth understanding of how technology, buying behavior, competitive profiles, channels, and so forth have changed and the implications of those changes for industry-wide profitability.

The second section of the book focuses on the strategic dilemmas of the central players in information technology. This section has five parts: competitive strategy, government and globalization, finance strategies, marketing strategies, and manufacturing strategies. The cases on competitive strategy—Intel, Microsoft, Apple, MIPS, and McCaw—revolve around the problems of setting standards and vertical and horizontal integration. The most important questions include: What is the appropriate scope of the firm in industries undergoing rapid changes in technology? What determines the appropriate strategy for forward integrating downstream into your customers' businesses? What activities should be done in-house versus subcontracted to alliance partners? And how far into related businesses and technologies do the core skills and capabilities of firms like Microsoft and Apple reach? The cases on globalization and government—Motorola and Japan and the Semiconductor Industry Association and the Trade Dispute with Japan—look at the issue of how to manage cross-border competition and the inevitable role in electronics played by governments around the world. Finally, the finance, marketing, and manufacturing strategy cases on Intel, Sun, and Sony offer opportunities to delve more deeply into functional policies on how to finance explosive growth (Sun Microsystems), how to create an appropriate capital structure (Intel 1992), how to manage the new marketing challenges associated with rapid obsolescence (Intel Overdrive), and how to manage product and technology development (Sony Corporation).

The last module in the book examines the problems of general management in information technology firms. There are striking contrasts in management style in firms like IBM, Apple, Microsoft, and Intel. The roles of the CEOs, the use of organizational structures, measurement schemes, and incentives vary dramatically. In addition, the cases on Acer and Sharp explore the problems of managing information technology businesses in different cultures: Acer's human resource systems and Sharp's mechanisms for coordination across business units offer important lessons for American and non-American managers.

Major Themes

Despite the variety of topics and scope of industries covered in this book, I have identified five major themes that cut across most or all of the cases. These themes are (1) global geographic scope; (2) blurring industry boundaries; (3) blurring firm boundaries; (4) lock-in and lock-out effects; and (5) mastering technology.

Geographic Scope

Perhaps the most obvious feature shared by all information technology industries is their *global geographic scope*. None of these industries are able to operate successfully within autarkic national boundaries. While the reasons vary somewhat across the businesses, all the industries share a relatively common set of customer requirements that behoove any competitor to expand beyond their own territory. Furthermore, in some industries like semiconductors and telecommunications, scale economies for re-search and development as well as manufacturing make it an absolute necessity to serve multiple geographic markets. All the firms in telecommunications equipment which remained at home in the 1980s went bankrupt or required large government subsidies and joint ventures to survive. No market in the world, not even the United States or Europe, is large enough to support the costs associated with developing a digital switch. The same has been true in semiconductors since their inception. With capital expenditures averaging close to 30 percent of sales and R&D at 15 percent most semiconductor manufacturers have always viewed the world as their market.

Blurring Boundaries

A second theme is that *technology has blurred the boundaries between the industries and across industry segments*. For decades analysts have

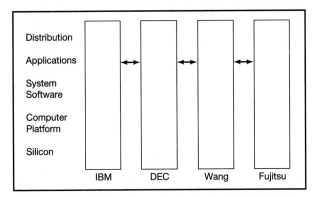

Figure 1 *The "Old" Computer Industry: Vertically Integrated Firms Competing Across All Segments. (Adapted from Intel documents and the Economist)*

discussed the merging of different information technology industries. NEC's entire strategy, for instance, was premised on "C&C," computers and communications. But the promise of merging technologies was only a promise until the 1990s.

Historically, firms and industries had clearly defined boundaries. Within the computer industry, vertically integrated firms like IBM, DEC, and Fujitsu used to dominate the competition. According to IBM estimates, one could identify only about 250 firms in the information processing industry in the 1960s, and most of them manufactured their own components and sold systems with all the necessary software. The CEO of Intel, Andy Grove, has called this structure the "old" computer industry, where competition was across all segments (see Figure 1).

In the 1990s, however, these vertically integrated firms are disintegrating, while independent vendors like Intel in semiconductors,

Microsoft in software, and Compaq, IBM, and Apple in personal computers are vying for market share within their horizontal segments (see Figure 2).

The blurring of industry boundaries goes well beyond personal computers. One way to look at the core industries in information technology is to view semiconductors as components, computers and central office switches as systems, and software as components or applications that make a system work. Yet the trend is that it is becoming harder and harder to distinguish between and among these segments. Within computers, as more and more functionality is put on standard CPUs and stand-alone machines are integrated into broad networks, the differences between PCs, workstations, minicomputers, and mainframes are collapsing. At the same time, very highly integrated semiconductors, like advanced microprocessors offered by Intel, Sun, MIPS, and Motorola, are difficult to distinguish from a fully integrated system. And no matter where you are located in the food chain in information technology, *everyone* is developing capabilities in software. Moreover, telecommunications and computers *are* merging in the 1990s. The hottest area of computing in the early 1990s has been networking, and the hottest area of telecommunications has been "value-added services," which generally means moving data and video across networks. As the cases on telecommunications equipment, networking software, Apple Computer, and McCaw (chapters 3, 4, 8, and 10) illustrate, the boundaries between industries are highly permeable at the edges in 1993 and will only get more intertwined by the end of the decade (see Figure 3).

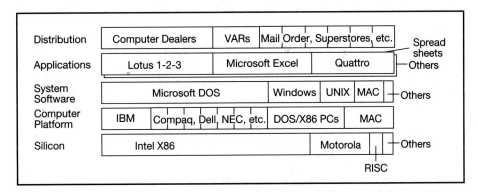

Figure 2 *The Personal Computer Industry: Fragmented, Horizontal Competition (Adapted from Intel documents and the Economist)*

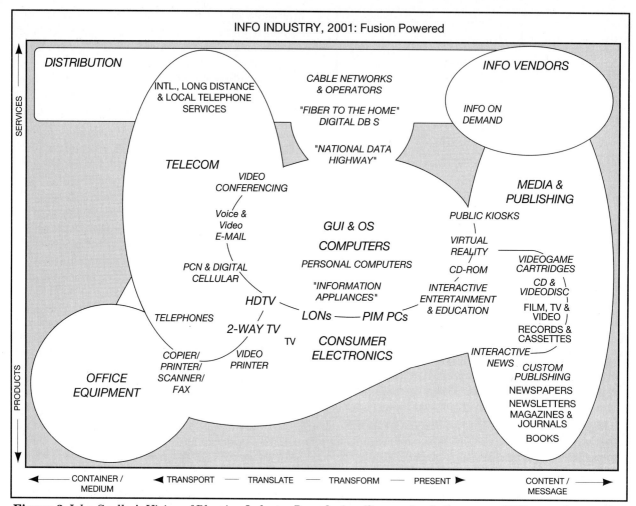

Figure 3 *John Sculley's Vision of Blurring Industry Boundaries. (Source: Apple Computer, 1992 case, chapter 8).*

Business, Industry, Government Alliances

The blurring of industry boundaries has been accompanied by a blurring of firm boundaries. *Alliances are everywhere.* As the note on The Global Computer Industry (chapter 2) illustrates, there has been an explosion of alliances, particularly across national borders (see Figure 4).

In semiconductors, computers, and networking equipment and software, a variety of new corporate forms have emerged. Perhaps the most extreme version can be found in the MIPS case (chapter 9), where MIPS relied almost exclusively on alliance partners to perform the most critical functions of the corporation except for circuit design. But alliances are pervasive in all parts of the industry with a wide range of possi-

ble partners. In this book, one can see alliances between business and government (e.g., the governments of Japan, Korea, and Europe worked closely with all of these industries, and in the United States, government intervention increased markedly in semiconductors); among entire industries [e.g., the Semiconductor Industry Association worked to build SEMATECH and generate sanctions against Japan (chapter 12)]; and among firms (e.g., Apple with IBM, IBM and Toshiba, McCaw with AT&T, Sharp with Intel.).

The motivation underlying these alliances ranged widely. But the most successful alliances seem to fall into a few categories: alliances with government; alliances on "pre-competitive" technologies within an industry; and risk-sharing alliances among firms. Alliances with government, for instance, tended to be most useful when they

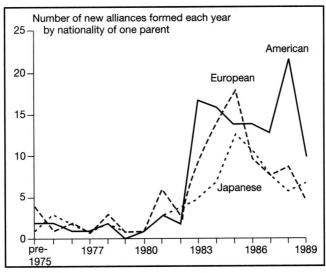

Figure 4 *International Alliances of Leading Computer Firms, 1975–1989. (Source: The Global Computer Industry note, chapter 2)*

offered firms an uneven playing field between their home base and their global competitors. In telecommunications equipment, for example, companies like Siemens, Alcatel, Northern Telecom, and the Japanese DenDen (NEC, Fujitsu, Hitachi, and Oki) benefited greatly from protected home markets which gave them sanctuaries at home (see chapter 3). By limiting stiff price competition in their largest markets, governments were effectively subsidizing their national champions, giving them more cash flow to support the enormous scale requirements in R&D. Similar benefits accrued to the alliances between Japanese and Korean semiconductor firms and their respective governments. However, protection or other forms of limited entry did not guarantee success. Since none of the national markets alone could support minimum efficient scale in these industries, only those firms which actively exploited the global market for their products thrived into the 1990s. European firms, such as Plessey in the U.K. which hid behind the walls of European protection, were never able to keep up with the dynamic technology challenges in information technology.

Industry-level alliances were most often successful when they focused on "pre-competitive" technologies. By pre-competitive, I mean before commercialization of products. Whenever industries tried to manipulate the market directly, as the U.S. industry did when it tried to control the prices of DRAMs in the late 1980s, inevitable distortions would creep in. On the other hand, firms could profit handsomely from collective efforts to build base manufacturing technology (e.g., SEMATECH), or create technical standards (e.g., CDMA versus TDMA in cellular communications in chapter 10, or DOS/Windows versus UNIX and System 7 in chapters 7 and 8). Once a standard was in place or new base technology was widely available, industry participants could compete on features that would benefit the customer. In the language of economists, whenever network externalities existed, industry-wide collaboration usually benefited firm and buyer alike.

At the firm level, alliances were most successful when they shared risk in situations with highly complementary assets. Novell and Sun Microsystems successfully leveraged their relationships with a variety of firms to build new standards and proliferate their products. But the cases in this book also suggest that widespread corporate alliances need careful consideration. Relatively few of the alliances were stable for more than a couple of years. AT&T's relationship with Sun Microsystems, IBM's relationships with many of its partners, and MIPS's relationship with Digital Equipment are but a few of the examples of strained alliances.

Lock-in and Lock-out

A fourth theme is that high technology industries suffer from or benefit from (depending on your point of view) *"lock-in"* and *"lock-out" effects*.[1] Lock-in effects means that once firms make a commitment down a particular path, it becomes increasingly difficult to change direction. For both suppliers of technology and consumers of products, information technology exhibits extraordinary switching costs. Once a firm started buying IBM's solution for mainframe computing in the 1960s, for example, it got locked-in for decades (see chapter 17). The reasons were fairly obvious: Information technology tends to have broad applications within a customer's business. As the IBM's customers began to build mission critical applications around the IBM mainframe, any effort to switch vendors or technologies would be costly. If a mistake was made, an entire business might come to a halt; even if no mistakes were made, it would cost millions of dollars to change.

While IBM is perhaps the most successful example in the history of lock-in effects, it is by no means the only one. Digital switches for telecommunications networks, for example, are very costly to replace once a particular vendor is chosen: Only seven switch manufacturers have almost 80 percent of the world's digital switch market, and in the absence of a major technological breakthrough, few observers believe that new players can enter switching equipment or gain significant share over the next decade. Customers—in this case, Bell operating companies and PTTs—are locked-in, implying that shifts in market share are only likely at the margin. The same scenario has emerged in personal computers. Microsoft's Disk Operating System (DOS) and Windows have set the standard for machines based on Intel's X86 microprocessor. Both Microsoft and Intel have locked-in the majority of computer users because, like corporate investments in IBM's mainframes, so much time, money, and energy have been spent on buying X86-based hardware and training corporate personnel on

DOS or Windows-based software, few customers are eager to switch. Lock-in effects are so critical because the general rule of thumb in information technology businesses is that customers require a 10:1 improvement in price/performance before they are likely to switch into new technologies.

From the firm's perspective, the possibility of lock-out is an equally important strategic problem. If a firm is not part of a standard, it can be excluded from participating in the growth and enormous profits available to the IBMs and Microsofts who lock-in their customers. In addition, many of the investments required for a firm to be successful in any given technology generation are highly specific. A decision not to invest in the current generation may be impossible to reverse in the next generation. For example, when most American firms decided to exit the dynamic RAM business in 1985, that decision was largely irreversible: Those firms were locked-out of the market for DRAMs for years. In chapter 6, Intel management estimated that it would have cost Intel $400 million and several years to reenter DRAMs; and even then, it would have little assurance of success. When Intel exited DRAMs in 1985, it laid off most of its design teams and scrapped or converted the manufacturing capacity dedicated to DRAMs. The job of reversing the earlier decision to participate in the DRAM market was made even harder with Japanese firms investing aggressively in successive generations *and* learning more and more about how to increase yields and reduce costs.

There are several critical implications of lock-in and lock-out effects. Perhaps most important is the role of *first mover advantages*. The first to establish a standard, the first to move down steep learning curves, the first to build economies of scale in segments where lock-in effects exist usually reap the lion's share of the profits. The history of information technology is littered with examples of second movers failing: Zylog and National Semiconductor in microprocessors, Digital Equipment and Wang in PCs, Apollo and Sony in UNIX-based workstations, to name a few. However, one should also note several caveats. Being first is no guarantee for success, as Digital Research—the inventor of the CPM operating system—and Visicalc—the inven-

[1]For a general discussion of lock-in and lock-out, see Pankaj Ghemawat, *Commitment: The Dynamics of Strategy* (New York: Free Press, 1991).

tor of PC spread sheet programs—clearly found out. Both companies dominated the early personal computer market but could not make the transition to the IBM PC. In addition, second movers can overcome their initial disadvantages if they offer some new twist or technology that creates added value for the customer. Dell, for instance, was a latecomer to the PC industry but nonetheless emerged as a leading manufacturer of personal computers by offering customers better service and lower prices through innovation in marketing. And finally, being the "first" mover does not necessarily mean being the very first to market. When industries are immature and fragmented, the first mover is the one who creates the standard. Thus, even though Apple pioneered the mass market for the stand-alone computer, it was IBM *five years later* that recognized its potential and created the standard; even though CPM existed before DOS, it was Microsoft that was the first to understand the need to build a loyal following among software vendors and therefore the first to create the market; and even though many firms had software designed to build networks of personal computers, it was Novell that first recognized and acted upon the potential (see chapter 4).

A second implication of lock-in and lock-out is recognizing that breaking new ground in an industry like information technology requires a return to the old adage: *try, try, and try again.* Because customers get locked in to a particular way of doing business, any change is difficult to engineer. While changing the rules is infrequent and difficult, companies willing to make big bets on innovation can make it happen. Apple Computer nearly went bankrupt when it tried to move its customer base from the Apple II to the Macintosh; Microsoft failed repeatedly over seven years to introduce Windows; the initial response to Intel's 486SX microprocessor was almost uniformly negative.[2] In each case, the companies endured, with spectacular results. What all these

examples share is a strong vision and commitment by senior management that their new product or service was the right direction for their companies and the computer industry. John Sculley at Apple believed that the Macintosh could change the way people use computers; despite its lack of compatibility with Apple's installed base, he was willing to bet the company that Macintosh would catch on if management was willing to stay the course. Similarly, Microsoft had many other opportunities beyond Windows in the mid-1980s which Bill Gates could have profitably pursued. But despite the vociferous criticism Gates received each time he introduced a new version of Windows before June 1990, he persisted. And Andy Grove at Intel saw a low-end 486 as a critical competitive weapon in his fight against imitators, despite the initial customer resistance and negative reactions from press. When AMD made significant inroads into the 386 market in 1992, Intel could use the 486SX as the new standard for entry-level computers. By early 1993, the 486SX was one of the world's largest selling microprocessors.

A third implication of lock-in and lock-out is the willingness to *cannibalize your business.* Perhaps the most difficult strategic move for any firm in any industry is to offer products or services which reduce the sales of existing product lines. Yet the history of information technology provides very clear lessons on this point: If you have the capability to cannibalize your own product lines and choose not to, someone else surely will. The danger of refusing to cannibalize your own sales is that when new products or technologies emerge as substitutes, they get locked-in and you get locked-out. The strategic question of cannibalization is not one of "if"; it is only a question of "when." Digital Equipment's refusal to pursue stand-alone workstations aggressively in the mid-1980s because they would cannibalize their minicomputer sales was a disaster; similarly IBM's refusal to use its best technology for its first technical workstation, the PC RT, for fear it would cannibalize its AS/400 sales was an unmitigated failure; AT&T's slow response to digital switching because it did not want to make its analog business obsolete cost AT&T 50 percent of the U.S. market, which it may never retrieve; and Apple Computer's preoccupation with not cannibalizing its high margin Macintosh busi-

---

[2]Microsoft's early versions of Windows were inferior products compared to Macintosh, and customers could not justify switching from DOS to Windows. Similarly, when Intel first introduced the 486SX, the product was a 486DX with some of the components disabled. Ultimately, Microsoft improved Windows to the point that it was a close substitute for Macintosh software, and Intel shrunk the die size of its 486SX chip, making it a truly different product that was cheaper to produce.

ness in the late 1980s led to a dangerous loss in market share, which took Apple several years to regain. In all of these cases, and many others offered in the book, firms that did not aggressively capitalize on new technologies found their businesses floundering and their market shares under attack. Whenever the technology was possible, other firms would find a way utilize it.

Mastering Technology

A fifth theme is that managing information technology businesses defies some of the standard wisdom about general management. Just being a good general manager may not be enough for IT firms: Excellent managers in information technology firms are invariably those who can *master technology*. The idea that a good manager can run any firm, regardless of the industry, hardly seems to apply in this sector. One of the critical jobs for any general manager is understanding how to allocate resources. In information technology, the possibilities for research, development and market expansion seem almost endless; it is tempting to invest in everything. Yet ultimately, successful firms must decide where and how to make their bets. This requires an in-depth understanding of technological trade-offs. As a consequence, financially-driven or marketing-oriented general managers, without a strong understanding of the technological frontier, usually have severe problems in trying to steer the course of an information technology business.

When John Sculley first arrived at Apple Computer, for instance, he was perceived as a strong general manager with good operating skills and marketing savvy. However, when Steve Jobs left, Apple was suddenly run by a man without much technical knowledge. Repeatedly in the late 1980s, Sculley found that he could not push Apple in the directions he believed to be the future: When he wanted Apple to make the Macintosh a leader in networking, he had to back down after he was besieged by engineers with all of the technological problems; when he wanted to port Apple's leading edge software to other platforms, he was told by engineers it was impossible. Yet in both cases, Sculley later discovered that he had been misled or misinformed, and the

impossible in 1987 suddenly became possible in the early 1990s. It was not until Sculley appointed himself chief technology officer at Apple in 1990 and committed himself to learning the technology that he was in a position to steer the company as a leader and general manager must do (see chapter 18).

Perhaps the most stark comparison between technical leader and general manager was Bill Gates of Microsoft and John Akers of IBM. Gates was the archetypical techie: He started by writing software code, and after he became one of the richest men in the world, he continued to involve himself at a deep technical level in most software products produced by his company. As the case *Bill Gates and the Management of Microsoft* (chapter 19) illustrates, Gates's effectiveness as a leader and a manager stemmed from his ability to allocate effectively corporate resources and his own time to highly valued projects that had the highest potential payoffs. Akers, by contrast, dealt with strategy and resource allocation at a much higher level of abstraction. As one sees in the *Transformation of IBM* case (chapter 17), Akers was the ultimate marketing/sales-driven CEO. If Gates was the archetypical techie, Akers was the archetypical IBMer: a marketeer who was meticulously dressed in a dark suit, white shirt, and conservative tie. Comparisons between Gates, Sculley, and Akers may be unfair; after all, IBM was a company 20 times Microsoft's size in the early 1990s and 10 times Apple's revenues. But the ongoing success of Microsoft and Apple was at least partly attributable to their high "hit rates" for turning R&D into successful products, and the trials and tribulations of IBM could be partly attributed to its low and declining hit rates on R&D. Although IBM spent more on R&D than most of the computer industry *combined*, many of their problems in the late 1980s and the early 1990s stemmed from their difficulty in turning R&D dollars into hit products. While Akers cannot be solely to blame, he clearly had responsibility for resource allocation.

Final Words

The challenges facing both managers and consumers of information technology are daunting.

There are few industries which match the rapid pace of change and the numerous risks and opportunities offered by the new information technologies. Similarly, there are few industries that require such constant renewal and organizational transformation. The companies represented in this book give the reader an opportunity to explore what has and has not worked in the last decade. From those experiences, hopefully you will be in a better position to deduce what will and will not work in the decades ahead.

PART ONE

Industry Notes

1. The Global Semiconductor Industry, 1987

In 1947, William B. Shockley and a team of Bell Laboratory engineers devised the solid state transistor, ushering into being the semiconductor industry—one of the most technologically dynamic industries of modern times. Over the next 40 years, semiconductor products would shrink in size, grow in power, and diminish in price. Semiconductors had become so pervasive in industrial and consumer products that they were being called the "crude oil of the 1980s." In 1987, however, the industry was in transition. After more than two years of global depression that led to $6 billion in corporate losses worldwide, demand and profits were finally picking up. In the meantime, the structure of the industry was evolving, as new leaders emerged.

History and Evolution of the Semiconductor Industry

After Shockley's team invented the transistor, companies focused on developing an efficient manufacturing process. Production was complicated because transistors, then made of germanium, were easily susceptible to contamination. In 1954, Texas Instruments discovered how to make transistors out of silicon, which quickly catapulted the company to a position of leadership. However, the power of transistors remained limited despite several further advances in production methods: scientists knew how to design a powerful computer circuit that would use 500,000 transistors, but wiring each circuit together was expensive and unreliable. The solution to this problem was discovered in late 1958 and early 1959 when TI and Fairchild independently filed patents for the integrated circuit (IC). The invention of the IC was of enormous importance. By putting transistor circuits directly on semiconductor material, elements no longer had to be wired together. As a result, it became possible to make highly complex and reliable electrical circuits.

The first marketable chips were not produced until 1961, but they were so expensive compared to transistors that they had no com-

Professor David B. Yoffie prepared this note with the assistance of Research Assistant Alvin G. Wint as the basis for class discussion.

mercial market. Nonetheless, the timing was fortuitous. President John F. Kennedy had just committed the United States to landing a man on the moon by the end of the decade. The new ICs would be critical to the space program's success and related military technologies. The U.S. government, and especially the Department of Defense, became the first major chip customer and constituted the entire market for ICs until 1964.

The willingness and ability of the government to purchase chips in quantity at premium prices allowed a growing number of companies in the industry to refine their production skills. Manufacturers continuously increased the number of elements contained on a single IC while significantly reducing costs. More than any other product in America's industrial history, the production of ICs benefited from an amazingly steep learning curve. In 1964, a chip containing about 64 components was priced at around $32. By 1971, the price of a chip containing over a thousand components was about $1. (See **Exhibit 1**.)

Another set of revolutionary innovations occurred in the late 1960s when Robert Noyce, and another eminent scientist, Gordon Moore, left Fairchild to start Intel. In 1971, the firm introduced an IC that permitted random access to information. This device, which could store 1024 bits in memory, was dubbed a 1K RAM (or Random Access Memory). In the same year, Intel made yet another breakthrough: the company created a single IC chip that performed all the central processing-unit functions of a simple computer and could therefore be programmed for a variety of jobs. This chip developed into Intel's first microprocessor, which ultimately led to the birth of personal computers. These plus other Intel inventions made the founders very wealthy and the firm an industry leader by the late 1970s.

The industry continued to generate increases in IC memory. The 1970s spanned two generations of chip technology: in the early part of the decade, a 4K RAM was introduced, ushering in the era of large-scale integration: and in the mid-to-late 1970s, the production of 16K RAMs followed by 64K RAMs began the period of very large-scale integration (VLSI). These increases in chip memory continued into the 1980s. By 1987, the 256K RAM was the standard: 1000K or 1 megabit RAMs were in volume production, and many firms had announced plans for 4 and 16 megabit chips.

Semiconductor Products

Semiconductor products included thousands of devices, ranging in complexity from the simple transistor that performed one function to the very complicated microprocessor that served as the brains for a computer. (See **Table A.**) By the mid-1980s, however, one could classify the semiconductor products into three distinct segments: discrete devices, which were mature products such as transistors; linear or analog ICs, which were also relatively mature components that would be used in a TV or radio; and digital IC's, which comprised almost 70% of the worldwide market and represented the fastest growth and most technologically innovative segment. The rest of this note focuses on digital ICs.

A digital IC acts as an on/off switch and comprises two basic categories of chips: memory and logic. Memory devices store information. The most popular memory ICs were dynamic RAMs (DRAMs)—chips that stored data that could be erased by simply turning off the power. DRAMs represented between 20% and 30% of the digital IC market and were primarily known for their central role in personal computers. The other most popular memories were SRAMs and EPROMs.[1]

Within each memory type, ICs were functionally identical and met industry-wide standards. This meant that all 16K DRAMs would store the same amount of information and that any company's 16K DRAM could be replaced by

---

[1]SRAMs stood for static RAMs; they differed from DRAMs because they were faster and they did not need a constant electrical charge to hold the memory. An SRAM could serve the same function as a DRAM, but it was more expensive to produce, making an SRAM most appropriate for specialized applications. EPROMs stood for erasable programmable read only memory. EPROMs could be erased with ultraviolet light, then reprogrammed. A typical use for an EPROM was in a computer keyboard.

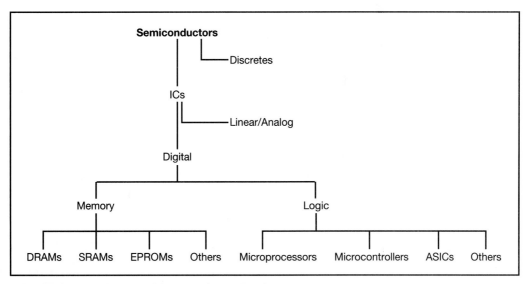

TABLE A *Family Tree of Semiconductor Products*

most any other firm's 16K DRAM.[2] At the same time, memories could be made in a myriad of ways, which allowed companies to offer similarly sized DRAMs that varied in speed, power consumption, and often quality and reliability. It was also cheaper for a computer company in 1987 to buy four 256K DRAMs at $2.50 a piece rather than a 1 megabit chip at almost $20. The four chips would perform the exact same function, but a single 1 megabit semiconductor took up less space on a circuit board, which lowered the cost of a computer.

Logic ICs could process information rather than only store it. Most logic devices were dedicated to particular functions. Very simple logic chips, for instance, would be programmed by the manufacturer to run a watch or calculator. More complicated logic chips were programmed to perform different tasks under varying conditions. For example, a logic chip known as a microcontroller might be used by Ford to regulate the air-fuel mixture in an automobile engine. Finally, microprocessors were the most complex logic ICs. Representing around 10% of digital IC revenues, microprocessors were programmable—software engineers could compose a variety of programs to run on a particular chip.

[2] There were rare exceptions to this rule. Memory products could be made incompatible if they had different pin structure, which could not plug into a standard socket, or if they used different electrical input signals.

Most logic products were interchangeable, albeit at a small cost. For example, similar firms' microcontrollers could perform the same function, but each might require a unique set of instructions and different circuit boards. Microprocessors were the least interchangeable because every family of microprocessors required their own operating language to run a program. In 1987, more than $10 billion of software had been written to run exclusively on the Intel family of microprocessors that powered IBM and compatible PCs, and about $1 billion of software had been written for the Motorola chips that powered Apple's Macintosh. If computer manufacturers switched vendors, the new PC or Mac would lose compatibility with previous machines. Nonetheless, analysts forecasted that innovations in software by the mid-1990s might make microprocessors as interchangeable as other logic products.

Firms were finding in the mid-1980s that product life cycles were shortening, especially in memory products. The 4K RAM was in production for almost ten years; the 256K RAM was likely to be in production for only three to four years. Technological advances were also producing chips so powerful that they were accounting for larger and larger shares of the total value of end products. A microprocessor that sold for under $100 in 1987 had the power of a 1970 mainframe computer that sold for $500,000.

EXHIBIT 1 Industry Experience Curve in DRAM Across Products (68% curve slope) (Source: HBS field study, Spring 1987).

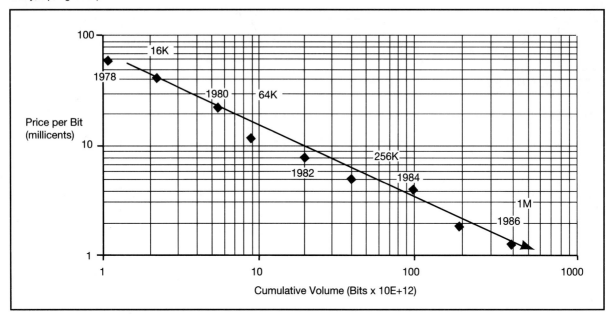

Designing Integrated Circuits

Circuit design was the first important step in making an IC: it was also the most time-consuming, skill-intensive, and costly phase in the production process.[3] Since engineers with the requisite skills tended to be in scarce supply, they commanded premium wages. However, despite the high costs, American firms found it difficult to keep designs proprietary. It was common for an American engineer with an idea for a new design to leave a firm and start his/her own company. These start-ups would frequently license their designs to established domestic and foreign merchants in exchange for capital or access to a particular market. Many of these fledgling companies would produce one moderately successful product, then go out of business. Chip designs spread rapidly in the 1970s for two further reasons: it was relatively simple to copy and commercialize a product with impunity, since patent protection was

weak; and, established manufacturers widely cross-licensed their technology. In areas where firms held significant patent positions, most managers viewed cross-licensing as a way to avoid costly, counterproductive court battles. Japanese firms, however, were able to license technology in the 1960s and early 1970s even when they lacked distinctive innovations. American companies that wanted to sell or invest in the rapidly growing Japanese market were required by Japan's government to license key technologies. The continual revolutions in technology through the 1970s made innovating firms confident that by the time licensees exploited the technology, a new generation would be in vogue.

Rising costs and complexity as well as the problems of pirated designs were leading to significant changes in the mid-1980s. To make the design phase of production more cost-effective and reduce design time, most firms in the United States and Japan were moving to automated tools such as computer-aided design (CAD) equipment. To prevent piracy, companies were

[3]Costs varied with the complexity of the chip. Three engineers could design a memory in a few months; dozens of engineers could take a few years to design a microprocessor.

turning towards the court. It became easier to protect chip designs after 1984 with the passage of the Chip Protection Act. Since a few landmark court cases forced some firms that were copying designs to discontinue sales or pay substantial royalties, analysts were predicting much more litigation over intellectual property.

Manufacturing Integrated Circuits

Producing ICs has been described as one of the most complex mass manufacturing processes in the industrial history of the world. The first stage was wafer manufacturing, which was usually performed by large diversified chemical companies. By 1987, most wafer manufacturers were located in Japan, with TI and IBM the only U.S. firms making wafers for in-house use, and Monsanto the only U.S. firm selling wafers. Wafer manufacturers grew silicon or gallium arsenide[4] crystals of high purity, then "pulled" the crystals into ingots that were sliced into thin wafers. Finally, the wafers were polished and coated with a layer of silicon dioxide. The standard wafer size in 1987 was six inches in diameter, but all semiconductor manufacturers were in a race to increase that size. The larger the wafer, the more chips that could be produced during a manufacturing cycle.

The next step was for engineers to transfer an IC design to a set of masks to be used in two lithography processes that imprinted the circuit patterns, layer by layer, onto a silicon wafer. The wafers had to be handled in a dust-free environment otherwise dust particles could contaminate the products. As semiconductor devices shrunk in size, even the smallest particle of dust could ruin a chip. This became especially problematic as the line width between circuits was being reduced to under one micron by the mid-1980s. To create a dust-free environment, firms built "clean rooms" with special air ducts to filter out impurities in the air, special water supplies, and workers who wore special clean room attire. The sensitive nature of the process led many IC manufacturers to automate their plants in the 1980s to reduce human interference.

The next stage in production involved testing to find defects, then separating each chip from the wafer. Finally, the chips were packaged so that their circuitry could be connected to external outlets. This labor-intensive process was frequently done in low-wage countries. By the mid-1980s virtually all U.S. semiconductor firms and most Japanese firms had low-cost assembly operations in developing countries. The final stage of IC manufacture involved performing a battery of computerized tests to ensure reliability.

The complexity and difficulty in manufacturing chips led to long lead times for plants to come on-stream. American and Japanese firms needed as much as 18–24 months to "ramp up": i.e., build the plant, install the equipment, and qualify the product's quality and performance.

Economics of the Industry

One of the most striking characteristics of the semiconductor industry was that production costs for most products would decline by 30 percent for every doubling of cumulative volume. One of the reasons that learning produced such

[4]Gallium arsenide, a material only recently commercialized for IC production, promised to be up to ten times faster than silicon. However, despite significant R&D efforts, this material had limited applications in 1987 because it was brittle and very difficult to use.

dividends was that semiconductor manufacturing routinely yielded more defective than sound products. For new products, yields as low as 10 percent for inexperienced manufacturers and 25 percent for experienced manufacturers were quite common. For more mature products, however, yields could be as high as 90 percent. The need to raise yields led firms to manufacture high-volume products that could act as "technology drivers." It was generally believed that skills learned in manufacturing large volumes of a simple product could be transferred to lower volume, higher value-added devices and help "drive" the firm down a very steep learning curve. Producing DRAMs was particularly well-suited for this task because they had a less complex structure than other ICs, which allowed firms to distinguish quickly between a flaw in the design and a flaw in the manufacturing process. The learning gained from making DRAMs or other high-volume products could be transferred rapidly to other memory or logic products.

Although semiconductor manufacturing was clearly capital intensive, it was difficult to calculate minimum efficient scale (MES) because of the enormous variations in yield. Nonetheless, many industry analysts estimated in 1987 that MES was at least 1,000, and probably closer to 2,000 wafer starts per week; at a cost of about $25,000 per wafer start for a state-of-the-art one micron plant, this represented an initial capital outlay for the fabrication facility of $40–$45 million. Since the plant required another $40–$60 million in equipment, total costs ranged from $80–$105 million. The rapid obsolescence of equipment (which was often outdated within 2–3 years) also led to huge, ongoing capital investments. In the mid-1980s, most large firms were building new IC fabrication facilities that cost over $150 million. While it remained possible in the 1980s to build low-volume plants for as little as $20 million, these were only useful for specialized producers that could charge big premiums for their unique chips.

Rising complexity of products and plants altered semiconductor firms' cost structure. Worldwide, the average semiconductor firm was projected to spend 15% of sales on R&D in 1987, a percentage that had been rising steadily for a decade. In addition, as much as 30% of sales was spent on capital equipment to prevent obsolescence. In the meantime, raw material costs were dropping: A polished wafer that cost $30 in the early 1980s could be purchased for only $6–$10 by 1987; labor costs were falling with the rise in automation; and distribution and transportation costs were tiny (1–2%). The entire production of the world's semiconductors in 1986 could fit in ten 747 jets.

The chip industry was highly cyclical. (See **Exhibit 2.**) Excess capacity and the practice of forward pricing ICs, especially by the Japanese, contributed to the enormous industry losses of the mid-1980s. Industry analysts estimated that between 1985 and 1986, U.S. companies lost about $2 billion, Japanese companies lost about $2 billion, and Korean and European companies each lost approximately $1 billion.

EXHIBIT 2 Growth in U.S. Semiconductor Consumption vs. U.S. GNP Growth (year-to-year percentage change) (Source: Dataquest, March 1987.)

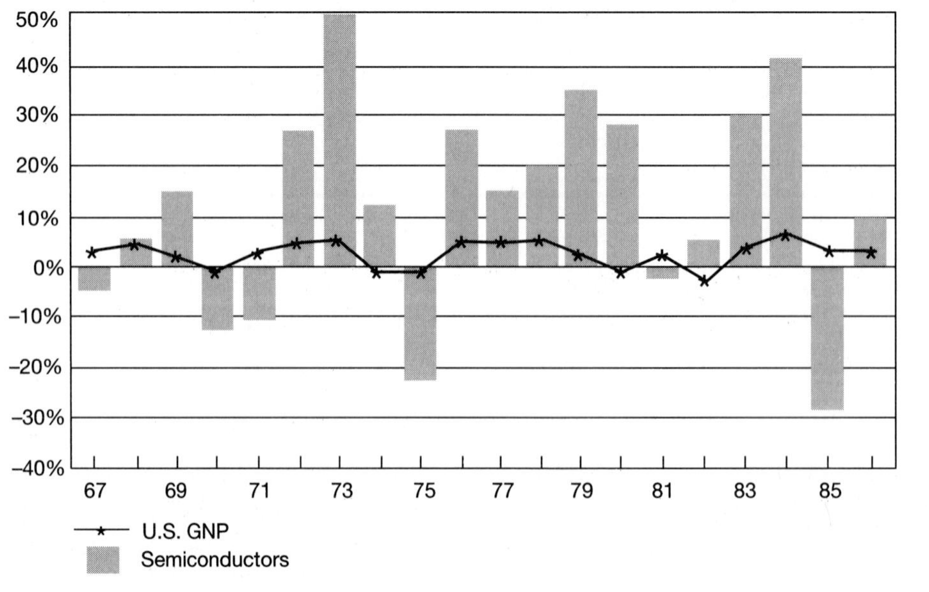

The continuous increases in IC memory and computing power combined with reductions in power consumption and price made ICs an essential component for all electronic and many industrial products. As a result, there were literally tens of thousands of chip buyers in all major markets, ranging from producers of computers to cars and VCRs. (See **Exhibit 3a.**)

The structure and growth of user industries varied by country. (See **Exhibit 3b.**) The United States had been the largest market for chips from the industry's inception. But demand in the United States slowed in the early 1980s while Japan's growth climbed through 1985. Although Japanese consumption fell in 1986 when measured in local currency, a 40% appreciation in the value of the yen made Japan the world's largest dollar market for chips.

When deciding on whose chips to buy, users of semiconductors focused on different factors. In the commodity memory chips, price was the overriding variable. It was easy for users to shop for discounts because manufacturers would usually publish a list price for standard products, and there were always multiple suppliers of any product. Occasionally, a buyer might purchase limited quantities of commodity products at higher prices in order to maintain or build a relationship with a particular vendor or simply for the convenience of one-stop shopping. In more advanced and highly specialized niches, relative performance was the crucial factor. One American computer buyer stated that "Price is irrelevant when you want to get performance leaders. In a specialty product, I'm willing to pay a higher price. There may only be two suppliers of a particular specialty chip, as opposed to several sources of satisfactory DRAMs."

In addition to price and performance, buyers were very sensitive to quality and delivery. For many electronics products, production lines would have to be shut down if chips were unavailable. Furthermore, the failure of a $300 microprocessor would render a $5,000–$10,000 computer unusable. Even the failure of a $2.00 chip could significantly reduce a machine's power: if the defect was not detected initially, it could cost up to $50–$100 to repair. Fearful of shortages, buyers frequently ordered in excess of their needs. It was also common for buyers to cancel bookings abruptly if their inventories swelled. Most users of chips were also well-informed. The Japanese reputation for delivering higher reliability gave them a significant edge in the early 1980s. U.S. firms subsequently focused attention and resources on improving quality and lowering the number of defects per shipment. By the mid-1980s, most buyers could not distinguish differences in quality based on national origin.

ICs were particularly important for computer companies. In early 1985, a personal computer costing $1,250 to manufacture included $300 of ICs. By 1988–1989, ICs were projected to account for 33% to 38% of the manufactured cost of a PC. The centrality of ICs led some users to backward integrate. (See **Exhibit 5a.**) While most big electronics firms in Japan built a large percentage of their ICs for internal use as well as for sale on the merchant market, the few American OEMs that built ICs did so for in-house consumption only.[5] IBM, for instance, which bought ,

EXHIBIT 3A Estimated 1987 Semiconductor Consumption by Application Market (Source: Adapted from Instat, Inc).

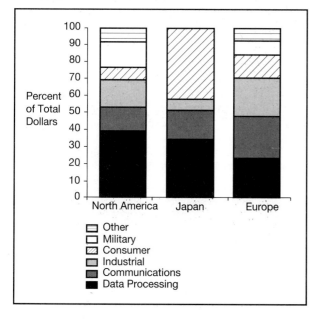

Percent of Total Dollars

- Other
- Military
- Consumer
- Industrial
- Communications
- Data Processing

(North America, Japan, Europe)

[5]There were exceptions. In the mid-1980s, for example, AT&T announced its intention to become a merchant semiconductor house. However, AT&T was not a low-cost producer and had not become a major merchant player. In 1987, for instance, AT&T was only the ninth largest DRAM supplier.

EXHIBIT 3B Total Solid-State Consumption Worldwide—ICs and Discretes (millions of dollars)

	1982	1983	1984	1985	1986	1987[a]
United States	$6,259	$7,763	$11,599	$8,091	$8,509	$9,823
Japan	3,985	5,534	8,034	7,598	10,451	11,117
Europe	2,998	3,319	4,738	4,541	5,344	6,387
Rest of world	822	1,152	1,586	1,250	2,052	2,496
Total world	**$14,064**	**$17,767**	**$25,956**[b]	**$21,479**[b]	**$26,355**[b]	**$29,823**
% Growth	NA	26.3%	46.1%	-17.2%	22.7%	13.2%

Source: Adapted from Instat, Inc.

[a]Estimate.

[b]Instat estimates are lower than Dataquest estimates reported in Exhibit 7a.

more than $2.5 billion worth of semiconductors in 1985, was the world's largest consumer of chips as well as the world's largest producer. Most captive manufacturers generally produced state-of-the-art, customized chips for their own use and bought commodity semiconductors on the open market. IBM and AT&T were also on the forefront of DRAM technology: both were global leaders in design and IBM, in particular, was among the most advanced in process technology.

Although there were thousands of buyers for a firm's chips, a large computer or telecommunications company would buy volume purchases directly from the manufacturer and it might account for 10% or more of a merchant's sales.[6] (See **Exhibit 5b.**) In the early stages of the industry, these large buyers often required their suppliers to create second sources for products. If a small or unproven semiconductor firm wanted to sell a new product the buyer insisted that the innovating firm license specific firms, either in the United States or abroad, to be second sources in the event of production problems or capacity shortages. Large customers also sought to avoid sole sources, especially from small, young companies. In some cases, second sourcing arrangements significantly reduced the innovator's revenues and profitability. Intel, for instance, was the world leader in microprocessors. But the company's second sources received more than 70% of the revenue from Intel's enormously successful 8086 microprocessor, which powered the original IBM and IBM-compatible PCs.

One of the most widely discussed trends of the 1980s was customization. The market for

custom and semicustom chips, known as ASICs (application specific integrated circuits), had grown from virtually nothing in 1980 to $6 billion in 1987. (See **Exhibits 4a and 4b.**) The emer-

EXHIBIT 4A Estimated World ASIC Consumption (Source: Adapted from Dataquest, January 1988).

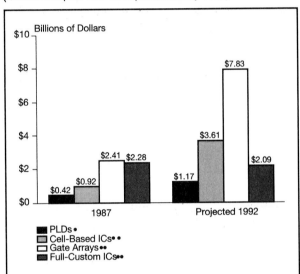

*PLDs are logic chips that can be programmed with software by the user. PLDs are the cheapest and fastest ASIC to design (usually within a few days), but the least versatile ASIC.

**Gate Arrays (GA) and Cell-Based Devices (CBD) are ASICs designed by the semiconductor manufacturer in collaboration with the user. A GA, which can be designed in only two to four weeks, has fixed circuits (transistors, resistors, and capacitors) which the ASIC designer interconnects to fulfill user-specific applications. In a CBD, an engineer selects standard semiconductor cells from a firm's library and then designs the chips to maximize efficiency and minimize space. CBDs are more versatile and efficient, but require up to 16 weeks to design. Full custom chips are the most efficient ASICs, but require up to 12

[6]Thirty percent of all semiconductors were sold via distributors. Distributors kept large inventories for immediate delivery, mostly for small customers.

EXHIBIT 4B Top 10 ASIC Vendors Worldwide in 1986 (millions of dollars)

| | % Growth | | Approximate Revenues by Segments | | |
Company	1985–1986	1986	Gate Array	Cell-Based	PLDs
1. Fujitsu	43.0%	$359.2	$309	$50	–
2. LSI Logic	38.9	194.3	192	–	–
3. AT&T	26.8	183.1	–	183	–
4. MMI/AMD[a]	19.3	176.7	–	–	$172
5. NEC	55.9	151.2	145	–	–
6. Toshiba	152.3	132.6	120	–	–
7. TI	40.0	99.7	38	42	20
8. Motorola	20.9	94.7	92	–	–
9. Hitachi	35.6	78.8	79	–	–
10. Signetics	3.7	76.0	–	–	50
Top 10 Vendors	**38.8%**	**$1,546.3**			

[a]MMI (Monolithic Memories) merged with AMD (Advanced Micro Devices) in 1987.
Sources: Adapted from Dataquest, *JSIS Newsletter*, May 1987.

gence of ASICs promised to change second sourcing practices in the 1980s. Most buyers used single sourcing for their ASIC purchases. Buyers often wanted their ASICs delivered in 3–4 weeks after an order versus the industry norm of 4–5 months; and many chips were simply not available from more than one supplier. Price was generally less important in the ASIC market as buyers sought extensive service, reliability, and advanced technology—both in the supplier's hardware for designing the products as well as in the designs themselves.

In the early 1980s, buyers relied heavily on specialty ASIC houses, which excelled in service and design. By 1987, buyers' choices were growing. There were four generic types of ASICs and much of the demand was moving towards chip-scalled gate arrays—chips that could be made in vast quantities and then specialized close to the last step in production. Rather than developing a chip from the ground up with a vendor, a buyer could, in a sense, "connect the wires" on a standard gate array to meet any number of requirements. With many analysts predicting that the worldwide gate array market would grow to $8 billion by 1992, more than 100 gate array suppliers were sacrificing profits in 1986 and 1987 in order to build share.

EXHIBIT 5A Estimated Semiconductor Production of U.S. Captive Manufacturers ($ millions)

Company	1981	1982	1983	1984	1985
IBM	1,500	1,680	1,932	2,318	2,600
AT&T	675	720	755	980	600
Honeywell	60	76	90	95	81
Delco	68	75	80	95	111
DEC	47	61	65	80	71
H-P (IC only)	116	118	134	165	180
Subtotal	2,466	2,730	3,056	3,733	3,643
Others	250	275	300	370	395
Total Captive	**2,716**	**3,005**	**3,356**	**4,103**	**4,038**
Total Merchant[a]	**7,607**	**7,694**	**9,509**	**14,244**	**11,103**

[a]Excludes intracompany sales of merchant firms, which averaged 5% from 1981 to 1985.
Source: Dataquest, July 1986.

EXHIBIT 5B Estimated Semiconductor Users Purchasing More than $100 Million

Year	Number of Companies	Total Semiconductor Consumption (billions of dollars)	Percent of Total Semiconductor Consumption
1976	1	$0.11	2%
1978	2	0.69	8
1980	12	1.80	17
1982	23	3.90	26
1984	36	5.80	28
1985	46	7.10	31

Sources: Adapted from Dataquest, *SUIS Industry Trends,* March 1987.

International Competitors

Globally, there were 150–200 firms making semiconductors in the mid-1980s. Total market sales of semiconductors, excluding those chips made by vertically integrated firms for their own in-house use, were approximately $27 billion in 1986. The top 50 merchant firms accounted for more than 90% of global merchant sales, and the top ten almost 60%. American firms held the world's largest market share through 1985. However, U.S. share of world semiconductor sales dropped to 43%, down from about 60% in 1980, while Japan's share rose from 33% to 45% over the same period. (See **Exhibits 6a and 6b.**)

THE U.S. SEMICONDUCTOR MERCHANTS In the United States, there were four types of competitors: independent merchant companies whose product lines were dominated by large-volume products sold to OEMs; design houses, which specialized in chip designs and subcontracted the manufacturing to foundries; process specialists, who specialized in narrow tasks, such as preparing masks or testing circuits; and semi-custom houses, who focused exclusively on products such as ASICs. In the late 1970s, a few large diversified firms had bought successful merchants. These combinations, however, had not worked well in the United States. Mostek, for example, was a leading DRAM manufacturer in the 1970s, but went bankrupt and was resold after being bought by United Technology; and Fairchild, an industry leader in the 1960s, lost money and market share after being purchased by Schlumberger, and was resold to National Semiconductor.

Despite the large number of firms in the industry, only five American merchants had been significant players in the wholesale market for chips since the mid-1970s: Texas Instruments, Motorola, Intel, National Semiconductor, and Advanced Micro Devices (AMD) accounted for 37.5% of U.S. merchant sales in 1986. The top four firms are briefly profiled below.

MOTOROLA Motorola was the largest American semiconductor merchant (30% of corporate sales)

EXHIBIT 6A Top Five Suppliers Across Technological Generations

1955 (Vacuum Tubes)	1955 (Transistor)	1965 (Semiconductor)	1975 (IC)	1985 (VLSI)
RCA	Hughes	TI	TI	NEC
Sylvania	Transitron	Fairchild	Fairchild	Motorola
GE	Philco	Motorola	National	TI
Raytheon	Sylvania	GI	Intel	Hitachi
Westinghouse	TI	GE	Motorola	Toshiba

Sources: Richard N. Foster, *Innovation: The Attackers' Advantage* (New York: Summit Books); Dataquest.

EXHIBIT 6B Preliminary 1986 World Semiconductor Market Share Ranking ($ millions)

1986 Rank	1985 Rank	1984 Rank	Company	1984	1985	1986	Percent Change '85–'86
1	1	3	NEC	2,251	1,984	2,638	33.0%
2	4	4	Hitachi	2,052	1,671	2,305	37.9
3	5	5	Toshiba	1,561	1,468	2,261	54.0
4	2	2	Motorola	2,320	1,830	2,025	10.7
5	3	1	Texas Instruments	2,480	1,742	1,820	4.5
6	6	6	Philips-Signetics	1,325	1,068	1,356	27.0
7	7	9	Fujitsu	1,190	1,020	1,310	28.4
8	10	12	Matsushita	928	906	1,233	36.1
9	11	10	Mitsubishi	964	642	1,177	83.3
10	8	8	Intel	1,201	1,020	991	-2.8
11	9	7	National Semiconductor[b]	1,263	925	990	7.0
12	12	11	Advanced Micro Devices[c]	936	615	629	2.3
13	14	15	Sanyo	455	457	585	28.0
14	13	13	Fairchild[b]	665	492	510	3.7
15	22	29	Sony	177	252	475	88.5
16	15	16	Siemens	450	420	457	8.8
17	16	20	Sharp	354	329	456	38.6
18	17	22	Thomson-Mostek[a]	301	324	436	34.6
19	19	19	Oki	362	307	427	39.1
20	23	24	Rohm	252	249	379	52.2
21	20	21	SGS	335	300	370	23.3
22	18	17	RCA	402	310	370	19.4
23	21	25	ITT	250	270	312	15.6
24	24	23	Harris	275	247	264	6.9
25	25	26	Analog Devices	210	226	232	2.7
26	31	32	Sanken	162	155	220	41.9
27	29	33	Telefunken Electronic	161	170	219	28.8
28	26	28	Hewlett-Packard	182	206	217	5.3
29	36	35	TRW	142	125	213	70.4
30	30	30	Fuji Electric	176	156	213	36.5
31	28	27	Monolithic Memories[c]	200	172	210	22.1
32	27	18	General Instrument	362	201	205	2.0
33	32	47	LSI Logic	84	140	192	37.1
34	41	57	Samsung	60	95	183	92.6
35	42	39	Seiko Epson	115	93	167	79.6
36	44	55	Honeywell	64	88	157	78.4
37	33	31	American Microsystems	164	140	155	10.7
38	34	38	International Rectifier	115	128	145	13.3
39	38	42	Siliconix	97	110	126	14.5
40	39	49	Plessey	82	99	112	13.1
41	48	53	VLSI Technology	69	78	110	41.0
42	n/a	n/a	Powerex	n/a	0	95	n/a
43	49	n/a	Burr-Brown	n/a	78	95	21.8
44	40	41	Ferranti	105	98	95	-3.1
45	45	48	Sprague	84	87	94	8.0
46	43	40	Unitrode	106	89	90	1.1
47	37	36	General Electric	136	118	89	-24.6
48	52	n/a	Precision Monolithics	n/a	68	81	19.1
49	46	34	Inmos	146	85	80	-5.9
50	50	46	NCR	85	75	80	6.7
Top 50 Total				**26,507**	**21,928**	**27,651**	**26.1%**

[a]Mostek and Thomson revenues were aggregated in 1986 but not 1984 or 1985.

[b]National and Fairchild merged in 1987.

[c]AMD and MMI merged in 1987.

Source: Dataquest, January 1987.

in 1986, one of the world leaders in mobile telecommunications equipment (40% of sales), and a manufacturer of computers and defense electronics. Motorola's semiconductor product line was among the most diversified in the industry: it was the world leader in discrete products (30% of semiconductor sales); second in microprocessors (advanced logic was 20% of sales); and a growing player in ASICs (10% of sales). TI and Motorola were the only American companies with 100%-owned manufacturing facilities in Japan. Although Motorola had abandoned the DRAM business in 1985, it entered a joint venture with Toshiba in 1986 that involved trading Motorola's microprocessor technology for Toshiba's DRAM process and product technology as well as greater access to Japanese customers. (See **Exhibit 7.**)

TEXAS INSTRUMENTS (TI) TI, the world leader in semiconductors until 1985, had fallen to fifth place in 1987. In addition to semiconductors (merchant sales of $1.8 billion and in-house sales of $300 million), the company produced defense electronics ($210 million in earnings on $1.7 billion in sales), computers, and electronic calculators. TI was considered by industry analysts to be technologically innovative and a broad-line, quality-oriented supplier with one of the lowest cost positions among American firms. TI typically sold standard volume products, and was the only large American manufacturer of DRAMs. Although the company had slipped from first to sixth among DRAM producers, it was seeking to regain leadership. In 1987, TI was the first to announce an operating 4 megabit DRAM. TI's strategy was to meet the Japanese challenge by becoming a leader in customer service, design automation and manufacturing processes. As part of this strategy it was aggressively targeting ASICs. In July of 1987, TI entered into an alliance with Intel to swap their libraries of chip designs. TI also had a unique position in Japan: it was the first U.S. firm to establish Japanese production facilities in 1968, and by 1987 it was that country's tenth largest semiconductor company.

INTEL Long considered the most technologically innovative company among the large merchants, Intel had pioneered many of the industry's standard products. Intel had dropped out of DRAMs,

but in 1987 it remained the world leader in its two dominant product lines: EPROMs and microprocessors. About two-thirds of Intel's revenues were derived from semiconductors and one-third was systems (e.g., computer boards and other assembled components). The company had a reputation as a relatively high-cost producer with poor customer service. Reversing that reputation became the company's top priority. Major actions included large layoffs and heavy investments in manufacturing and marketing. To bolster its small share of the ASIC business, Intel invested more than $100 million in CAD equipment and entered into agreements with IBM and TI to swap chip designs. Intel had various other alliances, including ones with Japan's Mitsubishi (for second sourcing EPROMs), Korea's Samsung (which supplied DRAMs that Intel marketed), and AMD (which second sourced manyIntel products, including microprocessors). In 1987 Intel decided to discontinue its second sourcing policy for its most advanced microprocessors. AMD sued Intel, while IBM negotiated a deal that allowed it to make a substantial portion of its own demand for advanced microprocessors by the early 1990s.

NATIONAL SEMICONDUCTOR Before National bought Fairchild in 1987, it was the fourth largest American producer of ICs with 72 percent of all sales coming from semiconductors. The company had a broad portfolio of products in memory, logic, and optoelectronic devices. National was largely a follower in product innovation. Although it was the first company to introduce a 32 bit microprocessor in 1984, it was still a distant third in the microprocessor market by 1987. National's reputation had been built on producing "jelly bean" ICs—i.e., standard, high-volume parts. Historically the firm had been weak in customer service, but compared to its American competitors, National was thought to be a relatively low-cost producer. In 1987, National was seeking a stronger custom IC business and greater leadership in design. For example, it signed a long-term deal with Xerox to provide ASICs in 1986. Xerox provided the system expertise, while National provided chip design, manufacturing and packaging. National made two further strategic moves in 1987: it was expanding its presence in Japan through international al-

EXHIBIT 7 Financials of Nine Leading Producers[a] ($ millions)

	1986	1985	1984	1983
Motorola				
Net Sales	5,888	5,443	5,534	4,328
Semic. Sales	1,880	1,728	2,240	1,612
Net Income/(Loss)	194	72	387	244
Semic. Operating Profit/(Loss)	87	(37)	373	205
R&D Expenses	492	457	489	392
Semic. Capital Expenditures	250	325	412	174
Total Assets	4,682	4,370	4,194	3,236
Long-term Debt	334	705	531	262
Equity	2,754	2,284	2,278	1,948
Return on Sales (Semi.)	4.6%	(2.1%)	16.7%	12.7%
Semi. Cap. Exp./Semi. Sales	13.3%	18.8%	18.4%	10.8%
Texas Instruments				
Net Sales	4,974	4,924	5,742	4,580
Semic. Sales	2,065	2,041	2,740	1,885
Net Income	29	(119)	316	(145)
Semic. Operating Profit	23	(89)	516	236
R&D Expenses	406	402	367	301
Semic. Capital Expenditures	232	281	472	232
Total Assets	3,337	3,076	3,423	2,713
Long-term Debt	191	382	381	225
Equity	1,727	1,428	1,540	1,203
Return on Sales (Semi.)	1.1%	(4.4%)	18.8%	12.5%
Semi. Cap. Exp./Semi. Sales	11.2%	13.8%	17.2%	12.3%
Intel				
Net Sales	1,265	1,365	1,629	1,122
Net Income	(173)	2	198	116
R&D Expenses	228	195	180	142
Total Capital Expenditures	155	236	388	145
Total Assets	2,080	2,152	2,029	1,680
Long-term Debt	287	271	146	128
Equity	1,275	1,421	1,360	1,122
Return on Sales (Semi.)	(13.7%)	0.2%	12.2%	10.3%
Semi. Cap. Exp./Semi. Sales	12.3%	17.3%	23.8%	12.9%
National Semiconductor				
Net Sales	1,478	1,787	1,655	1,210
Semic. Sales	842	1,156	1,107	788
Net Income	(91.5)	43	64	(14)
Semic. Operating Profit	(129)	62	110	10
R&D Expenses	222	205	158	115
Semic. Capital Expenditures	69	322	224	65
Total Assets	1,295	1,410	1,156	847
Long-term Debt	123	226	24	149
Equity	717	681	619	336
Return on Sales (Semi.)	(15.3%)	5.4%	9.9%	1.3%
Semi. Cap. Exp./Semi. Sales	8.2%	27.9%	20.2%	8.3%
LSI Logic				
Net Sales	194	140	84	35
Net Income	4	10	15	13
R&D Expenses	22	14	12	4
Capital Expenditures	70	40	NA	NA
Total Assets	451	372	318	211
Long-term Debts	107	82	67	21
Equity	251	232	206	176
Return on Sales (Semi.)	2.1%	7.1%	17.9%	37.1%
Semi. Cap. Exp./Semi. Sales	36.1%	28.6%	NA	NA

(continued)

EXHIBIT 7 Continued

	1986	1985	1984	1983
Fujitsu				
Net Sales	11,072	7,870	6,444	5,149
Semic. Sales	1,375	1,051	1,259	928
Net Income	92	181	366	285
Semic. Operating Profit	(204)	(153)	222	136
R&D Expenses[b]	1,099	730	547	438
Semic. Capital Expenditures	197	335	473	NA
Return on Sales (Semi.)	(14.8%)	(14.6%)	17.6%	14.7%
Semi. Cap. Exp./Semi. Sales	14.3%	31.9%	37.6%	NA
Hitachi				
Net Sales	32,086	23,302	20,630	18,583
Semic. Sales	2,586	1,953	2,222	1,532
Net Income	671	698	864	711
Semic. Operating Profit	(257)	(130)	444	226
Semic. Capital Expenditures	211	428	494	NA
Return on Sales (Semi.)	(9.9%)	(6.7%)	20.0%	14.8%
Semi. Cap. Exp./Semi. Sales	8.2%	21.9%	22.2%	NA
NEC				
Net Sales	16,224	10,860	9,292	7,498
Semic. Sales	3,125	2,051	2,453	1,809
Net Income	184	126	272	191
Semic. Operating Profit	(204)	(33)	329	136
Semic. Capital Expenditures	362	572	531	NA
Return on Sales (Semi.)	(6.5%)	(1.6%)	13.4%	7.5%
Semi. Cap. Exp./Semi. Sales	11.6%	27.9%	21.7%	NA
Toshiba				
Net Sales	21,230	15,688	13,757	11,519
Semic. Sales	2,217	1,391	1,523	1,013
Net Income	217	274	354	251
Semic. Operating Profit	(207)	(140)	198	72
R&D Expenses	1,316	884	720	600
Semic. Capital Expenditures	428	572	560	NA
Return on Sales (Semi.)	(9.3%)	(10.1%)	13.0%	7.1%
Semi. Cap. Exp./Semi. Sales	19.3%	41.1%	36.8%	NA

[a]Semiconductor sales figures reported by firms in their annual reports will not always correspond to Dataquest estimates in other exhibits. Most corporate fiscal years, for instance, do not correspond to the calendar years reported by *Dataquest*.

[b]Corporate R&D; semiconductor R&D figures were not available.

Sources: Prudential Bache Securities, 1986; Dataquest, *JSIS Newsletter*, December 1986; and annual reports.

liances, including contracting with a Japanese firm to manufacture and sell selected products; and by purchasing Fairchild, it became the largest supplier of semiconductors to the U.S. government. The merger with Fairchild was only the second time American merchants joined forces, and both mergers took place in 1987.

SMALL AMERICAN PLAYERS The large merchants had captured the lion's share of industry sales for more than a decade, but competition began changing in the early 1980s. The growing cost of IC designs and software, combined with increased availability of venture capital, con-

tributed to an explosion in start-ups specializing in the design or production of custom ICs. Excess capacity, especially in Japan, led many start-ups to subcontract their manufacturing, thereby avoiding huge investments in fixed assets. These factors produced niche players like LSI Logic, which grew from nothing in 1980 to over $200 million in 1987. Founders of the successful start-ups often became multimillionaires.

THE JAPANESE SEMICONDUCTOR INDUSTRY Japan was a late entrant into semiconductors, initially relying heavily on American technology. Two actions in the mid-1970s gave Japan its initial foothold in the U.S. market. First, U.S. firms cut their capacity expansion plans during the 1975 recession, while Japanese companies continued to invest. When the market turned up in 1976–77, American firms were caught short. Second, Japanese firms took the risk of investing in large-scale commercial production of the latest generation (MOS) circuits for desktop calculators at a time when U.S. companies were largely committed to the last generation (bipolar) technology. Over the next decade, Japanese firms became the global sales leaders and low-cost producers, dominating the commodity segments of the business, especially DRAMs and SRAMs. In 1987, the rising yen and intense Korean competition were pushing Japanese firms away from volume products towards more creative research in artificial intelligence, new materials, and new system architecture.

Most Japanese competitors followed strikingly different strategies compared to their American counterparts. In manufacturing, for instance, U.S. firms historically emphasized pushing products to their technological frontiers while Japanese companies focused more heavily on raising yields and reducing costs. Japanese firms also organized their factories differently and spent more money on plant and equipment. By 1986, Japanese firms had more automation, higher average yields, and two-thirds of their plants could produce state-of-the-art chips (line width under 2 microns), while only 50% of U.S. plants had that capacity.

Large Japanese manufacturers were highly diversified compared to American merchants. On average, around 50% of Japanese semiconductor production went to large captive markets, while semiconductor revenues averaged only 9% of corporate sales. Virtually all of the top semiconductor firms in Japan had big consumer electronics divisions, which used enormous volumes of ICs. In addition, a chip that did not meet the high performance standards for a computer or industrial product might find a market in the firm's consumer electronics division. For instance, a chip that was inadequate for a computer could be suitable for a TV.

Like the U.S. industry, only a few firms dominated Japan's domestic market: five suppliers accounted for 60.3% of domestic sales. The four largest firms are profiled below.

NIPPON ELECTRIC COMPANY (NEC) NEC, a member of the Sumitomo group, was a diversified firm that was the largest merchant semiconductor company in the world. Although the company's principal areas of competitive strength were in semiconductors and communication equipment, NEC was a big player in personal computers, consumer electronics, and selected industrial electronics. In semiconductors, NEC was considered a broad-line supplier of standard parts, an aggressive leader in process innovation, and a low-cost producer with a strong customer service orientation. NEC's multiple plants in the United States enhanced its service focus in the American market. Even though NEC was usually a follower in technology, it was the first Japanese company to design its own microprocessor. After second sourcing Intel's microprocessor, the company pioneered its V series chips in 1984.[7]

HITACHI Hitachi was a highly diversified, vertically integrated manufacturer of a full line of consumer, electronics, and heavy industrial products. A $32 billion company in 1986, it was often compared in size and product mix to the General Electric Corporation. In semiconductors, Hitachi was the second largest manufacturer in the world, deriving 9% of its revenues from chips. Analysts considered the company to have superior technological abilities, a strong low-cost position, and a moderately broad product line serving consumer, industrial, and automotive markets. In 1987, Hitachi was the world's largest DRAM supplier. The company had licensing arrangements with Motorola, Texas Instruments, and had long-term supply contracts with Olivetti and BASF. It also had offshore assembly plants in many developing and developed countries, including a plant in Texas. In 1986, the company announced a cooperative venture with Fujitsu to build a 32-bit microprocessor that company officials hoped would become the industry standard. Hitachi also had a five-year cross-licensing agreement on software with IBM.

TOSHIBA Toshiba, the second largest general electrical and electronic Japanese equipment

---

[7]In 1985, Intel filed a suit claiming that NEC's V 20 microprocessor had infringed Intel's copyright on its 8086 microprocessor. A loss in this case could lead to a ban of all NEC's V 20 series microprocessors from the U.S. market.

manufacturer, after Hitachi, was a member of the Mitsui group. Toshiba was also affiliated with the General Electric Co., which owned about 10 percent of its shares, and had strategic ties with LSI Logic, Siemens, Olivetti, Hewlett-Packard, and Motorola. Semiconductors averaged 10% of the company's sales, consumer electronics 31%, heavy-electric machinery 26%, and machinery and materials 10%. Toshiba was the Japanese industry leader in process technology, and second only to NEC in total MOS production. It was also a leading producer of discrete devices. Toshiba developed one of the first chips based on gallium arsenide technology. In 1987, Toshiba stated its intention to become the world's largest ASIC vendor. (See **Exhibit 4b.**) The company signed agreements with CAD makers and six different semiconductor firms to build its software capabilities and a library of chip designs. Toshiba was also rumored to be giving away design tools to customers to entice them to buy its ASICs.

FUJITSU Japan's largest computer manufacturer, Fujitsu was the second largest manufacturer of telecommunications equipment, and fourth largest IC manufacturer. The company oriented its semiconductor production towards computer and communications applications. It was a leading producer of memory ICs with competitive strength in both dynamic and static RAM. The company had pioneered research on high-speed switching techniques as part of the cooperative Japanese effort to develop a supercomputer. Fujitsu was considered to have a strong low-cost position and a major commitment to customer service. Fujitsu was a major second source for Motorola's 8-bit microprocessor family and Intel's microprocessors and microcomputers. In 1986, Fujitsu announced its intention of acquiring Fairchild Semiconductor from Schlumberger. Negotiations progressed until 1987 when Fujitsu abruptly withdrew its offer after U.S.

government officials indicated their opposition to the merger.

OTHER COMPETITORS Several European and East Asian firms were also involved in the production of semiconductors. By the mid-1980s, Korea, in particular, was emerging as a potent competitor in commodity businesses. Korean firms gained access to state-of-the-art designs and technology by reverse engineering or through licenses from U.S. and Japanese companies. Once the Koreans had the designs, they benefited from low labor and overhead costs, a supportive government, and the rising Japanese yen. Government subsidies, fewer safety and environmental standards, and low construction costs allowed the Koreans to "ramp-up" a new plant in six months at considerably lower cost than the Americans or the Japanese. In 1987, Korea had 6–7 percent of world semiconductor production capacity but only 2–3 percent of world market share. None of the five major. Korean manufacturers, Samsung, Gold Star, Korean Electronics, Hyundai, or Daewoo, were operating at or near capacity. In April 1986, Korea launched a Semiconductor Cooperative Research Project. Funded largely with government funds, this private-public partnership targeted $119 million towards producing 4 megabit DRAMs and entry into the logic markets, especially microprocessors and ASICs. Observers believed that Korea had some of the most modernfabs in the world and could capture 10% of the world market by 1990.

European firms had traditionally concentrated on discrete and optoelectronic devices, although in the mid-1980s some European firms were making inroads into the custom design segment of the world market. The industry was comprised of a few large, vertically integrated, diversified electronic equipment manufacturers. Major firms included: Philips, Siemens, SGS-Thomson, and AEG-Telefunken.

Suppliers of Semiconductor Manufacturing Equipment

The rapid growth of the semiconductor industry spawned the growth of semiconductor equipment (SME) firms. The SME industry, which included wafer processing, testing, and assembly, was generally a low-volume business, where scale economies were relatively unimportant. In the United States, the SME industry was not very concentrated in the mid-1980s with fourteen firms accounting for 56 percent of the sales. For certain important machines, however, there may have been only one or two suppliers. Most of the manufacturers had sales in the $10 to $50 million range.

Timely delivery of state-of-the-art equipment was critical for all semiconductor manufacturers. Any new equipment that could increase yield or reduce downtime could be an important source of competitive advantage. Historically, however, relations between U.S. chip and equipment companies were strictly arm's-length and usually adversarial. In boom times, SME firms would charge premiums and in downturns, the merchants were quick to cancel orders and demand steep discounts. This began to change in the United States after the economic downturn in the industry in 1985 put several American SMEs on the verge of bankruptcy. Fearing dependence on Japanese equipment suppliers, many U.S. semiconductor merchants started seeking greater cooperation. For instance, the SEMATECH project, discussed below, included several equipment manufacturers.

The United States dominated the world SME industry, but the Japanese were making substantial inroads. The Japanese SME industry consisted of about 500 firms producing wafer processing, testing, and assembly equipment. Despite the many firms in the industry, it was fairly concentrated with twelve firms accounting for 75 percent of sales. In some critical areas in 1987, such as steppers made by Nikon Camera, Japanese firms held virtual monopolies. Whereas the U.S. equipment manufacturers had historically been independent of the chip manufacturers, many important SME producers in Japan were subsidiaries of, or were financially linked to, Japanese chip manufacturers.

Government Policy

Governments around the world had been active in their semiconductor industries. European governments had intervened extensively through subsidies and joint R&D efforts. In 1987, for instance, Germany and Holland were in the midst of a $2 billion project to give Philips and Siemens an edge in the four-megabit DRAM and one-megabit SRAM market. By contrast, the U.S. government provided little direct support to the industry during the heyday of U.S. dominance. The major exceptions were the military's procurement program in the early years of the industry, and the Very High Speed Integrated Circuit program, established by the Pentagon in 1979 to provide R&D funding ($300 million) for the development of advanced ICs designed to meet specific military needs.

The U.S. government played an additional role by allowing the industry very limited antitrust exemptions. This led the Semiconductor Industry Association (SIA) to establish the non-profit Semiconductor Research Cooperative in 1982 to fund basic research at American universities. In 1983, a group of 21 firms created the Microelectronics and Computer Technology Corporation to sponsor long-term, applied research. By the mid-1980s, however, neither effort significantly altered the competitive balance between the United States and Japan.

In 1986–87, the U.S. government started to become more active. Japan's share of the U.S. market had reached almost 20% in the summer of 1986 when the United States negotiated a trade agreement with Japan. The accord required individual Japanese firms to stop dumping chips in the United States and third markets, and specified that America's share of the Japanese market would more than double to 20% by 1991. After apparent violations of the agreement, the Reagan administration retaliated against Japan in April 1987. In the fall of 1987, Congress allocated $100 million to support a consortium of computer companies, chip makers, and semiconductor equipment manufacturers. SIA firms made an equal monetary contribution, while IBM and AT&T donated advanced proprietary chip designs for DRAMs and SRAMs, respectively. The consortium would be called SEMATECH, and its goal would be state-of-the-art manufacturing techniques to help U.S. companies reestablish dominance in memory chips.

The Japanese government had been more actively involved in semiconductors, targeting the industry very early. Government support for the industry began in the 1950s in the form of financial assistance, R&D assistance, and a liberal antitrust policy. Japan's MITI orchestrated the government support, beginning with the administration of a series of laws, codified in 1957, that exempted the computer and semiconductor industries from antitrust prosecution. Government support of the industry continued throughout the 1970s and 1980s. It is estimated that between 1976 and 1982, the Japanese government pro-

vided at least $500 million in direct subsidies and loans to the industry.

The Japanese government also played a role in coordinating competitive strategies. In the mid-1970s, MITI targeted DRAMs and selected the five largest vertically integrated electronic firms for the project. While 60% of the budget came from the companies, MITI supported the effort with interest-free loans, government scientists, and a protected domestic market. Although quantitative restrictions on imports were eliminated in 1974 and tariffs reduced to zero in 1985, there was ongoing trade friction between the United States and Japan over whether American firms had truly free market access. In addition, government R&D support came from NTT, the government telephone monopoly prior to its privatization in 1985. Over the 1976–1980 period NTT invested $350 million in VLSI research, the results of which were available to all Japanese semiconductor manufacturers. In 1987, MITI was also guiding firms to cut production and increase purchases of American chips in order to comply with the U.S.-Japan semiconductor accord.

2. The Global Computer Industry

The computer industry's importance in the global economy has been remarkable, especially given its short history of four decades. During this time, it evolved from being the province of U.S. academia and government to permeating every aspect of modern life. Computers became critical to firm and national competitiveness in numerous sectors. In 1990 the industry represented more than $300 billion in sales annually—the largest in the information technology (IT) sector. Electronic data processing equipment accounted for 50% of the $660 billion in IT revenues worldwide. The next largest segments were software and services ($140 billion, or 21%), and telecommunication equipment ($120 billion, or 18%).

As computers were revolutionizing the business world, the industry itself was undergoing radical changes. Foremost among these were the appearance of new firms and massive shifts in patterns of international trade and competition. An industry dominated by the United States and by a handful of U.S. firms evolved into a truly international industry with intensive competition among diverse firms. Technological change, firm strategies, national development, and government policies all played a part in this evolution.

Industry Characteristics

Size and Scope

The computer hardware industry comprised the manufacture, sale, and maintenance of data processing equipment, including related peripherals such as printers and disk drives. It was closely linked to related sectors of the semiconductor and telecommunications equipment industries.[1] The United States has been the largest DP market,

[1]See David B. Yoffie and Alvin G. Wint, "The Global Semiconductor Industry, 1987," Harvard Business School case number 9-388-052 and Julie Herendeen, Willis Emmons, Richard H.K. Vietor, and David B. Yoffie, "The Global Telecommunications Equipment Industry," Harvard Business School case number N9-391-020.

Research Associate Maryellen C. Costello and Associate Professor Benjamin Gomes-Casseres prepared this note as the basis for class discussion rather than to illustrate either effective or ineffective handling of an administrative situation.

although demand in Asia and Europe has been growing rapidly (see **Exhibit 1**). The top 100 firms in the industry employed almost 2 million people worldwide, with about 1.2 million in the United States, 270,000 in Asia, and the rest in Europe.

The industry could be segmented in a number of ways, and its economics varied between segments. Peripherals could be separated from central processing units (CPUs), which in turn could be classified by size and cost. Sales of mainframe systems and personal computers (PCs) each accounted for 22% of the total in 1988, but the latter was growing two to four times as fast as the former. Sales of peripherals, such as disk drives and printers, also grew rapidly, partly because they were used with PCs. Peripherals represented about one-third of the total. Since about 1982, the minicomputer segment (14% of total) had been squeezed between booming PC sales and continued strong mainframe sales.[2]

IBM and Early Development of the Industry

While there had been research in the 1940s on electronic digital computers and production of a few one-of-a-kind machines, the commercialization of computers really got underway after the Second World War. Through the 1960s, U.S. firms, led by IBM, turned out increasingly sophisticated machines and dominated almost every market in the world. By 1971, IBM had a 62% share of the world computer market, other U.S. manufacturers combined had a 30% share, while European and Japanese producers had 4.1% and 3.4%, respectively. Europe's most important computer firm, the British ICL, had a 2.6% share and Japan's top two companies, Fujitsu and NEC, each had about 1%.

Despite many innovative management policies, analysts in the 1950s viewed IBM as a technologically conservative company, and its competitors regularly announced new and supe-

[2]In 1988, *Electronics* defined PCs as systems costing under $5,000, and mainframes as systems between $400,000 and $5 million. Minicomputers cost between $20,000 and $1 million.

rior technology. At the time, IBM sold six different and incompatible computer lines. This meant that software written for one machine could not be used on another; software represented about 40% of development costs for a new machine at the time. Also, different machines were designed specifically for scientific or business use.

To address these issues, IBM announced its System/360 line of computers in 1964. Named for the 360 degrees in a circle, it was designed to encompass all computing needs. For the first time, a broad "family" of compatible, multi-purpose computers was available, enabling users to upgrade without having to replace their existing databases or programs. This was also the first time transistors were used in computers, representing a leap forward from vacuum-tube and magnetic-core technologies. IBM took a big risk in launching this system—*Fortune* called it "IBM's $5,000,000,000 Gamble"—because of the enormous cost of engineering and producing it. After initial startup problems, the gamble paid off in increasing market share and profits. By 1970, IBM computers comprised 70% of the installed base of equipment in the United States. When IBM launched the System/370 in the early 1970s, its lead seemed insurmountable to General Electric and RCA, which soon abandoned their mainframe computer businesses. Across the Pacific and Atlantic, however, firms and governments launched aggressive programs to catch up with IBM.

Technological Change and Standards

The explosive growth of the industry occurred because of the technologies that reduced both the size and cost of computers. In the large systems era of the 1960s and 1970s, when mainframes were the norm, computers were built from the ground up with proprietary hardware architectures and unique components. New, standardized semiconductors introduced in the late 1970s were more reliable, smaller, faster, cheaper, and more powerful than earlier components. Through "downsizing," wholly new industry segments were created and came to threaten sales of the

EXHIBIT 1 Consumption of Dataprocessing Equipment, 1975–1990 (Sources: Compiled from *Electronics* and Gartmer Group, *Worldwide Yardstick*).

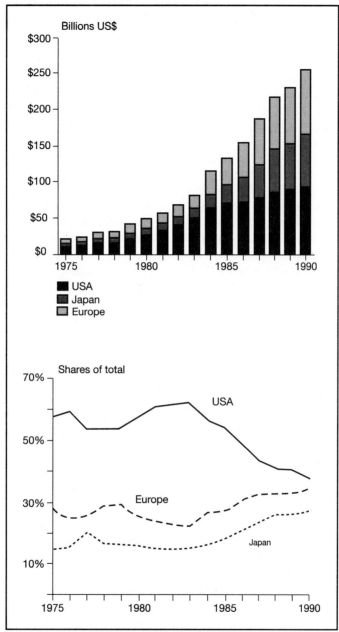

large systems. Minicomputers came to do the work of mainframes in the 1970s, and PCs and workstations (which in many cases could be made from readily available components) began to replace minis in the 1980s.

The large systems era was also the heyday of proprietary operating systems.[3] Originally, IBM and other mainframe vendors sold the operating system software bundled in with the hardware. As pressure from the U.S. Justice Department mounted, IBM began to sell unbundled hardware and software after 1969. This opened the door for other firms to produce and sell IBM-compatible hardware, so-called plug-compatible machines (PCMs). Even after 1969, however, IBM software was written specifically for a particular hardware architecture—in the case of System/360 for the whole family of computers. Although IBM's PCM competitors began to carve into its hardware market, IBM's architecture and operating system continued to dominate the large systems market.

The minicomputer industry also had proprietary operating systems, but while the most prominent was Digital's VMS, none was as dominant as IBM's in mainframes. The microcomputer revolution of the 1980s gave rise to "open systems," which allowed various hardware and software firms to make and sell products that would be compatible with each other. To achieve this, the operating system producers—Microsoft for MS-DOS and AT&T for UNIX—licensed to others to make compatible products. Furthermore, the PC hardware standard was open, too, since IBM—which introduced it in 1982—used off-the-shelf components and readily available Intel microprocessors. Apple's architecture and operating systems, however, remained proprietary and "closed": other than Apple itself, very few vendors were licensed to make compatible equipment or software.

Because of the "portability" of software applications resulting from open standards and the availability of standard components, some segments of computer hardware have become close to commodity businesses. According to *The Wall Street Journal*, "the [hardware] industry is condemned to ceaseless innovation, price cutting, and product cycles that are nasty, brutish and short."[4]

Production, Marketing, and R&D

The economics of the industry varied by segment and over time. The cost of goods sold was proportionately higher in PCs and peripherals than in mainframes. But selling expenses were lower for PCs and peripherals because they were usually sold through indirect channels. Mainframes required direct sales and substantial after-sales service. On average, about one third of the employees in leading computer firms worked in manufacturing, one quarter in sales, one tenth in research, and almost one fifth in maintenance and repair. Labor costs were not critical to competitiveness, though they could be important in the production of components. Even in PCs, direct labor accounted for less than 5% of total variable cost, and overhead for another 10%. More important were costs of components, such as semiconductors, printed circuit boards, and disk drives, which accounted for about three-quarters of variable costs.

From the outset, IBM leased its mainframe systems, setting the industry norm through the late 1970s. Leasing reduced the up-front cost to users and facilitated upgrading, while tying them to IBM service and support. This practice made entry difficult for firms too small to fund the up-front costs and strengthened the position of firms with large installed bases. But this pattern changed over time. At the U.S. government's insistence, IBM made equipment available for outright purchase in the late 1950s. Thus, when third-party leasing companies entered the market in the early 1970s, they were able to do so with IBM's machines. Digital Equipment Corporation (DEC) began selling minicomputers outright to the scientific and academic communities in the 1960s. By the late 1970s, IBM itself started emphasizing purchases over leasing. By the 1980s, PCs were being sold by mass-market retailers and mail-order discounters.

---

[3]An operating system was the software interface between the computer's hardware and the application programs. It managed files, memory, input and output, and other functions. For example, MS-DOS was the most popular operating system for PCs in the 1980s.

[4] *The Wall Street Journal*, September 5, 1991, p.1.

Aside from production costs and marketing, R&D was critical to competitiveness in computers, as it determined product features and computing power. Leading computer firms invested almost 10% of revenue annually in R&D, and another 10% in capital expenditures on new plant and equipment. Not surprisingly, PCs and mainframes were on opposite ends of this spectrum, too. Developing a new mainframe cost about $500 million and took five years; PCs required significantly less time and money, and designs of one firm could often be copied within months by others.

International Trade and Competitiveness

Demand and costs of production influenced the location of plants and sales worldwide, and thus the pattern of trade. These factors changed over time, and so accounted for some of the competitive shifts in the industry.

Early Trade Patterns

From the early 1960s, the United States was the largest exporter of computer products. Still, non-U.S. production grew quickly and major markets in Europe and Japan soon came to be served primarily by local production. Much of this local production, however, as well as what few exports these countries had, bore the logo of IBM. In 1960, IBM was already operating in 87 countries, had 19 manufacturing plants abroad, and employed 30,000 people outside of the United States. By 1972, IBM World Trade was active in 126 countries, with 22 manufacturing plants and 115,000 employees. Between 1967 and 1972, IBM World Trade's revenues had grown at 22% per year and represented 44% of IBM's total volume.

The pattern of trade in the 1960s and early 1970s, therefore, reflected IBM's international production strategy. Starting in the mid-1960s, the company pursued a goal of balanced trade in North America, Western Europe, and Japan.[5] IBM's booming foreign sales grew largely through local (or regional) production rather than by exports from the United States. IBM reportedly accounted for all of Japan's exports in 1972 and cross-shipments among IBM plants in Europe were thought to account for the bulk of exports registered by European countries in the mid-1960s. At this time, IBM accounted for three-quarters of the markets in West Germany, Italy, and France, half of the market in the United Kingdom, and about two-fifths in Japan.

Shifting Competitive Advantages

Overall, in 1990, world trade in data processing equipment and parts[6] amounted to about $70 billion, or one-quarter of consumption. The share of imports and exports in consumption varied over time and across regions, as did the composition of finished goods and parts (see **Exhibit 2**).[7] While U.S. imports and Asian exports grew robustly during the late 1970s and the 1980s, Europe remained the most dependent on imports and the least successful in exports. The difference in trade patterns between Japan and Europe has become more pronounced, as the trade balances in **Exhibit 3** show. While the United States continued to run a surplus in the industry, this surplus fell from $3.5 billion in 1978 to $2.5 billion in 1990, and as a share of total computer exports it declined from 80% to 10%.

[5]No region was meant to be self-sufficient. Rather, the aim was to balance any imports against exports. In fact, IBM Japan exported about 25% to 30% of its production and IBM Europe produced 90% of its sales in the region, implying imports of 10% of sales.

[6]"Parts" here excludes generic semiconductor and other components, but includes semi-finished equipment, printed-circuit boards, disk drives, and other electrical and mechanical components intended specifically for computers.

[7]Unless otherwise noted, the trade data for Europe exclude trade *among* Belgium, France, the Netherlands, the United Kingdom, West Germany, Italy, and Sweden; they thus represent an estimate of European trade with non-European countries. The data shown for NICs include only Hong Kong, Singapore, and South Korea; no comparable data were available for Taiwan.

EXHIBIT 2A Trade and Consumption of Computers and Parts, 1978–1990 (billions US$)

	1978	1981	1984	1987	1990	Annual Growth 1978–90	Trade as Share of Consumption				
							1978	1981	1984	1987	1990
Imports											
By USA	0.9	1.8	8.1	15.3	23.4	31%	5%	5%	12%	19%	24%
By Asia	0.8	1.7	3.2	5.2	12.2	25	15	19	17	12	17
By Europe	3.1	6.0	10.2	18.8	27.8	20	33	44	33	30	31
Total	**4.8**	**9.5**	**21.4**	**39.3**	**63.4**	**24**	**15**	**17**	**18**	**21**	**24**
Exports											
By USA	4.4	9.0	14.0	18.8	25.9	16%	26%	26%	21%	23%	26%
By Asia	0.8	2.0	8.5	18.9	33.3	36	16	22	44	42	47
By Europe	1.8	2.9	4.9	9.3	11.8	17	20	21	16	15	13
Total	**7.1**	**13.9**	**27.5**	**47.0**	**71.0**	**21**	**22**	**24**	**24**	**25**	**27**
Consumption											
By USA	17.1	35.0	65.8	82.1	97.8	16%					
By Asia	5.4	8.7	19.2	44.7	71.4	24					
By Europe	9.3	13.7	31.2	61.7	89.7	21					
Total	**31.8**	**57.4**	**116.2**	**188.5**	**258.9**	**19**					

Sources: Trade data from the United Nations (includes SITC 752 plus 7599); consumption from *Electronics* and Gartner Group, *Yardstick Worldwide*.

The underlying theme in these trends is the rapid development of Japan, and to a lesser extent the newly industrializing countries (NICs), into successful exporters of computers. At the same time, the position of the United States declined. A world industry dominated by U.S.-based production in the early 1970s had become one where the United States and Japan held more similar positions. The slow decline of Europe as a production site was less dramatic than that of the United States, since Europe never held a dominant position in the industry (see **Exhibit 4**).

Factor costs were only partly responsible

EXHIBIT 2B Parts as Share of Total DP Trade of[a]

	1978	1981	1984	1987	1990
Imports					
By USA	57%	61%	55%	52%	33%
By Japan	26	29	30	34	41
By Europe	27	29	31	28	29
By NICS	77	58	50	57	51
Total	**35**	**37**	**42**	**40**	**34**
Exports					
By USA	40%	44%	48%	51%	39%
By Japan	46	35	20	26	36
By Europe	34	36	41	41	33
By NICS	98	89	56	35	30
Total	**41**	**43**	**42**	**40**	**36**

[a] SITC 7599 divided by 752 + 7599

for these shifts. First, wages were a small component of production cost. Second, electronics wage differentials between Japan, the United States, and Europe had all but vanished by 1990. From the mid-1970s to the mid-1980s, Japanese wages were half those in the United States, but this gap had closed. European wages fluctuated around the U.S. level over most of this period. Labor costs remained low only in the Asian NICs, even though these too rose from about one-sixth to one-half those in the United States.

Only the Asian NICs have been successful in segments where labor costs were important. Most of the major computer firms have manufacturing plants there for labor-intensive components such as keyboards, printers, disk drives, and tape drives. In 1990, Taiwan alone exported $5.2 billion in computer products, making it the second largest Asian exporter behind Japan. Its exports represented 66% of world exports of PC system boards and 20% to 40% of monitors, power supplies, keyboards, graphics cards, and scanners. Thirty percent of these exports were made by subsidiaries of foreign firms, and 47% were sold by Taiwanese firms on an OEM basis to foreign firms.

The rise of Asian production and exports was also related to other factors. The volume and sophistication of demand for computers grew fast

EXHIBIT 3 Imports and Exports of Computers and Parts, 1978–1990 (in billion US$) (Source: Compiled from United Nations data. Includes SITC 752 and 7599).

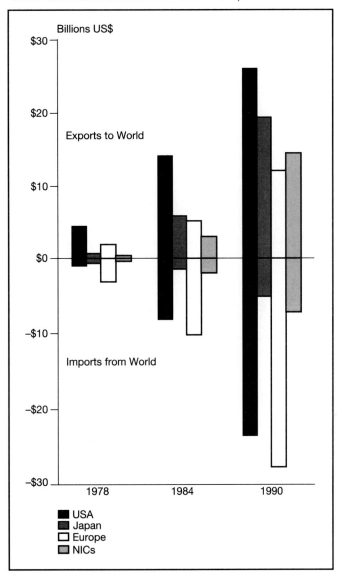

in Japan, and many of the leading-edge technologies (e.g., laptop computers) became popular there first. Related industries that fed directly into the computer industry, such as semiconductors, consumer electronics, and office printing and copying, blossomed in Japan. Japanese universities turned out large numbers of electronic engineers, and government as well as firms invested heavily in R&D.

The conditions behind the rising competitive advantage of the Asian NICs were somewhat different. Domestic demand was less important, and technology was usually acquired from the outside through licensing or foreign direct investment. But here, too, related industries played important roles, as skills first applied in simple consumer electronics were transferred to assembly of computer products. While they remained

EXHIBIT 4 Export Shares and Comparative Advantage by Region, 1978–1990 (DP equipment only) (Source: Compiled from United Nations data (includes only SITC 752).)

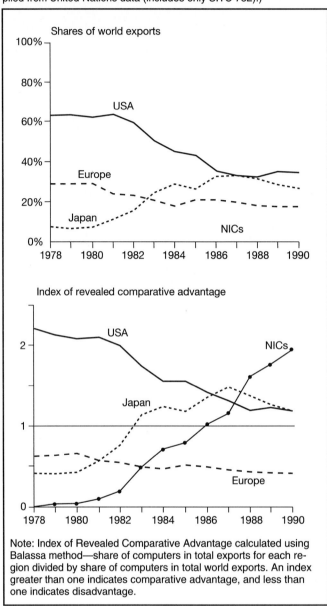

Note: Index of Revealed Comparative Advantage calculated using Balassa method—share of computers in total exports for each region divided by share of computers in total world exports. An index greater than one indicates comparative advantage, and less than one indicates disadvantage.

dependent on Japan and the United States for key components such as microprocessors and liquid-crystal display screens, the Asian NICs invested heavily in production of commodity semiconductors.

The destination of exports and the origins of imports—as distinguished from overall trade vol-

umes—also developed in distinct ways since the late 1970s, as shown in **Exhibit 5**. In short, the United States became the premier importer of Japanese and NIC goods and the dominant exporter to Europe and the rest of the world. By 1990, the United States ran $4 billion trade deficits with both Japan and the NICs, and an

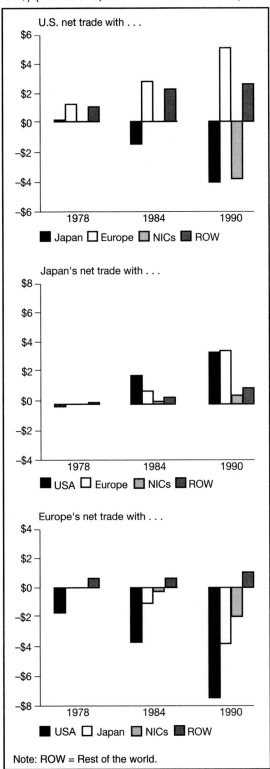

EXHIBIT 5 Computer Trade Balances by Region, 1978–1990 (bilateral balances in billion US$) (Source: Compiled from United Nations data).

U.S. net trade with . . .

■ Japan □ Europe ▨ NICs ■ ROW

Japan's net trade with . . .

■ USA □ Europe ▨ NICs ■ ROW

Europe's net trade with . . .

■ USA □ Japan ▨ NICs ■ ROW

Note: ROW = Rest of the world.

equally large surplus with the rest of the world. Japan, in turn, ran trade surpluses with all the regions, with Europe and the United States each taking $4 billion in net exports. The Asian NICs depended even more on the United States as a destination for their exports, and ran deficits only with Japan.

Trade, Foreign Investment, and International Strategy

One reason for this pattern lay in the role of firm-level strategy and competition in determining trade flows. From the Japanese firms' point of view, the United States was a larger, more accessible market than Europe, partly because these firms had experience exporting consumer electronics to the United States. Europe had traditionally been more closed to Japanese imports and internally fragmented. Several other factors made a presence in the U.S. market more important to these firms than a presence in Europe: the United States had more sophisticated demand, more advanced technology, and was home to the leading firms in the industry. This pattern changed during the 1980s, as Europe slowly became a more important destination for Japanese exports.

For the U.S. firms, Europe and Latin America were the traditional destinations of exports and foreign investment. The Japanese market was relatively closed to U.S. firms; IBM was strong in Japan only by virtue of its local production. As a result, more than 32% of the total sales of U.S. data-processing firms were in Europe in 1990, compared with 11% in Asia (see Exhibit 6).

Not all U.S. computer firms followed such foreign investment strategies, and those that did not often failed in foreign markets. Some entrants, like RCA and GE, never made a substantial commitment to foreign markets, preferring instead to export or license technology. Neither established a presence abroad, and both exited the business in the 1970s. Sperry invested more in foreign markets, including an early marketing joint venture in Japan that led to Nihon Unisys's strong position there. DEC's European production strategy was similar to IBM's: it produced most of what it sold in the region, and became a strong contender there.

Overall, U.S.-based computer firms were disproportionately active abroad. The assets of their foreign affiliates were $58 billion in 1986, or fully 20% of the total foreign assets of U.S. manufacturing firms. These assets represented 58% of the total assets of the parent firms, a higher share than for any of the other major industrial categories tracked by the U.S. Commerce Department. Furthermore, just over half of the foreign assets of U.S. computer firms were in Europe in 1986, down from 66% in 1982.

The role of foreign investment in supplying regional markets could be estimated by taking total consumption, and subtracting (a) sales in the local market by domestic firms and (b) imports from foreign firms abroad. The residual could be ascribed to local production by foreign firms. By this method, in 1990 local production by foreign firms accounted for only 6% of U.S. consumption, but 21% of Asian consumption, and 48% of European consumption. In both Japan and Europe, local production by foreign firms was twice as large as imports.

Government Policies

In addition to economic and technological trends, the policies of national governments affected thedevelopment of the industry worldwide. The large foreign investment by U.S. computer firms, for example, was partly motivated by host government pressure. Jacques Maisonrouge, CEO of IBM World Trade, said in 1973: "Political power is stronger than economic power when the two collide."[8] In accordance with this motto, IBM traded off responsiveness to local political constituencies for global efficiency: it continued to expand local production and R&D in Japan and the major European countries, even when exports from the United States or from a smaller number of plants might have been more efficient. In theory, competitive bidding among IBM plants determined the allocation of production, but a study by a former IBM manager noted: "The balancing act involved in assigning new production requirements often revolves around political factors that are little related to economics."[9]

Government policies affected competition in other ways as well. In particular, they often supported domestic firms against foreign competitors or encouraged technology development and diffusion. While American, European, and Japanese governments all influenced the development of the industry, the nature and effects of their policies differed.

Defense Spending and Antitrust in the United States

The U.S. military's support began in World War II and continued through the Cold War until the late 1960s, when the Vietnam War diverted funds. Most of the innovations in computer design and component technologies in the 1960s stemmed directly from government-supported R&D. The military funded the early, experimental, one-of-a-kind computers of the 1950s and continued funding leading-edge research through the 1980s. Between 1967 and 1975, the defense department and other agencies spent an average of $280 million (1982 dollars) annually on research in mathematics and computer science; this average rose to $380 million in 1975–1986. While government assistance often provided the early spark, private R&D targeted to the commercial market became the norm in the 1970s and later. For example, IBM's annual expenditure of internal funds on R&D climbed steadily from $676 million in 1972 to $4.1 billion in 1984, and $6.2 billion in 1990.

Through the 1970s and 1980s, 40% of U.S. government math and computer research budgets went to support work in universities. The Defense Advanced Research Projects Agency (DARPA) led this effort, but the Department of Energy (DOE), the National Science Foundation

[8]Quoted in Nancy Foy, *The Sun Never Sets on IBM* (New York: Morrow, 1974), p. 158.
[9]David Mercer, *The Global IBM: Leadership in Multinational Management* (New York: Dodd, Mead, 1987), p. 168.

(NSF), the National Aeronautical and Space Administration (NASA), and the National Institutes of Health (NIH) also participated. The NSF alone spent $200 million (1982 dollars) from 1956 to 1970. These programs were in addition to military and government procurement, the second most significant source of support for the industry. In 1953, federal agencies used an estimated 54% of the stock of general purpose computers; even by 1961, 15% of IBM's revenues and more than 50% of Control Data's came from sales of special products and services to U.S. government agencies. However, by the 1970s, federal installations accounted for only about 5% of the stock of computers in the United States, as the commercial market had grown dramatically. Still, through the 1980s, the federal government continued to buy about half the supercomputers made in the United States.

U.S. government policies also regulated domestic competition. The Justice Department initiated three major antitrust suits against IBM, which had important implications for the evolution of the industry. In 1956, IBM signed a consent decree that restricted its marketing practices and affected the dissemination of computer technology. In 1969, the company agreed to "unbundle" hardware and software. There was also much discussion in the early 1970s of whether and how to break up IBM as a remedy for its alleged monopolistic power. The biggest thorn in IBM's side was the suit beginning in 1969 that the Reagan administration finally determined was without merit in 1982. This suit was "stressful" for IBM, according to Thomas Watson, Jr., the company's CEO from 1956 through 1971:

> The government objected to virtually our entire way of doing business, from our use of total system sales—supplying customers with complete installations including hardware, software, engineering help, training, and maintenance—to the big discounts we gave universities. Strangely, none of these practices was illegal *per se* . . . Nothing in my experience prepared me for how treacherous the legal process can be when it gets out of hand.[10]

Industrial Policy in Japan

While Japanese research into computing began in the 1930s, governmental involvement remained minimal until MITI was granted extensive power over the computer industry in 1957. Over the next quarter century, Japanese computer firms benefited from government efforts to spur technology cooperation, R&D, and domestic demand, while being protected from foreign competition. As *Forbes* put it in 1977: "Systematically, doggedly, as they did in cameras, cars and TVs, the Japanese are mounting an attack on the worldwide computer market."[11]

The primary target of the Japanese government's actions in information technology was IBM Japan. In the late 1950s, IBM requested permission from MITI to produce computers locally. After three years of negotiations, IBM gained MITI's approval, but only in exchange for licenses to its basic computer patents as part of a cross-licensing agreement. In addition, IBM's local business was to be limited; MITI restricted the number and type of machines manufactured and IBM's market share, and required the firm to export about one third of its Japanese production. "The government really put some clamps on us that legislated against our progress," according to George Conrades, head of IBM Asia/Pacific Group.[12]

During the 1960s, Japan also imposed import duties of between 15% and 25% on computers, as well as import quotas. As part of a "Buy Japanese" program, prospective purchasers of computers from non-Japanese firms were subjected to government interrogation and social ostracism. The government also encouraged domestic demand through the Japan Electronic Computer Company (JECC). This leasing company used government money and low-cost loans to finance rentals of machines from Japanese manufacturers. Japanese customers would place orders with JECC, which would then buy machines from the Japanese vendors and lease them to customers at competitive rates.

NTT, Japan's telephone monopoly since

---

[10]Thomas Watson, Jr., *Father, Son & Co.: My Life at IBM and Beyond* (New York: Bantam Books, 1990), p. 376.

[11]"The Coming Japanese Computer Push," *Forbes*, May 15, 1977, p. 59.

[12]Quoted in Robert Sobel, *IBM vs. Japan: The Struggle for the Future* (New York: Stein and Day, 1986), p. 152.

1952, acted in concert with MITI in supporting domestic computer manufacturers. It did early research on computers and funded several major joint R&D projects from the 1970s through the 1990s. It bought only Japanese computers for its own operations, and had to approve any equipment linked to its communication network. These programs were funded partly through consignment fees and low-interest loans from the government.

But even with this government support, in the 1960s Japanese companies were dependent on American firms for technology. In 1961, Hitachi signed a technology transfer arrangement with RCA; NEC linked up with Honeywell in 1962, as did Mitsubishi with TRW; Sperry Rand was forced by MITI into a joint venture with Oki Electric in 1963; and Toshiba signed with General Electric in 1964. Only Fujitsu did not manufacture machines designed by a foreign partner; it was also the only one with a sizable research department. When IBM announced its System/360 line, Japanese computers were still far behind in technology, performance, quality and price; thus, MITI delayed production of the 360 series in Japan until 1966 and limited production volume.

IBM's announcement of the System/370 in 1970 was traumatic for the Japanese. Since most of their American partners exited the industry, the Japanese firms were in a quandary. MITI then formed three pivotal joint research projects, which were to shape the rise of the Japanese industry. One project involved Fujitsu and Hitachi, and was aimed to develop IBM-type mainframes and to challenge IBM's position directly. The second, between Toshiba and NEC, was to develop mid-size computers. The third, between Mitsubishi and Oki, was to focus on smaller computers and peripherals. This work was subsidized by MITI, whose contribution to industrial R&D in computers rose dramatically from 7% in 1970 to 84% in 1974. All together, the value of Japanese government subsidies, tax benefits and loans to the industry amounted to an estimated average $60 million annually between 1961 and 1969, $310 million annually between 1970 and 1975, and $635 million annually between 1976 and 1981.[13]

By the time the Japanese market was "liberalized" in 1975, domestic firms had gained a substantial share of the market and were moving to compete on a world scale. In addition, there remained strong incentives for domestic production: the government, which represented a quarter of the total demand, was still required to buy Japanese products. IBM was among the first to recognize the future role that Japanese firms would play in global competition. IBM World Trade's Management Committee warned in 1972:

> [T]he Japanese manufacturers have demonstrated commitment to an overseas marketing strategy. . . . In light of the Japanese Government's demonstrated support of this exporting strategy for computers, the effect of our action programs in Japan will be at best to delay the inevitable schedule by perhaps one year.[14]

Through the rest of the 1970s and the 1980s, MITI's role in the computer industry remained significant but declining. This was due in part to the opening of the Japanese market: although informal restrictions were still in place, continued overt protectionism and subsidies would not be tolerated overseas. The improving market position and financial strength of Japanese firms also created a shift in the balance of power towards the firms and away from MITI. MITI's objective shifted in the late 1970s to focusing Japanese firms on developing advanced semiconductor technology, so they could anticipate and compete with IBM's future offerings rather than imitate them. Other government-backed projects of the 1980s, including the Supercomputer and Fifth Generation projects, sought to end Japanese dependence on foreign technologies and software standards.

National Champions and Technology Collaboration in Europe

Aware of their lagging status even as early as the 1960s, European governments, individually and later in concert, attempted to close the gap in in-

---

[13]These values were equivalent to 188%, 168%, and 93% of the amount that the firms invested in R&D and plant and equipment during the same period, respectively.

[14]Minutes of February 28, 1972, quoted in Leo A. Morehouse and John W. Rosenblum, "IBM World Trade Corporation," Harvard Business School case number 374-303 (1974).

formation technology. In addition to funding R&D, they created "national champions" to achieve economies of scale in local markets. These firms were favored in government procurement and received subsidies in various forms. As late as 1992, there was controversy over the $1 billion that the French government was considering injecting into ailing Groupe Bull. But major scale economies were elusive— each nation supported its own champion, so that none was able to establish strong market positions across the whole region. Bull was strong only in France, Siemens in Germany, Olivetti in Italy, and ICL in Britain. And European markets were generally open to foreign investment and trade, allowing American firms to establish important positions everywhere.

European countries supported their firms with research funds as well. Average annual expenditures on computer and microelectronics programs in France, Germany, and Britain rose from $184 million in 1967–1975 to $356 million in the late 1970s. Until the 1980s, these national governments usually acted alone, and with differing philosophies. The "mission-oriented" countries—Britain and France—followed focused, centrally directed programs aimed at well-defined national goals and often tied to the military. The policies of "diffusion-oriented" countries—Germany and Sweden—were less targeted and attempted instead to spread technologies widely through product standardization and cooperative research.

While European countries had long cooperated in steel, aviation, and space, it was not until the early 1980s that the various governments began to act jointly on information technology. Prior to this time, most intra-European collaboration was driven by the private sector. One notable case was Unidata, a 1973 joint venture between Siemens, Philips, and the French CII (a predecessor of Bull's). It fell apart after only two years when the French decided to seek American partners. The three firms had been unable to resolve differences over technology and markets.

In 1982, the European Community (EC) launched the European Strategic Project on Information Technology (ESPRIT), a ten-year, multi-billion dollar program to promote cooperative R&D. It offered partial government funding for approved "pre-competitive" joint R&D projects among European firms. Results of this research were to be licensed on reasonable terms to all other ESPRIT participants and at no charge to a firm's partners on the project. Local subsidiaries of foreign firms could participate, but on limited terms, in these projects. However, ESPRIT innovations were to be applied only within Europe. By 1986, ESPRIT was funding 200 projects, involving 240 partners and 2,900 researchers, and had exhausted nearly its phase-one budget of $1.3 billion, half of which came from the EC.

Another cooperative research program was the European Research Coordination Agency (EUREKA), which targeted energy, new materials, and biotechnology, in addition to information technologies. This was not an EC program, but involved nineteen Western European countries. It funded cooperative R&D with commercial applications rather than basic research. After receiving qualification as a EUREKA project, the participants would negotiate with their national governments, who agreed to provide funds for approved projects. By the end of 1987, 600 companies were participating in 165 projects costing $4 billion, about 40% of which was public funding. About a quarter of this amount was for information technology.

Competition among Firms

The economics of the industry led to a classic oligopolistic structure. The mainframe segment was much more concentrated than others; its top four firms sold 77% of the world total in 1990, compared to 51% for microcomputers and 30% for peripherals. IBM alone accounted for 51%, 24%, and 10% of the sales in these segments. These shares were somewhat lower in the 1970s, but not by much. They indicate the great extent of the barriers to entry facing new firms.

U.S. firms dominated the world computer industry almost since its inception. Even in 1990, U.S. firms accounted for 64% of world computer sales and 88% of U.S. sales. Their position in Europe (62% of market) and in Asia (28%) was stronger than that of U.S. firms in most other comparable industries (see **Exhibit 6**). These foreign markets were, in turn, critical to the U.S. firms. The share of foreign sales in IBM's total, for example, grew steadily from 20% in 1960 to a peak of 54% in 1979; after that it declined and rose again to 59% in 1989.

The way computer firms chose to deploy their resources internationally could be crucial to their performance. The dominant U.S. firms in the 1970s organized themselves differently, pursued different strategies, and developed different capabilities (see **Exhibit 7**). While the European and, especially, the Japanese firms were still in their infancy, it took no exceptional strategies and management for U.S. firms to penetrate foreign markets. But by the mid-1970s, foreign firms gained capabilities and market position, first in their home country, and later, abroad.

EXHIBIT 6 Geographic Positions of Computer Firms, 1984–1990

Market Shares of Firms in Each Market (By nationality of firm)				Relative Weight of Geographic Markets in Each Firm's Sales (By nationality of firm)			
Total market sizes (billions US$)				Total sales (billiions US$)			
	1984	1990	CAGR		1984	1990	CAGR
USA	66	98	6.8%	IBM	43	65	7.2%
Europe	31	90	19.2%	All US	95	175	10.7%
Asia	19	71	24.5%	Japanese	14	64	28.1%
Other	8	16	12.6%	European	15	34	14.9%
World total	124	275	14.2%	Total	124	275	14.2%
Share of US market accounted for by:				Weight of US market in total for:			
IBM	39%	26%		IBM	60%	39%	
All US	94%	88%		All US	65%	49%	
Japanese	2%	6%		Japanese	10%	10%	
European	4%	4%		European	17%	13%	
				All	53%	36%	
Share of European market by:				Weight of Europe in total for:			
IBM	34%	27%		IBM	25%	38%	
All US	63%	62%		All US	21%	32%	
Japanese	3%	7%		Japanese	6%	10%	
European	34%	30%		European	72%	79%	
				All	25%	33%	
Share of Asian market by				Weight of Asia in total for:			
IBM	18%	13%		IBM	8%	14%	
All US	35%	28%		All US	7%	11%	
Japanese	61%	69%		Japanese	81%	77%	
European	4%	3%		European	5%	5%	
				All	15%	26%	
Share of other markets by:				Weight of other markets in totals:			
IBM	41%	38%		IBM	8%	9%	
All US	83%	79%		All US	7%	7%	
Japanese	6%	11%		Japanese	3%	3%	
European	11%	6%		European	6%	3%	
				All	6%	6%	
Share of world market by:							
IBM	34%	24%					
All US	76%	64%					
Japanese	12%	23%					
European	12%	12%					

Source: Compiled from Gartner Group, *Yardstick Worldwide*.

EXHIBIT 7 Product Positions of Computer Firms, 1984–1990

Market Shares of Firms in Each Segment (by nationality of firm)				Relative Weight of Geographic Markets in Each (by nationality of firm)			
Total Market Sizes (billions US$)	1984	1990	CAGR	**Total sales (billiions US$)**	1984	1990	CAGR
Mainframes	21	36	9.4%	IBM	43	65	7.2%
Minis	19	31	7.9%	All US	95	175	10.7%
Micros	14	43	20.4%	Japanese	14	64	28.1%
Peripherals	22	51	15.0%	European	15	34	14.9%
Software	10	29	20.0%	Total	124	275	14.2%
Other	38	85	14.3%				
Total	124	275	14.2%				
Share of Mainframe Market				**Weight of Mainframes in Total for:**			
IBM	67%	51%		IBM	33%	31%	
All US	85%	66%		All US	19%	15%	
				Japanese	17%	16%	
Japanese	11%	28%		European	4%	5%	
European	3%	6%		Total	17%	14%	
Share of Minicomputer Market				**Weight of Minis in Total for:**			
IBM	21%	21%		IBM	10%	9%	
All US	74%	72%		All US	15%	14%	
Japanese	14%	16%		Japanese	18%	12%	
European	12%	12%		European	16%	10%	
				Total	16%	13%	
Share of Microcomputer Market				**Weight of Micros in Total for:**			
IBM	43%	24%		IBM	14%	15%	
All US	82%	61%		All US	12%	14%	
Japanese	9%	24%		Japanese	9%	16%	
European	9%	13%		European	9%	16%	
				Total	11%	15%	
Share of Peripherals Market				**Weight of Peripherals in Totals:**			
IBM	23%	10%		IBM	12%	8%	
All US	64%	48%		All US	15%	14%	
Japanese	20%	38%		Japanese	30%	30%	
European	17%	13%		European	24%	21%	
				Total	18%	18%	
Share of Software Market				**Weight of Software in Total for:**			
IBM	33%	35%		IBM	7%	15%	
All US	76%	70%		All US	8%	12%	
Japanese	11%	18%		Japanese	7%	8%	
European	13%	11%		European	8%	9%	
				Total	8%	10%	

Source: Compiled from Gartner Group, *Yardstick Worldwide.*

When the Japanese government identified computers as a strategic industry, domestic manufacturers held less than 7% of their home market. Even by 1975, none of the world's top ten computer manufacturers were Japanese. However, by 1990, Japanese firms held 69% of the Asian market, and 23% of the world market, up from 12% in 1984. By then, four were among the world top fifteen firms (see **Exhibit 8**). Competition in Japan developed differently than in the United States or Europe. Although IBM had the largest sales before 1979, the top tier of the Japanese market was split four ways, and by 1989, Fujitsu, NEC, IBM and Hitachi each held between 12% and 15% of the market. By contrast, in the United States and Europe IBM led with

EXHIBIT 8 Top 15 Computer Firms Worldwide, 1975–1990

1975	1985	1990	1990 DP Rev. (billions US$)
IBM	IBM	IBM	64.6
Burroughs	DEC	Fujitsu	16.0
Honeywell	Sperry	DEC	13.1
Sperry	Burroughs	NEC	11.8
CDC	Fujitsu	Hitachi	10.8
NCR	NCR	Unisys	10.1
Bull	NEC	HP	8.3
DEC	CDC	Siemens-Nixdorf	7.0
ICL	HP	Olivetti	6.5
Nixdorf	Siemens	Bull	6.4
NEC	Hitachi	Apple	5.7
Memorex	Olivetti	NCR	5.4
HP	Wang	Toshiba	4.1
TRW	Xerox	Compaq	3.6
Olivetti	Honeywell	Philips	3.3
		Top 100	**275.0**

Source: Compiled from data from McKinsey & Co. and Gartner Group, *Yardstick Worldwide*.

about a 25% share, followed by a group of firms each with between 3% and 5%.

Thus, by the late 1970s, U.S. and Japanese firms dominated their home markets. The Europeans, on the other hand, were weak in their own region, with only 30% of the regional market in 1990. American firms, led by IBM, had established positions in these markets that could not be overcome easily by the smaller European firms, or, for that matter, the rising Japanese firms. Furthermore, the fragmented nature of the European market made it difficult for them to develop regional scale to challenge the substantial world scale of American firms.

The Role of International Alliances

A distinct feature of competition in the computer industry was the increasing importance of international alliances (see **Exhibit 9**). These alliances helped transfer technologies across national borders, facilitated market entry by new firms, and became competitive tools in battles over standards and market share. They were, at the same time, signs of the narrowing gap between the capabilities of firms from different nations and direct contributors to this trend.

A survey of press reports of the major international alliances formed by 24 top computer firms between 1975 and 1990 identified 226 deals.[15] These partnerships covered a range of structures and activities falling in the grey area between open-market purchases and internal company transactions. Forty-six percent of the deals were structured as supply agreements, 19% as technology licenses, 20% as joint R&D projects, and 21% as equity joint ventures or equity investments.

In the early 1980s, the computer industry was already third among a large group of industries in its use of alliances. After that came a rapid increase in the formation of alliances in computers, from fewer than four a year before 1980 to an average of 26 per year in 1985–1989. This rise was double that in world consumption of DP equipment, which rose from about $50 billion in 1980 to an average of $150 billion in the same period.

Computer firms used alliances in all parts of the value chain. About one-third were devoted to trading goods and components, another third to technology development and transfer, and about one-fifth to manufacturing. Over time, however, the role of technology development and transfer in alliances tended to increase; before 1984, 29% of the alliances were structured as

[15]For further details, see Benjamin Gomes-Casseres, "International Trade, Competition, and Alliances in the Computer Industry," Harvard Business School working paper number 92-044, (Rev. 1992).

EXHIBIT 9 International Alliances of Leading Computer Firms, 1975–1989 (Source: Survey of press reports; see Gomes-Casseres (1992).)

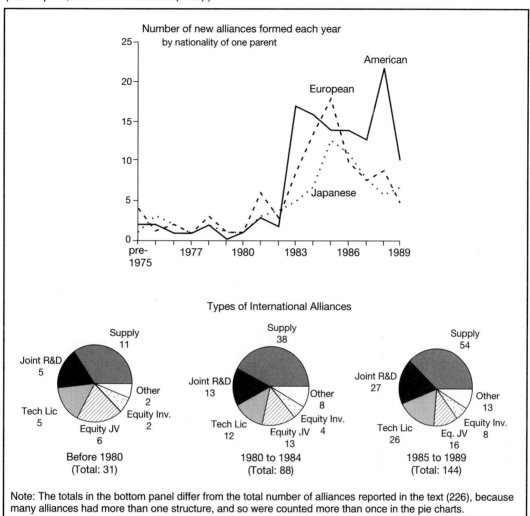

Note: The totals in the bottom panel differ from the total number of alliances reported in the text (226), because many alliances had more than one structure, and so were counted more than once in the pie charts.

joint R&D and technology licenses, compared with 37% in 1985–1989 (see **Exhibit 9**).

The alliances also varied by the contributions of the partners. Sometimes the partners exchanged technology for technology, at other times one contributed technology and other a market, and so on. There seemed to be some systematic differences across regions in the types of contributions made and sought by national firms (see **Exhibit 10**).

Selected Competitors

IBM IBM has been unique in the computer industry because of its size and early domi-

nance. It was traditionally a mainframe producer, although it became highly successful in PCs and also in minicomputers in the 1980s. It had the reputation of being more marketing-oriented than its competitors and of excelling at customer service. Many also argued that IBM's secret lay in its corporate culture, which, until the 1990s, included virtual lifetime employment and great employee loyalty. In 1991, it suffered its first annual loss ever, as it was rocked by recession and overcapacity in the industry. But it still held number one positions in a number of segments, including personal computers and mainframes. IBM attained its leadership through creative technology management in the 1960s, aggressive marketing, sheer finan-

EXHIBIT 10 Contributions of Partners in International Alliances (total number of alliances for 1975–1989, paired as shown) (Source: Survey of press reports; see Gomes-Casseres (1992).)

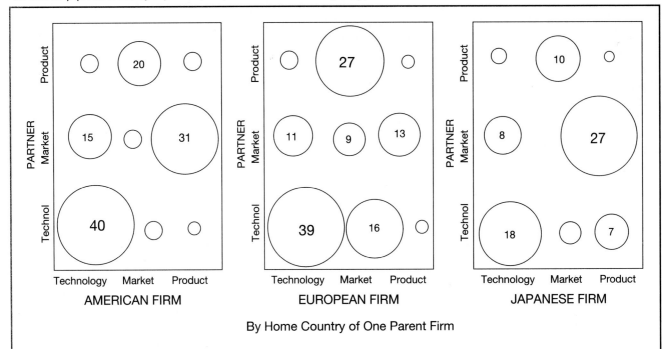

By Home Country of One Parent Firm

Note: This chart is to be read as follows: E.g., the left-hand panel shows that in 15 cases American firms contributed technology to an alliance in exchange for market access that was provided by the partner.

cial clout, and by extensive foreign production and sales. In 1991, it began a radical reorganization intended to decentralize operations and encourage greater market responsiveness in its businesses.

In foreign countries, IBM traditionally operated through wholly-owned subsidiaries. This approach was not always welcomed by host governments. In 1978, IBM pulled out of India rather than give in to the government's demand for a joint venture. In the 1980s, the company softened its insistence on whole ownership, and, in fact, became an active user of inter-firm alliances. This change stemmed from the gradual erosion of its market position in Japan and Europe, where local firms were aggressive in the new microcomputer segments (e.g., Olivetti in Europe) or had simply reached a stage where their products were good enough to challenge IBM's (Japanese firms). In response, the firm began to pursue alliances with local firms. In

1982–1984, IBM Japan formed only four alliances with local firms involving some equity investment; in 1987–1989, it formed 25 such alliances. Following this example, IBM Europe expanded its stock of equity-based alliances from six in 1987 to 150 in 1990. In the early 1990s, IBM even formed joint ventures in India and China.

OTHER U.S. MAINFRAME FIRMS The BUNCH group of companies comprised a second-tier of mainframe firms in the 1960s and 1970s—Burroughs, UNIVAC, NCR, Control Data, and Honeywell. This group plus GE and RCA (before they dropped out of the industry) had previously been known as the Seven Dwarfs and were the key challengers to IBM through the 1960s. On the whole, what was left of this group of once formidable potential has suffered declining performance and market share. In the 1980s, Burroughs and Univac merged to form Unisys,

Honeywell Information Systems was acquired by France's Bull, and in 1991 NCR was acquired by AT&T.

Aside from these broad-line firms, there were niche players in mainframes. In high-end mainframes, Control Data and Cray Research became the market leaders in scientific supercomputers. The manufacturers of PCMs were more direct competitors in IBM's heartland. Since 1975, Amdahl had been the most important player in this market. Gene Amdahl had been a lead engineer on IBM's System/360 and /370 projects, and set out on his own in the early 1970s, with the financial support of Fujitsu. In 1990, Fujitsu owned about 43% of Amdahl, and the two firms developed and produced computers together.

U.S. MINICOMPUTER FIRMS Digital Equipment Corporation, the strongest minicomputer maker in the 1970s and 1980s and the segment's pioneer, was started in 1957 by Kenneth Olsen (still the CEO) and Harlan Anderson. As a result of their favorable price/performance ratios, DEC's machines provided substantial competition to IBM's low-end mainframes. By 1990, DEC was the second largest U.S. computer manufacturer, with operations around the world; it was most successful with scientific and academic users, but less so with the business community.

Each minicomputer specialist—DEC, Data General, Hewlett-Packard, NCR, Prime, and Wang—had its own proprietary system architecture, and together they eclipsed IBM's share in this segment. But in the 1980s and 1990s they were all being threatened from below by workstations using open UNIX systems. Except for IBM and DEC, all more or less abandoned their proprietary systems by 1990 and were moving toward the less profitable open systems. Wang was hurt the most by this trend, and in 1991 began selling IBM hardware. Others had to downsize their operations and cut their workforces. In 1991, DEC suffered the first loss in its history.

U.S. MICROCOMPUTER FIRMS After IBM, Apple was the most important microcomputer maker in the United States. Its Macintosh system, introduced in the mid-1980s, pioneered the marketing of a friendly graphical user interface. Most other microcomputer producers sold "clones" of IBM's PC, using Intel X86 processors and Microsoft's MS-DOS operating system. The clone makers used marketing strategies and time-to-market advantages for differentiation in a cut-throat business. Compaq, established in 1982 and soon among the *Fortune 500*, was first to undercut IBM's prices, while still claiming a premium product. Dell, AST, Northgate, and Gateway grew rapidly in the late 1980s by selling exclusively through direct mail, cutting costs to the bare minimum.

U.S. WORKSTATION FIRMS Sun Microsystems was the archetypical workstation vendor of open systems. By contrast, workstation pioneer Apollo was taken over by Hewlett-Packard in 1989 after missing opportunities in open systems. Sun makes its own chips, but makes extensive use of alliances and liberal licensing to promote use of its RISC[16] design called SPARC. Sun produces systems and sells them under its own name through an aggressive sales force, while selling through so many OEM vendors in Japan (including Fujitsu, Toshiba, and Oki) that none is reportedly making any money on the business. Sun also invites clones, in another attempt to maximize the number of SPARC-based machines on the market.

American firms already well established in the computer industry—Hewlett-Packard, DEC and IBM—also used alliances in the workstation field, often to promote their own RISC architectures. DEC was an important ally of RISC designer MIPS Computer Systems, which in turn had a large network of partnerships. These firms joined Compaq, Microsoft, and others in the Advanced Computing Environment (ACE) consortium, formed to bring the MIPS architecture to the commercial desktop market. Hewlett-Packard, which had merged with Apollo, also began to push its PA-RISC architecture actively in the 1990s. Perhaps the most surprising, and potentially formidable, RISC alliance was that formed in 1991 by IBM, Apple, and Motorola. Together, these firms intended to promote a new "Power PC" based on IBM's RISC architecture,

---

[16]Reduced Instruction Set Computing (RISC) was a new type of processor design that yielded greater power than traditional designs.

Motorola's microprocessor manufacturing expertise, and Apple's software capabilities.

FUJITSU AND HITACHI In the MITI-sponsored projects of the mid-1970s, Fujitsu and Hitachi focused on challenging IBM's position in mainframes, partly through development of PCMs. Fujitsu was aided in this by its alliance with the U.S.'s Amdahl Corporation. Short of cash and unable to raise funding at home, Amdahl struck a deal with Fujitsu in 1972, taking in a 24% equity investment and providing technology and the permission for Fujitsu engineers to "look over the shoulder" of engineers at Amdahl. Amdahl began shipping its first plug-compatible CPU in 1975; two years later, Fujitsu announced that it would begin manufacturing the machines for Amdahl to sell in the United States.

By 1990, Fujitsu had the leading market share in Japan (23%) and was an important supplier of large computer and telecommunications systems to government and industry. It moved ahead of DEC in 1990 to become the second largest firm in the world when it acquired 80% of Britain's ICL. This climax to a ten-year technology sharing arrangement increased Fujitsu's overseas sales from 25% to 40% of its total.

Hitachi, which produced a broad spectrum of electronics products, was the third largest Japanese computer company. Hitachi was stung in 1982 by the FBI in an embarrassing corporate espionage case. Its employees attempted to fill "a long shopping list of IBM technologies" using "cloak-and-dagger" methods.[17] After this case came to light, Hitachi settled a suit with IBM and the two developed cross-licensing arrangements. Following a long dispute over intellectual property rights to IBM software, Fujitsu and IBM, too, reached an agreement in 1987 to allow Fujitsu to use IBM software under restricted conditions and pay IBM $833 million plus an annual fee.

NEC AND TOSHIBA With their greater capabilities in consumer electronics, NEC and Toshiba focused on small machines and peripherals. Pro-

duction cost was relatively more important in these segments than in the others, so these companies could enter and compete on low-cost strategies. In the early 1990s, these two firms still excelled in small computers, although NEC also competed in mainframes and supercomputers. NEC developed a proprietary microcomputer standard that grew to dominate the Japanese market with a 50% share in 1990. NEC had a long-standing relationship with Honeywell Information Systems, and came to own 5% of Groupe Bull after Bull bought Honeywell's business. NEC's strategy has been to focus on "C&C"—computers and communications. Toshiba was the fourth largest Asian computer firm. It was particularly strong worldwide in laptop and notebook machines, with 14% of the portable computer market in the United States in 1991.

EUROPEAN FIRMS European computer manufacturers were not much of a threat on a global scale. Even the largest, the merged Siemens-Nixdorf, was ranked eighth in the world in 1990. While European firms have some presence in the United States, they are negligible factors in Asia.

France's Bull and Britain's ICL were created through mergers of smaller firms to be their governments' national champions. Bull ended up with several incompatible product lines and with little incentive to be efficient. It attempted to expand internationally in the late 1980s by buying Honeywell Information Systems and Zenith Data Systems. Both moves gave it a strong U.S. presence and helped it move away from minis and mainframes toward smaller systems. Still, it had massive layoffs in the early 1990s and began reducing the size of its manufacturing operations. In 1992, Bull received a 5% equity investment from IBM, and began to sell IBM hardware through its channels. ICL, which was Europe's only profitable computer maker and excelled in software (particularly UNIX) and services, became a majority-owned subsidiary of Fujitsu in 1990.

The second largest computer maker in Europe after IBM was formed when Germany's two leading computer firms, Siemens and Nixdorf merged in 1990. Siemens had a strong proprietary mainframe line, and sold heavily in telecommunications markets. Unlike Bull,

[17]Marie Anchordoguy, *Computers Inc.: Japan's Challenge to IBM* (Cambridge: Council on East Asian Studies, Harvard University, 1989), p.1, 149.

Siemens made its own semiconductors, and had an important joint R&D project with IBM on semiconductor technology. Nixdorf had traditionally sold its own minicomputer systems to banking and small business markets, but had missed the transition to open systems.

Olivetti was the third largest European computer firm, and specialized mostly in PCs. It had several joint ventures with American and Japanese firms to make disk drives, displays, and computer systems. A joint venture with AT&T in the 1980s was shortlived, however, and failed to give the company the boost that it sought in the U.S. market. Finally, the Dutch-based Philips, which had long been a player in the European computer market, sold its computer division to DEC in 1991.

Competitive Conditions in the 1990s

As hardware manufacturers faced maturing markets, recessionary economies, rapid technological change, and excess capacity in the early 1990s, profits in the industry were sluggish or nonexistent. Operating income as a percent of revenue in the industry declined from 14% in 1984 to 8% in 1990 and dropped further in 1991. Turmoil and an uncertain future sent hardware manufacturers seeking solutions, but the crisis in profitability eroded firms' power and options. Foreign vendors continued to face barriers in Japan, which had the second largest market in the world and sophisticated users. While there were exceptions in the hardware segment, software and services showed potentially greater prospects for profit. Growth in these segments was expected to accelerate: spending on software was growing twice as fast as that on hardware, and computer services expenditures were projected by some sources to grow to $1.3 trillion by 1995.[18] While the future for many firms remained uncertain, change was sure to be a part of it. The question was how firms and governments could take action to prepare for it.

[18]IBM *Annual Report*, 1990, and "Why EDS Loves a Recession," *The New York Times*, October 20, 1991, Section 3, p. 1.

3. The Global Telecommunications Equipment Industry

Introduction

For nearly a century, most telecommunications equipment suppliers enjoyed comfortable, exclusive relationships with their national providers of telecommunication services. By the 1980s, however, the forces of deregulation, privatization and technological change had shaken international markets for telecommunications equipment. Given the increasingly competitive and complex business environment and the rising costs of R&D, firms were challenged to revise their traditional strategies for success.

This note surveys the global telecommunications equipment industry through the late 1980s, including recent technological developments, major product categories, regulatory trends and company-specific strategies. The note examines in greatest detail the roles played by central office switches and private branch exchanges (PBXs) in the global telecommunications industry.

Recent Technological Developments

Telecommunications technology has advanced considerably since the invention of the telegraph made possible long-distance communication by electric transmission over wire. This section summarizes several of the more significant technological advances affecting the dynamics of the global telecommunications equipment industry since the end of the 1970s, including the development of digital transmission technology, fiber optics, and cellular radio technology. The more general impact of innovations in computer technology on the telecommunications equipment industry is touched upon in subsequent sections of the note.

Digital Transmission Technology

Historically, telecommunications systems relied on analog technology for signal transmission. Analog systems transmit voice signals directly as

Research Associate Julie Herendeen prepared this note under the supervision of Professors Willis Emmons, Richard H.K. Vietor, and David B. Yoffie as the basis for class discussion.

sound waves, but can transmit data only after first converting them to wave form from their original digital form.

By the 1980s, digital technology, which converts both voice and data signals into electronic pulses for transmission, had become commercially available for use in telecommunications applications. Compared to analog systems, digital networks provide a much more efficient, accurate, and flexible means of signal transmission. As of 1987, approximately 55% of the signal transmission capacity of the U.S. regional Bell operating companies (RBOCs)[1] utilized digital technology.[2] It was projected that by the year 2000, the entire U.S. telecommunications network would be digitalized.[3] Outside of the United States, the shift to digital technology proceeded more slowly, with the notable exception of France, which had almost completely digitalized its network by 1990.

Fiber Optics

In the early years of telecommunications, simple copper wire served as the standard transmission medium. Over time, coaxial cable, a bulkier, higher volume transmission medium, replaced copper wire in applications requiring higher transmission capacity. Fiber optic technology, first commercialized in 1979, differs significantly from copper wire and coaxial cable technology. Instead of relying on electricity and conducting wires for transmission, fiber optics technology transmits signals via light waves through extremely thin glass fibers. These fibers are able to carry an immense amount of information while using only a fraction of the space required by wire-based trans-

mission media. However, in 1990, the cost of replacing existing copper wire and coaxial cable with optical fiber still outweighed the benefits in applications requiring only modest transmission capacity.

Cellular Radio Technology

In addition to land-based transmission media such as copper wire, coaxial cable, and optical fiber, air-based transmission via microwaves and radio waves has long been used in certain telecommunications applications. Microwave technology, commercialized after WWII, allows for signal transmission between unobstructed terrestrial antennae and via satellite. Traditional radio wave technology has provided a means for mobile communication, although limitations on the number of frequencies available has greatly restricted the number of users in any network. These limitations were eased considerably, however, with the commercialization of cellular radio technology in the 1980s.

Unlike traditional mobile radio, which serves users via a single central antenna, cellular radio divides a region into a honeycomb of cells, each with its own antenna. The capability of cellular technology to transfer signals easily between the multiple antennae and the public network has greatly increased the capacity of mobile telephone networks. By 1990, the application of digital technology and innovative signal compression techniques to cellular networks insured that the capacity of these systems would continue to grow, and created the possibility that these wireless systems might eventually serve significant user segments formerly dependent on land-based transmission media.

Major Product Categories

The telecommunications equipment industry can be divided into public network equipment and customer premise equipment (**Exhibit 1**). Public network equipment includes the central office switches and transmission media and electronics that telecommunications companies use to provide network services. The second segment, cus-

tomer premise equipment, includes everything from telephones to facsimiles to large private branch exchanges (PBXs).

Within these approximate boundaries, the most accurate estimate of worldwide telecommunications equipment sales was $120 billion in 1989.[4] Revenues grew at a compound average an-

EXHIBIT 1 World Telecommunications Equipment Market: 1989 estimated total: $120 billion (Source: *Telephony* (August 28,1989), p. 40.)

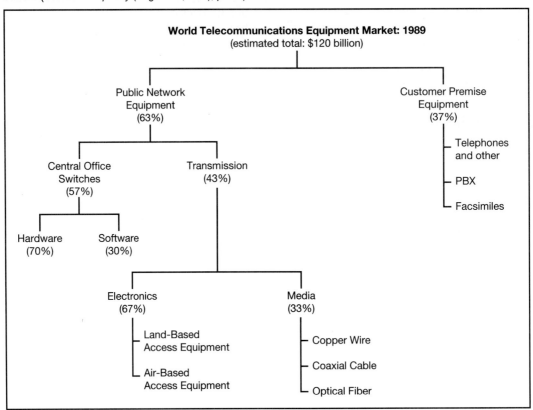

nual growth rate of 8.3% between 1984 and 1989.[5] During this period, the majority of equipment sales were concentrated in the developed world, with the United States accounting for 33%, Western Europe for 32%, and Japan for 12%.[6] In contrast, the market for telecommunications services exceeded $300 billion in 1989.[7] Voice services were predicted to grow at approximately 7% per year and data services at 25% to 30% per year in the 1990s.

Public Network Equipment

The public network equipment segment comprised slightly less than two-thirds of the world market for telecommunications equipment in 1989. Of this segment's total sales, central office switches constituted more than half, with transmission equipment accounting for the remainder (**Exhibit 1**).[8] Although end-users with very large private networks occasionally purchased public

network equipment, the principal customers were telecommunication companies that provided services for resale.

By the 1980s, a public network consisted of central office switches connected to transmission lines with highly sophisticated electronic equipment. Each switch was linked to hundreds or thousands of local lines that extended to the customer premises, where they connected to telephones, PBXs, and other terminal equipment. The switch, in other words, was the hub of the system; the transmission lines, the spokes; and the terminal equipment, the nodes.

TRANSMISSION EQUIPMENT Transmission equipment includes both transmission media and the electronics that control the movement of signals over the media. By the late 1980s, transmission media was generally a commodity business, with excess production capacity and thin margins, not only for copper wire and coaxial cable, where demand was declining, but also for optical fiber, where technology improvements had led to greater manufacturing economies, excess capacity, and increased price-cutting.

In the transmission electronics segment, major product categories include: microwave access equipment, satellites, multiplexers,[9] and digital access and cross-connect systems (DACS). In the late 1980s, margins were high in this technology-sensitive segment, and demand for the most sophisticated equipment was expected to remain strong through the 1990s as media were converted to optical fiber and as use of cellular radio systems increased.

CENTRAL OFFICE SWITCHES Central office switches vary in size and design according to the complexity of the network. Some switches are designed for special purposes, such as those that manage mobile cellular telephone systems. World central office switch revenues were predicted to grow at approximately 6.7% per year between 1987 and 1992, with the most rapid growth rate projected for Eastern Europe (**Exhibit 2**).[10]

Central office switches evolved technologically from electromechanical (pre-1960s), to analog electronic (1960s–1970s), to digital (1980s–1990s). Using complicated software (programs with millions of lines of code), digital switches not only can relay data and voice signals, but also can provide billing information and specialized services such as call forwarding and call waiting. With add-on devices and software enhancements, digital switches can provide more elaborate business features, such as conference calling and high-speed, high-quality data trans-

EXHIBIT 2 Central Office Switch Markets by Region: 1987–1992

	Market Share		CAGR
Region	1987	1992	1987–92
Asia	31%	28%	4.4%
North America	29	28	5.5
Western Europe	20	20	7.0
Eastern Europe	12	17	13.6
Latin America	4	4	8.1
Africa	2	2	6.9
Oceania	2	1	0.8
Total	100%	100%	6.7%

Source: Derived from Arthur D. Little Decision Resources, "Central Office Switching Equipment: Regional Market Opportunities and Issues" (June 1988), p.1.
Note: Projections are in 1987 dollars.

fer.[11] The market for these digital features was projected to expand rapidly from approximately $750 million in 1990 to nearly $2 billion by 1993.

The recent development of so-called "intelligent networks," however, has threatened to decouple many of these advanced digital features from the central office switch itself, placing them instead in a separate computer network. The long-term effect of intelligent networks may be to reduce the proprietary software requirements of switches, while increasing the competition between computer and telecommunication equipment firms for the lucrative features market.

RESEARCH AND DEVELOPMENT The development costs for digital central office switches were much higher than for previous switches.[12] By the mid-1980s, the development cost per model of an advanced digital switch was approximately $1 billion over an eight-year period. For four to five years before the introduction of a switch, about 60% of the R&D effort went into hardware development. Thereafter, the vendor would continue to spend $100 million to $200 million a year for about three years, 80% for modifying software.[13] Thus software represents a significant portion of the development cost of a switch, over 50% for a sophisticated digital switch. Some suppliers (Siemens, Plessey, and GEC) had a portion of these R&D costs underwritten by state-owned telecommunications providers or PTTs (postal, telegraph, and telecommunications entities). Others (Alcatel, Northern, NEC, and Fujitsu) received indirect subsidies through guaranteed long-term prices in protected home markets.

In addition to these R&D expenses, adapting a switch for a foreign market can cost up to $200 million, given the often significant differences in technical standards between countries. As an example of the difficulties faced in serving foreign markets, ITT spent over $100 million to adapt its System 12 switch for the United States before abandoning the market. Similarly, the Nippon Telephone and Telegraph (NTT)-sponsored D60/70 switch has been unworkable outside Japan. In contrast, Ericsson has usually designed its switches from the outset to adapt more easily to foreign markets.

Two developments may serve to reduce the costs of adapting switches for foreign markets over the long term. One is the spread of intelligent networks, discussed above, which should reduce the complexity of the switch itself as features are transferred increasingly to add-on computer systems. In addition, the International Telegraph and Telephone Consultative Committee (CCITT) has adopted a set of technical standards, known as ISDN (Integrated Service Digital Network), to promote compatibility across telecommunication networks. However, as of 1990, compliance with ISDN standards was voluntary, and many end users of telecommunication services did not require the high levels of technological sophistication provided by ISDN.

MANUFACTURING While central office switches are often produced in large-scale plants to take advantage of scale economies in manufacturing, their cost structure is similar to that of computers: little value-added comes from manufacturing, which mainly involves assembling computer chips (**Exhibit 3**). Both AT&T and Northern Telecom produce switches for the U.S. market at a single plant. However, there are plants that produce at a much smaller scale in both the United States and abroad, such as Ericsson's 700,000 line central office switch plant. One source has estimated that at least $400 million in investment is required for an optimally sized manufacturing plant.[14]

EXHIBIT 3 Cost Structure for Digital Switches: 1985

Manufacturing Costs	$ per Line
Labor	35
Purchased IC chips	55
Other material	45
Total manufacturing costs	135
Other Costs	
SGA allocation	35
R&D allocation	20–25
Total other costs	55–60
TOTAL COSTS	190–195
PROFIT MARGIN	15–20
SALES PRICE	210
Source: "The Central Office Switch Industry in 1985" (Harvard Business School Case No. 187-053, 1986), p. 33.	

SALES AND MARKETING The switch market is segmented by differences in the size and features of equipment, but above all, by national boundaries. In addition to local customization costs, potential vendors must participate in time-consuming and expensive testing and certification procedures. Then, assuming a contract is awarded, many national governments insist on the use of local manufacturing plants, often with ancillary R&D facilities. In addition, vendors are expected to provide extensive local service and engineering support.

In the late 1980s, central office switch prices ranged from about $160 to $1,000 per line. Although scale and features accounted for some of this difference, varying government procurement policies, subsidies, taxes, import duties, and the degree of competition in domestic markets accounted for most of it.[15] The United States and United Kingdom, which had the most openly competitive markets, had the lowest per line prices.

In 1990, distribution channels were relatively unimportant in the switch market since the customer base was narrow, centralized, and well-defined: government-owned or privatized telephone companies. The United States was the major exception, with 1,500 small, local telephone companies, 22 RBOCs, and GTE. In virtually all countries, exclusive procurement policies, endorsed by regulatory authorities, had led to long-term engineering relationships between vendors and buyers.

Customer Premise Equipment

At the other end of the telecommunications circuit is the vast and fragmented market for terminal equipment. Terminal equipment includes telephones, modems, recorders, facsimile machines, key telephone systems,[16] video and data terminals, and private branch exchange (PBX) switching systems. The customer base consists of residential buyers, businesses, and resellers, including telephone companies themselves. The total market for this equipment was approximately $44 billion in 1989 (**Exhibit 1**). PBXs accounted for the largest, but declining, share.[17]

PBXs (PRIVATE BRANCH EXCHANGES) PBXs are multiline, business telephone systems that route calls among extensions within a system, or between an extension and an external line. In essence, for a group of users, a PBX provides the same switching functions as the public network's central office switches.[18] The size of systems ranges from less than 100 to more than 1,000 lines. Dataquest reported that, in 1987, 35 manufacturers sold 130 PBX models in the United States alone.[19]

In the early 1980s, development of the digital PBX fueled growth in the PBX market by providing business customers with features not previously available from the public network, such as more precise billing and usage data, conference calling, call identification, and voice messaging. However, at the same time, the RBOCs in the United States had begun to offer PBX-like features to private users from the central office. The sophistication of these so-called "centrex" systems has been greatly enhanced by the digitalization of networks, along with the development of intelligent networks and ISDN. This accounts, in part, for the decline in PBX sales in the United States during the late 1980s and the increasingly intense price competition in this market. According to one source, only one manufacturer, Mitel, earned a profit in the U.S. PBX business in 1988.[20] The growth rate of the U.S. PBX market was projected to be .7% per year between 1987 and 1992.[21]

R&D AND MANUFACTURING The research and manufacturing of PBXs are quite similar to that of central office switches, but on a smaller scale. The same microelectronic components, circuit boards, wiring, and frames go into both PBXs and central office switches; at the high end of the market, only the software is different. In fact, some suppliers manufacture high-end PBXs and central office switches at the same facility. In the late 1980s, developing a competitive PBX required a $500 million investment over a three- to five-year period. Software development, marketing, installation, and service represented at least 50% of the value added by PBX suppliers.[22]

SALES AND MARKETING Distribution (marketing, sales, and service) is a major consideration in the PBX market. In the U.S. market, for example, there are hundreds of large customers and thousands of smaller customers. Different customer segments such as banks, hospitals, schools, and hotels each have different PBX needs, and distributors tend to be strong in particular segments. Some PBX suppliers contract with a variety of distributors to reach the broadest range of customers, while other multiproduct firms, like IBM and Northern Telecom, can distribute PBXs through existing computer or telecommunications equipment channels.

Access to foreign markets entails stringent certification requirements, customization costs, and, in some cases, competition from the PTTs. For smaller, less complicated models, the equipment to software ratio is higher, decreasing local customizing requirements.

Government Regulatory Regimes

With few exceptions, prior to 1980, national telecommunications markets were heavily regulated, closed to foreign competition, and dominated by state-owned monopolies. Telecommunication was universally deemed a public utility and particularly vital to defense and commerce. To make service widely available, rates were elaborately structured to generate cross-subsidies from long-distance to local services and from business users to residential users. Equipment suppliers were either vertically integrated with service providers or were virtually integrated through oligopolistic procurement arrangements, such as the Den Den "family" suppliers for NTT in Japan, Alcatel for France Telecom, and Siemens for the Bundespost in Germany.

Throughout the 1980s, rapid technological progress created entrepreneurial opportunities to bypass the central system, which threatened PTT control over the public network. As PTTs cut service prices to retain customers, margins fell, constraining their ability to subsidize local equipment suppliers. Ultimately, PTTs faced the possibility that, without competition in the home market, their domestic telecommunications equipment provider could become a technological laggard.

United States

The deregulation of U.S. telecommunications monopolies occurred first and had progressed farthest, as of 1990. Until the mid-1980s, AT&T was the only privately owned, national telephone system among the major industrial countries. It was also vertically integrated into equipment manufacturing.[23] Historically, the Federal Communications Commission (FCC) regulated AT&T's interstate service and its interconnect policies. State public utility commissions regulated intrastate and local rates.

Traditionally, AT&T, which served 82% of the local-service market and 100% of the long-distance market, had not allowed non-Bell equipment to be connected to its network. However, in 1968, the FCC ruled that AT&T could not arbitrarily prohibit interconnection of non-Bell terminal equipment. During the next 12 years, the remaining restrictions designed to protect the public network were replaced with a simple registration. In 1980, customer premise equipment was deregulated altogether, and price restrictions on AT&T's own installed base of telephones, keysets, and telex machines were removed.[24]

Similarly, in leased-line services and then in long-distance service, the FCC and the courts gradually allowed competitive entry. In a 1959 decision, the FCC allocated microwave frequencies to large users, and in 1969, it allowed MCI to sell leased-line services to third parties. By the late 1970s, several vendors were selling leased-line services, and MCI finally offered a switched, long-distance service in direct competition with AT&T. Although the FCC later opposed this development, MCI's move was upheld in the U.S. courts.[25] By 1989, MCI, Sprint, and other long-distance competitors had together gained 31% of the long-distance market.[26] As they struggled to become full-service vendors, these companies expanded into international long-distance service as well.

AT&T's alleged aggressive responses to competitive and regulatory changes led the U.S. Justice Department to bring an antitrust suit against the firm in 1974. In January 1982, apparently having exhausted efforts to gain legislative relief, AT&T agreed to divest its local operating companies and its cellular mobile communications service. AT&T retained Bell Labs (R&D division), AT&T Long Lines (long-distance service), and Western Electric (equipment manufacturing division), creating a new company with $34 billion in assets. The Justice Department dropped its suit and withdrew a previous consent decree that had prevented AT&T from entering the computer business.[27]

When divestiture took effect in 1984, the 22 Bell operating companies were reorganized into 7 regional holding companies (RHCs), each with about $11 billion to $14 billion in assets. Although the RBOCs were given the lucrative Yellow Pages, the Bell name, and a jointly owned piece of Bell Labs (renamed Bell Communications Corp.), they were restricted indefinitely from providing long-distance services across court-ordered market boundaries (called LATAs), from manufacturing equipment, and from providing information services.[28]

After the divestiture, the U.S. government implemented additional regulatory reforms. In 1986, the FCC required local telephone companies to begin to unbundle their tariffs and introduce "open network architecture" that would make access to the network fully competitive for all service vendors. At the same time, it freed AT&T from a previous requirement to keep services and equipment sales organizationally separate.[29] In September 1987, the courts ruled that RBOCs would be allowed limited entry into the information services market and unlimited entry into non-telecom businesses. Meanwhile, through legislative action, the RBOCs sought permission to manufacture telecommunications equipment as well.[30] In 1988, the FCC changed how it regulated AT&T's rates from a rate-of-return "cost plus" basis to a "price-cap" basis. This gave AT&T greater competitive flexibility and an incentive to operate efficiently.[31]

Japan

Prior to 1985, Japan's telecommunications system was a national monopoly, closed to competition in equipment and services. Under a series of laws enacted in the early 1950s, the Ministry of Posts and Telecommunications (MPT) had thorough regulatory control over Nippon Telephone and Telegraph (NTT)—a state-owned public utility that provided all local and domestic long-distance service in Japan. As in the United States, rates were designed to foster "universal service" via cross-subsidies from long-distance use and business customers to local residential service. NTT also maintained the Electronic Communications Laboratories (ECL), which conducted research with a "family" of four suppliers. These companies—NEC, Fujitsu, Hitachi, and Oki—provided virtually all of NTT's network equipment and much of the terminal equipment that NTT distributed under closed, market-sharing arrangements. A private monopoly, Kokusai Denshin Denwa (KDD), provided international service.[32]

In the early 1980s, trade frictions with the United States, complaints about high rates and inadequate service from large customers within Japan, and Ministry of International Trade and Industry (MITI) efforts to extend its computer industry jurisdiction into telecommunications precipitated an intense political debate over the direction of telecommunications policy. This culminated in late 1984 with the enactment of the Telecommunications Business Law and the Private Corporation Law.

The Telecommunications Business Law dramatically reorganized entry and licensing for domestic and international telecommunications services. Although provision of basic network services was liberalized, rates remained regulated, foreign capital was limited to one-third of the service provider's total capital, and licensing required MPT approval. For providers of "special" services such as data networks, only registration with the MPT was necessary. The Private Corporation Law mandated the privatization of NTT through a series of public offerings. MPT imposed no restrictions on relations between the regulated and unregulated units of NTT, and the firm organized more than 170 affiliates, many operating in less regulated or nonregulated businesses.[33] Although NTT cut costs and reduced rates, competitors and customers continued to complain of its bureaucratic operations, excessive costs, discriminatory access, and high rates. In 1990, the government was considering alternatives for the breakup of NTT.

The impact of these changes on competition was minimal. While competition increased for customer premise equipment, central office switch procurement remained mostly limited to NTT's family of suppliers. Foreign firms had made sales to NTT, but as a rule there was only one foreign supplier for each product segment: Northern in digital switches; AT&T in transmission equipment; Siecor (in which Siemens was a partner) in fiber; and Rolm in PBXs. Finally, Motorola, with the help of political pressure from the United States, became a significant player in Japan's cellular market.

Western Europe

Changes in public telecommunications policies in Europe, although gradual, were nearly as dramatic as those in Japan and the United States. Since 1987, the European Community had been moving towards integration and, by necessity, regulatory liberalization. Overall, the degree of liberalization varied widely among member states. In June 1987 the European Commission published a "Green Paper" on telecommunications, which recommended that, although national PTTs should retain jurisdiction over public networks and basic services, networks should be standardized and entry into all other services should be competitive.[34] In addition, the paper argued that PTTs should separate their regulatory and operational activities, reduce cross-subsidies, and open equipment procurement to competition.[35]

The Commission expressed two motivating factors for these changes. First, to achieve market integration within Europe, an integrated communications network was a prerequisite. Secondly, to achieve external competitiveness in scale-sensitive products such as central office switches, a home market of minimum efficient scale would be necessary. For example, there were seven different digital switching systems in EC countries in 1987, five of which were developed by EC firms that benefited significantly from national procurement policies and R&D subsidies. However, industry sources believed that with completely open markets, the EC could be served by two central office switch firms.[36]

Despite some delays, the Commission made remarkable progress, partly by twice using Article 90 of the Treaty of Rome to make PTTs comply with the treaty's competition rules in both service provision and equipment procurement.[37] When the Commission applied this article to terminal equipment in 1989, France, and several other member countries that were reluctant to liberalize their terminal equipment markets, challenged the Commission in the European Court of Justice.

UNITED KINGDOM   Until 1980, the British Post Office had a complete monopoly in providing telephone services in the United Kingdom. At that time, the British government, influenced by deregulation in the United States and the conservative Thatcher administration, published the Telecommunications Bill, which proposed dividing the Post Office into two organizations: Posts and British Telecom. In addition, telecommunications standards, formerly under the jurisdiction of the Post Office, were to be established by the British Standards Institute (BSI), and responsibility for testing would fall to the British Approvals Board for Telecommunications (BABT). In the following year, the legislation was approved, and two years later, 51% of British Telecom was privatized.

In 1981, a timetable was set, calling for full liberalization of telecommunications equipment by 1983. Also in 1981, the government recommended that private-sector suppliers have full freedom to use the national network to provide telecommunications services to third parties. A year later, the government licensed Mercury, a joint venture of Cable and Wireless (40%), British Petroleum (40%), and Barclays Bank (20%), to build and operate an independent telephone network. However, in 1984, the United Kingdom prohibited additional entry into basic telephone services. The duopoly approach was followed in other areas as well: mobile cellular service and international telecommunications were each limited to two carriers. However, by 1989, the duopoly system was under review to determine if increased competition would benefit the British market.

FRANCE   France repeatedly expressed reservations about the reform sweeping the EC, but it had one of the most technologically advanced and commercially successful telecommunications networks in the world. France Telecom, the national telecommunications service provider, was part of the powerful Posts and Telecommunications Min-

istry. In 1989, the government recognized that France Telecom needed more freedom to compete internationally and recommended that it become an autonomous public enterprise. France Telecom supported this approach because it would henceforth be able to prevent the government from using its budget to subsidize other government programs.[38]

According to plans for domestic liberalization, France Telecom would keep its monopoly in the basic network and telephone services but would allow foreign competition in terminal equipment and value-added services which had formerly been limited to domestic firms.

WEST GERMANY   Until 1989, the Deutsche Bundespost (DBP) was both the German telephone operating entity and the regulatory body. The DBP provided all telecommunications services in Germany, had a monopoly on first telephones, and distributed other terminal equipment, often competing with its own suppliers, mostly German firms. Unlike the PTTs in most other European countries, the DBP's responsibility for postal and telecommunications services was established in the Basic Law—Germany's constitution.[39]

Legislation to separate the operational and regulatory functions of the Bundespost was introduced unsuccessfully in the early 1980s. Nevertheless, with European integration on the horizon, the Minister of Posts and Telecommunications reorganized the Bundespost in 1988 into three separate operating units: Telekom, the telecommunications service division; Postdienst, the postal service division; and Postbank. Each entity would have its own supervisory board, yet still be broadly responsible to the Ministry. A separate entity would approve equipment and interconnect standards. The government stopped short of full privatization, partly to avoid amending the constitution.[40]

Terminal equipment was deregulated on July 1, 1990. Services were divided into two categories, basic network and competitive services. Telekom would be the sole provider of basic network services and could choose to enter competitive services, where foreign entry and investment were unrestricted. Subsidies between Telekom and Posts were to be phased out quickly, while subsidies among telecommunications services would be phased out more gradually.[41]

Eastern Europe/Soviet Union

By 1990, after decades of isolation, most Eastern bloc countries were ready to open their doors to the West. Yet the backwardness of their telecommunications infrastructure presented perhaps the single most important bottleneck to modernization. The substandard telecommunications networks were designed more to prevent communication than to facilitate it. The percent of population with telephones ranged from 10% in East Germany to 4% in the Soviet Union. In the Soviet Union, 93% of the international phone network was devoted to government and party officials.[42]

In most of these countries, basic voice and network services would remain the domain of the PTTs, while mobile telecommunications, data services, and telecommunications equipment would be provided competitively. Estimates of the cost of overhauling existing networks ranged from $6 billion in Hungary to $16 billion in East Germany. Each country had its own plans for raising the necessary funds. East Germany turned to West Germany for aid. Poland was expecting a $100 million World Bank loan, and the Deputy Minister of Communications was encouraging joint ventures between foreign firms and local Polish switch manufacturers. Hungary's government was also determined to overhaul its telecommunications systems, but, with a heavy foreign debt burden, at least half of the funds had to come from Hungarian Telecom's own resources.

Since World War II, CoCom, an organization that prevents Eastern bloc countries from obtaining sensitive technology with potential military applications, had restricted many telecommunications exports to Eastern Europe and the Soviet Union. However, in 1990, responding to political and economic liberalization in these countries, CoCom members voted to decontrol a long list of high-technology exports, allowing Western vendors to enter Eastern European markets.

With trade controls relaxed, joint ventures between Eastern European PTTs and foreign telecommunications firms proliferated. Alcatel was awarded the first round of contracts to modernize the East German telephone systems. Alcatel CIT had an arrangement with Telettra, a leading Polish manufacturer, to make digital switches in Poland. Negotiations were underway between other Polish producers and Siemens, Alcatel Sesa (Alcatel's Spanish subsidiary), and Ericsson for digital switches. Both Siemens and Alcatel had entered joint-venture agreements with Soviet firms to manufacture switches, and Siemens was also negotiating a deal with Czechoslovakia to produce central office switches.[43]

Many Eastern European countries, frustrated by the pace and cost of modernizing their public telecommunications network, turned to mobile cellular technology as a transitional solution. This was a cheap, rapid way to upgrade telephone systems without installing miles of new cable. For example, in 1990, Hungary and Czechoslovakia entered joint ventures with U.S. West, a U.S. Bell holding company, to develop cellular networks; Ericsson agreed to supply similar equipment for Hungary's network.

Industry Structure

Worldwide, the telecommunications equipment industry in the early 1980s consisted of some 200 manufacturing firms. However, the structural changes occurring in national telecommunications markets prompted numerous mergers, acquisitions, and joint ventures, significantly reducing the number of producers of central office switches and PBXs (**Exhibit 4**).

In public network equipment, a field of 16 firms in 1982 had narrowed to 7 by 1990. CGE acquired Thomson and then merged with ITT to form Alcatel; Ericsson acquired CGCT in France; AT&T acquired GTE's U.S. central office switch unit; and Siemens acquired GPT, the previous merger of GEC, Plessey, Stromberg-Carlson, and much of GTE's non-U.S. business. In addition to actual mergers, virtually all of these firms pursued strategic alliances and joint ventures as well. For example, AT&T entered a joint venture with Philips in central office switches and an alliance with Italtel of Italy to break into the European central office switch market.

EXHIBIT 4 Mergers, Joint Ventures, Strategic Alliances and Licensing Agreements between Major Telecommunication Equipment Suppliers: 1982–1989

Companies	Type	Year	SWI	TRM	CAB	PBX	TE
Alcatel – Ericsson(USA)	JV	1988			X		
Alcatel – ITT = Alcatel N.V.	M	1987	X	X	X	X	X
Alcatel – Nokia – AEG	SA	1987	1	1			1
Alcatel(SEL) – ANT – Newbridge	SA	1988					
AT&T – GTE(USA) = AG Comm. Sysm.	M	1988	X				
AT&T – Lucky Gold Star	JV	1984	X		X		
AT&T – Philips = APT–ANSI	JV	1983	X	X			
AT&T/ANSI – Italtel	JV	1989	X	X		X	X
Brit. Telecom – MITEL	M	1986		X		X	X
CIT - Alc. – Thomson = Alcatel	M	1985	X	X	X	X	X
Ericsson – GE	JV	1989	1	1			1
Ericcson – Hasler	LA	1983	X				
Ericcson – IBM	SA	1987	X				
Ericcson – Italtel	SA	1988	1	1			1
Ericsson – Kapsch	LA	1985				X	
Ericsson – Matra	SA	1987	1	1			1
Ericsson – Orbitel	SA	1987	1	1			1
Ericsson/Matra – CGCT = MET	JV	1987	X			X	X
Fujitsu – GTE(USA)	M	1987				X	
GEC – Plessey = GPT	M	1988	X	X	X	X	X
IBM – Rolm	M	1984				X	X
Motorola – DSC	SA	1987	1	1			1
Northern Telecom – Hasler	LA	1985				X	
Northern Telecom – STC	M	1987	X	X	X	X	X
Plessey – Stromberg	M	1982	X	X			X
Siemens – AT&T - PKI	SA	1988		X			
Siemens – GTE	M	1986	X	X		X	X
Siemens – IBM – Bell Atlantic	SA	1987	X				
Siemens – IBM/Rolm	JV	1989				X	X
Siemens – ISKRA = Iskratel	JV	1989	X				
Siemens – Italtel – Alcatel – Plessey	SA	1985	X				
Siemens – PKI – ANT/TN/Bosch	SA	1988	1	1			1
Siemens/GEC – Plessey (GPT)	M	1989	X	X	X	X	X

SWI	Public switching	JV	Joint venture
TRM	Transmission	M	Merger
CAB	Cables	SA	Strategic alliance
PBX	Private branch exchange	LA	Licensing agreement
TE	Terminal equipment	1	for mobile telephony

Source: Siemens Company Documents.

In PBXs, several of the world's largest vendors in 1982 were no longer independent by 1990: Rolm was acquired by IBM, then sold to Siemens; Mitel was acquired by British Telecom; Intecom was acquired by Wang, then sold to Matra; Telenoma was acquired by Bosch; Nixdorf by Siemens; GTE (PBX unit) by Fujitsu; and GPT by Siemens.

Despite these consolidations, fierce competition persisted in the central office switch and PBX markets, as stronger competitors moved into previously closed markets. However, technological incompatibilities, national political considerations, and the need to serve existing customers with established networks prevented significant integration of product lines. In 1990, one could still buy a GTE switch, a Thompson switch, an ITT switch, or a Rolm PBX—only under different corporate labels.

The following section briefly profiles the strategies and organizations of seven major telecommunications equipment vendors. (See **Exhibits 5** and **6** for market share data and **Exhibit 7** for company-specific financial summaries.)

EXHIBIT 5 Company Shares of Major Digital Switch Markets

A. World Market: 1982–1988

	1982	1984	1986	1987	1988
Alcatel	41.0%	31.4%	10.2%	15.4%	5.2%
ITT	*	2.4	3.7	—	—
AT&T	*	7.1	24.7	16.0	16.1
Ericsson	14.0	10.8	11.0	10.5	14.5
Fujitsu	*	2.7	4.0	3.8	3.5
GTE	2.0	11.5	6.0	3.6	3.2
NEC	5.0	10.0	7.2	8.5	7.9
Northern	29.0	4.9	20.1	14.8	15.3
Siemens	*	3.3	2.4	13.0	17.9
GEC	*	1.2	2.0	7.9	—
Plessey	5.0	2.7	2.9	—	—
Others	4.0	2.0	5.8	6.5	6.4
Total lines (000)	NA	12,632	23,061	NA	NA
Total revenues (M)	NA	$8,897	$10,960	$17,432	$19,047

Sources: 1987 and 1988 estimates are from McGraw-Hill/DRI.
1984–1986 estimates are from Northern Business Information.

C. Japanese Market: 1984–1987

	1984	1985	1986	1987
Fujitsu	35.0%	35.0%	40.0%	42.0%
Hitachi	5.0	15.9	19.2	16.2
NEC	57.9	30.6	24.3	23.3
Oki	2.1	18.5	16.5	18.5
Total lines (000)	140	712	1,293	6,001
Total revenues (M)	$455	$670	$907	$1,140

Source: Northern Business Information.

B. U.S. Market: 1982–1988

	1982	1984[a]	1986	1987	1988
AT&T	NA	20.0%	49.0%	47.2%	53.0%
GTE	3.0%	31.9	10.0	—	—
Ericsson	*	*	*	—	1.0
NEC	*	1.3	*	*	*
Northern	66.0	40.2	35.0	39.0	40.0
Siemens	*	*	*	*	5.0
Stromberg/GPT	2.0	NA	2.0	2.5	—
Others	29.0	6.6	4.0	11.3	1.0
Total lines (000)	NA	4,509	NA	14,600	9,400
Total revenues (M)	NA	$2,900	NA	$5,100	$5,050

D. Western European Market: 1984–1987

	1984	1985	1986	1987
Alcatel	70.7%	54.7%	34.0%	38.6%
ITT	3.5	8.5	12.0	—
Ericsson	13.1	16.0	19.7	17.5
GEC	3.2	6.4	9.0	25.3
Plessey	3.2	6.4	9.0	—
NEC	NA	NA	NA	1.5
Siemens	2.1	1.1	6.1	4.9
Other	4.2	7.2	10.2	12.2
Total lines (000)	4,748	4,681	5,000	6,123
Total revenues (M)	$2,742	$2,890	$2,705	$3,293

Sources: Robert Sayles Associates, Northern Business Information Datapro and Dataquest.

Source: Northern Business Information.

Note: Market shares based on number of lines shipped.

[a]Data for 1984 are for the United States and Canada.

*Denotes a market share of less than 1%, NA indicates that data were not available, — indicates that the firm's market share has been incorporated into that of the firm above it due to an acquisition or merger.

Competitor Profiles

ALCATEL Originally a subsidiary of CGE, Alcatel, the French electronics giant, merged with Thomson when CGE acquired Thomson in a consolidation of the French market in 1985.[44] In 1986, ITT, for years the number two supplier in the telecommunications equipment industry, entered a joint venture with Alcatel (61.5% was controlled by CGE, 37% by ITT, and 1.5% by Credit Lyonnais). The resulting company was involved in public network systems (25%), cable (28%), transmission systems (14%), business systems (21%), and other activities (12%).[45] In 1989, 82% of total revenues came from Europe, 29% of those from France and 17% from West Germany.

After the ITT merger, Alcatel restructured to consolidate product groups and divest unrelated businesses. The ITT acquisition guaranteed that Alcatel, with its E10 switch and ITT's System 12 switch, would be a major player in the European central office switch market, along with

EXHIBIT 6 Company Shares of Major PBX Markets

A. Principal Markets: 1987

	World	United States	Japan	Western Europe	West Germany
Alcatel	6.1%	*%	*%	16.9%	9.1%
AT&T	7.4	22.2	*	*	*
Bosch	4.8	*	*	12.0	24.1
Ericsson	4.1	1.3	*	8.0	*
Fujitsu/GTE	4.3	6.4	26.7	*	*
GPT	3.6	*	*	9.8	*
Mitel	6.4	9.9	*	5.3	*
NEC	7.2	8.6	44.8	*	*
Northern	10.6	17.2	*	4.2	*
Phillips	4.5	*	*	10.5	11.7
Rolm	7.5	14.5	1.4	*	*
Siemens	8.2	3.8	*	16.9	37.5
Toshiba	*	2.0	4.8	*	*
Others	25.3	14.1	22.3	16.4	17.6
Total (000 lines)	14,331	5,301	937	4,649	1,266
Total revenue (M)	$ 8,384	$3,086	$375	$2,368	NA

B. U.S. Market 1985–1988

	1985	1986	1987	1988
Alcatel	NA%	NA%	*%	NA%
AT&T	21.2	21.4	22.2	24.7
Fujitsu	2.2	2.4	6.4	5.6
GTE	3.9	4.3	—	—
Hitachi	1.9	1.9	1.9	1.9
Mitel	9.6	10.6	9.9	8.7
NEC	9.3	9.7	8.6	7.5
Northern	18.8	19.3	17.2	18.1
Siemens	4.0	3.8	3.8	19.1
IBM/Rolm	14.7	14.5	14.5	—
Toshiba	1.6	1.5	2.0	2.0
Others	12.8	10.6	13.5	12.4
Total (000 lines)	4,160	5,000	5,301	5,615
Total revenues (M)	$3,489	$3,105	$3,086	$2,843

Note: Market shares are based on number of lines shipped.

*Denotes a market share of less than 1%.

NA data were not available.

— Firm's market share incorporated into that of the firm directly above it due to an acquisition or merger.

Sources: North American Telecommunications Association, Northern Business Information.

EXHIBIT 7 Telecommunications Equipment Suppliers Financial Profiles: 1987–1989 (millions of U.S. dollars)[a]

Alcatel	1987	1988	1989	NEC	1987	1988	1989
Total revenue	13,021	13,061	14,058	Total revenue	19,756	20,566	22,020
Telecom. revenue	12,305	13,215	13,595	Telecom. revenue	5,644	5,741	5,732
Switch revenue	2,943	3,534	3,862	Switch revenue	1,588	1,683	1,784
Foreign revenue	11,100	11,320	10,969	Foreign revenue	5,607	5,648	5,552
Operating income	738	911	1,213	Operating income	744	855	944
Net income	366	425	525	Net income	121	192	461
Total assets	10,585	11,419	12,635	Total assets	22,306	22,007	23,903
Operating ROS	5.7%	7.0%	8.6%	Operating ROS	3.8%	4.2%	4.3%
Operating ROA	7.0%	8.0%	9.6%	Operating ROA	3.4%	4.0%	4.0%
R&D[b]	1,348	1,518	1,477	R&D[b]	3,072	3,280	3,471
AT&T				**Northern Telecom**			
Total revenue	33,768	35,210	36,112	Total revenue	4,915	5,408	6,106
Telecom. revenue	14,501	14,743	14,420	Telecom. revenue	4,854	5,246	5,910
Switch revenue	3,460	3,018	3,244	Switch revenue	2,577	2,910	3,258
Foreign revenue	433[c]	607[c]	1,000[c]	Foreign revenue	3,292	3,555	3,908
Operating income	3,476	(3,067)	4,278	Operating income	473	183	376
Net income	2,044	(1,669)	2,697	Net income	347	165	354
Total assets	38,426	35,152	37,687	Total assets	5,006	5,878	6,375
Operating ROS	10.3%	(8.7%)	11.8%	Operating ROS	9.6%	3.5%	6.2%
Operating ROA	9.0%	(8.7%)	11.4%	Operating ROA	9.5%	3.1%	5.9%
R&D[b]	2,453	2,572	2,652	R&D[b]	588	711	730
Ericsson				**Siemens**			
Total revenue	5,205	5,028	6,563	Total revenue	27,357	31,582	33,960
Telecom. revenue	3,679	4,969	5,926	Telecom. revenue[a]	3,435	3,571	3,770
Switch revenue	1,174	1,802	2,331	Switch revenue	2,558	2,712	2,874
Foreign revenue	4,049	4,115	5,533	Foreign revenue	11,953	15,159	18,155
Operating income	351	430	732	Operating income	559	368	551
Net income	(144)	(89)	(69)	Net income	678	740	876
Total assets	5,347	5,562	6,563	Total assets	29,194	31,711	35,776
Operating ROS	6.7%	8.6%	11.2%	Operating ROS	2.0%	1.2%	1.6%
Operating ROA	6.6%	7.7%	11.2%	Operating ROA	1.9%	1.2%	1.5%
R&D[b]	515	567	695	R&D[b]	3,451	3,600	3,819
Fujitsu							
Total revenue	14,315	15,506	18,987				
Telecom. revenue	2,162	2,460	2,844				
Foreign revenue	3,140	3,429	4,002				
Switch revenue	794	NA	NA				
Operating income	497	905	1,408				
Net income	311	319	528				
Total assets	15,985	17,550	19,886				
Operating ROS	3.5%	5.8%	7.4%				
Operating ROA	3.1%	5.2%	7.1%				
R&D[b]	NA	NA	NA				

[a]For conversion purposes the following exchange rates were used:

Yen/dollar: 125 (1987), 132 (1988), 140 (1989). Franc/dollar: 6.1 (1987), 6.0 (1988), 6.0 (1989). DM/dollar: 1.8 (1987), 1.8 (1988), 1.8 (1989). ECU/dollar: .86 (1987), .85 (1988), .91 (1989).

[b]R&D figures represent R&D for entire firm.

[c]Figures represent foreign sales for AT&T's Network Systems divisions only.

Sources: Corporate Annual Reports; Nothern Business Information,"The Telecom Strategy Letter" (February 1988); Arthur D. Little,"Spectrum" (December 1988).

Ericsson and Siemens. By 1987, it had a 39% share of Europe's digital switch market and a 70% share in France. The primary beneficiary of France's drive to rapidly digitalize its network, Alcatel controlled 90% of French digital switch sales in 1986. The firm also had a strong position in Eastern Europe and several developing countries and a minor presence in the U.S. central office switch market.

In 1989, Alcatel was the leading supplier of PBXs in Europe. It reached agreements with IBM in France and Siemens in Germany, guaranteeing compatibility between products. In the U.S. market, however, Alcatel had only a small share.

AT&T Even after the 1984 divestiture, AT&T remained the world's largest telecommunications equipment firm. As of 1988, AT&T's business divisions included telecommunication services (33%); business, data and consumer products (22%); network systems (19%); and other (26%). AT&T was perhaps the strongest brand name in the global telecommunications business, with a reputation for reliability and sophisticated technology.

Throughout the 1970s, AT&T consistently held 80% of the U.S. central office switch market. But in 1980, Canada's Northern Telecom began selling the first digital central office switch for the U.S. market four years before AT&T commercialized its digital switch. Although AT&T quickly rebounded after 1984, it had only half as many digital lines installed as Northern by the end of 1986.

After divestiture, AT&T's share was further diminished as the RBOCs, asserting their independence from AT&T, continued to ally with Northern and other new entrants in the U.S. digital switch market. The RBOCs complained that, among other things, AT&T had purposely minimized the centrex features of its switches to avoid competition with its PBX line.

Responding to increased competition at home and market opportunities abroad, AT&T reorganized to become a more aggressive, marketing-oriented competitor. The firm made each division a profit center and required operating divisions to contract with staff organizations for services. However, this separation of divisions resulted in reduced coordination across related product lines. Besides losing potential synergies across products, this lack of coordination caused confusion among AT&T customers, who reportedly often dealt with a different AT&T representative for each product in their network.

Internationally, AT&T pursued a strategy of aggressive expansion into Europe and Japan with the goal of generating 25% of its equipment revenues from non-U.S. sales by 2000. Recognizing its lack of international experience, AT&T launched a patchwork of strategic alliances: Philips, the Dutch electronics giant would help AT&T break into Europe's digital switch market; Olivetti would supply AT&T with PCs; a joint venture was signed with Spain's PTT, Telefonica, to make integrated circuits; Italy's SGS would distribute AT&T chips; a joint venture with Italtel would develop and sell public and private network equipment; Denmark's NKT would manufacture optical fiber under license from AT&T. In addition, a variety of distribution and joint-venture manufacturing agreements were signed throughout Asia, including a distribution arrangement with Toshiba to sell PBXs in Japan.

Once the world leader in the PBX arena, AT&T placed third after Northern Telecom and Siemens by 1988. However, AT&T did hold its position as the number one supplier in the United States, with a quarter of the market. While it marketed a full range of PBXs, its position was strongest in the medium and large PBX segments. AT&T was the second largest supplier of cellular systems in the United States after Motorola and the third largest supplier in the world.

ERICSSON Ericsson was among the smallest of the major central office switch vendors.[46] The firm's major telecommunications product groups included central office switches (43.6%), mobile telephone products (15.2%), business communications (11.3%), and media (8.9%).[47] Because of its small domestic market, this Swedish firm relied heavily on foreign markets, which accounted for 77% of Ericsson's total revenues and 91% of central office switch revenues. Industry sources described Ericsson as aggressive when entering new markets and willing to forgo short-term profitability in order to gain long-term market share.

Traditionally, Ericsson had focused on telecommunications in developing countries.

However, in the early 1980s, it shifted its efforts to information systems (computers and PBXs) in Europe and the United States. This strategy was unsuccessful because of a massive downturn in the computer industry and the slow convergence of computers and communications. Faced with rising R&D costs but without the financial resources of its competitors, Ericsson decided in 1987 to divest most of its computer business and refocus on telecommunications in the developed world, particularly central office and cellular switches. In fierce competition with AT&T and Siemens, Ericsson acquired the French central office switch supplier, CGCT, which gave it a 17.5% share of the West European switch market and a presence in all major European markets except Germany.

Despite a slow start in the United States, Ericsson had three RBOC central office switch contracts by 1990. Its success in the U.S. market was attributed to the sophistication and flexibility of the AXE, its "flagship" digital switch. In addition, it had increasingly located R&D in the United States to diffuse emerging technologies from the United States to markets abroad.

Although Ericsson's share of the world PBX market was small, the company was the world's largest cellular equipment vendor, with 40% of the world market in 1989. It was the largest supplier in Europe and close behind Motorola and AT&T in the United States.

FUJITSU Fujitsu produced computers (67%), telecommunications equipment (17%), and microelectronics (16%).[48] The firm controlled 42% of the digital switch market in Japan. Like NEC, Fujitsu had developed a separate switch for foreign markets. However, in 1988, it had only a 3.5% share of the world digital central office switch market, the bulk of its foreign sales coming from developing countries.

In the late 1980s, Fujitsu established a U.S. division, Fujitsu Network Switching of America, to design and implement its Fetex-150 digital switch. The firm was attempting to break into the U.S. market by technologically leapfrogging the competition into broadband switching.[49] Scheduled for sale in the U.S. market by 1991 or 1992, the Fetex was chosen by New England Telephone for a broadband trial in Boston in 1990.

In 1987, Fujitsu had a 26% share of the Japanese PBX market and a 4.3% share of the world market. With the purchase of GTE Business Systems in 1987, Fujitsu had increased its market share in the U.S. PBX market. Besides limited sales of transmission systems, Fujitsu had no appreciable market share in Europe.

NEC During the 1980s, the Japanese firm, NEC, sought integration in the fields of semiconductors, computers, and telecommunications equipment. It dubbed this strategy C&C—computers and communications.

NEC management recognized in the late 1970s that the digital switch was a disjuncture in technology that provided a significant opportunity to break into international markets. Before NTT started to develop a digital central office switch for the domestic market, NEC launched an independent R&D effort to design a digital switch to sell overseas. The result was the NEAX, a relatively simple, low-cost switch that sold well in the developing world.[50] Although NEC was one of the first (along with Northern Telecom) to export digital switches to the United States, sales remained stagnant as the switch failed to meet the technological and marketing requirements of the U.S. market.[51] By the early 1980s, NEC continued to lag behind AT&T in some basic telecommunications technologies, especially software, but excelled in others, such as low-cost manufacturing of high-volume components (e.g., the semiconductors and relays that are assembled into a switch).

In the late 1980s, NEC spent approximately ¥100 billion (about $770 million) to customize the NEAX switch for the U.S. market and invested in an assembly facility in Texas. Although NEC performed well in some market niches, NEC's share of the U.S. central office switch market had not risen above 1% by 1988. At home, NEC's share in the digital central office switch market declined precipitously in the 1980s as Fujitsu, Hitachi and Oki increased their shares.

NEC controlled about one-third of the Japanese PBX market throughout the 1980s. While capturing almost 10% of the U.S. market in 1986, poor distribution and increased competition caused NEC's share to deteriorate. In 1989, NEC was the largest supplier of cellular systems in Japan and fourth largest in the world, with most of its sales concentrated in Asia.

NORTHERN TELECOM In 1882, Northern Telecom was established as a manufacturer of telephones for Bell Canada, Canada's regulated telecommunications service provider. Originally a subsidiary of AT&T, this firm was incorporated under the laws of Canada in 1914 and became independent in 1956. Northern Telecom was 51.9% owned by Bell Canada Enterprises, which also owned Bell Canada. Northern's R&D activities, located primarily in Canada, were carried out by Bell Northern Research (BNR), which was jointly owned by Northern and Bell Canada.

Northern Telecom produced a full line of telecommunications equipment including customer premise equipment (36.8%), central office switches (36.6%), transmission equipment (15.7%), and media (10.9%).[52] Of total 1987 revenues, 90% came from North America, 60% from the United States.

In the late 1970s, Northern recognized, like NEC, that digital technology provided a significant opportunity to break into the U.S. market. Northern, however, was more successful at capitalizing on AT&T's slow response to digital switching technology than was NEC, perhaps due to its experience in the Canadian market which, in technical specifications, was vitrually identical to the U.S. market.

In 1988, Northern's share of the world digital central office switch market was 15.3%. Outside of North America, Northern had sold a limited number of central office switches in Australia, China, Japan and Turkey. Northern was the world's largest supplier of PBXs until 1988 when it was overtaken by Siemens/Rolm. To enhance its position, Northern formed strategic alliances with computer manufacturers, including Apple, DEC, ICL, Hewlett-Packard, Unisys, and Data General, to develop products with better computer interface. In addition, it entered into a joint venture with STC PLC, a British PBX supplier, in 1987. In cellular equipment, Northern was the fourth largest supplier in the world, primarily due to its strong position in the North American market.

SIEMENS A.G. Siemens was a widely diversified company with businesses including energy and automation (21%), semiconductors (3%), communication and information systems (17%), telecommunications networks and security systems

(17%), and other (42%).[53] Although the firm sold its products in 123 countries, approximately half of its sales were in the West Germany and three-quarters in Western Europe.

Siemens' close working relationship with the Bundespost, combined with limited competition in Germany for telecommunications equipment, allowed Siemens to generate a strong cash position (approximately $11.5 billion at the end of 1989), but it also caused the firm to be characterized as a "sleepy bureaucracy living off lucrative government contracts."[54] Protected from competition, Siemens could sell cordless phones through the Bundespost for $665, compared to $79 for a Japanese version in the United States.[55] The Bundespost paid an estimated $700 in 1989 for each telephone line while America's regional telephone operators paid about $160.[56]

European integration and the deregulation of telecommunication markets threatened Siemens' home market. In 1988, CEO Kaske promoted a flatter hierarchy and greater flexibility by rationalizing central operations, eliminating two management layers, reassigning 9,000 headquarters employees, and splitting seven operating units into 15 more specialized units, each with separate sales and marketing staffs. In the telecommunications area, for example, public communication networks (central office switches, transmission equipment, and media) and private communication networks (PBXs) were constituted as autonomous entities.[57] Despite Siemens' extensive social safety net, some of its 376,000 employees began to fear for their jobs.

Siemens tried to increase its share in the global central office switch market via direct investment and the acquisition of foreign suppliers. It maintained research, development, and manufacturing facilities for its central office switch, the EWSD, in the United States and marketed aggressively to increase its share at the expense of AT&T and Northern.[58] Its purchase of 40% of GPT gave Siemens a strong position in the United Kingdom's central office switch market and also provided Siemens with a 40% share in Stromberg-Carlson, GPT's central office switch subsidiary in the United States. This acquisition increased Siemens' share of the U.S. switch market to 5% by 1988.

Similarly, in the PBX business, Siemens was able to buy market share. By acquiring Nixdorf and GPT, Siemens gained dominant positions at home (45%) and in the United Kingdom (78%).[59] By buying Rolm, it gained access to IBM's large distribution network, increased its share of the U.S. market, and became the leading PBX supplier in the world.

OTHERS Other important firms in the telecommunications equipment industry included Bosch, Mitel, Toshiba, Hitachi, and Oki. Mitel, Toshiba, and Bosch were significant players in the PBX market. Hitachi and Oki were both major competitors in the Japanese PBX and central office switch markets, but had virtually no market share abroad. Toshiba and Mitel did not produce a central office switch and Bosch's participation in the switch market was limited to the joint development and production of the EWSD, under licensing agreement with Siemens, for the West German market.

End Notes

1. A Regional Bell Operating Company is one of the 22 Bell telephone companies whose primary business is providing local telephone service to customers.

2. "Fourteen Things You Should Know About ISDN," *Telecommunications*, December 1987, p. 39.

3. U.S. Congress, Office of Technology Assessment, *Critical Connections, Communications for the Future* (Washington, D.C.: Government Printing Office, 1990), p. 50.

4. *Telephony*, August 28, 1989, p. 40. Robert Sayles estimated the market at $140 billion in 1988, and Northern Business Information's estimate was approximately $55 billion in 1987. Discrepancies in estimates probably stem from alternative treatment of computer equipment and/or radio equipment by the source.

5. *Communication Systems Statistics* (Observatoire Mondial Des Systems de Communications, 1989), p. 12.

6. "Telecommunications," *The Economist*, March 10, 1990, p. 14; figures are for 1987.

7. *Communication Systems Statistics* (Observatoire Mondial Des Systems de Communications, 1989), p. 20.

8. *Telephony* (August 28, 1989), p. 40.

9. A multiplexer combines multiple signals for simultaneous transmission. This key product segment accounted for approximately $3 billion in sales in the United States alone in 1989. "Telecommunications," *The Economist*, March 10, 1990, p. 16.

10. Growth rate projection in real terms; J.M. Guite, Salomon Brothers, Inc., *Telecommunications Equipment: The United States Market*, February 1987, p. 14.

11. The Yankee Group, *Carrier Network Technology: The Next Generation* (Boston, Mass., June 1989), p. 48–49; U.S. Congress, Office of Technology Assessment, *Critical Connections: Communication for the Future* (Washington, D.C.: Government Printing Office, 1990), p. 46.

12. Northern Business Information, *World Public Switching Market, 1987 Edition* (New York: NBI, 1988), p. 95.

13. "The Central Office Switch Industry in 1985," Harvard Business School, Case No. 187-053, 1986, p. 7.

14. AT&T interview, 1989.

15. Paolo Cecchini, *1992, The Benefits of a Single Market* (Commission of the European Communities, 1988), p. 54.

16. Key telephone systems are multiline telephone systems designed to provide shared access to several outside lines through buttons or keys on the handset.

17. Northern Business Information, *World PBX, KTS and Centrex Markets: 1988 Edition,* p. 5.

18. NATA, *Industry Basics,* (Washington, D.C.: North American Telecommunications Association, 1990), p. 27.

19. Dataquest Inc., *PBX*, November 1988, p. 8.

20. *Washington Post*, August 11, 1989.

21. NATA, *Telecommunications Market Review and Forecast* (Washington, D.C.: North American Telecommunications Association, 1990), p. 12.

22. Peter Huber, *The Geodesic Network: 1987 Report on Competitiveness in the Telephone Industry*, (Washington, D.C.: U.S. Department of Justice, 1987), p. 16–21.

23. Bell Canada, which was divested from AT&T under an antitrust consent decree in 1956, was likewise privately owned; Northern Telecom, its exclusive equipment supplier, was a wholly owned subsidiary. Other American telephone companies, including nearly 1,500 independent exchange companies, were also privately owned. One of these firms, GTE, was also vertically integrated.

24. *Carterfone* 13 F.C.C. 2d 606 (1968); *Foreign Attachments Tariff Revisions*, 15 F.C.C. 2d 605 (1968); *Second Computer Inquiry*, 77 F.C.C. 2d 384, 390 (1980).

25. *Above 890 Mc.*, 27 F.C.C. 359 (1959); *Microwave Communications, Inc.*, 18 F.C.C. 2d, 953; *MCI Telecommunications Corp. v. FCC*, 580 F.2d 590 (D.C. Cir.), *cert. denied*, 439 U.S. 980 (1978).

26. *The New York Times*, August 5, 1990.

27. *U.S. v. AT&T*, C.A. No. 82-0192, "Modification of Final Judgment," August 24, 1982.

28. Richard H.K. Vietor, "AT&T and the Public Good: Regulation and Competition in Telecommunications, 1910–1987," in S. Bradley and J. Hausman, *Future Competition in Telecommunications* (Boston: HBS Press, 1989), p. 80–93.

29. FCC, Docket No. 85-229, *Third Computer Inquiry*, "Report and Order," June 16, 1986.

30. This had still proven unsuccessful as of 1990.

31. FCC, CC Docket No. 87-313, "Notice of Proposed Rule Making," August 21, 1987; *Communications Week*, March 20, 1989, pp. 1–52.

32. For more detailed description of Japan's telecommunications policies, see Tsuruhiko Nambu, Kazuyuki Suzuki, and Tetsushi Honda, "Deregulation in Japan," in Robert Crandall and Kenneth Flamm, eds., *Changing the Rules* (Washington, D.C.: The Brookings Institution, 1989), pp. 147–173; Youichi Ito, "Telecommunications and Industrial Policies in Japan: Recent Developments," in Marcellus S. Snow, *Marketplace for Telecommunications* (London: Longman Inc., 1986), pp. 201–230; Jill Hills, *Deregulating Telecoms* (Westport, Conn.: Quorum Books), chapter 4.

33. Harumasa Sato and Rodney Stevenson, "Telecommunications in Japan: After Privatization and Liberalization," *Columbia Journal of World Business*, Spring 1989, pp. 31–41.

34. Prior to 1987, the EC had adopted several resolutions, including establishment of a joint R&D program called RACE, a framework for standardization of telecommunications technologies, common standards for certain satellite broadcasting, and ISDN; and an important directive on the initial stage of mutual recognition of type approval for telecommunications terminal equipment; Commission of the European Communities, *Green Paper on the Development of the Common Market for Telecommunications Services and Equipment* (Brussels, June 1987), p. 5.

35. EC, *Green Paper*, pp. 14–16.

36. Paolo Cecchini, *1992, The Benefits of a Single Market*, The Commission of the European Communities, 1988, p. 22.

37. European Commission, "Commission Directive on Competition in the Markets in Telecommunications Terminal Equipment," Brussels, July 4, 1988; Article 90 allows the Commission to make certain laws without obtaining the approval of the Council of Ministers or the European parliament.

38. "Success Story of a Defender of the Public Service Ethic," *Financial Times*, April 19, 1990.

39. Commission of the European Communities, *Green Paper . . Appendices* (Brussels, June 9, 1987), Appendix 1, pp. 16–22.

40. "An Interview with Christian Schwarz-Schilling," *Telecommunications*, January, 1990, p. 29.

41. Deutsche Bundespost, *Recommendations in the Witte Report* (adoption schedule, 1989).

42. "The Paranoia Eases," *Financial Times*, April 19, 1990.

43. "Siemens, Soviets in C.O. Venture," *Telephony*, June 25, 1990, p. 3.

44. Arthur D. Little, "Central Office Switching Equipment: The Competitive Environment" (Cambridge, Mass.: December 1988).

45. Percentages represent share of revenue in 1988.

46. Arthur D. Little, "Central Office Switching Equipment: The Competitive Environment," (Cambridge, Mass.: December 1988).

47. Percentages represent share of revenue in 1988.

48. Percentages represent share of revenue in 1988.

49. "Nynex picks Fujitsu Switch for Boston Broadband Trial," *Telephony*, June 18, 1990, p. 8.

50. By the mid 1980s, NEC achieved dominant markets shares in New Zealand (100%), Thailand (80%), Malaysia (60%), Hong Kong (50%), Argentina (50%), China (35%), Brazil (32%), Venezuela (32%), and Chile (30%).

51. In the United States, NEC's NEAX was first installed at Rochester Telephone but, after major problems, the switch was taken out.

52. Percentages represent share of revenue in 1988.

53. Percentages represent revenue share in 1989.

54. "Siemens: A Plodding Giant Starts to Pick Up Speed," *Business Week*, February 20, 1989, p. 136.

55. Ibid., p. 137.

56. "War by Another Means," *The Economist*, December 17, 1989, p. 72.

57. Siemens Annual Report, 1989, p. 9.

58. According to the *Wall Street Journal* (March 22, 1989) p. A10, Siemens employed the unheard-of marketing technique of loading a $3 million switch into a van and driving it around the United States to show to potential buyers.

59. *The General Electric Company plc, Siemens AG and the Plessey Company plc,* A report on the proposed mergers, Presented to Parliament by the Secretary of State for Trade and Industry by Command of Her Majesty, April 1989, (London: Her Majesty's Stationery Office).

4. Note on the PC Network Software Industry, 1990

Personal computers (PCs) were initially stand-alone machines that did not communicate with other computers. As PCs became ubiquitous, organizations soon demanded networking capability. Initially companies wanted a network to connect multiple PCs to shared printers. For as little as $200 per PC, 10, 20, or more users could share a $10,000 printer. Over time, PC users also realized that networks were convenient ways to share information without copying a file onto a diskette and walking it to another desk. To meet these challenges, vendors had to offer a variety of hardware components combined with software. This note describes the evolution and structure of the PC networking software industry.

PC Network Technology

Special software was necessary to build a PC network because of the nature of the original IBM PC. DOS, the operating system software that controlled IBM-compatible machines, was used on roughly 80% of all PCs worldwide in 1990. The problem, from a networking point of view, was that IBM compatible PCs running DOS were not designed with networking in mind. They were designed for stand-alone computing.[1] To solve this dilemma, technology in 1990 offered two solu-

[1]The second-ranked operating system was the Macintosh, which held roughly a 10% share of global PCs. The "Mac" was designed with networking in mind, as Macs could readily communicate with one another and share printers. Traditional operating systems that controlled mainframes and minicomputers, as well as workstations running UNIX, had networking capability designed directly into the system.

Professor David B. Yoffie and Associate Fellow Toby Lenk prepared this note as the basis for class discussion.

tions: peer-to-peer networking and client-server networking. Peer-to-peer required that software and a computer board be added directly into every PC. A cable connected the computers to shared printers. This model was generally the easiest and cheapest solution as well as the most common in very small organizations or in work groups, where sharing printers was the main goal (see **Exhibit 1**).

The client-server model was a much more powerful solution, also involving new hardware and software on the PC. However, the bulk of the software was located on a PC dedicated to controlling the networks. This dedicated computer, called a "server," was the brains of the network, directing data traffic between individual PCs, called "clients." To perform this traffic cop role, servers required special software called a "NOS" (network operating system) that talked to the clients and handled all network functions. Unlike peer-to-peer computing, servers controlled by a NOS allowed users to more rapidly pass files between PCs. Users could also store directly on the server large files regularly accessed by several people. The higher performance client-server networks had become dominant in most medium and large companies by the end of the 1980s.

Originally, PC networks were common in small departments in geographically concentrated locations. It was unusual for more than 50 or 100 PCs to be connected in a group or local area network (LAN). A typical LAN might compose all of the PCs on one or two floors of a building, just sharing files and a few printers. By 1990, however, MIS departments and PC users were demanding new functionality. Of particular interest were wide-area capability, connectivity, and client-server applications.

WIDE-AREA NETWORKS As PC networks became widespread in corporations, users wanted to communicate with PCs on other LANs, sometimes in distant locales. This required additional technology called WANs—wide area networks—that connected computers that were geographically dispersed. In the 1980s, most WANs were based on mainframe or minicomputer technology. A common example of a WAN was an airline reservation system. An airline would maintain a computer control center with large mainframe computers. At airports around the world, ticket counter computer terminals were connected to the central computer. This particular application was mission critical for an airline: if the WAN did not work, the cost of downtime was prohibitive. WAN systems were usually developed over many years, and represented large investments by companies. By 1990, the power of microprocessors meant that development of WANs based on PCs was technically possible, but still inefficient and expensive.

CONNECTIVITY Beyond communicating with other PCs, users wanted to communicate with traditional mini and mainframe computer systems. Increasingly sophisticated end users wanted the capability to extract data from their company's central computers, through their PC network, and into their PC spreadsheets. By 1990, roughly one-third of PC LANs were connected to mini or mainframe computers.

CLIENT-SERVER APPLICATIONS (CSA) Client-server applications were one of the most important areas of development. Suppliers were attempting to make it easy for the industry to write applications software to run on the server. Just as Lotus had to write different versions of 1-2-3 for each operating system (DOS, OS2, MAC), CSAs were written for particular NOSs. Software vendors believed that, just as 1-2-3 helped sell PCs and DOS, client-server applications could help sell servers and NOSs. Electronic mail represented one example of CSA. A more complex CSA was Lotus Notes, a powerful program that ran on a server, but allowed everyone on the network to share information and build common data bases. Other than Lotus Notes, however, CSA development remained very limited through 1990. Few applications were running on client-server networks.

EXHIBIT 1 Peer-to-Peer PC LAN versus Client-Server PC LAN

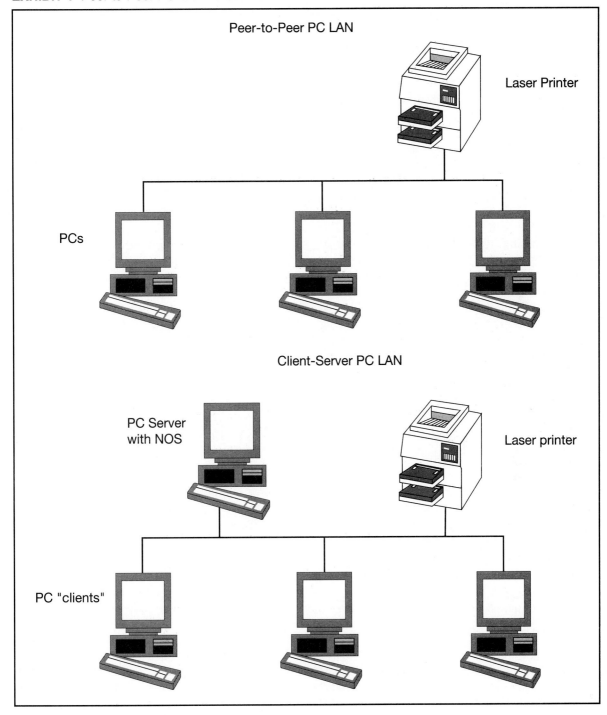

Market Development

The economics of network software were similar to many other segments of the PC software business. Vendors generally incurred huge upfront R&D costs, ranging from $5 to $10 million for a new application program, and up to $200 million for a new operating system. Since production costs were negligible, however, software programs usually generated gross margins of 80%. Volume and distribution costs were critical: for a typical shrink-wrapped desktop application program with a price tag of $100–$500, the program would be sold through retail or mail order, making advertising and shelf space essential. For desktop operating systems, hardware manufacturers usually bundled the software product with the computer. Selling peer-to-peer networking software packages (which included the computer board and cable) at about $200 apiece was akin to selling a shrink-wrapped application. But selling CSAs often required sophisticated reseller channels; and selling NOSs for client-server computing was even more complicated. PC network software suppliers generated revenues in several ways. First, they would sell a NOS license ($5,000 to $12,000 for up to 250 users) for a fee. This allowed an MIS manager to place the NOS software on a server, and connect a limited number of PCs. Second, customers could purchase add-on licenses to connect additional PCs to the server. Finally, suppliers could induce customers to replace their existing NOS with an updated or more powerful version. As the size of networks expanded, users often had to trade-up to a more powerful product.

By the end of 1990, more than 15 million PCs worldwide were connected to PC networks. This number was expected to rise to over 38 million by the end of 1993 (see **Exhibit 2**). A total of 1.5 million PCs acting as dedicated PC LAN servers controlled these networks. There were two factors driving growth: increasing installation of PCs worldwide and increasing network penetration. In 1990, 28% of networkable PCs in the world were connected to a network. Larger organizations, traditionally intensive users of computer technology, were also intensive users of networks. In large U.S.-based organizations (over 1,000 employees) an estimated 50% of PCs were connected to some sort of network in 1990. In organizations with fewer than 100 employees, this figure was less than 20% (see **Exhibit 3**).

Network software revenues grew from $190 million in 1987 to $850 million in 1990. Because of the various ways a supplier could earn rev-

EXHIBIT 2 World LAN Penetration and Forecast (all unit figures in 1,000s)

Region	1989	1990	1991	1992	1993
U.S. Installed PCs by End-Use Segment:					
Business/government	22,193	27,547	33,478	40,238	46,944
Education/home	24,904	29,354	34,496	40,620	44,056
Total	47,097	56,901	67,974	80,858	91,000
Potential market	22,193	27,547	33,478	40,238	46,944
Installed PC network nodes[a]	6,496	9,500	13,000	16,900	21,125
Rest of World Installed PCs by End-Use Segment:					
Business/government	21,720	28,474	36,394	45,310	54,550
Education/home	25,374	29,942	35,665	42,451	46,950
Total	47,094	58,416	72,059	87,761	101,500
Potential market	21,720	28,474	36,394	45,310	54,550
Installed PC network nodes	3,213	5,992	9,385	13,236	17,456
Penetration	15%	21%	26%	29%	32%

Note: It is assumed that the potential market encompasses business and government PCs. Education PCs, particularly in a university, also represent potential but are a very small portion of the education/home market.

[a]Nodes are defined as end points of networks. An end point could be a PC, printer, fax machine, etc.

Source: Sanford and Bernstein Research, "The PC Software Industry," and the International Data Corporation.

EXHIBIT 3 U.S. LAN Penetration by Organization Size, 1990

	Total	Small	Medium	Large	Government
Total potential PCs[a]	63,000	19,000	26,000	10,000	8,000
PCs installed	27,547	8,050	11,800	5,297	2,400
PC LAN nodes installed	9,500	1,500	4,550	2,650	800
LAN penetration	34%	19%	39%	50%	33%

Note: Small organizations are 100 employees or less; medium 100–1,000; large is over 1,000.

[a]This is equivalent to the number of white-collar workers for each size category.

Source: Dataquest, International Data Corporation (IDC). Sanford and Bernstein, casewriter estimates.

enue, forecasting the market was more complicated than forecasting networked PCs. Furthermore, the available market partly depended upon the rate at which customers retired old technology. In 1990, for instance, one-third of the growth in PC networks came from add-ons to existing networks, and two-thirds came from the creation of new networks. By 1993, add-ons were projected to be 50%. While analysts predicted that growth in networking would remain high, shipments of new NOS licenses were likely to slow. First, NOSs and servers in 1990 were growing more powerful and could support larger networks, decreasing the need for extra servers and NOS licenses. Second, upgrade and add-on shipments did not result in new licenses, though they generated revenue. **Exhibit 4** provides a demand model incorporating these market dynamics.

Market Segmentation

Network software suppliers identified three major segments: group, department, and enterprise. Although each segment had distinct product and marketing requirements, all three segments could, and often did, exist within the same organization.

EXHIBIT 4 World PC LAN Market Model and Forecast (unit figures in 1,000s)[a]

	1987	1988	1989	1990	1991[f]	1992[f]
Revenues ($ million)	$190	$373	$595	$850	$1,100	$1,380
Shipments:						
Net NOS licenses	172	283	345	415	475	520
Network nodes	1,371	2,982	4,945	7,033	9,055	11,033
New license nodes	1,254	2,406	3,466	4,703	5,668	6,369
Add-on nodes	117	576	1,479	2,330	3,387	4,664
Installed Base:						
Base nodes	1,280	2,572	5,339	9,709	15,492	22,384
New license nodes	1,254	2,406	3,466	4,703	5,668	6,369
Add-on nodes	117	576	1,479	2,330	3,387	4,664
Retired nodes	79	216	575	1,250	2,162	3,281
End-base nodes	2,572	5,338	9,709	15,492	22,385	30,136
Nodes Analysis:						
Add-on nodes	117	576	1,479	2,330	3,387	4,664
Greenfield nodes	1,175	2,190	2,891	3,453	3,506	3,088
Switched nodes[b]	79	216	575	1,250	2,162	3,281
TOTAL	1,371	2,982	4,945	7,033	9,055	11,033

[a]Definitions:
- Add-on nodes are nodes purchased to expand an existing LAN.
- New license nodes are purchased to start a new LAN.
- Retired nodes are, by definition, when one brand of LAN software is replaced by another brand.
- New license nodes go to replace retired or "switched" nodes, and to begin a first-time or "greenfield" LAN.

[b]Note: Much of the switching would be to replace old technologies, such as MS-NET.

[f]Forecast

Source: Sanford and Bernstein Research, "The PC Software Industry," and the International Data Corporation.

GROUP Group networks were small, typically under 10 PCs, which did not connect to other networks. The simplest group network allowed users to share printers only. It was critical that group networks be easy to install and use, since they were sold through retail computer stores without much technical support. A small law firm, for instance, would spend $25,000 to $30,000 for the hardware and software to network 10 computers. This price included the cost of the PCs. The NOS represented between 15% and 20% of total costs.

DEPARTMENT Department networks were larger, and might involve several servers and networks communicating with one another, with perhaps up to 100 or more users. Department networks were usually connected to mini or mainframe computer systems, allowing users to send messages and mail to people outside their PC LAN. Users typically shared files, storing larger word and data files on servers for common access. They were more complex than group networks, and were typically sold by skilled resellers specializing in networking. These resellers were capable of selecting, designing, installing, and troubleshooting a network. A typical network for this segment cost $75,000+ installed, in addition to a part or full-time LAN administrator to keep the network operating.

ENTERPRISE Enterprise networks connected departments and groups throughout an organization, across wide geographical areas. They were still quite new, because they depended on evolving PC-based WAN technology. Enterprise networks were only applicable to larger companies and involved long selling cycles with many parties. Parties included network product vendors, skilled resellers, and often big computer companies with a loyal following among the customer's internal computer management (MIS) staff. Enterprisewide systems were customized projects, costing millions of dollars. However, for any project over $200,000, the NOS usually represented roughly 2% of the total cost of the network.

Selling NOSs in 1990 was complicated by the industry's history. LANs did not develop in an orderly fashion: in a typical company, nontechnical PC users would buy a NOS without consulting the MIS staff. It was common to find up to 10 different PC LAN software brands inside one company. By the end of 1990, MIS departments in medium- to large-sized organizations were seeking standardization. They were choosing one or two software systems, and ordering a halt to purchases of all others. This was particularly true for department and enterprise networks. Therefore, suppliers were beginning to recognize there might be only two segments in the 1990s: department and enterprise LANs for medium- to large-sized organizations, or the *corporate market*, and group LANs, or the *low end*. Exhibit 5 estimates the 1990 market by segment.

Despite the desire for standardization, customers found it difficult to change existing LANs. End-users who were familiar with their network software resisted any change. Technical administrators who operated the network also resisted learning new systems. In addition, files and ap-

EXHIBIT 5 Estimate of 1990 World PC LAN Market By Segment

	Node Shipments (000s)	NOS Revenue ($ million)	Revenue per Node ($)
Corporate Segment:			
Department LANs	3,517	$425	$121
Enterprise LANs	422	85	200
Low-End:			
Group + small department LANs	3,095	340	110
TOTAL	7,033	850	121

Note: Corporate segment is medium to large organizations, including the government, purchases of department and enterprise PC LAN software. The low-end includes all group LANs, regardless of what size organization buys them, and department LANs bought by small organizations.

Source: Sanford & Bernstein, IDC, MIcrosoft and casewriter estimates.

plications were transferred at great cost, and sometimes could not be transferred at all. Specialized applications could cost up to $100,000 to rewrite for a new NOS. Finally, it was costly to transfer from one brand of software to another. Replacing old software on each PC typically required an average of one hour's labor, at $110–$135 per hour.

Competitors

The PC networking business started with many firms in the early 1980s, most supplying hardware and software components. On average, customers spent twelve dollars on hardware[2] for every dollar spent on software to build a PC network. However, hardware was generally not proprietary and firms that developed software found it increasingly difficult to manufacture the equipment competitively. The leading software firms, earning low or negative margins on hardware, were withdrawing from hardware in 1990.

When the PC network software industry began, many firms developed and marketed peer-to-peer products to connect IBM compatible PCs. However, with the emergence of client-server networking and increasing demands for more complex products from corporate customers, research and development requirements grew. In addition, the resellers who sold network software were themselves burdened, and could not invest in learning several network software products. An industry-wide shake-out left only a handful of significant competitors. One firm, Novell, achieved the largest position, with approximately 60% market share worldwide (**Exhibit 6**). IBM, Banyan, and Microsoft were the other leading players.

Novell

Situated at the foot of Utah's Wasatch mountain range in Provo, Novell emerged from near bankruptcy in 1983 to generate $497 million in sales in 1990. When Chairman Raymond J. Noorda, a 20-year veteran of General Electric, joined Novell in 1983, the firm produced hardware components with sales of less than $20 million. Noorda redirected the firm into products for networking DOS-based PCs. As Noorda reflected, "Initially, we just needed to pay some bills, and these PC network products were what we chose to get into." Since then, Novell's strategy has been the most focused in the industry: build and broadly distribute network operating system software.

Novell's global leadership in the PC network software industry was widely attributed to its 66-year-old chairman. A millionaire many times over, Noorda paid himself $35,000 a year and confined his work space to a windowless office just big enough for a desk and a chair.[3] A sometime golfer, Noorda patronized a course next to Novell's Provo headquarters: "They let us old folks in for nothing, and I take advantage of that." Described as folksy yet frugal and grandfatherly yet tough, Noorda developed the concept of "co-opetition" at Novell. Unlike his counterparts at rival firms, Noorda stressed the need to cooperate with all comers—even competitors—to make networking grow. Noorda viewed competitors as partners to an expanding industry and, in that capacity, as natural combatants to complacency. In reference to Novell's primary competitor, Microsoft, Noorda confessed, "[They] make us work harder and avoid that dominant mentality, which I hate." Competition, he stressed, "will simply make us better." Despite Noorda's widely-perceived "aw shucks" persona, competitors claimed that Noorda's down-home demeanor belied a steel core.

Novell's first products were relatively simple, meeting customer's early demands for basic printer and file sharing capability. As revenues

[2]This includes the PC server, cables, cards, routers and other associated equipment necessary to build a PC network. Hardware firms generally specialized within one category, and their equipment could generally be used interchangeably with any PC network software designed to connect IBM compatible PCs.

[3]At year-end 1990, Noorda owned 8,000,000 shares of Novell common stock, which closed at $32.125 on 12/28/90, making his stake worth approximately $281 million.

EXHIBIT 6 Worldwide PC LAN Market Shares of Leading Competitors, 1990

	Node Shipments (%)	Installed Base (%)
Novell	60%	55%
IBM		
(PC-NET, LAN Server)	11	13
Banyan	5	4
3Com[a]	5	12
Other	19	16

[a]3Com's shipment share was over 12% in 1989. The 1990 figure represents an estimate of their ongoing software support as they exit software.

Source: International Data Corporation, Sanford and Bernstein, casewriter estimates.

EXHIBIT 7 Novell's Product Line

Product	Segment	Retail Price[a]	Notes for Initial License	Total Number Possible Users
ELS I	Low end	$ 895	4	4
ELS II	Low end	1,895	8	8
Netware 286	Corporate	3,295	15	100
Netware 286 SFT[b]	Corporate	4,995	15	100
Netware 386	Corporate	7,995	25	250

[a]This was for the first NOS license—add-on nodes were purchased separately.
[b]SFT stood for "system fault tolerance" capability.

Source: Novell literature, Microsoft NBU

EXHIBIT 8 Novell Financial Performance, 1985–1990 (all figures in millions of $)

	1985	1986	1987	1988	1989	1990
Revenue	$45.2	$119.7	$221.8	$347.0	$421.9	$497.5
Cost of goods sold	18.9	47.9	90.8	152.0	152.4	132.3
Gross profit	26.3	71.8	131.0	195.0	269.5	365.2
Operating expenses:						
Sales and marketing	9.9	NA	57.4	93.0	131.6	142.8
Product development	4.1	NA	16.3	27.0	41.3	59.3
General and administrative	3.2	NA	16.3	21.0	25.2	28.9
TOTAL	17.2	46.6	90.0	141.0	198.1	231.0
Operating income	9.1	25.2	41.1	54.0	71.5	134.2
Net income	4.9	14.3	24.4	35.9	48.5	94.3
Net income per share	$0.21	$0.25	$0.39	$0.55	$0.73	$1.36
Cash and investments	2.2	10.5	53.3	80.1	129.8	254.8
Working capital	6.3	34.8	104.5	184.3	216.4	308.3
Total assets	19.2	67.1	171.9	280.3	346.6	494.4
Long-term debt	1.1	3.0	3.6	56.1	57.0	2.4
Shareholders' equity	7.7	42.8	133.2	174.6	235.8	398.3
Stock price:						
High	NA	5 1/4	14 7/8	15 5/8	19 1/8	29 1/4
Low	NA	3 1/4	5 1/8	7 5/8	11 7/8	12 3/8

Source: Company reports.

grew, Novell added functionality, partly by spending aggressively on R&D, and partly by buying small software companies that enhanced its technology. Almost every year, Novell came out with successive generations of more powerful NOSs. By 1990, Novell had become the leader in group and department networks, with an array of products under the name "Netware."

To distribute Netware in the United States, Novell relied upon 12,000 resellers of various types. A few could be classified as VARs (value-added resellers), who actually wrote supplemental software to work with Netware to solve particular customer problems. Still more were classified as highly skilled resellers who could sell and implement department LANs. The vast majority, however, were computer stores that stocked the simpler Netware targeted at the low end. Novell owed much of its success to its broad product line and distribution. Noorda summarized his strategy with the simple phrase "Netware anywhere, Netware everywhere." However, resellers complained that margins on Netware were razor thin; and a few customers complained that some resellers did not support Netware well. In response, Novell recently instituted a program to classify its distributors to avoid confusion and to reduce channel conflict. "Platinum" resellers were VARs and the more highly skilled resellers, of which there were 1,000. About 2,000 "gold" resellers formed the next tier, with the remaining thousands classified simply as "Netware certified." However, platinum resellers continued to complain, as they received little in the way of concrete benefits from their platinum designation. Distributors were not granted exclusive territories or given special leads.

In a characteristic display of toughness, Noorda noted that his competitors, Banyan and Microsoft, had both "screwed up" in networking. Noorda wanted them to do better so "they could help grow the industry" and "make sure our people do not become complacent." He also brushed aside any criticism about Novell's "over-distribution." Resellers often sold the software bundled with hardware, installation, and service, which allowed them to turn a profit. Noorda felt Novell's mission was to provide the best software as part of a broader solution, not to provide a superior standalone margin on Netware: "This (saturation) should not be a problem. The good

resellers don't even break out the price of Netware. And the bad ones, who complain, probably won't survive."

Novell had consistently moved its technology forward in terms of complexity and functionality, but early Netware lacked the emerging technologies of connectivity, client-server applications, and wide-area networking, all of which were demanded by the corporate segment. To strengthen Novell's position, Noorda purchased Excelan in 1989, a leading firm in connectivity technology. He then introduced an entirely new product, Netware 386, based on the powerful Intel 386 microprocessor. Netware 386 was designed as a general-purpose operating system for which other software firms could write client-server application software. Finally, Novell announced that it would deliver some crucial wide-area capability in future versions of Netware 386.

Novell's other weakness was its distribution to the corporate segment. Its strategy of relying on resellers made it difficult to sell more advanced networks inside larger companies. Noorda was seeking to build a direct presence within *Fortune 500* customers. Most large firms had Netware running someplace in their firm, but had never dealt directly with a Novell employee. Noorda had consistently sought, and failed, to strengthen his corporate distribution by entering into marketing relationships with larger computer firms, most notably IBM and DEC. These two firms distributed their own brands of PC network software, which they licensed from Microsoft.

Noorda was the driving force behind Novell, but his age, the lack of an obvious successor, and the growing need for scale economies in R&D led Novell's board to explore mergers with other companies in the late 1980s. In early 1990, Novell publicly announced that it would merge with the Lotus Development Corporation. This merger would produce a PC software firm with over $1.1 billion in revenue, equalling the size of industry leader Microsoft. Analysts felt the combination was a strong one, resulting in a competitor that could deliver networking and future networking applications. Lotus had already announced a new application, Lotus Notes, designed to run in a networked environment. Analysts also felt that the merged firms' scale would be an important factor, providing both a boost in competing with archrival Microsoft. However, the merger collapsed when Novell's board demanded equal representation in the merged company, and Lotus CEO Jim Manzi refused.

Banyan

When Banyan Systems was formed in 1983 with $3 million of venture funding it had a strong vision of the future for computer networking. The company developed a network operating system with a flexible architecture, based on UNIX,[4] designed to connect different types of computers running different operating systems to local and wide-area networks. According to CEO David Mahoney, "We address the needs of the corporate office, not small workgroups." Experts generally agreed that Banyan's "Vines" software was the most powerful and flexible solution for enterprisewide connectivity and mission critical applications.

The Vines target market was medium to large corporations that needed to connect hundreds or thousands of PCs as well as mainframes and minicomputers. Mahoney pointed out the key difference between Banyan and Novell: "Our business is not moving shrinkwrapped products through retail channels . . . we solve problems with a skilled and direct presence at the customer." Banyan's highly skilled and experienced representatives dealt with corporate MIS managers and referred sales to Banyan's 150 resellers. The selling cycle often required a year or more, but could result in an initial order up to a quarter-million dollars if the application involved multiple copies of Vines installed throughout a large and geographically dispersed company. Some customers had over 50 copies of Vines up and running. Customers paid Banyan on average $8,000 per copy of Vines—Novell generated an average of $1,000 per copy of Netware.

Banyan claimed leadership in enterprisewide networks, with sales growing from $10 million in 1985 to $100 million in 1990. Roughly 45% of sales were hardware, 45% software, and 10% service and support. Sales for 1991 were pro-

jected to remain flat, while net income was expected to drop from 1990's earnings of $4.7 million. Overall, Banyan accounted for about 5% of the installed base of networked PCs. While Banyan had a clear technical edge in enterprise networking, it was not clear how long the advantage would last. Both Microsoft and Novell were targeting new product development to mimic Vines capability, and were building direct selling staff to call on Banyan's traditional clients. Banyan was also slower to exit the hardware business compared to Novell: analysts estimated that proprietary servers and other computer hardware would constitute 30% of Banyan's revenue in 1991. Nonetheless, Banyan maintained a strong balance sheet at the end of 1990, with more than $20 million in cash and no debt. Mahoney hoped to take the company public in the 1991–2 timeframe. However, the company suffered from top management turnover, and at the end of 1990 lost its chief technologist to Microsoft. Some Banyan customers, doubting the firm's long-term viability, had ordered freezes on Vines purchases.

IBM

As part of its personal computer hardware and software line IBM offered PC networking software to customers and distributors. However, IBM relied upon its traditional software partner Microsoft for the technology. The original technology was called MS-NET, and was sold by IBM as PC-NET. The product, a simple peer-to-peer model, allowed basic file and printer sharing, and was quite successful. Microsoft's next generation networking product was OS/2, the operating system designed to succeed DOS, combined with a NOS called LAN Manager. LAN Manager for OS/2 was licensed to IBM, who sold it under the name LAN Server. To compete against Novell Netware, IBM sold customers OS/2 and LAN Server to run together on a PC server. The product was targeted at the corporate market. The cost and complexity of OS/2, which was a prerequisite for LAN Manager, precluded sales to the low end. LAN Server was sold directly by IBM's marketing organization; networking did not have a dedicated sales force.

---

[4]UNIX was an operating system developed by AT&T. It was very flexible in design and was well suited for networking.

Microsoft and Its Other Licensees

Historically Microsoft had not viewed networking as critical to its core business of providing PC operating systems and applications software. Networking software was provided to PC OEMs, such as IBM and DEC, typically for small license fees. When Microsoft released OS/2 and LAN Manager, it pursued this traditional strategy, licensing "LAN Man" to a variety of companies, including IBM, DEC (which used it for its minicomputers), and Hewlett Packard (which adopted it for use with UNIX). 3Com, a network firm that sold both hardware and software, entered into a joint development agreement with Microsoft. 3Com adopted LAN Man as its next generation of software and agreed to help fund on-going LAN Man development. By 1990, however, 3Com exited the NOS business to concentrate on networking hardware.

Others

While IBM, 3Com (along with other Microsoft LAN Man licensees), and Banyan competed against Novell in the corporate market, several smaller firms competed in the low end. The largest, Artisoft, developed and marketed a product called LANTASTIC, which was targeted exclusively at the low-medium end group market. LANTASTIC was viewed as the easiest product to install and use on the market, which contributed to its success in achieving roughly 35% share of the group market in the United States. Though it was second to Novell's low end offering, it was posing a serious challenge. Its sales had grown to roughly $50 million by the end of 1990. LANTASTIC was sold through retail channels in shrinkwrapped boxes and could be installed by nontechnical users. There were rumors that Artisoft was for sale for between $50 and $100 million.

5. Note on Microcomputers: Overview of PCs and Workstations

History of Computing

One of the first electronic digital computers was developed in 1941 and kept in absolute secrecy by a joint team of scientists from the United States and Great Britain. The ENIAC (Electronic Numerical Integrator and Computer) was a mainframe used in cryptology applications for deciphering enemy communication codes during World War II. The original ENIAC system weighed 30 tons, took three years to build, and cost nearly $500,000 to develop (in 1943 dollars). It contained 70,000 resistors, 20,000 vacuum tubes, and 3,000 neon lights.

Since the ENIAC, computers moved through a series of radical improvements in technology. The mainframes of 1950s were followed by minicomputers in 1962, microcomputers and supercomputers in the 1970s, and workstations and personal computers (PCs) in the 1980s. (See **Exhibit 1**.) During 1988, information processing amounted to over $150 billion in annual revenues, while expenditures in the technology sector accounted for over 40% of U.S. corporate capital spending. In its fifth decade of existence, the computer industry was the third largest in the United States, after only automobiles and petroleum.

Product Classification

Historically, computers have been classified by product features that include processing speed, materials technology, input/output performance, centralized versus distributed computing, memory capacity, number of users, and price. Traditional industry segments could be neatly categorized and broadly defined, as there were clear distinctions between mainframes, minicomputers, and microcomputers.

MAINFRAMES Mainframes were large-scale, batch-processing computers capable of supporting more than 128 concurrent users. Mainframes handled the central data processing needs of a large organization, or the needs of a smaller number of users performing computational-

Research Associate Ben Huston prepared this note under the supervision of Professor David B. Yoffie as the basis for class discussion.

EXHIBIT 1 (Source: *Business Week*, March 6, 1989.)

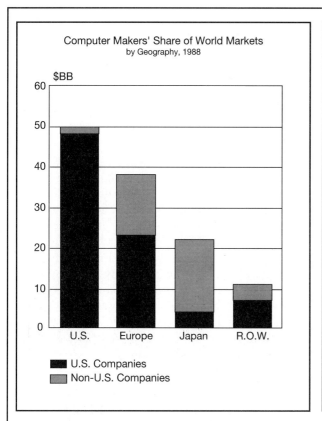

Computer Makers' Share of World Markets
by Geography, 1988

U.S. Companies
Non-U.S. Companies

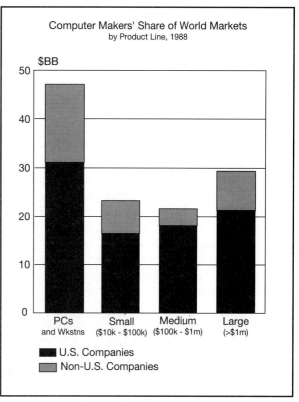

Computer Makers' Share of World Markets
by Product Line, 1988

U.S. Companies
Non-U.S. Companies

intensive applications. These computers usually required the service and support of dedicated maintenance personnel. By 1988, unit pricing for a mainframe typically exceeded $500,000.

MINICOMPUTERS Minicomputers were first developed in 1961 by the Digital Equipment Corporation (DEC), and ushered in the era of distributed computing (the simultaneous sharing of computer resources). These systems supported up to 64 concurrent users, and served the data processing needs of a large department within an organization, or the central data processing needs of a small organization with similar computing power requirements. These systems required limited service and support personnel, and ranged in price from $50,000 to $500,000.

MICROCOMPUTERS The development of the microprocessor in the 1970s eventually led to the

high concentration of computing power packed in small machines that would make up a new broad class of systems. Microcomputers were generally single-user systems that were originally dedicated to a limited number of applications. These systems were typically priced below $100,000, and required little on-site maintenance service.

By the mid-1980s, the long-standing definitions of the three major industry classifications were less clear. As semiconductors and microprocessors became more powerful and less expensive to manufacture, computer makers were increasingly able to build machines that performed across a broader spectrum of price and performance features. Technological advances in hardware, software, and connectivity eventually led to new systems that defied easy classification. The remainder of this note will focus on two of the newest computer systems: PCs and workstations.

Both PCs and workstations were desktop machines powered by microprocessors. Originally, PCs were designed with 8- and 16-bit CPUs (central processing units) (see **Exhibit 2**), while workstations processed data 32 bits at a time. PCs had commonly been employed in a wide variety of office automation roles, and were primarily used for word processing, spreadsheet, and database management applications. Workstations were used in more highly specialized and complex tasks such as financial modeling, computer-aided design and scientific calculation.

Worldwide sales of personal computers for 1988 were close to $40 billion, up from $30 billion in 1985. Greater than 60% of the personal computers sold in the domestic market were priced between $1000 and $5000, and business users accounted for a majority of unit and sales volumes. PC manufacturers sold through five main channels. (See **Exhibit 3**.) A survey of corporate volume buyers of PCs conducted by *PC Week* found that compatibility was most highly valued. (See **Exhibit 4**.) Knowledgeable users realized that hardware prices represented about 25%–30% of the cost of supporting a PC, while software,

training, and maintenance costs were the major expenses.

Manufacturing

High-volume, low-cost manufacturing had become critical in the PC business. This was particularly true for IBM PC clone-makers that sold computers at the low-end of the market, where markets became rapidly saturated and product life-cycles were short. Most IBM PC-compatibles were highly price competitive. Two-thirds of the cost of bringing a PC to market was tied up in advertising, distribution, and other overhead expenses. Materials and assembly costs accounted for the other third. Long production runs and automated assembly techniques characterized the manufacturing process. Manufacturers attempted to locate low-cost sources of reliable components from semiconductor and materials vendors anywhere in the world. Industry experts estimated that each dollar saved in manufacturing could amount to a $4 advantage in the retail channels.

EXHIBIT 2 Worldwide Personal Computer Market, 1981–1988 (million units)

	1981	1982	1983	1984	1985	1986	1987	1988
Total PCs								
Units shipped	1.7	5.4	9.0	11.7	11.5	12.6	14.6	17.4
Installed base	3.0	7.9	16.4	27.0	36.8	46.4	56.8	68.4
Intel Micro-based								
Units shipped	0.0	0.2	1.0	2.6	3.4	4.5	6.3	8.0
Installed base	0.0	0.2	1.2	3.7	7.1	11.4	17.4	25.1
8088								
Units shipped	0.0	0.2	0.9	2.4	2.8	2.9	2.7	2.4
Installed base	0.0	0.2	1.1	3.5	6.3	9.1	11.7	13.8
80286								
Units shipped	0.0	0.0	0.0	0.1	0.4	1.4	3.1	4.4
Installed base	0.0	0.0	0.0	0.1	0.5	1.9	4.8	9.2
80386								
Units shipped	0.0	0.0	0.0	0.0	0.0	0.0	0.3	1.0
Installed base	0.0	0.0	0.0	0.0	0.0	0.0	0.3	1.3
Motorola Micro-based								
Units shipped	0.0	0.0	0.0	0.5	0.7	0.9	1.1	1.5
Installed base	0.0	0.0	0.1	0.5	1.2	2.1	3.2	4.6

Source: *Infocorp*, 1988.

EXHIBIT 3 U.S. Microcomputer Unit Shipments— By Distribution Channel (000s)

	Mass Merchants	Computer Retailers	Wholesale Distribution	OEM/ VAR	Direct Sales
1983	2,332	1,626	867	434	163
1984	2,367	2,360	879	676	473
1985	2,085	2,641	765	834	626
1986	2,101	2,852	750	976	825
1987	2,037	3,097	815	1,141	1,059

Source: IDC, 1985.

Vendors

IBM In the late 1970s, IBM viewed microcomputers as a growing threat to its mainframe and minicomputer businesses. When IBM finally introduced its PC in 1980, the company departed from its traditional strategy of designing systems with proprietary technology. The first IBM PC used merchant semiconductor components, and included the Intel 8088 microprocessor. Microsoft Corporation's MS-DOS was selected as the standard operating system for IBM PCs. As a late entrant in the personal computer business, IBM published a detailed description of its system architecture in order to encourage independent application software and peripherals developers to support the IBM PC. This strategy allowed IBM to leverage its financial resources and reputation to dominate the growing market for personal computers. By 1984, the company claimed 71% of the total market for microcomputers.

In 1988, IBM remained the dominant, worldwide, full-line producer of computers, with an estimated $60 billion in revenues and 400,000

EXHIBIT 4 PC Buying Criteria (volume buyers of PCs)

	386 PCs	286 PCs
Compatibility	94%	95%
Reliability	94	94
Vendor support	80	77
Performance	79	75
Documentation	77	75
Reconfigurability	74	75
Relative Price	74	77
Easy to install	72	71

Source: *PC Week*, 1988.

employees. The company had an extensive sales and service organization, and its personal computers had a strong reputation for quality and reliability. IBM's domestic microcomputer hardware sales (PCs and workstations) accounted for $4.9 billion in revenues during the last four quarters ending in June of 1988. The company was one of the three manufacturers (in addition to Apple and Compaq) firmly established in computer retail channels. IBM was also the dominant vendor to large companies. In 1987, its share of PCs in *Fortune 1000* firms was 72%, while its closest competitors, Compaq and Apple, supplied 5% and 4%, respectively.

During 1987, IBM introduced a new generation of personal computers called the Personal Systems/2 (PS/2). Five out of six models in the PS/2 line incorporated a new, proprietary Micro Channel bus architecture (MCA), and each model ran Microsoft's OS/2 operating system. Models at the low end of the PS/2 line were designed with the Intel 80286 chip, while high-end models used the 80386 microprocessor. Some industry analysts predicted that the MS-DOS operating system would remain the dominant standard through the early 1990s due to its broad base of experienced users and existing software libraries. However, as users' needs shifted to graphics-intensive applications, IBM hoped that OS/2 would outsell MS-DOS.

One year prior to the PS/2 introduction, IBM's RISC[1] Technology (RT) workstations were unveiled as the company's first entry into the technical workstation market. These relatively inexpensive systems were designed with IBM's proprietary 32-bit RISC microprocessor chip, and were targeted for engineering and scientific installations seeking to distribute technical computing down to the desktop level. Most industry observers agreed that the RT's performance was not competitive with other available workstations. IBM's share of the U.S. workstation market was 4% in 1987.

APPLE COMPUTER Apple Computer offered an innovative product line of peripherals and personal computers. 1988 marked the beginning of Apple's second decade in the computer business,

---

[1]IBM pioneered much of the early research for Reduced Instruction Set Computing (RISC).

and featured the company's first billion-dollar revenue quarter. Total revenues in 1987 accounted for nearly 9% of the worldwide PC market. The company's proprietary Macintosh computers, accounting for 60% to 65% of Apple revenues in 1987, were designed using Motorola's 68000 family of microprocessors. The Macintosh product line featured a "friendly" graphics user interface that gave it the ability to represent information and programming with icons and symbols. The graphics user interface was similar and consistent across most software application packages. This helped to reduce the learning time required when users shifted from one program to another. A majority of Apple customers used the Macintosh for its high-end graphics capabilities in desktop publishing applications.

Apple held a 12% share of the office/professional market sector in 1988, up from only 6% in 1986. Apple sold almost exclusively through retailers, maintaining a strong position in the dealer channel. Hoping to become a more significant player in the business PC market, Apple was expanding its direct marketing efforts. Apple's corporate goals were to more than double the company's revenues from an estimated $4.1 billion in 1988 to $10 billion by the early 1990s.

COMPAQ COMPUTER Compaq was another company whose PCs could typically be found on computer retailers' shelves. During 1988, revenues were expected to increase by greater than 60%, to nearly $2 billion, which would account for nearly 9% of the U.S. PC market. The company also expected record earnings in 1988. (See **Exhibit 6**.) Compaq had a strong brand name, particularly among buyers that remained faithful to the MS/DOS operating system. Compaq's success could be partly attributed to its marketing skills and its early-mover strategy. Compaq had often been the first player in the PC business to use Intel's most advanced or newest microprocessors, such as the 80386 and 80386SX chips. Compaq's product strategy was focused on the high-profit, high-performance range of the personal compu-ter market. Compaq products were priced well above the clones, demonstrating the company's confidence in its technology. Secondly, Compaq was attempting to convince customers that Microsoft's OS/2 operating system could run just as well on its machines as it did on IBM's PS/2 systems that utilized the Micro Channel architecture.

OTHERS There were over 200 IBM PC clone makers worldwide. Most of these second-tier suppliers reported disappointing sales and earnings in 1988. Since the new generation of 32-bit PCs were designed to work more closely with mainframes and other computers on corporate networks, customers had become increasingly reluctant to rely on smaller suppliers. In addition, the industry had begun to mature, and distribution channels were saturated. Together, IBM, Compaq, and Apple accounted for nearly 66% of all personal computer sales through U.S. computer stores. Second-tier players had to compete on price (e.g., Wyse Technology with IBM clones) or look for a niche market (e.g., Toshiba with laptops).

Although independent computer stores handled nearly half of all PCs sold in the United States, there were other ways to reach customers. Zenith, for example, bid on large government PC contracts and competed aggressively in the OEM and university markets with its high-end laptop computers. Dell Computer used direct mail channels to become a $250 million company in less than five years. Also, Tandy used its own Radio Shack outlets to build a billion dollar PC clone business and had strength in the small business market.

Most Japanese and Korean computer companies served as original equipment manufacturers (OEMs) to domestic subsidiaries and independent U.S. computer makers that manufactured low-cost IBM PC clones. In 1988, Japanese producers were estimated to hold less than 30% of the U.S. personal computer market.

Trends in the PC Business

Analysts estimated that by 1990 more than $50 billion worth of personal computers would be in U.S. homes, offices and classrooms. About 29 million PCs would be installed in offices by the end of the decade, compared with only 9 million in 1985. At the beginning of 1988, penetration of the U.S. business PC market was nearly 25%, and was expected to reach 60% by 1992. (See **Exhibit 5**.) Also, international sales were becoming

EXHIBIT 5 U.S. Business PC Market Penetration (by end-user type, 1988—million units)

End-User	Total Available Market[a]	# of Installed PCs	Market Opportunity[b]
Large Company	10 MM	3.2 MM	6 MM
Medium Company	25	6.2	15
Small Company	18	4.3	11
Home Offices	4	0.5	2
Government	4	0.8	2
Total	61	15.0	36

[a]Defined as total number of white collar employees.

[b]Market opportunity figures are estimated.

Source: *Businessland*, 1988.

a significant factor in the overall PC industry picture. In 1988, nearly 10 million PCs, over 60% of the worldwide total, were estimated to be shipped in the United States. European shipments were 4 million units, while Japan and the rest of the world accounted for 2 million units each.

In 1988, there was heavy pressure on R&D expenses due to the transition to a more complex type of networked computing. Many of these R&D expenses were either directly or indirectly related to software development. The role of the PC was also changing. Personal computers had traditionally been sold for office automation and productivity applications. By 1988, however,

EXHIBIT 6 Selected Financial Statistics—1983–1988 ($ millions, except ratios and stock prices)

	Wyse Techology[bn]				Apple[f]			
	1988	1987	1986	1985	1987	1986	1985	1984
Revenues	457	260	166	78	2,661	1,902	1,918	1,516
Net Income	28	18	13	8	217	154	61	64
Liquid Assets[a]	391	292	111	50	1,872	1,617	1,159	803
Total Assets	383	229	108	51	1,478	1,160	936	789
Long-term Debt	116	86	5	3	0	0	0	0
ROS	6.1%	7.0%	7.6%	9.6%	8.2%	8.1%	3.2%	4.2%
ROA	8.4	10.8	13.9	14.7	16.4	14.6	7.0	9.4
ROE	10.1	22.0	21.9	41.5	28.3	24.6	11.9	15.1
Stock Prices ($/Share)								
High	26	40	19	15	60	22	16	17
Low	7	13	11	7	20	11	7	11
P/E Ratio	4	21-7	12-7	12-6	16-12	36-12	18-9	31-14
Market Valuation[c]	107	NA	NA	NA	4,223	1,744	1,367	
Book Value	167	94	64	25	1,188	836	693	552

	Compaq[f]				Zenith[d]			
	1987	1986	1985	1984	1987	1986	1985	1984
Revenues	1,224	625	504	329	2,363	1,892	1,624	1,716
Net Income	136	43	27	13	d19.1	d10.0	d7.7	63.6
Liquid Assets	813	317	317	217	1,110	969	694	698
Total Assets	901	378	312	231	1,373	1,235	927	909
Long-term Debt	149	73	75	0	315	272	165	172
ROS	11.1%	6.9%	5.3%	3.9%	NM	NM	NM	3.7%
ROA	19.8	12.3	9.8	7.2	NM	NM	NM	7.7
ROE	43.2	26.6	21.5	12.7	NM	NM	NM	15.5
Stock Prices ($/Share)								
High	79	22	14	15	34	30	25	29
Low	19	12	6	4	10	18	16	20
P/E Ratio	22-5	14-8	15-6	31-7	NM	NM	NM	13-7
Market Valuation	1,515	421	257		NM	NM	NM	
Book Value	400	183	137		489	432	437	

[a]Includes cash plus current assets.

[b]Results reported for year ended 3/31/88.

[c]Market Value = Average Stock Price * # shares outstanding.

[d]Zenith had 26 million common shares outstanding in 4088.

[e]Estimated using stock price @ $7 1/4 per share on 11/28/88.

Estimated book value for Apple at year-end 1988 were $1.2 billion and $5.0 billion, respectively; and, for Compaq at year-end 1988, they were $0.8 billion and $2.3 billion, respectively.

Source: *Value Line*, 1988.

high-performance personal computers, such as IBM's PS/2, Apple's Macintosh II, and Compaq's Deskpro 386, were becoming an accepted part of the technical workstation market. Segmentation of the workstation and PC markets below the $15,000 level was becoming increasingly difficult. The software base for both markets continued to grow, and fewer technical differences separated the two groups. Industry observers believed that PCs' increasing speeds, functional capabilities, and low unit prices were threatening sales of technical workstations. Also, an abundance of third-party add-on hardware and software had turned high-end PCs into tools for such demanding tasks as product design, simulation, and scientific problem-solving.

Workstations

Workstations were high-performance microcomputers built to accommodate complex applications processing in scientific, engineering, and commercial environments. Most of these machines featured powerful 32-bit microprocessors and ran either proprietary operating systems or versions of the UNIX operating system.[2]

The market for workstations had grown rapidly since their initial introduction by Apollo Computer in 1980. (See **Exhibit 7**.) Many former PC users were migrating upward from less powerful systems to machines capable of delivering more computational power, storage, and display capabilities. The increasing demand for workstations could also be attributed to a downward migration from mainframes and minis to the desktop. Individual workstations were endowed with the power of multi-user systems. By distributing demanding applications to networks of desktop and deskside systems, users had access to more processing power for department and workgroup-specific applications.

Product Strategy and Distribution

According to Dataquest, the workstation market was $4.1 billion in 1988, and the number of workstations installed worldwide was 450,000, which was more than three times the 1986 installed base. As competing systems began to proliferate, workstation vendors faced a number of critical product design and marketing decisions.

Compatibility, a function of the system architecture, was a key issue for both workstation vendors and their customers. Some workstation vendors elected to design and offer "closed systems," hardware and software with unique proprietary technology. Closed-systems manufacturers could protect their intellectual property through patents and copyrights, but were often willing to license their technology to other vendors for a royalty fee.

However, a growing number of vendors chose to build workstations for an "open-systems" environment, using off-the-shelf hardware and software components that adhered to industry standards or were widely employed in the marketplace. The use of merchant components enabled the vendor to reduce manufacturing and delivery costs. Research and development time and expense could also be reduced. Many work-

EXHIBIT 7 Technical Workstation Market—1985–1989

Year	Revenues ($000)	Unit ASPs ($)
1985	$ 938	$28,400
1986	1,563	25,500
1987	2,700	22,700
1988E	4,100	17,200
1989E	NA	13,000

Source: *Dataquest*, 1988 and 1989.

[2]UNIX was a preferred operating system of choice because it was a readily available systems tool and was easy to license from AT&T, saving vendors the expense of developing a proprietary operating system. Also, UNIX had intrinsic features well suited to software development, a task for which workstations were originally employed.

Note on Microcomputers: Overview of PCs and Workstations

station customers wanted nonproprietary solutions: open systems reduced the costs of moving to or from different computer platforms; increased the available base of applications software; and standardized computing across the organization. Software sales for open-systems (DOS, OS/2, and UNIX) were expected to increase from 34% of the U.S. market in 1987 to over 48% by 1991.

Throughout the 1980s, the average selling price (ASP) of workstations continued to drop. The increasing use of microprocessor chips such as the Intel 80386 drove the power of personal computers up into the technical workstation range. In response, high-performance workstation leaders, such as Sun Microsystems, Apollo Computer, and Digital Equipment Corporation, significantly lowered the price of entry-level desktop workstations so that prices were comparable with those of the so-called "technical PCs." Some of these workstations were priced below $7500, while others were below $5,000 without a hard disk.

Traditionally, workstation customers were volume purchasers, buying multiple machines configured in networks. As workstations were increasingly designed to serve commercial applications, they were expected to move through broader channels of distribution. By 1987, direct sales accounted for nearly 60% of their revenues. (See **Exhibit 8**.) Workstations were also commonly sold through value-added resellers (VARs) and OEMs. As selling prices fell, industry analysts expected workstation vendors to push their products through retail channels.

Workstation Vendors

SUN MICROSYSTEMS Founded in 1982 by four young Stanford graduates with virtually no prior business experience, Sun Microsystems was one of the fastest growing companies in the computer business. By the end of 1988, Sun claimed a 30% share of the workstation market and nearly $1 billion in annual revenues. (See **Exhibit 9**.) Sun offered a broad product line of workstations and servers, and targeted market segments within the business, professional support and scientific computing sectors. The company's innovative product design, aggressive pricing strategy, and its large network of value-added resellers contributed to Sun's success.

Sun's emergence as the leader in the workstation business could be attributed in large part to its open-systems approach. While the company built systems that adhered to existing software and hardware standards, it was also successful in getting many of its proprietary solutions accepted as new industry standards. One example was its RISC-based Scalable Processor Architecture (SPARC) microprocessor chip. Sun was the first computer company which aggressively sought to establish its internally developed microprocessor chip as a standard for other hardware competitors. Sun targeted its RISC-based SPARC chip for the workstation market, and had licensed the technology and manufacturing rights to several merchant semiconductor vendors. Industry observers speculated that the company's long-term goal was to establish its systems as the workstation industry standard of the 1990s. In January

EXHIBIT 8 Top Five Workstation Vendors (market share and distribution channels (%))

Vendor	1983 Market Share	Direct Sales	OEM	VAR/Vendor	Distribution
Apollo	21%	50%	49%	1%	—
DEC	20	55	35	1	9
Hewlett-Packard	12	65	33	2	—
IBM	4	70	15	15	—
Sun	29	58	41	1	—
Others	14				
Source: *Electronic Business*, 1988; IDC, 1988.					

EXHIBIT 9 Selected Financial Statistics—1983–1988 ($ millions, except ratios and stock prices)

	Sun Microsystems[b]					Apollo				
	1988	1987	1986	1985	1984	1988	1987	1986	1985	1984
Revenues		1,052	538	210	115		554	392	296	216
Net Income		66.4	36.3	11.9	8.5		21.7	9.6	d1.5	23.9
Liquid Assets[a]		660	613	183	95		333	293	169	216
Total Assets		757	524	182	84		447	367	258	217
Long-term Debt		125	127	4	7		117	117	29	1
ROS		6.3%	6.8%	5.7%	7.4%		3.9%	2.4%	NM	11.1%
ROA		10.1	9.7	9.7	14.8		5.3	3.0	NM	15.2
ROE		21.1	19.3	16.4	25.4		10.4	5.1	NM	19.4
Stock Prices ($/Share)										
High		41	46	24	NA		25	18	31	29
Low		27	22	11	NA		9	9	9	16
P/E Ratio		23-15	41-20	53-24	NA		41-14	68-34	NM	39-21
Market Valuation[c]	1,261	1,107	209	NA			352	654	480	NM
Book Value[d]	379	234	104	34			241	225	190	174

	DEC[b]					IBM				
	1988	1987	1986	1985	1984	1988	1987	1986	1985	1984
Revenues		11,475	9,389	7,590	6,686		54,217	51,250	50,056	45,937
Net Income		1,306	1,137	617	447		5,258	4,789	6,555	6,582
Liquid Assets[a]		9,094	8,319	7,217	5,718		37,987	35,006	31,692	24,737
Total Assets		10,112	8,407	7,173	6,369		63,688	57,814	52,634	42,808
Long-term Debt		124	269	333	837		3,858	4,169	2,955	3,269
ROS		11.4%	12.1%	8.1%	6.7%		9.7%	9.3%	13.1%	14.3%
ROA		14.1	14.7	8.8	7.4		8.7	8.7	13.7	16.4
ROE		18.9	19.1	11.6	10.3		14.6	14.5	22.4	26.4
Stock Prices ($/Share)										
High		145	200	109	69		176	162	159	129
Low		86	105	66	43		102	119	117	99
P/E Ratio	12-9	15-9	23-12	23-14	18-11			20-12	21-15	15-11
Market Valuation	17,225	16,038	8,783	5,992		71,260	86,562	85,277	80,768	
Book Value	7,512	6,293	5,727	4,554		40,563	38,263	34,377	31,990	

[a]Includes cash plus current assets.

[b]Year ended September 30.

[c]Market Value = Average Stock Price ∗ # shares outstanding.

[d]Book value = Book Value/Share ∗ # shares outstanding.

Source: *Value Line*, 1988.

of 1989, Solbourne Computer (a U.S. company with majority ownership held by Matsushita Electric of Japan) introduced the first Sun clones based on SPARC. Analysts expected many to follow Solbourne with Sun-compatible machines.

To tap the low-end workstation/high-end PC markets, Sun introduced its 386i workstation in 1988. Rather than use its SPARC chip, the 386i was an Intel 80386-based machine with an 80387 math coprocessor and high-resolution graphics displays. The 386i boasted three critical capabilities: 1) all networking was pre-installed and fully automatic; 2) the graphic icon-based interface in-

sulated the user from cryptic UNIX commands, and 3) the 386i ran DOS applications software in separate windows, and could even run more than one simultaneously.

APOLLO COMPUTER Apollo Computer, an industry pioneer, had once dominated the workstation market. By 1987, the company held second place behind Sun Microsystems with a 22% market share. In the early 1980s, Apollo targeted design automation and manufacturing applications as its primary market sectors. The company's workstation architectures were once almost exclusively proprietary. This closed-system approach made it difficult for users to port applications over from other vendors' systems, to connect other computers for information distribution, and to find appropriate software application systems for specific processing tasks. By 1988, however, Apollo had redefined its product strategy, responded to customer calls for systems with commonly available facilities, and repositioned its workstation line to compete in the business applications and software development markets. As Apollo lost market share, however, industry analysts speculated that the company might be for sale.

DIGITAL EQUIPMENT CORPORATION Digital Equipment Corporation, the No. 2 computer maker after IBM, entered the workstation market in 1984 and sold a variety of proprietary systems products. The VAXstation 2000, 3000, and 8000 workstations were designed to appeal to DEC's large, installed base of VAX[3] minicomputer users that wanted to add power at the desktop and workgroup levels. A number of these systems provided connectivity features as well as hardware and software compatibility that enabled smooth integration into existing VMS[4] operating environments. During 1988, DEC's

low-end VAXstation 2000 was the best-selling workstation in the industry based on unit volume. However, Sun and Apollo workstations had typically been purchased over DEC systems where standard UNIX requirements were specified. In January of 1989, DEC announced a low-priced, powerful workstation line designed to operate in an open-systems computing environment. The DECstation 3100 used a high-speed RISC microprocessor designed by MIPS Computer Systems and ran the industry-standard UNIX operating system.

OTHERS Several Japanese companies, including Hitachi, Sony, NEC, Mitsubishi, and Toshiba, had entered the workstation business by 1988. Most of these machines were based on Motorola microprocessors, and many used various versions of the UNIX operating system. Most Japanese vendors emphasized that these machines would serve an important role in the future of engineering networks. In 1989, Motorola announced its own technical workstation line, with products ranging in price from $28,000 to $80,000. Motorola's offering was based on its recently introduced RISC processor, which the company hoped would create a new standard.

---

[3]VAX, or Virtual Address Extension, was DEC's proprietary hardware platform.

[4]VMS was DEC's proprietary operating system designed to run the VAX hardware platform.

PART TWO

Competitive Strategy

6. Intel Corporation 1988

Sitting in one of the standard Intel cubicles, Andy Grove, Intel's president and CEO, told a newly hired consultant that "our most important challenge is how to use our momentum to continue our growth. Success must be based on a vision of the future, a strategy to optimize growth in promising areas." The consultant's job would be to assess Intel's present position and to offer recommendations on the company's future. The key question was: how should Grove position the firm for long-run growth vis-à-vis its more diversified and vertically integrated American and Japanese competitors?

The following account is a synopsis of the major issues in the consultant's report. In addition to reviewing company documents and interviewing key executives, she talked with customers, investment bankers, and competitors. Particular attention was given to the systems business. Generating around $800 million in revenue in 1988, the consultant thought that Grove needed to address the future of the systems division and its relationship with the rest of Intel.

The History of Intel

Intel was founded in 1968 by Robert Noyce and Gordon Moore, both pioneers in the semiconductor industry. Intel's original business mission was to "design, develop, manufacture, and market advanced memory circuits for digital equipment." Intel was one of the first companies to develop and commercialize the industry's three primary memory devices. In 1969, Intel introduced its first product, a static random access memory (SRAM) chip. Also in that year, Intel announced a 64-bit random access memory chip, and shortly thereafter, 256-bit and 1024-bit chips. Although Intel was not the first to introduce dynamic RAMs (DRAMs) in 1970, its DRAMs quickly gained a major share and became the industry standard. Within two years,

Research Associates Ralinda Laurie and Ben Huston, and Professor David B. Yoffie prepared this case as the basis for class discussion rather than to illustrate either effective or ineffective handling of an administrative situation.

Intel's DRAMs had become the largest selling semiconductor component in the world. In 1971, Intel introduced the first erasable programmable read-only memory (EPROM) chip. Although the true significance of this innovation did not become apparent for several years, EPROMs could be reprogrammed, and thus provided an alternative cost-effective means of storing information. Intel led the market for programmable memory devices with each successive generation of EPROMs. This high-volume product also helped the company to refine its manufacturing techniques and served as technology and process drivers for its future family of logic products.

While Intel continued to innovate in memory chips, its next important technological breakthrough was a logic product—the microprocessor. In the early 1970s, Intel proclaimed that their programmable microcomputer on a chip had "ushered in a new era of integrated electronics." Although these new microprocessors were clearly revolutionary, there were no existing markets for the products. Intel's response to the uncertainty in the marketplace was to educate the technical community, and to manufacture board level products which made microprocessors easier to use. Intel's second generation microprocessor, the 8080, led to the most successful microprocessor product families of the 1980s: the 8086 and 8088. Along with Intel's technological success came substantial financial returns. Starting with sales of $2,672 in 1968, both revenues and profits grew at compounded annual growth rates of nearly 65% from 1971 to 1980. (See **Exhibit 1**.) Intel became one of the fastest growing and most profitable merchant semiconductor firms in the world.

After more than a decade of continued prosperity, however, Intel's financial results suffered. Intel's initial strategy was to be the first mover, continually introducing new products for which it could demand premium prices. Intel would then withdraw from mature markets where products had become commodities. This strategy worked as long as the company had developed revolutionary products every few years. During the 1980s, however, Intel introduced fewer revolutionary products, and the company had made some mistakes. For instance, after failing several times to produce a competitive 256K DRAM, Intel fell so far behind Japanese chip makers that it decided to withdraw from DRAMs. A few years later, Intel stumbled into the Application Specific Integrated Circuits (ASIC) business. ASICs was expected to be a $9 billion market by 1989. These were semicustom chips which customers would create using Intel's design tools. After an enthusiastic, but late start in 1985, Intel signed a number of technology exchange agreements with other firms. Citing competitive pressures and the problems of being a late entrant, the company began phasing down its ASIC business in 1988.

Intel in 1988

Although the early 1980s were difficult, Intel made record profits in 1988. Most semiconductor firms also reported healthy profits during the year. (See **Exhibits 2** and **3**.) After a significant pruning of product lines and restructuring of manufacturing operations in 1985–1986, Intel had rededicated itself to being the leading "microcomputer" company. Featured on the cover of *Business Week* in September 1988, the press and the investment community were proclaiming Intel to be one of the premier American manufacturers of "electronic building blocks" used by original equipment manufacturers (OEMs).[1] Even the CEO of AMD, one of Intel's toughest competitors proclaimed 1988 the "glory year for Intel." Intel's biggest market was the computer industry, and its biggest customers included IBM (14.5% of Intel's sales), Ford Motor and Compaq Computer. Although the company's Product Guide listed well over 300 different product lines, these lines could be divided into three distinct groups: Memory Components, which manufactured EPROMs; Logic Products, such as microprocessors and microcontrollers; and Systems,

[1]Intel's reputation, symbolized in the *Business Week* cover story, was that the company had brilliant leadership at the top and many of the best chip designers in the world. However, investment analysts as well as some insiders expressed concern about the depth of Intel's management, especially since Andy Grove planned to retire in a few years, Gordon Moore had reduced his active management role, and Bob Noyce had left to run SEMATECH. Intel's strong internal culture, which emphasized decentralized responsibilities, openness, and constructive confrontation, created a family-like environment for insiders. This made it difficult for the company to assimilate newcomers at a very high management level.

EXHIBIT 1 Historical Financial Statistics (in millions)

	1978	1979	1980	1981	1982	1983	1984	1985	1986	1987[a]	1988
Net revenues	$399	$661	$855	$789	$900	$1,122	$1,629	$1,365	$1,265	$1,907	$2,875
Cost of sales	196	313	399	458	542	624	883	943	861	1,043	1,506
Research and development	41	67	96	116	131	142	180	195	228	260	318
Marketing/general administration	76	132	176	184	199	217	316	287	311	358	456
Operating income (loss)	85	149	183	30	28	139	250	(60)	(195)[b]	246	594
Net income (loss)	44	78	97	27	30	116	198	2	(173)	248	453
Cash and short-term investments	28	34	128	115	85	389	231	361	373	630	930
Long-term investments[c]										204	422
Inventories	52	79	91	97	122	152	219	171	198	236	366
Net investment in plant and equipment	160	217	321	412	462	504	778	848	779	891	1,123
Total assets	357	500	767	872	1,056	1,680	2,029	2,152	2,080	2,499	3,550
Short-term debt	44	19	12	32	75	81	66	89	112	195	200
Long-term debt	—	—	150	150	197	128	146	271	287	298	479
Shareholders' equity	205	303	433	488	552	1,122	1,360	1,421	1,275	1,276	2,080
Capital expenditures	$104	$97	$156	$157	$138	$145	$388	$236	$155	$302	$362
Number of employees	10.9	14.3	15.9	16.8	19.4	21.5	25.4	21.3	18.2	19.2	20.8
Average ROE	25.0%	30.6%	26.3%	5.9%	5.8%	13.9%	16.0%	0.1%	n.m.	19.7%	27.0%
Market valuation[d]	607	1,065	1,658	1,400	1,454	3,656	3,692	n.m.	n.m.	4,725	5,025
Book value[e]	206	303	283	487	552	1,126	1,363	1,420	1,275	1,304	1,838

[a]Among *Fortune* 500 companies in 1987, Intel ranked as follows: 200th in sales, 91st in profits, and 43rd in earnings per share.

[b]Includes $60 million for "restructuring of operation" in 1986.

[c]Long-term Investments are primarily liquid, and are stated at cost, which approximates market value.

[d]Market Valuation = Average Stock Price × # Shares Outstanding.

[e]Book Value = Book Value/Share × # Shares Outstanding.

Source: Intel Corporation annual reports and *Value Line*.

which included everything from boards to supercomputers. About one-third of Intel's revenues came from sales to electronics distributors who resold to tens of thousands of customers. Intel serviced its biggest customers directly with one of the largest technical sales forces in the industry (over 650 field engineers and salespeople worldwide). Since 1985, Intel also sold add-in products for personal computers through a network of over 1500 retail computer stores.

MEMORY PRODUCTS In 1988, Intel was active in only one type of memory products—EPROMs. The company, along with the entire semiconductor industry, had lost money in EPROMs and other memory segments since 1985. The July 1986 trade agreement between the United States and Japan in which the Japanese firms agreed not to dump semiconductors had a beneficial effect on EPROM prices. During 1987, Intel maintained its position as the world's number one supplier of EPROMs, with approximately 25% market share.

In March of 1988, Intel entered into a three-year marketing agreement with U.S. manufacturer Micron Technology to market DRAMs stamped with the Intel trademark. In the short run, Intel planned to sell these commodity products through its distribution channels. One analyst commented "before this move, Intel was like a supermarket without a dairy section." Intel had signed a similar marketing agreement for memory products with Samsung Electronics, a Korean firm, in 1987.

EXHIBIT 2a Estimated Revenues by Product Line ($ millions)

Intel Revenues	1983	1984	1985	1986	1987	1988	1989E
Semiconductor							
Microprocessor:							
8-bit, incl. 8086	315.8	418.5	95.2	24.4	11.7	4.5	2.0
80186/80286	27.7	282.2	444.4	410.9	475.5	450.0	334.2
80386	—	—	1.9	42.9	349.1	1,100.0	2,295.4
Subtotal	343.5	700.7	541.5	478.2	836.3	1,554.5	2,631.6
MOS Memory:							
EPROM	236.6	210.7	180.2	185.8	203.2	310.5	416.7
DRAM	66.2	61.1	25.1	—	—	—	—
SRAM	13.3	54.7	49.0	48.2	40.5	—	—
Other	18.9	65.6	58.0	25.3	23.0	24.0	24.0
Subtotal	335.0	392.1	312.3	259.3	266.7	334.5	440.7
Telecomm, ASIC, and other semiconductor	123.3	209.2	206.1	208.3	250.0	276.0	334.0
Total semiconductor	801.8	1,302.0	1,059.9	945.8	1,353.0	2,165.0	3,406.3
Systems	321.2	327.3	319.0	329.6	550.1	800.0	n.a.

Source: Prudential Bache Securities and casewriter's estimates; 1988 numbers slightly overestimated revenues.

LOGIC PRODUCTS While memory accounted for 90% of Intel's revenues in 1972, logic products accounted for approximately 90% of chips sales in 1988. Intel's strongest logic products were microprocessors—a business which took off after IBM chose Intel's 8088 for its personal computers in 1980. Intel's position as the industry standard was reinforced when IBM adopted the 80286 for its PC AT and the 80386 chip for its high-end PS/2 computers. In 1982, IBM went so far as to acquire a 20% interest in Intel to help ensure its survival. In 1987, however, IBM sold the last of its remaining shares in the company. By that time, the IBM and IBM-compatible PCs had grown to approximately 5.5 million units. Each of these computers incorpo-

rated one of three different types of Intel-based microprocessors, with approximately 46% using the 8088 (or a slight variant, the 8086), 49% using the 80286 chip, and the remaining 5% using the relatively new 80386 chip.

National Semiconductor, Motorola and AT&T successfully introduced 32-bit microprocessors up to two years before Intel, but the 80386 chip quickly captured the momentum. Produced over a four-year period at a total cost of about $200 million, the 80386 was becoming the new PC standard. As a member of Intel's 86 architectural family, the 386 ran all the software available for its 8- and 16-bit microprocessors, which amounted to $10 billion worth of programs

EXHIBIT 2b Estimated Profitability by Product Line ($ millions)

Intel Operating Profits	1985	1986	1987	1988E	1989E
Semiconductor					
Microprocessor:					
8-bit, incl. 8086	−$4.0	−$0.5	$0.0	$0.0	$0.0
80186/80286	14.1	5.5	92.4	79.9	76.0
80386	−11.5	−8.5	96.6	431.0	713.0
Subtotal	−1.4	−3.5	189.0	510.9	789.0
MOS Memory	−65.4	−123.7	3.4	30.0	54.0
Telecomm, ASIC, and other semiconductor	3.6	−4.8	15.1	32.9	56.9
Total semiconductor	−63.2	−132.0	207.5	573.8	899.9
Systems	3.0	−0.8	38.5	76.5	n.a.

Source: Prudential Bache Securities and casewriter's estimates.

EXHIBIT 2c Annual Revenues and Earnings for Year Ending 12/88

Company	Revenue ($M)	Net Income ($M)
AMD[a]	1,126.9	8.5
Cypress Semiconductor[b]	122.5	18.5
Intel	2,875.0	453.0
Motorola[c,d]	8,250.0	444.8
National	2,469.8	50.0
Siliconix	127.3	3.1
Texas Instruments[c,d]	6,300.0	323.2
VLSI Technology[c]	221.4	6.8
Western Digital	768.2	42.9

[a]Earnings reflect a $17.5 million nonrecurring charge for restructuring in 4Q88.

[b]Results reported for year ending 9/88.

[c]Estimates.

[d]Semiconductor revenues accounted for less than half of total revenues.

Source: Standard & Poors, Value Line, 1988.

by 1987. The 386 could also handle multiple tasks at one time, and run Microsoft's DOS and OS/2 as well as AT&T's UNIX.

Historically, the company was pressured by its customers, including IBM, to provide second sources for its microprocessors: by 1987, there were 12 second sources for the 8086, leaving Intel with less than a 30% share of the chips' revenues and profits. Royalties received by Intel for transferring this technology were insignificant compared to the lost revenues. For the 80286, Intel had limited the number of second sources to only four firms and, consequently, earned 75% of the revenues and profits. While it had granted IBM the sole license to manufacture the 80386 (ASP $250) for its own captive demand, Intel chose to be a sole source for the manufacturing and marketing of its 386 chip. Intel also introduced a low-cost version of the 386 in 1988, known as the 80386SX (ASP $150). Ultimately, Intel's decision to maintain a proprietary sole source position on the 80386 chips meant that the company would have to dedicate a significant portion of its existing production capacity to meet market demand. This included building new front-end fabrication facilities, which cost up to $200 million each.[2]

[2]Corporate profits were highly dependent upon the 386. When the company announced in November 1988 that supply had caught up with demand, customers who had been hoarding 386s immediately cut their bookings. For the short term, profits headed lower. One analyst speculated that "It looks like every dollar of sales [that Intel won't make on the 386] is a dollar of lost profit." (*Wall Street Journal*, 11/21/88, p. B4.)

Intel's next-generation design, the 80486, was expected to lead the new age of "personal mainframes." Produced at an estimated cost of around $300 million, the 486 would be introduced in 1989 and targeted for the workstation market. (See **Exhibit 3**.) The 80486 CPU would have one million transistors versus 275,000 for the 386, be fully compatible with 386, include a math co-processor (which increased a computer's computational capabilities), operate at speeds up to two to three times the 386, and run DOS, OS/2 and UNIX operating systems. The microprocessor's initial high price of close to $1,000 would restrict its use for the mass market. Desktop products using the 486 would probably sell for about $20,000. However, industry experts expected the price eventually to fall low enough for use in the broader desktop market.

Systems

Intel developed, manufactured, sold, and supported a broad line of subsystem and system level products built largely around its microprocessor technology and sold through the corporate sales force. The consultant concluded that corporate management had mixed feelings about the systems division, which included four relatively distinct businesses in 1988: OEM systems, which included boards, OEM PCs, software and hardware tools (analysts estimated sales to be around $400 million in 1988); PCEO (personal computer enhancement operations, with estimated retail sales of $200 million); a start-up operation in supercomputers; and a service business, which primarily serviced PCs (approximately $100 million sales). Although top management had stated for several years that systems should be 50% of corporate revenues, there remained considerable differences about the appropriate mission for systems, its general lack of visibility in the end-user market, and its lack of independent momentum. While systems, along with the rest of Intel, had a spectacular year in 1988, its growth was less than that for components.

OEM SYSTEMS The primary thrust of the system business had been to provide semiconductor technology to OEM customers at any level of integration. One departure from this strategy came

EXHIBIT 3 Product Evolution (Microprocessors vs. Application)

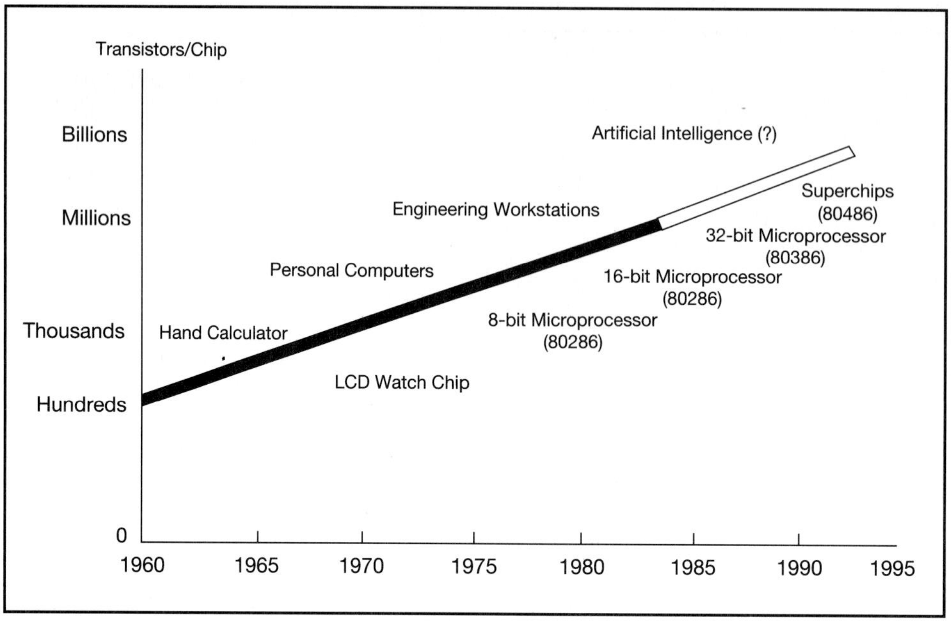

Source: *The New York Times*, September 14, 1988.

in 1972 when Intel acquired Microma, a small firm that had a prototype digital watch. Intel executives thought they had a sufficient repertoire of relevant production, technology, and assembly capabilities to compete in this market. However, the company soon exited because it lacked distribution channels, consumer marketing expertise, and the money needed to develop the requisite skills. Gordon Moore still wears his Microma watch. He claims that: "It is to remind me, if I ever find myself thinking of getting into other consumer products, of the trouble we'd be getting into."

To encourage sales of its 8080 microprocessor, Intel pioneered what some industry experts considered the world's first "personal computer," the Series 2 development system. Introduced in 1977, these systems, which were similar to the early Apple computers and sold for comparable prices, were primarily used for hardware design and software development. In the mid-1980s, Intel was selling its systems (prices ranging from $8,000–$30,000) to customers who were designing the 8086 microprocessor into their end products. At its peak in 1984, the development system business generated more than $200 million a year. By 1988, however, the commercialization of PCs, workstations, and other alternative design

techniques led to the virtual disappearance of this business. Another "missed opportunity" cited by insiders was the systems group's foray into database processing and transaction processing systems. One project manager noted Intel "was late to market," had "lousy execution, with an inferior product and technology, and used the wrong sales approach." The manager went on to explain that the systems group continually felt hamstrung by the component group and corporate management. "Santa Clara [corporate headquarters] is so concerned not to step on the toes of its major customers," he said, "that the systems group is like a fighter entering arenas with one hand always tied behind his back."

Microcomputer products for the OEM market represented the largest segment of the systems business. Intel offered a variety of building blocks for other computer OEMs. Intel's board business, for instance, enabled its customers to reduce development time for new products that incorporated Intel microprocessors and other related chips. According to Les Vadasz, general manager of the systems group, "We were so early in semiconductor memories and microprocessors, that many of our customers did not have the ability to use them. They didn't have the technical capabilities, nor could they really afford it. So we saw a business opportunity in board level products."[3]

One of Intel's largest OEM product lines was a recent offering: the 386 platform introduced in 1987. 386 platforms were fully functional PCs offered without the screen and keyboard[4] (see **Exhibit 4**). Sold at both the board and box levels, OEMs turned these platforms into finished computer products. Essentially a commodity business where high sales volume was critical, this type of operation required little manufacturing investment relative to the semiconductor business. By the early 1990s, the total market for 386 platforms was expected to be two million units (ASP $1500). Vadasz hoped that he could win 30% of this business. He cited as evidence of progress a very big contract to supply OEM PCs to AT&T.

Although the systems group was not treated differently from other customers of Intel's component division, Vadasz thought that he had two potential competitive advantages: economics of scale which could be realized in platforms; and close personal ties with Intel's microcomponent personnel. If systems engineers worked closely with component engineers, they could get board level products to market up to six months before many competitors. Thus when Intel announced the 80386, the systems group was the first to introduce a myriad of board level 386 products.

Relations between the components and systems, however, were not always smooth. Several managers interviewed from the systems group, which was located in Portland, OR, complained that customers such as Compaq and IBM often got better information and delivery. In addition, they complained that systems had a much harder time getting resources than its semiconductor counterparts. In the meantime, a few executives in the component division in Santa Clara, CA expressed a lack of confidence in the systems group,

EXHIBIT 4 Representation of Intel's OEM PC

and concern that systems was competing with its customers. While the two divisions operated at arms' length the systems group bought chips from the component group at its "best customer" price. Each division had its own P&L, and performance was assessed by various measures of profitability, with the most recent focus on return on assets.

PCEO PC enhancement products were another major product segment within the systems group. Started as an entrepreneurial venture in 1984, PCEO sold add-in boards and components directly to end users through the retail channel. PCEO's major product lines were memory expansion boards which often included no Intel silicon and math coprocessors (80387s). Management attributed the success of PCEO to Intel's strong name recognition among computer specialists and the company's ability to work with software vendors to establish its products as industry standards.

SERVICE AND SUPERCOMPUTERS Intel's systems group had two other divisions in 1988: a service business, whose primary function was to maintain the installed base of Intel's OEM systems;[5] and an experimental development program,

---

[3]One of the company's most successful board level products was its "bus" business. Intel's MULTIBUS products, which were boards that allowed the components of a system (central-processing-unit, input-output, peripherals, and memory) to be connected to each other, had become the industry leader in the OEM market.

[4]Occasionally, an OEM platform with an Intel nameplate, like the one pictured in **Exhibit 4**, would be sold by value-added sellers (VARs) to end users. Intel opposed these sales and was taking steps to prevent the unauthorized use of their label.

[5]About 25% of the service business revenue came from maintaining Intel's development systems; about 40% from servicing platforms sold to the U.S. army; and the remainder from networking and service Intel supercomputers, other PCs, and mainframes.

launched in 1986, in the supercomputer business. The company had designed fast computers using parallel processing technologies with Intel 286 and 386 microprocessors. The company's ultimate goal was to develop a new market for this class of computer, which would reach at least $100 million in revenue by the 1990s. By 1988, the supercomputer operation had broken even and Intel could boast the largest installed base of hypercube parallel processing supercomputers.

Confusion in the Market

While Intel alone sold 80386s in 1988, a variety of hardware and software threats were on the horizon. Theoretically, a semiconductor firm could clone the 386. Although technically difficult without violating Intel patents, several firms were working on clones. New software solutions could also eliminate Intel's lock on DOS-based machines. Unix could run on Intel and non-Intel systems, and future generation operating systems, forecasted to be available in the early 1990s, would be portable across different computers.[6] At most, Intel had three to five years before one or all of these technologies became a reality.

RISC　1988 also marked a new frontier for the battle over the microprocessor market. RISC, or Reduced Instruction Set Computing, began to gain momentum. RISC, a revolutionary microprocessor design technique first investigated by IBM in the 1970s, increased speed by streamlining the number of "hardwired" instructions that a semiconductor must process. RISC technology was said to compute faster than traditional CISC (Complex Instruction Set Computing) microprocessors, such as the 386. *Dataquest* predicted that RISC's share of the worldwide 32-bit microprocessor market would grow from 9% in 1988 to

nearly 39% by 1992. By and large, desktop systems designed using a RISC chip were entering the market with UNIX operating systems. A growing number of U.S. semiconductor and systems vendors, including Motorola, Sun Microsystems, and MIPS Computer Systems, were betting that workstations built around RISC semiconductor technology would take over that market within two years.

One of the greatest impediments to more rapid growth in RISC microprocessors was the lack of a software base. During 1988, several commercial RISC vendors had formed consortiums to recruit large software companies to write programs for their chips. While several other systems vendors had developed their own proprietary RISC CPU designs for internal consumption, the commercial RISC contenders were hoping that their RISC microprocessor chips would ultimately become the new industry-standard hardware platforms in a new age of fast computing.

In late 1988, Intel planned to introduce its own RISC chip for the high-end technical workstation market. This RISC processor would not be DOS-compatible or compatible with the 86 family architecture, but it would outperform other RISC chips presently available.

Competitive Environment

By 1988, Intel was the eighth largest semiconductor company in terms of revenue. In her report to Intel, the consultant noted several important trends in the industry that could affect Intel's future prospects. The first of these trends was the growing market for Intel's chips in Japan and the improved competitive position of vertically integrated Japanese electronics companies. Although the semiconductor industry began in the United States and was dominated by American firms for its first three decades, Japanese production surpassed the United States in 1986. Japan had targeted semiconductors as a strategic means for achieving dominance in a variety of downstream markets such as consumer electronics and computers.

Initially, Japanese companies licensed semiconductor technology. But as product innovations became more evolutionary rather than revolution-

---

[6]Beyond new operating systems, other technical solutions threatened the 386. A more direct threat, but technically very difficult, was emulation. It was hypothetically possible for a chip manufacturer to design a system with non-Intel-architecture processors and still have access to the PC software base with acceptable performance. Finally, binary compilation allowed existing programs to be translated into another processor's machine language while losing little of the efficiency of the original implementation. This would make it theoretically possible to convert PC programs to run at much higher speeds on a non-Intel architecture.

Intel Corporation 1988

ary, their skill at making incremental improvements in older technologies appeared to give the Japanese firms an increasing advantage in the mid-1980s. They had also set the standards in manufacturing efficiency by focusing on high-volume production, channeling significant financial resources to the development of production expertise, using dedicated instead of multiple-line plants, and continually innovating in process technology. In the words of one Intel executive, ". . . Japanese firms make investments in production technology that often cannot be justified on an ROI basis. They are often able to build larger plants that are better organized. Success in this industry is easier when a company has cash cows that support leading edge investments."

The consultant also noted that the biggest American firms, Motorola and Texas Instruments, were more horizontally integrated than Intel. Motorola's main business sectors included communications and semiconductor products for the commercial, industrial, nonprofit, governmental, and consumer markets. Motorola applied its expertise as an electronics manufacturer to computers, advanced military electronics, cellular radios and phones, and other products. Motorola was also preparing to enter the engineering workstation market in 1989 using its own RISC technology.

Texas Instruments focused on its semiconductor and defense electronics businesses, with semiconductors serving as the foundation for its other business activities. Recently, the company had invested in knowledge-based systems, industrial automation, and computer-aided software engineering. Through an agreement with Apple Computer, TI planned to deliver artificial intelligence capabilities to desktop computers. One observer argued that the company's objective was to "build on the synergy between its semiconductor and defense electronics businesses" in order to integrate its silicon and systems expertise.

Another persistent trend in the semiconductor industry was the formation of alliances. According to *Dataquest*, "The adversarial, contractual relationships of merchant semiconductor companies has tended to promote fragmentation and instability in the industry. Cooperation of buyers and sellers of products all along the product chain has become essential, and the concept of 'virtual vertical integration' has come into vogue. Its advocates urge that product development alliances be extended into joint-manufacturing agreements, long-term purchase contracts, and other relationships that help justify capacity expansions." In order for both component and systems companies to compete in this new business environment, many chose to combine their resources with other firms that could offer the necessary expertise. For instance, DEC signed joint technology agreements for network computing with Apple and Compaq in 1988. In another example, Sun Microsystems was one of the first players in the systems business to design and commercialize its own RISC microprocessor chip. Sun subcontracted the manufacturing of the silicon to merchant semiconductor houses. AT&T had also agreed to a partnership with Sun Microsystems to improve its UNIX operating system. Intel's most recent alliance was its formation of a joint venture in computers with Siemens.

The Intel/Siemens Alliance

In 1988, Intel announced the formation of a new company, BiiN (pronounced "bine") Partners, jointly owned (50%–50%) with Siemens AG, a West German electronics conglomerate. Analysts estimated that Intel and Siemens each spent more than $100 million on the joint venture as well as committed hundreds of design and engineering staff personnel to BiiN's Portland, Oregon headquarters. BiiN was to manufacture and market fault-tolerant computer systems for mission-critical markets, such as CAD/CAM, military applications, and on-line transaction processing (OLTP). (Fault-tolerant computers were specially designed to never crash or go down.) Intel and Siemens believed that existing computer architectures were inadequate for such tasks. The BiiN machines were based on a flexible, building block approach to hardware and software, which the partners believed would give them an advantage.

BiiN utilized proprietary microprocessor technology from Intel (that would not be sold to third parties). Although the volume was low, Intel had high yields on these microprocessors because they were manufactured with the same process and on the same lines as the 386. Eventually BiiN expected to develop its own design and technological capabilities. BiiN also anticipated significant benefits from its access to Siemen's European distribution and service network. As one analyst described BiiN: "Intel has been in the high-performance systems business for 12 years, but people still think of them as a chip company. This is another move in (expanding toward) that direction." BiiN shipped its first computers in the fall of 1988. The most optimistic projections suggested that BiiN would break even in two to three years and sell $500 million annually by 1992.

7. Microsoft's Networking Strategy

In the summer of 1990, Microsoft announced its intention to become the leader in PC network software. To achieve this goal, the company publicly promised a "networking crusade." With fanfare typical of a Microsoft product introduction, CEO Bill Gates announced that his company would make an investment, "both in dollars and in developmental effort, [that] represents the largest commitment Microsoft has ever made." Although no numbers were revealed, Microsoft would add 500 employees and attack industry leader Novell head-on. As usual, industry experts were impressed. Although they estimated that Microsoft's annual investment would be between $50 and $100 million, one noted, "we're encouraged by what we see . . . Bill Gates has a track record . . . he always accomplishes what he sets out to do. He's got a track record that proves he can do it."

The person in charge of making this a reality was Mike Murray, general manager of Microsoft's Network Business Unit (NBU). Murray, an engineer by training with an MBA from Stanford, was accustomed to such challenges. For four years in the early 1980s, he reported directly to Steve Jobs at Apple, where he was director of marketing for the Macintosh. After a brief hiatus with venture capital, Murray was offered jobs at Novell and Microsoft in 1988. Now, only 18 months into his new position, he had a mandate to become the industry leader by improving the product and expanding distribution. The very mild-mannered Murray confidently noted at the Microsoft press conference, "we intend to emerge as the leading vendor."[1]

Yet six months into their new strategy, Microsoft's traditional partner, IBM, dropped a bombshell. James Cannavino, IBM's vice president in charge of personal computing, stood arm in arm with Ray Noorda, Novell's president and chief executive officer, at the February 1991 PC networking convention in Boston. The two announced an agreement whereby IBM would market and support Novell's PC network software. Mike Murray was shell shocked. IBM had been the primary promoter of Microsoft's networking product, LAN Manager. Murray quickly had to resolve many critical questions. First, he had to assess what impact the IBM/Novell announce-

[1] All quotes on this page from *Lan Times*, September 1990, p. 1.

Professor David B. Yoffie and Associate Fellow Toby Lenk prepared this case as the basis for class discussion rather than to illustrate either effective or ineffective handling of an administrative situation.

ment would have on his strategy for selling LAN Manager to the corporate market. Second, he was in the middle of his firm's planning cycle, and he had to shape his longer-term networking strategy. Finally, he had to assess whether his current funding level was consistent with the answers to these issues. While most of Microsoft's other business units experienced double-digit growth, NBU was struggling to achieve its objectives. Murray had to decide whether to ask for additional investment beyond levels already committed. As Murray pondered these issues he could not help feeling that he had the most challenging job at Microsoft.

Brief History of Microsoft

Started in 1975 by Bill Gates, a dropout from Harvard College, and his high school chum, Paul Allen, Microsoft had become the dominant computer software company in the world. Under Gates' leadership, Microsoft's revenues surged 60% per year in the 1980s, double the industry's growth (see **Exhibits 1** and **2**). By 1991, the company's revenues were expected to approach $2 billion, making the 35-year-old Gates one of the richest men in the world. Thanks to a 40% stake in Microsoft, Gates had a net worth in excess of $4 billion.

The company's initial prosperity can be traced to its control over DOS, the operating system chosen by IBM in 1980 to run IBM-compatible PCs. Yet what ultimately distinguished Microsoft from other software companies was the breadth of its product offerings. While firms like Lotus and Word Perfect were still dependent on their first big hit, (spreadsheets and word processing, respectively) Microsoft successfully extended its product line in operating systems with Windows 3.0, and became the world's leading vendor of applications software with programs that included Word and Excel. Yet Microsoft rarely hit home runs with its initial product introductions: every one of its programs was considered poor or mediocre when it first hit the market; for instance, Windows, first introduced in 1983, was widely criticized for years as a poor imitation of the Apple Macintosh system. Each time, Gates overcame the limitations by persistence, by working closely with key partners, like IBM, and by exploiting technical disjunctures, like being among the first to write applications for the Macintosh and the first to provide a friendly graphical user interface for the IBM PC. The result was that Bill Gates built one of the most profitable and powerful companies in the history of the computer industry.

EXHIBIT 1 Microsoft Financial Performance, 1986–1990

	1990	1989	1988	1987	1986
Income Statement					
Net revenues	$1,183	$803	$591	$346	$197
Cost of revenues	253	204	148	74	41
R&D	181	110	70	38	21
Sales and marketing	318	219	161	85	58
General and administration	39	28	24	22	18
Operating income	$ 393	$242	$187	$127	$ 61
Selected Balance Sheet Numbers					
Cash and short-term inventory	$449.2	$300.8	$183.2	$132.5	$102.7
Total assets	1,105.3	720.6	495.0	287.8	170.7
Current liabilities	186.8	158.8	117.5	48.6	31.4
Stockholders' equity	918.6	561.8	375.5	239.1	139.5

Source: Microsoft Annual Report. Microsoft's fiscal year ends June 30.

EXHIBIT 2 Microsoft Revenues by Product, Channel, and Region

	1990	1989	1988	1987	1986
Revenue by Product Group					
Systems/languages	39%	44%	47%	49%	53%
Applications	48	42	40	38	37
Hardware, books, other	13	14	13	13	10
Total	100%	100%	100%	100%	100%
Revenue by Channel					
Domestic OEM	13%	14%	17%	21%	25%
Domestic retail	30	29	32	35	32
Total domestic	43%	43%	49%	56%	57%
International OEM	13	18	14	14	21
International finished goods	42	37	34	28	19
Total International	55%	55%	48%	42%	40%
Microsoft Press and other	2	2	2	2	2
Total	100%	100%	100%	100%	100%

Source: Microsoft Annual Report.

Microsoft Historical Strategy in Networking

Unlike desktop operating systems and applications, networking software had received relatively little attention during the early days at Microsoft. Gates' top priority was enabling the stand-alone microcomputer. Moreover, Gates did not want to sell networking software directly: he considered it a "systems products," software that required a good deal of support and service. These products were best distributed by OEMs like IBM and DEC, whose entire computer business was structured to sell and service them.

Microsoft's first networking product, MS-NET, was developed for IBM to link IBM PCs in corporate accounts. IBM sold it under the name PC-NET. Despite strong sales, neither IBM nor Microsoft invested heavily in the product, and PC-NET was soon eclipsed by Novell's Netware. Microsoft's next product, LAN Manager (LAN Man) for OS/2, was hastily developed towards the end of OS/2's development cycle and the initial release to OEMs contained many software bugs. In addition to this troubled introduction, LAN Man suffered a myriad of weaknesses. First, each OEM licensee took the basic LAN Man software code and added to and /or modified it. Then each used a different name for it (IBM/LAN Server, DEC/Pathworks, 3Com/3+Open, etc.). None of the final OEM versions were compatible with other LAN Man-based products. Second, of all the licensees only 3Com was dedicated solely to the PC networking, and it exited from the software side of the business in 1990. Finally, LAN Man was hurt by its dependence on the OS/2 operating system. OS/2 had sold only 300,000 copies between 1987 and the end of 1990, compared to over 60 million copies of DOS and 2.5 million copies of Windows 3.0.

A New Strategy

With the proliferation in PC networking, Bill Gates believed there was a great opportunity in the 1990s for Microsoft to move beyond stand-alone PC software. As the keynote speaker at the annual PC convention in 1990, he offered a new vision for his firm and the industry, called "information at your fingertips (IAYF)." Under IAYF, a PC user could be connected to most other computers and data inside his or her organization. More importantly, the user would be able to access the data quickly in a friendly and intuitive way to solve problems and answer questions.

A related concept was "downsizing": Gates believed that the increasing power of the microprocessor would allow PCs to do the jobs that larger, more specialized mini and mainframe computer systems performed. An example was wide-area enterprise networks. Microsoft itself had a 24-hour worldwide PC network that spanned several continents. Gates wanted Microsoft to develop and market the PC software that would enable downsizing to occur.

Microsoft's networking business was the first step towards the realization of Gates' vision. With the failure of the OEM-based strategy, Microsoft decided to develop and market LAN Manager directly. Management's goals were: 1) develop software for networked computing applications; 2) build Microsoft's in-house capability to sell and support this software to the *Fortune 1,000*; 3) make LAN Man the technical equal to Netware by 1991–1992 with a 30% market share, and surpass Novell in new sales by 1993; and 4) succeed in defending against the possibility that Novell might threaten Microsoft's PC operating system business. Microsoft managers felt that server-based operating systems represented a long-run threat to Microsoft's base business of providing PC operating systems. Some computer systems were designed so that the operating system and applications software all resided on a server. Sun Microsystems offered such a system based on the UNIX operating system. It was conceivable that Novell could offer either a DOS clone on the PC, or eventually add more and more of DOS's functionality onto its server-based operating system.[2]

In January 1991, Gates saw great potential for Microsoft. He stated that his vision for the networking business was based on several assumptions:

First, I believe that microcomputer-based servers will proliferate and there are great economics for Microsoft—$4,000 to $5,000 per server, plus unbundled service revenue. Every large company will have hundreds of these servers. Second, our selling costs will start high, but once our NOS becomes popular, they will decline dramatically. Third, our reputation gives us an advantage over all other players: people always go with the safe choice. Fourth, we can grow 30% per year. There is enough room for Microsoft and Novell in the short term. And fifth, over the long run, we can "out-Novell, Novell." We have the best R&D in the world. Ultimately, that will pay off.

Product Strategy: Short Term

Mike Murray and Bill Gates agreed on the short-term challenge for NBU: catch-up with Novell and Banyan (see **Exhibits 3** and **4**). Towards that end, NBU staff expanded rapidly in 1990, reaching 260 development and 400 sales and support personnel.[3] The new version of LAN Man, version 2.1, due out in 1991, would make up much ground. Although the LAN Man development group was working at a breakneck pace to catch up, they would not achieve visible leadership in the near term.

The one area where LAN Man had a distinct advantage was client-server applications (CSA).[4] The Netware operating system was not designed well for CSAs,[5] while OS/2 was widely regarded by customers as an excellent vehicle for client-server applications. Novell's newest product, Netware 386, was designed to improve Netware's CSA capability. It allowed outside software firms to write

---

[2]One company that did offer a DOS clone was Digital Research. Its product, DR DOS, generated about $50 million in revenues in 1990. Digital Research was rumored to be for sale, and Novell was rumored to be interested.

[3]Analysts estimated that each person cost Microsoft approximately $100,000 to $150,000 in overhead and associated expenses. But R&D and sales staff were generally fungible: good software engineers, in particular, were moved around between different software projects.

[4]Refer to the "Note on the PC Network Software Industry." Client-server applications (CSAs) were designed for multiple users, or workgroups, to share data and software to accomplish tasks. The software resided typically on the server, and interacted very closely with the NOS.

[5]The reasons for this were extremely technical. Essentially, Netware was designed to run networks very fast and efficiently—it did not have many of the normal safety features built into it that most general-purpose operating systems required. OS/2 was written as a full-fledged operating system. However, in some situations OS/2 and LAN Man were slower at moving information over a network than Netware. Analysts expected Novell to improve Netware's capability for CSA over time.

EXHIBIT 3 Comparison of Corporate Segment Product Offerings

Product Dimensions	Novell Netware	Microsoft LAN Man	Banyan Vines
1) Network features (file and printer sharing)	Strong	OK	Strong
2) Connectivity	Strong	Behind	Strong
3) Wide-area systems capacity (for WANs, etc.)	Weak	Weak	Strong
4) Client support (number of different PC systems can hook to: Apple, IBM, etc.)	Strong	Behind	OK
5) Client-server applications (CSA)	Weak (NLM strategy)	Strong (OS/2)	Weak[a] (UNIX)

[a]UNIX was a strong system for CSA, but Banyan, relative to others, lacked the market share to induce third parties to write client-server applications to Vines.

Source: Casewriter interviews with customers and VARs.

applications software that could be loaded in modular fashion onto a Netware server. These were dubbed Netware Loadable Modules (NLMs). Despite Netware 386's NLM capability, most customers agreed that OS/2 was superior for CSAs.

Microsoft itself had a separate CSA product group within NBU. The CSA group developed and marketed applications products that ran under the supervision of OS/2, located on a server. The flagship product was SQL Server. This software allowed users to access data bases on mainframe computers, format it, and pass it into a user's PC spreadsheet. A customer wanting to use SQL Server would typically have a server with OS/2 as the operating system, LAN Man performing the networking, and SQL Server handling the data application (see **Exhibit 5**). Dwayne Walker, general manager of CSA, described the logic of his business:

> Operating systems don't sell themselves or the computers. Applications sell operating systems and computers. People bought the original IBM PC, and DOS, because they wanted to use Lotus 1-2-3. It is the same logic for networked computing. People will buy servers and server operating systems to run applications like SQL Server.

However, Walker's mission was to succeed on a stand-alone basis—his primary job was not

to sell LAN Man. To this end, he felt it was necessary for his products to work well with Novell's Netware: "Most of the networks out there are Netware. About one-third of my SQL Server units run on a Netware network. Just as Lotus 1-2-3 was written to run with DOS, SQL Server was written to run with OS/2. So users who want both to keep their Netware and run SQL Server, have to buy a second server and load it with OS/2 and SQL Server. Because a significant enough number of customers want to do this, we felt it necessary to make SQL Server interoperate well with Netware." However, customers who used LAN Man with SQL Server saved the expense of an extra server and, under some conditions, achieved superior performance as measured by network speed.

Mike Murray knew that client-server applications were still nascent in 1991: they were one of tomorrow's trends. No one was certain how fast the market for them would develop. It was part of NBU's mission to educate customers about the benefits and potential of CSA, but the development of CSA networks depended on many other firms; applications had to be developed, sold, and implemented on networks. Murray was nonetheless confident that the shift to CSA would occur: "Today, we are a small part of PC networking, which consists of products that provide only network services, such as file and printer sharing. Novell is king of file and printer sharing, with over 60% market share. But the market will move to CSA based networks, and we will be king of those. We will grow CSA over the next three years, and we will lead it."

Product Strategy: Long Term

Over time, Microsoft would provide operating systems with networking inherently a part of the PC operating system. These were referred to as distributed operating systems. Jim Allchin, former chief technologist at Banyan, was a key figure in formulating and implementing this longer-term strategy. Allchin summed up the strategy: "In the long run there won't be any network operating systems, just operating systems. You won't need LAN Man or Netware."

Microsoft management acknowledged that this was a long-run plan, which might take 5–10

EXHIBIT 4 Corporate Segment Customer Survey Data: December 1990

Firm Product:	Microsoft LAN Man	Banyan Vines	IBM LAN Server	IBM PC-NET	Novell 286	Novell 386	3Com 3+Open	Digital Pathworks	Apple LAN	TOTAL
Question 1: Which PC LANS are in use at your firm today?	12%	22%	28%	12%	70%	54%	10%	10%	14%	232%
Question 2: Which PC LAN is dominant at your firm today?	2	14	8	5	44	20	2	4	1	100
Question 3: Which PC LAN will be dominant at your firm in three years?	10	8	26	0	2	42	2	10	0	100
Question 4: Which firms do you believe will be PC LAN "winners, doubtful as winners," and PC LAN "losers?"										
Number of mentions:	23	22	21	—	—	35	12	10	—	—
"Winner"	87	32	86	—	—	69	8	90	—	—
"Doubtful"	13	41	10	—	—	17	33	0	—	—
"Loser"	0	27	4	—	—	14	59	10	—	—

The survey was asked of 50 *Fortune 1,000* customers. Questions 1–3 answers are to be read "__% of the 50 surveyed companies." Question 4 asked people to name PC LAN companies, and classify them as long-run winners, doubtful, and losers. For Microsoft, 87% of the 23 respondents, or 20, believed Microsoft would be a long-run PC LAN "winner." The survey was generally asked to corporate MIS managers.

Source: Adapted from Forrester Research Reports, various issues.

years to evolve. Microsoft might develop its new distributed operating systems (to be called Windows NT) sooner, but it would probably take time for them to be adopted widely. It was likely that most personal computers would continue to be run by DOS, Windows, and OS/2 through much of the 1990s. For networking, NOS products like LAN Man and Netware would continue to be in demand.

Distribution

Microsoft planned to follow a different reseller strategy from Novell, focusing on "quality rather than quantity," according to Mike Murray. Many of Novell's resellers were unhappy about the number of Netware sellers in the market. NBU had, through the end of 1990, certified about 300 of Novell's top resellers as LAN Man dealers. Overall, NBU planned to target 1,000 worldwide in an attempt to build channel loyalty. This number would be significantly below Novell's 12,000 dealer network for another reason: many of Novell's dealers were retail computer stores that stocked low-end products. Microsoft did not have a low-end product.

Almost all dealers historically carried Netware, while a small percentage offered 3Com and other products. Leading competitors such as Banyan had focused on selling directly to corporate customers. At issue was the extent to which PC network software was a "push" product. For smaller and less sophisticated customers, resellers were very influential in the purchase decision. They had less influence on more sophisticated customers, whose MIS departments were better able to evaluate the network software alternatives.

An important element of Microsoft's distribution strategy was its own field organization. Corporate customers were increasingly demanding a direct presence by their PC network soft-

EXHIBIT 5 SQL Server CSA PC Network

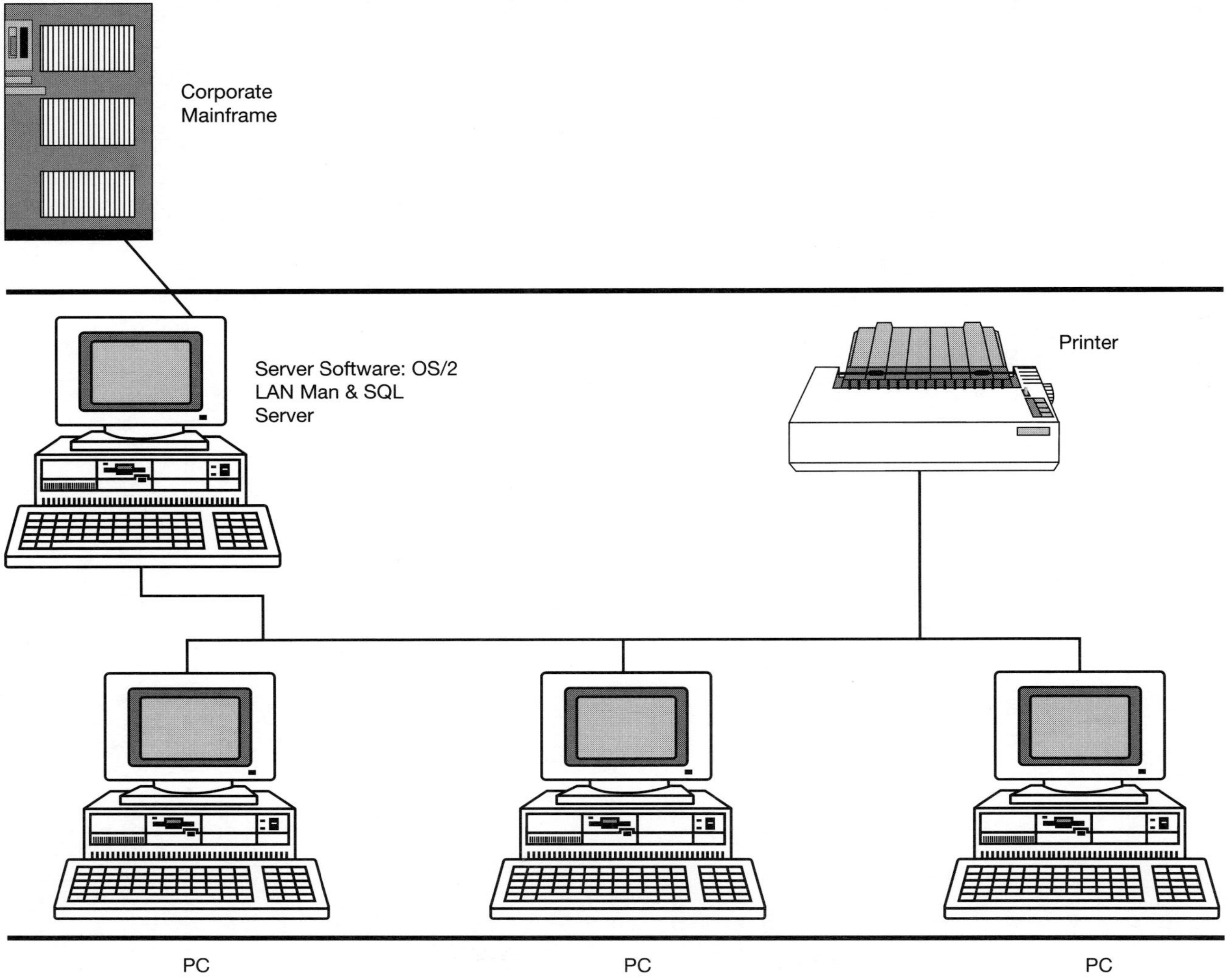

Corporate
Mainframe

Server Software: OS/2
LAN Man & SQL
Server

Printer

PC

PC

PC

Note: Each PC might run DOS & Windows with Lotus 1-2-3. The Server would act as a traffic cop controlling data to PCs on the network, allowing users to share information and a printer. In with SQL Server software on the PC Server, the PC user could access data from the corporate mainframe, which would then be formated into a PC spreadsheet.

ware vendors. Novell had very high ratings for its product, but corporate customers criticized the level of support and service that Novell provided. Customers believed that, with hundreds of their PCs networked with Netware, their problems and questions should be answered rapidly by Novell itself, and not by the resellers. Corporate customers preferred one vendor who could solve all problems, a role traditionally filled skillfully by IBM. With the growth of PC technology, many firms contributed technology to new PC based systems and customers often found service inadequate. To provide proper support Microsoft had invested significantly in building NBU's field organization. Their role was to generate sales, which would typically be credited to a local reseller, and to support customers. Bill Gates summarized the goal: "We want to build our direct presence and become a strategic partner to our corporate customers." Gates further noted the possible synergies with Microsoft's new but still quite small consulting organization. The mission of the consulting group was to help corporate clients with software choices.

Microsoft's new strategy to distribute LAN Man with its own field organization and qualified resellers would exist, at least in the short-run, side by side with OEM distribution. However, Microsoft would be in a competitive situation with its OEM licensees. For example, Microsoft found itself pushing PC-based networks against DEC, which would offer customers a VAX mini-computer-based network using Pathworks, DEC's version of LAN Man adapted for the VAX.[6] However, the most critical OEM relationship was with IBM.

IBM had a significant installed base of PC network software licensed from Microsoft, comprised of PC-NET (MS-NET) and LAN Server (LAN Man). As Microsoft invested aggressively in upgrading LAN Manager, and began to publicize its new strategy to market it directly, IBM's customers became somewhat confused about the difference between LAN Server and LAN Manager. They hoped that IBM and Microsoft would agree to make the two products interoperable, so that they could connect their LAN Server networks to

LAN Manager networks. IBM had, through the first half of 1990, actually been working with Microsoft staff to sell LAN Man in some corporate accounts. Micro soft's relationship with IBM was helpful for NBU field staff calling on *Fortune* 500 accounts.

Towards the end of 1990 Microsoft's relationship with IBM deteriorated; by early 1991, the two firms were publicly quarreling—the business press called it a war. Mike Murray had to contend with increasing strain between the two companies as he continued his efforts to cultivate large companies. This strain derived from Microsoft's success with a new PC operating system, Windows version 3.0. With the success of Windows, Microsoft had effectively reduced its support for OS/2 as a desktop operating system. IBM remained ardently committed to making OS/2 the next standard, succeeding DOS.

Mike Murray had more to worry about from the IBM-Novell alliance. Under the agreement, IBM would market Netware to its corporate customers and would write software that allowed Netware to interoperate with LAN Server. Novell would also provide Netware support for OS/2. This meant that in the future, corporate customers would be able to run OS/2 and Netware on one server. Furthermore, Netware would support most other IBM mainframe computer protocols and management systems. IBM stated that the agreement was the result of large business customers pressuring IBM to sanction and support Netware. After the agreement, IBM field reps who had been pushing the merits of LAN Server would now offer both LAN Server and Netware to customers. James Cannavino stated that IBM would sell both "without bias." Resellers also expressed a different view of Novell after the agreement. One noted, "IBM has blessed Netware . . . it is now considered safe in corporate America. This helps Novell's marketing in all segments."

The immediate impact of the announcement was to create additional confusion. Customers who had committed to purchasing LAN Manager were opening up the decision for additional review. Mike Murray had to face the prospect that IBM would actively sell Netware against LAN Manager. In addition, IBM might not agree to work to interoperate LAN Server with LAN Manager, while doing so with Netware.

[6]The Pathworks software resided on the VAX minicomputer, which would act as the server. With Novell Netware or Microsoft LAN Man, customers purchased a personal computer to act as the dedicated server.

Performance-to-Date

Bill Gates and top management were not looking for short-term returns in networking. Gates expected a cash drain and noted calmly, "we can afford it." But the first half of fiscal 1991 had not been as successful as management hoped. NBU's revenues were only running at 30% of forecasted expenditures. Mike Murray wondered— should he stay the course? Could he alter course after only six months? What other alternatives were available?

8. Apple Computer 1992

John Sculley, Apple Computer's charismatic CEO, sat in his small, interior glass office in Cupertino, California reading the year-end results for 1991. The computer industry had just experienced its worst year in history. Average return on sales plummeted to under 4% and the ROE was under 11%. For the first time, worldwide PC revenues actually dropped by almost 10%, despite rising unit volume. Although Apple continued to outperform the industry, the intensity of competition was putting acute pressure on Apple's margins. "Our challenge," noted Sculley, "is not only to stay ahead of our competition, but we have to find some way to change the rules of the game. If computer manufacturers continue to make and sell commodities, everyone in our business will suffer." Changing a $50 billion global industry, however, was no easy task. Yet Sculley believed that Apple was one of the only companies that could do it. For Apple's next strategy session, he asked his staff to address two key questions: 1) could Apple change the structure of the industry, and if so how? and 2) what other alternatives are available?

A Brief History of Apple

Apple's legendary story began when Steve Wozniak (Woz) and Steve Jobs joined forces to produce the Apple I computer in the Jobs family garage in Cupertino. College dropouts in their early 20s, they formed Apple Computer Inc. on April Fool's Day 1976. After selling 200 Apple I computers, mainly to hobbyists, they managed to obtain venture capital. Jobs sold his vision of making the personal computer easy to use for non-technical people. His stated mission, which permeated the firm through 1992, was "to change the world through technology." The concept was one computer for every man, woman, and child. When Jobs and Woz announced the Apple II in March 1977, they began a revolution in computing, which changed the company *and* the world.

Professor David B. Yoffie prepared this case with the assistance of Research Associates Jeff Cohn and David Levy as the basis for class discussion rather than to illustrate either effective or ineffective handling of an administrative situation.

Apple sold over 100,000 Apple IIs by the end of 1980, generating revenues over $100 million. Primarily selling into homes and schools, Apple was recognized as the industry leader. The company went public in December 1980, making the founders multi-millionaires.

Apple's competitive position changed fundamentally when IBM entered the personal computer market in 1981. While Apple's revenues continued to grow rapidly, market share and margins fell precipitously. Apple responded to IBM with two new products, the Lisa and Macintosh (Mac). These innovative computers featured a graphical interface and a windowing operating system that allowed the user to view and switch between several applications at once. They also used a mouse to move and point to positions on the screen, making applications easier to use. However, both computers were incompatible with the IBM standard and even with the Apple II. The technologically sophisticated, but expensive ($10,000) Lisa Computer was soon dropped. The Macintosh fared better, but suffered because of limited software and low performance. By 1984, the company was in crisis.

A year before the introduction of the Lisa and Macintosh, Apple hired John Sculley to be its president and CEO. Sculley, 44, an MBA from Wharton and previously president of Pepsi's beverage operations, had spent most of his career in marketing and advertising. Sculley was to provide the operational expertise, and Steve Jobs the technical direction and vision. But Jobs resigned from Apple in September 1985 after a well publicized dispute with Sculley and Apple's board of directors.

After its slow start, Apple's new Mac computer picked up steam. Between 1986 and 1990, Apple's sales exploded (see **Exhibit 8–1**). It introduced new, more powerful Macs that roughly matched the newest IBM personal computers in speed. Even more important, the Mac offered superior software and a variety of peripherals (e.g., laser printers) that gave Apple a unique market niche—the easiest computer to use in the industry with unmatched capabilities at desktop publishing. Apple's strategy of being the only manufacturer of its hardware and software made Apple's profitability the envy of the industry. By 1990, Apple had $1 billion in cash and more than $5.5 billion in sales. Return on equity, at 32%, was one of the best in the industry. Market share had stabilized at around 10%.

But the industry environment was changing rapidly. Rather than basking in success, Apple's management became convinced in the spring of 1990 that their position was unsustainable. According to Dan Eilers, V.P. of Strategic Planning at the time, "the company was on a glide path to history."

The Evolving Personal Computer Industry[1]

The personal computer was a revolution in information technology that spawned a $50 billion hardware business, with another $30 billion in software and peripherals by 1991. During its short 15 years, the industry evolved through three successive periods. During its first 5–6 years, it was characterized by explosive growth and multiple, small competitors vying for a piece of the market. IBM's introduction of the IBM PC in 1981 launched a second stage in desktop computing. Over the next five years, the industry became a battle for standards and retail shelf space. Three firms emerged as the clear leaders during this period: IBM, Compaq, and Apple. The third era was one of increasing fragmentation. From 1986 through 1991–2, new manufacturers of IBM clones from around the world grabbed share from the industry leaders as new channels of distribution emerged and product innovation as well as revenue growth slowed.

In some ways, the personal computer was a very simple device. Most PCs were composed of five, widely available components: memory storage, a microprocessor (the brains of the PC), a main circuit board called a mother board, a disc drive and peripherals (e.g., display, keyboard,

[1]The description of the industry will focus primarily on the U.S. market, which was the trendsetter in PCs in the 1980s. PC penetration was much deeper in the United States than Europe and Japan, and trends in areas such as software and distribution generally started in the United States and filtered to Europe, then Japan within 1–3 years.

EXHIBIT 8-1 Detailed Financials of Apple Over Time

	1991	1990	1989	1988	1987	1986	1985	1984	1983	1982	1981
Total revenues ($ millions)	$6,309	$5,558	$5,284	$4,071	$2,661	$1,902	$1,918	$1,516	$983	$583	$334
Cost of sales	3,314	2,606	2,695	1,991	1,296	891	1,118	879	506	288	170
Research and development	583	478	421	273	192	128	72.5	71	60	38	21
Marketing and distribution	1,740	1,556	1,340	908	655	477	478	399	230	120	55
General and administrative	224	207	195	180	146	133	110	82	57	35	22
Operating income	447	712	634	620	371	274	103	86	130	102	66
Net income	310	475	454	400	218	154	61.3	64.1	77	61	39
Property, plant, equipment and other	275	321	284	186	121	67	66	53	64	30	NA
Depreciation and amortization	204	202	124	77	70	51	41	37	22	16	NA
Cash dividends paid	56	53	50	39	15	—	—	—	—	—	NA
Cash and temporary cash investment	893	997	809	546	565	576	337	115	143	153	73
Accounts receivable	907	762	793	639	406	263	220	258	136	72	42
Inventories	672	356	475	461	226	109	167	265	142	81	104
Property, plant and equipment	448	398	334	207	130	222	176	150	110	57	31
Total assets	3,494	2,976	2,744	2,082	1,478	1,160	936	789	557	358	255
Total current liabilities	1,217	1,027	895	827	479	138	90	255	129	86	70
Total shareholders' equity	1,767	1,447	1,486	1,003	837	694	550	465	378	257	177
Permanent employees	12,386	12,307	12,068	9,536	6,236	4,950	4,326	5,382	4,645	3,391	2,456
International sales/sales (%)	45	42	36	32	27	26	22	22	22	24	27
Gross margin/sales (%)	47	53	49	51	51	53	42	42	49	51	49
R&D/sales (%)	9	9	8	7	7	7	4	5	6	7	6
ROS[a] (%)	4.91	8.55	8.59	9.83	8.19	8.10	3.20	4.23	7.83	10.46	11.68
ROA[b] (%)	8.87	15.96	16.55	19.21	14.75	13.28	6.55	8.12	13.82	17.04	15.29
Return on equity (%)	19	32	36	44	28	28	12	15	24	28	44
Stock price range	40.5–73.3	24.3–47.8	32.5–50.4	35.5–47.75	20.3–59.8	10.8–22	7.3–15.6	10.8–17.25	8.6–31.6	5.5–7.5	6.8–7.3
PE/ratio	12.9	10.5	12.9	13.6	20.3	11.6	22.1	26.7	30.6	16.1	24.3
Market value[c]	6,751	4,150	5,166	5,033	4,914	2,004	1,360	1,694	2,368	742	1,320

aROS = net income/total revenues.
bROA = net income/total assets.
cYear-end stock price times the number of shares outstanding.
Sources: Apple Annual Reports and Value Line.

mouse, printer, etc.). Most manufacturers also bundled their PC hardware with critical software packages, especially an operating system (the software required to run applications). But from the beginning, PCs have been available in almost infinite variety. They could vary in speed, amounts of memory and storage, physical size, weight, functionality, and so on.

During the early years of the industry, venture capital in the United States encouraged the entry of new firms, which offered products in every conceivable shape and size. By 1980, new entrants flooded the market, promoting distinct standards and unique technical features. Almost every firm had a different configuration of hardware and software, making communication or sharing applications between machines virtually impossible. The first PCs introduced by Commodore and Apple had relatively little speed or memory. However, even these early computers allowed managers to perform tasks that were either very time consuming or reserved for expensive ($50,000 to >$1 million), multi-user mini and mainframe computers. For under $5,000, anyone could now do spreadsheet analysis and word processing.

Before IBM entered the market in 1981, most products were considered "closed" or proprietary systems. A closed system, like mainframes, minicomputers, and Apple's PCs, could not be copied or cloned because it was protected by patents or copyrights. However, closed systems typically rendered the computer incompatible with competitor's products. IBM's entry in 1981 changed the playing field by offering an "open" system. The specifications of IBM's PC were easily obtainable, allowing independent hardware companies to make compatible machines and independent software vendors (ISVs) to write applications that would run on different brands. Open systems had a big advantage for customers because they were no longer locked into a particular vendor's product, and they could mix and match hardware and software from different competitors to get the lowest system price. And as long as manufacturers could buy the key components, particularly Microsoft's DOS (disk operating system) and Intel's X86 family of microprocessors, they could manufacture a product that could piggyback on IBM's coattails. Between 1982 and 1986, the majority of the industry consolidated around IBM's MS-DOS/Intel X86 microprocessor standard. Among the various proprietary PC systems, which had included names like DEC, Xerox and Wang, only Apple thrived.

Although IBM had created an open system that fostered imitators, few firms were capable of competing head-to-head with IBM. On the strength of its brand name and product quality, IBM captured almost 70% of the *Fortune* 1000 business market during its first four years. In addition, the personal computer was still a relatively new machine through the mid-1980s, and users were uncertain about quality, compatibility, service, and reliability. Concerns over the bankruptcies of companies, like Osborne and Leading Edge, as well as the occasional incompatible machine, led the majority of corporate buyers to buy brand name computers through respected, high service retail channels, such as ComputerLand. Most retailers, however, only had space on their shelves for four or five major brands. In the mid-1980s, the typical retailer carried three core, premium brands: Apple, which was the leader in user-friendliness and applications like desktop publishing; IBM, which was the premium priced, industry standard; and Compaq, which built IBM compatible machines with a strong reputation for quality and high performance. The multitude of smaller clone companies had to compete for the remaining one or two spaces on the retailer's shelf.

The early growth in PCs was built partly on rapidly changing innovative hardware and partly on exciting software applications. In its first five years, IBM and compatibles went through four major hardware product generations—the PC (based on Intel 8088), PC XT (based on 8086 and a hard drive), PC AT (based on Intel 80286), and 80386 PCs; in the meantime, Apple went from the Apple II to Macintosh—a major breakthrough in user-friendliness and functionality. The PC explosion was also fueled by software applications. Programs like Lotus 1-2-3 and WordPerfect were nicknamed "killer apps" because they were so powerful compared to their predecessors, everyone wanted them. Most of the best programs for business applications were written for the IBM standard, while Apple dominated educational applications and graphics.

The late 1980s saw revolution turn into evolution in both hardware and software. On one front, the IBM PC standard became the MS-DOS/Intel compatible standard. IBM tried to make PCs more proprietary in 1987 with the introduction of its PS/2 line of computers. Old IBM PC boards could not be plugged into the PS/2. Many customers, however, did not want to give up any compatibility with their prior purchases. As a result, IBM faltered, losing almost half its market share. Since Intel and Microsoft provided all manufacturers with identical parts, it was IBM's clones that offered compatibility with the installed base. A new generation of PC clone manufacturers such as Dell and Gateway also found that most customers could no longer distinguish between low priced and premium brands. Finally, the greatest differentiation in the industry had been between standards—IBM versus Apple. However, when Microsoft introduced its "Windows" 3.0 graphical user interface in 1990, the differences in user-friendliness between MS-DOS/Intel machines and Macs narrowed significantly.

By 1992, the PC business had changed from a high growth industry to an industry with a few high growth segments. The installed base of PCs approached 100 million units. New products, like notebook computers, and traditional products sold through new channels, like direct mail, continued to sell at double digit growth rates. But the economics of PC manufacturing, sales, R&D, and software, were fundamentally different compared to the early and mid-1980s.

Manufacturing and R&D

A company could manufacture a personal computer box (with the most current, state-of-the-art microprocessor, but without a keyboard and screen) for as little as $540 in 1992. That box would typically carry a wholesale price of $600. PC boxes with a last generation microprocessor (i.e., an 80386) wholesaled for about $500. Firms, however, had different cost structures, which varied with their manufacturing strategy. Some firms were pure assembly operations, buying all of their components from independent vendors, while others designed and made their own computer boards. For under $1 million, an assembler could buy the equipment and lease enough space to make 200,000–300,000 PCs per year. It would cost that assembler about $480 for the boards, chassis, disk drives, and power supplies and another $60 in direct labor. If a firm designed and manufactured its own boards, the entry costs were somewhat higher. While you only needed one manufacturing line to be efficient, the initial capital costs for assembling computer boards was $5 million. One line would produce about 1000 boards per day. If the PC manufacturer produced its own boards, it could reduce the cost of the computer box by as much as $50. The price of the keyboard and monitor could add from $100 to more than $500 to the system's total costs, depending on the options. The costs of specialty PCs, like notebooks, were considerably higher. There were fewer standard components, the products required more special engineering, and there were only two major suppliers of LCD screens in the world, Japan's Sharp and Toshiba.

Location was another important variable in the manufacturing equation. Freight and duty costs for a complete system could be as much as 10%–15% of total cost. As a result, many companies manufactured their boards in low labor cost locations (like Southeast Asia), then did final assembly near their market. The lowest cost producers in the world in the early 1990s were probably the Taiwanese. Their advantages went beyond having low-cost labor. For instance, they designed their products for the lowest possible costs. Companies like Compaq, IBM, and Apple typically designed a PC to last up to 50 years, while Taiwanese engineers used a 10–15 year horizon. In addition, their overhead was usually minimal: manufacturing was often set up in warehouses rather than fancy air-conditioned factories.

R&D expenditures closely tracked a firm's manufacturing strategy. While the average R&D spending in computers was ~5%, PC manufacturers spent from 1% for a pure assembler to 8%–10% for companies like Apple, which designed their boards, chips, and even the ergonomics of the keyboards and boxes. Since R&D costs on many key technologies were rising, there was a growing trend in the industry in the early 1990s to license technology from third parties, work collectively in consortiums, and whenever possible, buy off-the-shelf components and software, rather than develop from scratch.

Distribution and Buyers

Buyers of PCs could be roughly divided into three broad categories: business/government; education; and individual/home. Each customer had somewhat different criteria and different means for purchasing computers. The largest segment was business, with roughly 60% of the units and 70% of the total revenue. During the 1980s, personal computers were most often bought by individuals or small departments in corporations, without much input from a corporation's MIS staff. Individual business PC buyers were usually unsophisticated about the technology, and worried most about service, support, and compatibility. Brand name was especially important and full service computer dealers, such as Businessland and ComputerLand, built billion dollar businesses servicing these customers.

By the early 1990s, individual business consumers had become more knowledgeable about the PC; in addition, more computers were purchased by technically trained MIS staff, who were operating under tight budgets. (See **Exhibit 8–2**.) Full-service dealers suddenly became an expensive channel. Demand exploded at "superstores" like CompuAdd and Staples as well as at mail order outlets, which offered computers and peripherals at 30%–50% off list price. Even Kmart, Costco, and other mass merchandisers started to sell large volumes of PCs. (See **Exhibit 8–3**.) Since business organizations were increasingly demanding that their PCs be networked, another channel evolved, called value-added resellers or VARs. Most VARs were low overhead operations that could buy computers in volume, package them with software or peripherals, and then configure the PCs into networks. Finally, some computer manufacturers bypassed third-party distribution entirely, selling directly through the mail with phone support for customer service.

EXHIBIT 8-2 PC Consumer Preferences—Major Brands (Tier I) versus Other Secondary Companies—Baseline Study (March 1991–May 1991) *(Source: Compiled from Intellitrack data, 1991.)*

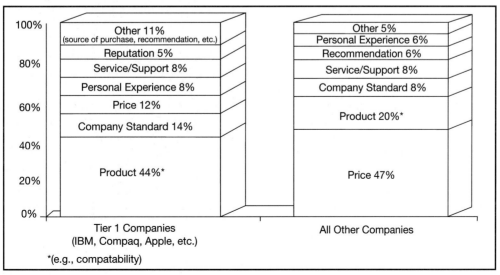

EXHIBIT 8-3 PC Distribution Channel Breakdown[a]

	Direct	Dealer	Superstore	VAR	Mass Merchant	Consumer Electronics	Mail Order
(%) of Total Unit Shipments							
1987	17.4	58.9	0	11.3	3.4	4.1	4.3
1988	12.3	61.7	0	12.4	3.9	4.3	4.8
1989	8.6	63.2	0	13.9	4.1	4.7	4.8
1990	8.0	58.3	1.1	14.7	5.2	5.2	6.1
1991	7.9	55.7	2.0	15.2	6.4	6.4	6.2
1992[b]	8.3	51.6	2.9	15.7	7.5	7.5	6.2
(%) of Total Value Shipments							
1987	31.0	49.0	0	13.2	1.4	1.8	2.3
1988	25.3	52.9	0	14.3	1.7	1.9	3.2
1989	17.3	56.9	0	17.1	1.9	2.1	3.7
1990	18.4	52.7	0.7	18.0	2.9	2.5	5.1
1991	14.7	51.7	1.6	18.7	3.9	3.7	4.6
1992[b]	14.4	50.0	2.5	19.0	4.1	4.0	4.9

[a]Estimated sales do not equal 100% because of rounding.
[b]Projected figures.
Source: Compiled from International Data Corporation data, 1991.

The education and individual/home markets were driven by different channels and somewhat different criteria. In the early 1990s, education accounted for roughly 9% of units and 7% of revenues. While most schools had limited budgets for computers, the primary concern for most educators was the availability of appropriate software. The individual/home market comprised about 31% of units and 23% of revenues; however, the market was a complicated mixture of people who bought computers for business work at home, and those who bought the computer for home uses. Most of these consumers bought PCs through mail order or other high volume, low-priced channels.

PC Manufacturers

In 1991, the four largest PC manufacturers were IBM, Apple, NEC and Compaq, collectively accounting for roughly 37% of the world market. (See **Exhibit 8–4.**) But PCs were a truly global business, with more than 200 players from a dozen countries.[2] While U.S. firms had more than 60% of global revenues, small Taiwanese companies, like Acer, were gaining share in the very low end and Japanese firms were the biggest players in portable computers, the fastest growing PC segment. Toshiba, a huge Japanese conglomerate, dominated laptops (26% share in 1990), followed by NEC (15%). The United States was also the largest market for computers (39%), followed by Europe (36%) and Asia (25%).

In general, the majority of buyers could not easily distinguish between IBM and no-name PC brands in 1992. As a consequence, price competition had become the rule. For instance, on the same day in February of 1992, Apple and Dell Computer both slashed prices by almost 40%. Within a week, other competitors were cutting prices. "386" clones retailed for as little as $999.00 and "486" clones were selling for $1,600.00. Analysts repeatedly talked about a shake-out in the computer industry, yet there were no indications when and if a shake-out

[2]Different geographic areas had different configurations of competitors: in North America, IBM, Apple, Compaq and Dell had approximately 70% market share. In Japan, NEC had a proprietary standard, with almost 50% of the market. NEC had a relatively low share outside of Japan. The European market was dominated by U.S. competitors, with national champions, such as Bull, Siemens, and Olivetti commanding large shares of their domestic markets.

EXHIBIT 8-4

Estimated PC Worldwide Market Share Ranked by Manufacturer Revenue[a]

Rank	Company	1981	1982	1983	1984	1985	1986	1987	1988	1989	1990	1991
1	IBM	6.04%	11.47%	21.34%	29.96%	29.04%	25.28%	25.27%	21.54%	18.65%	17.94%	16.05%
2	Apple	8.82	7.34	7.10	10.10	8.78	7.98	7.99	8.83	9.98	10.22	10.49
3	NEC	3.92	4.30	4.79	4.64	6.33	6.70	7.11	6.04	5.65	5.81	5.79
4	Compaq	0.00	0.00	0.73	1.52	2.25	2.48	3.47	4.93	5.36	4.77	4.44
5	Olivetti	2.27	2.08	1.76	1.28	2.63	3.37	3.14	3.12	2.79	2.92	3.10
6	Toshiba	0.60	1.68	0.94	0.46	0.24	0.74	1.32	1.58	1.68	2.44	2.72
7	Epson	0.00	0.01	0.41	0.62	0.66	0.96	1.26	1.81	2.11	2.39	2.67
8	Tandy	10.57	10.42	7.22	3.92	4.32	3.66	3.14	2.81	3.28	2.38	2.57
9	AT&T	0.63	0.35	0.39	0.98	3.18	3.24	2.95	2.70	2.13	1.92	2.09
10	Zenith	2.03	1.65	1.30	1.24	1.71	2.31	2.78	3.05	2.60	1.70	1.79
11	Philips	0.73	0.59	0.97	0.98	1.33	1.70	1.45	1.25	1.60	1.83	1.75
12	Siemens	0.00	0.00	0.01	0.05	0.26	0.62	1.14	1.45	1.51	1.58	1.62
13	HP	2.66	2.25	2.26	2.66	2.70	2.20	1.44	1.74	1.81	1.67	1.58
14	Acer	0.27	0.63	0.25	0.21	0.28	0.53	0.92	1.28	1.29	1.34	1.30
15	Packard Bell	0.00	0.00	0.00	0.00	0.00	0.01	0.04	0.13	0.72	1.05	1.20
16	Unisys	0.64	2.57	2.27	2.74	2.87	2.27	2.01	1.81	1.58	1.36	1.11
17	Dell	0.00	0.00	0.00	0.02	0.11	0.23	0.46	0.63	0.74	0.99	1.10
18	Other	60.83%	54.66%	48.26%	38.62%	33.30%	35.71%	34.13%	35.29%	36.54%	37.68%	38.18%

Estimated PC Worldwide Market Share by Installed Units[a]

Company	1981	1982	1983	1984	1985	1986	1987	1988	1989	1990	1991
IBM	1.35%	2.73%	4.60%	8.64%	11.09%	12.07%	13.12%	13.68%	13.68%	13.36%	12.81%
Apple	8.85	6.65	6.09	7.80	8.27	8.22	8.23	8.21	7.98	7.63	7.90
NEC	4.28	3.55	3.77	4.53	5.23	5.53	5.63	5.51	5.35	4.97	4.79
Compaq	0.00	0.00	0.27	0.70	1.08	1.37	1.66	2.04	2.38	2.57	2.74
Olivetti	1.78	1.03	0.78	0.68	0.99	1.25	1.50	1.69	1.79	1.72	1.66
Toshiba	0.29	0.86	0.84	0.74	0.68	0.77	0.83	0.98	1.18	1.59	1.98
Epson	0.00	0.01	0.18	0.38	0.50	0.70	0.95	1.36	1.85	2.18	2.40
Tandy	0.00	0.00	0.00	0.00	0.00	0.12	0.33	0.48	0.64	0.80	0.89
AT&T	0.26	0.10	0.09	0.25	0.79	1.08	1.24	1.34	1.33	1.24	1.20
Zenith	0.98	0.66	0.53	0.56	0.80	1.14	1.60	2.02	2.18	2.05	1.96
Philips	0.20	0.19	0.22	0.25	0.38	0.53	0.62	0.76	0.91	1.03	1.08
Siemens	0.00	0.00	0.00	0.02	0.06	0.14	0.27	0.41	0.53	0.61	0.68
HP	1.29	1.00	0.96	1.08	1.19	1.20	1.07	1.04	0.92	0.84	0.84
Acer	0.21	0.20	0.13	0.16	0.25	0.44	0.76	1.12	1.37	1.55	1.68
Packard Bell	0.00	0.00	0.00	0.00	0.00	0.00	0.02	0.07	0.34	0.58	0.80
Unisys	0.18	0.33	0.36	0.46	0.51	0.60	0.71	0.75	0.76	0.70	0.65
Dell	0.00	0.00	0.00	0.01	0.05	0.11	0.23	0.30	0.38	0.47	0.59
Other	80.32%	82.69%	81.18%	73.73%	68.14%	64.73%	61.23%	58.24%	56.43%	56.12%	55.34%

[a]Market share includes all computer sales under $12,000. Commodore and Sharp have been included in the "other" category even though their share exceeds 1%. However, both companies derive a large percentage of their revenues from nontraditional computer products (e.g., palmtop computers, organizers, and computers designed primarily for entertainment), which are not directly comparable to IBM PCs and Macs.

Source: Adapted from InfoCorp data.

would occur. A few large mergers had taken place in the early 1990s, such as Groupe Bull's purchase of Zenith, and AT&T's purchase of NCR. But the worldwide PC business was more fragmented in 1992 than 1985. Despite the variety of competition, Apple's rivalry in the PC industry could be typified by three players: IBM—the worldwide leader; Compaq—the premium-priced leader in the MS-DOS/Intel segment; and Dell, a low-priced clone.

IBM IBM's position in PCs was characteristic of many broad line computer companies in the world, ranging from Digital Equipment to Siemens. Like its competitors in mainframes and minicomputers, IBM had a large installed base of customers that were tied to the company's highly profitable, proprietary technology. However, like most mini and mainframe companies, IBM was also a relatively high cost producer of PCs that was struggling to create a unique position for itself in the 1990s. Despite suffering its first loss in history in 1991, IBM was still the world leader in computers, with $64 billion in revenue and the #1 market share in PCs, minicomputers and mainframes (see **Exhibit 8–5**). IBM's trademark was its sweeping horizontal and vertical integration. One of the largest manufacturers of semiconductors, IBM had the largest direct sales forces in the computer industry, and sold more types of computers, software and peripherals than any company in the world. IBM's R&D budget of $6.6 billion exceeded the *revenues* of all but a few competitors. Nonetheless, IBM's market share had steadily declined in the PC business since 1984. IBM's products lost much of their differentiation, as clones successfully attacked IBM with cheaper (and in a few cases, technically superior) products; and after a dispute with Microsoft, IBM appeared to lose control over the operating system software (discussed below). To regain the initiative, IBM launched a blizzard of alliances in the 1990s, ranging from jointly developing the next generation memory chips with Siemens and flat panel displays with Toshiba, to working with Apple on a next generation operating system and with Motorola on microprocessors.

COMPAQ Compaq got its start by selling the first successful IBM clone portable. In its very first year, Compaq generated $100 million in sales, making it the fastest growing company in history. Compaq's subsequent growth and profitability was based on offering more power or features than comparable IBMs, usually at slightly higher prices. When Compaq launched the first PC with an Intel 80386 microprocessor, it became a trend-setter rather than just another clone. Compaq generally engineered its products from scratch, developing and manufacturing many custom components. However, Compaq did not make semiconductors, like IBM, nor did it develop software or manufacture peripherals, like Apple. Compaq was a pure PC hardware company that sold its products through full service dealers. In 1991, however, Compaq's position weakened considerably. Clones were quickly copying Compaq's PCs and even beating Compaq to market with some new products. The most damage was done by Dell Computer, which ran full page ads in newspapers around the world, suggesting that Dell offered comparable value at 50% off Compaq's list price. Although Compaq rarely sold its computers at list, the campaign had a devastating impact. Compaq was put on the defensive with its customers, causing it to cut prices and streamline costs. Compaq's board fired the CEO and embarked on a new strategy of reducing costs and offering low-priced products through lower cost channels.

DELL COMPUTER Michael Dell, a dropout from the University of Texas, started Dell Computer in Austin in 1984. The company's first product was an IBM PC/XT clone that it sold through computer magazines at one-half IBM's prices. From 1985 to 1990, Dell became the fastest growing computer company in the world. By 1991, it was a half billion dollar company, offering a full line of PCs through direct mail. What made Dell distinctive was its unconditional money back guarantee within 30 days, its toll-free customer service number, and a one year contract with Xerox to provide next day, on-site service within 100 miles of nearly 200 locations. Dell could bypass dealers because utilizing computer technology (i.e., running PCs with software tools that could tell the customer quickly how to fix a PC) could offer customers comparable or better service at much lower prices than a local dealer. Moreover, Dell generally copied Compaq or IBM's basic design while assembling the products with standard components. Yet even Dell was feeling pressure from lower priced clones in 1992. Companies such as ALR, Packard Bell, and Gateway were doing to Dell what Dell had done to Compaq: copying the strategy with an even lower expense structure and lower prices. Packard Bell, for instance, grew larger than Dell in 1990 by selling cheap clones exclusively through mass merchandisers; in the meantime, ALR started offering Dell clones with similar service at lower prices. Since ALR's overhead was only 14% of sales, with R&D of only 1.5%, Dell was forced to look for new ways to differentiate its products. By 1992, Dell was introducing new PCs every three weeks; its oldest product was 11 months old. Dell also planned to offer on-site service within four hours.

Suppliers

There were two categories of suppliers to the personal computer industry in the early 1990s: those supplying products that had multiple sources, like disk drives, CRT screens, keyboards, computer boards, and memory chips; and those supplying products that came from only one or two sources, particularly microprocessors and operating system software. The first category of suppliers were all producing products that had become commodities by 1992. Anyone in the world could buy memory chips or disk drives at highly competitive prices from a large number of companies, often from a wide variety of countries. Microprocessors and operating system software, on the other hand, were dominated by a small number of companies.

Every PC needed a microprocessor, which served as the brains of the computer. While several companies offered microprocessors, two companies dominated the industry: Intel, which was a sole source for the latest generation (386, 486, Pentiums) of chips for the MS-DOS standard; and Motorola, which supplied 100% of Apple's needs.[3] (See **Exhibits 8–5** and **8–6.**) Microprocessors were critical to the personal computer because in 1992, the leading software operating systems (OSs) could only run on specific chips. Most new OSs conceived since the late 1980s were developed for multiple microprocessors. But Apple's OS was originally written in the early 1980s and would only run on the Motorola chip, and Microsoft's MS-DOS would only work on Intel's X86.

Similarly, there were only two major suppliers of OSs for the PC market—Apple and Microsoft (see **Exhibit 8–5**). Since application programs like word processing or spreadsheets would have to be rewritten to run on a different operating system, even the huge PC market could not support multitude OS standards. In the early 1990s, analysts estimated that more than $40 billion in software was installed on the Intel/Microsoft standard and $4.5–$5.0 billion on the Motorola/Apple standard. For computer users to switch standards, they had to buy new hardware and software as well as incur substantial retraining costs. The economics of operating systems also made it difficult for multiple players to survive. While the marginal costs of producing software were negligible, it cost an estimated $500 million to develop a new generation operating system, plus substantial ongoing development cost. Microsoft's dominance in this arena was based on its ability to sell to the huge installed base of Intel's X86 microprocessors, even though MS-DOS (and Windows) were widely acknowledged to be inferior to Apple's System 7. Microsoft typically received about $15 from a manufacturer for every PC sold with MS-DOS, and approximately another $15 if the PC was sold with Windows. Finally, OSs were of little value without application programs written by independent software vendors (ISVs). The market share of an OS was critical in influencing an ISV's decision. A program written for MS-DOS, for instance, had a potential market of more than 80 million PCs; a program written for Apple's OS had roughly one-tenth the potential; and programs written for some of the other OSs, discussed below, had only one-tenth of Apple's possible market.

[3]Apple worked closely with Motorola to design their microprocessor. In addition, since Apple did not allow other vendors to make compatible products, Motorola was essentially a captive supplier to Apple.

EXHIBIT 8-5 Selected Competitor/Supplier Financial Statistics—1982–1992 ($ millions)

	1991	1990	1988	1986	1984	1980
IBM						
Revenues	$64,792	$69,018	$59,681	$51,250	$45,937	$26,213
Cost of goods sold	32,474	30,723	25,648	22,706	18,919	10,149
R&D expense	6,644	6,554	5,925	5,221	4,200	1,520
Selling, general and administrative	24,732	20,709	19,362	15,464	11,587	8,804
Net income	−2,827	6,020	5,491	4,789	6,582	3,563
Total assets	92,473	87,568	73,037	63,020	42,808	26,703
Long-term debt	13,231	11,943	8,518	6,923	3,269	2,099
Stockholders' equity	37,006	42,832	39,509	34,374	26,489	16,453
ROS %[a]	−4.4	8.7	9.2	9.3	14.3	13.6
ROA %[b]	−3.1	6.8	7.5	7.6	15.4	13.3
ROE %[c]	−7.6	14.8	14.9	14.4	26.5	22.7
Stock prices ($/share)						
High	139.8	123.1	130	162	128.5	72.8
Low	92	94.5	104.5	119	99	50.4
P/E ratio	21.2	10.4	11.9	18	10.6	10.4
Market valuation[d]	50,285	64,523	70,210	72,720	75,399	39,115

	1991	1990	1988	1986	1984	
Compaq						
Revenues	$ 3,271	$ 3,598	$ 2,066	$ 625	$ 329	
Cost of goods sold	2,054	2,058	1,233	361	232	
R&D expense	197	185	75	27	11	
Selling, general and administrative	721	706	397	152	66	
Net income	131	455	255	43	13	
Total assets	2,826	2,717	1,589	378	231	
Long-term debt	73	74	275	73	0	
Stockholders' equity	NA	1,859	815	183	109	
ROS %[a]	4	12.6	12.3	6.9	3.9	
ROA %[b]	4.6	16.7	16	11.3	5.6	
ROE %[c]	6.9	30	42	26.8	12.9	
Stock prices ($/share)						
High	74.3	68	33	10.8	7.3	
Low	29.9	35.5	21	5.8	1.8	
P/E ratio	28.2	10.3	8.9	11.7	14.5	
Market valuation[d]	2,244	4,859	4,312	1,026	325	

	1992	1991	1990	1989	1988	1987
Dell Computer[e]						
Revenues	$ 890	$ 546	$ 389	$ 258	$ 159	$ 70
Cost of goods sold	608	364	279	176	109	54
R&D expense	33	22	17	7	6	2
Selling, general and administrative	180	114	80	50	27	10
Net income	51	27	5	14	9	2
Total assets	560	264	172	167	56	24
Long-term debt	42	0	0	0	0	0
Stockholders' equity	274	112	80	75	9	3
ROS[a]	5.7	4.9	1.3	5.4	5.7	28.6
ROA[b]	11.9	10.2	2.9	8.4	16.1	8.3
ROE[c]	18.6	24.1	6.3	18.7	100	66.7
Stock prices ($/share)						
High	NA	36.3	18.8	10.6	12.6	NA
Low	NA	15.8	4.6	5	7.7	NA
P/E ratio	NA	13.2	8.3	26	12.5	NA
Market valuation[f]	900	614	339	108	187	NA

EXHIBIT 8-5 (continued)

	1991	1990	1988	1986	1984	1982
Intel						
Revenues	$4,778	$3,921	$2,875	$1,265	$1,629	$ 900
Cost of goods sold	1,898	1,638	1,295	687	774	467
R&D expense	618	517	318	228	180	131
Selling, general and administrative	765	616	456	311	316	NA
Net income	818	650	453	−173	198	30
Total assets	6,292	5,276	3,550	2,080	2,029	1,056
Long-term debt	363	345	479	287	146	197
Stockholders' equity	4,558	3,592	2,080	1,275	1,360	552
ROS %[a]	17.0	17.0	16.0	−14.0	12.0	3.0
ROA %[b]	13	12.3	12.8	−10.3	9.8	2.8
ROE %[c]	20.4	18.1	21.8	−16.3	14.6	5.4
Stock prices ($/share)						
High	59.3	52	37.3	21.5	29	13.8
Low	37.8	28	19.3	10.9	16.5	6.9
P/E ratio	11	12.3	11.4	NA	21.2	48.7
Market valuation[d]	10,045	7,600	4,344	3,717	4,788	5,032
Microsoft	**1991**	**1990**	**1988**	**1986**	**1984**	**1982**
Revenues	$ 1,843	$ 1,183	$ 591	$ 197	$ 98	$ 25
Cost of goods sold	363	253	148	41	23	NA
R&D expense	235	181	70	21	11	NA
Selling, general and administrative	596	357	185	76	35	NA
Net income	463	279	124	39	16	4
Total assets	1,644	1,105	493	170	48	15
Long-term debt	0	0	0	2	1	0
Stockholders' equity	1,350	1,105	493	171	31	8
ROS %[a]	25.1	23.6	20.9	19.7	16.3	16.0
ROA %[b]	28.2	25.2	25	22.9	33.3	23.3
ROE %[c]	40.8	37.7	40.3	40.5	70	62.1
Stock prices ($/share)						
High	115	53.9	23.5	8.5	NA	NA
Low	49	28	5.2	6.5	NA	NA
P/E ratio	22.6	19.9	25.2	19.5	NA	NA
Market valuation[d]	19,380	12,788	8,533	NA	NA	NA

[a]ROS = net income/total revenues.

[b]ROA = net income/total assets.

[c]ROE = net income/total stockholders' equity.

[d]Number of shares outstanding (*Value Line* 1992) times the year-end stock price (NYSE and OTC daily stock price reports).

[e]Fiscal year ends in February.

[f]Market capitalization as of March 17th.

Sources: *Value Line* and companies' annual reports.

Events in the early 1990s suggested that the configuration of players in both microprocessors and operating systems might be changing. First, several new players entered the microprocessor arena, including imitators of Intel's chips as well as new competitors, such as IBM (with its RS6000 chip), Sun Microsystems, MIPS, and DEC. Most of these chips were designed in special ways, called RISC, which gave them some initial performance advantages over Intel and Motorola's existing products.[4] These RISC chips, however, could not run software directly compatible with Intel or Motorola in 1992. Second, there was an emerging battle over new operating systems. Microsoft's graphical user interface (GUI),

[4]RISC stood for reduced instruction set computing. RISC chips were designed for greater speed than the traditional chips made by Intel and Motorola, known as CISC or complex instruction set computing. Intel was investing aggressively to narrow the gap.

EXHIBIT 8-6 Shipments and Installed Base of Various Microprocessors, 1981–1991 (million units)

	1981	1982	1983	1984	1985	1986	1987	1988	1989	1990	1991
Intel X86 Microprocessors Shipments											
Units shipped	0	0.2	1	2.6	3.7	5.5	10.2	14	16.1	18.3	20.2
Installed base	0	0.2	1.2	3.7	7.4	12.9	23.1	37	53.1	71.4	91.6
Motorola Microprocessors Shipments											
Units shipped	0	0	0	0.5	0.7	0.9	1.2	1.6	1.8	2.9	3.3
Installed base	0	0	0.1	0.5	1.3	2.2	3.4	5	6.4	9.3	12.6
RISC											
Units shipped	0	0	0	0	0	0	0	0	0	0.2	0.4
Installed base	0	0	0	0	0	0	0	0	0.1	0.3	0.7

Source: Adapted from InfoCorp, 1992.

Windows 3.0, worked on top of MS-DOS. Windows sold 10 million copies from its introduction in June of 1990 through March 1992, and was selling one million copies per month. Since Windows mimicked Apple's operating system, the differences between the Apple environment and the Microsoft/Intel world were less obvious.[5] Windows was also attracting the greatest ISV attention in the early 1990s. In the meantime, several companies were trying to compete directly with Microsoft by rewriting their operating systems to work on Intel's X86 chips. These firms included Sun and Steve Job's new company, NeXT. In addition, after IBM broke with Microsoft, it spent $1 billion to offer its own OS in 1992, called OS/2 2.0. While other vendors were not offering OSs compatible with the installed base, IBM hoped to stall Microsoft's momentum with a superior OS that would maintain compatibility with MS-DOS and Windows. Finally, both Microsoft and Apple were developing new OSs. Microsoft promised that its next product, Windows NT, would be available in late 1992. Microsoft claimed that Windows NT would match or exceed competitive products, be backward compatible with MS-DOS and Windows, and run on Intel, MIPS, and DEC microprocessors.[6] Apple's new OS, discussed below, was scheduled for release in 1994.

[5]Apple had sued Microsoft over infringing its copyrights. Analysts did not expect Apple to win the law suit.

[6]Microsoft helped form the "ACE"—advanced computing environment—consortium in 1991 to help generate a coalition around the Windows NT OS. More than 80 computer companies originally committed to the standard; 12 months later, however, several of the leading firms broke ranks, including DEC and Dell.

Alternative Technologies

Like many high-technology businesses, there was a variety of substitutes either available or on the horizon. The most direct substitutes for PCs were technical workstations, powerful stand-alone computers that were used primarily by engi- neers for scientific applications, graphic-intensive applications, like designing airplane wings, and number-intensive applications, like financial transactions on Wall Street. Workstations comprised a highly competitive business, dominated by four companies: Sun, DEC, Hewlett-Packard, and IBM. Each of these companies used their own RISC chip and incompatible OS. Historically, workstations were not only more powerful than PCs, but they were also much more expensive. By the early 1990s, all of the major workstation vendors had proclaimed that they, too, wanted to sell cheap versions of their computers for the mass market. In 1992, prices of low-end workstations dropped to less than $5000, making them competitive with high-end PCs and Macs.

Many analysts thought that much faster growth would come from other alternative technologies, like pen-based computers, palm-top computers, and mobile computing. All of these technologies were in their nascent stages in 1992. Pen-based computers allowed the user to point a stylus on a screen rather than use a keyboard. Both hardware and software innovations were required to make pen-based systems cost-effective. Microsoft had already announced a version of Windows for pen-based machines that was expected to compete with alternative OSs from a variety of start-up companies and Apple.

Hewlett-Packard and Japan's Sharp were the early entrants in the palm-top market. Their products were relatively primitive computers that could do very simple operations, like spreadsheets, word processing, as well as keep calendars and address books. Their advantage was size and price: these computers sold for a few hundred dollars and could be carried in a shirt pocket. Sony also announced that it would offer for under $1000 portable "computer players" in 1992: book size devices with CD audio capability that displayed text and video, and ran Microsoft's MS-DOS software. Finally, several observers expected that all forms of computers would be networked in the 1990s, many with cellular phone connections. While analysts had talked about the merging of computer, telecommunications, and consumer electronics technologies for more than a decade, many industry executives believed that the integration of computers, phones and videos would be a reality by the mid-to-late 1990s. Many consumer electronic products, like televisions, were beginning to use digital technologies, while computers were becoming sufficiently powerful to encode and manipulate video, sound, and data.

Apple's Position in October 1990

Apple held a peculiar position in the computer industry as it entered the 1990s. It was the only existing alternative hardware and software standard for PCs other than the MS-DOS/Intel standard. It was also unique because it was more vertically and horizontally integrated than any other PC company, with the exception of IBM. Historically, Apple designed its products, usually from scratch, specifying unique chips, disk drives, monitors, and even unusual shapes for its chassis. While it never backward integrated into semiconductors, it manufactured and assembled most of its own products in state-of-the-art factories in California, considered among the most automated and modern in the industry. In addition, Apple developed its own operating systems software for the Mac, some of its applications software, and many of its peripherals, such as printers. About half of Apple's revenues came from overseas, and roughly half the U.S. sales were to education, where Apple had more than a 50% market share.

Analysts generally considered Apple's products to be easier to use, easier to network, and more versatile than comparable IBM machines. In many core software technologies like multimedia (integrating video, sound, and data), Apple had a two year lead on vendors such as Microsoft.

Since Apple controlled all aspects of the computer, from board design to software, it could offer a better computer "system," where all the parts—software, hardware, and peripherals—interacted in a coherent way. If someone bought an IBM and a clone, they could never be sure if one computer could be easily connected to another or whether two software programs from different vendors would lead the system to crash. Apple, on the other hand, gave customers a complete desktop solution. Hardware and operating system software were sold as a package, bundled together. This made Apple's customers the most loyal in the industry. As one analyst commented, "the majority of IBM and compatible users 'put up' with their machines, but Apple's customers 'love' their Macs."

Trouble started brewing, however, in the late 1980s. Apple had not aggressively lowered prices during the price war among competitors in the Microsoft/Intel standard. In addition, Apple's image as a performance leader was damaged in 1990 when Motorola, its sole source for microprocessors, was delayed in shipping its newest products. Suddenly Apple's computers looked overpriced and underpowered. And those were not the only problems, according to John Sculley:

We were increasingly viewed as the "BMW" of the computer industry. Our portfolio of Macintoshes were almost exclusively high-end, premium-priced computers that our market research suggested would continue to have limited success in penetrating the corporate marketplace. Without lower prices, we would be stuck selling to our installed base. We were also so insular that we could not manufacture a product to sell for under $3000. We constantly fell into the trap of "creeping elegance" with our NIH—not invented here—mentality. We spent more than two years, for instance, designing a portable computer that had to be "perfect." But in the end, it was a disaster—it was 18 months late and 10 pounds too heavy. Our distribution was also an issue. Five large dealers were selling 80% of our products. Given the evolution of the computer industry, we concluded that drastic action was necessary; there could be no sacred cows. The result was a dramatic shift in Apple's strategy and culture. We still want to change the world, but we have to transform the company and industry for it to work. We cannot permit the commoditization of this industry to continue.

The New Apple

In October of 1990, Apple began a process of repositioning its entire business. This repositioning included new financial and manufacturing policies, a new marketing mix (new products, pricing, and distribution), and new relationships with other companies, including its own subsidiaries, IBM and a variety of Japanese firms.

NEW MARKETING MIX   The key to Apple's ongoing business, noted John Sculley, was that "Apple could no longer be a niche player. We were going to enter the mainstream with products and prices designed to regain market share." With that philosophy, Apple embarked on an ambitious strategy of expanding its product portfolio to include low-cost, low-priced computers for the larger business and individual market. With the introduction of the Mac Classic with a street price of $999 in October of 1990, Apple would be competing head-on with the clones and go for volume (see Exhibit 4). Sales of Macs rose from 9.8% of U.S. computer stores' unit sales in Q2 1990 to 17% market share, one year later.

But Sculley did not believe that volume was enough. In 1990, he also appointed himself the chief technology officer, and made it a priority to get products out faster and extend the hardware and software product lines. "To build on our core differentiation," commented Sculley, "we will bring out a series of 'hit products' through the first half of the 1990s." "Hit products" were defined as new products and derivations of older products that could be produced with very rapid cycle times. Sculley believed that product turns would have to be every 6 to 12 months. By the end of 1991 he noted with pride that 80% of Apple volume was coming from products introduced in October of 1990. In the previous year, only 35% of revenue came from new products. Two more hit products were introduced in late 1991 and early 1992. The first were aggressively priced notebook computers, called Powerbooks. Notebook computers were the fastest growing segment of the computer market since 1989, but it was a segment where Apple had previously failed. When the Powerbook shipped in October 1991, it got rave reviews. Analysts predicted the Powerbook might generate a billion dollars in revenue in its first year. Sculley's second effort was unveiled shortly thereafter. In January 1992, Apple introduced a new software product, called Quicktime, which put Apple at the forefront of multimedia technology. One month later, Apple announced software that would allow Macs to respond to commands from the human voice, without special hardware or training. In both areas, Apple was probably 12–18 months ahead of the competition.

To complement the hit products strategy, Sculley also proclaimed that Apple would restructure its distribution strategy. Apple maintained a direct sales force of approximately 300, one-third covering large corporate accounts, two-thirds focused on education and other markets. Most products, however, were still sold through computer stores. Bob Puette, president of Apple USA, described the problem succinctly, "how do we move to the Dell model, without killing our existing business?" In late 1991, Apple decided that it would sell its products through superstores and started to offer limited direct end-user telephone support.

FINANCE AND MANUFACTURING Apple's historical financial model was based on one simple principle, Sculley's "50-50-50" rule: If Apple could sell 50,000 Macs a month, with a gross margin of 50%, Apple will have a stock price of $50. In 1987, Sculley wrote in his autobiography, "it was critical to have high gross margins to pay for the huge research and development expenses to support a proprietary technology." And until 1990, Apple followed these policies religiously, achieving all of Sculley's objectives.

New, low-end products designed to gain market share as well as 'hit products' with short product life cycles could not operate on the same principle. Joe Graziano, Apple's CFO remarked, "We have no choice. We must bring down our expense structure, raise our productivity, and fundamentally alter the way we do business." If Apple wanted to match the computer hardware industry's average (see **Exhibit 8–7**), it would have to cut costs drastically. Yet Apple was also a software company, which meant that Apple had less flexibility than other PC companies in cutting certain expenditures, especially R&D. Sculley nonetheless decided to trim Apple's entire cost structure before a crisis emerged. In May of 1991, Apple reduced its work force by 10% or 1,560 people. But as Kevin Sullivan, S.V.P. Human Resources, explained, the cuts went much deeper:

> This was not a drive to lower expense rates in response to temporary market conditions, but rather to get cost out of the system permanently. We had to change the way we did our work . . . we attacked how we spent our money rather than reducing our expenses. Actions ranged from consolidating buildings, cutting away cafeteria subsidies, charging for the use of the Fitness Center, subcontracting the management of the Child Care Center, etc. . . . In addition, we cut some projects and activities that some people felt were important to us, especially in sales and marketing. We let people go who were very talented and doing great work, but we chose not to do that work any more. We also stated that we were going to be moving jobs out of California. . . . The Campus was no longer the Center of the Universe. . . . Finally, we changed many of our relationships with the channel, large accounts and developers. We got much tougher on selecting who they were and what kind of service or response they would get from us. We were building a new Apple that had to be leaner and swifter. Finally, we had to do layoffs, and layoffs are layoffs, any way you cut it.

Part of Apple's greatest challenge was in manufacturing, which historically was a center-

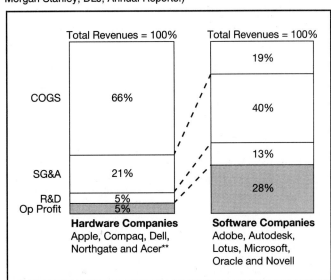

EXHIBIT 8-7 Average Operating Ratios in 1990* (Sources: Morgan Stanley; DLJ; Annual Reports.)

*Unweighted average of 5 hardware and 6 software companies.

**Acer was a Taiwanese clone manufacturer and Northgate was a mail-order clone manufacturer based in Minnesota.

piece of Apple's sole source strategy. In the past, virtually *everything* was done in-house. But now manufacturing had new instructions: anything that could be bought on the outside should be subcontracted rather than developed. NIH was no longer acceptable. At the same time, manufacturing facilities were expanded to build a greater variety of products that could be ramped faster to global volumes.

RELATIONSHIPS WITH OTHER COMPANIES To get a better understanding of the competitive environment, Sculley and his COO, Michael Spindler, spent nine months in 1990 visiting with the senior executives of major computer companies, including Sun, Hewlett-Packard, IBM, DEC, as well as the large Japanese and European companies. Sculley said, "We discovered that we were out of touch. We did not really understand open systems, how to penetrate big corporations, and we did not realize that firms like IBM had big leads in semiconductor technology." Sculley's conclusion was that Apple should build a "federation" of alliances with partners that could help leverage Apple's strengths in software, especially user-friendliness, multi-media, and networking. He said, "We have to have partners; we have to become more open; we have to penetrate a broader market or our application developers will abandon us; we have to license technologies in and be willing to license technologies out." A key to the federation concept was that the core Macintosh business would be largely separate from the new ventures and product groups. Spindler would run the Mac business, while Sculley could operate the alliances and federation like Silicon Valley start-ups. (See **Exhibit 8–8**.) However, Apple shocked the world when it chose its first significant alliance partner—its long-time nemesis, IBM.

THE APPLE-IBM JOINT VENTURES During the summer of 1991, IBM and Apple formed two joint ventures—Taligent and Kaleida. Sculley listed four major objectives in working with IBM:

> First, we had to overcome the resistance of MIS managers in large corporations to buying Apple computers. We called this our Enterprise Systems effort. The alliance attacked this problem in three ways: 1) we got IBM's stamp of approval; 2) IBM's sales force would offer Mac communication products; and 3) we both committed to achieve "interop-

erability" (seamless connections between the varying IBM and Apple computers). Second, our current microprocessor technology from Motorola would not carry us through the 1990s. We saw IBM's RS6000 RISC microprocessor as the best technology in the industry. Since IBM also agreed to work with Motorola as a second source for the technology, we reduced our vulnerability from being dependent on a sole source. We would call this new generation of computers the "PowerPC." Third, we formed Taligent to develop our next generation OS, which we internally called Pink. Pink will be a major breakthrough in software technology.[7] However, to pay for Pink, we needed money and a broader market. IBM and Apple together would have the resources and large installed base. In addition, Pink would be written to run on Apple's installed base of Motorola chips, the new IBM chip, as well as the Intel X86 chips. Lastly, we formed Kaleida to create standards in multimedia technologies, like putting full motion video on the personal computer.[8]

The underlying concept of the IBM-Apple relationship was that both companies could share the costs and risks of developing new technologies, but ultimately, the parents would compete in the market place for computers. The JVs would operate independently, shipping their software products to both parents at agreed upon transfer prices. IBM would provide the semiconductor technology while Apple would provide most of the software technology and personnel. Six months after the JV was formed, the parents appointed a CEO from IBM and COO from Apple.

CLARIS To help create a supply of applications for the Mac in the mid-1980s, Apple created a software subsidiary called Claris. Claris was responsible for many of the important programs for the Mac, like MacDraw and MacWrite. However, in an effort to reduce potential conflicts of interest with Apple's ISVs, Sculley decided to spin-off a portion of Claris to the public. Although Apple

[7]This new technology, known as "object-based systems," was so complicated that it would take several hundred million dollars and at least three years to complete the project. Pink promised to increase significantly a computer user's productivity by making the writing of customized software applications very easy. If on schedule, Pink would probably give IBM and Apple at least a two-year lead on Microsoft. In a parallel, independent effort, Apple was developing the follow-on OS to System 7. This follow-on OS could be designed to run on multiple microprocessors, such as the RS6000.

[8]A fifth objective was highly technical—creating a joint Apple-IBM version of UNIX, which was another OS that both companies wanted to use for certain large corporate applications.

ultimately decided to keep 100% of Claris in 1990, it kept Claris operationally independent (see **Exhibit 8–8**). By 1992, Claris was the second leading supplier of applications to the Mac with 15% of the market (compared to Microsoft's 30% share of Mac applications) and was in the top 15 application software companies in the world. Analysts estimated that Claris had broken even on roughly $100 million in sales in 1991. As part of Sculley's strategy to be a more open computer company, Claris would not have to dedicate itself in the future to Mac applications. It could write applications for DOS, Windows, OS/2, as well as the Mac. Although Claris was behind other companies, like WordPerfect, Lotus, and Microsoft, its goal was to be in the top 5 software companies by the mid-1990s.

ALLIANCES WITH JAPANESE FIRMS Beyond reinvigorating its core business with the IBM alliance and expanding its application software sales, Sculley believed that Apple had to break out of the mold set by other computer companies and look for major innovations that would change the way people used computers. In the near future, Sculley argued, computers would be pervasively networked. His vision of the year 2001 saw computers, telecommunications, consumer electronics, publishing, and a variety of other technologies merging together (see **Exhibit 8–9**). Apple, he believed, had unique software technology that could exploit these linkages. Rather than everyone using general purpose PCs in the future, computing would be increasingly specialized.

Sculley announced to the world at the Consumer Electronics Show in January of 1992 Apple's intention of creating a new era of "personal electronics" with "personal digital assistants (PDAs)." In describing the product concept, Sculley recalled the words of Dr. Edwin Land of Polaroid, who said, "we really don't invent new products, but the best ones are there already, only invisible, just waiting to be discovered." In this vein, Apple would introduce an executive organizer that would fit in the palm of your hand and keep track of telephone numbers, calendars,

EXHIBIT 8-8 Apple's Federation Concept (Source: Casewriter's Representation.)

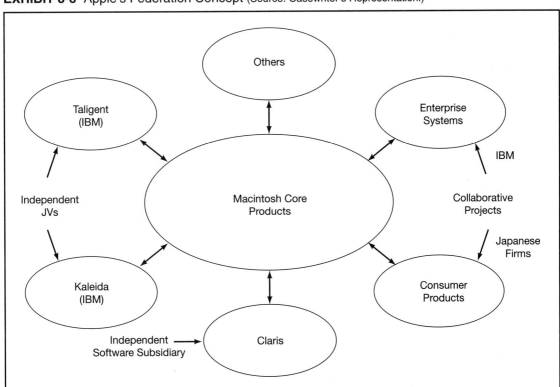

EXHIBIT 8-9 Info Industry, 2001: Fusion Powered

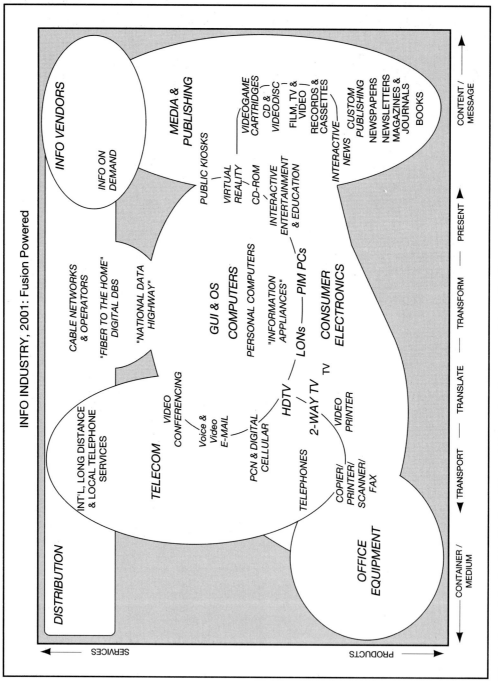

INFO INDUSTRY, 2001: Fusion Powered

Source: Presentation by John Sculley at Harvard University—Program on Information Resources Policy, 1991.

etc. It would have built-in wireless communications, and have the capability of displaying best selling book titles. Other products would include portable MultiMedia Players that used computer and CD technology, and a portable pen-based computing product. Sculley even suggested at the public gathering that Apple would license its GUI and operating systems for other companies' consumer electronic products, possibly including digital television.

These types of computing and consumer electronics products, however, required expertise that exceeded Apple's core skills and competencies. While Apple could pioneer the computing hardware and software technologies, it lacked distribution and marketing expertise for consumer electronics, LCD display technology needed for hand-held computers, and very low-cost manufacturing for miniaturized products. For these new technologies to be successful, analysts speculated that they would have to be priced under $500. Given the ambitious nature of these projects, Sculley also believed that no one company could pursue all of these avenues by itself. Sony had already manufactured one of Apple's new portable computers, and a number of other Japanese companies might be candidate partners to work with Apple in this new realm.

Going Forward in 1992

Sculley told his sales force in late 1991, "the industry must once again become innovation driven, move away from commodity status, and provide value-added products and services. I believe Apple has a chance to make the difference. In fact, Apple may be one of the few great hopes for turning things around." The question Sculley posed in March 1992 was: can our actions to date achieve the objective of changing the industry structure? Would other steps be necessary? Was it even required that Apple change the industry structure to be successful in the future? And were there other alternatives that Apple might consider?

9. Mips Computer Systems (A)

Our mission is to make the MIPS architecture pervasive worldwide.

MIPS ANNUAL REPORT, 1990

On April 9, 1991, twenty computer hardware and software firms announced the formation of an industry alliance centering around a new, and as yet untried, microprocessor from Mips Computer Systems. Due out at the end of 1991, the R4000 microprocessor from Mips was chosen as part of an attempt by some of the industry's leading firms to establish hardware and software standards in the divided market for personal computers (PCs) and workstations. Uniting such firms as Compaq Computer, Microsoft, and Digital Equipment Corporation behind the Mips chip, the Advanced Computing Environment (ACE) consortium had the potential to affect significantly the position of industry-leaders Sun Microsystems, Motorola, Intel, Hewlett-Packard and IBM. For Mips, the newest player in the industry, it meant a major endorsement of its technology.

Headquartered in Sunnyvale, California, Mips designed and developed high-performance Reduced Instruction Set Computing (RISC) chips and systems. In 1985, Mips was the first company to bring a viable RISC design to the marketplace; by the late 1980s, the struggle for dominance in the RISC-based segment of the marketplace involved all the major computer companies and semiconductor firms worldwide. A lot was at stake; it was estimated that RISC chips had the potential to capture as much as 95% of the global workstation market by 1993, and also significantly affect the much larger markets for PCs and minicomputers.

In 1990, Mips had sales of just over $152 million and 775 employees worldwide; it was among the smallest players in the industry. Its size, however, belied a larger market effect. Since 1987, the company had promoted its technology worldwide through a network of alliances with semiconductor manufacturers and large systems developers. In addition, it provided technology licenses to dozens of original equipment manufacturers (OEMs) and value-added resellers (VARs). Mips chairman and CEO Robert Miller, who came to Mips from minicomputer maker Data General in 1987 and then led the start-up company out of the red, set his sights high:

There have only been three successful standard architectures[1] in the computer industry: the IBM

Krista McQuade and Professor Benjamin Gomes-Casseres prepared this case as the basis for class discussion rather than to illustrate either effective or ineffective handling of an administrative situation.

360 in mainframes, the DEC VAX in minicomputers, and the Intel X86 in personal computers. Each company has made a ton of money. At Data General I used to argue that it was too late to stop VAX from being the standard. Instead, we had to be on the forefront of the next wave. That is what we are doing at Mips and why we need to make the Mips architecture pervasive worldwide.

RISC Technology

RISC technology was essentially a streamlined approach to microprocessor design. Traditional microprocessor design, called Complex Instruction Set Computing (CISC), was based on the theory that the more complex the instruction set embedded in the chip's design, the more efficiently the computer operated. RISC challenged this premise, claiming that, in practice, only 20% of conventional instructions were called upon to perform 80% of a computer's functions. RISC designers set out to increase processing speeds by reducing and simplifying the instruction set. In RISC, many of the more complex commands and functions included in conventional designs were transferred to the compiler[2] and the application software.

Besides seeing advantages in terms of performance, RISC designers thought that there were cost and time-to-market advantages to their approach. With simpler instruction sets, RISC chips were implemented using less circuitry. This typically resulted in a shorter design and initial testing phase, as well as in lower manufacturing costs. Just as in CISC, however, the viable manufacture of RISC chips required a high level of capital investment and volume production. Throughout the 1980s, a debate had raged about the technology's commercial potential.

Although RISC technology was invented at IBM in 1975, ten years later not one major chip manufacturer or computer firm had introduced a RISC-based product. Ridge Computer Systems and Pyramid Computer had both introduced early RISC designs,[3] but had been unsuccessful in converting many customers to their technologies. Major U.S. chip manufacturers Intel and Motorola were slow in developing chips with the new technology, due to the firms' reluctance to cannibalize their existing CISC-based product lines. Hewlett-Packard (HP), DEC, and IBM had all established RISC R&D programs; however a lack of confidence in the market's acceptance of RISC kept these projects on "wait and see" status. The major drawback to RISC was that software developed for traditional CISC systems was incompatible with RISC systems. IBM was said to have dropped its early RISC program in the late 1970s because it estimated that writing programs to attract customers to RISC would require 1,000 employee-years.[4] This lack of application software, many believed, would keep RISC a theoretical concept, or at best a niche technology.

Mips was instrumental in changing the industry's opinion of RISC technology. In 1985, Mips brought a RISC chip to the marketplace that represented a ten-fold increase in processing power at a fraction of the price of a CISC chip. This demonstration of RISC's commercial feasibility caused other firms to launch full-blown RISC development programs, and by 1991 seven different RISC architectures competed in the marketplace. The major designers of RISC microprocessors in 1991 were Sun Microsystems, Mips, Hewlett-Packard, and IBM.

[1]Computer "architectures" generally referred to the technical design of components, such as the microprocessors, as well as to the way in which components were linked to make the whole system. "Standard" architectures were those with substantial, or dominant, shares of the relevant market.

[2]Compilers translated language commands into machine-readable instructions. In RISC designs, the speed and efficiency of program execution was substantially determined by the quality of the compiler.

[3]These early RISC products were not considered "pure" RISC. That is, although their design incorporated some RISC principles, some complex instructions were left in the design to avoid the complicated problems of redesigning system and compiler software.

[4]IBM reentered the RISC field in 1986, as discussed below.

RISC in the Marketplace

One of the advantages of RISC processors was that their architecture was "scalable," meaning that it could be used in large and small computer systems. Unlike the IBM 360 architecture, for example, RISC architectures could be used in PCs, workstations, minicomputers, mainframes, and even in supercomputers. RISC processors first became widely used in workstations, and in the early 1990s were still largely confined to this segment and certain minicomputer segments. One reason for the early application of RISC in workstations were the price-performance advantages of RISC. Other reasons were the rapid growth of the workstation segment, and the existence of well-established standards in PCs, minicomputers, and mainframes.

RISC's future success in penetrating any of these markets depended on the establishment of an operating system standard.[5] Nearly every RISC architecture on the marketplace in 1991 used Unix, an operating system originally developed by AT&T that was prevalent mainly in the workstation segment of the industry. In 1990, nearly half of all workstations used Unix; by 1994, this percentage was expected to rise to 80%. In the market for personal computers, however, Unix was not popular. In part, this was because there were many versions of Unix; hundreds of versions had been developed since the 1970s, when AT&T began to license this operating system. Furthermore, most Unix systems were difficult to use.

In an attempt to clear up the confusion, Sun Microsystems collaborated with AT&T in May 1988 to combine two versions of Unix that were popular in the workstation industry. Fearing that Sun would gain an advantage in the marketplace through early access to new AT&T versions, a group of competitors aligned themselves to form the Open Software Foundation (OSF). OSF established its own version of Unix, which it called OSF/1, to compete against the AT&T/Sun version. By 1991, OSF numbered over 200 members, including DEC, IBM, HP, Groupe Bull, Nixdorf, and Siemens. In December 1988, AT&T and Sun formed their own broad industry alliance—Unix International—in response to the OSF. Key members included Intel, Motorola, Unisys, NCR, Fujitsu, and Control Data.

WORKSTATIONS In 1991, the greatest penetration of RISC-based computer systems was in the workstation segment of the marketplace. Originally purchased for computationally-intensive scientific and engineering applications, workstations were gaining popularity during the late 1980s in commercial markets such as electronic publishing and business graphics. In 1989, revenues from sales for commercial applications represented just over 7% of total workstation revenues, and industry analysts expected this to rise to one-third by 1994. Potentially, commercial applications represented a much larger market for workstations than technical applications. In 1991, the workstation market was dominated by three vendors—Sun Microsystems, HP/Apollo,[6] IBM, and DEC. Thirteen other firms manufactured workstations, including niche players such as Silicon Graphics (3D graphics) and Intergraph (military applications). Still, the whole workstation market was smaller than the PC market (**Exhibit 9–1**).

Workstations were the fastest growing segment of the computer industry; between 1990 and 1994, workstation revenues were expected to grow at a compound annual rate of 53%. In 1990, sales of U.S.-based vendors hit $8.5 billion, up from $6.8 billion in 1989, and $4.5 billion in 1988. But experts disagreed about the potential for growth of RISC workstations; in 1990, their forecasts for 1993 of the proportion of RISC in total workstations sold ranged from 95% to less than 50%.

---

[5]An operating system was the software code that controlled the computer and provided interface between application software, the user, and the microprocessor. DOS and Unix were both operating systems common in desktop computers. Traditionally, computer companies had attempted to protect their markets by developing proprietary operating systems and software to match. IBM's 370 operating system had long dominated the market for mainframes, for example, while DEC's VMS held the majority of the minicomputer market. "Open" systems, in contrast, allowed hardware and software made by different companies to be used, and promised greater competition between vendors.

[6]In 1989, HP acquired Apollo, one of the pioneers in the workstation segment.

EXHIBIT 9-1 Worldwide Market Shares of Leading PC and Workstation Vendors in 1990

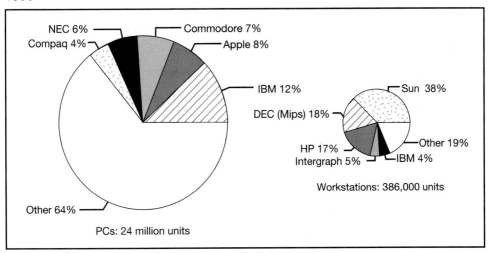

Source: Compiled from Dataquest information appearing in *Electronics*, November 1991, p. 59.

One reason for this wide variance was uncertainty about how established CISC customers and producers would react over the long term. Despite 50%–75% annual gains in performance expected from RISC architectures, compared to 30% annual gains for CISC, not all end users would find switching feasible or desirable. Some large CISC customers, such as banks, department stores, and airlines, had invested billions of dollars in software over the years. For smaller customers, the selection of third-party software available was much greater for CISC than for RISC, making a strong case for staying with the former. In addition, faced with the RISC threat, CISC developers were increasing the performance of their chips, and lowering prices. Paired with CISC's overwhelming advantage in software applications, improved price/performance from CISC put it in a position to compete with RISC. Intel's 80586 chip, due out in 1992, would combine RISC principles for improved performance with the original Intel design, and so would be compatible with existing software designed for the X86 family.

Several trends were expected to increase the demand for RISC and Unix. First, increasingly complex applications such as 3D graphics and large database management required increased amounts of processing power, and RISC offered significant performance boosts without large increases in price. Second, a market had de-

veloped for network computing, providing connectivity between incompatible computer systems so that a variety of users—workstations, personal computers, and terminals for example—could access specific services at the same time. These network computing environments also required increased processing power. Third, customers' demand to protect their investment in software and gain independence from proprietary operating systems led to an increasing acceptance of Unix as an industry standard. Unix was well-suited to RISC implementations, and Unix and RISC together could operate across the entire spectrum of computing, from desktop workstations to mainframes.

INTERNATIONAL MARKETS Although all of the major workstation manufacturers were based in the United States, firms in both Europe and the Far East were entering the workstation business. U.S. firms, for their part, were also continuing to expand their international operations. In 1990, non-U.S. markets surpassed the U.S. market for the first time. Technical workstations, however, were still most popular in the United States. In Europe, commercial workstation applications were widespread, perhaps due to the popularity of Unix in that market. Many European producers embraced Unix in an effort to increase their independence from the operating systems controlled by IBM, DEC, and other U.S. leaders.

Unix represented one-third of the total European computer market in 1989, and was expected to grow 40% per year into the 1990s.

RISC technology was also dominated by U.S. firms in 1991—not one European or Pacific Rim firm had introduced a RISC design, other than of the U.S. vendors. Instead, these firms were licensing RISC technology from U.S. firms in large numbers. Mips had been the most successful in attracting companies to its RISC technology in Europe, with the giant German firm Siemens-Nixdorf Informationsystems and French Groupe Bull as its flagship licensees. In Asia, Mips, Sun, and HP competed for distribution channels. Toshiba, Fujitsu, and Daewoo had lined up behind Sun; NEC and Sony, behind Mips; and Samsung and Hitachi, behind HP. While the U.S. firms welcomed foreign licensees, critics decried how easy it was for foreign firms to gain access to advanced microprocessor technology developed in the United States.

Company Background

Mips began as a Stanford University research project led by three professors, who went on to found the company in 1984. They obtained $22 million in financing from a Silicon Valley venture capital firm and concentrated on research and product development during the first two years. Mips developed the first commercially available RISC microprocessor (the R2000), RISC compiler software, and a RISC-based computer system; volume shipment of its chips and systems began in the last quarter of 1986. At this time, the production of chips and boards was contracted out, while Mips's manufacturing department assembled complete computer systems. A small sales force sold Mips products directly to the end user.

But by early 1987, despite several design wins,[7] Mips had accumulated a deficit of $16 million, and less than $1 million of the original venture capital was left. The company was in precarious financial shape (**Exhibits 9-2** and **9-3**). Although its leadership in RISC technology was widely acknowledged, customers were hesitant to invest in a new technology when they could not be sure that the young company would survive. Also, Mips had no clear strategic vision. Robert Miller recalled: "When I was senior VP at Data General, Mips tried to convince us to adopt their microprocessor. We didn't do so, in part because Mips did not pass the strategy test. They had no clear idea of where they wanted the company to go and how to get there."

[7]The selection of a particular technology for a new product line was termed a "design win" for that technology. In the computer industry, this was a widely used measure of the success of a new technology.

Mips's Strategic Turnaround

Miller was trained in electrical engineering and worked 15 years at IBM before joining Data General in 1981. He was highly regarded in the industry as a savvy and experienced manager. In time, he hired equally seasoned executives for his team (see **Exhibit 9-4**). Observers were soon calling Mips the million-dollar company with a billion-dollar management.

Miller's first concern at Mips was to return the company to secure financial footing. First, he led a crash effort to reduce cash outflows. In the three months before his arrival, the company had spent $3 million; in the two-and-a-half months after that, it spent only about $150,000. He then raised $14 million from the venture capital community, half of it from existing Mips investors.

Next, the question of the company's strategic direction was addressed in a four-day, off-site meeting of top executives. What emerged was a plan to change Mips's basic business approach. Miller explained: "Mips had wanted to build semiconductors. It thought it could compete with the likes of Intel and Motorola, but it could not. It was paying foundries on a wafer-by-wafer basis to produce its chips, but with its small volume, it was getting second-hand treatment." Instead, Miller proposed to license Mips's technology to leading semiconductor firms who could manufacture Mips chips using leading process technology, and help market the product. By the end of 1987, he had succeeded in signing on three small California firms—LSI Logic, Integrated Device Technology, and Performance Semiconductor.

EXHIBIT 9-2 Mips Income Statement, 1985–1991 (in thousands $)

	1985	1986	1987	1988	1989	1990	1991 (Q1 & Q2)	1991 (Q3)
Revenues	0	7,882	13,902	39,383	101,862	152,347	88,502	32,727
of which:								
Product	—	7,882	13,902	32,032	70,032	105,703	60,681	29,514
Technology	—	—	—	7,383	31,830	46,044	27,821	3,213
of which:								
USA	—	7,882	13,485	35,144	79,994	124,407		
Europe	—	—	417	4,239	13,789	22,288		
Pacific Rim	—	—	—	—	8,082	5,652		
Costs and Expenses								
Cost of revenue	—	3,986	7,554	16,069	41,877	67,331	43,678	20,213
R&D	3,593	7,334	8,801	12,910	18,982	27,828	17,285	8,749
SG&A	2,684	5,848	8,223	15,123	33,349	53,166	29,329	13,871
Restructuring costs	—	—	—	—	—	—	—	25,500
Total costs and expenses	6,277	17,078	24,578	44,102	94,208	148,325	90,292	68,333
Operating income	−6,277	−9,196	−10,676	−4,719	7,654	4,022	−1,790	−35,606
Interest income	290	171	176	1,977	2,091	6,219	1,840	597
Income before taxes	−5,987	−9,025	−10,500	−2,742	9,745	10,241	50	−35,009
Provision for income taxes	—	—	—	240	2,749	3,127	23	2,287
Net income from continuing operations	−5,987	−9,025	−10,500	−2,982	6,996	7,114	27	−37,296
Discontinued operations	—	—	—	−736	−4,065	—	—	—
Net income	−5,987	−9,025	−10,500	−3,718	2,931	7,114	27	−37,296
Per share information ($)								
Income from continuing operations	−1.06	−1.03	−.92	−.19	.36	.28	.00	−1.55
Net income	−1.06	−1.03	−.92	−.24	.15	.28		
Memo Items on Technology Revenues (end of year; in millions $)								
Technology revenues reported above			—	7.4	31.8	46.6	27.8	3.2
Accumulated deferred income[a]			4.8	14.4	17.0	8.5	11.7	~12.8
Identifiable sources of technology revenues:[b]								
Kubota								
up-front fee			2.4					
received			2.4			c		
DEC								
up-front fee				15.0				
received				11.7	3.3			
NEC and Siemens together								
up-front fee					21.5			
received					17.0	4.5		
Nonmonetary transactions[d]						6.5		

[a]Technology fees received, but not yet reported. See balance sheet note (a).

[b]Identified in Mips annual and press reports. Financial details of licenses to Bull, Sony, and others have not been identified. Up-front license fees from LSI, IDT, and Performance Semiconductor (1987) were reported to be insignificant.

[c]Mips reported that a new license and manufacturing agreement with Kubota in the third quarter had a significant impact on technology revenues.

[d]Three separate agreements where technology and services were acquired by Mips in exchange for architecture licenses, which Mips ordinarily sells. These transactions were reported as technology revenue and as purchased assets.

Source: Mips annual reports, IPO Prospectus, and 1991 unaudited quarterly reports.

EXHIBIT 9-3 Mips Balance Sheets, 1985–1991 (end of year; in thousands $)

	1985	1986	1987	1988	1989	1990	1991 (Q1 & Q2)	1991 (Q3)
Balance Sheet								
ASSETS								
Current Assets								
Cash and cash equivalents			} 30,584	} 38,292	} 91,732	42,005	31,449	} 52,394
Short-term investments						18,303	26,103	
Accounts receivable			4,379	10,753	26,820	40,108	47,965	41,276
Inventories			1,704	10,028	17,888	33,050	27,098	25,396
Prepaid expenses and other			676	2,220	1,773	4,458	4,620	5,908
Total current assets			37,343	61,293	138,213	137,924	137,235	124,974
Property and equipment, net			5,406	8,700	17,954	34,134	32,495	29,478
Other assets			2,313	4,907	9,777	21,131	26,517	5,730
Total Assets	**6,390**	**16,659**	**45,062**	**74,900**	**165,944**	**193,189**	**196,247**	**170,182**
LIABILITIES								
Current Liabilities								
Accounts and notes payable			3,076	9,776	12,048	16,548	12,654	14,030
Accrued compensation			461	1,550	3,122	6,051	7,131	} 22,502
Other liabilities			2,599	1,712	4,979	8,901	7,238	
Total current liabilities			6,136	13,038	20,149	31,500	27,023	36,532
Deferred revenue[a]			4,834	14,430	16,990	8,540	11,701	} 12,772
Long-term convertible debt	672	2,101	378	—	1,500	1,521	1,567	
Other			—	2,630	2,630	—	—	—
Total Liabilities	**1,997**	**9,098**	**11,348**	**30,098**	**38,639**	**41,561**	**40,291**	**49,304**
SHAREHOLDERS' EQUITY								
Total Equity	**4,393**	**7,561**	**33,714**	**44,802**	**127,305**	**151,628**	**155,956**	**120,878**

[a]Deferred revenue is up-front technology licensing fees that have been received, but that have not yet been recognized as income.

Source: Mips annual reports, IPO Prospectus, and 1991 unaudited quarterly reports.

Mips executives also agreed to build up a systems business to complement technology revenues. Remaining simply a design house for RISC technology, they thought, would not provide the marketing clout needed to convince software developers to write applications. The company thus began forming alliances with computer companies that had strong marketing and service capabilities. The companies acted as resellers for Mips systems products, either licensing its technology for use in their own systems, or purchasing computer systems products from Mips.

In September 1988, Mips entered into a key alliance with DEC. The minicomputer maker paid $15 million for access to all current and future Mips architectures, designs, and related systems software. It also invested an additional $10 million for a 5% equity stake in Mips, with the option to purchase another 15%, and the right to elect one of Mips's six board members. In addition to strengthening the company's financial footing, the DEC alliance provided credibility in the industry for Mips technology, and helped Mips sign agreements with other major firms, such as NEC and Siemens (see below). It also provided access to DEC's strong engineering customer base. In the fall of 1988, DEC announced plans to design its new generation of workstations around the Mips RISC chip. It was the first time that DEC had gone to outside technology for its products. DEC did so because its own proprietary RISC project—code named Prism—was running behind schedule. This internal project was canceled when DEC decided to use the Mips chip.

Early on, Mips recognized the importance of a strong international presence. "Companies like

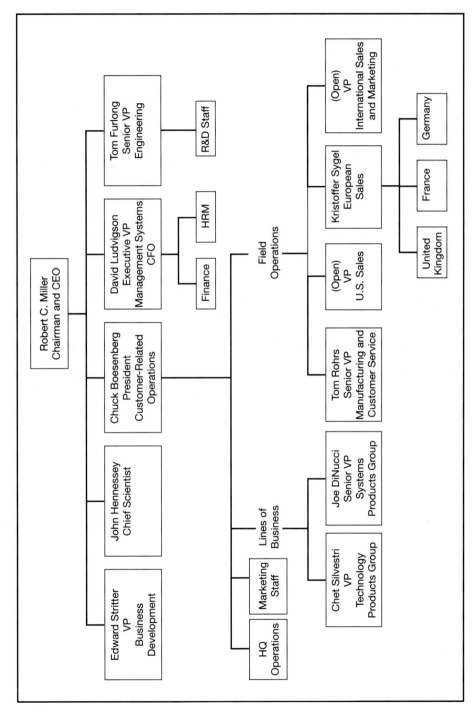

EXHIBIT 9-4 Mips Organizational Chart, December 1991 Source: Mips.

to buy locally," explained Miller. "The computer industry is a global business supported by domestic suppliers." In addition, the best technology, process manufacturing, and marketing capabilities for semiconductors were often located abroad. In order to succeed at attracting regional system vendors and OEMs, Mips's strategists thought, an indigenous supply of chips was critical. In addition, the company benefited from reseller alliances with international firms. Still, Mips's early offers of partnerships were turned down, as the foreign firms found a relationship with Mips too risky. After Mips signed DEC in 1988, however, there was more interest than Miller could accommodate.

On the strength of the company's new strategy, its growing network of alliances, and its improving financial situation, Miller took Mips public in December 1989. The public was offered 24% of the company's stock at a price of $17.50 per share. The offer was oversubscribed and Mips's share price rose rapidly after that to a peak of $24 in April 1990.

Mips Business Model in 1991

By 1991, Mips had established itself as a one-stop shop for RISC technology, designing RISC microprocessors, compiler and operating system software, board products, and RISC systems (see **Figure A**). All of Mips's products were based on a single, compatible RISC architecture. Chip and software designs were licensed for production to six semiconductor partners, who in turn marketed these products. Mips licensed its system products (including software, board products, and systems architecture) to system developers, OEMs, resellers, and integrators and also sold them directly. Chester Silvestri, Mips vice president for technology products, summed up this business model:

> The foundation of our strategy is that one customer can buy at any level of integration. We attract them at either part of the food chain. Sometimes they begin with a chip and move up, or they begin with a box and move down to the boards. Once we begin a relationship, we build a business strategy around selling to them at all levels.

By 1991, Mips had introduced three generations of 32-bit RISC microprocessors—the R2000 (1985), R3000 (1988), and R6000 (1990)—and one 64-bit one, the R4000 (1991). With each introduction, Mips set performance records in the industry. In addition, Mips had brought seven systems products to the marketplace by 1991. Manufacturing of these products was limited, consisting mainly of box assembly and testing. The manufacture of boards was contracted out.

FIGURE A Mips's Business Approach

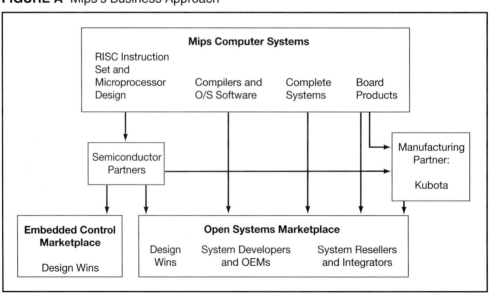

Only approximately $1 million had been invested in manufacturing since the company's inception. Seventy-five percent of manufacturing costs were for material costs and components. The manufacturing division employed only 100 people.

Mips did not develop application software; its customers either developed their own, adapted popular software, or purchased from third parties. In 1988, Mips had invested in a separate software business, Synthesis Software Solutions, in order to acquire, port, and distribute third-party software for Mips systems. It sought out software of interest to two or more of its customers and tried to arrange joint ventures to split the cost of porting it to Mips systems. But the plan did not work well, and Synthesis was dissolved in 1989. Mips then began to sign independent software developers to pursue specific applications, such as database management and desktop publishing. By the end of 1990, RISCware—the name Mips gave to software available to its systems—numbered nearly 1,000, compared to 2,000 software packages available for Sun's RISC design.

Mips sold its last microprocessor in the first quarter of 1988. From then on its revenues were divided between the sales of systems products and income from technology licenses. There were significant differences between these two businesses. Technology revenues were a mix of initial licensing fees and continuing royalties; while initial fees had outweighed royalties in 1989 and 1990, the company expected that from 1991 on, royalties would make up the larger percentage share. Systems sales had average gross margins of 45%, while gross margins from technology licensing were closer to 85%. Mips predicted that 10% of its systems sales would eventually come from software sales and customer service. Twenty percent of R&D expenditures were dedicated to semiconductor design, 20% to operating system software and basic chip software, 30% to system software, and 30% to system hardware. Mips's long-term business model aimed for revenues split 80%-20% between systems and technology licensing, giving the company overall gross margins of 50%–55%.

In 1990, 72% of Mips product sales were for commercial applications. The company believed that it was better positioned than its competitors to take advantage of the expected swelling of demand in commercial segments; only 9% of Sun's sales, for example, came from this segment.

Mips's Alliance Strategy

"Making Mips architecture pervasive," explained Miller, "means seeing that it is implemented across companies, across applications, and across geography." Since 1987, the formation of partnerships and alliances worldwide had been the key element in Mips's strategy to achieve market pervasiveness (see Exhibits 5 and 6). Mips president Chuck Boesenberg, whom Miller hired from Apple, explained that there were important differences in Mips's relationship with its semiconductor partners and the system resellers:

> I think we're getting a bit too schmaltzy in American business in using words like partners and alliances. What we do with our semiconductor partners is provide them with the design in return for a royalty, and leave it to them to do the manufacturing and marketing. They can't survive without us, nor we without them; there is a great amount of mutual dependence. Our OEM resellers are more like customers. We sell them a board or complete system and then we each go our own way. We depend on them to market the product, not to build it.

Kubota

Mips did not seek out its first license. Only a few months after his arrival at Mips, Miller was approached by Kubota Ltd., a $5.2 billion Japanese agricultural equipment manufacturer that was interested in diversifying into new technologies. Kubota had already provided financing to several other U.S. firms, among them California start-up Ardent Computer Corporation. Ardent planned to build a line of supercomputers around the Mips RISC chip, and Kubota thus had a direct stake in the survival of Mips. In an agreement signed in September 1987, Kubota purchased a 20% equity stake in Mips, worth $20 million. For

EXHIBIT 9-5 Main Alliances of Mips in 1991

Type	North America	Europe	Far East
TECHNOLOGY LICENSING PARTNERS			
Semiconductor Partners	LSI Logic Integrated Device Performance Semiconductor DEC[a]	Siemens	NEC
Other Semiconductor			Sony Tosihiba NKK Daewoo
Manufacturing License			Kubota Computer
SYSTEMS RESELLERS			
OEMs[b]	Control Data	Groupe Bull	Daewoo
Technology	Evans & Sutherland Prime Computer Pyramid Technology Tandem Computer Wang Laboratories	IN2 (Siemens) Siemens-Nixdorf Olivetti	Kubota Computer Sumitomo Electric
VARs	American Airlines Bachal Telematique Computer Dynamics Dynix Corporation Falcon Microsystems Gain Communications	TIS Metrologic S.A.	Hitachi-Zosen Systems
Distributors	Comperex Texas Instruments		Kubota Computers
Systems Integrators	Bolt Beranek & Newman Sylvest Management Sys.	GEI Rechnersysteme	

[a]DEC had a license to manufacture Mips processors for its internal use, but had not exercised it as of 1991.

[b]OEM resellers also have software licenses from Mips.

Source: Mips Computer Systems.

an additional $5 million, Kubota helped to fund a high-end systems development program at Mips in return for the exclusive right to sell that product in the Far East. Kubota also agreed to build a $100 million computer factory in Japan. Mips, in turn, agreed to restrictions on its ability to grant additional manufacturing licenses in the territory covered by the agreement, and agreed to source a certain percentage of its sales to OEMs through Kubota.

In time, Kubota purchased further, non-exclusive manufacturing rights to other Mips products, and Mips appointed the company a distributor of certain semiconductor products in its territory. The company also began to purchase some components directly from Mips—those that were hard to source in Japan, although no finished boards. In 1991, one product made up 90%

of Kubota's manufacturing for Mips, while Kubota products represented 20%–25% of Mips's revenues.

Semiconductor Partners

Mips's semiconductor partner strategy was formed when Mips switched from being a chip manufacturer to a chip design house. The first three small U.S. licenses were signed soon after management's off-site strategy meeting in 1987, when it decided to seek a maximum of six partners. Mips would promise these firms that no other semiconductor partners would be added until 1992. Miller explained that Mips "had as an ideal to sign one of the top three semiconductor firms in the United States, one of the top three

EXHIBIT 9-6 Major RISC Alliances of Mips, Sun, HP, and IBM: 1987–1991

		Mips	Sun	HP	IBM
1987	Q1				
	Q2	jt R&D Prime and SiGraphics			
	Q3		lic Fujitsu, Cypress, and Bipolar		
	Q4	lic LSI Logic, and Performance	equity invest. from AT&T		
1988	Q1	lic Integrated Device Tech.	jt R&D Unisys / lic LSI Logic		
	Q2	equity invest. from Kubota	design win ICL / lic TI		
	Q3	equity invest. from DEC	OEM Toshiba / design win TI and Solbourne		
	Q4		OEM and lic Seiko	stop jt R&D IBM	stop jt R&D HP
1989	Q1	lic Siemens and NEC	jt R&D Toshiba	lic and jt R&D	
	Q2	OEM Pyramid	design win Tatung and other Taiw. firm	Hitachi lic/OEM Samsung	
	Q3	lic Bipolar	lic Philips		
	Q4	OEM Bull, Nixdorf and CDC; lic Sony	design win Goldstar		
1990	Q1	manuf lic Kubota	design win Hyundai		lic from SiGraphics
	Q2		design win Twinhead		
	Q3	design win Prime	x-lic IBM / mktng Compuadd		x-lic Sun
	Q4	design win AT&T and Daewoo	design win Matsushita and Taiw. firm		
1991	Q1	OEM Wang	design win Tandon		
	Q2	consortium ACE, with Compaq, DEC, 18 others.		consortium with Hit., Sams., and Sequioa	OEM Wang
	Q3	lic Toshiba			JV Apple and lic Motorola

Notes: lic = license to
    x-lic = cross-license
    OEM = OEM sales to

Source: Press reports, compiled by casewriter.

in Japan, and one of the top three in Europe." (See **Exhibit 9–7** for rankings of global semiconductor firms.) Three other U.S. firms—Motorola, Advanced Micro Devices (AMD), and National Semiconductor—were approached by Mips, but refused. Motorola and AMD were unwilling to give up their own RISC development efforts, which was a Mips requirement, while National Semiconductor would not agree to marketing and sales obligations.

In September 1988, DEC became the fourth licensee of Mips semiconductor technology when it signed the equity deal with Mips, although as of 1991 DEC was not manufacturing the chip. For the two remaining slots, Mips sought international partners. Siemens A.G., of West

EXHIBIT 9-7 Rankings of World's Top Semiconductor Vendors in 1989–90

A. Ranked by Share of Whole Semiconductor Market

Rank	Company	1990 Share of World Market	RISC Ally
1	NEC	8.4%	Mips
2	Toshiba	8.4	Sun[a]
3	Hitachi	6.7	HP
4	Motorola	6.4	IBM
5	Intel	5.5	
6	Fujita	5.0	Sun
7	Texas Instruments	4.4	Sun
8	Mitsubishi	4.0	
9	Philips	3.5	Sun
10	Matsushita	3.3	Sun
11	National Semiconductor	3.0	
12	SGS-Thomson	2.5	
13	Sanyo	2.4	
14	Sharp	2.3	
15	Samsung	2.3	HP
16	Siemans	2.1	Mips
17	Sony	2.0	Mips
18	Oki	1.9	
19	AMD	1.8	
20	AT&T	1.5	Sun

B. Ranked by Share of the Microprocessor Market

Rank	Company	1990 Share of World Market	RISC Ally
1	Intel	53.2%	
2	Motorola	13.3	IBM
3	AMD	5.1	
4	Hitachi	3.6	HP
5	NEC	3.5	Mips
6	National Semiconductor	2.7	
7	SGS-Thomson	2.3	
8	Toshiba	2.1	Sun[a]

[a]In the fall of 1991 Toshiba also became a Mips licensee.

Note: Total market size for all semiconductors (Table A) was approximately $58 billion in 1990. The world microprocessor market was about $6 billion.

Source: Dataquest.

processors, and the company was willing to commit exclusively to Mips's RISC. "Because of the NEC connection, we are almost bigger than life in Japan," added Boesenberg.

The terms of these semiconductor licenses, which Mips called Level III licenses, were similar to second-source agreements, with the exception that Mips would not be a competitor. The firms were granted licenses to Mips's second generation RISC chip, the R3000. Mips provided each firm with the RISC instruction set and VLSI[8] design, or layout, for this chip, as well as licenses to all applicable system software. The licensees, for their part, agreed to an up-front payment of about $10 million, and royalties of approximately 5% based on the selling price of each unit sold. Mips believed that the up-front payment was close to the actual cost for the technology being transferred. Mips provided exact technical specifications for the R3000, and tested all products for pin-compatibility.[9] Mips's "seal of approval" assured customers that chips from different manufacturers were fully interchangeable. The licenses lasted 5 to 10 years, during which time Mips guaranteed that it would provide access to new generations of its technology, each time for an additional up-front fee. Beyond 10 years, the licensees had complete rights to continue to use the architecture covered by the license in perpetuity, but there was no guarantee of access to future technology.

Bob Miller explained that, although Sun Microsystems also licensed its SPARC chip widely, its approach differed from that of Mips:

Mips completely designs its microprocessor, down to the mask level. So when we sign our semiconductor partners, we give them everything, and they can be in production faster than licensees of other designs. Sun provides only the instruction set and licensees have to do all of the designing themselves; as a result, it can take them up to two years to reach the production phase. For this reason, Mips can command much higher up-front fees and royalty payments.[10] Furthermore, SPARC chips made by different firms are not pin-compatible.

[8]VLSI stood for Very Large Scale Integration.

[9]Pin compatibility meant that the functions of each of the pin connectors of a chip was identical, regardless of manufacturer. The chips were thus functionally and physically completely interchangeable in computer systems.

[10]In 1991, Sun licensed SPARC for $15,000, with no royalties.

Germany, had had its own RISC project going, but the Mips chip would allow them to reduce to one-quarter the time-to-market with a RISC chip. Also, since Siemens was DEC's largest supplier of semiconductors in Europe, DEC Europe welcomed the deal. NEC, the largest semiconductor manufacturer in the world, signed on in Japan. Through a former agreement with Intel, NEC had experience making and selling micro-

But, Mips's dependence on its allies was not without risks. The R6000 chip, which was of a different type than the R2000, R3000, and R4000, had been licensed to only Bipolar Technologies, a small U.S. firm. Problems with supply cost, reliability, and quantities resulted in substantial delays in commercializing the product. While it was announced and demonstrated in the fourth quarter of 1989, the product was not shipped in large volumes until 1991. This delay, in turn, affected Mips's sales of R6000-based systems. Aside from this dependence, managing the interests of five semiconductor partners could be challenging, as Bob Miller explained:

> The key ingredient to our semiconductor partnership program is perseverance. Keeping five companies on the same strategic path can be difficult; it takes diplomacy, time, and energy at the senior level. Chuck Boesenberg and I spend a lot of our time resolving issues to keep us all in the same line.

Other Technology Licensees

By 1991 Mips had also created two other types of semiconductor licenses, which allowed it to continue to promote its technology without creating competition for its first six semiconductor partners. Level I semiconductor licensees had access to the Mips instruction set for internal use only—for example, for research purposes to build systems around the Mips chip—but could not sell chips. Level II semiconductor licensees were allowed access to the Mips instruction set without the VLSI design, in order to build their own version of the Mips chip. These chips could be used for special "embedded control" applications, which were estimated to account for half the total market for RISC chips. For embedded control applications the microprocessor was slightly redesigned and built into a system other than a general purpose computer. In 1990, for example, Sony became a Level II licensee from Mips to use modified versions of Mips chips in an array of consumer products.

Finally, Mips also created licensing agreements for its operating system (RISC/os) and compiler software. Mips allowed licensees to modify the software for their products and applications, and in turn, license these to third parties. As before, however, third parties needed to execute a licensing agreement with Mips for the original software. Mips believed that by optimizing all of a RISC system's components—chip, operating system, and complier software—and licensing it all, its architecture would maintain technological superiority in the marketplace.

Alliances for Marketing System Products

Mips's distribution strategy for system products grew out of the realization that Mips could not singlehandedly create the volume that would make Mips a major player in the RISC marketplace. In 1989, the company began to develop sales relationships with OEMs, distributors, value-added resellers (VARs), and systems integrators. Many of Mips's largest OEM customers were ailing makers of minicomputers, the segment of the market most directly threatened by the rise of RISC workstations. The company avoided competition with these parties by deemphasizing its direct sales efforts. In 1990, Mips's direct customer contact was mainly with advanced technical end-users, such as universities.

Systems were marketed both under Mips's brand label, and under the brand labels of the company's OEM customer. Prime Computer, Control Data, Wang, Bull, Nixdorf, and others purchased system products manufactured by Mips, packaged in various configurations. This approach gave the systems vendors a range of options. They could purchase complete Mips systems, add their company logo, and achieve quick time-to-market advantages. Or, they could purchase products at the chip, board, or subsystem level and add their own value to the design before selling them to end-users and resellers. Finally, they could design their own products using a combination of these integration options. Boesenberg explained how varied and dynamic these OEM relationships could be:

> We often begin working with an OEM to fill a gap in their product line, say, by providing workstations to complement their minicomputers. In time, the more successful they are in reselling our systems, the more likely they are to want to design and build them from the microprocessor up, with the result that our sales to them would decline. So our challenge

enge is to keep replenishing these OEMs with new products.

VARs typically would purchase complete system products from Mips, and then bundle them with their own application software; they often specialized in specific vertical markets. Since these VARs did not build systems, they were not likely to replace Mips machines with their own. Systems integrators, still another type of reseller, purchased products from Mips, and incorporated them into customer-specific systems and networks. They provided custom end-user system design and management. Distributors were mainly used for sales to end-users, often in international markets where Mips had no direct sales presence.

From 1988 to 1991, Mips's system products were sold increasingly through VAR channels. At the end of 1988, for example, Mips reseller contracts were divided nearly equally between VARs, OEMs, and systems integrators/distributors. By the end of 1990, however, Mips had signed 136 VARs, compared to 34 OEMs and 27 systems integrators. Mips, like its competitors, looked increasingly to new channels, as competition in the RISC/Unix market heated up. In 1990, nearly 250 computer dealers started to carry workstation products of Mips and others.

Mips's Main Competitors

Mips had four main competitors in 1991: the three companies that had developed commercially successful RISC processors (Sun, HP, and IBM[11]) and Intel, which dominated the desktop market with its CISC processors. Among these competitors, Mips was the only one exclusively selling RISC systems, but not the only one using alliances to spread its technology worldwide (see Exhibit 6). In addition, while in 1991 DEC was still an important Mips ally, the company was rumored to be planning the introduction of its own RISC processor in 1992.

Sun Microsystems

Sun Microsystems, like Mips, was formed out of computer science research at Stanford University. Sun's strategy was to manufacture computers based on open standards and purchasing readily available components. Sun started in the workstation business using off-the-shelf Motorola CISC processors. Through aggressive selling and championing of the open systems concept, the company's sales soared—in 1987 its revenues passed then market leader Apollo (which also used Motorola chips), and by 1990 Sun held over 30% of the workstation market.

In 1987, Sun entered the market for RISC-based workstations with the Sun-4, based on the company's proprietary RISC architecture, SPARC. Sun's first licensee was Solbourne Computers, a small U.S. firm controlled by Japan's Matsushita. By 1991, Solbourne had produced a SPARC clone, and was competing against Sun in the marketplace. Other major licensees were Unisys, AT&T, Xerox, Prime Computer, ICL, Philips, Fujitsu, Toshiba, and Matsushita itself. As of March 1991, a total of 30 vendors had announced SPARC-based systems. Still, in 1990, Sun itself supplied 95% of the SPARC systems sold. In 1991, *Unix World* characterized Sun's alliance strategy as follows:

> [Sun] has tried to set an industry microprocessor standard and let companies clone the technology, but so far there's only one winner: Sun. Despite Sun's posturing as an "open systems company," the company has made progress difficult for SPARC-compatible vendors. . . . Earlier this year, Sun issued an edict to its VARs barring them from selling Sun clones. It also lowered its prices to undercut the least expensive SPARC clone machines. Sun's paranoia about the potential success of SPARC-compatible vendors is jeopardizing the very market Sun is trying to create, say analysts.[12]

---

[11]A fourth company, Intergraph, also had a proprietary RISC design on the market, but it focused almost exclusively on the military market.

[12] Gary Andrew Poole, "Sun in Their Eyes," *Unix World*, October, 1991, p. 79.

Hewlett-Packard

Although HP's traditional strength lay in minicomputers, decreasing sales in this market led the company to turn toward higher-growth segments of the industry. In 1985, it entered workstations using Motorola chips, with systems that complemented its minicomputer lines. In 1989, it acquired ailing workstation leader Apollo Computer for $500 million; this propelled HP into second place in the industry, and first place among suppliers of Motorola-based workstations.

HP's first RISC machine was a minicomputer, based on the company's proprietary Precision Architecture (PA-RISC). This was followed by its first RISC workstation, introduced in February 1991. Introduced at a price that undercut Sun's comparable RISC workstation and marketed with aggressive advertising, this machine claimed to offer twice the performance, for half the price. This machine turned out to be a hot seller and helped drive HP's excellent financial results in 1991, one of the few bright spots in the performance of global computer firms in that year. By 1991, HP had also completed the merger with Apollo, having moved the former Apollo customers to the PA-RISC architecture, which by then had become the company's core architecture.

Compared to Sun and Mips, HP had formed few international alliances in the RISC field, but it did joint research with Hitachi and licensed Samsung to make low-end PA-RISC workstations. Observers expected HP to become more aggressive in pushing its PA-RISC architecture.

IBM

In 1991, IBM, too, was poised to become a major competitor in the RISC workstation marketplace. Its first RISC workstation line—the RT family—was introduced in 1986 based on its proprietary RISC architecture. Widely considered overpriced and underpowered, the RT line was not successful. In 1990, however, the company entered the fray in a big way with its RS/6000 line of Unix RISC workstations. The performance of these machines temporarily leapfrogged Sun's entire RISC product line. Twenty-five thousand units were sold in the first six months of production, and the line accounted for some $750 million of IBM's $1 billion in workstation sales that year. With its vast market power and pool of application software, IBM was a serious threat to its smaller competitors.

In October 1991, IBM announced a major alliance with Apple and Motorola that included collaboration in the RISC field. IBM and Apple agreed to develop a new operating system that would function, among others, on a future generation of IBM's RISC processor. The RS/6000 processor actually consisted of seven chips used together, and was therefore much more expensive than the single-chip designs of Mips and Sun. As part of the new alliance, IBM agreed to redesign its RISC processor to fit onto one chip, and granted Motorola a license to manufacture the new chip. Motorola had been the CISC supplier for all Apple computers, and had not developed a widely used RISC chip. IBM and Motorola announced that they intended to license the new RS/6000 chip widely.

Intel

Even though RISC was rapidly penetrating the Unix workstation market, Intel's X86 CISC architecture continued to dominate the personal computer world. The company had not developed a commercially successful RISC chip, although it had a special-purpose RISC processor and planned to incorporate RISC principles in its design for the 80586, due out in 1992. In 1991, Intel redoubled its development efforts on the 80586. Because Intel-based PCs dominated the desktop, Intel's executives did not seem overly concerned about the threat posed by the new RISC competitors. As Intel chairman Gordon Moore explained:

> As to the people ganging up on us—the Mips thing, for example—one thing you have to look at is the relative market size you are serving. We'll ship more 486 processors this quarter than all the RISCprocessors in all the designs shipped from the beginning of time.[13]

[13]Samuel Weber, "Waging War on Intel: The RISC Crowd Moves In," *Electronics*, November, 1991, p. 58.

DEC

Probably the biggest wild card for Mips was DEC's decision around 1990 to revive its project for a proprietary RISC chip, this time under the code-name Alpha. By the end of 1991, it was expected that DEC would come out with this new chip within a year, and would use it as the core of its new minicomputer lines. DEC intended to port its VMS operating system to run on Alpha, and in time would help its customers migrate from the old VAX architecture to the new RISC-based systems. But it was unclear what DEC would do about its involvement with Mips. Since 1988, it had used Mips chips successfully in its line of Unix workstations. There was a possibility that the company would continue to use the Mips architecture for its low-end machines and would move to the more expensive Alpha architecture for its high-end systems.

The ACE Consortium

Late in 1990, Compaq Computer, the third largest PC maker behind IBM and Apple, announced that it was investigating the possibility of a new RISC-based high-end PC line. It was rumored that Compaq's search had been narrowed to Mips and Sun. Working in Mips's favor was a previously announced alliance with software developer Microsoft Corporation. Microsoft had agreed to adapt its Windows operating environment to run on Mips's RISC architecture.

By February 1991, it was clear that an alliance was forming around Mips's R4000 chip. Under development since 1989, the R4000 was expected to be available by late 1991. Led by Compaq, the alliance announced support for two hardware platforms—Mips's R4000 RISC chip and the Intel X86 microprocessors that dominated the PC market—as well as two operating systems—a "unified" version of Unix, based on a version from the Santa Cruz Operation, and the "Windows New Technology" (NT) from Microsoft. In this way, alliance members hoped to create new hardware and software standards for desktop and laptop computers, as well as capitalize on the huge installed base of Windows application programs, which would be recompiled to run on Windows NT, even though they would not exploit its most advanced features. By the time the alliance was formalized in April, over 21 firms had joined. Key members included DEC, Control Data, Silicon Graphics, Prime, Wang, and Pyramid Technology of the United States; Olivetti, Siemens-Nixdorf, and Bull/Zenith of Europe; and NEC, Sony, Sumitomo, and NKK of Japan. Robert Miller summed up the challenge for Mips: "At the end of the day, the winner—a relative term, anyway—will be the one who gets the customers' desktops converted. Our new mission is to provide as much enabling technology to the ACE members as possible."

ACE membership continued to grow rapidly to over 60 in July and almost 200 in October. Many of these new members were foreign clone makers and small software firms. But, on October 15 Mips announced a new semiconductor partner—Toshiba. Like the other semiconductor partners, Mips licensed Toshiba to make, sell, and develop Mips R3000 and R4000 chips, and incorporate these into its systems. The signing of Toshiba was particularly noteworthy because the company had been one of the first licensees of Sun's SPARC technology. The status of Toshiba's relationship to Sun remained unclear.

The Future of Mips and ACE

While ACE and the Mips architecture seemed to be gaining momentum in the second half of 1991, Mips's financial prospects began to look less promising. The company incurred a loss of $597,000 in the second quarter of 1991, which compared unfavorably with the $624,000 profit in the first quarter, and the $4 million profit of the second quarter of the previous year. Mips executives attributed this trend to the general slowdown in computer sales and to the changing mix of Mips's product line, which showed technology revenues declining relative to product revenues. Furthermore, Miller warned that significant restructuring of the company's operations was needed to reduce costs and address ACE's goals and the needs of its members. He said that "the company expects to incur significant costs related to these actions."

The third quarter of 1991 was not kind to Mips and ACE. "Mips Computer has a beautiful future behind it," wrote *Business Week* in October, in an article that reported an expected loss of $15 million for the quarter. By then, investors had already driven Mips stock down to $11 per share, from $21 in March, 1991.

Part of the blame for the loss lay with disrupted relations with resellers that followed Mips's decision to phase out high-end systems in favor of ACE-compliant desktop systems. Groupe Bull was among the resellers reportedly unhappy with this shift, as was Wang, which became a reseller of IBM workstations. It began to look as if Bull, too, might follow that route: in December the company was considering adopting IBM's RS/6000 or HP's PA-RISC to replace Mips.

The ACE consortium began to exhibit other cracks. DEC was reported to be close to introducing the Alpha chip, and consortium members forced the group to accept a second version of Unix, which competed with the Santa Cruz version. Furthermore, the early momentum behind ACE spurred competitors to action. As IBM, Apple, and Motorola began to work together, Sun began offering a version of its Solaris operating system for Intel-based computers, and Compaq was reportedly one of the PC makers considering breaking ranks and offering Solaris as an option. Intel, for its part, reported good progress on its 80586 chip.

When Mips announced its third quarter results (Exhibits 2 and 3), they were even worse than *Business Week* had projected. Revenues fell 27% from the second quarter, and the company incurred a net loss of $37.3 million, which included a $25.5 special charge for corporate restructuring. The drop in revenues was largely attributable to a decline in technology income from $11.6 million in the second quarter to $3.2 in the third. "Our technology revenue is influenced significantly by new technology licensing agreements which are often the result of long sales cycles," explained CFO David Ludvigson. He expected that new licensing programs in the fourth quarter would increase technology revenue.

The one-time restructuring charge included severance costs related to a 10% reduction in employment, write-downs of capitalized software, inventory and equipment, and a provision for idle facility costs. Mips expected that the 1991 cash impacts of this charge would be minimal, and that the restructuring would reduce operating costs. Miller added: "Mips remains a strong company. We have substantial capital resources and remain a leader in our core technologies."

As the year drew to a close, observers wondered what would become of Mips and of ACE. Whatever the answer to this question, it was bound to have implications for firms joining the popular trend to stake their future on inter-firm alliances and industry consortia. Were these strategies the road to riches or to ruin? And was Mips's management of its alliance network an example to follow or to shun?

10. McCaw Cellular Communications, Inc. in 1990

In 1984, it seemed unlikely that a small family-run business could compete successfully with the multibillion-dollar regional Bell operating companies in the emerging cellular communications business. By 1990, however, McCaw Cellular Communications, Inc. was the largest cellular telephone service company in the United States. This family-built company, headquartered in Kirkland, Washington, had more than 70 million potential customers (or POPs, in industry parlance) in its service areas, 963,000 existing customers, and more than $500 million in 1989 revenues. Craig O. McCaw, the company's 40-year-old chairman and CEO, was described by competitors as the entrepreneur of the 1980s. His vision was to build a seamless national cellular phone system and to charge premium rates for top-quality service.

First offered in 1983, cellular phone service had more than 4.4 million subscribers in the United States by 1990. This subscription growth rate indicated that cellular phones had won acceptance faster than televisions, videocassette recorders, or facsimile machines had. Experts predicted there could be 25 million cellular customers in the United States by the year 2000. Revenues had risen from $300 million in 1985 to $3.2 billion in 1990, with experts predicting an increase to $15 billion by 1995. Observers called cellular service a victim of its own popularity; in some urban areas, the volume of calls strained capacity.

Industry History

Since the 1927 Radio Act, the U.S. government had regulated use of the radio spectrum to reduce problems of interference. Long before cellular phone service had emerged, parts of the radio spectrum were allocated to private radio systems for uses such as police, ambulance, taxi, law enforcement, and industry communications. In 1990, parts of the spectrum were allocated also to

Professor Elizabeth Olmsted Teisberg prepared this case with research assistance from Business Information Analyst Sarah R. Collins as the basis for class discussion rather than to illustrate either effective or ineffective handling of an administrative situation. All information is drawn from public sources.

televisions, baby monitors, garage door openers, and remote paging systems.

In 1981, the Federal Communications Commission (FCC) determined that it would award cellular service licenses to two companies in each of 306 Metropolitan Statistical Areas, or MSAs, (which included 75% of the U.S. population) and 428 Rural Statistical Areas, or RSAs (which included 80% of the U.S. land area). According to the FCC rules, one license would be given to the local wireline (traditional noncellular) phone company and the other would be awarded in a lottery; the licenses could be resold, but no entity could control more than one cellular system within a service area. More than 90,000 applicants participated in the lotteries. The first two cellular phone service networks began operations in Chicago and Baltimore in 1983. By 1990, all of the MSAs had cellular service; the last of the RSA lotteries had been completed, and the first 22 RSA systems had begun operations.

The process of qualifying to compete in the FCC lottery for cellular service licenses and completing the application was estimated to cost $250,000. Once a company won (or purchased) a license to a service area, it could apply for a construction permit. After the permit was granted, the company had 18 months in which to begin building a system. If it did not build a system in parts of its service territory within three years, its license for the unbuilt areas reverted back to the FCC. Sale of licenses and permits was common.

Cellular Communications

To make cellular phone calls, callers had to be within the range of one of the service areas. Then they could call any location in the world where regular or cellular service was available. Signal quality was not as good as on standard telephones. Voices sometimes faded in and out, and connections were occasionally lost if the radio signal was blocked by a bridge, building, or forest. Cellular phones could have all of the services standard phones had, such as voice mail, call forwarding, and data transmission, but data transmission such as portable facsimile transmission was slower.

Cellular communication required a cellular telephone, battery, antenna, and a subscription with a cellular service company. Manufacturers offered three kinds of cellular phones: mobile, transportable, and portable. Mobile phones were installed in cars or trucks, using power from the vehicle's battery; its own antenna was mounted on the outside of the vehicle. Transportable phones could be moved from car to car or could be used in a boat, in the field, or in the house. They drew power from a vehicle's cigarette lighter or from a battery pack. In 1990, a mobile or transportable cellular phone, battery, and antenna cost $100 to $700; one that cost $3,500 in 1983 could be purchased for $300 in 1990. Portables were one-piece phones that operated on lower power from a built-in rechargeable battery. The newest portables, which could be folded to pocket-size and weighed as little as ten ounces, cost $400 to $1,500. Portable and transportable phones accounted for about 50% of the market in 1990.

For people concerned only with status or appearances, a small California company called Faux Systems sold a $16 ($9.95 on sale) nonworking replica of a car phone and antenna called the Cellular Phoney. In 1990, 40,000 Cellular Phoneys had been sold in California.

Cellular phone transmission service was provided by a network of low-power radio transceivers called cell sites, or base stations, each transmitting and receiving signals in a 1- to 25-mile radius known as a cell. Smaller cells led to increased system capacity because the same airwave channel could be used simultaneously for different calls in different cells. When a cellular call was made, the voice was transmitted in the form of continuous radio waves to the transceiver at the cell site, and then it was transmitted through the regular telephone network to the number being called. The cell switch periodically monitored the signal strength of calls in progress. If the signal strength fell to a predetermined level, the switch determined if the signal quality was greater at an adjacent cell site, and, if so, it passed the call to that cell site. The transfer took a fraction of a second and was not noticed by the calling parties. However, if the switch at the adjacent site was made by a different manufacturer, the hand-off would not necessarily work because different manufacturers used different hand-off protocols. If the hand-off failed, the call abruptly disconnected.

When a cellular phone customer "roamed," or drove into the service area of another company, the call was passed to an adjacent cellular service with which the subscriber's company had a billing agreement Effectively, the United States had two cellular networks because wireline companies shared billing agreements and nonwireline companies shared billing agreements, but calls were not passed between wireline and nonwireline companies. If there was no cellular service where the customer roamed, or if there was not a billing agreement, the call was disconnected. Customers could place calls when they were away from their regular service territory by dialing a 10-digit access code before dialing the call. To receive calls on a cellular phone away from one's service territory, subscribers had to phone the access number and location to the home service company; then if the two territories had compatible switches, calls could be received.

Fully digital networks (which in 1990 were under development) would transmit voices in the form of a series of pulses representing the zeros and ones of computer language. With digital technology, more calls could fit on a single channel and the speed of cellular data transmissions for portable fax machines or laptop computers could increase to match the speed of the regular telephone system. The possibility of an all-digital network also created the possibility of a standardized network in which telephone numbers could be associated with individuals (wherever they traveled) instead of with places. Customers would no longer need access codes for calls when they were out of town. A standardized national digital network would make it possible even for small cellular service companies with few service areas to offer national calling benefits to their customers.

Other portable communication options were increasing in 1990. Remote pagers allowed customers to receive messages, but not to make or receive calls. The market for pagers was 7.8 million units in 1988 and growing at a rate of 30%

per year. Some customers used both pagers and mobile phones.

Personal communications networks (PCNs), which were under development, used a type of cellular phone that was pocket-sized and less powerful. Instead of using relatively few cells spread widely (as other cellular systems did), they used thousands of microcells spaced more closely so that users would never be far away from one of them. Some telecommunications experts believed that PCNs would become the primary wireless telephone service in urban areas; others argued that microcells' limited range would make other technologies dominant. In 1990, the FCC granted experimental licenses to firms to use a different radio frequency than the cellular service companies and build PCN systems in Washington, D.C., Detroit, Chicago and White Plains, New York.[1]

Satellite phone systems also were under development. For example, Motorola's "Iridium" project was a plan to use 77 low-orbit satellites to bring wireless telephone service to every point on earth. Motorola described it as a complement to cellular service. The system, which would cost $2.3 billion, was scheduled to begin service in 1996. Hand-held phones for the Iridium system would cost about $3,000, and calls would cost $1 to $3 per minute, plus a $50 monthly service charge. Hughes Network Systems also was developing a satellite system.

Customers

The Cellular Telephone Industry Association and many analysts predicted that the number of subscribers would grow at 40% to 50% per year for the next five years. Revenues from cellular service for the first half of 1990 were $2.13 billion, up 10% from six months earlier. A few observers believed that cellular phones would entirely replace wireline phones soon after the turn of the century. In spite of such optimistic projections, cellular service company stock prices dropped 50% during 1990 amid fears of recession. **Exhibit 10–1** shows U.S. industry growth statistics from 1984 to 1990.

[1]The United Kingdom had already licensed a PCN company to compete with cellular service.

EXHIBIT 10-1 U.S. Cellular Telephone Industry Growth

Date	Subscribers	Revenues	Cell Sites	Employees	Total Capital Investments[a]	Systems Operating	Resellers
Dec. 84	91,600	$ 178,000,000	346	1,404	$ 354,760,500	32	107
June 85	203,600	$ 176,231,000	599	1,697	$ 588,751,000	65	211
Dec. 85	340,213	$ 306,197,000	913	2,727	$ 911,167,000	102	224
June 86	500,000	$ 360,585,000	1,194	3,556	$1,140,163,000	129	213
Dec. 86	681,825	$ 462,467,000	1,531	4,334	$1,436,753,000	166	240
June 87	883,778	$ 479,514,000	1,732	5,656	$1,724,348,000	206	230
Dec. 87	1,230,855	$ 672,000,000	2,305	7,147	$2,234,635,000	312	285
June 88	1,608,697	$ 888,075,000	2,789	9,154	$2,589,588,000	420	247
Dec. 88	2,069,441	$1,073,472,000	3,209	11,400	$3,274,104,000	517	211
June 89	2,691,793	$1,406,463,000	3,577	13,719	$3,675,473,000	559	252
Dec. 89	3,508,944	$1,934,132,198	4,169	15,937	$4,480,141,752	584	303
June 90	4,368,686	$2,126,362,078	4,768	18,973	$5,211,765,025	592	372

[a]The capital Investment per subscriber appears lower than the data in the section on Transmissions Systems because those data include installation and frequency planning expenses.

Source: Cellular Telephone Industry Association, 1990.

The average cellular customer in 1990 was college educated, was married, and had a household income of $66,000. Use was reported to be 75% business calls and 25% personal. In 1990, more cellular phones were installed in pick-up trucks than in any other type of vehicle. Three years earlier, the average customer was a 55-year-old CEO earning more than $90,000, and only 11% of use was personal. The average monthly bill by a cellular subscriber was about $81 in the first half of 1990, down from about $87 in 1989 and from more than $100 in 1986. In general, average monthly bills were higher in rural than in metropolitan service areas, although the Los Angeles area had average monthly bills of about $140 in 1990.

In high-volume markets such as Los Angeles and New York, callers sometimes had to wait several minutes for a dial tone; about 20% of rush-hour callers in these markets were unable to place calls on the first try. Overcrowded systems also had higher numbers of accidentally disconnected calls. Some observers believed that the first company to enhance its capacity in overcrowded systems might win a large share of the market and create loyal customers.

Market research showed that a subscriber's choice of service company was based on the breadth of service coverage and the quality of customer support. Companies competed fiercely to offer broad coverage. Participants said that because no firm had dared to experiment with narrow coverage, no one knew if customers would avoid a company that serviced a small area. Bell operating companies often had marketing advantages based on their reputation as large, stable phone companies.

Marketing and Distribution

The costs of marketing and advertising were $400 to $600 for each new subscriber attracted. Factoring in "churn rate" (i.e., the percentage of customers who canceled their subscriptions within six months), these costs were $600 to $900 for each new long-term subscriber. Most cellular service companies used a variety of distribution channels to attract and support customers, including dealers, sales agents, direct sales forces, retailers, and resellers.

Dealers and agents were independent companies that contracted to market one cellular service exclusively. They received a commission for each subscription and an additional commission after the customer had been with the service for six months. Dealers and agents were estimated to account for as much as 60% of service companies' sales.

Service companies' direct sales forces called on major corporate accounts, which required a sales process that could last six months. Direct sales forces typically accounted for about 30% of sales. Industry participants explained that marketing to large customers did not yet—in 1990—result in significant marketing economies because of the time and effort required to sign big customers, and because these customers tended to start with relatively small numbers of uses and add volume slowly over time. In the future, cellular service companies hoped that the marketing cost per user might be an order of magnitude lower for major corporate accounts than for individuals.

Retailers such as Sears, Caldor, Highland, Whole Earth Access, and Radio Shack also sold subscriptions for cellular service. Cellular service companies often trained retail sales representatives and paid commissions for each contracted customer. Retailers tended to change service company affiliations if they could earn a more favorable commission; commissions had risen to $200 to $800, up from $50 a few years earlier. One industry report estimated 30% of the volume of cellular equipment sales was made at retail stores in 1990, with projected growth of up to 60% or 70% by 1995. However, service companies reported that less than 10% of their service revenues were from customers who subscribed at retail stores.

Resellers bought cellular airtime in bulk at a discount (usually about 20%) and sold it to customers at rates similar to those of the cellular service company. The cellular service company had no direct link to the customer, who was billed by the reseller, which, in most areas, accounted for less than 10% of cellular service sales. In northern California, however, resellers constituted about 40% of sales.

PROMOTIONS AND ADVERTISING   It was common for dealers and retailers to apply a large fraction of their commissions to customer discounts, reducing equipment prices by up to several hundred dollars; in the late 1980s, customers could get a virtually free phone, battery, and antenna when signing up for service. Other promotions included free long-distance calling on weekends,

free voice mail for a month, and free tickets for two to Hawaii when signing up for cellular service for a year.

Cellular service companies' advertising tended to focus on technological capabilities. For example, McCaw advertised its seamless network with smooth hand-offs of calls from one cell to the next, preventing customers from being disconnected midcall. NYNEX Mobile Communications claimed 25% more calling channels than its competitors.

Pricing and Billing

Rates for cellular phone service were regulated in many states; usually, regulation meant simply that a public tariff had to be filed before rates could be changed. By 1990, about 20 states, including California, had stopped rate regulation for cellular service companies, in part because the service was viewed as a discretionary purchase.

The charge for cellular service was usually a one-time activation fee ($35 to $40), a flat rate per month ($19 to $45), and an air charge for each minute of both incoming and outgoing calls. The rate was 40¢ to 60¢ per minute for peak calling times (7:00 a.m. to 7:00 p.m. weekdays) and about 25¢ to 40¢ per minute for off-peak times. In addition, there were land charges for connecting to the local phone company lines, unless the cellular service was owned by the local phone company, and applicable long-distance charges.

Most cellular service companies bought long-distance service at a discount and resold it to their customers at retail rates. Wireline phone companies were legally required to offer equal access to all long-distance providers. Some non-wireline companies such as McCaw offered only one long-distance provider in some markets to increase the volume of long-distance purchases from that company. The size of price discounts to cellular service companies was negotiated, and companies involved were unwilling to disclose the terms of deals they had struck.

Transmission Licenses

Licenses to provide cellular service (and associated transmission systems, if built) were bought and sold among industry participants as each sought to build or consolidate its network. The market value of a license to operate a transmission system in a given area was usually expressed by the price per person in the area, or price per POP. In 1990, the value of a POP was hotly debated in the industry. Some analysts claimed that a market was worth $200 per POP to a service operator that could sign up 8% of the population within 10 years. Assuming no new regulation and few competing technologies, Morgan Asset Management Inc. projected that if 15% of Americans used cellular phones by the year 2000, and if efficient operations generated 65¢ of cash flow for every dollar of revenue, then each POP would be worth $424.

The price per POP in the early 1980s was as low as $4 to $6. Prices increased in the late 1980s and peaked in 1989 with McCaw's $350 per POP purchase of premium properties in New York and Los Angeles. Three months later, Contel paid $215 per POP for East Coast properties. In July, Pacific Telesis paid $190 per POP in Cleveland and Cincinnati, and in October, Crowley Cellular Telecommunications paid $165 per POP for Illinois properties.

Transmission Systems

Cumulative capital invested in U.S. cellular transmission service in 1990 was more than $5 billion. Industry participants estimated that building even a small system cost at least $750,000. The capital cost per customer was about $1,500, including equipment, installation, and frequency planning. Because cell size was not fixed, most service areas initially used cells 8 miles in radius in more populous areas and 25 miles in radius in rural areas. As demand increased, the cell could be split into three to six smaller cells, but beyond this point the cost and complexity of further subdivision became prohibitive. Each time a new cell was added to a network, the frequency use plan for the entire network had to be redesigned so that no two adjoining cells shared the same frequency. If adjoining cells did share a frequency, calls in these cells would interfere with each other. Although frequency planning was uncomplicated in flat, open country, it was a time-consuming engineering

task when many hills, trees, or buildings required a complicated mosaic of cells.

Industry participants said that an efficient transmission system was one with enough cell sites to cover the marketing and use region and with enough transmission channels to meet demand for cellular phone use in the region. However, in 1990, no one could characterize an efficient system in terms of customers per cell site or customers per transmission channel. Observers watched the activity levels of cellular companies' engineers and the service quality to customers to estimate which regions had system capacity well matched with demand.

The operating cellular phone network in 1990 used analog technology. To increase system capacity, service companies planned to replace analog transmission technology with one of two new digital technologies: Time Division Multiple Access (TDMA) or Code Division Multiple Access (CDMA). New transceivers, amplifiers, and controllers would be required, but the new equipment would fit on the same racks as analog equipment had. Although both new technologies were compatible with analog transmission, the two possible digital technologies were incompatible; consequently, if adjacent cells used different digital transmission technologies, callers moving from one cell to the other would have to be switched using the analog setting. If no analog channel was available, or if the caller's phone was digital only, the call would be disconnected. In 1990, cellular phones were analog or analog and digital, but in the future, digital-only phones, expected to be smaller, lighter, and less expensive, would be available. Some industry participants believed that in the future software would be created to make the two digital technologies compatible.

TDMA, the standard in Japan and in some European countries, had been chosen in February 1989 by the Cellular Telecommunications Industry Association as the U.S. standard for first-generation digital cellular technology. Expected to be available for installation in the United States in 1991, TDMA was referred to by proponents as a proven technology; it was widely licensed and was being developed by many cellular telephone equipment manufacturers. TDMA offered a threefold increase in capacity, and thus the capital cost per customer was estimated to be about $500 (one-third of the $1,500 per customer analog capital cost). Requiring channels to be set aside for digital transmission, TDMA would therefore reduce the analog capacity in systems in which it was installed. Experts expected TDMA technology to reduce system maintenance costs by 10% to 25%. They also expected the first TDMA/analog phones to be bigger and heavier than analog cellular phones and to cost 10% to 15% more. Developers believed that improvements in TDMA would offer a sixfold or tenfold increase in capacity (relative to analog capacity) by the late 1990s.

CDMA, a proprietary technology of Qualcomm, Inc., was projected to allow a tenfold to twentyfold increase in capacity. Although it had been used in some military communications since World War II, it had not been proved technically feasible for use in cellular phones until late 1989. Some observers believed CDMA could be available for use by late 1991 or 1992, but others were skeptical about its being ready before the mid-1990s. CDMA was described as more flexible, because in theory it could be overlaid on cells still serving analog users without disrupting the analog calls, and because its cells all operated on the same frequencies and thus did not require frequency plans. CDMA was described also as leading the industry closer to a generation of technology that would enable individuals to carry hand-held telephones with them anywhere. Furthermore, CDMA was predicted to have cost advantages both in installation and operation because it required fewer transmitters and combiners than did TDMA. Proponents argued also that because CDMA used the spread spectrum and covered many frequencies, interference would be reduced, sound quality would be enhanced by more robust signals, and privacy would be increased by reduced interception problems. But detractors argued that improvements in sound quality and privacy were benefits of any digital technology.

A new analog technology called Narrow Advanced Mobile Phone Services (NAMPS) was announced by Motorola in October 1990. NAMPS broadcast on a smaller band width, enabling triple the 1990 capacity without adding cells. Field tests were scheduled to begin in January 1991, and Motorola announced availability for mid-1991 for companies needing a short-term ca-

pacity enhancement before investing in digital technology. The cost of new NAMPS transceivers was projected to be "significantly less" than digital transceivers, but more precise price estimates were not yet available in late 1990. Installation would require redesign of frequency planning because NAMPS tripled the number of channels in each cell. Customers in NAMPS systems would need new phones, which Motorola planned to market at a $100 price premium over other cellular phones.

Procurement

Cellular service companies bought transmission equipment in large-volume purchases from equipment suppliers. Small rural cellular service companies usually purchased equipment jointly with an adjacent metropolitan service company to gain the advantages of volume discounts. The metropolitan companies benefited from this arrangement because they were then assured that the adjacent companies had compatible switches.

Motorola had 32% of the $627 million U.S. market for cellular switches and cell site transmission gear. AT&T had 30% and Ericsson 22%. Northern Telecom, General Electric, Nippon Electric Company, Astronet, NovAtel, and CTI/E.F.Johnson shared the remaining 16% of the market. All of these companies made analog switches, and most were expected to offer TDMA technology in 1991. Ericsson and Motorola reportedly were preparing to produce large quantities of TDMA equipment. A Motorola spokesperson noted that when cellular service companies upgraded to digital networks, "the deck would be shuffled among suppliers."[2]

Only Qualcomm offered CDMA technology in 1990. Qualcomm had contracts with PacTel, NYNEX, and Ameritech Mobile Communications to initiate testing of CDMA transmission, and with AT&T to make CDMA phones. Each of the companies that contracted with Qualcomm stated to the press that they were not abandoning TDMA and pointed out the importance of technological innovation in the industry and the

[2]Quoted by John J. Keller in *The Wall Street Journal*, March 11, 1990, p. B13.

excitement with which they viewed the potential capabilities of CDMA.

International Markets

Although the concept for cellular phones was first developed in the United States, other countries began cellular service earlier. Industry observers had attributed the U.S. delay to legislative lags in allocating the radio spectrum and in licensing service companies. Japan began commercial cellular service in 1979 and, by 1984, had 20,000 subscribers to networks in Tokyo, Osaka, and five other cities. Norway, Sweden, Denmark, and Finland began commercial service in 1981 and, by 1984, had more than 75,000 subscribers. Cellular systems were in place also in Saudi Arabia, Indonesia, and Spain before they were in the United States.

In 1990, cellular service was available in more than 70 countries and had more than 6.5 million subscribers (more than half in the United States). The highest penetration levels were in Norway, Sweden, Iceland, Denmark, and Finland. Most countries had a single cellular service system rather than competing service companies. National standards often differed among countries, resulting in incompatible systems. Europe had eight incompatible regional and national systems, but plans had been made for a pan-European network based on TDMA technology to begin service in 1992. It was hoped that the uniform standard would increase manufacturing volumes and lower costs of cellular phones.

Competitors

By law, each service area in the United States was served by two companies, one of which was the local phone company for that area. To combat the name recognition of the local phone companies, the new operators created a nationwide image with the shared trademark, "Cellular One." The Cellular One service mark was licensed by Southwestern Bell (which acquired it in 1987 with the purchase of most of Metromedia Inc.'s cellular phone business) to other companies for a minimal fee. The license was perpetual, subject to compliance with service quality standards. In 1990, the Cellular One brand was used in 300 U.S. nonwireline markets covering 85% of the population. (Wireline service companies could not use the Cellular One brand within their wireline service territories.) Each company using the brand remained independent.

In 1990, a number of service companies built large service networks. **Exhibits 10–2** and **10–3** show the number of POPs served by the largest companies, and the licensed operators in the largest markets. **Exhibit 10–4** shows financial results for leading competitors. Operating cash flow margins from cellular service were estimated to be just under 50%.

Industry observers believed regulators might allow additional competition in each region in the future. In New York, petitions had been filed for a third license. In addition, some firms were lobbying for permission to offer mobile telephone service on frequencies reserved for other uses. This section briefly profiles five selected cellular service companies, illustrating different strategies, as well as Fleet Call, a company that had petitioned to create a third cellular system in several major cities.

GTE MOBILNET, INC. GTE Mobilnet, Inc., a subsidiary of GTE Corporation, was a wireline company in parts of the southwestern and midwestern United States. It had sold its Sprint long-distance telephone service for $500 million in April 1990. The Mobilnet subsidiary was incorporated in 1981 to provide cellular phone service and related equipment. In 1984, in a limited partnership with Ameritech, Hancock Rural Telephone, and Monrovia Telephone, it launched the second operational cellular system in the United States, serving the Indianapolis area. In 1988, GTE Mobilnet was the fifth-largest U.S. cellular service company, with $84 million in cellular sales. Through a series of acquisitions, including the 1990 purchase of the Providence Journal Cellular ($710 million for 3.5 million POPs) and Contel Cellular Communications ($6.2 billion for 22.3 million POPs), GTE Mobilnet became the second largest U.S. cellular service company (as measured in POPs).

GTE Mobilnet was targeting national business accounts as a way to increase profitability. A spokesperson said it planned "to be the first cel-

EXHIBIT 10-2 Largest U.S. Cellular Operators

Operator	MSA #	Major Markets Served (top 30 only)	Total Population Served[a]
McCaw Cellular Communications, Inc. (includes LIN Broadcasting)	1	New York, N.Y.	60,887,000
	4	Philadelphia, Pa.	
	9	Dallas, Tex.	
	10	Houston, Tex.	
	12	Miami, Fla.	
	13	Pittsburgh, Pa.	
	15	Minneapolis, Minn.	
	19	Denver, Colo.	
	20	Seattle-Everett, Wash.	
	22	Tampa, Fla.	
	24	Kansas City, Mo.-Kans.	
	30	Portland, Oreg.	
GTE Mobilnet, Inc. (includes Contel and Providence Journal)	7	San Francisco, Calif.	40,680,000
	10	Houston, Tex.	
	16	Cleveland, Ohio	
	22	Tampa, Fla.	
	27	San Jose, Calif.	
	28	Indianapolis, Ind.	
	30	Portland, Oreg.	
BellSouth Mobility, Inc. (includes American Cellular Communication Corp.)	2	Los Angeles, Calif.	30,705,000
	12	Miami, Fla.	
	17	Atlanta, Ga.	
	29	New Orleans, La.	
PacTel Cellular	2	Los Angeles, Calif.	30,083,000
	5	Detroit, Mich.	
	7	San Francisco, Calif.	
	17	Atlanta, Ga.	
	18	San Diego, Calif.	
	27	San Jose, Calif.	
Southwestern Bell Mobile Systems	3	Chicago, Ill.	28,545,000
	6	Boston, Mass.	
	8	Washington, D.C.	
	9	Dallas, Tex.	
	11	St. Louis, Mo.	
	14	Baltimore, Md.	
	24	Kansas City, Mo.-Kans.	
NYNEX Mobile Communications	1	New York, N.Y.	25,076,000
	6	Boston, Mass.	
	25	Buffalo, N.Y.	
Ameritech Mobile Communications	3	Chicago, Ill.	20,271,000
	5	Detroit, Mich.	
	23	Milwaukee, Wis.	
	23	Cincinnati, Ohio	
Bell Atlantic Mobile Systems, Inc.	4	Philadelphia, Pa.	16,369,000
	8	Washington, D.C.	
	13	Pittsburgh, Pa.	
	14	Baltimore, Md.	
U.S. West Cellular	15	Minneapolis, Minn.	14,881,000
	18	San Diego, Calif.	
	19	Denver, Colo.	
	20	Seattle-Everett, Wash.	
	26	Phoenix, Ariz.	

EXHIBIT 10-2 (Continued)

Operator	MSA #	Major Markets Served (top 30 only)	Total Population Served[a]
Centel Cellular Company			12,332,000
Metro Mobile CTS	26	Phoenix, Ariz.	9,747,000
Cellular Communications, Inc.	16	Cleveland, Ohio	9,519,000
	23	Cincinnati, Ohio	

[a]Total population, not just those in the top 30 markets, served by the company.

Source: CTIA, *State of the Cellular Industry*, Spring 1990.

EXHIBIT 10-3 Cellular Operators in the Largest U.S. Cities

Rank	City	Population	Cellular Service Operators[a]
1	New York, N.Y.	14,696,685	NYNEX Mobile Communications LIN Broadcasting Corp. (McCaw)
2	Los Angeles, Calif.	10,968,394	PacTel Cellular American Cellular Communication Corp.[b,c]
3	Chicago, Ill.	7,103,624	Ameritech Mobile Communications Southwestern Bell Mobile Systems
4	Philadelphia, Pa.	4,716,818	Bell Atlantic Mobile Systems, Inc. LIN Broadcasting Corp. (McCaw)
5	Detroit, Mich.	4,618,161	Ameritech Mobile Communications PacTel Cellular
6	Boston, Mass.	3,853,177	NYNEX Mobile Communications Southwestern Bell Mobile Systems
7	San Francisco, Calif.	3,250,630	PacTel Cellular GTE Mobilnet, Inc.
8	Washington, D.C.	3,060,922	Bell Atlantic Mobile Systems, Inc. Southwestern Bell Mobile Systems, Inc.
9	Dallas, Tex.	2,974,805	Southwestern Bell Mobile Systems LIN Broadcasting Corp. (McCaw)
10	Houston, Tex.	2,905,353	GTE Mobilnet, Inc. LIN Broadcasting Corp. (McCaw)
11	St. Louis, Mo.	2,356,460	Southwestern Bell Mobile Systems CyberTel Cellular Telephone Co.
12	Miami, Fla.	2,643,981	BellSouth Mobility, Inc. McCaw Cellular Communications, Inc.

[a]Wireline companies are listed first, followed by the nonwireline competitor.

[b]ACCC is owned by BellSouth Corp.

[c]ACCC owns 60% of the L.A. nonwireline license; LIN owns 40%.

Source: CTIA, *State of the Cellular Industry*, Spring 1990.

lular concern to offer businesses one-stop shopping nationwide for service and equipment."[3] Where it could not buy or develop cellular operations, GTE Mobilnet was acquiring resale rights from the licensed service providers.

In late 1990, GTE Mobilnet announced plans to replace Motorola with AT&T as its major

[3]Janet Guyon, quoted in *The Wall Street Journal*, May 5, 1989.

equipment vendor. A spokesperson said the company wanted the future flexibility to install either TDMA or CDMA switches, and Motorola's digital equipment could support only TDMA.

PACTEL CORPORATION   PacTel was a subsidiary of Pacific Telesis Group, one of the regional Bell operating companies. In 1990, PacTel was the third-largest cellular operator in the United

EXHIBIT 10-4 Financial Data for Selected Competitors ($ thousands)[a]

	FYE 12/31/89	FYE 12/31/88	FYE 12/31/87	FYE 12/31/86	FYE 12/31/85
AMERICAN INFORMATION TECHNOLOGIES CORP.					
Net sales	10,211,300	9,903,300	9,547,500	9,384,800	9,021,100
Cost of Goods	2,539,800	2,516,000	2,365,000	2,465,500	1,646,900
SG&A Expense	3,720,200	3,497,700	3,076,700	2,789,300	3,482,500
Income Before Tax	1,784,900	1,818,600	1,905,800	2,067,800	1,897,400
Net Income	1,238,200	1,237,400	1,188,100	1,138,400	1,077,700
Return on Sales (ROS)	12%	12%	12%	12%	12%
Return on Assets (ROA)	6%	6%	6%	6%	6%
Return on Equity (ROE)	16%	16%	16%	15%	14%
Total Debt to Equity	73%	63%	64%	62%	64%
% of Sales by Cellular Subsidiary	1.5%	N/A	N/A	N/A	N/A
GTE CORP.					
Net Sales	17,424,360	16,459,852	15,421,030	15,111,528	14,371,659
Cost of Goods	N/A	N/A	N/A	N/A	N/A
SG&A Expense	14,235,130	13,408,299	12,268,365	11,873,480	11,170,925
Income Before Tax	2,064,062	1,840,962	1,751,950	2,090,611	(162,386)
Net Income	1,417,270	1,224,681	1,118,817	1,184,312	(161,091)
Return on Sales (ROS)	8%	7%	7%	8%	−1%
Return on Assets (ROA)	4%	4%	4%	4%	−1%
Retun on Equity (ROE)	18%	15%	14%	15%	−2%
Total Debt to Equity	N/A	N/A	111%	108%	108%
% of Sales by Cellular Subsidiary	N/A	0.52%	N/A	N/A	N/A
NYNEX CORP.					
Net Sales	13,210,600	12,660,800	12,084,000	11,341,500	10,313,600
Cost of Goods	3,375,000	3,303,100	2,268,400	2,185,700	2,119,500
SG&A Expense	5,762,000	4,965,400	5,392,700	4,984,800	4,450,800
Income Before Tax	1,073,500	1,688,200	1,954,700	2,105,000	1,891,100
Net Income	807,600	1,315,000	1,276,500	1,215,300	1,095,300
Return on Sales (ROS)	6%	10%	11%	11%	11%
Return on Assets (ROA)	3%	5%	6%	6%	5%
Return on Equity (ROE)	9%	14%	14%	14%	13%
Total Debt to Equity	69%	66%	68%	62%	65%
% of Sales by Cellular Subsidiary	1.5%	N/A	N/A	N/A	N/A
PACIFIC TELESIS GROUP					
Net Sales	9,593,000	9,483,000	9,156,000	8,977,000	8,498,000
Cost of Goods	1,870,000	1,966,000	2,068,000	1,534,000	1,676,000
SG&A Expense	3,360,000	3,179,000	3,243,000	3,443,000	3,331,000
Income Before Tax	2,038,000	1,972,000	1,614,000	1,979,000	1,739,000
Net Income	1,242,000	1,188,000	950,000	1,079,000	929,100
Return on Sales (ROS)	13%	13%	10%	12%	11%
Return on Assets (ROA)	6%	6%	4%	5%	5%
Return on Equity (ROE)	16%	15%	12%	14%	13%
Total Debt to Equity	70%	69%	73%	74%	82%
% of Sales by Cellular Subsidiary	5.21%	N/A	N/A	N/A	N/A
METRO MOBILE CTS INC.					
Net Sales	111,295	55,983	19,490	7,856	3,454
Cost of Goods	46,705	27,221	9,756	4,853	3,369
SG&A Expense	56,091	41,333	19,073	18,518	4,025
Income Before Tax	(47,276)	(37,108)	(17,791)	(11,487)	(5,198)
Net Income	(46,589)	(36,845)	(17,596)	(11,315)	(5,129)
Return on Sales (ROS)	−42%	−66%	−90%	−144%	−148%
Return on Assets (ROA)	−13%	−15%	−8%	−13%	−8%
Return on Equity (ROE)	N/A	N/A	−11%	−110%	−26%
Total Debt to Equity	−347%	−989%	37%	725%	51%

[a] 1990 data were not yet available.

Source: Lotus OneSource.

States (as measured in POPs) and was estimated to have a 10% national subscriber share. Revenues rose 47% between 1988 and 1989 to $453 million. Industry analysts estimated its return on investment at 40%.

Leading a trend toward consolidation and regionalization, PacTel made an agreement with Cellular Communications Incorporated (CCI) to merge the two companies' Ohio and Michigan holdings to improve customer support and regional marketing power. The agreement enabled PacTel to buy CCI after five years, giving PacTel 15 million POPs and a 27,000-square-mile territory in that region. One observer explained, "What we're seeing is basically telephone companies reclaiming an aspect of the industry which had temporarily been claimed by nontelephone interlopers."[4]

Although PacTel's president first urged the Cellular Telephone Industry Association in 1989 to adopt TDMA as an industry standard, the company (working with Qualcomm) completed the first successful test of CDMA less than a year later. Following this test, PacTel announced that CDMA was far superior to TDMA and had potential benefits too great to ignore. Faced with a dire need to increase capacity in its Los Angeles market by late 1991 or early 1992, PacTel announced it would use CDMA switches.

Some observers said PacTel's choice would compel the industry to follow; others said the firm might lose its leadership in the Los Angeles market by risking incompatibility with adjacent TDMA systems that might be installed. PacTel's director of advanced technology asserted, "We will stay compatible with the industry, but if we go with CDMA first and the industry goes with TDMA, we would implement both systems in Los Angeles."[5]

In Los Angeles, PacTel's rival was L.A. Cellular, jointly owned by McCaw and BellSouth Corporation. Since L.A. Cellular had taken over the Los Angeles license in 1987, PacTel's market share had fallen from 69% to 57%. Analysts noted that Los Angeles Cellular had higher quality ratings than PacTel in 9 of 12 quarters. The number of Los Angeles subscribers was growing in both companies.

NYNEX MOBILE COMMUNICATIONS COMPANY INC. NYNEX Mobile, a subsidiary of NYNEX Corporation, began cellular service operation in New York City in early 1984. By 1990, the company had become the fifth largest cellular operator in the United States (as measured in POPs), with sales of $200 million. Unlike the other big cellular operators, NYNEX did not pursue expansion through acquisition. Instead, it concentrated on expanding usage in its own regions, particularly the New York to Boston region. According to Charles Many, NYNEX Mobile's president, "Our fundamental philosophy is to get the basic business running and then build off the core. We prefer to stay in the Northeast because we can really make that system hum and make it profitable."[6]

By the end of 1991, NYNEX planned to have the first operational CDMA personal telephone system (PTS) for pedestrians, with 200 microcells covering Manhattan Island. The system would use AT&T equipment and Qualcomm digital phones (both in the prototype phase in 1990) and would cost $100 million. Unlike personal communication networks, which required the FCC to reallocate space in the radio frequency, the PTS would use 5 MHz (megahertz) of NYNEX's existing spectrum. Service options would include two-way calling, outgoing calling only, or outgoing calling plus paging service.

NYNEX had not decided which digital standard it would support for its cellular service. A spokesperson explained: "That is a political decision. We have to consider the rest of the industry as far as roaming is concerned."[7] NYNEX had applied to test CDMA and TDMA in areas of New York City, Boston, and White Plains, New York, with equipment from AT&T and Qualcomm.

AMERITECH MOBILE COMMUNICATIONS One week after the FCC began licensing cellular operators, in October 1983, American Information Technologies turned on the United States's first available cellular phone service in Chicago. Later that year, Ameritech Mobile Communications

---

[4]Herschel Shosteck, quoted in *Telephone Engineer & Management*, September 1, 1990, p. 28.

[5]*Mobile Phone News*, November 23, 1989, "Qualcomm, PacTel Complete First CDMA Mobile Call."

[6]Maribeth Harper, "Will the RHCs Devour the Cellular Industry?" *Telephony*, July 11, 1988.

[7]*Industrial Communications*, August 10, 1990.

was incorporated. By 1990, it had become the sixth largest cellular operator by acquiring licenses throughout the United States.

In 1990, Ameritech Mobile decided to allocate spectrum for the testing of both CDMA and TDMA mobile transmission, using AT&T and Qualcomm equipment and telephones. By the end of 1991 or early 1992, it hoped to introduce a telephone that would transmit over traditional analog channels as well as CDMA. The new device was expected to be priced at a 20% premium over all-analog or all-digital phones. The company planned also to continue to support TDMA technology.

Another large-scale project at Ameritech Mobile was the two-year test of a microwave personal communication system. The test, to be held in Chicago, was scheduled to try out three versions of the service: the first version would allow the subscriber to make out-going calls near any public base station; the second version would include a pager signifying incoming calls; the third version would allow two-way calling, with roaming capability. Ultimately, Ameritech wanted subscribers to be able to change services without owning multiple phones and pagers and without paying for all three services when using only one.

METRO MOBILE CTS, INC.

Metro Mobile was a nonwireline cellular service company founded in 1980 by George Lindemann. By 1990, the company owned and operated cellular telephone systems in 17 markets located in three regional clusters: Massachusetts/Connecticut/Rhode Island, the Carolinas, and Arizona/New Mexico. It had approximately 140,000 subscribers as of September 1990.

Metro Mobile explained its "three interrelated strategies" as (1) obtaining cellular interests in areas with favorable demographics or population growth, indicating substantial potential for cellular phone use, (2) clustering cellular systems in proximate areas for economies of scale and efficient operation and marketing, and (3) controlling (rather than having a minority interest in) all of its systems. Metro Mobile was one of the first companies to institute the concept of "calling party pays," in which the person placing the call, rather than the owner of the cellular phone, paid. It used this billing system in parts of its Southwest region and was discussing imple-

mentation in other areas with the local land-line telephone companies.

Metro Mobile had no announced plans to expand its capacity with digital technology. Management had indicated that the company was not a going concern for the long term and would consider purchase offers. No transaction was imminent in late 1990.

FLEET CALL

Fleet Call was a taxi dispatch service with $30 million in revenue in 1989. In 1990, it applied to the FCC for permission to upgrade its taxi dispatch service to include cellular phone service, by dividing its service areas into cells and installing new digital transmission equipment. Cellular service companies described Fleet Call's effort as an attempt to create a third cellular system in the markets it would serve, seeing it as a viable option for those customers who did not need the roaming capability of cellular service.

Fleet Call was founded in 1987 by a former FCC staff lawyer and a former executive of a cellular and paging company. In the ensuing three years, the company spent about $250 million acquiring 1,600 dispatch channels in New York, Los Angeles, Chicago, San Francisco, Dallas, and Houston. It paid an average of about $5 per MHz, compared with $166 per MHz that McCaw had paid for a part interest in a Los Angeles cellular system.[8] Fleet Call's president explained that the company already completed mobile calls for some customers at a charge amounting to $15 for 75 minutes, compared with a $100 charge for the same length call on a cellular service. If the FCC approved the application, as Fleet Call expected, the firm planned to spend $500 million to construct its system, which would be fully operational by 1995.

Many industry analysts expected FCC approval for Fleet Call's plans, arguing that regulators were unlikely to object to a third party that would compete on price and lower industry rates. However, several large cellular service companies were lobbying against Fleet Call. For example, McCaw hired a former FCC chairman as its lawyer to work against the rule change.

[8]There were no dollars per POP comparisons because Fleet Call was buying access to the radio spectrum (without the right to use that spectrum to serve cellular phone customers) while cellular companies were buying access to the radio spectrum *and* a license to provide cellular service in a specified region.

McCaw Cellular Communications

Craig O. McCaw began his communications career in high school, selling subscriptions for his family's fledgling cable television company. When his father died, in 1969, the family business was deeply in debt. In 1973, Craig McCaw graduated from Stanford with a degree in history and joined the family business, McCaw Communications, a cable system in Centralia, Washington. In 1978, at the age of 28, he became the head of the company.

In 1983, when the FCC began issuing licenses for cellular phone operations, McCaw budgeted $3.5 million to enter the business. Shortly thereafter, it began buying franchises for top dollar (then about $5 per POP) in what one competitor described as a "piranha frenzy" of acquisitions. At the same time, McCaw expanded into the paging business; in 1986, it paid $122 million for MCI's cellular and radio paging operations. McCaw sold the paging business for $75 million and kept the seven million cellular POPs, which effectively cost just over $6 per POP.

By 1987, McCaw had rights to build cellular systems serving 94 markets. To raise the necessary cash, it sold its cable television operations for $755 million and 11% of McCaw Cellular Communications to the public. McCaw then put up the cash and junk bond financing for additional cellular operating rights from coast to coast. By 1988, it owned more U.S. cellular phone franchises than any other group, and it had about 35 million POPs, with 38% of them in the 30 biggest markets.

In December 1989, the company won a tough bidding battle with BellSouth Corporation for the acquisition of a majority of LIN Broadcasting Corporation. The LIN acquisition gave McCaw control of an additional 25 million POPs, including controlling interests in licenses in Los Angeles, New York, Philadelphia, Dallas, and Houston, which McCaw referred to as gateway cities. For these markets, McCaw paid about $3.4 billion. Analysts calculated a price of $350 per POP. As part of the deal, McCaw had committed itself to buy the remaining LIN shares at "private market value" (the price paid by a buyer seeking control of a company) or to sell its 52% stake within five years.

LIN had $226 million in revenues in 1989, more than $100 million of which came from its TV stations and publishing operations. Its cellular division was reported to have 50% operating profit margins, in spite of a reputation for poor service in its New York City network. Craig McCaw acknowledged that the LIN acquisition could result in losses during the next several years of more than $1 billion. But, he said to an interviewer, "The key to having dreams is to make sure they come true. Waking up in a cold sweat is not what you want. . . . Debt is clearly not a challenge we want today."[9]

Craig McCaw had been referred to as a strategic visionary. He explained, "We are certainly aware of changing times. You make decisions on long-term planning, not on short-term changes in the environment."[10] Managers who had worked for him for years said, "He thinks so far down the road that his ideas are out of context for the rest of us."[11] Under his guidance, the company's assets had grown from $27 million in 1980 to $4.6 billion in 1990. In 1989, Craig McCaw, who owned 9.8% of the company, earned almost $54 million, including a salary and bonus of $289,000 plus $53.6 million from the exercise of stock options on 1.5 million shares awarded to him in 1983 and 1986.

Marketing

McCaw stated that it aimed to sell high-quality cellular phone service, including add-ons such as voice mail and call waiting, at a premium price. To boost the number of calls on the network, the company planned also to sell information services (which the regional Bell companies were prohibited from selling). Services under consideration included stock quotes and local weather and traffic reports.

Craig McCaw was known as a meticulous manager with a fetish for quality. Industry

[9]*New York Times*, May 6, 1990, p. D6.
[10]*New York Times*, May 6, 1990, p. D6.
[11]Brian J. McCauley, former McCaw vice president, quoted in *Business Week*, December 5, 1988, p. 140.

observers said it was not unusual for him to fly his own Lear jet into a city, rent a car, and test the local cellular system. After one such test (in 1987), he decided that McCaw's marketing was too aggressive, because the company's billing, accounting, and transmission systems were not growing as fast as the subscriber base. Credit policies were tightened, commissions were slashed, advertising was cut, rates were raised, and a number of new managers were hired. As a result of disagreements about these decisions, the executive vice president, the Western Operations vice president, and the head of National Accounts left the company.

McCaw had a 750-person direct sales force targeting national accounts, which it expected to provide more than a third of company revenues within ten years. In 1990, major national accounts included IBM, with more than 1,000 cellular phones (mostly for sales people), and Consolidated Freightways, with 800 phones. McCaw also had a partnership with AT&T to provide national cellular service as part of AT&T's multibillion-dollar contract to rebuild the federal government's telecommunications network. In 1990, 12% of McCaw's sales were to companies with more than 1,000 employees, up from 2% in 1988.

Transmission Systems

McCaw sought to develop regional clusters of cellular operations, each built around a core metropolitan area. In Florida, McCaw served the contiguous Miami, West Palm Beach, and Fort Pierce markets; in Colorado, it served the contiguous markets of Denver, Colorado Springs, Fort Collins, Greeley, and Pueblo; in the Pacific Northwest, it served Seattle, Tacoma, and Portland.

One observer claimed McCaw had efficient systems in the Northwest, Florida, and northern California, based on the activity level of its engineers and the absence of overcapacity problems. The LIN systems were large enough to cover their marketing and use regions, but observers were not sure if the systems were efficient. In other areas, McCaw's holdings were dispersed. John E. DeFeo, president of rival U.S. West New Vector Group, explained, "This business is about

local traveling areas, and McCaw is spread out all over God's green earth."[12] In 1990, including the LIN systems, 65% of McCaw's POPs were in the 30 biggest markets.

Craig McCaw said, "Automatic, effortless call delivery anywhere in North America has long been among our most important strategic objectives."[13] To do this, McCaw needed compatible switches throughout the continent. The company pursued control of licenses in many major metropolitan areas throughout the United States and sought to convince many rural service providers to join the Cellular One network, of which McCaw was a part. To induce rural operators to join and purchase compatible switches, McCaw offered marketing and technical support and, in some instances, financial support (or equity investment). In return, it planned to charge a fee on calls made on those systems to adjoining systems.

In 1990, the LIN system in the Northeast used Motorola switches, the Pacific Northwest system used AT&T switches, the California and Florida systems used switches supplied by a joint venture of Ericsson and General Electric, and still other areas used switches supplied by Northern Telecom Ltd. McCaw estimated that replacing the switches in the company's major markets with new ones would cost about $250 million over a period of five years. The cost would not include modernizing the systems in the central United States; they would need to have upgraded software to enable them to communicate with the new switches in other parts of the system. Some industry analysts estimated that capital expenditures would cost closer to $800 million over the next several years.

Extensions of Cellular Service

McCaw applied for FCC authorization in 1990 to test new wireless technologies in Orlando, Florida, and Seattle, Washington. The planned tests included two types of cordless telephone equipment for communications in offices, shopping malls, or other localized areas. McCaw said

[12]*Business Week*, December 5, 1988, p. 151.
[13]John J. Keller, quoted in *The Wall Street Journal*, October 4, 1990, p. B1.

it would work with vendors to develop prototype equipment that would enable customers to use a single handset to make or receive calls employing one or more technologies, with the goal of potentially linking these localized systems to McCaw's network.

Also in 1990, McCaw formed a partnership with Hughes Network Systems to construct and operate in-flight cellular phone and data services on commercial airlines. Unlike users of GTE Airfone, customers would be able to receive calls as well as make them. Alaskan and Northwest Airlines had agreed to carry the service, and agreements with other airlines were under negotiation.

Finance

In 1981, McCaw formed a partnership with the cash-rich publisher of the Boston Globe, Affiliated Publications Inc. At the time, McCaw was anxious to expand its cable business, and Affiliated's chairman wanted to diversify into more venturesome businesses. During the 1980s, the publisher invested almost $1 billion in McCaw, of which it owned 43%. Although Affiliated held several seats on the board, it did not try to set directions for McCaw. "One of the keys to his success has been our willingness to let him run the show," an Affiliated executive explained.[14] Affiliated's strong balance sheet provided credibility for McCaw with bankers and institutional investors. Affiliated spun off its McCaw holdings in May 1989.

In 1987, McCaw sold its cable business for $755 million to help fund its cellular system acquisitions. The same year, Drexel Burnham Lambert Inc. helped take McCaw public, offering 13,050,000 Class A common shares (12% of outstanding shares) for $21.75 each. The same year, McCaw raised $600 million with Triple C-rated bonds. McCaw's monthly closing stock price moved from $16.13 in December 1987 to a high of $43.75 in May 1989. It then dropped to $11.50 by October 1990. In 1990, Craig McCaw and his three brothers owned 32% of the company and 88% of the voting stock.

As McCaw moved into the 1990s, it faced

[14]Arthur Kingsbury, quoted in *The Wall Street Journal*, July 31, 1987, p. 6.

EXHIBIT 10-5 McCaw Cellular Communications Income Statement ($ thousands) and Financial Ratios

	1989	1988	1987	1986	1985	1984
Income Statement						
Net Sales	504,138	310,826	196,420	68,665	7,372	297
Cost of Goods	169,290	130,967	111,815	31,818	7,657	254
Gross Profit	334,848	179,859	84,605	36,847	−285	43
SG&A	282,709	186,844	145,406	44,525	7,784	229
Income Before Depreciation	52,139	−6,985	−60,801	−7,678	−8,069	-186
Depreciation and Amortization	202,876	156,358	80,804	16,912	749	4
Nonoperating Income[a]	101,709	53,054	108,874	12,385	−479	241
Interest Expense	238,740	199,137	108,055	29,566	3,582	N/A
Income Before Tax	−287,768	−309,426	−140,786	−41,771	−12,879	51
Provision for Income Tax	760	−12,431	−52,081	N/A	N/A	N/A
Net Income Before Extraordinary Items	−288,528	−296,995	−88,705	−41,771	−32,879	51
Extraordinary Items	N/A	N/A	138,383	N/A	N/A	N/A
Net Income	−288,528	−296,995	49,678	−41,771	−12,879	51
Financial Ratios						
LT Debt to Equity	1.75	−164.6	3.55	−8.90	11.16	N/A
Total Assets to Equity	3.03	−186.6	5.30	−9.91	36.63	N/A
Interest Coverage	−0.21	−0.55	−0.30	−0.41	−2.6	N/A
Gross Margin %	66.40	57.9	43.1	53.7	−3.9	14.5
ROS %	−57.20	−95.6	25.3	−60.8	−174.0	17.2
ROE %	−28.70	N/A	16.8	N/A	−525.0	N/A
ROA %	−9.50	−14.3	3.2	−6.6	−14.3	N/A

[a]Includes gains on sales of assets, interest income, and increases in equity of unconsolidated interests.

EXHIBIT 10-6 McCaw Cellular Communications Balance Sheet ($ thousands)

	1989	1988[a]	1987	1986[a]	1985
Assets					
Cash and Marketable Securities	897,653	505,917	424,867	42,663	1,625
Other Current Assets	98,020	55,067	260,010	142,814	4,541
Total Current Assets	995,673	560,984	684,877	185,477	6,166
Net Property Plant and Equipment	630,264	491,851	292,902	121,765	22,497
Investment and Advance Payments	358,326	73,344	84,980	35,663	21,297
Intangibles	928,603	920,814	491,682	208,850	37,935
Other Noncurrent Assets	128,478	28,760	14,228	79,950	1,914
Total Assets	3,041,344	2,075,753	1,568,669	631,705	89,809
Liabilities					
Total Current Liabilities	222,256	193,571	154,353	215,810	59,480
Long-Term Debt	1,738,896	1,821,663	1,032,760	402,781	27,351
Other Long-Term Liabilities	47,780	32,641	26,000	12,750	N/A
Total Liabilities	2,008,632	2,047,875	1,213,113	631,341	86,831
Minority Interest	28,743	38,998	59,724	64,123	526
Shareholders' Equity	1,003,969	−11,120	295,832	−63,759	2,452
Total Liabilities and Shareholders' Equity	3,041,344	2,075,753	1,568,669	631,705	89,809

[a]Restated as required by SEC.

considerable financial uncertainty. Stock analysts were unwilling to make explicit projections of sources and uses of funds due to the high level of uncertainty surrounding McCaw Communications and the cellular communications industry. **Exhibits 10–5** and **10–6** show McCaw's income statement and balance sheet from 1985 to 1989. **Exhibit 10–7** gives projections of revenues, net income, and funding needs from 1900 to 2000.

On the sources side, McCaw had a number of alternatives. It had a $1.6 billion line of credit,

and further bank financing was a possibility. It could elect to sell assets. In 1990, for example, the company raised $1.2 billion on a gain from the sale of 6.1 million POPs in Tennessee, Kentucky, and Alabama to Contel Cellular. McCaw could raise funds also through a public offering or private placement. It had raised $1.37 billion in 1990 from the sale of 20% of the company to British Telecommunications PLC, which was limited by law to owning not more than 20% of any U.S. cellular carrier.

EXHIBIT 10-7 Projected Financial Results for McCaw Communications, Inc. Pro Forma 1990–2000 ($ thousands)

	1990	1991	1992	1993	1994	1995
Total revenues	555,498	771,972	1,013,874	1,279,156	1,563,293	1,860,108
Net income	(469,783)	(462,307)	(346,731)	(137,365)	66,839	299,373
Available funds	(1,872,972)	(187,909)	(126,705)	23,636	259,930	544,969

	1996	1997	1998	1999	2000
Total revenues	2,164,125	2,470,530	2,775,138	3,074,356	3,366,985
Net income	582,373	569,967	759,766	912,835	1,091,012
Available funds	889,065	915,027	1,121,641	1,290,793	1,482,265

Notes: 1. Pro forma performance results are for McCaw Communications on a stand-alone basis.
      2. Effects of the LIN acquisition are not shown here.
      3. Ceilings for the LIN and warrants purchase obligations are $5 billion in 1995 and $81 million in 1997, respectively.

Source: Donaldson, Lufkin & Jenrette, Inc.

On the uses side, McCaw was committed to acquiring all outstanding LIN stock by 1995 or selling its stake in LIN; one balloon payment in 1995 was expected to cost $5 billion, but the company could begin acquiring additional stock before 1995. Between 1991 and 1997, it had to repurchase any warrants still outstanding that it had issued for one of its previous acquisitions; this obligation could cost up to $81 million. The firm also had debt service projected to total $2.4 billion between 1990 and 1995. And, McCaw faced the uncertain expenses of updating its switches and creating a compatible national network.

PART THREE

Globalization and Government

11. Motorola and Japan (A)

Japanese industry promotion policies have evolved in form over the last 30 years. They remain effective in semiconductors, telecommunications, and computers. In other words, the Japanese government is continuing to target as a national priority all of Motorola's major businesses.

MOTOROLA EXECUTIVE

In late 1981, Motorola executives held a series of meeting at their headquarters in Schaumburg, Illinois to hammer out a response to intensifying Japanese competition. To date, all of Motorola's efforts to gain significant sales of semiconductors and mobile telecommunication products in Japan had been disappointing. Moreover, Motorola's management had evidence that some Japanese manufacturers were dumping telecommunication products in the American market. Bob Galvin, Motorola's Chairman and CEO, knew that something had to be done, but what?

Business Lines

Motorola in 1981 was balanced on an integrated technology triad of semiconductors, communications, and computers. Motorola's products included two-way radios, pagers, cellular telephones and other electronic communications systems, semiconductors, defense and aerospace electronics, automotive and industrial electronic equipment, and data communications and information processing hardware and software. In 1981 the company registered sales of $3.5 billion (**Exhibit 11-1**). Galvin was pleased with the structure of the company, noting that "We like to perform all the functions of our business under our own aegis. We control our own designs, our own processing and manufacturing and our own distribution and marketing, which includes service and sales. If we

Professor David B. Yoffie and Research Associate John J. Coleman prepared this case as the basis for class discussion rather than to illustrate either effective or ineffective handling of an administrative situation.

EXHIBIT 11-1 1977-1981 ($ millions)

	1981	1980	1979	1978	1977
Net sales	$3,336	$3,086	$2,700	$2,212	$1,850
Cost of sales	2,028	1,545	1,625	1,340	1,140
SG&A expenses	855	773	672	549	426
Depreciation	173	145	111	83	73
Net interest expence	28	37	22	19	19
Income tax	77	88	105	95	85
Net earnings	175	186	154	125	107
R&D expenditures	229	200	167	133	NA
Semiconductor sales	1,278	1,209	991	718	582
Semiconductor operating profit	131	187	170	107	80
Semiconductor capital expenditure	184	177	159	72	53
Communications sales	1,422	1,257	1,118	965	823
Communications operating profit	162	144	140	111	131
Communications capital expenditure	88	78	57	46	55
International sales	1,213	1,181	1,056	816	598
International operating profit	58	76	65	50	41
Total assets	2,399	2,112	1,903	1,657	1,420
Working capital	773	743	709	620	567
Long-term debt	352	336	296	198	200
Stockholder equity	1,288	1,152	1,004	886	788
Current ratio	2.25	2.42	2.35	2.20	2.47
Return on equity (%)	14.3	17.3	16.3	15.0	14.3
Return on sales (%)	5.3	6.0	5.7	5.7	5.8
Year-end employment (000)	76	72	75	68	68

Source: Annual and 10-K reports

were heavily in consumer products we would be at the mercy of retailers."[1]

Motorola had long been considered a powerhouse in land-mobile communications, and in 1980 it was one of the largest suppliers of two-way radios and assorted mobile electronic communications equipment in the world, with market share estimates of 65–75%. Motorola, General Electric (GE), and E.F. Johnson controlled about 85% of the U.S. two-way radio market, with the remainder going to very large, diversified Japanese firms such as NEC, Matsushita, and Fujitsu. In some categories, such as communications gear for police departments, Motorola accounted for approximately 90% of the total U.S. market. The company expected major growth to come from cellular radio. Bill Weisz, the vice chairman and chief operating officer, estimated that by 1983 Motorola would spend about $150 million in developing the technology, and he expected it to bring in $1 billion worth of revenues before 1990.

About half of this total would come from equipment for major stations that would transmit the radio signals and half from the smaller terminals that individuals would use to communicate with one another.

The primary customers for Motorola's communications products included public safety agencies, utilities, transportation companies such as taxicab operators, institutions such as schools and hospitals. Product development pressures in communications were high and increasingly stressed the use of advanced electronic components. Competitive factors facing communications firms included price, product performance and quality, and quality and availability of service and systems engineering. Because the equipment configurations demanded by its customers were diverse, Motorola found that none of these factors was dominant overall.

Motorola's product sales and leasing took a number of forms: mostly through a company distribution force, but also through independent distributors and commission agents, and through

[1] *International Management*, March 1978, p. 113.

Motorola and Japan (A)

licensing of independent companies. One important variable affecting the firm's telecommunications operation was government regulation. In the United States, the Federal Communications Commission's allocation of frequencies could significantly affect the two-way radio business, particularly in congested urban areas.

The semiconductor industry was a rapidly growing, highly fragmented industry. Motorola faced intense competition from domestic firms, which were largely small (under $1 billion sales) merchants,[2] and larger, vertically integrated Japanese firms. Motorola's semiconductors were used in a variety of products, including mass-market video and audio receivers, computers, automotive controls, industrial automation systems, and defense equipment. Like most companies in the industry, Motorola's sales were heavily oriented toward original equipment manufacturers and were typically channeled through both in-house distribution forces and independent distributors. Chips were supplied to other operating units within the company, a common practice at other diversified companies. Although its semiconductor sales tended to be sharply cyclical, Motorola had one of the most diversified semiconductor product lines in the industry. Along side of its advanced line of microprocessors and memory products, almost one-third of Motorola's semiconductor sales consisted of relatively stable discrete components.

Restructuring and Organization

Motorola's early history strongly emphasized consumer products. Founded as the Galvin Manufacturing Corporation in 1928 by Paul V. Galvin, two years later the firm introduced the first commercially manufactured car radio under the brand name Motorola (Motor + Victrola = Motorola), and subsequently (in 1947) adopted that name for the corporation. Over the next 40 years the company was involved in several consumer lines (as well as its communications and semiconductor businesses), including car and home radios and televisions. But starting in the early 1970s the company's focus shifted to high-technology industrial electronics, including advanced mobile telecommunications (e.g., cellular phones) and advanced semiconductors (e.g., microprocessors).

Motorola's leap from the consumer electronics field was unusual. As one business analyst noted, "What must be appreciated is that Galvin did this proactively. There was no crisis at Motorola; the company and the industry appeared to be in good shape. Galvin did something highly unusual for an American executive—he anticipated the need for future change even though the company was not in any imminent trouble."[3] Galvin decided, in effect, to "bet the company" and make Motorola number 1 in semiconductors and retain the top spot in two-way communications over the next ten years. The overhaul at Motorola involved putting in place a mix of high-growth businesses, decentralizing the company allowing each division substantial autonomy while building up internal controls, establishing a long-term oriented New Enterprises operation, introducing new personnel programs, and committing employees to very high quality—the formal goal was zero defects.

The company was run by the triumvirate of Galvin, Weisz, and John Mitchell, the President and Chief Operating Officer. These three men retained independent spheres of authority with responsibility to make any decision that had to be made in the corporation. If conflicts reached a stalemate, Galvin tipped the scales one way or the other. But the company had a democratic flair and had traditionally been a first-name organization. New employees were told to call the CEO "Bob." Galvin noted that "my style is a participative one. I relegate a good deal of the operation today to others who are clearly more expert in certain details of operation than I am and put my emphasis on what I call leading the institution."

[2]Several large U.S. companies were involved in the manufacture of semiconductors exclusively for internal use, including GE, GTE, Rockwell, Western Electric, and IBM. These so-called "captive" producers posed no direct competitive threat to Motorola's semiconductor business lines.

[3]James O'Toole, *Vanguard Management: Redesigning the Corporate Future* (Garden City, N.Y.: Doubleday & Co., 1985), p. 91.

Evolution of Motorola in Japan

In the 1950s President Eisenhower advised American business to increase its business dealings with Japan. Galvin took Eisenhower's suggestions seriously and encouraged Motorola to purchase electronic components from Japan and help Japanese companies set standards and improve quality in consumer electronic businesses such as car radios, home radios, and televisions. But things had changed drastically by the late 1970s. Motorola officials had witnessed strong Japanese inroads in the electronic components, portable radio, stereo system, car radio, brand name television, and citizens' band radio industries. "We can see the writing on the wall," one said, and "we know that the firm's survival will depend on how we confront the Japanese challenge. Japan has the second largest market in the world for our products [semiconductors and telecommunications] and some of the biggest and best competitors." Yet Motorola had run into one road block after another in Japan in the 1970s. Each division had attempted for years to sell into the Japanese market, but thus far they had little success.

TELECOMMUNICATIONS By the end of the 1970s, changes in U.S. regulatory policies ended the prohibition against plugging non-AT&T equipment into the U.S. telecommunications system. This shift in policy led to increasing inroads by foreign firms into the U.S. telecommunications market at a time when foreign countries retained strict clamps on their telecommunications sectors. To redress the growing trade imbalance in telecommunications equipment, the U.S. government negotiated a bilateral agreement with Japan in December 1980. The basic point of the agreement was that NTT, Japan's state-owned telecommunications monopoly, would "for each proposed procurement, invite applications from the maximum number of domestic and foreign suppliers consistent with the efficient operation of the procurement system." The agreement stated that foreign firms responding to requests for proposals (RFPs) would "be treated in a manner no less favorable than those domestic [firms] responding to

the NTT-issued RFPs."[4] NTT was also obligated to supply complete information on both the product and the procurement process in the RFP and in supplemental documentation. A bilateral dispute settlement mechanism was set up to enforce the agreement, and the United States agreed not to bring any disputes to an international forum.

Galvin decided in 1979 that Motorola had to do all it could to enter the Japanese pager market—a market thought to be growing by as much as 10% a year. Before the bilateral agreement was penned, Motorola had made inquiries to NTT. Motorola had 50% of the worldwide market for pagers, so company officials were certain they had the highest volume and probably the lowest cost in the world. Galvin also recognized that telecommunications systems were part of the lifeblood of advanced industrial countries, but pagers were a modest technology which NTT could not object to on grounds of national security.

Initially, Motorola's telecom group was unable to schedule an appointment to see the people at NTT and had to ask the United States Trade Representative to send cables just to get the appointment. The first meeting was not fruitful and convinced people at Motorola that they were going to need additional assistance from the American government. "We had no idea what the specifications were, how to make a proposal, or how to sell a product to NTT, and NTT wouldn't tell us," Motorola's vice president of communications reported. Even after the bilateral agreement was signed, he reported, things did not get any easier:

> A senior NTT executive told us we were wasting our time, because the United States wouldn't be satisfied with any NTT agreement with Motorola. He said that such a deal wouldn't even fit into the bilateral agreement. Even after [Secretary of State] Cyrus Vance personally confirmed that a pager deal would fall within the bilateral, NTT still hedged. We were told the specifications were considered proprietary and, in fact, they weren't even written down, they were just worked out with the manufac-

[4]Cited in Stefanie Ann Lenway, *The Politics of U.S. International Trade: Protection, Expansion, and Escape* (Boston: Pitman Publishing, 1985), p. 188.

turers. If we wanted to get a bid we'd have to work with NTT for several years, talk with them, get to know the specifications, and relay all specific questions to them. But it's a bit difficult to ask specific questions when you're starting from ground zero.

When the specifications were eventually released, company officials soon discovered that NTT emphasized product design as well as product performance. At the time, Japanese pagers were built to last 20 years, while Motorola's were built to last five. NTT also expected designs to be followed explicitly, regardless of whether there were alternative ways to do the same thing. When Motorola originally proposed to change the electrical current used from the battery in pagers, NTT refused. After prolonged negotiation, this change was eventually allowed. Motorola ran into another problem because it used a microprocessor that recirculated a timing mechanism every 11 times the pager performed a certain task rather than every 10 as listed in the specifications. NTT considered the request to allow such an exemption a very poor reflection on Motorola and was firm in its opposition despite the negligible influence the change would have on the pager's performance.

The communications division ultimately received a contract for $9 million worth of pagers in late 1981, 18 months after the first contact. The initial NTT contract was for 50–60,000 units. After providing NTT with an acceptable product, Motorola still had to undergo long negotiations on price and share. Historically, NTT reserved 60% of the market for NEC and Matsushita, the prime suppliers. Four other firms were to divide up the remaining 40%.

Motorola had experienced other problems in entering the telecommunications market. Middle managers didn't want to "buy American" because they looked to retire to the big "family firms" like NEC, Fujitsu, Oki, and Hitachi. Moreover, NTT made no multiyear purchases. This was important because Japanese companies would enter a nominal bid to design a particular product, being reasonably certain that if they got that one contract from NTT they would get subsequent business. But a U.S. firm had neither an assurance that there would be follow-up work nor a commitment on future prices if they got a design contract. Companies had to take NTT on faith.

Motorola was willing to take the risk because of its commitment to selling to NTT. For example, Motorola set up a separate pager production line for selling to NTT at a significant cost. (Japanese specifications for telecommunications products frequently differed from worldwide standards.) Indeed Motorola expected it would take several years to show a profit with the pagers.

The company also had a long history of difficulties with the Ministry of Post and Telecommunications (MPT), which disallowed some of the services offered in other countries around the world. Japanese companies on MPT committees were not interested in rocking the boat by pushing for changes in the frequency allocation. Another problem was that standards tended to be set by MPT and a committee of Motorola's competitors, and MPT wouldn't allow competition on standards. This process gave Motorola's competitors a year's edge in getting from design to manufacturing.

Motorola had found it extremely difficult to crack other markets. While there were few discriminatory barriers, a major problem was that advanced products were regulated out of the market. This included products such as alphanumeric display pagers, digital voice privacy radios, "intrinsically safe" portable radios, and portable computer terminals with built-in modems. Several of these products had higher frequencies than the frequencies allowed in Japan. In product areas that were permitted, Motorola salespeople also found that strong social pressure and pressure from Japanese companies was placed on organizations considering foreign goods.[5] Motorola had achieved a very substantial share of the U.S. market in police two-way radios, but its police radios were invisible in Japan, despite extensive sales efforts.

SEMICONDUCTORS Disputes in semiconductors dated back to the mid-1970s, starting with the founding in the United States of the Semiconductor Industry Association (SIA) in 1977. Articles such as "The Japanese Spies in Silicon Valley" charged the Japanese with using unethical means

---

[5]The owner of a trucking company told Motorola salespeople that "we would not buy a pager unless [Prime Minister] Nakasone himself called me and said it was worthwhile."

to gather intelligence on U.S. production methods and set a bitter tone early on.[6] Later, American producers complained that while the U.S. share of the Japanese market had remained mired at about 10% for over a decade, the Japanese had managed to increase their share of the American market steadily in a few years, rising to over 12% of the noncaptive U.S. market in 1981.

One major difference between Japanese and U.S. firms was that Japanese semiconductor manufacturers tended to be very large and diversified while their U.S. counterparts were more likely to be specialized semiconductor companies. In fact, the Japanese firms challenging Motorola in semiconductors were for the most part the same firms challenging it in telecommunications. In semiconductors, however, firms such as NEC, Matsushita, Fujitsu, and Hitachi were major customers of Motorola as well as major competitors (**Exhibit 11–2**).

SEMICONDUCTOR MANUFACTURING   Motorola decided in 1979 to buy a Japanese company as a way to advance its position in the Japanese semiconductor market. Local manufacturing in semiconductors would serve two purposes: it would provide local support for local problems and it would help promote an image that Motorola's products were Japanese products. According to Mitchell, the further down the technology curve in the semiconductor industry the more important it was that manufacturing be done in a local market. Customers were increasingly demanding that there be local manufacturing in order to support their local production operations. TI, the foreign market-share leader in Japan and Motorola's major U.S. challenger in semiconductor components other than microprocessors, had four Japanese factories and publicly expressed satisfaction with its access to Japanese customers (**Exhibit 11–3**).[7]

Galvin, Weisz, and Mitchell shared a general preference for a wholly owned strategy because the company had bad experiences with joint ventures in earlier years in a number of countries. In 1980, Motorola's head of strategic planning

[6]*Fortune*, 27 February 1978

[7]TI invested in Japan before all other American manufacturers (1968). However, TI paid a high price for its rights to produce locally. The Japanese government demanded, and TI agreed to provide, licenses to all Japanese companies for some of its leading edge technology.

identified Toko as a potential company in which Motorola might get involved. Toko had a semiconductor subsidiary (Aizu—Toko) involved in MOS wafer processing but didn't have the financial resources to fund these operations. A joint venture agreement was reached in November 1980 that included buyout options for both partners. Motorola was responsible for design and manufacturing, the Japanese were responsible for people matters, and both firms were to share sales and finance responsibility. However, by the end of 1981, it was already becoming clear that Toko was not going to be able to contribute their 50% of the capital spending.

Motorola's vulnerability to Japanese competition was becoming most apparent in D-RAMs in 1981. While Japan's share of global semiconductor sales rose from 20% in 1975 to 30% in 1981, in 64K D-RAMs the Japanese had 70% world market share.

The Problem in the U.S. Market

Motorola executives were concerned about the effects of Japanese industry-promotion policies on competition in the United States. The Japanese policies that most concerned Motorola were identified by Weisz as a "set of differences, the sum of which gives them a major competitive advantage that can't be matched by U.S. companies." Weisz considered differences in three categories to be especially crucial: government-supported activities; the Japanese financial system and environment; and the actions of the industrial companies themselves (see **Exhibits 11–5** and **11–6**). Weisz noted that Japanese firms' willingness to use marginal-cost pricing and cross-subsidies to push those products was becoming particularly problematic in 1981. Motorola had collected evidence that Japanese firms were dumping in the United States. A year earlier, Motorola supported the successful dumping suits filed by E.F. Johnson in CB radios and in mid-1981, it was filing its own case on copyright and patent infringements against Japanese pagers. Motorola executives also believed that two Japanese firms were now dumping pagers (simple beepers) in the United States. However, the appropriate response was unclear. Japanese price cutting was leading to a rapid deterioration in market share, but at the

EXHIBIT 11-2 Financial Data for Selected Competitors ($ millions)

	1981	1980	1979	1978	1977
NEC[a]					
Net sales	$4,433	$3,637	$3,712	$3,450	$2,396
Net income	93	62	36	35	29
R&D expenditures	214	186	162	108	70
Total assets	4,869	4,176	4,269	4,131	3,032
Long-term debt	798	734	931	949	737
Equity	736	550	453	431	321
International sales	1,338	1,080	943	935	612
Communications sales[b]	1,581	1,367	1,363	1,311	923
Semiconductor sales[c]	1,023	781	627	580	443
Matsushita					
Net sales	$14,563	$12,304	$10,827	$10,296	$7,280
Net income	661	526	451	428	291
R&D expenditures	538	428	389	369	257
Total assets	12,432	10,458	9,801	9,073	6,370
Long-term debt	150	248	312	96	166
Equity	5,381	4,609	4,224	3,973	2,734
International sales	6,662	4,911	2,782	2,781	1,982
Communications sales	1,813	743	636	563	374
Semiconductor sales[d]	1,321	522	433	398	284
Fujitsu					
Net sales	$2,931	$2,114	$2,021	$1,859	$1,225
Net income	114	66	49	39	35
R&D expenditures	239	208	212	212	NA
Total assets	2,804	2,115	2,027	1,931	1,444
Long-term debt	303	507	498	507	397
Equity	855	542	521	467	349
International sales	443	335	296	228	140
Communications sales[e]	556	495	501	444	285
Semiconductor sales[f]	426	240	131	97	45
General Electric					
Net sales	$27,240	$24,959	$22,461	$19,754	$17,909
Net income	1,652	1,514	1,409	1,230	1,088
R&D expenditures	1,690	1,600	1,440	1,270	1,156
Total assets	20,942	18,511	16,645	15,036	13,697
Long-term debt	1,059	1,000	947	994	1,284
Equity	9,128	8,200	7,362	6,587	5,943
International sales	10,190	9,597	4,997	4,379	3,973
Consumer products[g]	4,202	3,998	5,448	4,865	4,215
Texas Instruments					
Net sales	$4,206	$4,075	$3,224	$2,550	$2,047
Net income	109	212	173	140	117
R&D expenditures	373	344	134	111	96
Total assets	2,311	2,414	1,908	1,494	1,255
Long-term debt	212	212	18	19	30
Equity	1,260	1,165	953	821	724
International sales	1,984	1,498	1,494	1,127	873
Semiconductor sales	1,532	1,899	1,527	1,192	958

EXHIBIT 11-2 (Continued)

	1981	1980	1979	1978	1977
Intel					
Net sales[h]	$789	$855	$663	$401	$283
Net income	27	97	78	44	32
R&D expenditures	116	96	67	41	28
Total assets	872	767	500	357	221
Long-term debt	150	150	0	0	0
Equity	488	433	303	205	149
International sales	191	233	245	141	60

[a]One yen-dollar exchange rate used for each year to translate yen into dollars for all three Japanese companies. May not match exchange rate used to translate yen figures in individual company annual reports.
[b]Telecommunications.
[c]Electron devices.
[d]Lighting equipment, tubes and semiconductors.
[e]Communication, measuring and special equipment.
[f]Telephone exchanges and telephone sets plus radio and carrier transmission equipment.
[g]Includes communications products, excludes major appliances.
[h]All sales from semiconductors.

Source: Annual and 10-K reports

same time, Motorola was still negotiating with NTT over its own pager contract.

Galvin's Dilemma

Motorola had been one of the most successful American firms in mobile telecommunications and semiconductors over the previous two decades. For every previous problem, ranging from the company's consumer radio business to color TVs, Motorola had devised a strategy to remain independent and profitable. But Galvin sensed that this Japanese challenge was different. So he called together his entire top management team, asking "what are the range of strategic options, and how should Motorola respond?"

EXHIBIT 11-3 1980's Top Ten Semiconductor Merchants Worldwide (rank in $ millions)

Company	1980 rank	1975 Rank	1966 Rank
Texas Instruments	1	1	2
Motorola	2	4	3
Philips/Signetics	3	5	4
NEC	4	NA	NA
National	5	3	NA
Toshiba	6	NA	NA
Hitachi	7	NA	NA
Intel	8	5	NA
Fairchild	9	2	1
Siemens	10	NA	NA

Source: Office of the Secretary of Defense, "Report of the Defense Science Board Task Force on Semiconductor Dependency-Action Memorandum," December 31, 1986, p. 51; Electronics, April 2, 1987, p. 60.

EXHIBIT 11-4 History of Motorola in Japan

1960	Tokyo office opened as Motorola's first office in Far East.
1961	Motorola Service Company Ltd. established as Consumer Products Division purchasing office. Automotive Products Division purchasing functions added in following years.
1967	Automotive Products Division/Alps joint venture established to manufacture automotive radios.
1968	Motorola Semiconductors Japan Ltd. established.
1969	Osaka branch sales office opened.
1973	Communications Division's two local representatives added to Motorola Service Company's payroll. Semiconductor Products Division/Alps joint venture established and began construction of N-MOS plant at Morioka.
1974	Consumer Products Division's television business sold to Matsushita.
1975	Motorola/Alps semiconductor joint venture dissolved, Motorola semiconductor production in Japan suspended, and Morioka facility sold to Alps Electric Co. Motorola Communications Japan was established and assumed responsibility for sales operations.
1976	In November the new Motorola Semiconductor Japan started.
1978	CODEX Tokyo office opened in January (Information Systems Group, data-processing hardware). Motorola/Alps auto radio joint venture dissolved in August. Asia/Pacific Design Operations began.
1980	Motorola/Tokyo joint venture established as Aizu-Toko Corporation Inc. for MOS wafer processing capability.

Source: Company documents.

EXHIBIT 11-5 Excerpts from Japan's Public Law No. 84, July 1978

Article 1. Purposes The purposes of this law are to develop specific machinery and information industries by promoting, among other things, improvement of manufacturing technology and rationalization of production thereof, and thus to contribute to the sound development of the national economy and improvement of national standards.

Article 3. Advancement Plan The Competent Minister must set up a plan concerning advancement . . . with respect to the following industries . . . :

(a) those industries manufacturing such Electronic Machines and Tools specified by government order, the manufacturing technology of which has not yet been established in Japan and which especially require the promotion of experiment and research . . . ; (b) those industries manufacturing such Equipment and Tools specified by government order, the industrial production of which is not conducted in Japan or the production quantity of which is extremely small, and which especially require the promotion of the commencement of industrial production or increase of production quantity; (c) those industries manufacturing such Electronic Machines and Tools specified by government order, which especially require the promotion of rationalization of production, such as improvement of performance or quality or reduction of production costs, etc . . .

Matters to be set forth in the Advancement Plan for those industries described in (a) include content of the experimentation and research and the target year of its completion; matters concerning funds necessary for the experimentation and research . . . ; With respect to the industries in (b), such matters which are fundamental for the promotion of the commencement of industrial production or increase of production quantity, including . . . the production quantity for the final target year; the kind and numbers of facilities to be newly established . . . ; With respect to industries in (c), such matters which are fundamental for the promotion of rationalization of production, including target of rationalization, such as target of performance or quality, production costs, etc. for the final target year; kind and number of facilities to be newly established; matters including proper scale of production, introduction of cooperation of the business or specialization of the kinds to be produced; matters concerning funds necessary for rationalization; and other important matters concerning promotion of rationalization.

Article 5. Procurement of Funds The government shall make efforts to procure the necessary funds set forth in the Advancement Plan.

EXHIBIT 11-6 Extract from Bill Weisz Memo, 1981

Specific Actions, Differences by the Japanese—Past and Present

1. Higher tariffs (some recently reduced)
2. Prohibition on almost all 100% non-Japanese ownership acquisition of a Japanese company for many years (some now allowed but culture is very anti)
3. Cartelization of Japanese companies promoted and required (Public Laws #17 and #84)
4. Japanese government support of direct commercial activities
5. Protection of Japanese "infant" industries
6. Joint research by various means
7. Focused country-wide goals and targeted industries for worldwide dominance
8. Low interest loans to industry, many never repaid
9. Rebate of excise tax on exports
10. Japanese companies allowed a deductible "overseas market development reserve"
11. "Old boy" network in government and industry
12. No external pressure on companies for substantive earnings
13. Low profit margins acceptable, 10 to 20% dividend rate on *par* value of stock acceptable
14. High debt to equity leverage
15. Bank and government support of big companies substantially eliminating risk of their failure and providing a continuous effectively guaranteed flow of capital
16. Industrial grouping with interlocking ownership including banks who own about 60% of industrial companies shares
17. Low interest financing on exports
18. Alleged division of customers among Japanese companies
19. Alleged use of incremental pricing/dumping in order to increase penetration of markets and sustain export growth. Examples:

Past

Citizen Band Radio—Reckless price reduction killed the market for all. U.S. ITC action found injury to U.S. industry and raised tariffs, but too late to save companies

TV Dumping—Most Japanese companies found guilty *years* ago and fines levied but none paid to date. The appeal process continues

Current

Semiconductors
    16K RAMS—Price collapse
    64K RAMS—Price collapse on new product just *beginning* its life cycle
Communications
    Radio Paging—35% price reductions overnight

20. Massive continuing increase in certain semiconductor manufacturing capacity even though world over capacity is estimated by independent observers
21. Restricted access to NTT market (recently improving)
22. NTT past favored supplier concept provided closed market that allowed build-up of competence and volume by the suppliers
23. Difficulty of foreign companies to hire, for employment in Japan, experienced Japanese people, and on Japanese college campuses

12. The Semiconductor Industry Association and the Trade Dispute with Japan (A)

Semiconductor firms do well politically because we tell a good story. We have never paid a dividend, we have contributed significantly to the growth of employment, we have desirable jobs and a good mystique. Also, our naivete has been one of our major advantages: We have few lobbyists; the CEOs go directly to Washington. You have to remember that the whole semiconductor industry is small compared to General Motors.

ROBERT N. NOYCE, VICE-CHAIRMAN, INTEL CORPORATION

The U.S. government decided several trade cases in the American semiconductor industry's favor in the first half of 1986, most significantly an unfair trade practices case filed by the Semiconductor Industry Association (SIA) under Section 301 of the Trade Act of 1974. In July 1986, the Japanese and American governments inked an agreement that promised foreign firms (as a group) a doubling of their Japanese market share and elimination of any Japanese dumping into U.S. and third country markets. But now, in March 1987, member firms of the SIA were convinced that the Japanese were violating the agreement. Industry officials had to decide what the SIA and the government should do next.

The decision on an appropriate response would come from the SIA's Public Policy Committee (PPC), headed by George Scalise. Scalise, chief administrative officer of Advanced Micro Devices (AMD) and a 30-year semiconductor industry veteran, played an important role in the SIA's political activities after assuming the PPC chair in 1982. He considered the forging of consensus to be perhaps his most important task as head of the PPC and believed that achieving internal agreement had allowed the SIA to take on controversial issues and move fast and effectively. Yet finding a consensus on whether and how the United States should retaliate against Japan would be no easy task.

John J. Coleman prepared this case under the supervision of Professor David B. Yoffie as the basis for class discussion rather than to illustrate either effective or ineffective handling of an administrative situation.

The Semiconductor Industry Association

Consisting of five members when founded in 1977, the SIA had 48 firms on its membership rolls in 1985 (Exhibit 1). Collectively, these firms produced 95% of the semiconductors fabricated annually in the United States. Although the association's primary objective was to coordinate the political action of the semiconductor industry, the SIA was engaged in a number of other activities as well. These activities included the collection of statistics related to occupational health and safety, the environment, and industry market trends. This latter project, known as the Worldwide Semiconductor Trade Statistics program, assembled and analyzed data submitted voluntarily by most American, European, and Japanese semiconductor companies. The SIA also published several monographs relating to economic aspects of the industry. Politically, the SIA's agenda included trade concerns, export controls, intellectual property rights, capital formation, research and development, and antitrust issues.

Unlike most trade associations, the SIA was not staff-driven. Only six professionals ran the association, two handling government affairs. Instead the SIA relied on the initiative of the people in the individual companies who sat on the various SIA committees. CEOs and high-level executives, whether on the committees or not, played a very important role in defining and promoting industry positions in Washington. The SIA also tried to leverage outside expertise. For instance, Scalise believed that the SIA had a good idea of what the government would and wouldn't do for the industry because of the real-world experience of the SIA's outside legal counsel.

This combination of maximizing company involvement, leveraging outside expertise, and using the SIA staff to coordinate a common front to the government, resulted in a number of successes. Of six goals set in 1983, five clear victories were obtained over the next three years. The SIA won an amendment to the Trade Act of 1974 which made clear that "denial of fair and equitable market access" could be the subject of a trade petition. The SIA also successfully eliminated semiconductor duties in the United States and Japan. Passage of the Semiconductor Chip Protection Act, which offered intellectual property protection to chip designs and encouraged foreign countries to reciprocate, was another achievement. The National Cooperative Research Act eased antitrust restrictions on joint R&D projects. An amendment to the Export Administration Act helped streamline export licensing procedures. Finally, one partial success was the 1986 extension of the R&D tax credit, which would have otherwise been phased out.

The Section 301 Case

Firms in the SIA had thought about what trade actions to adopt for many years before actually filing the 301 case in 1985.[1] The central American charge was that Japan was a protected market. This protection prevented U.S. firms from improving their position in Japan, gave the Japanese the opportunity to dump chips abroad, and altered the industry's pricing structure dramatically. The American firms argued that their share of the Japanese market in no way approximated their overall position in the world semiconductor market (**Exhibits 12–2** and **12–3.**)

Early Activities

From 1979 to 1983, the association informally urged the government to take trade action of some

[1]Section 301 cases considered trade practices deemed to be "unfair:" acts, policies, or practices of a foreign government that violated or denied benefits to the United States under a trade agreement or were considered unjustifiable, unreasonable, or discriminatory and a burden or restriction on U.S. commerce. Unlike the more judicial proceedings used to decide antidumping and countervailing duty cases, Section 301 cases were notable for their political orientation. The flexibility given to both the USTR (who need not investigate a submitted petition) and the president (who could fashion almost any, or no, response to a finding of unfair practices) differed sharply from the more structured procedures for antidumping and countervailing duty cases.

EXHIBIT 12-1 SIA Members, 1985

Merchant Producers	Represented On[a] Board of Directors	Public Policy Comm.	Products Sold[b]	Projected Sales ($ mil)
Advanced Micro Devices	x	(2)	IC	500–1,000
AT&T			Both	N/A
California Devices			IC	10–50
Cherry Semiconductor			IC	10–50
Digital Equipment		x	IC	10–50
General Electric			Both	100–300
General Instrument			Both	100–300
General Semiconductors			D	10–50
GigaBit Logic			IC	<10
Gould AMI	x		IC	100–300
GTE Communication Systems			IC	10–50
Harris	x	(2)	IC	300–500
Intel	x	x	IC	>1000
Int'l Microelectronic Prod.			IC	10–50
International Rectifier		x	D	100–300
ITT			Both	100–300
Linear Technology			IC	10–50
LSI Logic			IC	50–100
Microwave Semiconductor			D	10–50
Monolithic Memories	x		IC	100–300
Mostek	x	x	IC	N/A
Motorola	x	(3)	Both	>1000
National Semiconductor	x	(2)	Both	>1000
NCR			IC	50–100
NEC			IC	500–1000
Precision Monolithics			IC	50–100
Raytheon			Both	N/A
RCA			Both	300–500
Rockwell International	x	(2)	IC	100–300
Siemens Components			Both	10–50
Signetics		x	IC	500–1000
Silicon Systems			IC	50–100
Solid State Scientific			IC	50–100
Sprague Electric			Both	50–100
Telmos			Both	N/A
Texas Instruments	x	x	Both	>1000
Thomson-CSF Components			Both	10–50
Unitrode			Both	100–300
VLSI Technology			IC	50–100
Westinghouse			D	10–50
Xilinx			IC	>10
Zilog			IC	50–100
ZyMOS			IC	10–50

Captive Producers

Burroughs				
Control Data				
Hewlett-Packard	x	(2)		
IBM	x	x		
Northern Telecom				

[a]Numbers represent the number of representatives on the committee. An (x) indicates one representative.

[b]IC = integrated circuits; D = discrete semiconductors.

Source: Semiconductor Industry Association, *1985-86 Yearbook and Directory*.

EXHIBIT 12-2 U.S.-Based Semiconductor Companies' Worldwide Sales ($ billions)

1975	1976	1977	1978	1979	1980	1981	1982	1983	1984	1985	1986
2.6	3.4	3.9	4.8	6.6	8.4	7.8	8.0	9.6	14.0	10.6	10.7
(Pretax Income as Percent of Sales)											
NA	NA	NA	NA	NA	13.4	4.7	−0.1	7.9	15.0	−6.5	−6.0
(Percent Worldwide Market Share—U.S.-based Firms)											
61	57	62	55	60	61	57	57	55	54	50	43
(Percent Worldwide Market Share—Japan-based Firms)											
20	26	25	29	27	28	30	33	36	37	40	45

Source: World Semiconductor Statistics.

sort against Japan. At the same time, however, the SIA was internally divided over the exact tactics and demands to employ. A 1979 International Trade Commission probe of the U.S.'s semiconductor position in Japan and Europe, which was encouraged by the U.S. industry, declared that the United States would maintain its lead in semiconductors despite targeting and trade barriers. In 1982, Motorola asked the government to conduct an informal study of Japanese pricing policies in 64K DRAMs, with a view to possible antidumping action. The SIA was split on whether to participate in a 64K DRAM dumping case, with

Motorola and IBM the primary proponents of the pro and con views, respectively. Ultimately, the SIA did not approve any particular plan to combat Japanese marketing practices in 64K DRAMs.

The idea of a 301 suit was first discussed in 1982. When the possibility of a 301 action was mentioned to United States Trade Representative (USTR) Bill Brock in 1982, he advised against it, suggesting that the case did not seem strong. Instead, Brock pursued a route of negotiations by pressing for the formation of a U.S.-Japan High Technology Working Group (HTWG). The HTWG agreement reached in 1983

EXHIBIT 12–3 U.S. Share of Japanese Market Versus Japanese Share of U.S. Market

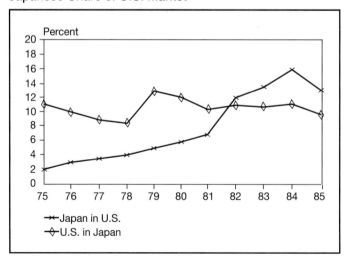

Source: Adapted from Dataquest, August 1987.

called on the Japanese government to promote actively the purchase of U.S. semiconductors.

For the first half of 1984, the HTWG agreement seemed to work. American sales in Japan increased faster than the overall increase in the Japanese market, pushing the U.S. market share over 12%. The U.S. share of the Japanese market was 10.1% and 10.8% in 1982 and 1983, respectively. But this increase was at least partly due to the shortage of chips in Japan during the unprecedented boom of 1983–84. By late 1984 worldwide demand for semiconductors was decreasing. The U.S. share in Japan for 1984 finished at 11.4%, and in 1985 it returned to its pre-HTWG rate of about 10%. The severity of the market decline made the lack of penetration of Japan even more costly. Semiconductor sales dropped 20% in the world market in 1985, with a 30% drop in the United States. At this point, according to the SIA's legal counsel, "the decision to file a 301 case was largely a tactical decision in response to the violations of the HTWG Agreement. Firms had no patience for any further negotiations."

Deciding to File a Section 301 Case

George Scalise thought a 301 case would validate the SIA's claims about the Japanese market, show that it was willing to commit real resources to prove its point, and establish a way to deal with similar issues in the future. From January to June 1985 Scalise sought to build a consensus within the SIA for a 301 petition. The first step was estimating the costs of a case as accurately as possible, because the SIA was resource-constrained and any 301 action was going to be paid by a special assessment on SIA members. Another important step was getting the support of major semiconductor consumers within the association. Scalise noted that companies such as IBM, Hewlett-Packard, and Digital Equipment Corporation (DEC) were important enough within the SIA that they could have vetoed a decision to move forward. Ultimately, "these companies passed the word that 'we won't stand in the way.'"

The SIA also had to work out a common position among firms with different inclinations to-

ward political involvement and different economic interests. Intel, AMD, Motorola, DEC, Rockwell International, and Harris were among the firms most active politically. On the other extreme was Texas Instruments (TI), which had declined to even join the association until 1984.[2] While firms such as IBM wanted to move cautiously, a few, including Motorola, were much more aggressive. By the time the semiconductor boom of 1984 had turned into the bust of 1985, many firms within the SIA had moved closer to Motorola's position.

Economic factors differentiated the firms as well. Merchant firms had proposed embargoes on certain products such as EPROMs, and the imposition of high tariffs and fines. Semiconductor customers within the SIA, including IBM and DEC, opposed any embargo. TI, a major customer and producer, opposed the imposition of any tariffs or quotas. The SIA ultimately reached a consensus that asked for: (1) an increase in the U.S. firms' market share in Japan somewhat more commensurate with their worldwide performance; and (2) a monitoring procedure that would ensure that Japanese chips were not being dumped in the United States or in third countries.

Scalise also tried to build consensus for the case outside the SIA. One important endorsement came from the American Electronics Association (AEA). The effort to gain AEA support highlighted some of the concerns customers had about the 301 case. Customers in the AEA noted that: (1) less market share did not necessarily mean discrimination; (2) there might be competition in some semiconductors but not others; (3) any kind of required market percentages could not be enforced; and (4) U.S. semiconductor firms were perhaps not as vigorous as they needed to be in the Japanese market. "But there was absolute agreement that there was lack of fair access," an AEA official noted, "and most of our members felt that something should be done to send the Japanese a message." The AEA ultimately wrote a letter to the USTR supporting the SIA's objectives in the 301 case.

The SIA submitted its 301 petition in June 1985, organizing its evidence around four central themes: Japanese market barriers, the structure of the Japanese market, Japanese government

[2]TI subsequently became quite active in the 301 case.

policies, and the promotion of a positive environment for dumping. Speaking specifically about market share, one of the key SIA players in Washington described the industry's position this way: "Despite changes in the dollar/yen ratio, despite changes in tariffs, despite new product introductions by American firms, there was at no point a change in market share over a ten-year period between the United States and Japan" (**Exhibit 12–4**). The association stressed that the U.S.'s relative position in almost all product areas was trending downward. The vaunted job-creating ability of high-tech industries was also portrayed as vulnerable: 65,000 U.S.-based chip company positions were lost worldwide by the end of 1985.

Political Strategy and Tactics

According to Scalise, the SIA's 301 case had two overriding strategic goals. First, the SIA wanted to build the broadest case possible in order to enhance its bargaining position. Second, the chip firms wanted to ensure that the case did not disadvantage any of their customers in any of their markets. "If the customers were hurt," Scalise noted, "no one would win."

Within these broad strategic goals, the SIA employed several political tactics. The SIA decided to focus considerable energies on the Congress, much in contrast to the track followed by the Japanese industry's representatives in Washington; the Japanese industry focused its attention and energy almost exclusively on the executive branch. Because U.S. trade deficits with Japan (and overall) were at historical peaks, interest in trade issues on Capitol Hill was growing. New and tougher trade bills were introduced almost weekly, and some political observers suggested that if one of these bills were to pass, a presidential veto stood a strong chance of being overridden.

To establish a base in Congress, the SIA formed the Congressional Support Group, a group of sympathetic legislators consisting of ten Representatives, ten Senators, ten Republicans, and ten Democrats. The SIA wanted to use this group to "energize" the Executive branch by sending letters and making phone calls. All twenty of the group signed a letter to Brock's successor as USTR, Clayton Yeutter, requesting that his office

become more involved in the semiconductor case. Eventually, five of the group met with Yeutter. This group of legislators was often needed simply to get access to Cabinet-level and sub-Cabinet level people. The SIA got 180 members of Congress to write letters to the Executive branch, including entire delegations from California, Illinois, New Mexico, Arizona, and Texas. The California delegation also met with the Japanese ambassador to the United States (**Exhibit 12–5**).

Although the SIA's political tactics were channeled predominantly through the Congress, the SIA did not form a Political Action Committee to contribute to congressional campaigns. And while member companies made some candidate endorsements, the SIA did not attempt to encourage grassroots or constituency (employees, shareholders, etc.) letter-writing. Scalise worried that these tactics "might taint the legitimacy of our arguments a little bit. Representatives and Senators are smart enough to know that most voters would have very limited understanding of and interest in this issue."

Scalise believed that going through the Congress provided, ironically, the best way for the industry to express its case to the Administration. He was concerned about the attitudes within the executive branch. He found the most resistance initially coming from within the State Department and the Defense Department, although other agencies were opposed as well. State and Defense were eager to shore up the U.S.-Japan relationship as allies and saw cases of this kind as a threat to bilateral cooperation. Indeed, the SIA's legal representative noted that "one big problem with a 301 case is that it is quite dependent on the president taking action, and that means you risk raising larger foreign policy questions unintentionally." Indeed, the SIA found that raising these larger questions brought a number of executive agencies into the decision-making process. Scalise found it necessary to hold inter-agency progress meetings covering developments in the Departments of Defense, Labor, Treasury, State, and Commerce, in addition to the Central Intelligence Agency, the National Security Council, the Council of Economic Advisors, and the Office of Management and Budget.

Despite the opposition of State and Defense and the wavering of the USTR, segments of the Administration were supportive. When the SIA

EXHIBIT 12-4 "Liberalization" Measures, U.S. Investment Attempts, and Yen Appreciation Have Had Little Effect on U.S. Merchant Firm's Penetration of the Japanese Market.

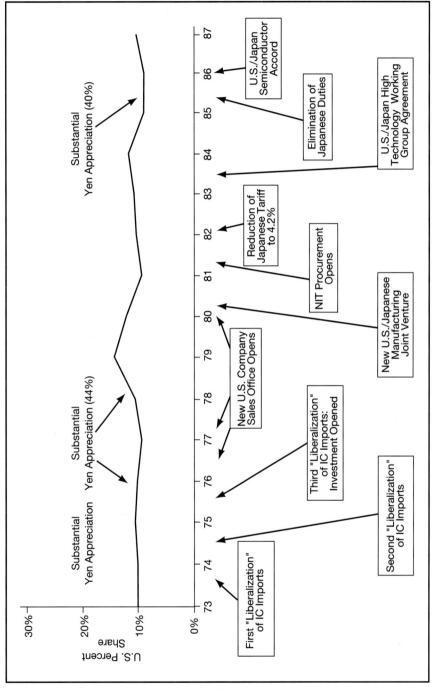

Source: SIA.

189

Exhibit 12-5 U.S. Semiconductor Employment, 1984

State	Percent of Total U.S. Semiconductor Employment	Semiconductor Industry Employment ('000s)
Arizona	11.5	31.7
California	32.4	89.0
Florida	3.2	8.7
Massachusetts	4.2	11.5
New Jersey	2.2	6.0
New York	9.6	26.2
Oregon	3.0	8.2
Pennsylvania	5.3	14.5
Texas	14.1	38.8
Utah	3.2	8.7
Vermont	3.2	8.7
12 other states (<2% each)	7.1	21.9
Industry total	100	274.0
Total merchant	46	127.0
Total captive	54	147.0

Source: *U.S. Census of Manufacturers,* 1982; U.S. Bureau of Labor Statistics.

managed to get some time with Secretary of State George Schultz, Schultz took particular interest in a page of comparative pie charts showing the dominant U.S. market share in the United States, Europe, and the rest of the world, and the relatively meager market share gained by U.S. firms in Japan.[3] "This tells me all I need to know," he reportedly declared as he tore the sheet from a bound document. "The cash registers have to start ringing over there [Japan]." The SIA also had some success dealing with the working-level people in the Commerce Department, but had trouble with higher ranking free-trade economists in other agencies. "It was frustrating," Scalise sighed, "trying to convince them that you can't have free trade without a free market."

Another step in the SIA political plan was to maintain good relations with the press by distributing literature and holding briefings for major national media and local media in Silicon Valley. SIA also distributed basic background information on the issues to a wide array of groups. And the SIA hired a public relations firm based in Washington to help the SIA get media contacts, ensure that they knew how to write press releases,

[3]The United States heavily outsold Japan in all regions other than Japan. Between 1982 and 1986, the United States averaged 53% of Europe's market, and 47% of all other markets, while Japan averaged only 10% and 28%, respectively.

and so on. Scalise felt that the industry's educational campaign "started in a good position because we had already been discussing these issues in an incremental, nonextreme way for more than three years before the 301 petition was even filed."

The SIA allocated less than one million dollars annually to cover legal expenses and other operating costs associated with the 301 campaign. More significant than the financial cost, however, was the contribution of time. Three to four labor years were devoted to the case by the staffs of Motorola, Intel, and Rockwell. George Scalise spent roughly one-third of his time on the project. And the CEOs and high-level executives of several SIA companies, including AMD, National Semiconductor, TI, Intel, and Motorola, devoted much time to speeches, testimony, and interviews on the subject.

Other Trade Actions

Trade action against Japan in semiconductors was not limited to the 301 case. By the end of 1985, three suits had been filed charging Japanese firms with selling semiconductors in the United States below their cost of production. In late June, soon after the 301 petition was filed, Micron Technology charged Japanese semiconductor firms with dumping 64K DRAMs. Then, in late September, Intel, AMD, and National Semiconductor claimed that Japanese firms were dumping EPROMs. (TI, a large EPROM firm, declined to join this suit.) Finally, in a rare move, the Department of Commerce "self-initiated" a case in early December and charged Japanese firms with dumping 256K and up DRAMs. Although most U.S. firms had already abandoned the 256K DRAM market, this case held particular importance for Texas Instruments, the last major U.S. merchant producer. In all three cases, the petitioners argued that Japanese prices had fallen far too sharply in short periods of time to be explained by superior production methods (**Exhibit 12–6**).

All three petitioners recognized that their dumping suits would interact indirectly with the Section 301 case. Intel felt that the EPROM case and the 301 case increased American bargaining power, and hoped that the Japanese would want to settle everything at once—the 301 and the EPROM dumping suit. Intel officials also hoped they could get specific provisions on EPROMs built into an agreement; they believed that such a specific provision was highly unlikely without the pressure of the dumping suit. (Intel executives noted that the United States could supply enough EPROMs to make up for any embargo on Japanese EPROMs coming into the United States, thereby minimizing any inconvenience to users.) Intel proposed that financial penalties paid by Japan go to the Semiconductor Research Corporation, an organization that distributed research funds to U.S. universities. The concern for Intel, AMD, and National was that they retain EPROMs as their "technology driver:" a chip they could produce in high quantities that would encourage both design innovations and manufacturing efficiencies. Intel absorbed the financial costs of the case, while Scalise spearheaded the issue in Washington.

EXHIBIT 12-6 256K DRAM Regional Pricing

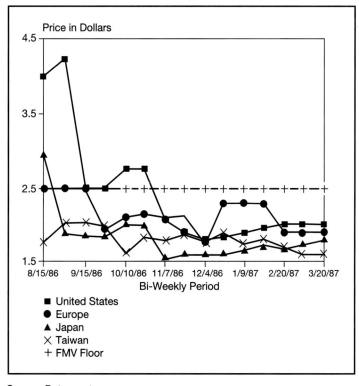

Source: Dataquest.

U.S.-Japan Semiconductor Negotiations

Once the USTR announced in early 1986 that he supported the SIA's position in the 301 case, President Reagan had until July 1, 1986 to determine a U.S. response to the unfair trading practices (later extended to July 30). Once the positive finding in the 301 case was issued, U.S. and Japanese government negotiators began meeting to work out a solution to the trade problems in semiconductors. The U.S. position was strengthened considerably by preliminary positive findings during Spring 1986 on all three of the dumping suits that prescribed dumping duties of up to 188%.[4] Scalise explained that "those decisions gave us some bargaining leverage. The Japanese firms knew that dumping duties would be imposed as a result of the three dumping cases. The preliminary margins were already published, and their application was automatically provided for in the trade laws. Furthermore, sanctions could be imposed because of the 301 case itself. At a time of sharp trade tensions, they couldn't just assume that these sanctions would be weak. They could already see that we had built some high-level support in the Administration."

During the negotiations no actual figure for the Americans' desired Japanese market share was specified by the SIA, but the industry argued that in the absence of trade barriers, the U.S. semiconductor industry should have had between 20% and 30% of the Japanese market.[5] As one company official noted, "the key became that the Japanese had to guarantee a market share in the 20's. It had to have 'a two' in front of the number in order to be acceptable."

In August 1986 the United States and Japan announced that the two countries had reached an accord on semiconductor trade.[6] The Japanese agreed to increase their purchase of foreign-made chips to slightly over 20% of the Japanese market over a five-year period, effectively doubling U.S. semiconductor sales in Japan. Japan intended to establish an organization that would provide sales assistance for foreign semiconductor manufacturers. The Japanese also agreed to have the Ministry of International Trade and Industry (MITI) monitor export prices on a wide range of semiconductor products, including EPROMs, 256K DRAMs, and 8-bit and 16-bit microprocessors, to prevent Japanese chipmakers from selling at less than fair market value in the United States or in third countries. The United States reserved the right to add or drop products from this list in the future.

The U.S. Commerce Department was responsible for determining the foreign market values (FMVs)[7] for each Japanese company's chips and monitoring production costs and prices of Japanese-made chips. These prices varied for each firm depending on their costs of manufacture (**Exhibit 12–7**). (In their rebuttals to the SIA stance during the 301 case, the Japanese firms sharply criticized the "cost-price" method of determining fair selling values, arguing that it overlooked market conditions.) Firms were prohibited from selling chips below the specified price in the United States and third country markets. Prices in Japan were not bound to the FMVs, but Japanese firms were expected not to "undercut" the agreement in Japan. Chips produced in the United States were not subject to the FMVs, even if produced by the subsidiary of a Japanese firm. The FMVs were to be adjusted quarterly. This specific targeting of individual Japanese companies was highly unusual; the more common procedure was to issue one overall ruling for a country as a whole and let the foreign government work out the details of implementing the policy company-by-company.

For its part, the United States agreed to suspend the existing dumping suits against Japan and the 301 case. The United States retained the right to reactivate the suits if Japanese firms were found guilty of selling at less than

---

[4]The margins were 11% to 35% of the retail price in 64K DRAMs, 21% to 188% in EPROMs, and 19% to 108% in 256K and up DRAMs. The duties levied varied by firm.

[5]The SIA kept an industry advisory team available to the negotiators for assistance in technical negotiations. Available on-site for consultation, this team could tap a network of experts. Aside from the assistance in technical matters, the government found the quick industry feedback on its reactions to various proposals to be helpful in its negotiations.

[6]The announcement of the agreement was one week prior to a scheduled House of Representatives vote to override President Reagan's veto of the Jenkins Bill—a bill that would have significantly cut textiles imports.

[7]The term "fair market values" was used during dumping proceedings. The term "foreign market values" was employed after the signing of the 301 agreement.

EXHIBIT 12-7 Determination of Foreign Market Values

The Department of Commerce used a formula to construct the quarterly Foreign Market Values (FMVs). This formula (A+B+C+D=Foreign Market Value) was made up of the following four parts:

A. Material costs, including some R&D
B. Fabrication costs
C. General sales and administrative expenses, including some R&D (not less than 10 percent of the above two costs)
D. Profit (not less than 8 percent of the above three costs)

The formula was applied on a company-by-company basis using proprietary cost information to determine the minimum price of each company's products. This method used real-time fabrication cost data in determining FMVs. The capacity utilization of a given company at a given time determined in large part what that company's FMV would be. A company running at 80 percent capacity would have lower fabrication costs per unit than a company running at 50 percent capacity. The initial capacity utilization rate used could determine which companies would be continually competitive and which would continue to be uncompetitive, since a profit always had to be added to a higher manufacturing cost.

Source: Excerpted from Dataquest, *User Update,* October 1986.

---

fair value. For the dumping suits, this meant that duties could be reimposed; for the 301 case, President Reagan would have to determine the U.S. government's response. If either country were concerned about possible violation of the agreement or other matters pertaining to the agreement, immediate consultations would be held and last for a maximum of two weeks.

Reaction to the agreement in the press and among some semiconductor customers was strongly negative. Scalise was taken aback by the vociferous opposition the pact had engendered. Press reaction predominantly portrayed the agreement as protectionism instigated by an American industry that no longer wanted to accept the verdict of the marketplace. Some customers argued that U.S. producers had caused their own troubles by misreading the market in the late 1970s and early 1980s and by failing to keep pace with Japanese improvements in manufacturing. Others saw the agreement as effectively charging customers a premium in order to make the U.S. industry competitive again. In Japan, firms and MITI were unhappy with the agreement but contended that they would abide by the new regulations. European manufacturers accepted the anti-dumping provisions for the U.S. market, but expressed concern that the U.S. industry was being granted discriminatory access to the Japanese market. The European manufacturers submitted a complaint with GATT that the accord violated multilateral international trade agreements. Scalise spent time in Europe explaining the trade case to major customers and attempting (unsuccessfully) to get the GATT complaint withdrawn. He felt that it was important that the Europeans knew that the agreement called for "foreign capital affiliated firms" to get 20% of the Japanese market, not just U.S. firms.

In early September 1986, several semiconductor customers met with Commerce Department representatives to argue that the semiconductor agreement was forcing them to consider moving production overseas. These customers reported that prices of 256K DRAMs in the United States had risen anywhere from two to eight times the pre-agreement price and argued that these prices would make U.S. computers and other electronic products noncompetitive in world markets. Indeed, many member firms in the AEA, especially the smaller firms, reacted negatively to the trade agreement and predicted tremendous offshore movement by U.S. companies. In response, the SIA set up a subcommittee within the AEA to deal with user concerns. Scalise felt that the greatest opposition came from firms that did not make their own semiconductors and were not in the SIA.

One AEA official noted that the organization supported the negotiated agreement but was "appalled" by the FMVs issued by Commerce in August. Expressing surprise at the prices, he noted that "we thought they'd use high FMVs as a negotiating tactic, but we never imagined they'd actually put them into effect." Anger in the user community, he reported, was aimed primarily at the price of DRAMs; users had much less trouble with the EPROM prices. Tempers cooled somewhat when the FMVs were adjusted in October. And by March 1987, managers in charge of semiconductor purchasing at several larger computer firms reported that the revised FMVs were not too far off what the market itself would have produced. While they could live in the existing environment, however, several reported that they were "determined to see that things don't go any further."

Impact of the Agreement

In March 1987, seven months after the chip accord was signed, SIA members were convinced that the Japanese were violating the agreement by selling below fair value in third countries and failing to increase purchases from U.S. semiconductor manufacturers (**Exhibit 12–10**). They charged that chips were being bought up cheaply in Japan and then resold in "gray markets." Moreover, they argued that despite substantial commitments by U.S. companies to the Japanese market, both before and after the agreement, there was little impact on sales.[8] The question facing the SIA was what to do next.

Political Environment

The U.S. semiconductor industry seemed surrounded by bad news since the signing of the agreement. In 1986, for the first time, the Japanese market for chips was actually larger than the American, and Japanese firms in total had a larger worldwide semiconductor market share than the Americans.[9] A Japanese firm was the world's largest semiconductor merchant for the first time in 1985, and by 1986 the top three firms were Japanese. Japanese firms held seven of the top ten spots in 1986, up from five in 1982.

The U.S. Congress had become increasingly concerned in the early months of 1987 about the country's trade "competitiveness" and the growing U.S. trade deficits, particularly with Japan. Tension over the alleged violations of the semiconductor agreement was especially high: semiconductor trade had become one of the dominant issues confronting the United States and Japan. A major trade bill which toughened several trade provisions but still retained presidential flexibility in implementing penalties was working through committee hearings. In more focused actions in early March, the House of Representatives voted unanimously and the Senate voted 93–0 to encourage the Administration to apply sanctions on Japanese chips.

In the executive branch, the Defense Department's Defense Science Board issued a report in early February that pointed with alarm to the declining U.S. competitiveness in semiconductors and in semiconductor manufacturing equipment. The report called for $1 billion to be provided over five years to shore up American manufacturing ability in semiconductors and painted the loss of the American semiconductor industry as a major national security issue. Another $1 billion was recommended for semiconductor laboratory research. Cabinet-level officials were scheduled to meet to decide what action, if any, to take.

The response from the Japanese government to the U.S. concerns was mixed. On one hand, MITI requested two reductions in Japanese semiconductor production—the first by an average of 10% and the second by another 11%.[10] These requests were designed to increase prices in Japan

[8]Dataquest's *User Update* reported in October 1986 that expected FMVs of $2.50 to $4.00 for 256K DRAMS were apparently undercut in Taiwan, where "prices have remained at $2.00 or less."

[9]These changes were attributable partly to actual growth in Japan and partly to foreign exchange fluctuations caused by the sharp decline of the dollar in relation to the yen.
An SIA memo noted that "the average U.S. share in the first month of a quarter in 1986 (i.e., January, April, July, and October) was 7.9%, a level equal to the January 1987 level. Similarly, the gain in share in February 1987 over January 1987 was consistent with the pattern observed within a quarter in 1986. These figures are consistent with our belief that there has been no gain in U.S. market access in Japan."

[10]The reductions reflected comparisons to the previous quarter. The 10% cut recommended for the first quarter of 1987 resulted in an actual production cut of nearly 23%. The 11% cut was for the second quarter of 1987.

EXHIBIT 12-8 Story on Kyodo (Japan) Newswire

Japanese Strongly Concerned about Senate Call On Chips

Tokyo, March 20, 1987—Japan has reacted with strong concern about the U.S. Senate resolution calling for retaliation against Japan for failing to honor the bilateral pact on orderly trade in semiconductors. Hajime Tamura, Minister of International Trade and Industry, personally asked representatives of 10 major Japanese chipmakers to ensure there are no exceptions to the agreement which calls for chip prices to be maintained at fair market prices in Japan, the United States, and third countries. He said allegations of dumping in third countries at well below the Japanese and U.S. prices must not be allowed and he called on presidents, vice presidents, and managing directors of 10 major Japanese users of microchips to step up their own buying of semiconductors from U.S. manufacturers. The 10 represent some 40% of the Japanese market for semiconductors.

Prime Minister Yasuhiro Nakasone also stepped into the fray and ordered Tamura to ensure there are concrete results from the pact. . . MITI is to announce a guideline on April-June chip production in Japan soon and is expected to call for a 20 to 30% reduction in Japanese output. Japanese chipmakers also expressed concern about the Senate resolution which passed 93-0 and indicated they will follow MITI production guidelines when they are set, probably next week.

in an effort to thwart the gray market (**Exhibit 12–8**). On the other hand, the Japanese government also argued that the American firms were not realistic about how quickly their sales in Japan could increase. Moreover, USTR Yeutter, while supporting the U.S. industry's position, noted that the Japanese had become particularly aggressive in trade disputes, largely because of the damaging effects a rapidly rising yen was having on production, sales, and employment. Hints in the press suggested that the Japanese might retaliate if the American government took new measures in semiconductors.[11] The Japanese were also known to be concerned about the pricing threat in memory chips presented by firms in South Korea and Singapore.

Determining the SIA's Response

Scalise believed the SIA needed to move quickly in this environment of high trade tensions, especially since he felt that the press was now largely in favor of the SIA's position. In early March, the SIA Board approved plans for a multifirm collaborative project known as SEMATECH. Spearheaded by Charles Sporck, president of National Semiconductor, and strongly supported by IBM, SEMATECH was conceived as a laboratory and small production facility where American manu-

facturing processes could be enhanced and then distributed to the member firms. The SIA Board feared that the United States was falling behind in semiconductor technology, primarily because of deficiencies in process technology (**Exhibit 12–9**). Funding of SEMATECH in the SIA plan was to be 50% industry and 50% government. Annual costs were expected to reach $200 million.

The SIA still faced the issue about what to do next in its trade dispute with the Japanese. Several decisions needed to be made. One decision was whether to propose a tariff (duty), a quota, or an embargo. These policies could be applied to semiconductors themselves, to products containing semiconductors produced by the highly diversified Japanese semiconductor companies, or even to unrelated products. If products containing semiconductors were selected, there remained a choice between mass market items such as video cassette recorders and color televisions, which the Japanese dominated, or markets such as mainframe computers where they were seeking to build market share. Even the party to target with retaliatory action was not clear. Should the SIA favor company-specific penalties against Japanese firms or propose instead that an overall penalty be imposed on Japan?

Scalise believed the association should act quickly: He was concerned about Reagan's upcoming meeting with Japan's Prime Minister Nakasone within six weeks and the yearly summit talks among the largest industrial nations

[11]*New York Times* 24 March 1987, p. D5.

EXHIBIT 12-9 Status and Trends of U.S. Semiconductor Technology Relative to Japan

	Japan Lead	U.S.-Japan Parity	U.S. Lead
Silicon Products			
DRAMs	<		
SRAMs	<		
KPROMs		•	
Microprocessors			<
Custom, Semicustom Logic			<
Bipolar	<		
Nonsilicon Products			
Memory	<		
Logic	<		
Linear			•
Optoelectronics	<		
Beterostructures	<		
Materials			
Silicon	<		
Gallium Arsenide	<		
Processing Equipment			
Optical Lithography		<	
K-Beam Lithography			<
X-Ray Lithography		<	
Ion Implantation Technology			
Chemical Vapor Deposition		•	
Deposition, Diffusion, Other		•	
Energy-Assisted Processing	<		
Assembly		•	
Packaging	<		
Test	<		
CAE		•	
CAM		<	

< U.S. Position Declining.

• U.S. Position Maintaining.

Source: Interagency Working Group on Semiconductor Technology.

EXHIBIT 12-10 U.S. Sales in Japan, Calendar Year 1986 ($000)

	Q1	Q2	Q3	Q4	Total
U.S.-based sales	178,730	223,960	241,890	230,800	875,370
Japan market	2,235,000	2,563,000	2,905,000	2,769,000	10,472,000
U.S. share	8.0%	8.7%	8.6%	8.3%	8.4%

Source: World Semiconductor Trade Statistics; Japanese Ministry of International Trade and Industry; Japanese Ministry of Finance.

scheduled for early June. In addition to weighing the pros and cons of these specific choices, Scalise, as head of the Public Policy Committee, had to determine the answers to several more general questions: What would the U.S. government accept? What types of action would lead the Japanese to enforce the agreement? And what would be an acceptable consensus among SIA members?

PART FOUR

Financial, Marketing, and Manufacturing Strategy

13. Intel Corporation, 1992

In late December of 1991, Intel's co-founder and Chairman of the Board, Gordon Moore, was rethinking the company's capital-structure and cash-disbursement policies. The company had just completed an extremely successful five-year period during which annual revenues had grown almost fourfold. Now, the firm found itself with cash balances (net of long-term debt) of $2.4 billion—well over a third of total assets of $6.3 billion. With a market capitalization of almost $9 billion, Intel had become one of the largest firms in the U.S. to have never paid a dividend.[1] Moore wondered whether the firm he founded in 1968 had grown sufficiently mature to begin returning some of its cash to investors, perhaps by beginning to pay dividends or repurchasing shares of stock.

While returning cash was a worthwhile goal, Moore recognized that cash-availability was an essential component of the firm's overall strategy and that future cash needs were very uncertain.

He knew that the company faced considerable competitive pressure over the next few years. Imitations of Intel's proprietary microprocessor products had recently obtained substantial market share. Furthermore, the production and development of new Intel products required ever-larger up-front expenditures. In 1992 alone, Intel was expecting to spend over $700 million on research and development and approximately $1.2 billion on new plant and equipment. The rapid rate of innovation in Intel's business meant that it would be extremely costly—perhaps even fatal—to delay or scrimp on these expenditures.

Moore was also concerned with the stock market's response to recent competitive pressures. Intel's stock had over the last few weeks been trading at a price of $42.50—a price-earnings (P/E) ratio of under 11, far below the P/E of about 20 for the S&P 500. Some outside analysts seemed to be pessimistic about Intel's ability to keep its profits high. Notwithstanding these concerns, Moore asked Intel's CFO, Harold Hughes, and Treasurer, Arvind Sodhani, to determine whether Intel's current capital structure was appropriate. Moore also wanted to know what alternatives might be available for disbursing cash to shareholders.

---

[1] The largest firm in all of U.S. history to have never paid a dividend was Digital Equipment Corporation, which in 1987 had a market capitalization as high as $26.6 billion. However, by December 1991, DEC's market capitalization had fallen below Intel's, to $6.7 billion.

Professor Kenneth A. Froot prepared this case as the basis for class discussion rather than to illustrate either effective or ineffective handling of an administrative situation.

Intel was founded in 1968 by Moore and the recently-deceased Robert Noyce (co-inventor of the integrated circuit and Vice Chairman of Intel until 1988). The company quickly established a reputation as a leading innovator in the design, development and manufacture of semiconductors. In 1969, Intel produced the world's first static random access memory (SRAM). This was followed by the 1024-bit dynamic random access memory (DRAM) in 1970. Intel DRAMs (which rapidly grew in capacity) quickly became the industry standard, and were by 1972 the largest selling semiconductor component in the world. In addition, Intel introduced in 1971 the first erasable programmable read-only memory (EPROM) chip. This was an important innovation, as it created a versatile and inexpensive data-storage medium. Intel soon was the leading supplier of successive generations of EPROMs.

Intel's most important early breakthrough, however, came in the early 1970s. That breakthrough was the microprocessor, a logic product that ultimately would become the "computer inside the personal computer." Upon its development, Intel proclaimed that microprocessor chips would "usher in a new era of integrated electronics." Yet the innovation came years ahead of the development of its most popular end-use product—the personal computer. (Indeed, Intel itself underestimated the importance of its technology, missing the opportunity to commercialize its early stand-alone personal computer to compete with Apple, whose first 8-bit machine was introduced in 1978.)

Throughout the 1970s, Intel continued to innovate, creating a second-generation of micro processors, the i8088™ and i8086™. In 1980, the i8088 was chosen as the computational centerpiece of IBM's first microcomputer, the PC. Later, IBM decided to base its more advanced AT computer on Intel's i80286™, and its even more advanced PS/2 on Intel's i80386DX™. IBM's sheer size and open-architecture policy quickly made its PC and AT important standards, in turn propelling Intel's microprocessors into a position of dominance.

During its first 15 years, Intel's record of innovation had been impressive. According to one observer, Intel was responsible for 16 of the 22 major breakthroughs in microelectronics between 1971 and 1981. The pace of the firm's technological innovation was exemplified by "Moore's Law," which had become an industry-wide benchmark. The law held that the number of components on a chip doubled every two years. To fund this continuing innovation, Intel's strategy had been to withdraw from product segments that had matured, and to redirect resources toward new products which sold at premium prices.

However, the focus on rapidly developing product markets with steep learning curves created risks. A major mistake or delay in a product could result in Intel falling permanently behind its competitors. In one example, Intel's failure to produce a viable 256K DRAM product in the mid-1980s (after being the world leader in DRAMs in the 1970s) led to its permanent withdrawal from DRAM design and production activities.

In spite of such lapses, by 1991 Intel had become the world's second largest manufacturer of integrated circuits (with estimated 1991 integrated circuit revenues of almost $4.1 billion), and the world's largest metal-oxide-silicon (MOS) manufacturer.[2] **Exhibit 13–1** reports revenue data on Intel's largest competitors. Although based in the United States, Intel operated 40 major manufacturing and development facilities on three continents, and had 90 sales offices in over 21 nations. Gordon Moore, with his gentle and deferential manner, had become perhaps the most respected figure in the semiconductor industry (in addition to one of its richest, with holdings of about 7 percent of Intel's stock). **Exhibits 13–2** and **13–3** provide recent financial information on Intel.

[2]MOS was the newer, and more efficient, of two processes for making integrated circuits.

EXHIBIT 13-1 Top Integrated Circuit Manufacturers, Worldwide Revenues ($ millions)

1976	$MM	1981	$MM	1987	$MM	1991	$MM
TI	135	Intel	491	NEC	2,006	NEC	4,742
Intel	132	NEC	438	Toshiba	1,566	Intel	4,059
NEC	74	Motorola	372	Intel	1,473	Toshiba	3,910
Gen'l Inst.	68	TI	350	Hitachi	1,236	Hitachi	3,587
National	67	Hitachi	288	Fujitsu	1,014	Motorola	3,096
Hitachi	63	National	255	Motorola	986	TI	2,667
AMI	59	Toshiba	250	Mitsubishi	811	Mitsubishi	2,121
Mostek	56	Fujitsu	218	TI	784	AMD	1.185
Motorola	55	Mostek	210	Matsushita	593	VLSI Tech.	165
Rockwell	50	Gen'l Inst.	141	OKI	566	Chips & Tech.	158

Source: Dataquest, 1992.

Products

In 1991, Intel's mission was to be the leading "building-block supplier to the new computer industry." To fulfill this mission, management believed the firm had to invest in the design, development, and manufacture of a variety of advanced microcomputer components and related products at various levels of integration. **Exhibit 13–4** gives details on sales and operating margins for Intel's various product lines.

Memory (10 percent of sales)

Intel supplied a broad line of memory components, including EPROMs, DRAMs and SRAMs (both produced in recent years by subcontractors for Intel), and flash memories (introduced by Intel in 1988). Flash memories were easier and faster to update than EPROMs because they could be reprogrammed after installation.

Microprocessors and coprocessors (52 percent of sales)

Processor and logic products performed the central and peripheral data processing functions for microcomputers. Intel produced several families of processors for personal computers (see **Exhibit 13–5**). The higher performance microprocessors in the 32-bit i386 and i486 families were also powerful enough to be used in minicomputers, parallel processing systems, and engineering workstations. The most recent addition to the i386 family was Intel's i386SL, a microprocessor designed for portable computers and introduced in 1990. It incorporated a power management unit which extended battery life up to 10 hours. The high-performance i486 family was introduced in 1989. Intel was also developing two even more advanced processors, the P5 (referred to by analysts as the i586) and the P6. These chips were expected to include networking and digital-video-interface circuitry directly on the microprocessor, and were scheduled to become available in mid-1992 and late-1993, respectively.

In addition to these processors, Intel produced the i860 microprocessor (introduced in 1989), which was designed for high-speed multiprocessing systems and technical workstations. Intel also made coprocessors for various applications: graphics, disk drives, keyboards, printers, networks, and high-speed mathematical calculations.

Microcontrollers, peripherals, and systems (38 percent of sales)

Microcontrollers were designed to be embedded within an application, and to be programmed to control the operation of that application. They typically integrated a central processing unit, memory, and other features on a single chip, and were used in computer and communications sys-

EXHIBIT 13-2 Annual Income Statements

	December 1991(E)	December 1990	December 1989	December 1988	December 1987	December 1986	December 1985	December 1984	December 1983	December 1982	December 1981	December 1980
Sales	4,779	3,921	3,127	2,875	1,907	1,265	1,365	1,629	1,122	900	789	855
Cost of goods sold	1,898	1,638	1,440	1,295	872	687	784	774	539	467	395	350
	2,881	2,283	1,687	1,580	1,035	578	581	855	583	432	393	504
SG&A, of which:	1,383	1,133	849	775	618	540	482	496	359	329	301	272
R&D	618	517	365	318	260	228	195	180	142	131	116	96
advertising expense	121	94	55	55	28	28	30	24	16	14	14	12
Operating income before depreciation	1,498	1,151	838	805	417	38	99	359	224	103	93	232
Depreciation, depletion, and amortization	418	292	237	211	171	174	159	109	85	75	63	49
Operating profit	1,080	858	601	594	246	(135)	(60)	250	139	28	30	183
Interest expense	105	102	102	78	66	39	26	15	17	17	15	8
Interest income	194	203	154	102	61	42	53	57	46	18	21	9
Other nonoperating income	26	27	(70)	11	46	(42)	27	6	10	2	5	0
Pretax income	1,195	986	583	629	288	(175)	(5)	298	178	30	40	185
Total income taxes	376	336	192	176	112	9	(7)	100	62	0	13	89
Income before extraordinary items and discontinued operations extraordinary items	819	650	391	453	176	(183)	2	198	116	30	40	185
	0	0	0	0	73	10	0	0	0	0	0	0
Net income	819	650	391	453	248	(173)	2	198	116	30	27	97
Earnings per share (fully diluted)	3.62	3.19	2.06	2.51	1.38	-0.99	0.01	1.13	0.70	0.22	0.20	0.74
Common shares outstanding	208.99	199.65	184.52	180.54	168.33	176.66	174.12	170.75	167.55	136.09	131.30	128.21
Book value per share	21.14	17.99	13.81	11.52	7.76	7.22	8.16	7.97	6.60	4.06	3.72	3.38
Market to book ratio (end of year)	2.01	2.14	2.50	2.06	3.41	1.94	2.39	2.34	4.18	3.19	2.02	3.97

Source: Intel Corp. 1991 figures include casewriter estimates.

EXHIBIT 13-3 Annual Balance Sheet ($ millions)

	December 1991(E)	December 1990	December 1989	December 1988	December 1987	December 1986	December 1985	December 1984	December 1983	December 1982	December 1981	December 1980
Assets:												
Cash and equivalents	2,277	1,785	1,090	971	619	373	361	231	389	85	115	128
Net receivables	698	710	569	506	439	298	364	354	303	221	180	196
Inventories	422	415	347	366	236	198	171	219	152	122	97	91
Other current assets	207	209	157	126	138	154	128	154	89	100	67	32
Total Current Assets	3,604	3,119	2,163	1,970	1,431	1,024	1,024	958	933	528	460	447
Gross PP&E	3,723	2,814	2,249	1,898	1,536	1,364	1,338	1,165	801	697	591	447
Accumulated depreciation	1,560	1,156	965	775	645	585	490	386	297	236	179	126
Net PP&E	2,163	1,658	1,284	1,122	891	779	848	778	504	462	412	321
Long-term investments[a]	480	561	508	422	262	264	267	272	217	51	0	0
Other assets	46	38	39	36	13	13	12	21	26	16	0	0
Total Assets	6,292	5,276	3,994	3,550	2,597	2,080	2,152	2,029	1,680	1,056	872	767
Liabilities:												
Long-term debt: current portion	0	86	16	0	117	0	4	0	0	0	0	0
Notes payable	173	193	140	217	335	112	84	66	81	75	32	12
Accounts payable	245	209	165	153	115	62	57	80	79	39	32	12
Taxes payable	152	241	167	156	25	15	3	40	18		0	4
Accrued expenses	536	464	337	308	206	118	85	117	73	56	46	55
Deferred income on shipment to distributors	122	121	96	100	83	67	72	88	74	52	53	46
Total Current Liabilities	1,228	1,314	921	934	882	374	307	390	326	223	172	147
Long-term debt	363	345	412	479	298	287	271	146	128	197	150	150
Deferred taxes	144	126	111	56	105	132	134	113	89	68	44	23
Investment tax credit	0	0	0	0	6	12	19	20	15	17	18	14
Equity:												
Common stock + capital surplus[b]	1,411	1,404	1,011	861	540	757	730	671	631	177	143	128
Retained earnings[b]	3,007	2,188	1,538	1,219	766	518	691	689	491	375	345	305
Common equity	4,418	3,592	2,549	2,080	1,306	1,275	1,421	1,360	1,122	552	488	433
Put warrants	140	0	0	0	0	0	0	0	0	0	0	0
Total Equity	4,558	3,592	2,549	2,080	1,306	1,275	1,421	1,360	1,122	552	488	433
Total Liabilities and Equity	6,292	5,376	3,994	3,550	2,597	2,080	2,152	2,029	1,680	1,056	872	767
Capital Expenditures:	948	680	422	362	302	155	236	388	145	138	157	156
(Cash + Long-term investments – Long-term debt) / assets	0.38	0.37	0.30	0.26	0.22	0.17	0.17	0.18	0.28	-0.06	-0.04	-0.03

[a]Long-term investments are held almost exclusively in investment-grade bonds.

[b]Surplus on common stock and retained earnings accounts are restated from company reports in order that the retained earnings account above be consistent with the income statement in Exhibit 1.

Source: Intel Corp. 1991 figures include casewriter estimates.

203

EXHIBIT 13-4 Analysts Estimates of Market Segments 1987-1991 ($ millions)

	1987	1988	1989	1990	1991
Segment Sales:					
EPROMS	130	220	265	252	228
SRAM	103	180	140	116	113
Other	102	137	120	133	131
Memory	335	537	525	501	472
8086 Family	69	39	29	18	12
80286	275	202	98	63	41
80386	210	538	822	1084	1361
80486	0	0	22	338	713
80586	0	0	0	0	0
i860	0	0	18	70	65
Coprocessors	81	175	163	233	255
Other	37	35	22	48	54
Microprocessors	672	989	1174	1854	2501
8-bit microcontrollers	200	255	245	223	195
16-bit microcontrollers	67	110	120	143	177
Microcontrollers	267	365	365	366	372
Processor Support	94	145	160	159	222
Graphics/Disk Controllers	58	73	80	79	122
Communications	53	84	75	63	117
Peripherals	205	302	315	301	461
OEM PC	0	0	45	175	295
Other Systems	428	682	702	723	723
Systems	428	682	747	898	1018
Total	1907	2875	3126	3920	4824
Operating Profit:					
Memory	41	81	50	57	51
Microprocessors	97	275	262	500	776
Microcontrollers	25	71	68	62	46
Peripherals	23	50	61	65	91
Systems	60	117	116	174	123
Total	246	594	557	858	1087
Operating Margin:					
Memory	12%	15%	10%	11%	11%
Microprocessors	14%	28%	22%	27%	31%
Microcontrollers	9%	19%	19%	17%	12%
Peripherals	11%	17%	19%	22%	20%
Systems	14%	17%	16%	19%	12%
Total	13%	21%	18%	22%	23%

Source: Analyst estimates, Morgan Stanley

tems, automobile control applications, robotics, electronic instrumentations, home video machines, and other applications.

Intel's technological leadership in microprocessors gave it certain competitive advantages in designing and marketing integrated microcomputer systems based on Intel products. Intel microprocessors were also at the heart of the company's design and development of parallel-processing supercomputers, which began in 1986.

Intel Corporation, 1992

EXHIBIT 13-5 Intel Microprocessor Product Line

Chip Name	Introduction Date	Clock speed	Mips	Price Per chip (1)	Internal bus	External bus	Number of transistors	Typical use
i8086	June 1978	5MHz	0.33	$5.50	16-bit	16-bit	29,000	Portable computing
		8MHz	0.66	$6.00				
		10MHz	0.75	$16.00				
i8088	June 1979	5MHz	0.33	$3.00	16-bit	8-bit	29,000	Portable computing
		8MHz	0.66	$4.00				
i286	February 1982	8MHz	1.20	$8.00	16-bit	16-bit	130,000	Portable computing
		10MHz	1.50	$8.00				
		12MHz	2.66	$8.00				
i386DX	October 1985	16MHz	6.00	$156.00	32-bit	32-bit	275,000	Desktop computing
	February 1987	20MHz	7.00	$156.00				
	April 1988	25MHz	8.50	$156.00				
	April 1989	33MHz	11.40	$195.00				
i386SX	June 1988	16MHz	2.50	$57.00	32-bit	16-bit	275,000	Entry-level desktop and portable computing
	January 1989	20MHz	4.20	$85.50				
i386SL	October 1990	20MHz	4.21	$135.00	32-bit	16-bit	855,000	Portable computing
	September 1991	25MHz	5.30	$189.00				
i486DX	April 1989	25MHz	20.00	$428.00 (2)	32-bit	32-bit	1,200,000	Desktop computing and servers
	May 1990	33MHz	27.00	$428.00				
	June 1991	50MHz	40.70	$644.00				
i486SX	September 1991	16MHz	13.00	$214.00(3)	32-bit	32-bit	1,185,000	Desktop computing
	April 1991	20MHz	16.50	$242.00(4)				
	September 1991	25MHz	20.00	$333.00(5)				

Notes: (1) Based on purchase of 1,000 chips; (2) low-power version costs $471; (3) low-power version costs $235; (4) low-power version costs $266; (5) low-power version costs $366.

Source: Intel Corp. and *PC Week,* November 1981.

Intel's Microprocessor Competitors

In the late 1970s, before a standard microprocessor technology had emerged, semiconductor producers typically cross-licensed products with competing companies. Intel's sales contracts often stipulated that Intel facilitate the develop ment of second sources for its i8088, i8086, and i80286 microprocessors. The company therefore licensed the i8088 and i8086 to 12 competitors and the i80286 to 4. These competing producers commanded a substantial fraction of industry microprocessor sales. Indeed, by the end of 1990, Intel had garnered only 19 percent of i8088 unit sales (against 51 percent by Advanced Micro Devices (AMD) and 13 percent by Siemens), 23 percent of i8086 family unit sales (against 23 percent by AMD and 37 percent by NEC), and 41 percent of i80286 unit sales (against 37 percent by AMD and 10 percent by Siemens).

Meanwhile, the design, development, and production costs of successive generations of microprocessors were rising rapidly. In just a few years, Intel's development expenses went from $100 million for the i386, to $300 million for the i486, to an estimated $500 million for the P5, and to perhaps $600 million for the P6. The costs of building state-of-the-art fabrication facilities (fabs) and equipment capable of producing 32-bit (and beyond) processors were increasing even more rapidly. Intel's capital spending on plant and equipment rose from $422 million in 1989 to

$680 million in 1990, to an estimated $948 million in 1991, and to an expected $1.2 billion in 1992 (see **Exhibit 13–3**). These setup costs also represented an ever-increasing fraction of total production costs. For example, analysts estimated that Intel's marginal costs for the i486 would fall from about $75 per unit in 1990 down to about $6 per unit by 1993, as more sophisticated fabs were employed and learning-by-doing effects made existing processes more efficient. Such dramatic declines in marginal costs were very common for new microprocessor products.

The economics of microprocessor production combined with the emergence of the X86 family as the dominant industry standard gave Intel the strategic leverage it needed to change its licensing policies. Beginning with the i386 family (which was introduced in 1986), the company refused to grant second-source contracts to customers other than IBM, which retained the right to manufacture the i386 for some of its own machines. Demand for Intel's i386 microprocessors seemed to be less price sensitive than that of earlier processors because there were no competing suppliers. Partly as a result, Intel's operating margins for microprocessors began to rise beginning in 1987 as the i386 product cycle moved into its "ramp-up" phase (see **Exhibit 14–4**). Net income increased from a loss of $203 million in 1986 to an expected $819 million in 1991.

Intel's decision to exclusively produce its newer microprocessors raised competitive challenges. One source of competition came from imitations (commonly, but inaccurately, called "clones") of Intel's products. Intel had already seen imitations of its mathematics coprocessors take considerable market power and market share away. In general, imitations were much less expensive to develop than the original processor, and tended to appear after demand for the original had already ramped-up. This timing allowed imitators to avoid the costly development and market-acceptance phases of the life cycle, and to align their product features with more recent changes in demand. **Exhibit 13–6** depicts the time profile of a typical microprocessor life cycle. (Industry ana-

EXHIBIT 13–6 Microprocessor Product Life Cycle (Source: Dataquest and case writer estimates.)

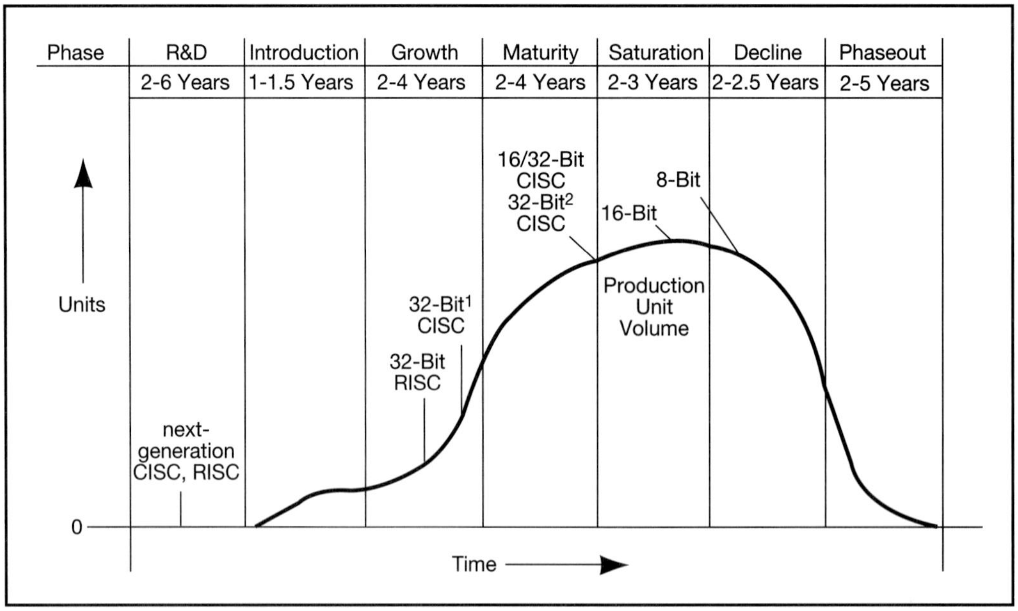

Phase	R&D	Introduction	Growth	Maturity	Saturation	Decline	Phaseout
	2-6 Years	1-1.5 Years	2-4 Years	2-4 Years	2-3 Years	2-2.5 Years	2-5 Years

Notes: 16/32-Bit CISC includes i386SX, 32-Bit CISC includes i386DX, 32-Bit CISC includes i386SL and i486 family, and next-generation CISC includes Intel's P6 microprocessor.

lysts believe that life cycles for newer processors are considerably shorter than that shown in **Exhibit 13–6**.) In Intel's experience, imitators tended to enter when (and if) the product reached the "growth" or ramp-up phase. **Exhibit 13–7** presents time-series data on both shipments and the installed base of various microprocessors.

In one example of a late-entry imitation, AMD began shipping its i386SX-and i386DX-compatibles in December 1990, almost five years after Intel introduced the originals. By that time, the i386 family was roughly in between the "growth" and "maturity" phases of the life cycle (see **Exhibit 13–6**), with Intel's i386 sales having reached an annual rate of about $1.2 billion on volume of about 12 million units. AMD's chips, however, had somewhat higher operating speeds and better power usage than comparable Intel processors. With a selling price slightly below Intel's, AMD's share of monthly i386 shipments had shot up to about 30 percent at the end of 12 months time. AMD sold approximately $145 million worth of imitation i386s in the last quarter of 1991 alone (about 27.5 percent of the last-quarter's market of $2.1 billion in annualized sales). See **Exhibit 13–7** for data on the industry-wide number of units shipped. Late entry into successful markets was W.J. Sanders' (AMD's flamboyant chairman and CEO) strategy. He kept AMD focused on high-volume products and well behind the cutting edge.

By the end of 1991 the number of companies which sold imitation products had grown dramatically. Chips and Technologies had recently announced a group of chips that mimicked the functions of the i386, and Cyrix was expected to do the same in the near future. AMD and Nex-

EXHIBIT 13-7 Shipments and Installed Base of Various Microprocessors (MM units), 1981-1991

	1981	1982	1983	1984	1985	1986	1987	1988	1989	1990	1991
Intel Micro-based											
Units shipped	0.0	0.2	1.0	2.6	4.6	6.1	8.8	11.9	15.7	18.6	20.7
Installed base	0.0	0.2	1.2	3.7	9.2	15.1	23.5	34.4	47.8	62.6	77.7
8088, 8086											
Units shipped	0.0	0.2	0.9	2.4	4.1	4.5	5.1	5.0	4.7	3.4	2.3
Installed base	0.0	0.2	1.1	3.5	8.7	13.1	17.9	22.0	24.7	24.7	22.8
80286											
Units shipped	0.0	0.0	0.0	0.1	0.4	1.6	3.3	5.7	7.6	7.2	6.8
Installed base	0.0	0.0	0.0	0.1	0.5	2.0	5.2	10.9	18.4	25.3	31.2
80386											
Units shipped	0.0	0.0	0.0	0.0	0.0	0.0	0.4	1.2	3.3	7.8	10.3
Installed base	0.0	0.0	0.0	0.0	0.0	0.0	0.0	1.5	4.7	5.5	12.5
80486											
Units shipped	0.0	0.0	0.0	0.0	0.0	0.0	0.0	0.0	0.0	0.1	1.3
Installed base	0.0	0.0	0.0	0.0	0.0	0.0	0.0	0.0	0.0	0.1	1.3
Motorola Micro-based											
Units shipped	0.0	0.0	0.0	0.5	0.7	0.9	1.2	1.6	1.8	2.6	3.0
Installed base	0.0	0.0	0.1	0.5	1.3	2.2	3.4	5.0	6.4	8.4	10.7
RISC											
Units shipped	0.0	0.0	0.0	0.0	0.0	0.0	0.0	0.0	0.0	0.2	0.3
Installed base	0.0	0.0	0.0	0.0	0.0	0.0	0.0	0.0	0.1	0.3	0.6

Source: *Infocorp,* 1992.

Gen Microsystems were expected to introduce i486-compatible processors during 1992. Imitating an existing processors' functions was less expensive and time-consuming than designing the original—analysts reported that Chips and Technologies created its imitation i386 for about $50 million, which is reported what AMD needed to spend on each of its i386-and i486-compatibles. **Exhibit 13–8** reports general financial information as well as data on net cash assets for several of Intel's competitors.

Another competitive threat was posed by alternative central processing units (CPUs) which did not attempt compatibility with Intel products. Motorola's 68000 family of CPUs, used principally on Apple machines, had for several years been a potentially threatening alternative. Furthermore, several high-performance reduced-instruction-set-computing (RISC) processors had recently been introduced: the ACE consortium would use a product of NEC and Siemens, the MIPS chip; Fujitsu had built the SPARC chip for Sun Microsystems; and a recent Apple/IBM alliance would use the Motorola-built, IBM-designed RS6000 series as a platform. Some informed observers believed that these processors might have performance advantages over Intel's X86 microprocessors. Furthermore, there was concern that the large Japanese companies might price their RISC processors very aggressively in order to gain market share.

Intel's response to these competitive challenges was fourfold. First, Intel used the legal system to defend vigorously what it believed to be infringements of its intellectual property rights. In early 1991, Intel sued AMD for illegal use of Intel's microcode in its processors. The case was originally to come to trial in February of 1992, although AMD had filed for a continuance to delay the trial until April 1992. In January 1991, Intel had also filed a preliminary injunction in the U.S. District Court in Sherman, Texas against Cyrix Corporation (a Texas-headquartered firm), which sought to prohibit Cyrix from shipping its "cloned" math coprocessors and claimed that Cyrix was infringing on Intel's patents. The case was not expected to go to trial until 1993. Intel was also pursuing actions against several companies (such as USLI and Cyrix) which had allegedly copied patented Intel circuits in their microprocessors and which were not licensed by Intel to do so. These companies argued that they could employ Intel circuits without violating the patent law, provided that they used fabs owned by companies which *were* licensed by Intel. Court decisions in these cases were expected soon.

Second, Intel responded to "me-too" competitors with a major advertising thrust (see **Exhibit 13–2** for advertising expense data). The "Intel Inside" campaign, which would cost almost $100 million per year, attempted to gain better premium-brand recognition. In addition, Intel tried to exploit its continuity as a producer of microprocessors in its "pull" campaign. This was intended to attract consumers to the i486's easy-upgradeability feature—a feature which no other supplier currently offered.

Intel's third competitive response was to speed up the product cycle by switching consumers to its "second-wave" 32-bit microprocessors, the i386SL and i486 family. Analysts anticipated that the newer i386SL, with its advanced power-management circuitry, would displace a substantial portion of the demand for first-wave i386 imitations. First-wave 386 processors were increasingly used in the large and rapidly growing portable-and laptop-computer market, where power-management features were crucial. However, due to a certain software bug, demand for Intel's i386SL had thus far been disappointing. Intel also began to encourage vendors and OEM manufacturers to switch from 386 processors to Intel's new 1.2-million-transistor i486 family through price cuts and greater availability. Demand for i486 processors had begun to accelerate, but was hampered by some observers' skepticism about the chips' performance. (See **Exhibit 13–7** for data on shipments.) In spite of these delays, one analyst expected shipments of the i386SL to rise from a negligible number of units in 1990 to 1.8 million in 1992, and those of the i486 family to rise from 0.3 million units in 1990 to 3.7 million in 1992. In addition to accelerating the life cycle for existing processors, Intel had recently moved up the introduction date of the P5 and P6, further shortening future life cycles. Intel's forecast of microprocessor sales by type is reported in **Exhibit 13–9**. It predicts a rapid decline in shipments of 8-and 16-bit processors in the near future.

Intel attempted to counter the competitive threat from RISC-based chips by emphasizing performance and portability. It was believed that high-speed i486 and P5 chips would at least match the performance of recently introduced RISC products. Furthermore, Intel had an advantage over other microprocessor platforms in the sheer size of the previously installed base—85 million existing X86-based PCs, with more than 50,000 software applications and $40 billion invested in software. **Exhibit 13–10** shows that, as of 1991, all major operating-systems for microcomputers ran (or were soon to run) on Intel designs. No other type of microprocessor had more than two operating systems designed for it. The result was that Intel architecture had become the "port of choice," according to Andrew Grove, Intel's CEO.

Intel's final strategy for confronting potential competitors was its aggressive spending on R&D, equipment and fabs to produce its chips. The company wanted to be strong in process technology and production capacity, and to use those strengths together with its design capability as competitive weapons.

In spite of Intel's responses, many informed observers worried about the company's ability to continue its rapid growth and sustain its generous margins. Analysts argued that if AMD could successfully "clone" the i486, others could (and would) do so as well. Rumors were already circulating that AMD would announce its 486-compatible chip earlier than expected and soon thereafter would raise substantial outside money for additional fabs. Even if AMD failed to build its own facilities, suitable state-of-the-art fabs could be rented from companies which produced less profitable semiconductors (such as DRAMs and EPROMs). Analysts also knew that while the best known names in the PC business—Compaq, IBM, Dell, NEC, and Toshiba (together representing about 30 per cent of microcomputer sales)—had thus far purchased microprocessors only from Intel, it was not clear whether they would continue to do so.

The stock market seemed to treat the competitive threats to Intel with increasing seriousness. From the time of the announcement of the i386 in early 1986 until the recognition that AMD was successfully shipping its imitation in mid-1991, Intel's stock price rose from approximately $13 to $59. By the fall of 1991, however, the stock had fallen to the low $40s. (See **Exhibit 13–11** for information on stock prices.) Given 1991 anticipated earnings of $819 million, Intel's price-earnings ratio (P/E) was less than 11. Intel's management had become concerned about the market's increasingly negative view of Intel's competitive positioning.

Financial History

Intel became a public corporation in 1971, the year in which it recorded its first net profit. Even at that time, Intel carried almost no debt on its books (as of December 31, 1971, Intel's net worth and total assets were $13,456,344 and $14,839,755, respectively). The firm's policy was to issue debt only when and if the terms were attractive. For example, in the fall of 1983 Intel issued $110 million of 20-year adjustable- rate industrial revenue bonds, with an average interest rate of just under 8 percent.[3] In connection with these bonds, Intel was obliged to spend $110 million to finance expansion in Puerto Rico. To ensure that adequate debt financing would be available if suddenly needed, the company and its subsidiaries kept lines of bank credit in place—currently allowing for over $900 million in borrowing capacity.

Intel's debt issues often contained equity-linked components. For example, in August 1980 the firm issued $150 million in 20-year 7-percent convertible subordinated debentures. These debentures were called on September 14, 1983, and one month later the bonds were converted into 5,000,000 shares at approximately $30 per share. Intel also issued 10-year notes in May 1985 and April 1987 ($236.5 million of zero-coupon, 11.75-percent notes and $110 million of 8.125-percent notes, respectively). Both sets of notes were sold with detachable warrants (which yielded an additional $27.1 and $90.4 million in cash, respectively). The warrants from the note issues were

[3]During that year the average U.S. Treasury medium-and long-term bond yields were 10.45 and 11.11 percent, respectively.

EXHIBIT 13-8 Selected Financial Data, 1987-1991

	Advanced Micro Devices					Chips and Technologies				
	1987	1988	1989	1990	1991	1987	1988	1989	1990	1991(E)
Sales	997	1,126	1,105	1,059	1,175	80	141	218	293	225
Net income	(48)	19	46	(54)	(59)	13	22	33	29	(10)
Cash flow	105	173	182	75	188	14	24	38	29	2
Capital expenditures	138	132	159	304	142	2	7	5	14	9
Cash	235	287	279	115	128	30	48	59	72	38
Total assets	1,114	1,081	1,122	1,112	—	51	95	141	202	159
Long-term debt	136	130	126	131	155	1	3	6	9	7
(Long-term debt - cash)/ market value of equity (%)	-0.13	-0.23	-0.24	0.04	—	-1.09	-0.17	-0.16	-0.21	-0.30
Years of cash[a]	0.7	1.2	1.0	-0.1	-0.2	18.5	6.8	10.8	4.7	3.6
Return on equity (%)	-7.3	3.0	6.7	-8.4	—	48.8	33.2	31.4	1.9	-8.4
Cash dividend	0	0	0	0	0	0	0	0	0	0
High price	24.88	16.88	10.50	11.38	—	37.75	21.25	26.25	23.50	13.25
Low price	7.50	7.13	7.13	3.63	—	8.25	10.75	13.25	5.25	6.00
Book/share	6.21	5.91	6.39	5.63	6.70	2.03	4.79	7.30	9.31	8.51
P/E ratio	—	78	18	—	—	14	8	7	10	—
Market value	775	690	639	401	—	322	261	339	306	103
Shares (millions)	78.51	79.95	81.14	82.34	83.60	13.01	13.92	14.44	14.39	13.44
Beta	1.96	1.90	1.94	1.69	1.92	—	—	2.13	1.92	2.12

	Intel					IBM				
	1987	1988	1989	1990	1991	1987	1988	1989	1990	1991(E)
Sales	1,907	2,875	3,127	3,921	4,779	54,217	59,681	62,710	69,018	64,700
Net income	248	453	391	650	819	5,258	5,806	3,758	5,020	2,425
Cash flow	347	664	628	943	1,215	8,785	9,362	7,998	10,237	8,696
Capital expenditures	302	477	422	680	873	4,304	5,390	6,414	6,509	6,580
Cash[b]	881	1,393	1,598	2,346	2,757	6,967	6,123	4,961	4,551	4,700
Total assets	2,597	3,550	3,994	5,376	6,292	63,688	73,037	77,734	87,568	—
Long-term debt	298	479	412	345	363	3,858	8,518	10,825	11,943	11,991
(Long-term debt - cash)/ market value of equity (%)	-0.13	-0.21	-0.19	-0.26	-0.49	-0.05	0.03	0.11	0.11	—
Years of cash[a]	1.9	1.9	2.8	2.9	2.7	0.7	-0.4	-0.9	-1.1	1.1
Return on equity (%)	13.4	21.8	15.3	18.1	22.8	13.7	13.9	9.8	14.1	—
Cash dividend	0	0	0	0	0	2.654	2.609	2.752	2.774	2.803
High price	41.83	37.25	36.00	52.00	59.00	175.88	129.50	130.88	123.13	—
Low price	13.83	19.25	22.88	28.00	37.00	102.00	104.25	93.38	94.50	—
Book/share	7.76	11.52	13.81	17.99	21.14	64.09	66.99	67.01	74.96	74.60
P/E ratio	19	9	17	12	11	13	13	15	11	—
Market value	4,461	4,288	6,366	7,687	8,882	68,960	71,875	54,094	64,567	—
Shares (millions)	168.33	180.54	184.52	199.65	208.99	597.05	589.74	574.70	571.39	572.14
Beta	1.67	1.74	1.68	1.70	1.75	0.75	0.81	0.85	0.75	0.74

LSI Logic Corp. / Motorola, Inc.

	LSI Logic Corp. 1987	1988	1989	1990	1991	Motorola, Inc. 1987	1988	1989	1990	1991(E)
Sales	262	379	547	655	—	6,707	8,250	9,620	10,885	11,400
Net income	11	25	(25)	(33)	—	308	445	498	499	450
Cash flow	50	77	63	67	—	802	988	1,148	1,289	1,267
Capital expenditures	174	101	114	62	—	689	873	1,094	1,256	1,128
Cash	267	204	153	159	—	258	340	433	577	627
Total assets	699	787	765	784	—	5,321	6,710	7,686	8,742	—
Long-term debt	188	192	204	190	—	344	343	755	792	794
(Long-term debt - cash)/ market value of equity (%)	-0.20	-0.03	0.18	0.12	—	0.01	0.00	0.04	0.03	—
Years of cash[a]	0.5	0.1	-0.4	-0.5	—	-0.1	-0.0	-0.3	-0.2	-0.1
Return on equity (%)	3.5	7.2	-8.4	-12.3	—	10.2	13.2	13.1	11.7	—
Cash dividend	0	0	0	0	—	83	87	99	100	100
High price	17.25	13.63	12.38	13.00	—	74.00	54.63	62.50	88.38	—
Low price	6.50	7.25	6.25	5.13	—	34.50	35.88	39.50	49.13	—
Book/share	7.70	8.20	7.24	6.55	—	23.26	26.02	28.16	32.32	35.05
P/E ratio	37	19	—	—	—	21	15	12	14	—
Market value	395	435	293	263	—	6,433	5,447	7,612	6,898	—
Shares (millions)	40.05	40.46	41.07	42.06	—	129.30	129.70	130.40	131.70	131.95
Beta	2.30	1.95	1.76	1.48	1.71	1.47	1.49	1.55	1.48	1.49

Texas Instruments / VSLI Technology

	Texas Instruments 1987	1988	1989	1990	1991	VSLI Technology 1987	1988	1989	1990	1991(E)
Sales	5,594	6,295	6,522	6,567	6,600	172	221	288	325	410
Net income	309	366	292	(39)	(170)	8	7	1	(13)	9.5
Cash flow	637	756	745	502	398	32	36	38	36	57
Capital expenditure	463	628	863	909	500	50	55	39	35	50
Cash	663	780	637	412	416	103	75	55	35	41
Total assets	4,256	4,427	4,804	5,048	—	271	303	318	327	—
Long-term debt	487	624	618	715	950	81	84	85	89	100
(Long-term debt - cash)/ market value of equity (%)	-0.04	-0.05	-0.01	0.10	—	-0.09	0.04	0.17	0.48	—
Years of cash[a]	0.4	0.2	0.0	-0.3	-1.0	0.4	-0.2	-0.8	-1.5	-1.2
Return on equity (%)	14.9	21.3	14.9	-2.1	—	5.7	4.5	0.3	-8.7	—
Cash dividend	55	58	59	59	59	0	0	0	0	0
High price	80.25	60.00	46.75	44.00	—	20.25	11.38	10.13	12.25	—
Low price	36.25	34.50	28.13	22.50	—	7.13	5.88	6.38	3.00	—
Book/share	21.95	21.36	24.10	22.46	17.10	6.15	6.40	6.42	5.86	6.30
P/E ratio	15	10	12	—	—	36	29	369	@NM	—
Market value	4,383	3,306	2,924	3,108	—	246	200	178	113	—
Shares (million)	78.62	80.65	81.50	81.78	81.99	22.86	23.48	24.17	25.11	25.81
Beta	1.09	1.31	1.50	1.43	1.58	2.11	1.84	1.69	1.63	1.99

[a] Years of Cash reports the number of years of current investment expenditures which can be funded by net cash balances — (Cash - Long-term Debt) / Capital Expenditures.

[b] Cash balances for Intel include Long-term Investments.

Sources: Value Line and Standard and Poors.

Exhibit 13–9 Intel X86 Family Sales

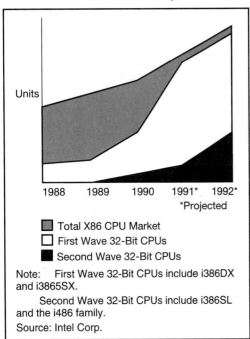

Units

1988 1989 1990 1991* 1992*
*Projected

■ Total X86 CPU Market
□ First Wave 32-Bit CPUs
■ Second Wave 32-Bit CPUs

Note: First Wave 32-Bit CPUs include i386DX
and i3865SX.

   Second Wave 32-Bit CPUs include i386SL
and the i486 family.

Source: Intel Corp.

tives to strengthen Intel's balance sheet. In June 1987, however, IBM was persuaded to terminate its investment in Intel, and Intel repurchased and retired 13,350,000 shares from IBM for $361.6 million, or about $27 per share. In August of 1987, Intel also issued 9 million one-year warrants for $63.3 million. In August 1988, the warrants were exercised (at a price of $30 per share), yielding Intel another $268.6 million in cash net of fees. **Exhibit 13–11** shows the timing of these equity-linked transactions.

The company also maintained several liberal stock option plans which generated cash through the exercise of employee options and direct share purchases. During 1990—which was not an atypical year—options were exercised on 2.9 million shares, generating approximately $42.0 million in cash. In that year, employees also purchased an additional 1.4 million shares under Intel's stock participation plan, resulting in an additional inflow of $39.3 million.

In an effort to offset the steady dilution from the stock purchase and option plans, in August 1990 management authorized the repurchase of up to 20 million shares. Repurchases would be performed by the Treasurer and would take place in the open market or in privately negotiated transactions. After consulting with Moore and others, Arvind Sodhani soon executed the repurchase of approximately 3.2 million shares at a total cost of $102.4 million. However, as management was hesitant to buyback shares at a price much above $40, the repurchase activity soon came to a halt. With the stock currently stalled in the low $40s, some analysts began to interpret Intel's reluctance to re-

exercised in 1990, resulting in the issuance of 14.15 million shares at an average price of $27.80 per share.

Intel had also issued stock during the last decade, although never publicly. On February 7, 1983, IBM purchased 12.5 million newly issued shares in Intel (equivalent to approximately 13 percent of previously outstanding shares) for $250 million. IBM, which accounted for 8.6 percent of Intel revenues in 1983, had clear incen-

Exhibit 13-10 Portability of Various Microprocessor Platforms

	Microprocessor Platform				
	X86	68000	MIPS	SPARC	RS/6000
Operating System Software:					
DOS	X				
Windows	X				
32-Bit OS/2	X				
UNIX	X	X	X	X	X
Microsoft Windows NT#	X		X		
Apple/IBM New OS#	X	X			X
Sunsoft Solaris 2.0#	X			X	
Source: Intel Corp.					

EXHIBIT 13-11 Stock Price History and Recent End-of-Month Stock Prices

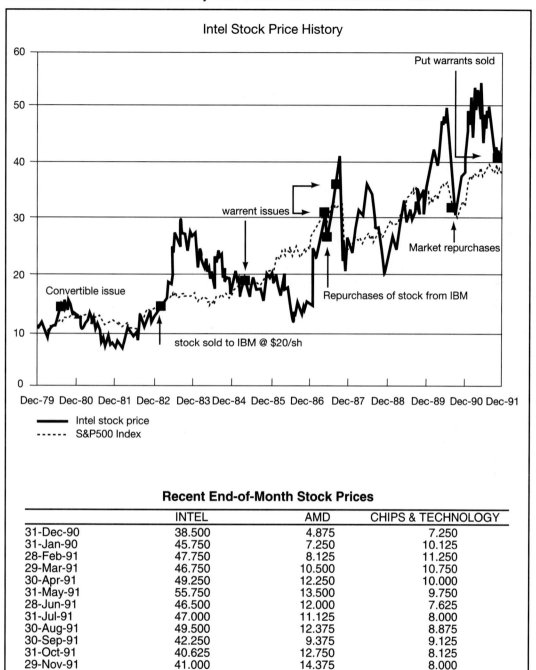

Intel Stock Price History

Legend:
— Intel stock price
- - - - - S&P500 Index

Annotations visible on chart: Put warrants sold, warrent issues, Convertible issue, Repurchases of stock from IBM, Market repurchases, stock sold to IBM @ $20/sh

Recent End-of-Month Stock Prices

	INTEL	AMD	CHIPS & TECHNOLOGY
31-Dec-90	38.500	4.875	7.250
31-Jan-90	45.750	7.250	10.125
28-Feb-91	47.750	8.125	11.250
29-Mar-91	46.750	10.500	10.750
30-Apr-91	49.250	12.250	10.000
31-May-91	55.750	13.500	9.750
28-Jun-91	46.500	12.000	7.625
31-Jul-91	47.000	11.125	8.000
30-Aug-91	49.500	12.375	8.875
30-Sep-91	42.250	9.375	9.125
31-Oct-91	40.625	12.750	8.125
29-Nov-91	41.000	14.375	8.000
20-Dec-91	42.500	17.000	7.750

Intel Corporation, 1992

purchase as a negative signal about the firm's future prospects.

While Sodhani did not repurchase additional shares directly, he did perform a kind of conditional repurchase in November 1991. That is, Intel privately sold about 3.5 million tradeable put warrants to some of its institutional investors for approximately $14 million. Each warrant gave its holder the right to sell one share of common stock back to Intel at $40 per share in one year's time. The repurchase was "conditional" because investors would not (rationally) elect the repurchase unless the stock price were below $40 on the warrants' expiration date.

In April 1989, Intel undertook several steps to strengthen its independence and to protect it from potential hostile acquirers. Specifically, Intel issued to its existing stockholders a set of common-stock-purchase Rights, which would trade in a one-to-one ratio with existing shares of common stock. The Rights could be exercised or traded separately from the shares of stock they represented only if certain events occurred. For example, under one of the Right's provisions, at any time after an entity acquired more than 20 percent but less than 50 percent of Intel's stock, Intel had the option to exchange the Rights (other than those held by the acquirer) for shares of common stock, with an exchange ratio of one to one.[4] This gave Intel the ability to dilute substantially a potential acquirer's holdings and therefore created a large disincentive to attempting a hostile takeover.

During the 1980s, Intel's net cash position grew steadily. Between 1980 and 1982, the ratio of long-term debt to total assets stood at approximately 20 percent, and the firm's cash position was negligible. After IBM's stock purchase and the 1985 issuance of 10-year notes, Intel's cash and equivalents plus long-term investments (which consisted of liquid investments in bonds rated AA or higher) less long-term debt rose to approximately 15 percent of total assets in December 1986. By December 1991, this ratio had grown to approximately 38 percent. This was in spite of the fact that, during the 1986-to-1991 period, Intel had experienced very rapid growth, with revenues increasing at a compound annual rate of over 30 percent. Intel's competitors kept proportionately much smaller cash balances (see **Exhibit 13–9**), although several large firms in the industry, such as IBM, held larger absolute amounts.

[4]The statuary and case law pertaining to such Rights issues was highly developed in the State of Delaware, where Intel was incorporated beginning in mid-1989.

The Decision

As Moore contemplated these developments, he wondered whether Intel's cash balances had grown unnecessarily large. At $2.4 billion, the firm could fund its planned investment expenditures out of cash for almost two and one-half years without using any cashflow from operations. While there remained great uncertainty about the level of these flows, earnings estimates from analysts suggested that operations would continue to generate cash—indeed, perhaps in substantial amounts. **Exhibit 13–12** presents cash flow forecasts based on several analysts' expectations of future earnings.

Harold Hughes and Arvind Sodhani weighed the arguments for and against a change in cash disbursement policies. Both believed that Intel's cash was an important competitive weapon and that, with the economy in recession, "cash was king." It seemed to Hughes and Sodhani that the costs of holding cash were small, especially in view of the high returns Intel's treasury had earned on its cash balances. For several years, Hughes and Sodhani had posted returns of approximately 170 basis points over U.S. Treasury bills without investing in securities rated below AA (see **Exhibit 13–2**). This "excess" income after tax in 1990 alone came to about $18 million. Nonetheless, Hughes and Sodhani started to explore several cash-disbursement options that were open to Intel.

First, Intel could continue or expand its market repurchase program. In practice, however, open-market repurchases were executed

EXHIBIT 13-12 Estimates of Future Cash Flows

Depreciation Worksheet	1991	1992	1993	1994	1995
Earnings estimates from analysts:					
Average	819	862	1,028	1,166	1,339
Pessimistic	819	485	595	700	900
Capital Expenditures:	(948)	(1,200)	(1,380)	(1,587)	(1,746)
Land and Buildings	(237)	(240)	(276)	(317)	(349)
Machinery and Equipment	(711)	(960)	(1,104)	(1,270)	(1,397)
Depreciation Expense	418	666	971	1,044	1,235
Net Additions to PPE	(530)	(534)	(409)	(543)	(511)
Decrease in Net Working Capital	(58)	(11)	(42)	(35)	(43)
Shares issued, @$40, 3M/yr	120	120	120	120	120
Put warrants issued	14	0	0	0	0
Paydown of Long-Term Debt to 0	0	(91)	(91)	(91)	(90)
Annual Change in Cash*:					
Average	365	346	606	617	815
% of Estimated Revenues	8%	9%	12%	11%	12%
Pessimistic	365	1	198	221	426
% of Estimated Revenues	8%	0%	2%	3%	4%
Cash Balance plus Long-Term Investments less Long-Term Debt:					
Average	2,394	2,740	3,346	3,964	4,779
Pessimistic	2,394	2,395	2,593	2,815	3,241
Total Assets	6,292	7,169	8,309	9,335	10,694
Total Cash/Total Assets:					
Average	38%	38%	40%	42%	45%
Pessimistic	38%	33%	31%	30%	30%

*Note: Annual change in cash is equal to estimates Earnings and Net additions to PP&E + decrease in net working capital + proceeds from shares and warrants issued + cost of paying down long-term debt.

Capital Expenditures are assumed to grow at 15 percent per year.

Depreciation: Straight line over 3.5 years for machinery and equipment and 25 years for plant and property.

Capital spending is also depreciated for six months in the year made. Net working capital: calculated as current assets - current libailities - cash and cash equivalents. In 1990 and 1991 NWC was 28% and 24% of earnings, respectively.

Estimates for 1992-95 assume that NWC remains at 25% of average estimated earnings.

Source: Intel Corporation and casewriter and analyst estimates.

only when management could agree that the stock price was unduly low. Hughes and Sodhani knew that such consensus was difficult to achieve. One alternative was to undertake a formal fixed-price tender offer, in which Intel would publicly announce an offer to buy back shares at a given price. Another repurchase possibility was a Dutch-auction, in which shareholders submitted schedules that reported the number of shares they would tender at each price across a range of shares it wanted to repurchase by picking a single price at which to buy.

A second alternative was for Intel to declare a $0.40 per share ($84 million total) annual dividend on its common stock. Dividends were controversial within Intel. While some favored dividends, others, such as Hughes and Sodhani, opposed them because dividends were a tax-disadvantaged means of disbursing corporate cash, and because a dividend represented an ongoing commitment that could be potentially difficult to maintain. Indeed, Hughes and Sodhani speculated that the market might react negatively to a dividend, perhaps pushing the stock price down even further. Nevertheless, dividends would give shareholders income on their holdings without having to sell shares.

A final alternative was a package of two less conventional securities. For the first, Intel would dividend to shareholders a two year put warrant, one warrant for each share of stock. Each warrant would be tradeable and gave its holder the right to sell 0.1 shares of stock back to Intel at the end of two years time at a price of $50 per share. Thus, for example, if Intel's stock price was $40 in two years, Intel would be obliged to buy back 208.99/10 = 20.9 million shares at $50 each (or a total of $1.0 billion) from those who held the warrants. Investors who were not interested in holding the warrants could sell them in the open market at an expected price of about $0.60 per warrant. The second security in the package was $1.0 billion of 10-year convertible subordinated debentures with a 5 percent coupon. The bonds would be convertible at the end of two years into 13.3 million shares of Intel common stock at a conversion price of $75 per share.

Moore wondered about the implications of these measures for the company's future competitive position and for shareholder value.

14. Sun Microsystems, Inc., 1987 (A)

Joe Graziano, the recently appointed chief financial officer of Sun Microsystems, considered the challenges unfolding before him and his company. The date was May 29, 1987, and Graziano had barely settled into his new office. Sun's chief rival, Apollo Computer Company, had just indicated to the press that it would soon introduce its next generation product, the Domain 4000. Sun could counter by introducing the Sun-4, a computer workstation family based on a reduced instruction set computer (RISC) chip, a revolutionary microprocessor architecture. (The appendix gives a technical overview of workstations and supporting products.)

The Sun-3, introduced in September 1985, had taken Sun from quarterly sales of $50 million and a 22% market share (second in the industry) to quarterly sales of $200 million and first place in the market with a 26% share. Historically, Sun would price a new computer line at the same level as the old line, and halve the price of the old line. Graziano wondered how the stock market would react to the cannibalization of the phenomenally successful Sun-3 family, a product likely to yield a healthy revenue stream in the absence of the Sun-4. He knew, however, that Sun would have to introduce the Sun-4 in the near future in order to remain competitive in a fast-paced industry.

Graziano could not ignore the stock market's view of the company. In the past fifteen months, Sun had issued $45 million in an initial public offering (IPO), an additional $75 million in common stock, and $100 million in convertible, subordinated debentures. At its present rate of growth, Sun would need additional funds by the end of 1988. Graziano worried that a new equity issue would massively dilute Sun's existing shareholders. (See Exhibits 1–3 for Sun's latest financial statements.)

Research Associate Jack Soll prepared this case under the supervision of Professor Carliss Baldwin as the basis for class discussion rather than to illustrate either effective or ineffective handling of an administrative situation.

EXHIBIT 14-1 Sun Consolidated Statement of Income (In thousands, except per share amount)

	Years Ended June 30			Nine Months Ended, March 27
	1984	1985	1986	1987
Net revenues	$38,860	$115,249	$210,104	$348,552
Costs and expenses:				
Cost of sales	21,309	61,697	101,965	174,233
Research and development	4,813	15,193	30,649	43,490
Selling, general and administrative	9,022	24,103	56,894	82,604
Total costs and expenses	$35,144	$100,993	$189,508	$300,327
Operating income	3,716	14,256	20,596	48,225
Interest income (expense), net	$ 286	$ (14)	$ 378	$ 255
Income before income taxes	4,002	14,242	20,974	48,480
Provision for income taxes	1,344	5,709	9,025	23,028
Net income	$ 2,658	$ 8,533	$ 11,949	$ 25,452
Income per common and common equivalent share	$ 0.13	$ 0.36	$ 0.46	$ 0.82
Common and common equivalent shares used in the calculation of income per share	21,051	23,766	26,217	31,496

The Sun Strategy: Systems Based on Standards

For many years computer vendors sold systems based exclusively on proprietary architectures. This strategy provided insurance: if a company lost its technological advantage, customers could not change brands unless they replaced all their machines.

In contrast, from its inception, Sun embraced open systems, architectures already accepted as industry standards.

In 1981 Andreas Bechtolsheim, a Stanford graduate student in computer science, built the first Sun computer using off-the-shelf parts. Bechtolsheim then joined forces with two recently-graduated Stanford MBAs, Scott McNealy and Vinod Khosla. The three founders obtained venture capital financing, which allowed them to make and market the first generation Sun-1.

McNealy, president and CEO of Sun in 1987, compared manufacturing a computer based on standards to the assembly line process developed by Ford Motor Company. Standards were the functional equivalent of interchangeable parts; each company in the highly fragmented workstation industry served as part of the production line. Although Sun designed and assembled its machines, it purchased components such as microprocessors, monitors, and disk drives from outside suppliers.

Without standards, Sun could not have purchased hardware devices as commodities. Instead, it would have had to design and manufacture the parts itself, or subcontract out production. Thus reliance on standards saved Sun valuable capital.

In addition, using a standard microprocessor and a standard operating system enabled Sun computers to run readily available software. Therefore, in its early days Sun did not suffer from the lack of software that often plagued new computer manufacturers.

Finally, Sun's founders discovered that the *users* of workstations attached great value to sys-

EXHIBIT 14-2 Sun Consolidated Balance Sheet (In thousands, except per share amount)

| | Years ended June 30 | | Nine Months Ended, March 27 |
	1985	1986	1987
Assets:			
Current assets:			
Cash and cash equivalents	$29,552	$ 49,666	$216,993
Accounts receivable, net of allowances	16,464	40,359	90,212
Inventories	17,852	38,752	87,428
Other current assets	1,269	3,832	7,721
Total current assets	65,137	132,609	402,354
Property and equipment:			
Machinery and equipment	$16,734	$ 42,538	$ 75,122
Furniture and fixtures	3,191	8,211	11,890
Leasehold improvements	2,364	7,751	11,487
	22,289	58,500	98,499
Accumulated depreciation and amortization	(5,855)	(12,989)	(27,167)
Net property and equipment	16,434	45,511	71,332
Other assets:	2,598	4,171	6,946
	$84,169	$182,291	$480,632
Liabilities and Shareholders' Equity:			
Current liabilities:			
Notes payable	$ 4,362	$ 14,960	$ 31,727
Accounts payable	8,619	29,664	46,165
Accrued payroll expenses	1,277	3,178	14,473
Accrued liabilities	2,651	5,806	10,743
Deferred credits on sale and leaseback arrangements	947	1,988	1,988
Long term debt due within one year	1,600	1,600	—
Obligations under capital leases	231	373	489
Income taxes payable	6,914	7,521	11,912
Deferred income taxes	1,061	2,013	7,506
Total current liabilities	$27,662	$ 67,103	$125,003
Deferred credits on sale and leaseback arrangements	1,615	2,159	668
Long term debt	5,323	2,223	125,000
Obligations under capital lease, less current portion	1,191	1,839	2,434
Shareholders' equity:			
Convertible preferred stock; 884,369 shares outstanding in 1985	35,218	—	—
Common stock, 27,179,428 shares outstanding in 1986 and 9,100,897 shares in 1985	6	18	22
Additional paid in capital	2,070	86,318	178,375
Retained earnings	11,715	23,664	49,116
Shareholder notes receivable	(651)	(832)	(519)
Foreign currency translation adjustment	20	(201)	533
Total shareholders' equitny	$48,378	$108,967	$227,527
	$84,169	$182,291	$480,632

tems based on standards. Proprietary communications networks and operating systems prevented the interlocking of different vendors' machines within the same network. Users wanted to pick and choose among the vendors for each hardware item, and also wanted to be able to change vendors without overhauling their entire system. Moreover, a user locked into a pro-

prietary system could only use software developed for that system. In contrast, systems based on standards offered the user a wide range of standard software products.

UNIX AND AT&T A key standard incorporated into Sun's workstations was the UNIX operating system. The operating system is software code

EXHIBIT 14-3 Sun Statement of Changes in Financial Position (In thousands)

	Years Ended June 30			Nine Months Ended, March 27
	1984	1985	1986	1987
Sources of Working Capital:				
Working capital provided from operations:				
Net income	$ 2,658	$ 8,533	$11,949	$ 25,452
Depreciation and Amortization	1,493	4,060	5,596	13,756
Working capital provided from operations:	4,151	12,593	17,545	39,208
Additions to obligations under capital leases	76	748	1,058	1,019
Proceeds related to deferred credits on sale				
and leaseback arrangements	—	1,893	2,082	—
Proceeds from long term debt	3,028	4,472	—	25,000
Proceeds from convertible				
subordinated debenture	—	—	—	100,000
Issuance of preferred stock, net	10,911	19,768	250	—
Issuance of common stock,				
net of repurchases	459	950	46,198	91,078
Repayment of shareholder receivables	—	—	913	313
Tax benefit related to ESOP	—	—	—	983
Issuance of warrants	230	—	—	—
Total Sources of Working Capital	$18,855	$40,424	$68,046	$257,601
Uses of Working Capital:				
Additions to property and equipment	$ 5,090	$14,931	$36,211	$39,999
Increase in other assets	173	2,198	1,573	3,844
Payment of obligations under capital leases	100	282	410	424
Payment of long term debt	332	1,845	1,600	2,223
Increase in deferred charge resulting from				
warrants issued	230	—	—	—
Foreign currency translation adjustment	—	(20)	221	(734)
Total Uses of Working Capital	$ 5,925	$19,236	$40,015	$ 45,756
Increase in working capital	$12,930	$21,188	$28,031	$211,845

that controls the computer and provides interfaces between the software, the human user, and the microprocessor.

In the mid-1980s, UNIX, an operating system developed by AT&T's Bell Labs, became the system of choice for many academics and engineers. Initially, as a regulated telephone monopoly, AT&T was prohibited from entering the computer market. Thus it licensed UNIX at low cost to all comers.

UNIX users in turn often adapted it to their own needs or added new features. For example, Sun's operating system, SunOS, was based on Berkeley 4.2, a version of UNIX developed at the University of California. Bill Joy, a world-renowned UNIX expert, served as Sun's vice president of research and development.

In the mid-eighties, after the breakup of the Bell system, AT&T sought to re-establish control over the development of UNIX. AT&T's System V

was not compatible with SunOS, and thus, in 1985 AT&T and Sun agreed to integrate the best features of their different systems. If the resulting UNIX version caught on, a single program could run on a wide spectrum of machines.

However, each company had projects with higher priority, and thus the unification of UNIX proceeded very slowly. In 1987 the two companies had continuing joint development programs, but their operating systems were still not compatible.

In early 1987 Sun attempted to combine its quest for a single version of UNIX with the promotion of its new SPARC chip as an industry standard (see below). Sun believed that an alliance with AT&T would stimulate market acceptance of both UNIX System V and SPARC.

The company approached John Scanlon, a vice president in AT&T's Business Markets group, to propose a technological joint venture to

Sun Systems, Inc.,1987 (A)

link SPARC to System V, with sophisticated software known as an applications binary interface. However, AT&T refused to consider Sun's proposal.

THE DEVELOPMENT of SPARC Initially, Sun relied on standard microprocessors manufactured by Motorola, one of the largest independent producers of "chips." However, in designing the Sun-4, it abandoned the Motorola microprocessor series, and instead used the Scalable Processor Architecture (SPARC) chip, its own proprietary reduced instruction set computer (RISC) design.

In developing the SPARC design, Sun departed from its former policy of relying solely on standard hardware components. Sun developed the SPARC microprocessor because it feared that the independent chip makers would be slow to adopt the new RISC architecture (see appendix). Their delay in turn would retard the technological progress of Sun workstations.

Although the market for RISC-based chips was potentially very large, Sun chose not to enter it. Instead, Sun licensed the SPARC design to several microprocessor manufacturers, notably Fujitsu, Cypress Semiconductor, and Bipolar Integrated Technology.

Sun's decision to license SPARC, rather than developing it as a new product, surprised many in the industry. However, McNealy believed that diversification into the microprocessor business would divert needed resources from the company's primary focus on workstations.

Competition

The fiercely competitive computer workstation industry required heavy investment in research and development and frequent new product introductions. Initially, in 1982, when workstations emerged as a separate market, hundreds of actual and potential competitors were poised to fight for market share.

By 1987 four companies—Sun, Apollo Computer, Hewlett Packard and DEC—dominated the industry. In addition, there were about a dozen companies with the technical or marketing skills to enter the market if they chose. Exhibit 4 lists the major workstation manufacturers and potential entrants as of 1987.

APOLLO COMPUTER The early leader in the technical workstation market was Apollo Computer Company, based in Chelmsford Mass. In late 1984 Apollo had nearly half the $615 million total installed value of workstation and slightly over half the $420 million in industry revenue for that year.

Although Apollo dominated the workstation market in the early 1980s, the company had difficulty keeping up with the market's rapid growth. A sharp downturn in demand and production difficulties caused it to lose money in 1985. Building on the success of the Sun-3, Sun grew faster than Apollo in 1986, and in the first quarter of 1987, Sun's revenues surpassed Apollo's for the first time in its history. Exhibit 5 summarizes Sun's and Apollo's new product introductions and financial moves from 1980 through early 1987.

IBM In 1984, when Apollo's market share and profitability peaked, several major computer manufacturers had yet to enter the market. For example, IBM Corporation did not then have a technical workstation product, even though workstations had penetrated IBM-dominated fields such as office automation and desktop publishing.

IBM made its move in January 1986 with the introduction of the RT PC, a computer that incorporated many, but not all, aspects of the RISC microprocessor. Surprisingly, the machine failed to match the capabilities offered by Sun and Apollo. In 1987, IBM languished in eighth place in the workstation market with a 3.9% market share.

DEC Digital Equipment Corporation also made its first serious bid for the market in January 1986 with the VAXstation II/GPX. Unlike IBM, Digital had a history of serving technical customers well. But at $35,000, the GPX lacked the price/performance ratio necessary to compete effectively.

EXHIBIT 14-4 Actual and Potential Workstation Manufacturers in 1987

Company	Workstation Revenue (1986)[1] (in millions)	Market Share[1] (in millions)	Total Assets (in millions)[2]	Internal Cash Flow[3]	Fiscal year end[4]
Present Competitors					
Apollo Computer	$ 361	23.1%	$ 367	$ 82	1/3/87
Sun Microsystems	316	20.2	182	48	6/30/86
Hewlett Packard	310	19.8	6,287	1,661	10/31/86
Digital Equipment	213	13.6	7,173	1,815	6/28/86
Silicon Graphics	52	3.3	107	115	6/30/87
IBM	38	2.4	57,814	13,326	12/31/86
Others	274	17.5			
Total	1,564	100.0			
Potential Entrants[5]					
AT&T	0	0	38,883	6,342	12/31/86
Apple	0	0	1,160	333	9/26/86
Intel	0	0	2,080	218	12/28/86
Next	0	0	N/A	N/A	N/A
MIPS	0	0	N/A	N/A	N/A
Matsushita	0	0	2,690	N/A	3/31/87
NEC	0	0	18,944	3,802	3/31/87
Sony	0	0	8,951	1,494	10/31/86

[1]Workstation revenue and market share information drawn from "The Technical Workstation Market: 1987 Results, 1988 Trends", Dataquest Incorporated (1988). Revenue data may differ from company annual report figures because definitions of the fiscal year 1986 vary.

[2]Total asset information taken from company annual reports.

[3]Internal cash flow information from company annual reports. Internal cash flow, or internally generated funds, is the sum of net income, depreciation and amortization, research and development spending, and paper losses such as inventory writedowns or loss carryforwards.

[4]Lists dates of annual reports used to compile this exhibit.

[5]Some companies listed in this section may have small workstation revenue and market share. Zeros are entered for want of data.

In late April 1986 Digital introduced an entry-level, monochrome workstation, the VAXstation II/RC, priced under $15,000. Digital also reduced the price of the GPX to $30,500, the first in a series of price moves designed to gain market share. In 1987 Digital, had a 20% market share, and was third in the industry behind Sun and Apollo.

HEWLETT-PACKARD Hewlett-Packard Company entered the workstation business in 1985 with the HP 9000 Series 300 family. While HP accounted for nearly 20% of the industry in 1986, it sold mostly to specialized "niche" markets. For example, HP packaged the 9000 with medical monitoring equipment.

AT&T AT&T did not have a product in the technical workstation market in 1987. However, virtually every workstation manufacturer had shifted to a UNIX operating system. AT&T, the creator and licensor of UNIX, had recently published protocols which would allow different version of UNIX to run the same software. (See appendix.)

AT&T's managers believed a huge network would eventually connect computers distributed throughout the country. They felt AT&T had the resources to dominate this new field of distributed computing and communication. The company had acquired networking technology through its years as the telephone monopoly. Its engineers had developed sophisticated UNIX software. Finally, with over $30 billion in assets and $6 billion of internal cash flow, AT&T's financial resources were unmatched by any in the industry except IBM.

Notwithstanding these advantages, AT&T's first attempt to enter the highly competitive computer market was unsuccessful. AT&T would not divulge the figures, but analysts estimated that in 1985 and 1986, AT&T's computer division lost nearly $2 billion on sales of $4.5 billion.

The company did succeed in capturing 5% of the personal computer market with its PC6300, an IBM compatible. However, AT&T did not manufacture this machine. The PC6300 was designed and built by Olivetti, an Italian electronics firm in which AT&T held 22% ownership. AT&T earned very little by selling the Olivetti machines, but netted hundreds of millions in capital gains as Olivetti stock skyrocketed. In late 1986, AT&T recruited Vittorio Cassoni, director of Olivetti's North American computer business, to head up its computer division.

Financial Strategy: Sun vs. Apollo

Sun's financial strategy had contributed to its newly secured leadership in the technical workstation market. Graziano believed that financial choices, as much as technology and marketing, would determine which companies would survive the next rounds of competition.

INTERNAL FINANCING For high-tech companies that invest considerable amounts in R&D, internal cash flow may be defined as the sum of net income, research and development spending, depreciation, and other non-cash charges such as deferred taxes and inventory writedowns. In a high-growth market such as computer workstations, these funds fuel investments in working capital, expenditures on research and development, and investments in new plant and equipment. Exhibit 6 presents Sun's quarterly sources and uses of funds, balance sheets, and selected financial ratios. Exhibit 7 does the same for Apollo.

In September 1985 Apollo led the workstation market with third quarter net sales of over $55.2 million, compared to $33.7 million for Sun. However, an industry-wide slump hit Apollo harder than expected, and caused the company to lay off temporarily 3,700 employees in August 1985, and to fire another 300 in September. Thus, although Apollo's third quarter sales exceeded Sun's, they were down 37% from the second quarter. The company reported an after-tax loss of $18.5 million in the quarter (see Exhibit 7).

Apollo faced a further challenge in the third quarter of 1985: Sun had just started to ship the Sun-3 family, based on the Motorola 68020 chip (see Exhibit 5).

Despite these problems, in 1985 Apollo still had higher internal cash flow than Sun. In the fourth quarter of 1985, Apollo generated $16 million internally (including R&D expenditures) compared to Sun's $9 million.

However, between September 1985 and April 1987, Apollo failed to match Sun's impressive growth rate. The Domain 3000 series, Apollo's main product simply did not sell as well as the comparable Sun-3 series. By the first quarter of 1987 Sun had drawn even with Apollo in sales, profits, and internal cash flow.

DEBT FINANCING Sun used significant amounts of straight debt to fund its growth during this period. It typically maintained a senior debt ratio (senior debt/(total debt + equity)) between 17% and 21%. By the end of the third quarter of 1987, Sun had nearly $70 million of senior debt on its balance sheet.

Apollo maintained a more conservative capital structure. Unexpected losses and high research and development costs forced it to borrow $20 million in the third quarter of 1985, and another $10 million in the following quarter. However, the company repaid this straight debt in the beginning of 1986 with proceeds from a $100 million convertible, subordinated debenture issue. From then on, in contrast to Sun, Apollo limited debt to only a few million dollars, mostly in the form of capital leases. Apollo's senior debt ratio generally fell below 2%.

EXHIBIT 14-5 Sun and Apollo Chronology

Date	Sun	Apollo
1980		Apollo incorporated
February 1982	Sun Microsystems incorporated	
March 1983		$51 million initial public offering
July 1983	Technology and OEM agreement with Computervision	
August 1983		Secondary offer
October 1983		DN660 and DN460 introduced
November 1983	Sun-2 family introduced	
October 1984		$63 million common stock issue
November 1984	Kodak buys 7% interest in Sun for $20 million	
August 1985		Apollo temporarily lays off 3,700 employees
September 1985	Sun and AT&T agree to resolve operating system differences Sun-3 family introduced	Apollo reports an $18.5 million net loss
February 1986		$97 million convertible subordinated debenture issue Domain Series 3000 introduced
March 1986	$45 million initial public offering	
August 1986	Sun-3/200 introduced	
November 1986	$75 million common stock issue	
February 1987	$98 million convertible subordinated debenture issue	

EQUITY FINANCING   From 1985 to 1987, Sun's external financing through common stock and convertibles also surpassed Apollo's. Before going public, Sun obtained equity from venture capitalists and customers. In November 1984 Eastman Kodak, a major customer that accounted for 12% of Sun's revenue, purchased 7% of Sun stock for $20 million in a private placement. Sun granted Kodak a seat on its board of directors, but the contract limited Kodak to 15% of Sun stock, except in the event of an attempted takeover.

In March 1986 Sun sold 11.4% of its outstanding shares to the public for $45 million (additional proceeds of $16 million went to the existing shareholders). Sun followed this offering with a $75 million issue of common stock in November 1986 and a $100 million convertible subordinated debenture issue in February 1987. Thus, including the initial public offering, the company issued $220 million in stock and convertible debentures in three issues between March 1986 and February 1987, compared to $100 million for Apollo.

Through these equity and convertible debt issues, Sun had built up a war chest of over $200 million of cash (see Exhibit 6). Graziano and Mc-Nealy felt that this liquidity was only prudent, however, for as Sun's sales rose, its cash needs would increase as well. If Sun continued to spend at its present rate, the $216 million in the bank would run out in late 1988 or early 1989.

The repeated issues of new equity and convertible debentures did little to dampen the stock market's enthusiasm for Sun. Sun's shares traded in the range of $40 to $44 in late May 1987. This was almost three times the initial public offering price set only a year before. Exhibit 8 shows Sun's and Apollo's stock prices from March 1986 through May 29, 1987.

SPENDING   To keep up with technology and growth in the technical workstation market, Sun and Apollo spent liberally on research and development, plant and equipment, working capital, and other assets. Neither company paid dividends.

Bob Smith, Graziano's predecessor as chief financial officer of Sun, had compared Sun's and Apollo's spending patterns through the first quarter of 1987. The comparison revealed that the two companies invested about the same amount in research and development as a percent of sales. However, Apollo invested in capital much more intensively than Sun did. Apollo held about twice as much property, plant, and equipment relative to sales. (See Selected Financial Ratios in Exhibits 6 and 7.)

Apollo also used more working capital than Sun. Since its troubles in the fall of 1985, Apollo had an average collection period of 80 to 90 days, while Sun's average collection period ranged from 48 to 67 days. Apollo's days of inventory peaked in the third quarter of 1985 at 178 days, but averaged around 130 days in later quarters. Sun's inventories had been lower (around 95 days) but over the last four quarters had increased to 112 days.

Although differing in the details, prior to 1986, Sun and Apollo each spent two to three times as much as it generated internally on working capital, property, plant and equipment and other assets.

However, after the losses reported in late 1985, Apollo, under a new, cost-conscious CEO, adopted a more conservative financial policy. In its 1985 Annual Report, Apollo announced that it planned to reduce capital expenditures in the forthcoming year. The report emphasized that "good internal control is a basic management responsibility."

The success of the new internal controls was evidenced in Apollo's cash flow figures. Its quarterly internal funds deficit dropped from a high of $37.8 million in September 1985 to less than $10 million in the latest quarter.

Sun's quarterly internal funds deficit peaked at $25 million, in September 1986. Significantly, this was the quarter in which Sun introduced the Sun 3/200, a new high end workstation series. As the new product gained market acceptance, the internal funds deficit shrank. By March 1987, it had fallen to $9.6 million per quarter. However Sun was poised to introduce its *next* product—the Sun-4.

The Impact of a New Product Introduction

Graziano considered Sun's probably response to the upcoming introduction of the Apollo Domain 4000. If Apollo acted as it had in the past, it would not seek to obsolete its entire product line. Instead, it would most likely introduce one or more high-end products incorporating new capabilities.

In principle, Sun's managers had some flexibility in tailoring their company's response. They could introduce the new generation products without fanfare and at high prices. This might delay customers' conversion to the Sun-4. Sun could then preserve its gross margins and slow its growth rate. Business might continue as usual for a few months; Sun could use this breathing space to nail down additional financing for the next generation.

However, Graziano felt that other members of Sun's management team would favor a dramatic new product introduction, a substantial price decrease on older machines, and a rapid ramp up in production and inventory. In this case, Sun could continue to grow at the rapid pace of 25% to 30% per quarter for the next six to eight quarters. Gross margins would drop initially and then, if all went well, return to their present level. In addition, Sun would require $40 million to $50 million in new working capital in the quarter of the new product introduction.

If Sun pursued this strategy, it would most probably continue to grow faster than cash-constrained Apollo and other close competitors. However, the strategy would expose Sun to the risks of manufacturing disaster and of a sales decline in existing products. For example, if customers were eager to purchase the new Sun-4's and if Sun could not deliver them, customers would simply hold off on any orders until the new products were available. In these circumstances, Sun's sales might decrease by 25% and costs

EXHIBIT 14-6 Sun Financial History (Thousands of dollars unless otherwise shown)

	Quarter Ended 6/30/85	Quarter Ended 9/27/85	Quarter Ended 12/27/85	Quarter Ended 3/28/86	Quarter Ended 6/30/86	Quarter Ended 9/26/86	Quarter Ended 12/26/86	Quarter Ended 3/27/87
Sales	$37,322	$33,690	$42,173	$57,578	$76,663	$91,572	$115,275	$141,705
Cost of Goods Sold (CGS)	N/A	17,183	20,578	28,041	36,163	45,601	57,614	71,018
R&D	N/A	5,289	6,299	7,928	11,133	10,833	13,899	18,758
Internal Sources								
Net Income	2,086	978	1,684	3,386	5,901	6,745	8,515	10,192
Depreciation and Amortization	1,214	582	1,343	1,512	2,159	3,647	4,313	5,796
Funds Provided from Operations	3,300	1,560	3,027	4,898	8,060	10,392	12,828	15,988
Uses								
PP&E	6,041	4,076	3,805	8,273	20,057	9,878	13,234	16,887
Other Assets	1,182	188	435	1,364	(193)	1,163	297	1,650
Working Capital (excl cash & notes)	(13,532)	4,802	7,314	2,689	(6,888)	24,961	12,477	7,080
Total Uses	(6,309)	9,066	11,554	12,326	12,976	36,002	26,008	25,617
Net Internal Funds Surplus (Deficit)	9,609	(7,506)	(8,527)	(7,428)	(4,916)	(25,610)	(13,180)	(9,629)
Capital Sources								
Debt	2,419	498	631	(93)	(493)	(487)	25,648	99,507
Equity	423	59	383	47,105	401	51	86,695	4,332
Net Capital Inflows (Outflows)	2,842	557	1,014	47,012	(92)	(436)	112,343	103,839
Change in Cash Balances	12,451	(6,949)	(7,513)	39,584	(5,008)	(26,046)	99,163	94,210
Ending Cash Balances	29,552	22,603	15,090	54,674	49,666	23,620	122,783	216,993

	Quarter Ended 6/30/85	Quarter Ended 9/27/85	Quarter Ended 12/27/85	Quarter Ended 3/28/86	Quarter Ended 6/30/86	Quarter Ended 9/26/86	Quarter Ended 12/26/86	Quarter Ended 3/27/87
Selected Ratios								
Growth Rate in Sales	9%	(10%)	25%	37%	33%	19%	26%	23%
Gross Margin	47%	49%	51%	51%	53%	50%	50%	50%
R&D as a % of Sales	N/A	16%	15%	14%	15%	12%	12%	13%
Net Income as a % of Sales	6%	3%	4%	6%	8%	7%	7%	7%
Depreciation / Sales (%)	3%	2%	3%	3%	3%	4%	4%	4%
Other Asset Outlays / Sales (%)	3%	1%	1%	2%	0%	1%	0%	1%
Total Uses / Funds Provided from Operations	N/A	5.8	3.8	2.5	1.6	3.5	2.0	1.6
Balance Sheet								
Cash	$29,552	$22,603	$15,090	$54,674	$49,666	$23,620	$122,783	$216,993
Current Assets	35,585	42,044	74,752	77,020	82,943	124,665	157,373	185,361
Net Property, Plant, & Equipment	16,434	19,939	17,147	28,110	45,511	51,246	59,670	71,332
Other	2,598	2,775	3,301	4,242	4,171	5,318	5,172	6,946
Total	$84,169	$87,361	$110,290	$164,046	$182,291	$204,849	$344,998	$480,632
Notes Payable	4,362	5,673	8,476	11,596	14,960	19,283	22,086	31,727
Other Current Liabilities	23,300	23,646	41,074	42,696	52,143	64,581	82,009	93,276
Long Term Debt (including lease obligations)	8,129	8,627	9,258	7,210	6,221	5,238	29,404	128,102
Net Worth	48,378	49,415	51,482	102,544	108,967	115,747	211,499	227,527
Total	$84,169	$87,361	$110,290	$164,046	$182,291	$204,849	$344,998	$480,632
Selected Balance Sheet Ratios								
A/R / Sales (%)	44%	66%	73%	76%	53%	74%	71%	64%
Days Receivable	40	60	66	69	48	67	65	58
A/P / CGS (%)	N/A	66%	63%	87%	82%	76%	80%	65%
Days Payable	N/A	60	58	79	75	69	72	59
Inventory / CGS (%)	N/A	106%	100%	104%	107%	115%	121%	123%
Days Inventory	N/A	96	91	95	98	105	110	112
Ending Net PPE / Sales (%)	44%	N/A	N/A	49%	59%	56%	52%	50%

EXHIBIT 14-7 Apollo Financial History (Thousands of dollars unless otherwise shown)

Quarter	Quarter Ended 6/29/85	Quarter Ended 9/28/85	Quarter Ended 12/28/85	Quarter Ended 3/29/86	Quarter Ended 6/28/86	Quarter Ended 9/27/86	Quarter Ended 1/3/87	Ended 4/4/87
Sales	87,548	55,232	70,675	82,021	88,382	100,408	120,874	123,420
Cost of Goods Sold (CGS)	42,054	38,657	38,188	45,920	47,274	53,178	63,617	61,020
R&D	11,520	10,855	9,888	10,923	10,666	10,831	12,230	13,822
Internal Sources								
Net Income	7,365	(18,459)	732	539	1,041	2,476	5,275	6,430
Depreciation and Amortization	3,756	5,254	4,917	7,139	6,844	7,404	6,930	9,947
Deferred Income Taxes	2,833	(993)	(48)	(1,735)	(2,653)	3,200	(1,895)	(862)
Funds Provided from Operations	13,954	(14,198)	5,601	5,943	5,232	13,080	10,310	15,515
Uses								
PP&E	31,552	12,934	11,023	11,093	8,411	8,434	13,598	14,040
Other Assets	(991)	(256)	883	5,181	2,251	5,699	1,598	4,888
Working Capital (excl cash & notes)	12,055	10,931	5,302	12,364	5,200	8,987	2,304	6,024
Total Uses	42,616	23,609	17,208	28,638	15,862	23,120	17,500	24,952
Net Internal Funds Surplus (Deficit)	(28,662)	(37,807)	(11,607)	(22,695)	(10,630)	(10,040)	(7,190)	(9,437)
Capital Sources								
Debt	11,050	21,452	14,498	89,624	(20)	(15)	(41)	(82)
Equity	1,604	441	931	1,107	963	1,281	1,092	2,262
Net Capital Inflows (Outflows)	12,654	21,893	15,429	90,731	943	1,266	1,051	2,180
Change in Cash Balances	(16,008)	(15,914)	3,822	68,036	(9,687)	(8,774)	(6,139)	(7,257)
Ending Cash Balances	18,825	2,911	6,733	74,769	65,082	56,308	50,169	42,912

	Quarter Ended 6/29/85	Quarter Ended 9/28/85	Quarter Ended 12/28/85	Quarter Ended 3/29/86	Quarter Ended 6/28/86	Quarter Ended 9/27/86	Quarter Ended 1/3/87	Quarter Ended 4/4/87
Selected Ratios								
Growth Rate in Sales	7%	(37%)	28%	16%	8%	14%	20%	2%
Gross Margin	52%	30%	46%	44%	47%	47%	47%	51%
R&D as a % of Sales	13%	20%	14%	13%	12%	11%	10%	11%
Net Income as a % of Sales	8%	N/A	1%	1%	1%	2%	4%	5%
Other Asset Outlays / Sales (%)	N/A	N/A	1%	6%	3%	6%	1%	4%
Total Uses / Funds Provided from Operations	3.1	N/A	3.1	4.8	3.0	1.8	1.7	1.6
Balance Sheet								
Cash	$ 18,825	$ 2,911	$ 6,733	$ 74,769	$ 65,082	$ 56,308	$ 50,169	$ 42,912
Current Assets	143,885	157,584	155,740	167,016	177,511	191,017	192,557	198,886
Net Property, Plant & Equipment	85,261	86,489	93,311	95,049	97,713	103,043	110,905	117,172
Other	1,257	1,230	1,850	8,783	10,464	11,813	12,934	16,815
Total	$249,228	$248,214	$257,634	$345,617	$350,770	$362,181	$366,565	$375,785
Notes Payable	0	0	0	0	0	0	0	0
Other Current Liabilities	59,682	61,456	54,278	51,860	54,472	62,131	59,486	58,847
Long Term Debt (including lease obligations)	664	15,042	29,395	117,861	117,619	117,372	117,162	117,008
Net Worth	188,882	171,716	173,961	175,896	178,679	182,678	189,917	199,930
Total	$249,228	$248,214	$257,634	$345,617	$350,770	$362,181	$366,565	$375,785
Balance Sheet Ratios								
A/R / Sales (%)	71%	105%	92%	103%	103%	105%	91%	88%
Days Receivable	65	95	83	94	94	95	83	80
A/P / CGS (%)	77%	58%	52%	48%	55%	58%	34%	32%
Days Payable	70	53	47	43	50	53	31	29
Inventory / CGS (%)	185%	196%	175%	136%	146%	143%	117%	133%
Days Inventory	168	178	159	124	133	130	107	121
Ending Net PPE / Sales (%)	97%	157%	132%	116%	111%	103%	92%	95%

might rise by 20% for one or two quarters while the production engineers worked out the problems in the system.

Conversely, customers might not accept the new and unproven technology embedded in the Sun-4's SPARC microprocessor. Sun had developed variations of the Sun-4 based on Motorola and Intel microprocessors to insure itself against this risk. However, each microprocessor type required extensive hardware design and software development. The introduction of multiple versions of the Sun-4 would further strain Sun's financial resources.

Even in the best of circumstances, assuming a trouble-free transition to the Sun-4, at its present rate of growth Sun would use up its cash in approximately six quarters. Thus it would almost certainly have to raise new equity before the end of the Sun-4's product life.

Sun's main source of equity at this point in its history was the public stock market. If the market responded favorably to the Sun-4, Sun could then call its existing convertible debentures and issue new convertible debt or equity.

The market's ability to absorb large convertible debt or equity issues had grown dramatically in recent times. The largest equity issue through mid-1987 was Conrail's $1.65 billion initial public offering in March of that year. MCI had issued a record $1 billion in convertible debentures in 1983. And Sun's own history proved that a reputable company could issue equity and convertibles several times a year if its growth warranted the funds infusion.

However, Sun's prior experience with new product introductions suggested that the company could not necessarily expect a positive market response to the Sun-4 introduction. On August 5, 1986, Sun introduced the Sun-3/200. Between the first and the eighth of August, Sun stock plummeted nearly 20%.

EXHIBIT 14-8 Sun and Apollo Stock Price 3/4/86–5/29/87

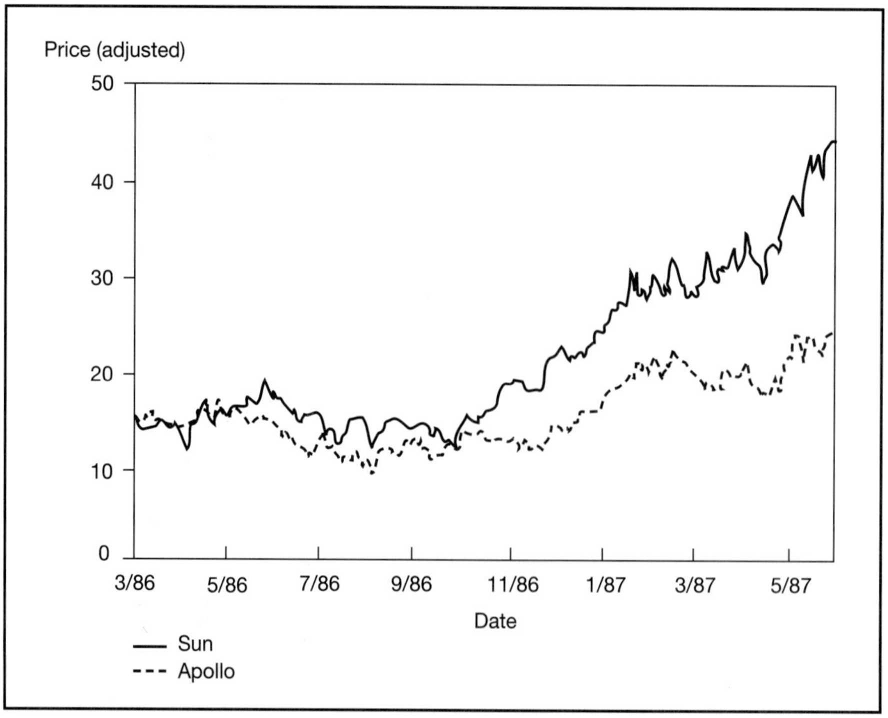

Sun Microsystems: 1987

Sun Systems, Inc., 1987 (A)

Sun's Alternatives

As Sun's new chief financial officer, Graziano felt that he needed to understand how Sun's financial decisions might affect its future success in the workstation market. To clarify his thinking he defined two very different financial strategies.

First, Sun could continue to rely on the public stock market to fund its growth. Under this strategy, Sun would simply raise cash whenever market conditions were favorable. If the market turned sour, Sun could issue debt or, perhaps, raise prices and slow growth. The greatest risk of this strategy, Graziano felt, was that if Sun's stock price dropped, or flattened for some time, successive new equity issues would dilute existing shareholders. The company's competitive goal of dominating the technical workstation market might then come into conflict with the financial goal of maximizing shareholder wealth.

Alternatively, Sun could seek a strategic partner. Other companies in capital intensive businesses with high growth rates had managed to obtain financing from corporate investors with "deep pockets." For example, MCI and Rolm had each sold large blocks of shares to IBM. Several large brokerage and investment firms were in the process of selling equity to well-capitalized firms such as American Express, the Equitable Insurance Company, and General Electric. And Sun itself, before going public, had obtained financing from Kodak, a large customer.

In Graziano's eyes, the main objections to a strategic partnership centered around the issue of control. Not only would a large block investor require more information than public shareholders, but it would almost certainly demand a seat on the Board, and would seek to influence company policy. Graziano wondered if such an arrangement would be the first step in a takeover that would end with Sun's absorption into a much larger company.

Appendix: Technical Workstations

Product Definition

In the early 1980s, the technical workstation emerged as a distinct type of computer, combining the best features of the dedicated minicomputer and the timesharing mainframe. The dedicated minicomputer afforded high speed to a single user, but failed to provide simultaneous access. Timesharing systems allowed users to share files and peripheral devices, but at the expense of speed as more users logged into the network.

When interconnected within a network of computers and peripherals, workstation provided the economy of shared files and peripherals with the power previously available only on machines dedicated to one user.

As the 1980s progressed, personal computing power grew rapidly. Workstation prices fell amid stiff competition between vendors for the best price/performance ratio.

The performance of high-end personal computers and low-end workstations also began to converge. Beginning in 1987, many personal computers at the high end used the same powerful 32-bit microprocessors as workstations. Hard disks with expandable storage capacity upwards of 60 megabytes became commonplace in PCs. Cheaper and improved video technology enabled developers to integrate high-resolution monitors into relatively inexpensive computers. A few personal computers even ran the UNIX operating system.

Nevertheless, some important differences between workstations and personal computers remained. First, most personal computers did not utilize a sophisticated operating system such as UNIX. Second, workstation vendors designed and supported complex networking systems. A user could always add new computers to a workstation network, regardless of the number of machines already hooked up. Users did occasionally network personal computers, but they received little support from the vendors. Moreover, personal computer networks generally could support only a limited number of machines.

Value-Added Resellers

The typical workstation manufacturer distributed nearly half its sales through value added resellers (VARs). The VAR would in turn market a total system, a complete solution that bundled specialized software with a distributed network of computers configured to perform the functions desired by the customer. Workstation manufacturers also sold computers and networks directly to end users. In comparison, personal computers were most often sold through retail chains as single units.

Customers of VARs wanted to be able to expand their networks at will. Unless the VAR guaranteed a compatible line of products from low-end to high-end, customers would go elsewhere. Thus workstation vendors had to offer a full range of computers for a distributed network, from desktop units to $200,000 file servers.

UNIX

By the late eighties, the non-proprietary UNIX operating system dominated the workstation market. Customer demand had forced companies like Apollo, which started with a proprietary operating system, to switch to UNIX.

Scientists at AT&T's Bell Labs developed UNIX in the mid-seventies. Bell engineers wrote UNIX entirely in the C language, and any machine fitted with a C compiler could run UNIX.

At first, because of its status as a regulated telephone monopoly, AT&T was legally constrained from commercial exploitation of UNIX. Thus it licensed UNIX at low cost and with few restrictions to anyone who asked. The system's portability and multitasking capabilities led to its quick acceptance in academic circles.

However, many licensees tailored UNIX to their own needs and, as a result, the original UNIX evolved into over thirty variations. For example, Sun used Berkeley 4.2, a popular version among engineers.

The 1984 breakup of the Bell system allowed AT&T to enter the computer market. Its managers soon found that many users avoided AT&T computers based on the UNIX System V operating system because of an insufficient supply of software. Furthermore, potential customers in the engineering and scientific communities preferred the Berkeley version offered by Sun and others. Among its advantages, Berkeley offered support for virtual memory and a full-screen text editor.

AT&T believed that a convergence of some of the more popular UNIX versions would encourage software houses to develop more UNIX applications. As an initial step toward merging the major UNIX versions, AT&T published the System V Interface Definition (SVID) protocols designed to ensure consistent interfaces across UNIX versions. Op erating systems conforming to SVID could run the same software, and thus applications developers could write programs for UNIX, as opposed to only for a particular version of UNIX.

Although SVID set standards for software interfaces, it did not do the same for device drives, the interfaces standing between the operating system and the peripherals. Standardizing peripheral interfaces was a much more complex task than standardizing software interfaces. Peripherals were an oddball collection of devices ranging from dot matrix printers to hospital monitoring equipment, and encompassing fields as diverse as satellite telecommunications and geophysics. Each UNIX version interacted with each peripheral in its own way. The lack of standards for device drivers created huge problems for users seeking to purchase machines from multiple vendors: the different UNIXes appeared as entirely different operating system for those who owned highly specialized peripherals.

Network File System

UNIX's limitations caused Sun Microsystems to depart from its original policy of using only previously established standards. In 1984, with a single UNIX standard apparently years away, Sun realized that truly open systems, with different brands of machines communicating with one another, would require software that did not yet exist. Sun developed the Network File System (NFS) to meet the needs of a heterogenous computing environment.

In May 1985 Sun published the NFS protocols, source code, and object code, and issued a statement encouraging the adoption of NFS as an industry standard. NFS was the first system software to allow the transparent sharing of files in a heterogenous environment.

Sun designed NFS as an independent system. In theory it could run with any microprocessor, operating system, or network configuration. In practice, however, NFS supported only UNIX-based operating systems, Digital's VMS, and PC-DOS.

At the time Sun introduced NFS, industry practice was to keep solutions to technical problems proprietary. Sun departed radically from this practice by publishing the codes and protocols of NFS and promoting this solution as an industry standard.

Microprocessors: CISC vs. RISC

The microprocessor performs the binary operations that are the basis of computing. Motorola and Intel, two of the largest independent chip manufacturers, supplied most of the microprocessors used in technical workstations and personal computers.

Motorola and Intel based their products on a complex instruction set computer (CISC) architecture. CISC was highly efficient in processing complicated code, but it failed to perform some of the simpler, more frequently used, instructions in just one clock cycle.

In contrast, proponents of reduced instruction set computer (RISC) architecture argued that overall processing time could be shortened by eliminating the complicated instructions and devoting more processing space to the primitive commands. A RISC chip executed simple instructions in just one clock cycle, but could only perform more complex instructions by combining the primitives. In 1987, computer experts were heatedly debating the merits of these two architectures.

15. Intel Corporation: Going Into OverDrive™

On May 26, 1992, Intel Corporation's Folsom, California-based End User Components Division (EUCD) announced the immediate availability of two versions of OverDrive Processors—one for 16- and 20-MHz Intel486™ SX CPU-based systems and the other for 25-MHz Intel486 SX CPU-based systems. The insert on the previous page is an extract from the press release accompanying the product announcement.

The May 26 press release also included in-formation on Intel's benchmark tests on a 20-MHz Intel486 SX CPU-based system: the new processor was found to be 62% faster when running WordPerfect Corporation's WordPerfect 5.1 word-processing software, 77% faster with Borland International's Paradox database-management software, and 481% faster in the case of Lotus Development Corporation's Lotus 1-2-3 spreadsheet software. When running Lotus 1-2-3, the OverDrive processor was also 67% faster than the Intel487™ SX math coprocessor, a performance-enhancing processor that the user could (and might) have installed in the vacant socket intended for the OverDrive Processor. These speed improvements at the processor level promised up to a 70% improvement in the speed of the complete personal-computer system.

EUCD expected to announce the availability of OverDrive Processors for Intel486 DX CPU-based systems in late 1992 and Intel486 DX2 CPU-based systems in 1993. Industry observers saw the new OverDrive processors as part of a new trend at Intel: microprocessor upgradability, with each new microprocessor being followed some time later by an OverDrive Processor. An important motivation for the new processor was the chorus of end-user demand for a cost-effective way to enhance the computer-system performance without having to invest every so often in entirely new systems. The *cause célèbre* of the end-user demand was the relentless pace of product improvement in the personal-computer industry: the different industry players were introducing "new-and-improved" products every two to three years, and this was at least twice as fast as the normal asset depreciation and replacement cycles for most corporate end users. Prior to the OverDrive Processor, a number of systems manufacturers who used Intel microprocessors in their systems had introduced upgradable systems, but the performance-enhancement solution differed from manufacturer to manufacturer, and there was no "standard" way that was cheap, easy, and nondisruptive. Intel, with the new OverDrive

Processor, was offering an industrywide solution that was less expensive ("$500 range" *vs.* "$800 to $2,000"), easy ("depending on system design, . . . in five minutes"), and nondisruptive ("adding a single chip [in a vacant OverDrive Processor socket], without upgrading or modifying any other system components").

If the OverDrive Processor strategy proved to be a winner, it would have a significant impact on Intel and its relationship with its customers: the microprocessors that would be "overdriven" were the company's main line of business (and the responsibility of the Microprocessor Products Group, or MPG—a separate products group that was older, larger, and more "powerful" than EUCD); the original-equipment manufacturers (OEMs) who employed these microprocessors in their personal-computer products were MPG's most important customers; MPG and its OEM customers had well-defined product design, pricing, positioning, and evolution strategies; and the new OverDrive Processors called into question some, if not many, of these strategies. Furthermore, the new processors launched Intel into an entirely new line of business—OverDrive Processor sales to end users owning systems made by MPG's OEM customers. EUCD—and not MPG—was responsible for OverDrive Processor sales, and, as the newly appointed general manager of EUCD, it was Mike Fister's responsibility to develop the OverDrive Processor business such that it was congruent with—and not in opposition to—the strategic interests of MPG and its relationships with the OEM customers.

Intel Corporation—An Overview

Santa Clara, California-based Intel Corporation was founded in 1968 "with the vision of designing and manufacturing very complex integrated circuits, or silicon 'chips.' . . . In 1971 Intel introduced the world's first microprocessor, a development that changed . . . much of the industrial world. . . . Today, . . . [m]ost of the company's activities are focused on extending and enhancing the worldwide business computing hardware standard that started with the introduction of the Intel microprocessor-based IBM PC ten years ago. . . . Intel's mission is to supply the

building blocks that allow this 'new computer industry' to grow."[1]

One of the most important building blocks was the microprocessor, the "brain" that served as the computer's central-processing unit (CPU), and where all computer-program instructions were executed. Intel was the world's leading supplier of microprocessors, and microprocessors were

[1]*Annual Report 1991* (Santa Clara, CA: Intel Corporation, 1991), p. 6. Much of the information in this section is based on the "Intel in Brief" discussion on page six of the annual report.

a significant part of the company's business (contributing an estimated 55% of Intel's sales and the bulk of its profits).[2]

As important as *microprocessors* were as a product category, they were not the only building blocks that Intel offered to the PC industry. The company's other building blocks for the industry were:

microprocessor peripherals, which worked with microprocessors and handled specific functions such as the control of disk drives and memory devices;

multimedia products, which brought multimedia capability to PCs; and

PC enhancement products, including add-in boards, PC-networking products, components for boosting PC computing power ("math coprocessors"), and selective software. Over-Drive Processors were PC enhance ment products.

Just as microprocessors were not Intel's only PC products, PC products were not the company's only major product offerings. Intel's other products were:

flash memory devices and "*EPROMs*," which stored programs for microprocessors and microcontrollers and retained data even when power was turned off;

microcontrollers, which were microcomputers programmed to perform specific functions in automobile engines, laser printers, disk drives, home appliances, consumer-electronic equipment, household appliances, and so on;

OEM modules and systems, which were based on Intel components and sold to OEMs for integration into their products; and

supercomputer systems, which were high-performance computers based on "massively parallel" processing on many microprocessor modules.

Intel sold the above products through a number of distribution channels:

original equipment manufacturers, who incorporated Intel's microprocessors, microcontrollers, components, modules, and systems into their products;

electronics distributors, who sold replacement microprocessors, microcontrollers, components, modules, and systems for the OEM customers' products;

retail computer stores, which sold Intel's enhancement products (the company distributed these products through a network of over 8,400 retailers); and

end users, who directly purchased Intel's supercomputers and centain net working products.

For the year ending December 31, 1991, 49% of the company's sales were in the Americas, 22% in Europe, 19% in Asia Pacific, and 10% in Japan.

Exhibit 15–1 presents Intel's financial highlights for the five years 1987–91.

Intel was organized in a "matrix" form, with products and functional groups. **Exhibit 15–2** identifies the different groups in the corporate organization. The two products groups directly relevant to this case study—the Microprocessor Products Group and the Intel Products Group—are identified in boldface EUCD was one of five divisions in the Intel Products Group (the other four divisions were Networking Products, PC Enhancement Products, OEM Modules and Systems, and Supercomputer Systems). Mike Fister, general manager, EUCD, reported to Frank K. Gill, senior vice president and general manager, Intel Products Group. Fister was new to EUCD. When the OverDrive Processor was first conceived and the decision was made to go ahead, Dennis L. Carter was the general manager of EUCD; by May 1992, however, Carter had moved to a different position in the Intel organization.[3]

---

[2]Microprocessors were used, not only in personal computers, but also in a wide range of consumer-electronic, household, industrial, telecommunications, and transportation equipment. In this case study, the term "microprocessors" refers to microprocessors used as central-processing units in personal computers. The revenue share estimates for Intel's different product groups are drawn from the article "Inside Intel," *Business Week*, June 1, 1992, pp. 86–94. The article quotes a Robertson Stephens & Co. estimate of $3.1 billion in microprocessor sales in a total 1992 revenue estimate of $5.5 billion. The revenue estimates for the other product groups mentioned in the case were other chips (principally microcontrollers), $1.4 billion; flash memory, $200 million; personal computers, $380 million; PC enhancement products, $310 million; and supercomputers, $150 million.

[3]Vice president and director of marketing in the Architecture Marketing & Applications Group.

EXHIBIT 15-1 Intel Corporation: Financial Highlights

Five Years Ended December 28, 1991	1987	1988	1989	1990	1991
Net revenues ($ in millions)	1,907	2,875	3,127	3,921	4,779
Cost of sales ($ in millions)	1,044	1,506	1,721	1,930	2,316
Net income ($ in millions)	248	453	391	650	819
Return on average stockholders' equity	19.7%	27.0%	16.9%	21.2%	20.4%
Research and development ($ in millions)	260	318	365	517	618
Employees at year end (in thousands)	19.2	20.8	21.7	23.9	24.6

Intel Microprocessors and Math Coprocessors

The Microprocessor[4]

The microprocessor was where the action was in a personal computer: it was the computer's central-processing unit (CPU), the module in which all the instructions of a computer program were executed, including numerical processing, logical operations, and timing functions. The microprocessor consisted of three functional units: registers, which provided temporary storage for memory addresses, status codes, and information used during program execution; an arithmetic/logic unit, which performed all the numerical processing and logical operations; and control circuitry, which used a clock input to coordinate activity and maintain the proper sequence of operations in program execution.

For the personal computer to work effectively, the microprocessor had to be correctly and efficiently linked with the computer's memory (where programs and data were stored), and input/output devices (keyboard, display monitor, printer, floppy disk, and so on). The link was achieved through "buses," and one of the most important bus was the data bus, which was used for transporting data. There were two types of data buses: (1) the internal data bus, which carried data inside the microprocessor, and (2) the external data bus, which shuttled data between the microprocessor and the other parts of the computer.

The "width" of the data bus was an important determinant of performance: the wider the bus, the more "powerful" the computer. Data-bus width was measured in bits (an abbreviation for *bi*nary dig*its*, the smallest unit of information in computers), and the smallest width in personal computers was 8 bits (1 computer "word"). While internal and external buses were typically of the same width, they did not have to be so: microprocessor manufacturers often followed up a new-generation chip with an entry-level, low-cost version that had the same internal bus width but a narrower external bus width. The Intel386™ SX microprocessor is a good example: it was introduced over two-and-a-half- years after the nearly three times as expensive Intel386 DX microprocessor, it had the same internal bus width as the DX version (32 bits), but it had a narrower external bus width (16 bits *vs*. 32 bits). In general, the less-expensive version was less powerful than its more-expensive counterpart, but more powerful than a previous-generation microprocessor.

As the microprocessor executed a program, data were transferred from one subsystem of the computer to another. Each instance of data transfer was called a bus, or machine, cycle. Cycle timing was kept by a microprocessor clock signal, and the frequency of the signal (the number of cycles per unit of time) was another determinant of computer performance. Clock frequencies for Intel microprocessors ranged from 5 MHz to 50 MHz (1 MHz = 1,000,000 cycles per second).

---

[4]This section draws on the discussion in the chapter "Introduction to Microcomputers," *8086/8088 User's Manual* (Santa Clara, CA: Intel Corporation, 1989).

EXHIBIT 15-2 Intel Corporation: Different Groups in Corporate Organization

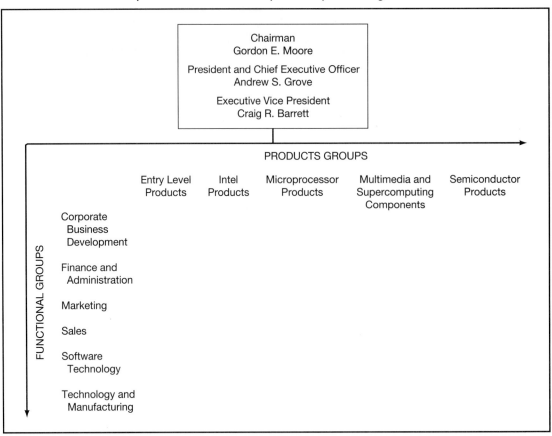

The Evolution of Intels Microprocessors: 8086/88 to Intel486 SX

Intel introduced its first 16-bit microprocessor for the personal computer—the 8086 "chip"—in 1978, but it was a later 8-bit chip—the 8088—that made its way into the first IBM PC, the computer that set the IBM PC-compatible standard and led the personal-computer revolution of the 1980s. The 8088 chip had an 8-bit external bus width, a 16-bit internal bus width, and—in its initial version—a 5-MHz clock frequency. It was a fairly advanced microprocessor for its time.

In subsequent years, Intel "improved" the 8086/8088 microprocessor line in two ways: (1) it introduced new versions with higher clock frequency (8 MHz and 10 MHz in the case of the 8086, and 8 MHz in the case of the 8088); and (2) it

introduced a next- generation 80286 in February 1982. As the product-line evolution information in **Exhibit 15–3** indicates, the company followed the same two-pronged product-improvement strategy for the 80286 chip. Thus, there were faster versions of the 80286 (up from 8 MHz to 10 MHz and 12 MHz) and, in October 1985, the Intel386™ DX.

The evolution of the Intel386 series was different from that of the previous two generations (8086/8088 and 80286) in one very important respect: in June 1988, Intel introduced the Intel386 SX, a lower-performance, lower-priced chip that would bring the new Intel386 technology to entry-level systems (for which the DX version was too expensive). Now, Intel had a three-pronged product-improvement strategy: continuing improvements in the speed of the up-market DX microprocessor, continuing improvements in the speed of the entry-level SX microprocessor, and,

EXHIBIT 15-3 Evolution of Intel's Microprocessors Product Line

Chip Series	Date of Introduction	Clock Frequency	Internal Bus	External Bus	Number of Transistors	Typically Used in
8086	June 1978	5 MHz 8 MHz 10 MHz	16-bit	16-bit	29,000	Portable computing
8088	March 1979	5 MHz 8 MHz	16-bit	8-bit	29,000	Desktop computing
80286	February 1982	8 MHz 10 MHz 12 MHz	16-bit	16-bit	130,000	Portable computing
Intel386 DX	October 1985 February 1987 April 1988 April 1989	16 MHz 20 MHz 25 MHz 33 MHz	32-bit	32-bit	275,000	Desktop computing
Intel386 SX	June 1988 April 1989	16 MHz 20 MHz	32-bit	16-bit	275,000	Entry-level desktop and portable computing
Intel386 SL	October 1990 September 1991	20 MHz 25 MHz	32-bit	16-bit	855,000	Portable computing
Intel486 DX	April 1989 May 1990 June 1991	25 MHz 33 MHz 50 MHz	32-bit	32-bit	1,200,000	Desktop computing and servers
Intel486 SX	April 1991 September 1991 September 1991	20 MHz 16 MHz 25 MHz	32-bit	32-bit	1,185,000	Desktop computing

in April 1989, the introduction of yet the next-generation microprocessor. In October 1990, the company added a fourth prong to the Intel386 strategy: the Intel386 SL for low-power consumption (and, therefore, ideal for the new breed of portable personal computers).

The Intel486 series added another variation to the product-evolution theme. Like the Intel386 series, the company increased the speed of the DX version and introduced an entry-level SX version. Five months after the 20-MHz SX was introduced, Intel added to the SX line in two opposite directions—a slower 16-MHz version and a faster 25-MHz version.

While the Intel486 SX and Intel386 SX were similar in that they were entry-level versions of the corresponding DX chips, the two were realized in dissimilar ways. In the case of the Intel386 SX, the chip had the same 32-bit internal bus as the DX chip, but a narrower 16-bit external bus (instead of 32 bits for the DX). The Intel486 SX was based on a totally different approach: it eliminated the Intel486 DX's "float-ing-point unit," a module that gave the DX an extra zip when performing numerical analysis.[5]

Until March 1991, Intel microprocessors—either manufactured directly by Intel or manufactured under license by large OEM customers and other chip manufacturers—were the only microprocessors used in IBM PC-compatible personal computers. One chip manufacturer producing Intel microprocessors under license was Santa Clara, California-based Advanced Micro Devices (AMD). In March 1991, AMD introduced its own version of the 386 microprocessor—a version that

[5]In fact, when the Intel486 SX was first introduced, the die for manufacturing the new chip was not ready, and Intel made the chip by disabling the floating-point unit in the DX. When word of the disablement reached the press, the company was criticized for offering a less-expensive version of the DX chip that was a DX chip with the floating-point unit disabled. Once the SX manufacturing die was ready, subsequent Intel486 SXs were manufactured without the floating-point unit. Perhaps because of this controversy, the Intel486 SX chip acquired the reputation of being a "hobbled" chip and was not popular—until, that is, plans were announced for a forthcoming "upgrade"; demand was also spurred by a substantial reduction in the processor's price.

AMD claimed was up to 32% faster than Intel's.[6] The new processor proved especially popular among the low-price IBM PC clone manufacturers and grabbed an estimated 30% of the 386 market in the fourth quarter of 1991. AMD was also working on a clone of the 486 chip, though shipment was not expected until the fourth quarter of 1992, by which time Intel was expected to be selling its next-generation "P5" microprocessor.

AMD's entry foreshadowed a number of other competitive entries:

> . . . Led by . . . [AMD], cloners of Intel chips are denting its bottom line. In May [1992], the No. 3 U.S. chip-maker, Texas Instruments Inc., announced two souped-up microprocessors. MIPS Computer Systems Inc. and [Mountain View, California-based] Sun Microsystems Inc. have new designs that outrace Intel's—and will even run the same huge library of programs. Even IBM, Intel's No. 1 customer, has joined with Apple Computer Inc. and Motorola Inc., maker of Apple's microprocessors, to build a new desktop brain. . . .
> . . . [Milpitas, California-based] Cyrix Corp. and [Richardson, Texas-based] Chips & Technologies Inc. have re-created—and improved—Intel386 without, they say, violating copyrights or patents.[7]

Intel Math Coprocessors

One reason why Intel did not choose to realize the Intel386 SX chip in the same way as the Intel486 SX was that the Intel386 DX chip did not have a floating-point unit (and, therefore, there was no question of coming up with a version without the floating-point unit). The 8086/8088 and 80286 series did not have a floating-point unit either, and this was a problem when it came to numerical computations. To overcome this deficiency, from the very beginning, Intel had offered a separate "math coprocessor," a single-chip floating-point microprocessor that interfaced with the main microprocessor. Thus, there was the 8087, the

80287, the 80387 DX, and the 80387 SX (for the 8086/8088, the 80286, the Intel386 DX, and the Intel386 SX, respectively). The Intel486 DX did not need a math coprocessor. Finally, the Intel486 SX was an entirely different story. When it announced the chip, Intel also introduced the 80487 SX. But, for all practical purposes, the 80487 SX was the Intel486 DX—since all that differentiated the Intel486 SX from the Intel486 DX was the absence of the floating-point unit in the former.[8]

While Intel's math coprocessors complemented the company's corresponding microprocessors, the two product lines were managed by two different products groups. The Microprocessor Products Group (MPG) managed the microprocessors line; the End User Components Division (EUCD), the math coprocessor line. Harry Laswell, marketing manager, EUCD, talked about the math coprocessor business:

> You might think that the math coprocessor business was some brilliant strategy on Intel's part. It wasn't; the business just happened. The motivation for a separate chip with a floating-point unit came from our microcontrollers for factory-automation equipment. Even then, the chip was never intended for the PC. But IBM introduced a vacant socket in the PC, and there you have it: a math coprocessor market developed.
> Now that we had the market, we had to manage it. The math coprocessor was not a branded product; price competition was intense; a number of competitors were promising a superior socket-compatible product; and, with the Intel486 DX architecture, we foresaw the eventual death of the product category.
> As early as 1989, we were thinking about what to do with the math coprocessor line. Then, the question was, how to increase the coprocessor's performance to compete effectively with the imitators. We had two options: "add more transistors" and/or "make the transistors run faster." We couldn't choose the second option in 1985, when the 80387 came out. But, by 1991, we could. That realization had a major impact on our plans for the Intel486 SX: yes, we could worry about the math coprocessor for the chip; but now, we were onto something more important: the OverDrive Processor.

---

[6]The information in this and the next two sentences is drawn from Yoder, Stephen K., "Intel-AMD Clash Is Close to a Climax," *The Wall Street Journal*, January 31, 1992.

[7]*Business Week, op. cit.*, pp. 86–87. Cyrix was also taking another page out of Intel's book: in August 1992, Jim Chapman, Cyrix's vice president of marketing, was quoted as saying that the company was working on a clock- doubling line of 386 chips; "clock-doubling" was the technology that Intel had employed in the OverDrive Processor to soup up its performance.

[8]This was even more reason for dissatisfaction among the initial Intel486 SX buyers: at least initially, they were already buying the DX chip, albeit with its floating-point unit disabled; in the 487 SX, they would have to buy what was effectively another DX chip so that the original SX chip would perform like the DX chip—which, in a sense, it already was.

The OverDrive Processor

Genesis

Until mid-1991, Dennis Carter was general manager, EUCD. In that capacity, he too was concerned about the future of the division's math coprocessor business. Carter remembered talking about this with Laswell and Bill Rash, then a marketing manager in the Microprocessor Products Group:

> Until the 80387, Intel's math coprocessor business was good, but not great. The 80387 did well. But what next? With the advent of the floating-point unit in the Intel486 DX, there was no need for a math coprocessor. Even in the resulting shrinking market, there was an increasingly strong competition from look-alikes. What would happen to this business? What could we do?
>
> And then, Harry [Laswell] and Bill [Rash] came up with this idea of *speed doubling*. Harry can explain it better than I can; basically, their idea was to improve—enhance— microprocessor performance by doubling the speed inside the processor. Harry actually thought of speed doubling in the context of the math compressor. Later, Bill argued, if we can pull off this trick in the math coprocessor, why not in the microprocessor itself? This thought led to two new chip series: the OverDrive Processor, and the Intel486 DX2 microprocessor. But, MPG was not ready for the DX2, and we had to hold off.
>
> It was the OverDrive Processor that caught EUCD's imagination. We had surveyed many customers and corporate MIS [management information systems] managers about our math coprocessors, and we had some very interesting data. When asked why someone purchased a math coprocessor, the answer was not "for the ability to do floating-point arithmetic." Most customers didn't even know what floating-point arithmetic was. Most were buying a math coprocessor for "better" performance. Indeed, most customers were comparing the math coprocessor with other enhancement products, and it soon became clear to us that the math coprocessor was mispositioned.
>
> The same MIS managers also told us they were concerned about the rapid pace of product improvement. Microprocessors improve significantly every couple of years, while most corporations depreciate their PCs over five years—a mismatch that caused many users to look for some way to upgrade their systems without having to scrap the system before its depreciation life has expired.
>
> There were plenty of upgrade options around: one could upgrade the graphics, one could add in modules to accomplish specific tasks, one could add memory, and one could even upgrade the central processing unit. A number of system vendors offered the last option in their "upgradable" systems. These vendors designed CPU-level upgradability in one of three ways: swap system boards, add "turbo" cards, or install new, proprietary CPU modules. All three methods were risky. Each system vendor offered its own proprietary upgrade scheme; imagine the plight of the MIS manager supporting systems supplied by ten to fifteen different vendors. Furthermore, upgrading required the end user (or a special service facility) to tinker with the CPU. Some call the CPU the computer's heart; some call it the brain; in either case, a transplant is very risky. Finally, at $800 to $2,000, upgrades were expensive.
>
> So, we asked, why not an upgrade processor that would fit into a separate "upgrade-ready" socket? This would assuage the MIS managers' concern about doing a heart or brain transplant with the original microprocessor and yet offer the end user a standard way to upgrade to an increased performance level across all applications. The OverDrive Processor was the solution. Of course, we had not coined the term Overdrive Processor yet. The brand name would come later.

"The basic idea of speed doubling is quite simple," said Laswell as he explained the speed-doubling concept alluded to by Carter. Laswell elaborated:

> Take the 80387 math coprocessor. It has two clocks: one for coordinating communications with the Intel386 microprocessor, and the other for the floating-point unit. We couldn't do anything to the first clock, but supposing we ran the second clock faster. That would soup up the coprocessor. As math coprocessors go, that would differentiate our product. There was only one problem: in the time frame of the 80387 coprocessor, we were already pushing the two clocks as fast as we could, and the only way to enhance the math coprocessor's performance was by increasing the number of transistors.
>
> The same logic did not apply when the Intel486 SX came along. By then, semiconductor process technology had advanced so we could speed up—double—the second clock. The result: a souped up 80487 SX coprocessor [see "Example" in **Exhibit 15–4**].
>
> Of course, the Intel486 SX was a bad example to begin with: the chip was made possible by [first disabling and then] eliminating the floating-point unit in the Intel486 DX, and the unsouped-up 80487 SX was essentially the Intel486 DX. If we souped up the 80487 SX, then the Intel486 SX-80487 SX combination would outperform the Intel486 DX. In any case, if we could soup up the original 80487 SX, and

EXHIBIT 15-4 Speed-Doubling Technology

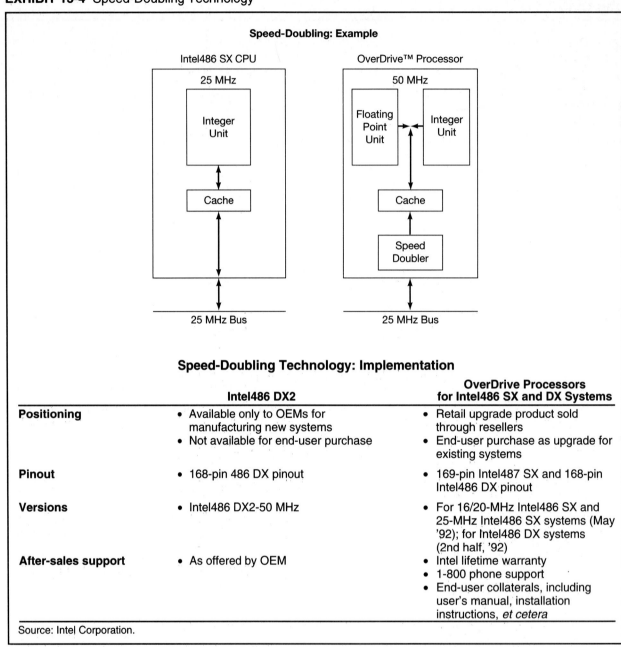

Speed-Doubling: Example

Intel486 SX CPU

25 MHz

Integer Unit

Cache

25 MHz Bus

OverDrive™ Processor

50 MHz

Floating Point Unit — Integer Unit

Cache

Speed Doubler

25 MHz Bus

Speed-Doubling Technology: Implementation

	Intel486 DX2	OverDrive Processors for Intel486 SX and DX Systems
Positioning	• Available only to OEMs for manufacturing new systems • Not available for end-user purchase	• Retail upgrade product sold through resellers • End-user purchase as upgrade for existing systems
Pinout	• 168-pin 486 DX pinout	• 169-pin Intel487 SX and 168-pin Intel486 DX pinout
Versions	• Intel486 DX2-50 MHz	• For 16/20-MHz Intel486 SX and 25-MHz Intel486 SX systems (May '92); for Intel486 DX systems (2nd half, '92)
After-sales support	• As offered by OEM	• Intel lifetime warranty • 1-800 phone support • End-user collaterals, including user's manual, installation instructions, *et cetera*

Source: Intel Corporation.

if this was essentially the Intel486 DX, then we should be able to soup up the latter chip as well. By now, Bill [Rash] was really into the *bigger* picture. "Why," he argued, "can't we speed up the Intel486 DX and make way for an Intel486 DX2?"

Rash's idea of an DX2 chip made sense for another reason: there was a performance gap in Intel's product line between the then fastest DX chip and the forthcoming "P5" chip series, and the DX2 chip could fill the gap.

Interregnum: The Intel486 DX2 Microprocessor

Laswell's and Rash's analysis suggested two implementation paths for the speed-doubling technology: a new Intel486 DX2 microprocessor, and upgrades for the Intel486 DX and SX. As sensible as the analysis appeared, it posed all kinds of im-

Intel Corporation: Going Into OverDrive™

plementation problems. One of them was that the Microprocessor Products Group (MPG) was not ready for the Intel486 DX2: the new chip would throw a monkey wrench into their and their customers' product-evolution plans (and the customers' upgradable systems product offerings); the new chip would divert design, development, and manufacturing resources; and, in any case, it takes time to launch a new product that must fit into someone else's systems product. Intel's Management Committee gave its go-ahead for the Intel486 SX and DX OverDrive Processors in March 1991, but until MPG was ready to go public with its plans for the DX2, EUCD could not officially announce the OverDrive Processors for the Intel486 SX and DX.

The introduction of the Intel486 DX2 in the context of the SX and DX OverDrive Processors also posed some knotty marketing problems. For the same clock speeds, there was not much to differentiate a DX2 chip from the corresponding SX or DX-plus-OverDrive Processor combination; in which case, how should the DX2 be positioned, and why would MPG's OEM customers even bother building systems around the DX2 chip? Would a gray market develop for the new chips? What about the differences in after-sales support for OEM and retail products? The lower half of **Exhibit 15–4** offers some answers.

OverDrive-Processor Implementation: Architecture and Road Map

While the pieces were being positioned for the Intel486 DX2 chip, EUCD was planning the eventual implementation of the OverDrive Processor concept. Carter, Laswell, and others realized that they could not test the concept with the Intel486 DX: while this would be the logical place to start (rather than the SX chip), the chip was first issued before the OverDrive Processor concept was articulated, and, therefore, the OEMs had not designed their PCs with an empty socket. The only way to install the OverDrive Processor in these PCs would be by pulling out the old chip and replacing it with a new chip—precisely the kind of transplant that end users had cautioned against.

That left only one alternative: to introduce the concept with the Intel486 SX chip. While this

introduced a new set of product-positioning problems (the SX-plus-OverDrive *vs.* the DX), it was an especially viable alternative because many SX systems already had an empty socket for a math coprocessor.

The decision to use the math coprocessor socket for the OverDrive Processor raised a new set of questions. The socket had 169 holes for the math coprocessor's 169 pins. This was one hole (and one pin) more than the main microprocessor socket. The extra pin was originally added on the math coprocessor to make sure that the coprocessor was oriented correctly (the locator pin was on one of the four corners of the coprocessor). Since EUCD decided to make the Intel486 SX OverDrive Processor pin-compatible with the 80487 SX, it could not serve as an OverDrive Processor for Intel486 DX systems (which were not intended to have a vacant socket) or for those Intel486 SX systems where the OEM vendors had decided not to include a vacant socket; these required a 168-pin connector.

Finally, once the idea of OverDrive Processors as enablers of upgradability had gained currency, it quickly transcended the speed-doubling concept: speed doubling was a solution that applied to the Intel486 DX and SX; other chips might warrant other solutions. For example, the Intel486 DX2 chip already had speed doubling and, therefore, could not be further upgraded by speed doubling. As EUCD envisioned it, there would be an OverDrive Processor for the DX2 chip, but performance enhancement would be realized in that case by the use of next-generation technology. **Exhibit 15–5** illustrates EUCD's OverDrive Processor strategy for the Intel486 series.

OverDrive-Processor Implementation: Getting the Systems Manufacturers' Buy-In

Bob Bennett, OverDrive Product manager, was responsible for working with the systems manufacturers so that their systems would be designed with an OverDrive Processor in mind. Bennett talked about the challenges in getting the systems manufacturers to buy into the concept:

> For starters, we couldn't even talk to them about the OverDrive Processor. We told them "something"

EXHIBIT 15-5 OverDrive Processor Strategy: A Roadmap

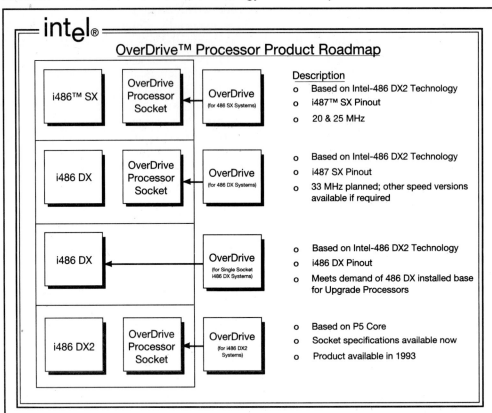

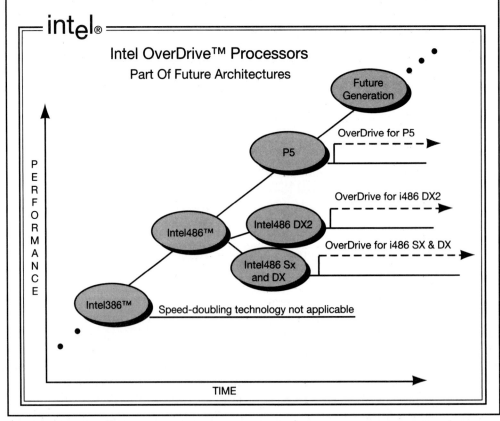

Source: Intel Corporation.

was in the works, but we could not be specific until MPG went public about the DX2 chip. And even then, it was not clear they would be exactly happy about the OverDrive Processor idea: the microprocessor upgrade would threaten *their* upgradable products. Of course, we could talk about the 80487 SX math coprocessor, but there was already a lot of confusion about the positioning of the Intel486 SX.

The OEMs were also not enthused about giving away premium real-estate space on a rapidly shrinking CPU board to a vacant socket for which Intel was promising—wink, wink, nudge, nudge—"something." And it was not only a matter of space. With speed doubling, the OverDrive Processor would generate a lot of heat. Would there be enough space for cooling? What about product warranties and other issues? Who would be responsible if an end user makes a mistake when installing the OverDrive Processor and damages the system? In any case, was the OverDrive Processor a consumer product or an OEM product?

To see why the last point was relevant, consider pricing. The OEMs typically dealt with MPG, which had an established pricing "formula": a price schedule that offered discounts depending on the quantity purchased (for the OverDrive Processor, we would only have two prices: distributor cost and manufacturer's suggested list price): MPG practices dynamic pricing, where a chip starts off with a high price and then drops in price as it gets older and new-and-improved chips come along (in the retail market, you can't drop prices every quarter); and, given the vast increase in the offering of equivalent products (for example, a 50-MHz Intel486 DX2 was equivalent to a 25-MHz Intel486 SX with an OverDrive Processor), how are we going to maintain price equivalence to minimize arbitrage opportunities?

Then, take product positioning. How were we going to position the OverDrive Processor? If we positioned it as a CPU upgrade, then we would be pitting it directly against the systems manufacturer's upgrade scheme. If we positioned it as akin to a math coprocessor, then Intel would not get the maximum impact from the new product. Or should we position it as a performance booster?

Cesar Pun was compatibility manager, EUCD. It was his job to make sure that once a systems manufacturer signed on, its vacant socket was mechanically and logically compatible with the OverDrive Processor. Pun talked about his challenge:

Things became easier once we could discuss our plans openly with the systems manufacturers. But, for the older systems—especially the Intel486 DX CPU-based systems, which were designed before even we knew about the OverDrive Processor—compatibility was a major concern.

On the mechanical side, we had to test for heat emission, air flow, heat sinks, insertion forces, and what have you. Even if we could get mechanical compatibility, there was logical compatibility to worry about. Individual systems and microprocessors have their own windows of tolerance when it comes to electronically interacting with each other, and the windows must have a large enough overlap for the PC to function effectively. Some systems, especially inexpensive ones supplied by down-market OEMs, have narrow tolerance windows, and while the system might be jury-rigged to work with DX or SX microprocessors, it might experience difficulty with the OverDrive Processor. For example, of the eighteen 25-MHz DX systems we tested, three or four failed.

We have established a Compatibility Council and have been testing systems on the basis of their market shares, but there are issues we haven't settled yet. For example, who should pay for the testing: Intel, or the systems manufacturers? How does the answer change if the OverDrive Processor concept catches on, and it is in the systems manufacturers' interest to have their system qualified for compatibility? For our part, we plan to regularly publish a list of qualified vendors [see **Exhibit 15–6** for a list as of May 26, 1992].

Cheryl Beninga was product manager for a future DX2 OverDrive Processor. Being responsible for a future rather than an existing or past product, her relationship with the systems manufacturers was different than that of Bennett and Pun. Like Bennett, Beninga was new to EUCD (and to Intel; Bennett joined the company in early 1991; Beninga, in November 1991). Beninga talked about her job, the relationship between EUCD and the systems manufacturers, and the challenge of managing the OverDrive Processor line in the long run:

I work with Intel's engineering team on product design and the OEMs on the design of the OverDrive Processor socket. The Intel486 DX2 microprocessor was released in March 1992, and the volume build-up has been quite good. I believe that a full 75% of the new DX2 systems will be designed with an OverDrive Processor socket. Ideally, we would like a branded, "OverDrive Ready" socket in all systems.

You have probably heard a lot about OEMs and the OverDrive Processor. But, if you think of it, we need the OEMs. They are our channel to the market: if they don't include a socket, we can't sell the OverDrive Processors. Perhaps the best way to encourage the OEMs to include an OverDrive socket is to generate end-user enthusiasm for the concept.

EXHIBIT 15-6 Intel486 SX CPU-based Systems Supporting OverDrive Processors*

Intel486™ SX CPU-based Systems that Support the OverDrive Processor*

U.S. System Manufacturers

3D Microcomputers	ECS	PC and C Computer Corporation
ALR	Eltech	PC Designs
Altos	Epson	Philips
AMI	Everex	Reply
ARES	Fountain Technologies, Inc.	Rogentech
AST	Fujikama	Sceptre Technologies
Austin	Hewlett-Packard Corporation	Sefco East
BCC	IBM	Swan
Blackship	Kama	Tandon
Cemtech	Leading Technology	Tandy
Club American	Micronics	Tangent
Commodore Business Machines	Mylex	Touche
Compaq	Mynix	Tri-Star
Compuadd Computer Corporation	NCR	Tricord
Cumulus	NEC Technologies, Inc.	Vtech
Dell Computer Corporation	Northgate	Win Labs, Ltd.
Digitial Scientific	Novas	Zenith Data Systems
Easy Data	Packard Bell	Zeos International

European System Manufacturers

Actebis	ITOS	Schneider
Akhter GMBH	NCR	Siemens Nixdorf
Apricot Computers	NEC Technologies, Inc.	Tandon
Aquarius System Int'l GMBH	Normerel	TCI Trident Computer GMBH
ASEM	Olivetti	TMC Technology Electronics GMBH
ECS Germany	Opus Technology PLC	Triumph-Adler
Elonex PLC	Osicom	Tulip Computers
Escom Computer Vertriebs	Peacock Computer GMBH	Viglen LTD.
GMBH	Philips PCS	Worx
Hewlett-Packard Corporation	Research Machines	Zenith Data Systems
ICL Personal Systems	Schmidt Computer GMBH	

Asia Pacific System Manufacturers

ACER	ECS	Juko
ACT	FIC	Micro Computer Systems
Altos	GES	Mitac
Arche	GVC	SVT
Asus	Handjade	Tatung
CAF	HCL	Trigem
Copam	Infocom	Twinhead
DTK	Informtech	Videotech
		Wipro

Rest of the World System Manufacturers

Itautec Informatica S.A.	Microtec S.A.	Monydata Teleinformaticia LTDA.

*Partial list as of May 1992.

Source: Intel Corporation.

OverDrive-Processor Implementation: Reaching Out to the End User

Two people in the EUCD organization were charged with the responsibility for generating end-user enthusiasm for the OverDrive Processor concept: Kristin Bailey, marketing communications manager, and Bill Bidal, acting worldwide channel marketing manager. Bailey talked about the marketing communications support for the OverDrive Processor concept:

The OverDrive Processor concept was supposed to apply to all three lines in the Intel486 series—the DX, the SX, and the DX2—and we had a different problem in each case: DX was an older chip, and most DX CPU-based systems did not have an OverDrive socket; the SX was introduced in April 1991

Intel Corporation: Going Into OverDrive™

EXHIBIT 15-7 OverDrive Processor: An Installation Guide

OverDrive™ Processor Quick Installation Card

The instructions on this card pertain only to computers with an empty OverDrive Processor socket. If your computer does not have an empty OverDrive Processor socket, see the *User's Guide*.

■ The diskette included with your OverDrive Processor contains an animated installation demonstration. You may wish to see this before proceeding. Read the diskette label for instructions.

■ This *Quick Installation Card* is for customers who are familiar with installing computer upgrade products; other customers should use the more detailed instructions in the *User's Guide*.

1

Remove the cover from your computer. Be sure to ground yourself.

Warning! Danger to you! Turn off the computer's power switch and unplug the power cord from the wall outlet. If you don't you could electrocute yourself.

2

Check the pins.
Examine the connector pins on the OverDrive Processor. If any pins are bent, carefully straighten them as shown. Note that the 25 MHz and the 33 MHz Over-Drive Processors have heat sinks attached to insure proper heat dissipation; the 16/20 MHz version does not need a heat sink.

OverDrive Processor 16/20 MHz version   OverDrive Processor 25 MHz version 33 MHz version

LIF or standard socket

ZIF sockets

3

Find the empty OverDrive Processor socket.
Some typical socket types are shown here. If your system does not have an empty OverDrive Processor socket, see *Installing the OverDrive Processor* in the User's Guide.

4

Orient your OverDrive Processor correctly.

A keyed socket will have three rows of pin holes and a key pin hole. Match the key pin on the chip with the key pin hole on the socket.
If your socket has less than or more than three rows of pin holes, or does not have a key pin hole, your computer may still be upgradable with the OverDrive Processor. Contact your computer dealer or manufacturer for more information.

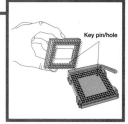
Key pin/hole

Pull lever to unlock; push to lock.

LIF or standard socket; push firmly and evenly as shown here.

5

Insert the OverDrive Processor in the empty socket.
If your computer has a Zero Insertion Force socket like the ones shown here, be sure to unlock or release the socket before inserting the chip. After inserting the chip, close the lock/unlock lever or turn the lock/unlock screw (or hex-head screw) to the closed position. If your system does not have a Zero Insertion Force socket you may have to press firmly to "seat" the pins in the socket. Your computer's system board should not bend under the pressure of inserting the OverDrive Processor.

6

Set jumpers or switches on the system board.

You may need to set switches, jumpers, or both on your computer's system board to let the computer know you've added an OverDrive Processor. Refer to your computer's manual for information.

7

Put the cover back on the computer.

Reconnect all the cables and cords, and plug the power cord into the wall outlet. Turn on the computer. If your computer requires it, run the computer's setup or configuration program.
If you have problems with your computer after installing the OverDrive Processor, *see Troubleshooting* in the User's Guide.

8

Test your OverDrive Processor.

Use the diagnostics included on the utilities diskette. If you already installed the Installation Demo, you *do not* need to reinstall the diagnostics. To install the tests, insert the disk in drive A (drive B on some computers) and type:

    A: Enter
or
    B: Enter
Then type
    install Enter
Follow the directions on the screen. After installation is complete, type overdrive and press Enter to start the programs.

intel.

Source: Intel Corporation.

with a math/OverDrive socket in mind, but the chip had acquired a reputation as a hobbled chip; and no one was ready to talk about the DX2 until early 1992. Indeed, we couldn't even talk in specific terms about the OverDrive Processor until MPG was ready to announce the DX2 chip. What do you tell people?

Furthermore, whom do you tell? How do you tell them? And when do you tell them? The OEM customers read publications like *Electronic Design* and *EDN*; the end user reads *PC Magazine, Byte*, and *PC World*. People typically purchased math coprocessors—the product with which EUCD has lots of experience—at the time of system purchase, but we expect them to purchase the OverDrive Processor one to two years after purchasing their PC.

There was an additional element of confusion as marketing communications go. We had to decide whether to launch the DX2 and the OverDrive Processor at different times or at the same time. If the answer is "at different times," which should come first? Whichever way you cut it, there was bound to be some confusion. It was decided that MPG would introduce the DX2 in March [1992] and we would follow with the OverDrive announcement in May. In a sense, the DX2 served the role of placating the system manufacturers; announcing the OverDrive before the DX2 would have defeated that goal.

We began advertising a "Vacancy" slot beginning September-October 1991. Since we couldn't talk about the OverDrive Processor at this time, the advertisement was subtle: we promised the audience that Intel will have "something" next year for the slot, and that "something" will be of value and help protect the system-owner's investment in the system. The "Vacancy" ads were specifically targeted to the nontechnical audience. We placed them in *The Wall Street Journal, Business Week*, and so on. In January [1992], we even had TV commercials during the Super Bowl [American professional football finals].

If it was Bailey's job to make the systems manufacturers, the end users, and the distribution channels aware of the OverDrive Processor product, it was Bidal's job to make sure that the product was "correctly" priced, the distribution channels got the product, and it was packaged so that it was indeed easy for the end user to install. Bidal commented on these aspects of his functions:

> Let's start with price. Actually, price is not something I decide: Mike [Fister] and Harry [Laswell] worry about that. But it affects channel marketing, and I worry about it. From the outset, we had decided that something in the $500 to $600 range

made sense: it was cheaper than the end user's other options, and it was within the purchase-requisition authority of many end users. We didn't want people to have to go to their bosses or an executive committee just to buy an OverDrive Processor.

As for distribution channels, in the United States our "customers" are (1) OEMs like Dell and Gateways [discount PC vendors], who have indicated their desire to sell the OverDrives through their channels; (2) 40 direct accounts; and (3) national distributors (the major 3), regional distributors, direct resellers, superstores, and so on. We are reaching these channels directly and also through the usual catalogs that the different distributors use. In Japan, the strategy is somewhat different. There, most of our customers are the systems manufacturers, though we also distribute through a few resellers. In Europe, we rely more on distributors, who are seen as partners in making the OverDrive business happen.

Finally, product packaging. Here's what we have come up with [he said, holding a 6" by 8 1/2" envelope]: a small box ["Chip Removal Kit"] containing the OverDrive Processor and a chip-removal tool [in case the socket in which the processor would go was not empty], a *Quick Installation Card* [see **Exhibit 7**], a *User's Guide*, a *Utilities* diskette, a *Warranty Registration Card*, and some after-sales support and promotional materials.

Given Intel's matrix organization, EUCD did not directly handle the sales function for the OverDrive Processor—or, for that matter, the math coprocessor or any other product. Sales for all five Intel Products Group divisions (EUCD, Networking Products, PC Enhancement Products, OEM Modules and Systems, and Supercomputer Systems) were centralized at the group's headquarters in Portland, Oregon.

Concluding Comments

Mike Fister, general manager, EUCD, commented on the OverDrive Processor's broader implications for Intel: "MPG has microprocessor product-line evolution, positioning, pricing, *et cetera*, down to a science. Over the last couple of years, they have also adopted an aggressive "Intel Inside" branding strategy. How will OverDrive affect the MPG business? Also, how will it change the way people perceive of CPUs, computer obsolescence, and Intel's role in managing the consequences of rapid change in microprocessor technology?"

16. Sony Corporation: Workstation Division

In July 1989, Dr. Toshi T. Doi, general manager of Sony's Workstation Division, was reviewing a proposal to split hardware design engineering into two separate departments. Isao Yamazaki, manager of the hardware design engineering department, had proposed the split to help alleviate the pressures of extremely rapid growth while maintaining past strengths in product development, and to make workstation designs more manufacturable.

In just over three years since its founding, the Workstation Division had grown to annual sales of approximately 6,200 units, giving it the largest share in Japan's workstation market. Furthermore, sales were expected to double again in 1989.

This rapid growth created stress in all areas of the division, including the hardware design engineering department. Yet because Sony's development cycle had traditionally been much shorter than that of most competitors, Doi wanted to avoid any changes that might have an adverse effect. An efficient product development effort was crucial in an industry where life cycles were measured in months rather than years. Any decision on Yamazaki's proposal would have to take that fact into account.

Sony Corporation History

The Tokyo Telecommunications Engineer Company (later renamed Sony) was founded in 1945 immediately after the end of World War II by Masaru Ibuka, who was soon joined by his friend (and later chairman), Akio Morita. During its first four decades, Sony concentrated almost solely on consumer electronics, introducing a wide range of products, starting with the first

---

Geoffrey K. Gill prepared this case as the basis for class discussion rather than to illustrate either effective or ineffective handling of an administrative situation.

Japanese tape recorder and continuing with the world's first transistor radio, the Trinitron color TV, the Walkman line of portable radios and tape recorders, and the Camcorder video camera. Because of such products, Sony Corporation had become a recognized leader in the consumer electronics field, with 1988 worldwide sales of more than $16 billion.

Throughout this growth period, Sony relied on innovative products that created new markets. As Morita explained the firm's philosophy: "We don't believe in doing market research for a new product unknown to the public. So we never do any. We are the experts." During the 1970s, one of the most promising new products to be developed at Sony was the Betamax VCR. Unfortunately, several of Sony's competitors adopted the VHS standard and, after a long and costly battle, Sony admitted defeat by introducing a VHS model in 1988.

The Betamax disaster forced Sony to rethink its strategy in several ways. The company began to pay more attention to expanding its markets in existing lines in addition to developing totally new products. For example, it entered low end markets for equipment such as Walkmans. It also started cooperating more with competitors, developing standards for products such as compact disks. Perhaps the most fundamental shift was a move away from total dependence on consumer electronics. When Norio Ohga became president in 1982, he set a goal of 50% of sales from nonconsumer products.

The Workstation Division

One side effect of Sony's preoccupation with the video business was that its computer business had been largely ignored. Although Sony had some success in the computer game market, its first entrants in the computer market were 8-bit machines (the SMC-70 and SMC-777, introduced in 1982 and 1984, respectively), which failed quickly in competition with 16-bit MS-DOS systems (e.g., the IBM PC). Sony considered developing a 16-bit microcomputer but it soon abandoned the idea because that market had already matured.

When Doi took charge of the project to develop a new computer in 1984, he recruited 11 top-flight engineers to form the team. Doi established three basic guidelines for the development: (1) the computer should be 32 bit; (2) it should be multipurpose; and (3) the project should be completed as soon as possible. The engineers, however, decided that they wanted to design a machine (an engineering workstation) that would help them in their own engineering work rather than a multipurpose machine. Doi approved their plan, but he required that it be finished in six months.

The initial development effort, named the IKKI project, began to move quickly. The hardware prototype was completed in three months, and the operating system was installed three months later—meeting the aggressive schedule set by Doi. This speed was in sharp contrast to the two years of development typical for a project of this kind at Sony. As Doi recalled the development period:

> . . . [the design team] had little consciousness of producing a marketable product . . . they first wanted to create a computer they could use themselves . . . I decided that what the Sony engineers wanted was probably what other engineers also wanted, and went ahead . . . [W]e showed this machine to Mr. Koichi Kishida from SRA (Software Research Associates), which had brought Unix to Japan, and he was elated . . . The developers at Sony created something they themselves wanted and a developer from another company was elated. This was very simple and no market research was necessary.[1]

Despite its technical success, the computer division (which was focused primarily on optical disks and game computers) was slow to proceed with the IKKI project. It was reluctant to terminate any of its other projects to squeeze out enough money to pursue IKKI as a new business. When the computer division proposed a market introduction of 1988, Doi felt that date was unacceptable and he persuaded Ohga to let him develop the workstation business as an in-house venture.

Developing a business was a challenge to Doi, who had been primarily a manager of R&D. He had to implement prototyping for commercialization, develop standard operating procedures, recruit dealers and applications software vendors, and create promotional materials. Doi saw the new venture as very much in the tradition of

[1] From *The Computer* magazine, June 1988.

the "original Sony"—a small and dynamic venture business, whereas the "current Sony" was an established organization suffering from bureaucratic stagnancy and a lack of entrepreneurial spirit.

The new workstation computer, called NEWS™ (NEtWork Station), was introduced in October 1986 at the Tokyo Data Show. It was a remarkable success, generating over 1000 inquiries at the show. In a few months, investment in the new venture was fully recovered. Since that time, Sony's workstation sales had doubled each year.

In June 1987, all the computer-related divisions were incorporated into one internal venture, including Workstation, CD-ROM Development and Home Interactive (which worked with game computers and portable word processors), which became the Super Micro Group.

Current Workstation Products

At the highest level, workstations were systems consisting of several different components. Although the exact configuration varied somewhat, a typical workstation had a main system unit (including the mother board), a cathode ray tube (CRT) display, a keyboard, a hard disk drive for permanent storage that could be accessed at any time, a floppy disk drive to allow data to be carried from one computer to another, and a network interface that allowed the workstation to communicate with other computers on a local area network (LAN). The heart of the workstation was the main system unit; the other components were called peripherals.

The primary component of the main system unit was the mother board. This printed circuit board (PCB) typically contained the electronics required to perform all major functions of the computer: the central processor unit (CPU), the random access memory (RAM), the bus control logic, and the read only memory (ROM), as well as some peripheral control functions such as a network controller. These terms are explained further in Appendix I.

Sony's workstation product line was segmented into three categories and marketed under the NEWS™ trademark (see **Exhibit 16–1**). The low end, the Series 700, had developed from the

original IKKI workstation[2] which was based on the 68020 chip and did not have a hard disk. The mid-range, the Series 1500 and Series 1700, were based on a single 68030 microprocessor and did have hard disk capabilities. The high end, Series 1800 and 1900, also were based on the 68030 but had a special dual processor architecture in which a second 68030 handled all the input/ output (I/O) tasks. This architecture increased the processing speeds by about 25% over the mid-range products. Although the Workstation Division was still small (with approximately $140 million of Sony's $16 billion in sales), by July 1989, it was the company's most profitable division.

Each computer within a given series used the same basic mother board and differed from other offerings in the same series only by the peripheral devices that were attached. For example, the 1550 workstation, the initial offering in the 1500 series, had a black and white display, whereas the 1560, a subsequent line extension, had color. (See **Exhibit 16–2** for a description of the 1500 Series and optional peripherals.)

The workstation product strategy had not been based on leadership in either price or performance (see **Exhibit 16–3**); its systems were in the middle to upper range in both categories. The performance leaders were Sun Microsystems and Hewlett-Packard/Apollo, both of which had recently introduced a workstation based on a RISC (Reduced Instruction Set Chip) microprocessor. While Sony was researching a RISC-based workstation, it was not yet ready to organize a product development effort whose output would be a marketable product.

Because the Workstation Division felt that it lacked the marketing power to create entirely new markets, it concentrated on creating a competitive workstation by making use of Sony's capabilities in manufacturing and other technologies such as optical disks and video to exploit niches. It concentrated also on the Japanese market where U.S. workstation firms were at a disadvantage because of the complexity of the characters in the Japanese language.

Although Sony's strategy had worked in the early stages of its entry into the workstation market, to grow further it had to expand its tra-

[2] The IKKI workstation was marketed as the 800 Series, which was soon to be phased out.

EXHIBIT 16-1 Product Line

The NEWS family of Sony workstations not only offers compact high performance but also leads the way in network computing. The Open Distributed Processing capability of these workstations helps build a heterogeneous, easily expandable network of shared resources. The dual-processor architecture demonstrates its power in I/O-intensive applications, delivering a constant CPU processing speed regardless of I/O loads and application programs. Furthermore, the NEWS family encompasses a wide range of products to meet the diversified needs of software engineers and technical professionals.

Open Distributed Processing

The NEWS workstations allow networking of various machines from different manufacturers, as well as efficient file sharing and distributed processing among these machines.

The key to this networking flexibilty is the adoption of the latest version of the industry standards or defacto standards. All NEWS workstations use Sony's implementation of UNIX 4.3BSD, NFS Rel. 3.2 and X Window System Ver. 11, combined with CGI graphics libraries and a number of languages such as C, Fortran 77, Franz Lisp and Pascal. Network interfacing is based on the standard IEEE802.3 Ethernet and TCP/IP and XNS protocols.

Dual Processors

The NEWS/1800 and 1900 Series of workstations feature Sony's unique dual-processor architecture. They use two MC68030's—one for the main processor and the other as a dedicated I/O processor. Equipped with a 256K byte static RAM and a real-time multitask monitor, the I/O processor handles all I/O processing (except the VME bus) and direct memory access, freeing the CPU power to run applications.

This means that the processing speed of the main processor can be maintained despite the increase in I/O loads caused by color graphics, network communications and disk access. The dual-processor NEWS can perform much faster in actual applications than single-processor workstations with the same MIPS value.

High-Speed X Window System

Established as the industry standard, the X Window System is one of the most important human interfaces available for workstation users. With this in mind, Sony has placed a high priority on the implementing of the X Window software on NEWS workstations. In addition to the software, the X Window System used in NEWS workstations owes its speed to specifically designed display boards which make possible high-speed bitblt (bit boundary block transfer) and raster operation. Furthermore, a dedicated high-speed bus is employed between the CPU and the display board, in order to maintain the high performance of the CPU during window operations. This combination of software and hardware found in NEWS workstations has resulted in one of the fastest and most reliable X Window Systems in the industry.

Versatile Product Lines

NEWS workstations come in a variety of configurations: deskside file servers, desktop power machines, cost-effective disk-based workstations, and color/monochrome diskless nodes. The wide line-up enables installation of the right machine for the right job, making it possible to achieve maximum efficiency at minimum network cost. Taking advantage of over 40 years of experience as a total electronics manufacturer, Sony also offers a wide selection of option units including high-resolution display monitors and an ultra-capacity MO disk drive unit.

	700 Series			1500 Series			1700 Series			1800 Series		1900 Series	
Model	NWS-711(UC)	NWS-712-(EK)	NWS-721	NWS-1510(EK)	NWS-1530(EK)	NWS-1580(EK)	NWS-1720	NWS-1750(UC)	NWS-1750(EK)	NWS-1830	NWS-1850	NWS-1930(UC)	NWS-1930(EK)
CPU	MC68020 (16.67MHz)	MC68020 (20MHz)		MC68030 (25MHz)									
I/O Processor	—											MC68030 (25MHz)	
Floating-Point Coprocessor	MC68881 (16.67MHz)	MC68881 (20MHz)		MC68882 (25MHz)									
Main Memory	4MB	4MB (expandable to 8MB)		4MB (expandable to 16MB)			4MB (expandable to 32MB)			8MB (expandable to 32MB)		16BM (expandable to 32MB)	
Cache Memory	—						16KB					64KB	
Streamer	—						125MB			—		125MB	
3.5" FDO (formatted)	—			1.44MB									
Hard Disk (formatted)	—			40MB		170MB	156MB	286MB		156MB	286BM	286MB x 1 (expandable to x 4)	286MB x 2 (expandable to x 4)
Power Requirements	AC100-120V	AC220-240V	AC100-120V or AC220-240V	AC220-240V			AC100-120V or AC220-240V	AC100-120V	AC220-240V	AC100-120V or AC220-240V		AC120V	AC220-2240V
Standard Software	• Operating System: NEWS-OS (UNIX 4.38SD + X Window System Ver. 11 + NFS. Rel. 3.2) • Communications: TCP/NP, XNS • Languages: C. Fortran 77, Franz Lisp, Pascal •Graphics CGI												

- UNIX is a registerd trademark of AT&T in the USA and other countries.
- NFS is a product created and developed by Sun Microsystems, Inc. and is a trademark of Sun Microsystems, Inc.
- X Window is a trademark of MIT.
- Ethernet and XNS are trademarks of Xerox Corporation.
- The MIPS value is determined in comparison with the performance of VAX 11/780 measured using the Dhrystone program. VAX is a registered trademark of Digital Equipment Corporation.
- NEWS is a trademark of Sony Corporation for their Workstation.
- UC models are available in the areas with AC100—120V, while EK models are available for the areas with AC220—240V. Those models with no suffix are designed for use in both areas.
- The NWS-1510/1530 are installed with part of the NEWS operating system.

EXHIBIT 16-2 1500 Series and Optional Peripherals

1500 Series
The Perfect Low-Cost Choice for Any Network

NWS-1510(EK)

System Connection

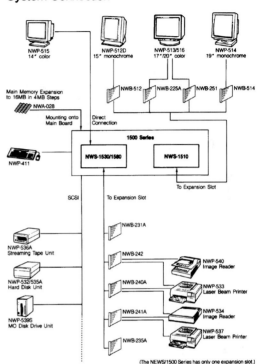

(The NEWS/1500 Series has only one expansion slot.)

The NEWS/1500 Series is an ideal way to reduce the network cost without affecting its efficiency. Based on the 25MHz MC68030 CPU and the 25MHz MC68882 floating-point coprocessor, the 1500 Series packs 3.9 MIPS processing power in a unit that's smaller than a personal computer. It is priced in the range of diskless machines but has its own local disk, making it possible to start up faster and operate faster.

The NEWS/1500 Series consists of three models, all featuring the extremely compact dimensions of 355 × 341 × 110mm. The NWS-1530(EK)/1580(EK) are equipped with a high-resolution color bitmap interface board. Up to 256 colors from a 16.7 million color palette can be displayed at once on the 1024 × 768 dot NWP-515 14″ (13″ viewable) color display designed specially to match these machines. The bitblt (bit boundary block transfer) function is implemented in hardware to realize a high-speed, multi-window display.

The NWS-1510(EK) has no display interface and thus can be connected to any color or monochrome display of your choice using the appropriate bitmap interface board.

The capacity of the main memory is 4M bytes for all models and is expandable in 4M byte steps to a maximum of 16M bytes with the use of the optional NWA-028 expansion RAM kits.

The capacity of the internal hard disk is 170M bytes for the NWS-1580(EK) and 40M bytes for the NWS-1530(EK) and 1510(EK). The SCSI bus enables the addition of external storage options. The RS232C ports accept up to two personal computers, modems and printers. There is also a parallel interface for connection to a Centronics compatible unit.

Specifications

Model Name	NWS-1510(EK)	NWS-1530(EK)	NWS-1580(EK)
CPU		MC68030 (25MHz)	
Floating-Point Coprocessor		MC68882 (25MHz)	
MIPS		3.9	
Main Memory		4MB (expandable in 4MB steps to 16MB with NWA-028)	
Hard Disk		40MB (formatted)	170MB (formatted)
3.5″ FDD		1.44MB (formatted)	
Standard Interfaces	Ethernet, SCSI RS232C (×2), Centronics Parallel	Ethernet, SCSI, RS232C (×2), Centronics Parallel, Color Bitmap Display	
Expansion Slot		1	
Power Requirements		AC220—240V	
Power Consumption		330VA (220V)	
Dimensions		355(W) × 341(D) × 110(H)mm (14 × 13½ × 4⅜″)	
Weight		10kg (22 lb 1 oz)	
Operating System		NEWS-OS (UNIX 4.3BSD + X Window System Ver. 11 + NFS Rel. 3.2)	
Communications		TCP/IP, XNS	
Languages		C, Fortran 77, Franz Lisp, Pascal	
Graphics		CGI	

NOTE: Because of limited internal storage capacity, the NWS-1510(EK)/ 1530(EK) are installed with part of the NEWS operating system.

Sony Corporation: Workstation Division.

EXHIBIT 16-3 Sony and Sun Microsystems
Product Introductions

First Product to Use New Microprocessor

Micro-processor	Sun Microsystems		Sony	
	Product	Date	Product	Date
68000	Sun-2	11/83	—	—
68010	Sun-2/160	11/84	—	—
68020	Sun-3	9/85	800 Series	1/87
68030	Sun-3/60	7/87	1800 Series	9/88
RISC	Sun-4	7/87	?	?

ditional role to become more of a leader. In particular, the U.S. market was more competitive because Sun and HP/Apollo did not have to face the difficulties of the Japanese language in the U.S. (See **Exhibit 16–4** for a comparison of Sony and U.S. workstations.) On the other hand, Sony management felt that manufacturing expertise and costs would become more important as the industry matured, and Sony's size and experience in electronics manufacturing would give it a competitive advantage.

New Product Development in the Workstation Division

The division's development process had evolved somewhat since Doi had assembled 11 maverick engineers and given them free rein. In 1989, the development process had three stages: (1) basic architecture specification, (2) product design, and (3) first lot production. During each phase, a different group (or groups) had primary responsibility for the development effort, although their responsibilities tended to overlap for a considerable amount of time and people were transferred across groups as projects moved through the process. (See **Exhibit 16–5** for the organization of the SuperMicro

Group and **Exhibit 16–6** for a flow chart of how the process was intended to work.)

The basic architecture stage occurred before a specific product was targeted. The R&D department would examine new and existing technologies to determine the basic hardware and software on which Sony should develop its line. The R&D department would then study the technologies it had chosen by developing a prototype workstation based on the new technology. While this prototype was not directly connected to a particular product line, it gave R&D engineers "hands-on" experi-

EXHIBIT 16-4 Comparison of the 1500 with Competitors' Workstations

	Sony	Sun	HP/Apollo
Model	1520	3/80	DN2500
CPU	68030/25 MHz	68030/20 MHz	68030/20 MHz
Coprocessor	68881	68882	68882
MIPS	3.9	3.0	4.0
Amount of Main Memory	4–16 MB	4–16 MB	4–16 MB
Hard Disk	40 MB	104 MB	100 MB
Floppy Drive	3.5" 1.44 MB	3.5" 1.44 MB	5.25" 1.2 MB
Standard Interfaces	Ethernet, SCSI, RS232C, Centronics	Ethernet, SCSI, RS432	Ethernet, Tokenring, RS232C
Operating System	NEWS-OS (UNIX 4.3BSD + X Window System Ver. 11 + NFS 3.2)	Sun OS 4.1 (UNIX 4.3BSD + System V, NeWS, SunView, NFS)	Domain/OS (Aegis UNIX System V, 4.3BSD NFS, X Window DM)
Display	15" Monochrome (816X1024)	16" Monochrome (1280X1024)	15" Monochrome (1024X800)
Price	$7,860	$8,720	$5,420
Date of Introduction	December 1988	January 1988	Announced (to be introduced in Dec. 89)

EXHIBIT 16-5 Workstation Division Organization Chart

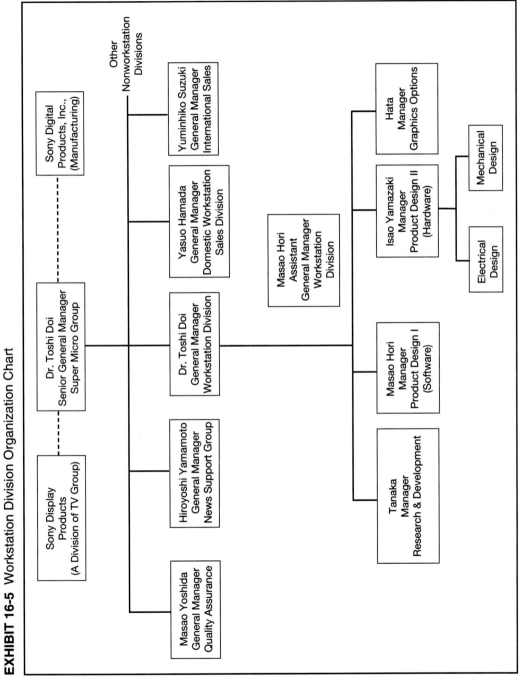

Sony Corporation: Workstation Division.

EXHIBIT 16-6 Flow Chart of Prototyping in the Development Process

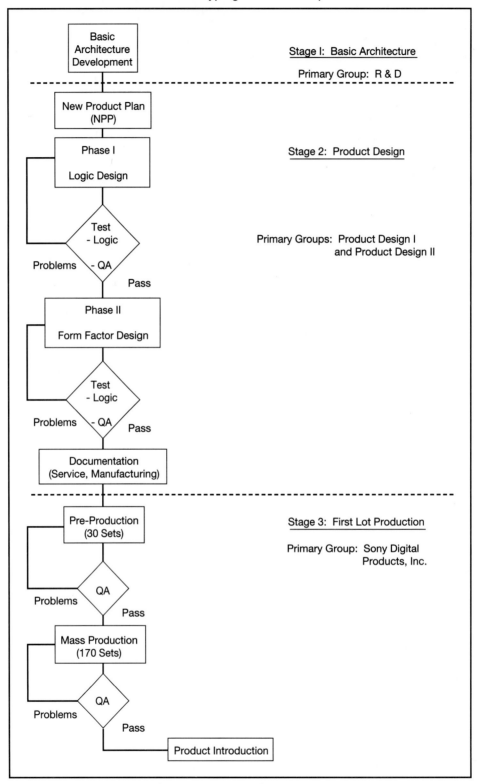

Sony Corporation: Workstation Division.

ence with the new technology. With this experience, they would develop a basic architecture for the workstations which would form the core or platform projects in the product line.

The R&D group was continually working on the basic technologies that would be used in the top-of-the-line next generation systems. For example, after studying the 68020, several engineers were transferred from R&D to the two design engineering groups to lead the design ef-

fort when the time came to develop an actual product. The R&D group then studied the 68030 chip and later a RISC microprocessor from MIPS Computer Systems Inc. for the division's next generation products (see **Exhibit 16-7**).

The second stage in the development process was the actual product design effort, which started with the generation of a New Product Plan (NPP). While one person was assigned to write the NPP, it was a collaborative effort by

EXHIBIT 16-7 Transfer of Products from R&D to Design, and Product Families

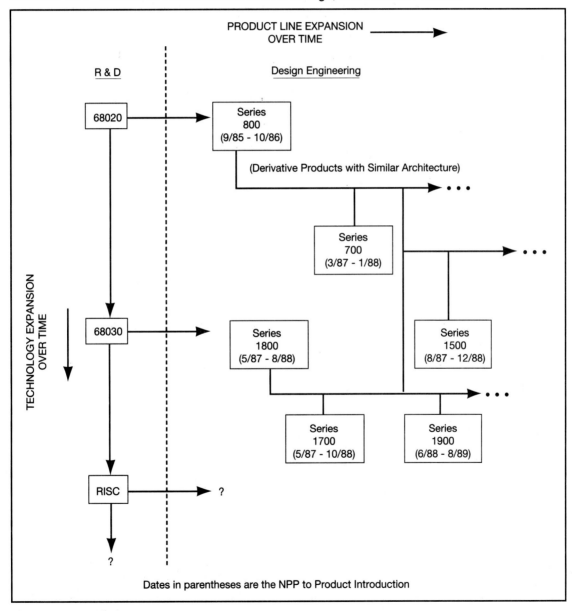

Sony Corporation: Workstation Division.

people in the Planning, R&D, and Design Engineering departments. The primary author could be a member of any of the relevant departments, although normally he or she was in the hardware design engineering department. The NPP included a description of the proposed product, a brief competitive analysis, cost and schedule projections, and a summary of other relevant business and technical data (see **Exhibit 16–8**).

After the NPP was formulated (and approved by Doi), two design engineering groups became involved. Most product-specific work was done by the hardware design engineering department managed by Isao Yamazaki (Design Engineering II). The majority of the software development effort was based on the Unix kernel and the creation of the low level routines that made up the operating system. Relatively little effort was devoted to applications programs (e.g., a spreadsheet or word processing program), although some work was done on applications that would be common across the entire NEWS™ product line. A very small subset of hardware-dependent software (e.g., the operating system) was developed by five or six software engineers from Masao Hori's department (Design Engineering I), which employed a total of 25 software engineers. The software design engineering department's primary task was porting[3] Unix and Sony's application programs to the new computer.

The hardware development task—designing the main system board for the computer—was divided into two phases, each of which culminated in building and validating a prototype. In Phase I, the system's logic was designed and checked. Toward the end of this phase, the format of the board was specified to fit into the overall system design (e.g., to make sure the board would physically fit into the housing) and a few sample boards were built and tested. In Phase II, several prototype printed circuit boards (PCBs) with the final format were produced, tested, and debugged.

The R&D group and both design engineer-

EXHIBIT 16-8 New Product Plan (NPP) Data Requirements

1. Product Concepts and Main Features
2. Competitors' Products
3. Sales and Distribution Channel
4. Target Market Segments
5. Target Price Points
   a. List
   b. FOB
6. Competitors' Prices
7. Cost of Material
8. Production Cost
9. Maintenance Information
   a. Technical
   b. Warrantee Length
   c. Special Services (Periodic Maintenance, etc.)
10. Applicable Safety Regulations (UL, CSA, FCC, etc.)
11. Other Regulations (EMI, EBU, etc.)
12. Manufacturing Plants to be Used
13. Product Lifecycle
14. Estimated Sales
    a. Monthly
    b. By Geographic Region
    c. Market Share
15. System Concept
    a. Monitor
    b. Computer
    c. How to connect the peripherals, network, etc.
16. Accessories (Power Cords, etc.)
17. Anticipated Product Line Evolution
18. Approvals
    a. Planner
    b. Plant Manager
    c. Design Leader
    d. Design Manager
    e. Senior Manager
    f. Accounting Manager
    g. Department Manager
    h. General Manager

ing groups were located in two adjacent buildings in the Shinagawa section of Tokyo. Each of the three departments had one large room where everyone (including the manager) worked. There were no partitions or doors and because this arrangement kept the manager well informed, Sony did not rely very much on formal project reviews. However, each department had one or two rooms that could be used for meetings so that the rest of the group would not be disturbed.

The third and final stage of new product development was first lot production, for which the manufacturing division, Sony Digital Products Inc., had primary responsibility. This division, a

---

[3]Porting software was the technical term for modifying a software program so that it would run on a different type of system. Unix was highly modularized in order to ease the porting tasks; applications programs that ran under Unix tended to need very little, if any modification to run under Unix on a different computer.

wholly owned subsidiary of the Sony Group, produced CD players, optical disks and other digital products for several Sony divisions. Its plant was located in the mountains, four hours (by train) from Tokyo.

Project Management in the Workstation Division

At Sony, a project manager was assigned after the NPP approval. Based on merit and availability rather than seniority, this assignment did not confer special status on the project manager—at least not permanently. An engineer who served as manager on one project might be a regular member on the next. Often the project manager was a member of the R&D department who was transferred to a design engineering department when an NPP for the area in which he or she had been working was written, and the project was sent to design engineering for development. This procedure was adopted to make the transfer of knowledge from R&D to design engineering as quick and effective as possible.

The project manager was in fact more of a senior engineer than a manager. Because the teams were so small (typically three or four hardware engineers), the need for many of the traditional management tasks, such as coordinating within the team, essentially disappeared. The engineers typically had to split their time among two or three projects, although they were generally assigned only one major project (such as a new workstation) at a time. The major project tended to take about 70% of an engineer's time with the other 30% divided up among smaller projects. In general, the major project took precedence over the minor ones, although there were occasional conflicts over priority (which were settled by Yamazaki).

Doi felt strongly that senior management's role in a project should be to build a team, establish broad objectives, and then leave it alone. He believed managers should remain outside the project, perform miscellaneous tasks for it, and remove any obstacles to it. High-level managers also had a role in developing strategy and monitoring the project, but not in the day-to-day operations of the project.

Doi's management approach was successful in part because of the skills and abilities of the engineers in the Workstation Division. Although the division had grown from the original 11 to over 100 engineers in 1989, the original 11 still formed the technical core for the division. The newer engineers had been brought in from a variety of sources. While some had been hired straight out of college, many had been transferred from other Sony divisions, and some had even been hired away from other companies. This diverse mix had given the engineering function a breadth and depth of experience unusual in a Japanese company.

The 1550 Project (August 1987 to December 1988)

One of the division's recent major development projects had been the 1550, a general purpose workstation positioned in the middle of the Sony line. Although every project had some unique aspects, the 1550 development was fairly typical of an initial offering in a next generation product series. (A time line is shown in **Exhibit 16–9**.)

The first stage, specification of the basic architecture and concepts, typically was done by the R&D department for "core" products. For the 1550, however, the basic architecture was well understood because the division had developed several computers based on the same microprocessor chip. Therefore the project began directly with an NPP written in August 1987 by a senior hardware engineer, Takashi Yoshida.

Because he had written the NPP, Yoshida was the logical choice to manage the second stage of the development effort on the 1550. Joining Yoshida for the project team were three other electrical engineers, who worked on designing the mother board while one software engineer (from Hori's group) was responsible for the product-specific programming to be included in the ROM on the board. An overview of workstation technology is found in Appendix II.

EXHIBIT 16-9 Time Line of the 1550 Project

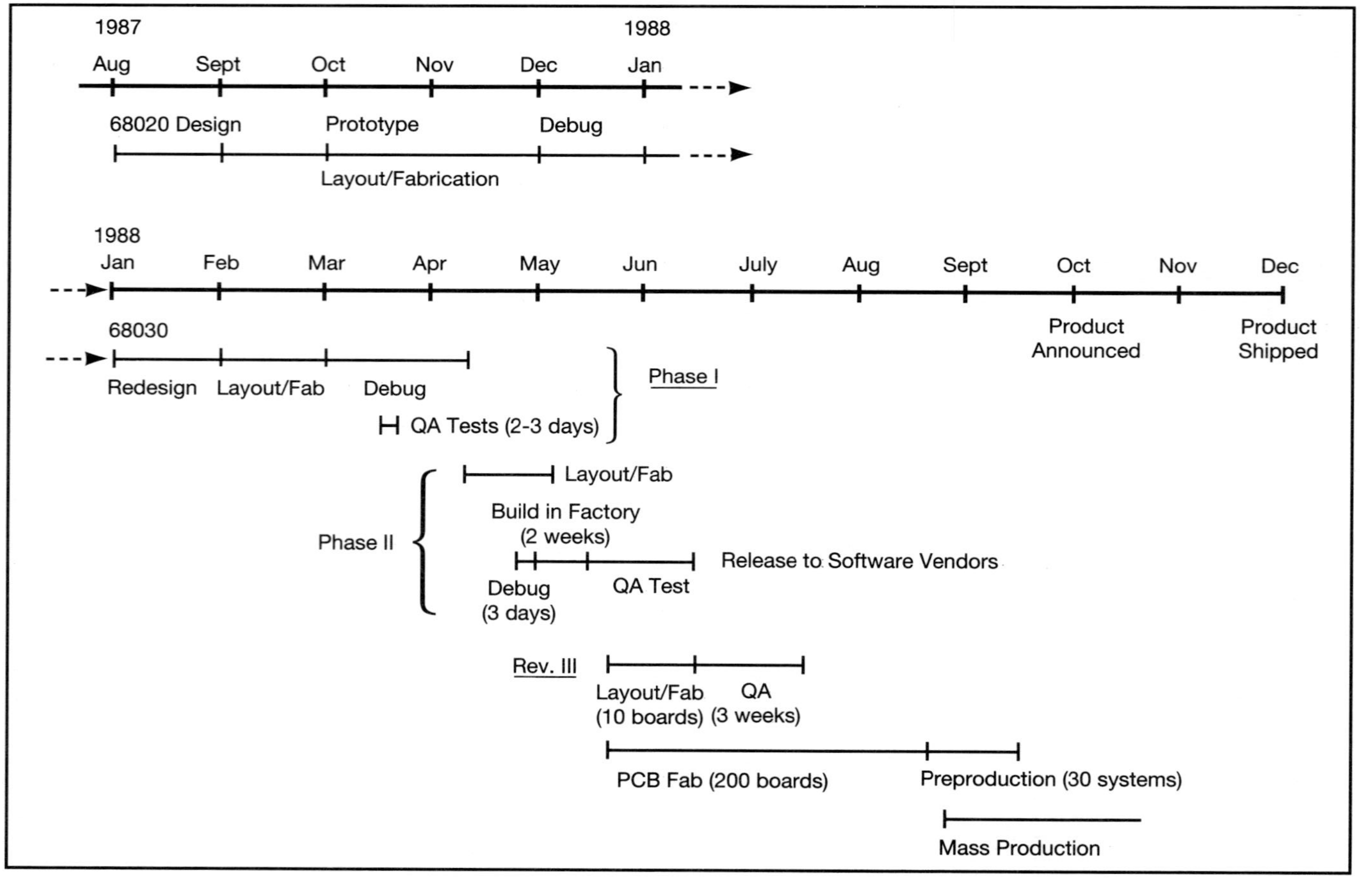

Sony Corporation: Workstation Division.

Phase I

The first task in any development effort was creating a detailed design of the logic for the mother board. The logic design determined how the computer would function, although the details of the PCB (e.g., dimensions, number of layers, and routing of wires) were left until later. The logic functions were determined by choosing the components (e.g., chips, resistors, and capacitors) and specifying how they would be connected. The final output of this task was a set of schematics (engineering drawings) that showed each of the components and the wires connecting them.

Because wires on the same layer of a PCB could not cross one another (such crossing would cause a short circuit), specifying the logic of how all the chips were to be connected did not complete the design. The position of the chips, the number of layers, and the physical routing of the connecting wires on the PCB also had to be determined. Because of the many connections necessary and the desire to minimize the number of layers on the PCB, this process was quite complex. When there was no way to connect one point to another without crossing a wire, a new layer had to be added, even though doing so increased the board's production cost considerably.

After the schematics were completed, a layout was developed so a first prototype could be built. Because of the Workstation Division's small size, it did not have the resources either to develop the layout or to fabricate the prototype PCB in-house. Instead, the schematics were sent to one of several outside vendors who developed the detailed board layout. This process generally took four to five weeks the first time it was done. Subsequently, when changes were made to a previous design, much of the layout stayed the same and the time for developing the remainder was reduced to as little as two to three weeks.

After the board layout was completed, it was sent to a vendor who would fabricate a batch of boards. Often the same vendor would do both the layout and fabrication, but sometimes a different subcontractor would be used. Fabrication took an additional two to three weeks; typically, a batch of ten prototype boards would be made in Phase I.

Thus, the total time required from the time

the schematics were finished until the prototype board was returned was usually about six to eight weeks. During this waiting period, the engineers were able to catch up on their smaller projects.

For the 1550 project, the NPP called for the system to be based on a 68020 microprocessor, and by mid-October 1987, Yoshida and his project team had developed a set of schematics for the main board. The board was then sent to Oki, an outside vendor who not only developed its layout but also fabricated it. By early December, the 10 units of the Phase I prototype had been made and Yoshida's small team of engineers had started their debugging procedures.

It took about one month for the first prototype board of the 1550 to be 90% debugged. However, further work was terminated when management decided that, because Sun Microsystems had just introduced a competing machine based on the 68030, a newer and more powerful microprocessor, the 1550 should be based on the 68030 instead of the 68020. Although the 68030 was very similar to the 68020, much of the design did have to be redone. The primary difference between the chips was that the 68030 contained its own memory management unit,[4] making the memory management unit designed for the 68020 irrelevant and an unnecessary cost for the 1550.

Phase I on the 1550 therefore needed to be repeated, and the first several weeks of 1988 were spent redesigning the mother board to use the 68030. The new schematics were then sent to Oki, and six weeks later 10 revised prototype PCBs were delivered to Sony. Next, the hardware design engineers hand-inserted the chips into the boards and started the low-level hardware checks, which included testing the data and address buses to ensure the voltage levels were in the required range, and testing that the clock and reset waveforms had the right shape. Software to drive a monitor was then placed in ROM so that a

---

[4]A memory management unit was the electronics that controlled a high speed memory cache. A cache, a high speed memory bank for frequently accessed data, was used because the microprocessor was much faster than main memory. This dual memory system allowed the computer to utilize low-speed memory without much loss in performance yet without the extremely high cost of using very high speed memory exclusively.

CRT could be connected to the serial port[5] on the board. Because of the similarity with the 68020 version of the 1550, the "terminal driver" software needed only slight modifications from the previous version. By the end of the first week, the engineers were able to test memory by typing commands from a keyboard.

After the low-level tests were completed, the more complicated tasks of debugging the various interfaces (e.g., interfaces to disk controllers, networks, and displays) began. The software to test these interfaces was written on three levels: the top-level shell, the middle-level controller, and the low-level device drivers. Usually, when altering the basic architecture of the interface, higher level code did require modifications. When modifying the software from an existing workstation, however, only the device drivers needed to be changed. Thus, modifying the 1550's software structure to work on the new system could be done quickly. For example, although the test code for the disk controller contained approximately 4,000 lines of assembly language, adapting it to the new system took only two to three days.

Debugging the various interfaces for the 1550 mother board took approximately one month, during which several software engineers worked closely with the hardware engineers. Once the system was debugged (by the end of April 1988), the software people who were converting application software were given several of the debugged boards on which to continue their work. Three of the remaining boards were given to the quality assurance division (which performed QA for the entire SuperMicro Group) to test for electromagnetic interference (EMI) and to complete other Phase I tests. The final form factor (e.g., size and shape) of the board also was determined during the final portion of Phase I. This task was performed in conjunction with an outside vendor who was designing the box into which the mother board and all the other electronics were to be placed. Once these tasks were completed, the electrical engineers then spent a couple of days documenting changes in the circuits before returning the updated schematics

back to Oki for layout and manufacture of the Phase II prototype boards.

The purpose of Phase I was to ensure that the logic of the design worked properly. If the problems with the PCB design were excessive, another Phase I prototype cycle would be performed. Fortunately, on the 1550 project the problems were not that severe, and in most cases only one Phase I prototyping cycle was necessary. After the Phase I debugging was completed, the components with long lead times were ordered and a date was set for first lot production. (Most of the long lead items were semiconductor devices that had to be ordered three or four months in advance.)

Phase II

In Phase II, the size and shape of the PCBs were adjusted to meet the form factor requirements that had just been established at the end of Phase I. Phase II also provided an opportunity for the manufacturing division (Sony Digital Products, Inc.) to start learning about the new product and preparing its manufacturing processes.

Because the 1550 was the first computer in the 1500 series, 100 boards were ordered in the Phase II prototype cycle so that third-party software vendors could be given beta-test systems to use in developing their applications. Oki finished the 100 boards by mid-June, having taken approximately six weeks to redo the layout and fabricate the boards. Five boards were sent directly to the hardware engineering team, and the remaining 95 were sent directly to the Sony Digital Products factory, where the chips were inserted using the automatic chip insertion machines. Normally, the hardware engineers would have debugged and corrected the prototype boards before sending the batch to the factory. In this instance, however, the switch from the 68020 to the 68030 had delayed the project several weeks and the capacity had been scheduled months in advance—making it impossible to delay or reschedule.

This schedule put a great deal of pressure on the engineers to debug the Phase II prototype board quickly, because any cuts of connecting wires (i.e., electrical paths) had to be made before

[5]A serial port was one of several interfaces to external devices on a computer. It allowed the computer to communicate with devices that sent and received data in a serial fashion (e.g., terminals, plotters, and some printers).

the chips were inserted. Adding jumper wires—additional connections—was done afterwards. On the 1550, the hardware and software people had only three days in which to debug the prototype mother boards before the factory inserted the chips.

There were usually very few logic bugs at this point because they had been removed in Phase I, but noise and EMI problems could appear. Noise problems occurred when chips could not react fast enough to handle the speed at which the computer was run. EMI problems occurred when the computer's internal signals emitted radio waves that interfered with other equipment (such as TV and radio receivers).

Fortunately, in the 1550 project, there were no noise or EMI problems and only a couple of minor logic errors. Through a great deal of effort, the hardware team managed to find the problems, which were solved by one cut and two jumpers. Sony Digital Products was then able to begin production of the batch of prototype boards on schedule.

While the hardware design engineers were debugging the system, several manufacturing people had been present to learn about the system and to help wherever possible. After the boards were debugged, the engineers went to the factory with the manufacturing people to help with the production of the 95 prototype boards. The engineers remained at the factory for a week, of which three days were spent making the logic changes to the PCBs and an additional day was spent inserting and soldering some special components.

Approximately 70% of the boards worked after the first pass through production, that is, at the end of the fourth day. The engineers remained through much of the night to determine the problems with the other 30%. Most of the problems involved soldering- and manufacturing-related issues and by the next morning 90% of the boards were working. The boards were assembled into complete systems the next day, and on day six, the remaining boards were fixed and completed.

Several of the completed systems were sent to quality assurance for special tests: EMI, UL, FCC, and other environmental concerns. The Phase II QA tests were more extensive than in Phase I and included testing under extreme conditions of temperature, humidity, and vibration, and with wide voltage swings (+/-10%).

The other systems were distributed with the majority (approximately 50) going to software vendors, who were writing third-party application software. The balance was divided among the two design engineering groups and the R&D department, with a few systems sent to marketing for customer presentations.

First Lot Production

After returning from the Sony Digital Products plant, the hardware engineers documented the Phase II design changes and sent them to Oki, which was to do a final layout for the boards in anticipation of first lot production. Because the changes were so small, Oki was able to build 10 of these "Prototype III" boards in three weeks (including one week for layout). These boards were used by the project team to ensure that all the changes had been made properly before the first lot production boards were built. By the second week in August, following Sony's companywide vacation week (August 1 to 7), the Prototype III systems had passed QA tests. The remaining 200 boards for the first lot production were then ordered from Oki.

After the Prototype III boards passed QA's tests, the hardware engineers expanded the system's documentation, writing maintenance manuals, test procedures for manufacturing, and other instructions. Throughout this period, the engineers also had to help maintain the prototype systems that had been sent to the software houses.

The first lot production of the 1550 was scheduled to start in the third week of October at which time the hardware design engineers returned to the factory for a couple of weeks to help with ramp-up and testing, and to troubleshoot any problems. The first lot production was done in two phases. The first batch, pre-production, sent 30 systems through the production line.

Because of the large number of products manufactured at Sony Digital Products, the plant operation was extremely flexible. There were 10 lines for automatic chip insertion as well as a couple of manual insertion lines for especially difficult insertion tasks. The plant automatically inserted over 90% of the chips onto approximately 2,500 PCBs a day. About 600 different PCBs, all made by subcontractors, were run through the various insertion lines in a typical month. In addition to the traditional chip insertion machines, a new Sony-designed machine for placing surface mount chips had recently been installed.

After the chips were inserted into the PCBs, the boards passed through wave soldering twice to improve the soldering's quality and yield. (Most problems with PCBs could be traced to bad solders.) The boards and other components then were assembled into the final system. Although the plant had several traditional assembly lines (with conveyor belts and each worker performing a precisely defined task), workstation volumes were too small for an assembly line to be efficient. The workstations were therefore assembled off-line by two workers, each of whom did half the tasks.

After the 30 pre-production systems were completed, they were tested intensively and again debugged. At this time, any remaining systematic errors were found and corrected and then the balance of the first lot production units were produced. In the 1550 project, no major problems were found and the factory continued producing the remaining systems. The product was announced at the end of October, and shipments started on December 21, 1988.

Yamazaki considered the development process at the Workstation Division quite successful. He attributed its success to several factors: very little time was wasted passing project responsibility from group to group; the project teams tended to be small groups of very expert engineers who took the development of a new computer from the NPP all the way through to manufacturing; the project team was typically formed around either an R&D person who had worked on the system's basic concept or a person who had experience with a similar system; and this same team eventually ended up on the manufacturing plant floor, helping to ramp-up production.

Comparing Workstation Development Processes

From what Doi knew about similar PCB-based product development efforts at different Sony divisions as well as at other companies, the Workstation Division's development effort was very efficient. Its usual development cycle time was 12 months, while product development cycles at other workstation companies usually lasted 18 to 24 months.

In the number of prototyping cycles, Sony's advantage was even more obvious: competitors typically went through 6 to 8 (although there was a wide variation from about 4 to 12 depending on the company and the project). Sony's development process typically required only two to four cycles.

Although Sony had far fewer prototyping cycles on average, the time for each cycle tended to be about the same as at other companies—approximately two months. The time at Sony, however, was spent very differently. In general, other companies did their own board layout with automated CAD/CAM systems. Sony had placed little emphasis on CAD/CAM tools and instead subcontracted the layout task to a variety of small firms that specialized in PCB layout design.

Most companies in the workstation business did focus on getting the prototypes back quickly. Often these companies would go to a board prototyping house that, for an extra fee, might be able to fabricate the boards in a week. When the boards returned from the prototyping vendor, the chips would be inserted by an internal model shop. Because these tasks were handled by groups other than hardware or software design, the design engineers at other companies were able to focus exclusively on their primary design tasks.

There were also differences in the philosophy of developing new workstations. Most companies divided the development process into three phases: Engineering Verification Test (EVT), Design Verification Test (DVT), and Production Verification Test (PVT). The EVT stage verified that the board logic worked properly; the DVT stage verified that the board worked in its final size and shape; and the PVT stage verified that the factory's fabrication process could produce that board in volume and on specification.

Sony's development process consisted of

Phase I, which was essentially EVT, but then seemed to combine DVT and PVT stages into the Phase II prototyping step. In Phase II, not only was the board reduced to its final size and shape, but the factory was involved in inserting the chips and assembling the board into complete systems. While there was an element of testing in the first lot production stage, the primary purpose was to produce systems that were sold to customers.

Yamazaki's Proposal

Although the development process at the Workstation Division was efficient, changes were needed. The principal problem was that too much was required of the hardware design engineers. Small teams were more efficient but they required that each engineer be able to handle the complete range of design tasks, from high-level architecture down to minor details. Furthermore, because the same engineer dealt with all the issues—from logic design to manufacturability—the procedure required a great breadth of knowledge. Thus the engineer's skills and knowledge had to be both broad and deep. Even the current, experienced engineers had trouble with these requirements; getting new engineers with this combination of skills appeared almost impossible. New engineers would have to be trained, and that could take years.

The current system also required an almost superhuman effort by hardware engineers, who typically worked 60–70 hours a week, and even more during a crisis. Yamazaki was afraid that some of them would burn out after only a few years at such a pace.

Another problem with the current procedure was that the designs were not optimized for manufacturability. Because hardware design engineers were unfamiliar with all of the manufacturing concerns, they often missed simple redesigns that could make manufacturing far more efficient. For example, the size of a hole could be changed slightly to allow easier insertion of a component, or the orientations of the components altered to better fit the capabilities of the particular insertion machines used by Sony Digital Products. Even when these problems were brought to the attention of the design engineers, they lacked time to go back and fix them.

Masao Hori, the assistant general manager of the Workstation Division, stated the problem succinctly:

The current process is not so bad, because it is very quick. It is very difficult to separate technology into neat little steps and for this reason it takes time to transfer technology. Because the workstation market is so competitive there is no time to do this transfer. On the other hand, design engineering does not have enough manpower or expertise to support manufacturing properly, especially as our product line and the number of development projects continue to grow.

Yamazaki's proposal involved adding a Manufacturing Engineering Section (MES) between the hardware design engineering department and manufacturing (at Sony Digital Products, Inc.). This new section would have five responsibilities: (1) representing manufacturability issues and concerns early in the development process; (2) supporting manufacturing during ramp-up; (3) doing follow-up engineering and redesigns necessary after first lot production; (4) developing minor upgrades, extensions, and enhancements to the product; and (5) supporting field service and providing analysis of recurrent problems in the field.

MES would get involved with a development project in Phase II, playing a support role in building and testing the prototypes and preparing design documentation. By first lot production they would take over primary responsibility for supporting manufacturing. Given MES involvement, the design engineers would have to spend less time supervising prototyping and less time at the factory during first lot production. In some instances, MES could probably itself handle the manufacturing support required during first lot production.

After product introduction, MES would perform any redesigns requested by manufacturing (for example, a chip from a certain vendor might have too high a defect rate and a small redesign might be necessary to switch to a different vendor). Under the current system, these tasks were delayed or not completed at all because the hardware design engineering department was overloaded.

MES would also design small upgrades to existing systems. For example, for the 1500 Series, MES would perform the minor redesigns of the mother board needed so it could interface with a high resolution graphics display.

Support of field service was another area in which MES would fill an important gap. In addition to pure technical support when field service could not solve a problem, MES could analyze the different types of failures and determine their root causes. They could then redesign the product to prevent similar failures in the future.

By transferring tasks to MES, design engineering's workload would be significantly reduced, and the remaining tasks would be completed in a more timely fashion. The hardware design engineering department would also be able to spend more time designing new systems, thus reducing the development cycle. Furthermore, the design engineers could become more specialized because MES would handle most of the manufacturing issues.

Because the tasks proposed for MES involved only minor adjustments in existing design and manufacturing knowledge, the MES engineers would not require the same breadth of knowledge as the design engineers. They would not be required to design the architecture of the workstations or even do major design tasks. Hiring relatively young, less experienced engineers for MES would be much easier than hiring the type of people currently required for the hardware design department. Furthermore, because design would become more focused, even hardware engineers would be easier to find.

Yamazaki proposed that the new section be located in Tokyo, near the hardware design engineering department, and report to him. It would eventually need 10 engineers, but the section could be started with fewer (a minimum of five) because it would have responsibility for only a limited number of products. Of course, as it took responsibility for more and more products, the staffing would have to be increased.

Although Doi understood and agreed with many of Yamazaki's points, he was worried about the effects on Sony's development process of implementing the proposal. He did not want the Workstation Division to fall into the big-company mode like the rest of Sony, yet he knew that growth necessitated some changes. If he merely tried to add engineers to the current structure, those engineers would probably begin to specialize anyway.

Appendix I: Selected Workstation Terminology

The CPU (central processor unit) formed the "brains" of the computer, interpreting the software commands and controlling all the other components of the computer. At the heart of the CPU was a microprocessor, a single chip for arithmetic, input and output data, and similar operations. In 1989, most workstations used a microprocessor from the Motorola 68000™ family (the 68000, 68020, 68030, etc.). There was, however, a distinct trend toward using Reduced Instruction Set Chips (RISC). Although the RISC microprocessors had many fewer functions, they were optimized for speed, thus improving the total system performance.

The RAM (random access memory) consisted of all the memory chips that provided fast, temporary storage for data that the computer used while running. Because data in RAM were lost if the power were turned off, workstations needed permanent storage as well, and that was provided by the hard disk(s). Data were stored magnetically on disks and remained even when the power was turned off. However, being mechanical devices, hard disks were much slower than RAM.

The ROM (read only memory), like RAM, was a collection of chips that provided memory. Unlike RAM, however, ROM could not be altered after the chips were fabricated and programmed. Furthermore, ROM did not lose its data when the power was shut off. For this reason, ROM was used as a place to store a small "kernel" of software that the computer used when it was first turned on.

The CPU communicated with these devices, as well as with peripherals, through the bus. The bus, like a telephone junction box, was a collection of wires that ran through the computer system. Two buses existed: the address bus and the data bus. The address bus contained the signal from the CPU that determined which device should respond. The data bus carried information (data) to be communicated. To make sure that the signals were sent and received properly, some chips (the bus controller) performed logic functions to test for data validity.

Appendix II: Workstation Technology (1989)

All the chips to be included in a workstation were located on a PCB. The circuit board was a sheet of plastic on which alternating layers of wires and insulation were placed. Within the same layer, spaces were left between wires so that they did not short-circuit the electrical signal. The wires could cross between layers because wire layers were separated by insulation. (The green insulation gave the boards their green appearance.) Because the wires on each layer were laid down using a printing process, the cost of a board was related directly to the number of layers. The manufacturing process also became more difficult when more layers were added, further increasing the cost, complicating the debugging process, and making it more difficult to achieve consistently high quality. There was, therefore, a great incentive to reduce the number of layers.

Historically, once a board was fabricated and appropriate holes were created, chips were inserted into those holes and soldered on the bottom side. While this could be done by hand, using an automatic chip insertion machine was much more efficient. After the chips were inserted, they had to be soldered into place. Again, this could be done by hand, but a more efficient method was wave soldering: the protruding "legs" of the chips that had been pushed all the way through the board were passed over a "river" of molten solder. This technique uniformly soldered all the chips on a board at one time.

A newer method for attaching chips to a board was called surface mount. In this method, the chips were connected only to the surface of the board, without going through holes. Soldering by hand was much more difficult and sometimes impossible with surface mount chips. Because surface mount reduced the size of a board by three-quarters or more, the electronics industry was adopting this technology quite quickly.

Mistakes found in the design of a PCB usually could be corrected by hand; if a new connection were needed, a short wire could be hand-soldered onto the board, connecting the two points desired. Such a hand-soldered wire was called a jumper. If an extra connection between two components had to be made, the wire often could be cut by finding a space on the board where no other wires crossed the offending wire and then cutting through the layers until the connection was broken. Because these hand fixes were difficult, time consuming, and not fully reliable, all such design problems normally were corrected before regular volume production began.

Another problem often occurring in workstations was noise from the signals changing so rapidly. Noise had two manifestations. The first was "external" noise or electromagnetic interference: the wires in the computer started acting like little antennae, producing radio signals that could disrupt nearby television and radio reception. In the United States, the amount of EMI permitted was regulated by government agencies such as the FCC. The second, "internal," noise, was caused when some of the chips did not respond fast enough to the signals they received, resulting in misread data. So, computers that worked perfectly when run slowly, sometimes failed when operated more quickly. Because many things affected the ability of the chips to respond quickly (e.g., temperature, strength of the signal), these problems were often sporadic and very difficult to find. Much QA testing during product development focused on discovering such problems before the product was delivered to customers.

PART FIVE

General Management

17. The Transformation of IBM

IBM had a very good year in 1990. John Akers had guided his company through three major rounds of corporate restructuring since 1985, and he was proud of IBM's accomplishments. Recent product introductions were being hailed as technical breakthroughs with great market potential, the stock price had recovered, and internal morale was improving. Akers was determined that IBM be viewed as *the* world-class competitor in its field, and all the signs were pointing in the right direction—profits were growing again and IBM remained the market share leader in each of its businesses.

But after an outstanding fourth quarter, Akers had to tell his shareholders in March 1991 that operating profits would be down sharply in the latest three months as a result of lower sales in the U.S. and Europe. Concerned about the magnitude of the downturn, the competitive Akers was growing impatient with the time it was taking to transform IBM, especially the vexing problems of meeting deadlines and getting the organization to be aggressive in solving quality issues and delivering on commitments. Akers challenged his senior management team: "How do we respond to this latest decline? Should we restructure ourselves to anticipate lower growth? And how do we improve our execution?" Akers made it clear that all options should be on the table.

History of the Company

IBM's first president was the legendary Thomas J. Watson, Sr. After joining the Computing Tabulating and Recording Company in 1914, Watson changed the company's name to International Business Machines in 1924 and began building one of the most successful corporations in modern history. Among Watson Sr.'s most prescient strategies was seeing the whole world as IBM's market. Between World Wars I and II, the company erected plants in Germany, France, and the U.K. and established agencies in Latin America and Asia. From the beginning, national compa-

Professors David B. Yoffie and Andrall E. Pearson prepared this case as the basis for class discussion rather than to illustrate either effective or ineffective handling of an administrative situation.

nies were run by locals and given leeway in deciding product mix and pricing policies. Over the years, IBM's established global presence gave it a huge international installed base and the capability to tap the best human resources worldwide.

Perhaps most important to Watson Sr. was his belief that people were IBM's most valuable assets. He replaced foremen with managers who were instructed to treat workers with respect, listen to their ideas, and encourage innovation. IBM provided its employees with healthy paychecks, free insurance, and numerous benefits. Watson developed the principle of continuous learning and brought teachers into the company to help workers improve their education. Watson Sr. and his successor, Thomas Watson, Jr., went on to create a work environment that rewarded winners and sought the highest possible standards of performance.[1] To build organizational excellence, IBM developed its "contention management" style. Every staff unit would be asked to "concur" or "non-concur" with each operating unit's plan. Dual teams were also set up to present conflicting views on key issues, after which a "shoot-out" would take place before top management. To further harness its human resources toward the development of a new product or technology, IBM established multiple groups to focus on the same project. Management then chose the winning project.

This competitive, results-oriented environment produced functional excellence. IBM became especially strong in marketing and distribution; it outmaneuvered its competition with a superior sales force that built close ties to corporate data processing managers. The IBM brand name became so powerful in the postwar period that it became a cliche to say that "no one was ever fired for buying IBM." Service, in particular, became a fetish for IBM. The company won customers by standing prepared to perform any amount of assistance the customer needed.

---

[1]One offshoot of the Watson philosophy was the stress on the importance of integrity and loyalty and his insistence that salespeople be well-informed, in good physical shape, and well-groomed. These guidelines led to the widely commented-on "IBM uniform," consisting of a dark blue suit, white shirt, and subdued tie. While not a formal requirement in 1990, all of the executives and salespeople interviewed for this case maintained the tradition.

SYSTEM/360 Despite all of these advantages, many analysts in the late 1950s viewed IBM as a conservative company that rarely pioneered new technologies. Facing an onslaught of challenges from many computer companies that were announcing newer, faster machines with lower prices, IBM changed its strategy. To counter the growing competitive threat, Watson Jr. announced the System/360 in 1964, a "bet the company" move. This system provided software compatibility across the entire family of products and enabled IBM to implement its now-famous migration strategy, moving customers up the product line without the expense of changing computer systems every time more capacity was required. It also reduced the likelihood that customers would change vendors during the upgrading process. The 360 was a bold move because it rendered obsolete IBM's highly successful 7000 and 1400 series computers—much to the chagrin of prized customers. The project cost $5 billion over four years—the most expensive privately financed program in history. But the move was a giant success: it established IBM as *the* technical leader. The 360 stimulated significant new demand for large computers, and IBM captured almost 70% of the American market by the end of the decade. The 360 also fueled global expansion: by the early 1970s IBM had local manufacturing in every major part of the world.

SUCCESS, SUCCESS, SUCCESS IBM was the epitome of a growth company. By the 1980s, it was making more profits in most years than any other corporation in the world and had the highest market value (see **Exhibits 17–1** and **17–2**). The company could invest more in R&D, marketing, software, distribution, etc. than most of its competitors combined. It had become a world-class manufacturer, and a powerful global marketer. Moreover, IBM would come to be regarded as one of the best run companies in the world—a company with detailed financial and operational measurement systems that carefully monitored all aspects of the organization. IBM also became famous for its practice of full employment. It retrained rather than laid off employees; in 1990 alone, IBM spent $1.1 billion on educating its work force. As a consequence of these and other policies, IBM built an unusually loyal and com-

EXHIBIT 17-1 History of IBM's Finances ($ in millions)

	1970[a]	1980[a]	1984[a]	1985[a]	1986[a]	1987[a]	1988[b]	1989	1990	Three Months Ending 3/31/90	Three Months Ending 3/31/91
	Financial Records for the Year Ending December 31,										
Total revenues[c]	7,504	26,213	45,937	50,056	51,250	54,217	59,681	62,710	69,018	14,185	13,545
Cost of prods, svcs, rentals[c]		10,149	18,919	21,103	22,706	24,610	24,648	27,701	30,723	6,328	6,337
Research & development		1,520	4,200	4,723	5,221	5,434	5,925	6,827	6,554	1,395	1,500
Selling, gen'l & admin.		8,804	11,587	13,000	15,464	16,431	19,362	21,289	20,709	4,326	4,699
Operating income[d]	1,882	5,740	11,231	11,230	7,859	7,742	8,746	6,893	11,032	2,136	1,009
Net income	1,018	3,562	6,582	6,555	4,789	5,258	5,491	3,758	6,020	1,037	(1,731)[g]
Cash, equivs & mktable secur.	1,339	2,112	4,362	5,622	7,257	6,967	6,123	4,961	4,551	5,458	6,828
Inventories	374	2,293	6,598	8,579	8,039	8,645	9,565	9,463	10,108	9,844	10,056
Net inv'ment in fixed equip	4,740	15,017	16,363	19,680	21,268	22,922	23,426	24,943	27,241	24,941	26,009
Investments & other assets[e]	410	1,761	6,070	6,884	8,797	9,746	14,268	16,916	21,407	17,417	20,258
Total assets	8,539	26,703	42,808	52,634	57,814	63,688	73,037	77,734	87,568	77,227	83,925
Current liabilities	1,877	6,526	9,640	11,433	12,743	13,377	17,387	21,700	25,276	21,130	23,023
Long-term debt	573	2,099	3,269	3,955	4,169	3,858	8,518	10,825	11,943	10,696	12,131
Shareholders' equity	5,947	16,453	26,489	31,990	34,374	38,263	39,509	38,509	42,832	38,615	39,195
Capital expenditure	2,160	6,592	5,473	6,430	4,620	4,304	5,390	6,414	6,509	1,343	1,407
Total employees	269,291	341,279	394,930	405,535	403,508	389,348	387,112	383,220	373,816	NA	NA
Return on avg. equity[f]	18.1%	22.7%	26.5%	22.4%	14.4%	14.5%	14.9%	9.6%	14.8%	NA	NA

NA—Not available.

[a] Data in 1970, 1980, 1984–87 have not been restated to show 1988 change in accounting principles, (FAS 94).

[b] 1988 net income does not include $315 million credit for accounting change, (FAS 96).

[c] IBM's revenues have, since before 1970, been comprised of equipment sales, services and rentals.

[d] Operating income is defined here as earnings before interest and taxes.

[e] Investments shown here include two major categories of financial reporting items:
1. Nonfixed long-term assets such as software development costs, sale-type leases, and goodwill.
2. Capital invested in the securities of other corporations, governments, and municipalities.

[f] Return on average equity is calculated here as net income in each year, divided by the average shareholder's equity in that year and shareholder's equity in the previous year.

[g] Net income for three months ending 3/31/91 reflects the adoption of new accounting rules relating to the reporting of employee benefits. Without the extraordinary item, net income for that period would have been $532 million.

Sources: IBM Financial Reports—Forms 10-k and 10-q; 1970, 1980, 1984–1989, Q1 1990, Q1 1991.

EXHIBIT 17-2 Revenues By Classification of Products and Services (in millions of dollars)

	1986	1987	1988	1989	1990E
Processors					
Mainframe	$ 8,587	$ 9,256	$10,365	$11,352	$12,091
Est. % Gross Margin (GM)	67.5%	68.0%	68.5%	68.2%	65.5%
Midrange	4,465	4,727	4,712	4,735	5,320
Est. % GM	53.8%	52.0%	55.5%	57.3%	56.3%
PC's & Workstations	9,436	10,439	11,484	12,261	13,529
Est. % GM	48.0%	47.5%	51.5%	52.2%	51.7%
Peripherals	10,807	10,186	11,280	11,021	11,941
Est. % GM	52.2%	51.0%	58.7%	58.0%	59.0%
Maintenance	7,413	7,691	7,347	7,070	7,203
Est. % GM	58.8%	55.6%	53.2%	50.1%	50.1%
Software	5,514	6,836	7,927	8,424	9,910
Est. % GM	72.9%	71.4%	73.4%	68.4%	68.9%
Other	5,829	6,121	6,566	7,847	8,511
Est. % GM	34.4%	31.8%	30.9%	29.8%	29.4%
Total Revenues	52,051	55,256	59,681	62,710	68,505

Revenues And Earnings By Geographic Location (in millions of dollars)					
	1986	1987	1988	1989	1990
UNITED STATES					
Revenues	$28,420	$29,498	$30,271	$31,221	$37,132
Net Earnings	1,603	1,936	1,408	(325)	1,459
EUROPE/MIDDLE EAST/ AFRICA					
Revenues	17,774	20,596	22,555	24,271	27,234
Net Earnings	2,267	2,209	2,349	2,676	2,977
ASIA/PACIFIC					
Revenues	6,745	8,341	10,661	10,875	9,564
Net Earnings	603	780	1,394	1,296	1,151
AMERICAS					
Revenues	3,665	4,104	5,227	6,054	5,088
Net Earnings	314	341	328	173	420
ELIMINATIONS					
Revenues	(5,354)	(7,283)	(9,033)	(9,711)	(10,282)
Net Earnings	2	(8)	12	(62)	13
CONSOLIDATED					
Revenues	51,250	55,256	59,681	62,710	69,018
Net Earnings	4,789	5,258	5,491	3,758	6,020

Sources: Revenue Breakdown by Classification: Sanford C. Bernstein & Co. Earnings Estimates dated 6/90.
Revenue Breakdown by Geographic Location: IBM Annual Reports, 1986–1989.

mitted work force. Employees throughout the corporation referred to "the IBM Company" with an attitude that bordered on reverence. In fact, the company was regarded by its peers as one of America's most effective recruiters and developers of workers and managers. A 1990 survey of 142 human resource executives rated IBM the leader in every personnel area assessed, ranging from compensation to recruiting. According to the *Wall Street Journal*, "no other company came close."

Between Watson Jr. and Akers, IBM had had only three CEOs. Each was regarded, in the IBM tradition, as a strong leader and each contributed in his own way to the company's continued growth and development. T.V. Learson, who succeeded Tom Jr., served just two years. He was a skillful, tough operator who had earlier led the launching of the System/360. Frank Cary, who served as CEO for eight years, was credited with getting IBM into the PC business, starting the decentralization process in IBM, refocusing IBM

World Trade, and shepherding the company through its disruptive antitrust suit. He also had the vision to invest in production capacity that enabled IBM to fill the burst in demand that occurred after his retirement. John Opel's four-year tenure as CEO saw the company through the transition from mainly leasing to mainly selling its products. Contemporaries regarded him as a skillful strategist and a strong implementer. Collectively, these CEOs had built a company whose dominance in products, technology, marketing, and distribution was so pervasive that one analyst observed in the 1970s, "IBM isn't the competition, it's the environment."[2]

IBM's Products and Competition

By the late 1980s IBM was the largest full-line producer of computers in the world. It sold about 10,000 computer hardware, software, and peripheral products in more than 130 countries. IBM was also a leading producer of typewriters, copiers, and other office equipment. One of the distinguishing characteristics of IBM was its sweeping vertical integration: its huge scale allowed it to invest more in semiconductors and software technologies than most of its competitors combined. This vertical integration gave IBM the ability to respond rapidly to shifts in technology or market trends; in addition IBM could build most of its computer product lines with proprietary technology, which produced gross margins often in excess of 70%. While IBM's hardware could be highly segmented along a dozen dimensions ranging from processing speed to price, most analysts divided the firm's product lines into three big categories:

MAINFRAMES   Almost half of IBM's business (and as much as 70–80% of its profits) came from mainframe computers, related software, and peripherals. Mainframes were large-scale computers capable of supporting large numbers of concurrent

---

[2]One consequence of IBM's dominance was an antitrust suit filed in 1969 by the Justice Department in the United States; the European Community began a similar investigation in 1977. The United States dropped its suit in 1982, and the EC settled with IBM in 1984.

users and handling the central data processing needs of a large organization, or the needs of a smaller number of users performing extensive computations. These computers usually required the service and support of dedicated maintenance personnel. In the early days of the industry, IBM faced competition in this segment from "the Seven Dwarfs"—Sperry Rand, Control Data, Honeywell, Burroughs, General Electric, RCA, and National Cash Register. By the late 1970s IBM's competition came from the BUNCH—Burroughs, Univac, NCR, Control Data, and Honeywell. In 1990 a mainframe's price typically exceeded $500,000. Industry analysts predicted that growth of mainframe computer revenues would slow from 5% in the 1980s to 3% through 1996.

MINICOMPUTERS   A second large segment of the computer industry was minicomputers, pioneered in 1961 by the Digital Equipment Corporation (DEC). Minis supported fewer concurrent users and served the data processing needs of a large department within an organization, or the general computing needs of a small firm. These systems required limited service and support personnel and ranged in price from $25,000 to $500,000. IBM minicomputers (which were incompatible with its mainframes) along with DEC were the market share leaders in this segment through the 1980s, with a host of smaller competitors such as Prime Computer and Data General vying for niches. Minicomputer sales grew about 13% annually in the second half of the 1980s, but analysts predicted that revenues would shrink (and according to some, disappear) in the 1990s.

MICROCOMPUTERS   Microcomputers were single-user systems that were originally dedicated to a limited number of applications. IBM entered the PC market in 1981 and quickly became the standard setter (see **Exhibit 17–3**). As PCs declined in price, volumes expanded exponentially (74% CAGR, 1984–89), creating the largest segment of the global computer market (over $50 billion) by the end of the 1980s. The processing power of microcomputers also took off in the late 1980s, especially as desktop computers, known as workstations, invaded the technical engineering

EXHIBIT 17-3 Global Market Share Estimates

	1985	1986	1987	1988	1989
Mainframes					
IBM	55.4%	51.4%	41.6%	40.1%	44.0%
Fijitsu	6.4	8.8	12.3	13.8	11.6
NEC	4.8	8.1	11.5	13.3	8.5
Hitachi	3.3	4.9	6.9	8.3	11.1
Unisys	7.5	7.8	5.3	3.9	4.3
Minicomputers					
IBM	20.8	17.5	18.4	18.2	29.4
Digital Equipment	9.5	11.7	15.0	15.5	11.6
Hewlett-Packard	6.3	6.4	5.6	6.2	3.3
Wang	5.2	4.7	4.2	3.8	2.5
Fijitsu	2.6	3.6	3.7	4.1	5.7
Workstations					
Sun Microsystems					21.3
Digital Equipment					17.6
H-P/Apollo					12.2
Matsushita					11.8
IBM					8.7
Personal Computers					
IBM	35.9	29.3	29.7	25.5	22.3
Apple	10.5	9.2	9.6	10.5	9.6
Compaq	3.3	3.2	5.2	7.4	7.7
Olivetti	5.8	6.6	5.0	5.1	4.1
Tandy	5.2	5.2	4.8	4.4	3.6
NEC	2.2	3.6	4.0	4.3	8.3

Source: *Datamation Magazine*, June 15 issues in 1986–1990.

market.[3] Prices of micro or desktop computers ranged from under $1,000 to $50,000.

The New Computer Technology

By the mid-1980s technological change began to blur product segments. PCs, technical workstations, and networks of PCs and workstations began encroaching on markets previously reserved for minis and mainframes. The driving force in this change was semiconductor technology, which became more powerful, less expensive, and widely available. Rather than every computer company in the world designing and building its own proprietary parts, independent suppliers provided standard building blocks. As a consequence, a wide array of companies could build machines that performed across a broad spectrum of price and performance features. Furthermore, advances in semiconductor technology came so quickly that improvements in price/performance were expanding almost fourfold every three years in the 1980s.

These developments threatened IBM's market position in multiple ways. To begin with, the new technologies required new skills. Shortening product life cycles, for example, necessitated very rapid cycle times. Next, the economic scale needed to build a computer declined, which produced an explosion of competition. Two types of competitors emerged: hundreds of small niche players; and four or five big Japanese firms. The niche players, epitomized by companies like Apple Computer, Sun Microsystems, and Compaq, were generally started and led by young, technical entrepreneurs who quickly capitalized on the new technologies in growth segments. Bolstered by creative marketing, many of these firms set speed records for reaching $1 billion in sales and climbing the *Fortune* 500 ladder. Collectively,

[3]Workstations were purchased primarily by engineers for projects that required modeling or high resolution graphics. The core technology for workstations was known as RISC (reduced instruction set computing); RISC allowed for faster processing speed compared to a PC. IBM pioneered RISC technology in the 1970s, but Sun Microsystems developed the market. Workstations used an "open" operating system, called UNIX, originally developed by AT&T. Growing from a small base, workstation sales expanded 1,093% from 1984 to 1989.

The Transformation of IBM

these niche firms were a major new force in the computer industry.

The Japanese challenge, coming from firms like NEC, Fujitsu, and Hitachi, was fundamentally different. Each firm was a huge, diversified company with ample resources to compete with IBM on a global basis. Partly sponsored by their government, giant Japanese firms attacked IBM head-on. While the computer divisions of these Japanese conglomerates remained small compared to IBM (Fujitsu was the closest with $17 billion in computer-related sales), in 1990 they were collectively the largest semiconductor producers in the world, with market share greater than IBM in computers. In general, Japanese firms were dedicated to driving down costs and prices while improving speed and performance. Despite their size, Japanese firms remained innovative by organizing their huge businesses into small profit centers and using corporate-level "off-line" task forces extensively for major development projects. They also placed much more emphasis on harnessing existing technologies to produce better products, rather than trying to develop new technologies, the thrust of much of the U.S. computer industry's R&D efforts. While IBM insiders were impressed by the skills of the niche competitors, they were much more concerned about the threat posed by the resourceful, technically strong Japanese.[4]

Some competitors, especially those fighting for the desktop market in North America and Europe, promoted their hardware and software products as "open" systems rather than proprietary systems. The concept of an open system was that computers used operating systems software that conformed to industry standards, that applications were interchangeable and data could be shared among different manufacturers' systems. Open systems allowed customers greater opportunities to establish networks of different vendors' hardware and software.

[4]Not all Japanese firms had the same strategy: Hitachi and Fujitsu focused primarily on mainframes that were compatible with IBM but faster and cheaper, while NEC, Toshiba, and others attacked IBM in PCs. Japanese companies also grew faster (25%) than the world information processing and services market (15%). If calculated in yen, Japanese sales expanded 21%. Japanese firms also spent an average of 15% of sales on R&D.

Consequences of the New Technology

The move toward desktop computers and open systems had the most significant implications for computer customers. By the 1980s computers were no longer black boxes: customers increasingly understood the technology, which allowed them to place greater demands on computer manufacturers. In addition, the PC revolution put computers on the end-users' desks; gone were the days when a handful of data processing professionals in huge corporations made all the decisions. Customers were also demanding total solutions to their information needs, not just new, faster computers. The result was that growth in software and services outpaced hardware sales. By 1988 hardware was 57% and software and related services were 43% of customer spending on information processing. IBM estimated that by 1994 software and services would be 52% of spending. Finally, the geographic distribution of the computer-related sales shifted. The United States was almost half the world market for computers in the 1980s, but estimates suggested that the United States would account for only 39% of the market by 1994, while the Asia-Pacific region would be 22%, Europe 34%, and the rest of the world 5%.

The emergence of new technologies and different customer needs drastically altered the economic, technical, and human requirements for competing in the computer industry. The gap between IBM and its competitors had been narrowed significantly. At the same time, the interwoven complexities of the marketplace, customer needs, and technology made IBM a much more difficult company to manage. While spending billions on R&D, IBM was finding it increasingly hard to pick the promising growth segments, design the right products, and get them out on time. The highly centralized functional organization that served the company well in an earlier era was straining to cope with these rapid changes. Resource allocation had become a major challenge, even for a company with comparatively huge resources like IBM.

Yet despite these threats, IBM had four of its best years between 1980 and 1984. Sales reached a record of $45.9 billion in 1984, and PAT soared to $6.6 billion. According to some analysts, IBM's profits represented 70% of the global information industry's profits. When Opel retired as CEO in 1985, the corporation's outlook called for revenue of $100 billion in 1990 and $185 billion by 1994 while maintaining market share. To prepare for the boom, the company spent over $16.5 billion on new facilities and equipment in the early 1980s, while the work force ballooned (see **Exhibit 17–1**). The plan called for continued investment in new plants to allow for the trebling of turnover. The company appeared poised for yet another burst of growth.

As Akers recalled, "I inherited in 1985 a business that was successful beyond our wildest expectations. We had a centralized, prudent, cautious organization that no one wanted to change." However, within 18 months of taking over, Akers found that change was not only desirable but a necessity. The go-go years of the early 1980s abruptly came to an end: in 1985, industry growth slowed to under 10% and IBM's growth stagnated. IBM was left with unsold inventories and under-utilized plants. As a result, its asset turnover dropped sharply, and profit margins were cut in half, compared to 1980 levels.

It became clear to Akers in 1986 and early 1987 that his company was afflicted with many of the same ailments that had plagued other large American companies in the global competition. Products were coming to market more slowly than its smaller, nimbler competitors; Japanese firms were making serious inroads into a variety of IBM's markets; the firm's cost structure, premised on 15% growth, had become uncompetitive; several products, like IBM's PCjr and its first technical workstation (the PC RT), were either poor products or inferior to other offerings; serious quality problems began to surface in both manufacturing and design; employee surveys suggested declining morale; long-standing relationships with customers were weakening; and resources seemed out of balance—industry growth was weighted toward software and markets outside of North America, but IBM's product mix in 1988 was 71% hardware with the majority of its assets, 60% of its people, and most of its R&D activities in the United States. Some features of IBM's full line also haunted management. IBM had developed its products over time, and none of its major computers systems was compatible. As IBM President Jack Kuehler com-

mented, "It was disturbing when *Business Week* ran a cover story in 1986, saying that DEC computers worked together, and IBM's didn't."

Akers summed up the situation this way: "In the mid-1980s we asked ourselves, 'How well are we positioned?' Our answer: 'Not well at all!' Our market strength was in large hardware, whereas the market growth was taking place in software, services, and smaller machines (i.e., PCs and workstations). Furthermore, we were organized around hardware, not markets, so we weren't well set up to solve customer problems. It was clear that we needed to change IBM and find ways to facilitate constant transformation."

The Succession of John Akers

Like all of his predecessors, Akers was a product of IBM's management development process. He joined the company as a sales trainee, but early on he was identified as a potential star. In 1971 Akers was chosen to be the administrative assistant to Frank Cary, soon to be IBM's CEO. For the next ten years, Akers served in a succession of increasingly important management assignments in the product and marketing groups. By 1981 Akers rose to group executive in charge of IBM's nonmainframe businesses, and in 1985, at age 50, he was tapped to replace John Opel as the youngest CEO since Tom Watson Jr. When he assumed the role of CEO, Akers recalled, "I was particularly concerned with overhead, staff size, and the slow decision-making process. My personal experiences—my background in sales and marketing, my sense that headquarters was doing a lot of work but providing very little value added—all suggested that we needed to do things differently. But there was a pervasive attitude of 'don't tamper with success.' Initially, it was very difficult to force dramatic action in the absence of a major crisis."

Yet Akers was clearly the leader in forcing change at IBM. Over the second half of the 1980s, outsiders came to admire Akers for his openness, candor, and hands-on management style. Inside IBM, he was perceived as an attentive listener who asked tough questions. An IBM board member described him as "personable, forthright, while very strong." One IBM executive explained, "People like to work for John; he is a natural leader and has a great feel for our business." A voracious reader, Akers interacted with IBMers by orally responding to memos and presentations; he rarely wrote memos or letters. Not a strong believer in formal systems, he preferred to make decisions in an informal, collegial environment with his Management Committee (MC)[5] and directly with 10–15 senior IBM executives. Akers worked comfortably with his three MC colleagues: they obviously respected one another and communicated freely as a group. He relied on them to supervise their particular areas of responsibility and to contribute their thinking on broad corporate policies. According to Kuehler, "One of John's greatest strengths is his ability to pick the best people for a particular job, give them very simple instructions, and let them figure out how to get the job done. He also follows up to see that the job is done well."

STARTING THE TRANSFORMATION Beginning in late 1986, Akers embarked on an ambitious program to transform the company. His basic goals over the next four years remained consistent and straightforward—"enhance customer relationships; improve product competitiveness; and strengthen structural efficiency"—without abrogating IBM's historic full employment practice. To implement this strategy, he initiated three major "rounds" of action.

In Round One, begun in 1987, Akers took steps to streamline the product line, reduce capacity, and realign human resources. As part of this process, 10,000 U.S. employees opted for early retirement in 1987, representing a savings of $500 million in personnel costs; IBM also closed a number of U.S. factories and redeployed another 8,000 U.S. employees into new jobs, mainly in sales and customer contact. Akers also launched a campaign entitled "The Year of the Customer" the preeminent feature of which was a series of forums where key customers were informed and consulted on IBM's plans. Customers responded candidly to these conferences. Many were posi-

tive, but complaints ranged from IBM's need for "more integrated systems" to the "disruptiveness" of constant changes of IBM sales personnel.

Complementing this effort was Akers' soul-searching process of trying to uncover why IBM was no longer growing as it had been in the early 1980s. After more than six months of in-depth study, the conclusion was that IBM was largely responsible for its own downturn, and the biggest problems were in the United States. IBM senior management concluded that the key problem was ineffective execution and the inability to offer "complete business solutions."

During Round Two in early 1988, Akers enacted a sweeping reorganization of the entire company. The new organization, which can be seen in **Exhibit 17–4**, was designed to put more emphasis on markets and less on hardware, improve coordination, fix responsibility for results, and decentralize authority. In this way, Akers hoped to speed up the process of selecting the right target markets, develop competitively superior products (and services), and get products to market sooner than the competition.

The major changes involved in the reorganization were:

- Creating three product development lines of business (LOBs) called Personal Systems, Application Business Systems, and Enterprise Systems with primary responsibility for worldwide R&D and U.S. manufacturing. While each LOB had its own hardware responsibility—essentially PCs, minis and mainframes—their overriding job was to develop IBM's position in their assigned market segments. These three LOBs became cost, quality, and technology centers.
- Forming three LOBs that would provide software and components to the product development LOBs. The Communication Systems and Programming Systems LOBs developed tools that integrated IBM's product lines,[6] and the Technology Products LOB was re-

---

[5]The MC was a long-standing feature of IBM management, dating back to the mid-1950s. In 1990 the MC was made up of IBM's top four executives: John Akers; IBM President Jack Kuehler—regarded as IBM's leading technologist; Mike Armstrong—a former marketer in charge of IBM World Trade, which covered all of IBM's non-U.S. business; and Frank Metz, the CFO, whose background was in finance and operations.

[6]The communications group developed software and hardware tools that would allow IBM products to "talk" with each other. The programming systems group developed data base programs and devised software protocols, including SAA (Systems Application Architecture), which would allow programmers to write applications that could be transferred among IBM machines.

EXHIBIT 17-4A Abbreviated IBM Corporate Organization Chart, 1985

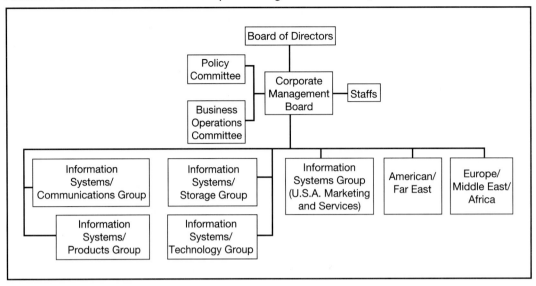

EXHIBIT 17-4B Abbreviated IBM Corporate Organization Chart, September 1990

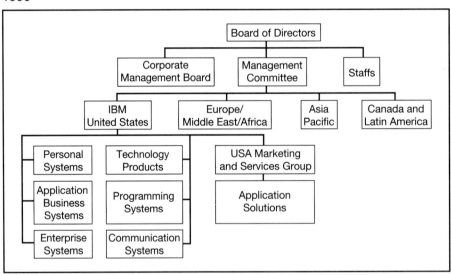

sponsible for developing and manufacturing semiconductors (for internal IBM use). All three were expected to maintain IBM's technical leadership in their assigned areas.

- Creating the U.S. Marketing and Services Group (US-M&S), which would have sales and profit responsibility for all IBM hardware and software products sold in the U.S. Within this group, an Applications Solutions (AS) LOB was set up to serve two key world-

wide functions: (1) provide optimum customer solutions by either making, buying, or allying with outside vendors; and (2) translate customer needs into product requirements.

- Appointing an assistant general manager (AGM) of marketing to each of the product development LOBs to facilitate greater coordination between marketing and R&D. The AGM's job was to make sure that worldwide

The Transformation of IBM

marketing and service were working cooperatively with the LOBs on IBM's top priorities.

- Keeping IBM's international operations largely intact, with three geographic units responsible for sales, manufacturing, and profits of all IBM products in their assigned territories. Akers felt that country managers were generally more profit-conscious and results-oriented than their domestic counterparts.

- Redefining the corporate staff's role to serve as the MC's personal staff and put less emphasis on second-guessing, staff approvals, and contention. The size of the staff was cut by 75%.

Ideally, Akers and his key associates would have preferred a simpler organization with a few self-contained profit centers. However, they were unable to divide IBM's broad product line in that way because of the tight interdependence among the various product and service groups. For example, Technology Products serviced all three product development LOBs; if each LOB made or purchased its own semiconductors, scale economies would be lost.

The role of the MC also changed in this new organization. The head of IBM US—not the MC—would be responsible for resolving conflicts among the LOBs. To further force decentralization, Akers cut the number of MC meetings to about two half days per week. Very few operational issues were now debated; the MC primarily focused mainly on strategic issues, finance and resource allocation, major product and marketing issues, and human resources (see **Exhibit 17–7B**). In addition, the MC met monthly with the heads of the three largest geographic regions, and every 90 days with the senior LOB executives. The purpose of the reviews, as Akers described them, "was to have an informal setting to report on what problems they encountered, what problems they had solved, and what help the MC could be." Kuehler emphasized that "we not only expect to hear about issues, we also expect that the LOBs are already taking the initiative to deal with them." This new organization delegated downward more responsibility, including flexibility on pricing and packaging of systems. At the same time, the hope was to stamp out bureaucracy and create more local innovation and entrepreneurial behavior.

Finally, Round Two involved more downsizing and shifting of personnel out of staff jobs: since 1986, total employment had dropped by 20,000 through attrition and more early retirements, while the total marketing, programmers, and other "direct" employees were up 21,000. ("Direct" was defined as "those who design, develop, build, sell and service and their first line managers." "Indirect" was considered overhead.) Akers made speeches around the company, telling his employees, "The jobs that are the most fun in IBM are those which contribute directly to added value, and if you don't have one of those jobs, you'd better find one." This process improved productivity per employee to $154,000 in 1989. (By comparison, Fujitsu, Hitachi, and NEC's sales per employee were $182,000, $186,000, and $238,000 respectively; Apple, Compaq and Sun's sales per employee were $364,000, $296,000, and $173,000.)[7]

Round Three, begun in 1989, sought to execute these changes in a way that would make IBM "a genuinely market-driven company." Despite a dominant market position, a huge sales and service group, and over $6 billion annually invested in technology, IBM was still not meeting Akers' goal to be the unquestioned leader in technology, quality, or service. He felt the company had become too inwardly focused. So he sought to articulate a new IBM, a market-driven company that revolved around four principles: (1) The customer (not IBM management) is the "final arbiter"; (2) "understand markets"; (3) "commit to leadership in those markets we choose to serve"; and (4) "execute with excellence across our enterprise." Akers' goal was to put IBM at the forefront of quality and customer service. The principle was to optimize the total corporation rather than individual divisions, delegate responsibility, and empower the employees. This involved several concrete steps. First, this meant greater involvement by customers and IBM's field force in defining product and service needs and quality requirements. Then new measurement systems were created throughout the corporation that were designed to emphasize quality at all levels.

[7]Part of the explanation for the difference between IBM and its smaller domestic competitors was that no US desktop manufacturer was vertically integrated, and Apple subcontracted much of its production.

Historically, IBM had been a pioneer in quality: it had established a Quality Institute and created programs that required every new product be equal to or better than existing ones. Dissatisfied with these efforts, Akers broadened the quality initiatives in Round Three. Using Motorola's success with quality as a model, IBM installed a statistical system, called six sigma, which limited defects to 3.4 per million in any product, any process, or any activity. The goal was to be a six sigma company by 1994. Moreover, IBM made it a corporate priority to win the Malcolm Baldrige National Quality Award, the U.S. government's recognition of quality. In addition to the six sigma quality program, the new measurement systems included customer satisfaction surveys, competitive benchmarks of IBM versus the competition, revenue growth, market share, employee morale and involvement, and various profitability measures, such as ROE and ROA. To give lower-level managers more profit incentives, Akers broadened the number of employees covered by stock options and bonuses. In 1990 all executives in the corporation were brought into an incentive compensation plan based on company or unit performance.

Akers also wanted to change IBM's planning system to reflect decentralization and the desire for faster decision making. According to Peter Schavoir, IBM's director of strategy, "the strategic planning process was too long, involved too many people (sometimes into the thousands), and inevitably involved too much trivia. Starting in 1990, we cut the cycle time almost in half and dramatically reduced the number of staff and line participants. We also moved away from a rigid numerical planning system to one where we offered alternative scenarios, which each geographical region had to respond to." Akers also eliminated much of the contention system. He noted that abolishing the "contention system had costs—there was less debate and higher risk— but we have had faster decision making. We simply can't spend so much time debating things and duplicating efforts in today's competitive environment."

In the process of focusing resources, IBM sold to Siemens the manufacturing and research operations of Rolm, a telecommunications subsidiary, and decided to divest copiers, satellite transmission, educational publishing, and retail stores. According to an IBM board member, Akers made it clear that "nothing is being taken for granted any longer." In August 1990 Akers took this program one step further; he announced that IBM would restructure and spin off 90% of one of its oldest businesses—typewriters, keyboards, and low-end printers. This potential spinoff illustrated the problems of breaking up IBM's interrelated product line. These products were produced in mixed plants, sold by the IBM salesforce, and accounted for as part of IBM's total product line. Most of their sales were in-house to IBM itself. Thus the new spinoff would, at least initially, need to market IBM-branded products, draw on IBM technology, and rely mainly on sales to IBM to sustain its volume.

The AS LOB also developed a set of about 20 industries and product areas, like computer-aided manufacturing, where IBM would concentrate its resources. Recognizing the critical importance of mastering emerging technologies, IBM spent $6.8 billion on R,D&E in 1989 alone, not including $2 billion in software spending that was capitalized. Management considered its investment in software and services (38% of R&D) and advanced chip manufacturing techniques its top priorities and vital to its long-run success.

Thus by the end of 1989, IBM had shifted its strategy to focus major attention on software and services, but not at the expense of hardware. They had also reduced the scope of operations, selected target markets, and stressed product quality and innovation as IBM's key strategic drivers. Despite its streamlined business scope, however, IBM remained by far the broadest-based computer company. Company executives were convinced this broader scope and scale were significant competitive advantages.

Akers also continued the massive redeployment of thousands of employees to new direct assignments rather than laying them off. Indirect labor (47% of the work force) and the number of managers (11.4%) were further reduced. The stated goal was to bring management down another 1.4% and ultimately make 60% of the employees direct by 1993. Throughout the process of reducing and refocusing the work force, IBM's top management was committed to maintaining the full employment practice. Each MC member stressed the conviction that full employment was not just a matter of fairness; it was a key element of IBM's distinctive work environment. They freely conceded that it resulted in extra short-term personnel costs. But they were convinced this approach gave IBM a significant competitive advantage through greater worker commitment and productivity. They stressed that full employment meant no group layoffs but did not guarantee anyone a job. Implementing rigorous performance standards would ensure that poor performers were weeded out of the organization. Furthermore, to be eligible for full employment employees were expected to demonstrate flexibility (i.e., willingness to relocate, retrain, or change careers). So, in 1990 the MC planned to continue the practice as long as business results permitted and as long as it provided a competitive advantage.

In the management of technology, while Akers had delegated the main responsibility for identifying new fields to enter and developing new technologies to the LOBs, he and the MC remained broadly in charge of allocating resources among the businesses. They also, of course, decided on IBM's basic technological direction, as well as how the company would compete in each field. Akers said he felt comfortable making these kinds of decisions, despite his lack of formal technical training, because of his long experience in data processing and his ready access to technical experts like Kuehler. One of the transformation's biggest surprises to outsiders was that IBM management abandoned a hallmark of the corporation, its NIH—not invented here—philosophy. Borrowing extensively from some positive experiences of IBM Japan, LOBs began engaging in wide-ranging alliances, including equity investments, joint R&D, and licensing of technology. IBM joined forces with Siemens to develop 64 megabit DRAMs, with Toshiba to make flat panel displays, and with Motorola to develop new semiconductor production techniques, to name just a few. Starting from virtually nothing in 1988, IBM had more than 75 equity alliances by 1990. According to Kuehler, "Only five years ago, it took months of agonizing at the highest levels of the corporation before IBM would make an equity investment in one company; look at what we have done in a year, largely at the LOB level."

AKERS' MANAGEMENT STYLE Akers' program had clearly attacked IBM's highly centralized, somewhat lethargic *modus operandi*. He emphasized his sense of urgency by a series of formal and one-on-one sessions where he and the MC had a chance to identify slippage or unnecessary delays. Yet Akers also tried to lead by personal example. He refused to allow his day to be consumed by meetings; he enjoyed talking with customers and employees in the field. While at headquarters, he worked a disciplined nine-plus-hour day, arriving at 8 a.m., leaving by 5:30 p.m., and not taking a full briefcase home on weekends. He also traveled extensively (one or two days a week) around IBM worldwide, asking managers at all levels what was going on within their operations to make them a market-driven company (see **Exhibit 17-7A**). These were not symbolic site visits, according to Akers, because he got into details; as he put it, "I asked local managers to tell me precisely their quality story and tell me precisely your product plan and where they stand." In 1990 he visited most of IBM's manufacturing and development locations.

Akers met twice each year with his entire top management team. He used these Strategic Planning Conferences as a major device to communicate new initiatives, reset priorities, and discuss IBM's performance and competitive standing. The conference themes reflected his perspectives and priorities. In recent years they focused on subjects like superior execution, market-driven quality, managing technology, revenue growth, and cost management. Akers also used these conferences to convey his sense of impatience with the progress of IBM's transformation. For instance, at a senior management meeting in February 1989 he told management, "Right at the outset let me make clear that we're talking not about a frill or a fad [when discussing market-driven quality] but about survival. We have no choice; reality has changed and we must change with it." Then at the January 1990 meeting, he made four key points:

1. Market-driven quality begins with education and ends with education—the majority of it on the job. It is everyone's job to teach it incessantly.

EXHIBIT 17-7A John F. Akers Representative Calendar—Fall 1990

Monday

8:30– 9:30	Strategic Planning Conference update
10:00–10:30	Review plans for T.J. Watson Jr. Annual Design Award
11:00–12:00	IBM Management and Measurement Systems
1:00– 1:15	Review Education speech
1:30– 2:00	Quality Update
4:00– 4:45	Preparation for Board meeting
5:25	Depart for New York City
6:30– 9:30	Dinner meeting–outside Board of Directors
	Overnight NYC

Tuesday

8:00– 9:00	Breakfast meeting
9:30	Depart for Washington
11:00–11:45	National Alliance of Business–Education meeting
12:00– 2:00	The Business Roundtable–Education Task Force
2:00– 8:30	The Business Roundtable–Board meeting
	Overnight Washington

Wednesday

8:15–11:45	United Way Executive Committee
12:15– 1:30	Travel Washington/Armonk
2:00– 5:00	Management Committee meetings
6:00	Depart for East Fishkill
	Overnight East Fishkill

Thursday[a]

3:30– 5:00	East Fishkill plant celebration–3rd shift
5:30– 9:15	Poughkeepsie plant/lab celebration–3rd and 1st shifts
9:35–10:30	Myers Corners lab celebration
11:00–11:50	East Fishkill plant celebration–1st shift
12:00	Depart for Armonk
2:00– 4:15	Management Committee meetings

Friday

8:15– 8:30	Board meeting agenda
8:30– 9:00	3rd quarter outlook
9:00–12:00	Management Committee meetings
1:15– 5:00	IBM–U.S. review

[a]It was the first customer shipment of the ES/9000 mainframe computer.

---

2. We are still not bringing products to the market fast enough.

3. Our goal of becoming a solutions company, as measured by software growth, remains very much ahead of us.

4. We haven't yet demonstrated that we are tough-minded enough in managing costs and expenses.

And, characteristically, he assigned responsibility for implementing improvements in each area.

Akers saw one of his most important jobs as being the "corporate skeptic." This task had become especially important in recent years. He said, "In our fast-changing business, we can't afford to be overoptimistic about our strategies or capabilities. We can no longer make a bet and hope it works out. We have to be realistic from the start. That's my job— to ask questions and raise doubts about proposals to help prevent us from going too far down the wrong road as we've sometimes done in the past. As long as I probe sensitively, people understand."

EXHIBIT 17-7B IBM's Management Committee Agenda, First Six Months 1990

Subject	Hours in 1990					
	Jan.	Feb.	Mar.	Apr.	May	Jun.
Finance and planning	4.00	3.00	3.00	2.75	4.75	2.50
Geographic units						
Business reviews						
—IBM U.S	6.00	0.50	0.50	6.50	0.50	0.50
—Europe, Mideast, Africa	0.00	2.00	0.50	0.00	1.25	0.50
—Asia-Pacific	0.00	2.00	0.50	1.00	0.25	0.50
Site reviews	6.50	3.50	4.00	12.50	10.50	10.50
Strategic issues	5.50	2.50	2.25	1.50	0.75	3.00
Technical product and						
marketing reviews	1.50	1.50	5.25	3.00	2.75	1.50
Human resources	0.00	1.00	2.75	3.25	0.00	0.50
Total hours/month	**23.50**	**16.00**	**18.75**	**30.50**	**20.75**	**19.50**

THE IMPACT OF AKERS' INITIATIVE   As the operating divisions began to implement Akers' initiatives, the pace of IBM's transition accelerated. Some examples:

The general manager (GM) of Personal Systems made a number of significant moves. He brought "fresh blood" into his management group (from inside IBM) and raised performance standards to weed out weak performers. He mounted major programs to shorten cycle times and materially improved quality standards. The GM also took the unusual step for IBM of appointing a cross-functional task force to "fast-track" a new laptop computer.

The president of Data Systems (mainframes) addressed the division's concerns about being too much of a boss-driven, top-down organization by mounting a major attack on the work environment. The result was to "turn the organization upside down" by putting the customer on top of the organizational pyramid and senior management at the bottom. As in Personal Systems, he also focused on improving quality and shortening cycle times.

The U.S. Marketing and Services GM focused his organization on sharply improving customer service. He gave the field organization greatly increased authority to cut prices and deal more flexibly with customers. Education spending was increased in 1989 to $400 million to upgrade the competence of the enlarged field force. The group was reorganized to reduce layers and flatten the management structure. Performance measures were revamped to focus local management on gross profit, market share, strategic priorities, and customer satisfaction—not just on sales. The GM stressed that his AS LOB—consisting of 30,000 people, 10,000 in software alone—was coming into its own. "No other company can match our commitment to offering customers hardware, software, and service solutions to their problems."

The president of IBM-Asia Pacific used the theme of market-driven quality (MDQ) to launch a number of programs. "After John Akers gave MDQ a sense of urgency in January 1989, we conveyed the message quickly. Today, measurement systems are in place and owners are responsible for MDQ initiatives. While we are currently number three in Japan (behind Fujitsu and NEC), I see an opportunity to be number two by the mid-1990s."

The president of IBM-Canada moved equally fast to improve his company's competitiveness. He redeployed staff people to line marketing jobs and focused them on new high-growth opportunities like small systems and software. He pushed down decision-making and eliminated three management layers. He set demanding ("breakthrough") goals and measured performance against them. Cross-functional off-line "rings" were set up to implement new ideas.

The Akers' initiatives were also beginning to have an effect at the regional and local levels in the United States. Empowerment (making lower-level managers feel greater responsibility for their actions and corporate performance) was especially noticeable. The GM of the Northeastern Area noted that his job was now "more like a country manager than strictly marketing. In the last year, I've become responsible for profits, not just revenues, and for the first time we are rewarding salespeople on market share and customer satisfaction." And two levels down, a branch manager expressed similar views. "Akers' vision," he said, "is being translated into the field. There is a sense of giving everyone greater responsibility and flexibility."

The View in 1990

Towards the end of 1990, IBM's top management could point to a number of accomplishments. Over the previous four years, manufacturing cycle times were down by as much as 50%; the time to produce the high-end mainframe was cut by two-thirds; and installation time for a mainframe went from a week to 16 hours. On the product front, IBM announced a new technical workstation (the RISC System/6000), which many acclaimed as a technological leader; IBM also introduced a new low-end computer (the PS/1), a user-friendly PC designed to give IBM leadership in home computers; IBM's targeting of the educational market produced significant gains against Apple (IBM's market share went from under 10% to more than 30% from 1986 to 1989); and IBM's minicomputer team was the winner of the 1990 Baldrige competition. For 1990 as a whole, shipments, revenues, and earnings all showed gains. As results improved, employee attitude surveys also reflected significant improvement, although not back to the record levels of the mid-1980s.

But naturally the transformation had its ups and downs, and IBM's visibility assured extensive press coverage of both. While many observers were favorably impressed with IBM's transition, others continued to challenge the company's effectiveness (**Exhibits 17–5 and 17–6**). Most criticism dealt with issues such as the pace of change and the cost of full employment rather than the substance of Akers' actions. Through 1990, Akers continued to fine-tune the transformation. To address nagging problems such as quality and cost control, he:

- Created three new staff positions to spearhead major aspects of IBM's business. First, he appointed the former GM of minicomputers to SVP-Quality; his job was to keep track of performance on MDQ worldwide and spread the best practices within IBM. Next, he appointed the former head of Technology Products to GM-Operations, IBM-USA; his job was to help allocate resources and set technological priorities for the LOBs. Finally, he appointed a corporate head of Environment to oversee IBM's company-wide efforts.

- Assigned the corporate SVP of Personnel the task of translating "market-driven quality" into operational terms and of setting up training and employee involvement sessions to convey his message deeper into the divisions. Employee surveys had indicated middle-level managers were unclear on what the term meant or what they were expected to do differently.

- Increased the incentives for early retirement in an effort to further reduce the size of the work force by as many as 10,000.

- Instituted MC "inspections" to heighten awareness at the operating level of key corporate priorities such as quality and competitiveness.

- Challenged IBM's management of technology at his Fall 1990 Strategic Planning Conference. Akers expressed dissatisfaction with the way new products were developed and brought to market. To spur innovation, Akers was intrigued by the notion of exploiting IBM's "core competencies." To pursue the idea, he brought in an outside consultant and assigned two senior managers the job of identifying and improving on IBM's core competencies—one in the area of technology and one for marketing.

- Shifted the responsibility for developing smaller products (e.g., laptops and notebook PCs) from the U.S. to IBM-Japan.

- Announced a new policy to sell IBM products to OEM competitors in virtually all products, services, and software. This was partly defensive against the Japanese who had long been selling to OEMs, partly to utilize excess capacity in the IBM system, but also to spur more innovation.

EXHIBIT 17-5 "Innovation: Advice on How IBM Can Retain Greatness"

To: John F. Akers

Because you are a realist, you know that this past year can be best described as a blend of frustration and disappointment. Key shipments in mainframe disk drives slipped, software sales from the highly touted applications systems division are growing at rates less than half the industry average. . . . The only people more confused about IBM's direction than Wall Streeters are your own employees and customers. . . . You're certainly saying all the right things, but IBMers and your customers aren't hungry for rhetoric. . . . They're hungry for the opportunity to push IBM to new levels of excellence. The challenge is how? How can IBM be great as a business and information technology innovator? . . . My fear is that, much like post-Oil Shock General Motors, IBM may be a great company on the verge of losing its greatness. . . .

1. **Stop treating your customers as consumers.** A decade ago, IBM marketing reps could saunter onto a customer site confident that they knew more about data processing than the customer. That's no longer true. Today, your customers know more about what they need than you do. . . . Nevertheless, many of your people still behave as if Big Blue is the font of all information systems wisdom. That's as annoying as it is untrue. It's particularly annoying because the typical IBM rep now has more than 2,000 product and service offerings to keep track of; they know less and less about more and more. . . . That's an inevitable byproduct of trying to be a full-service provider . . . . Start treating your customers as people whom you can learn from as well as sell to. Create sales and engineering teams that are rewarded not only for selling systems but also for getting customers to co-develop applications that can be used industrywide. . . .

2. **Be less strategic and more tactical.** IBM has more strategies than NATO and the Pentagon combined. Unfortunately, the company seems unencumbered by any tactical sense. One longtime IBMer remarks that you prefer to "steer the ship and see what the market does" rather than "let the market drive these things." That's not my idea of customer-responsive. The reason is obvious: IBM moves too slowly to be tactical. Big Blue still relies more on momentum than initiative. With the notable exception of the IBM PC, product development still takes years. Technical development is not treated as urgently as sales development. . . . Shouldn't IBM be prepared to crash develop products like laptop computers that clearly have become market staples? Shouldn't you publicly champion speed to market as a virtue and change your compensation system accordingly? . . .

3. **Opt for bold investments rather than bold acquisitions.** You've taken bite-sized equity stakes in lots of little software firms. That's smart. Do much more of it. . . . Have fun. Scare a few people. Why not buy 10% of Compaq Computer? Fifteen percent of Cray? Twenty percent of Stratus Computer? Buy a Macintosh software company. Send the message that you're prepared to invest in quality information technology firms anywhere in the world. You've got cash—use it. Emulate Olivetti; invest in networks of technology firms in Europe. Not only will these investments command attention, they'll give you a window on technology and management that you couldn't possibly build in-house. . . .

4. **Break up IBM.** It's better to be a Gorbachev than a Honecker. As recent events confirm, planned economies don't work as well as market forces. Right now, IBM's $60-billion annual economy resembles Kremlin econometrics more than Adam Smith. Ask any IBMer who works with customers and they'll tell you they spend more time coordinating things inside the company than with the outside world. That's bad. So make a virtue of necessity. "Deregulate" IBM. Ideally, you should set up a holding company (a la Citicorp in global banking) to coordinate—not control—the efforts of multibillion-dollar IBM-lettes. Keep the key technologies like semiconductor packaging and magnetic recording in the holding company (not to mention network and telecommunications standards) but spin out the entry systems division as a stand-alone company, as well as the mainframe group, the workstation-Unix people, and the AS400 minicomputer folds. Turn your semiconductor plants loose onto the marketplace. Lead IBM as a coalitition, not as a monolith. . . . Do you run the risk of creating half a dozen weaker IBMs? Yes, but only if you don't believe that your people can handle new responsibility and added competition. In your heart and mind, you know that competition from AT&T, Apple, DEC, and Sun has made IBM a better company in the 1980s. Why not lose market share to your own companies instead of someones else's in the 1990s?

By any measure, IBM is a national asset. You have managed to keep the company's full employment practice through difficult times and you have made major commitments to support this country's technology base. Look deep into your company and you will see talented people who want to add value to both IBM and their customers. Listen to your customers and you'll hear people tell you that IBM isn't as responsive as it can be. If you do that, I think you'll agree that you have the unique opportunity to turn IBM into several great global companies. You can be the steward of a great tradition or a leader who builds a new generation of companies upon that tradition. Either way, good luck.

Source: Copyright, 1989, Los Angeles Times Syndicate. Reprinted by permission. Excerpted from an article by Michael Schrage, November 16, 1989.

EXHIBIT 17-6 Excerpts of a Letter from a Large IBM Customer (April 1990)

. . . Until recently IBM's organizational structure has made it very difficult for the company to provide solutions to customers' information technology problems rather than just high capacity hardware. I know they're working very hard on this, but the impression is that they still have a long way to go. . . .

From my perspective the three primary problem areas are IBM's people, customer relations and products. I feel that the people issue has been IBM's most serious problem for some time and I do not see any major improvement on the horizon. . . . Beginning eight or nine years ago, experienced, knowledgeable salesmen were replaced . . . by young, inexperienced sales personnel. . . . we had a succession of young sales personnel on our account who just seemed to be passing through on the way to their next promotion. They knew nothing about [our business] nor did they attempt to learn much. During the late 1980's, IBM continued its policy of "full employment" but instituted several early retirement programs. As a result of these programs, IBM lost between fifteen and twenty-five thousand of its most senior, experienced personnel. IBM lost a significant pool of talent but to make matters worse, most of them went to work for IBM's competitors.

. . . I have [also] seen a significant change in IBM's relations with its customers. I would characterize this as the maturing of customers and the immaturing of IBM. . . . Prior to the 1980's IBM's account personnel, both sales and technical, were more knowledgeable than the customer's personnel. This knowledge leverage was used by IBM to effectively control the account . . . Times have changed and now the situation is reversed. Today the customer's personnel . . . are the more knowledgeable parties and the IBM personnel provide limited value-added. . . . For example, at least once a month, I receive a stack of IBM announcements (sometimes more than an inch thick) which describe in infinite detail new and revised hardware products. On numerous occasions, I have requested of our IBM sales team that they only send me those which they think would relate to [our business]. This has never happened because they do not know what relates to us.

[Lastly] . . . IBM is a victim of its own past success. In an effort not to alienate its customer base, IBM has been forced into support of and compatibility with technically and functionally outmoded hardware and software. This approach of being all things to all customers has created a huge IBM product line that no one can understand in any depth. What has been created is the proverbial aircraft carrier. With a huge product line and massive numbers of people and facilities who create and manufacture the products, IBM has a nearly impossible job of reacting to change. It is even difficult for IBM to recognize change. . . . IBM has immense capital, plant and people resources but these resources appear to be almost too large to be manageable in the short term and places IBM in a difficult position to react to important market changes.

IBM has lost its flexibility at a time when that is what the market demands . . . I feel these problems are probably irreversible but must be addressed for the longer term if IBM is to continue to be the leader in the world information handling market.

Dealing with the 1991 Downturn

At the end of 1990, Akers believed that IBM had come a long way. But despite a record year and strong fourth quarter, he was not complacent. He commented, "I think IBM is a very different company today compared to six years ago. We are proud of what we've done, but we think we have a helluva long way to go. Tens of thousands of people in IBM still do not appreciate how good you have to be to be a world leader in today's fiercely competitive environment. Our competitors are ferocious, yet our people still feel too comfortable. There are large companies and hundreds of small ones in Asia whose employees start every day focused on destroying IBM. Nonetheless, we remain the market share leader in the major segments of the computer industry. We've got new products in the pipeline that should bolster that position in virtually every market segment."

Yet Akers remained worried. Warranty, software, and service costs had reached record proportions in 1990, while asset turns and ROA had not improved. When soft demand cut operating profits in the first quarter of 1991, many of Akers' concerns crystallized. Moreover, IBM's profit decline caught Wall Street by surprise. As a result, the stock dropped sharply. Knowledgeable insiders, such as former CEO Cary, pointed out that IBM had periodically experienced similar "surprises" in the past. According to Cary, "When the economy slips, or there is a sudden uncertainty (e.g., Iraq war), customers often defer—and sometimes even cancel—their orders for new computers." Usually, according to Cary, these cancellations were reinstated after a few months.

Akers knew, of course, that IBM's transformation was a moving target, especially in the computer business, where technology was constantly changing and competitors were fast-moving and highly innovative. In fact, trade press reports of announced price cuts, new products, and product improvements—including those by IBM—seemed to have reached new highs, even for the always dynamic computer industry. So he was concerned that IBM's managers might not be responding as rapidly as necessary to environmental changes. Initial indications suggested that worldwide computer demand was indeed slowing, but IBM's sales had slowed more than the industry and IBM was not exploiting some of the promising growth segments, such as notebook computers and certain services.

Akers therefore asked his management to once again address the tough questions:

- Are we doing everything practical to achieve the right mix of businesses? Should we be downgrading or exiting from more slow growth segments?

- How can we better manage our resources, expenses, and assets? Have we done everything possible to streamline our cost structure? Should we retain our vertical integration? Should we adopt a global manufacturing strategy instead of our traditional localized approach?

Beyond these immediate issues, Akers also had a nagging concern about whether he and his team had done enough to ensure that IBM had in place the discipline, stress on innovation, and fast response required to be the undisputed leader.

18. Reshaping Apple Computer's Destiny 1992

In 1992, Apple Computer was going through its second revolution in only a decade. The first came in 1984, when Apple made the transition from the Apple II computer to the Macintosh (Mac). Apple emerged from that experience as the most profitable personal computer company in the world. But now the $80 billion PC industry was in crisis, and John Sculley, Apple's chairman and CEO, was again confronted with the task of reshaping the corporation. Sculley's first steps were to launch a new, ambitious strategy to gain market share and diversify into related technologies. In the process, Sculley broke all the old rules at Apple: he cut perks, brought in new senior managers, introduced formal quality and performance systems, entered alliances with former enemies, and started pulling resources away from Apple's core Macintosh business.

Through the summer of 1992, Apple's implementation had been almost flawless: market share was up, profits were up, and new products were coming to market as fast as any major competitor. But Sculley was fighting against time: cutthroat pricing in the PC industry was squeezing Apple's margins; one slip in execution could be disastrous. Sculley summed up his dilemma:

> We are running as fast we can, but we still have gaps between our human resource needs, our organization and our strategy. We have also gotten so lean at the top, we lack benchstrength. In addition, Apple seems to be one of the toughest organizations in the world to change. Our culture revolves around the Macintosh and building great products that will change the world. This culture is not only strong, it's like a religion—a theology. And this theology is so deeply rooted, I worry about how the organization will react to more systems, more cuts, and less resources. How can I engineer a revolution that will make Apple one of the best professionally managed companies in the world, while keeping up the pressure, keeping up the innovation, and keeping the key people at Apple?

Research Associate Johanna M. Hurstak and Professor David B. Yoffie prepared this case as the basis for class discussion rather than to illustrate either effective or ineffective handling of an administrative situation.

Sculley Takes Charge

John Sculley seemed an unlikely candidate to run the world's second largest PC company. Sculley held an MBA from Wharton Business School and a degree in architectural design from Brown University. Although non-technical by training, he tinkered in electronics as a youth, even filing a patent application for a TV picture tube. As one of the first MBAs hired by Pepsi, he began his climb to the presidency by driving delivery trucks. Rising rapidly in the firm, Sculley left his position as head of U.S. sales and marketing to take over PepsiCo's floundering international operations in 1973. He returned to Pepsi-Cola as president four years later, after transforming the unprofitable business into an efficient revenue generator.

During his six years as Pepsi-Cola's president (1976–1983), Sculley instilled a sense of accountability and discipline without dismantling Pepsi's existing, decentralized corporate structure. He was praised for building the infrastructure of Pepsi's fragmented independent chain of bottlers by establishing regional chain trading areas to manage distribution, sales promotion, and cost accounting. Sculley also masterminded the highly successful "Pepsi Challenge" and "Pepsi Generation" advertising campaigns. By 1983, many believed that Sculley was on the fast track to succeed Donald Kendall as PepsiCo's next chairman.

In April 1983, Apple's cofounder, Steve Jobs, lured Sculley from PepsiCo to take on the presidency at Apple. Sculley's challenge was to bring organizational and marketing discipline to Apple without sacrificing creativity and spirit. However, tensions mounted between Sculley and Jobs soon thereafter. Eventually Jobs resigned after a well publicized dispute with Sculley and the Board of Directors in 1985.

THE 1985 REORGANIZATION   To solidify his control over Apple's fractious organization, Sculley reorganized Apple in June, 1985. He combined the Apple II and Mac divisions into a single Product Operations Group, consolidated manufactur-ing, and reduced the workforce by 20% (1200) in Apple's first major layoff. Sculley's key decision, however, was to move Apple out of the home computer market and into the mainstream of business. Said Sculley, "we had to move away from building what engineers wanted to what the market wanted . . . We went after business because that's the biggest market with the highest profit and the fastest growth in the PC industry." Sculley focused Apple on a unique niche—desktop publishing. The Mac was particularly well suited to this task because of its sophisticated graphics and inherent ease of use.

In order to bring discipline to the organization, Sculley put in stronger financial controls and focused on key financial expenses. Apple's financial model was based on Sculley's "50-50-50" rule: sell 50,000 Macs a month, with a gross margin of 50%, to achieve a $50 stock price. To Sculley, the company's most important "number" was the gross margin. When he came to Apple in 1983, that figure was roughly 42%. By 1988, Sculley increased gross margin to 52%, the highest in the PC industry. However, below-the-line expenditures ballooned. There were few controls on R&D and little direct accountability. In addition, Sculley spent heavily on advertising to define Apple as an industry innovator.

PEOPLE AND CULTURE   Sculley came to a company renowned for its exciting and countercultural work environment, where employees often wore T-shirts that proclaimed "working 90 hours a week and loving it." Sculley described Apple as "the Ellis Island of American business because it intentionally attracted the dissidents who wouldn't fit into corporate America." Employees believed that they were the power of Apple and that management's role was to create an environment in which they could do wonderful things. People tended to garner influence by their charismatic personalities and leadership of successful technical projects. Employees dubbed this "the star system" and "management by celebrities."

Sculley was determined to preserve the positive elements of this culture, and later recalled, "in 1985, I consciously did everything not to change the work environment. Rather than reaching for experienced managers, I promoted people in the company who were closely identified with either the culture or the values or were regarded as prophets of the vision." He institutionalized the Silicon Valley traditions of off-sight meetings and beer busts, and made them "a fundamental way of doing business at Apple." One of Sculley's first attempts to alter Apple's direction was a 1986 speech calling for investment in computer networking technology. However, he quickly backed down when his office was besieged by a group of angry engineers. Sculley commented, "I made a mistake in not realizing how truly deep the company's link to its vision really was. They all really believed in the machine for the individual. When I first started pushing in the area of networking, I was stopped. I was simply pushing too far too fast."

Sculley likened joining Apple to pursuing a graduate degree at a university: "You select Apple because you think it can offer you an incredible, life-growing experience. Indeed, we seem to have become one of the country's most elite 'higher education' institutions, because there tend to be more than 50 applications for virtually every unadvertised job. People gravitate to us with the idea of staying three to five years and then going off to start their own companies." In return for asking people to "pour a part of [them]self into the success of the company," Sculley believed that Apple owed its employees "a chance to realize their quest to grow, to achieve, and to make a difference in the world." They were also rewarded handsomely, with salaries and benefits "in the 90th percentile."[1]

THE 1988 REORGANIZATION   As Mac sales exploded, Sculley announced yet another reorganization in 1988. He established four new divisions. Apple Products, headed by John-Louis Gassee, included all manufacturing, product development, product marketing, and the Advanced Technologies Group (ATG). ATG was created to explore revolutionary ideas and high-risk technologies. In addition, three regional sales divisions were created and several new managers were promoted to senior positions (see **Exhibit 18–1**). During this time, Sculley brought in experienced managers from other computer companies, including Allan Loren from Cigna Information as president of Apple USA, and Kevin Sullivan from DEC as V.P. of human resources. Sculley also hired more managers at operational levels—over 3,000 new employees during 1988—bringing the total to more than 9,000, only 75 of whom had been with the company at its inception. Yet the dedication to Apple values remained intact. Within six months, even former IBM and DEC employees would whole-heartedly embrace the Apple culture.

[1]"Wherefore Art Thou, Apple?," *Upside*, October 1991, p. 46.

Exhibit 18-1 Apple Computer Organization Chart, 1988

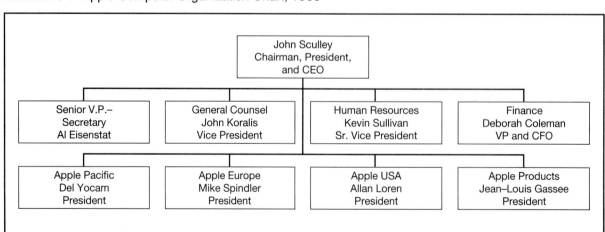

One of Sculley's greatest frustrations in the late 1980s is that his proposals for new directions in technology were often rebuffed by Gassee, the technical leader of the company. Gassee strongly believed that Apple should sell single-user, proprietary systems that had very high margins with premium prices. Indeed, under Gassee's direction, Apple raised the Mac's average selling price more than 60% between 1988 and 1990.

APPLE'S COMPETITIVE POSITION Apple held a peculiar position in the computer industry as it entered the 1990s. It was the only real alternative hardware and software standard for PCs other than the IBM standard. (See the **Appendix** for background on the PC industry.) It was also more vertically and horizontally integrated than any other PC company, with the exception of IBM. Apple designed its products, usually from scratch, specifying unique chips, disk drives, monitors, and even unusual shapes for its chassis. It assembled most of its own products in state-of-the-art factories, considered among the most automated and modern in the industry. In addition, Apple developed its own operating systems software for the Mac, some of its applications software, and many of its peripherals. Indeed, almost one-third of Apple's business was imaging products, like printers and scanners designed exclusively to support Macintosh computers. About half of Apple's revenues came from overseas, and roughly half the U.S. sales were to education, where Apple had more than 50% of the market.

Apple's products proved to be easier to use, easier to network, and more versatile than comparable IBM machines. In many core software technologies like multimedia (integrating video, sound, and data), Apple had a two year lead on vendors such as Microsoft. Since Apple controlled all aspects of the computer, from board design to software, it could offer a better computer "system", where all the parts—software, hardware, and peripherals—interacted in a coherent way. Unlike IBM and its clones, Apple gave customers a complete desktop solution. This made Apple's customers the most loyal in the industry. As one analyst commented, "the majority of IBM users 'put up' with their machines, but Apple's customers 'love' their Macs."

Trouble started brewing, however, in early 1990. While Gassee was raising prices, IBM PCs and clone prices fell precipitously. And that was not the only issue, according to Sculley:

> We were increasingly viewed as the "BMW" of the computer industry. Our Macintoshes were almost exclusively high-end, premium-priced computers that would continue to have limited success in penetrating the corporate marketplace. Without lower prices, we would be stuck selling to our installed base. We were also so insular that we could not manufacture a product to sell for under $3000. We constantly fell into the trap of "creeping elegance" with not invented here mentality. We spent more than two years, for instance, designing a portable computer that had to be "perfect." But in the end, it was disaster— it was 18 months late and 10 pounds too heavy.

Apple was also plagued with severe morale problems. An employee survey in 1990 indicated that most employees were still proud to work at Apple, but a majority thought that Apple lacked direction and that management was unaware of the challenges faced by employees. Many blamed Apple USA President Allan Loren, who would tell employees at communications meetings they were "stupid." And Apple's CFO, Joe Graziano, was quoted as saying, "We had a fundamental problem. Our own employees, even management, were complaining, "What's the direction of the company?"[2]

Sculley Builds a New Apple

While the company was still profitable and before a real crisis emerged, Sculley sought to redefine Apple. One of his first moves was to clean house. By February 1990, Sculley put a new executive team in place (see **Exhibits 18–2** and **18–5**). Loren resigned, Gassee resigned, and Sculley promoted Michael Spindler, a German and the former president of Apple's highly profitable European division, to be President and COO. This was an emotional transition because Gassee represented

[2]Upside Magazine, October 1991, p. 37.

Exhibit 18-2 Apple Computer Organization Chart, May 1992

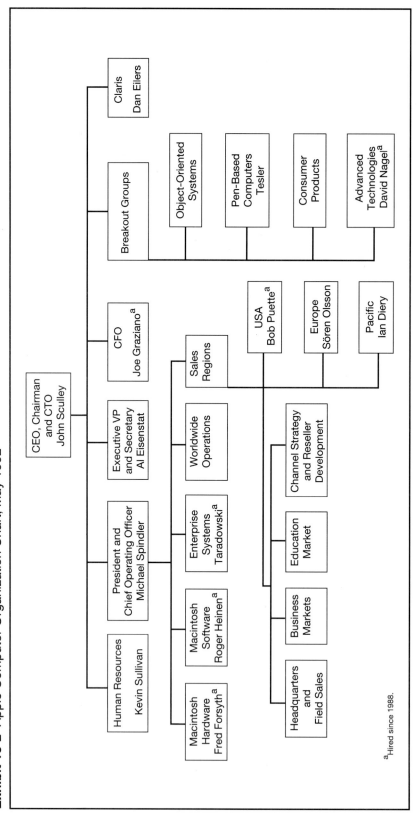

[a] Hired since 1988.

part of the old core of Apple—a charismatic manager dedicated to developing cutting-edge products. Perhaps most important, Sculley realized that he would continue to have difficulty shifting the company's direction unless he had a deeper understanding of the technical issues and how the bowels of the organization worked. He therefore appointed himself chief technology officer (CTO) and began to oversee R&D and product development. This last move was especially controversial, but Sculley saw no choice. He said, "the CTO does not have to be the chief scientist, but does have to make decisions on technology. Apple is a technology company and the most important business decisions are technology/product decisions." To bring himself up to speed, he met daily with engineers to discuss product plans and technology issues whenever he was not traveling. He said he did not want executive summaries—he wanted to learn the technology and become involved in technology choices.

Agreeing that high margins and proprietary technology were no longer part of a sustainable long-term strategy, the new team worked together to plan Apple's course. Four principles would drive the corporation into the 1990s: 1) get customer input upfront; 2) time-to-market was critical. Bonuses would be tied to meeting specific milestones. If people miss, they won't get fired, but they will no longer get extra compensation; 3) innovate at the lowest possible price point versus the old philosophy of create great technology (usually at the high end); and 4) no sacred cows—everything must be questioned. Moreover, the driving force behind Apple's new approach would be maximizing shareholder value. The financial markets were pricing computer hardware companies at roughly 10–12 times earnings, and software companies at 20–40 times earnings. Apple's stock had a PE of roughly 10 and Sculley was committed to getting Apple's PE closer to companies like Microsoft (PE of ~45) and Novell (PE of ~50).

To execute this philosophy, Sculley gave the CFO, Graziano, responsibility for developing a new financial model, and gave Spindler day to day operations. Sculley focused on new product development and technologies. Unlike prior management teams, this new executive staff maintained close personal ties; Spindler and Sculley, in particular, kept each other informed about their strategies and the actions, working in locked-step on every major issue.

New Financial Discipline

To regain market share and compete with the clone companies, Spindler and Graziano overhauled Apple's financial strategy to target gross margins in the low 40% range—with the same hoped-for pre-tax profits. According to Graziano: "We had the highest expense structure in the industry. If you look at the cost structure of Apple and its resellers, marketing and distribution costs more than production. If Apple was to survive, we had to get into a crisis mode."

To steer Apple toward lower gross margins, Graziano cut perks such as company cars and lavish parties—perks that had disappeared in the rest of Silicon Valley by the mid 1980s. Other symbolic cost-cutting measures included reducing subsidies to the company cafeterias and fitness center. By 1992, the joke was that everyone would have to time-share the vacuum cleaner to clean around their cubicles, because janitors would be the next to go. Apple's pay scales were also brought down from the 90th percentile to slightly above average for Silicon Valley.

To improve the return on Apple's R&D expenditures, Graziano tightened the R&D allocation process and established formal project reviews. R&D, which had no account ability by project, was restructured to track revenues on a project basis with bonuses tied to specific milestones. Graziano strove to push profit and loss responsibility as far down the company as possible. He expected corporate services to justify their existence and compete with outside vendors. Even after-sales support services, which had traditionally been handled through dealers and toll-free 800 numbers, were put on a profit and loss basis, and customers had to pay for telephone advice after 90 days through the use of 900 numbers.

While Graziano revamped the financial model, Spindler worked to improve operations and build accountability into the organization. Spindler, nicknamed "Diesel" by his colleagues for his tenacious management style, recalled the situation in early 1990: "The whole organization was built on abundance; there were no limits on resources. We had to explain why it's a dynamic, ruthless world." Spindler commanded universal respect among his direct reports. Unlike Gassee's staff meetings which were filled with theological discussions about computers, Spindler kept a

Exhibit 18-3 Apple Financials over Selected Years

Cost of sales	1,049	815	3,314	2,606	2,695	1,991	1,296	1,118	506	170
Research and development	131	140	583	478	421	273	192	72.5	60	21
Marketing and distribution			1,740	1,556	1,340	908	655	478	230	55
General and administrative	420	492	224	207	195	180	146	110	57	22
Operating income	263	228	447	712	634	620	371	103	130	66
Net income	166	151	310	475	454	400	218	61.3	77	39
Property, plant, equipment & other			275	321	284	186	121	66	64	NA
Depreciation and amortization			204	202	124	77	70	41	22	NA
Cash dividends paid			56	53	50	39	15	—	—	NA
Cash and temporary cash investment	988	984	893	997	809	546	565	337	143	73
Accounts receivable	973	853	907	762	793	639	406	220	136	42
Inventories	643	409	672	356	475	461	226	167	142	104
Property, plant and equipment	456	436	448	398	334	207	130	176	110	31
Total assets	3,745	3,157	3,494	2,976	2,744	2,082	1,478	936	557	255
Total current liabilities	1,271	1,072	1,217	1,027	895	827	479	90	129	70
Total shareholders' equity	1,923	1,545	1,767	1,447	1,486	1,003	837	550	378	177
Permanent employees			12,386	12,307	12,068	9,536	6,236	4,326	4,645	2,456
International sales/sales (%)	44	45	45	42	36	32	27	22	22	27
Gross margin/sales (%)		51	47	53	49	51	51	42	49	49
R&D/sales (%)	7	8	9	9	8	7	7	4	6	6
ROS[b] (%)	8.91	9.01	4.91	8.55	8.59	9.83	8.19	3.20	7.83	11.68
ROA[c] (%)	4.43	4.78	8.87	15.96	16.55	19.21	14.75	6.55	13.82	15.29
Return on equity (%)	9	10	19	32	36	44	28	12	24	44
Stock price range	53.5-59.5[e]		40.5-73.3	24.3-47.8	32.5-50.4	35.5-47.75	20.3-59.8	7.3-15.6	8.6-31.6	6.8-7.3
P/E ratio	20.3[f]		12.9	10.5	12.9	13.6	20.3	22.1	30.6	24.3
Market value[d]	6,522	6,751	4,150	5,166	5,033	4,914	1,360	2,368	1,320	

[a]Quarter ending 12/27/91.

[b]ROS = net income/total revenues.

[c]ROA = net income/total assets.

[d]Year-end stock price times the number of shares outstanding.

[e]Week ending 6/4/92.

[f]For 12 months ending 3/92.

Source: Apple Annual Reports and *Value Line*.

Monday
7:00–8:00   Meeting with staff assistants

tight focus on the issues at hand. He met weekly with six to ten critical people, where he continually stressed time-to-market issues and sought to resolve any operational conflicts.

To maintain operational discipline, Spindler reconfigured domestic operations to give profit and loss responsibility to smaller groups. He developed a new budgeting process with Graziano that laid out key operational goals and established accountability measures, through departmental budgets, marketing initiatives, and product calendars. Spindler noted that people were loyal to the product, not the company. He said "we need to realign people to work for the company not themselves." He made Apple's largely salaried-compensation structure more commission-based, and created performance-related incentives to reward good management. Spindler also selected the most experienced managers and established strong management teams at the operating level. In the Mac core, he created a team of five managers (three geographic heads—US, Asia Pacific, and Europe—along with manufacturing and software) with increased responsibility.

The clearest indication of Spindler's success came from the testimony of a manager in the advanced technology group: "A few years ago," he noted, "there were more projects than people and no clear responsibility. Projects used to take on a life of their own; if management tried to cut one, engineers would simply rename it, and carry on. Now, one person is in charge of each project, and there is an annual review process emphasizing measurable outcomes."

The New Strategy

Sculley, Spindler, and Graziano formulated a new strategy in 1990 and 1991 that had three key components: 1) reinvigorate the Mac business with a strategy to gain market share; 2) expand the Mac business into the world of enterprise computing (i.e., large corporations) through greater openness, and less emphasis on proprietary systems; and 3) diversify Apple into new technologies that leveraged Apple's strengths in software.

The strategy of gaining market share required Apple to do two critical things: lower prices *and* costs to attract a larger number of users; and reduce cycle time radically. By lower-

ing prices, Apple would match the competition. Apple also cut its workforce in a major layoff. However, Sculley noted that lower costs and higher volumes were not enough: Apple also had to bring out 'hit products' through the first half of the 1990s—i.e., new Macs and derivations of older products that could be produced every six to twelve months. The competition was becoming so intense, Sculley believed, Apple's best chance to keep the Mac profitable was to give customers more and more options, faster. The first hit product was the Powerbook, an aggressively priced notebook computer which Apple introduced in October of 1991. The Powerbook was a spectacular success, predicted to generate a billion dollars in revenue within 12 months of its introduction.

The second part of the strategy was to make Apple more "open"—both technically and organizationally. On the technical side, Apple would start to offer solutions that would work with other firms' computers. On the organizational side, Sculley believed that scale economies in key technologies were simply too great in the 1990s for any one firm to control them all in-house. A new operating system, for instance, could take five years to develop and cost $500 million in R&D. He therefore concluded that Apple should build a "federation" of alliances with partners that could help leverage Apple's strengths, especially in software. He said, "we have to have partners; we have to become more open; we have to penetrate a broader market or our application developers will abandon us; we have to license technologies in and be willing to license technologies out." However, Apple shocked the world when it chose its first significant alliance partner—its long-time nemesis, IBM.

THE APPLE-IBM JOINT VENTURES During the summer of 1991, IBM and Apple formed two joint ventures. Sculley listed four major objectives in working with IBM:

First, we had to overcome the resistance of MIS managers in large corporations to buying Apple Computers. We called this our Enterprise systems effort. The alliance attacked this problem in three ways: 1) we got IBM's stamp of approval; 2) IBM's sales force would offer Apple network products; and 3) we both committed to achieve "interoperability" (seamless connections between the varying IBM and Apple computers). Second, our current microprocessor technology from Motorola would not carry us through the 1990s. We saw IBM's RS6000 RISC microprocessor as the best technology in the industry. Since IBM also agreed to work with Motorola as a second source for the technology, we reduced our vulnerability from being dependent on a sole source. We would call this new generation of computers the "PowerPC". Third, we formed Taligent to develop our next generation OS, which we internally called Pink. Pink will be a major breakthrough for some customers because it will allow big corporations to customize their applications very easily. However, to pay for Pink, we needed money and a broader market. IBM and Apple together would have the resources and large installed base. In addition, Pink would be written to run on Apple's installed base, the new IBM chip, as well as Intel chips. Lastly, we formed Kaleida to create standards in multimedia technologies, like putting full motion video on the personal computer.

The underlying concept of the IBM-Apple relationship was that both companies could share underlying the costs and risks of developing new technologies, but ultimately, the parent companies would still compete in computers. The JVs would operate independently, shipping their software products to both parents at agreed upon transfer prices. IBM would provide the semiconductor technology while Apple would provide most of the software and personnel.

PERSONAL ELECTRONICS   The third leg of Sculley's strategy was to move beyond desktop and portable computers to a whole new generation of products. Sculley wanted Apple to participate in broader markets, including the mass consumer market. At the Consumer Electronics Show in January 1992, Sculley announced that Apple would create a new era of "personal electronics" with "personal digital assistants" (PDAs). PDAs would utilize Apple's most advanced software technologies. For instance, the first announced product was called Newton—a one pound device the size of a video cassette. Newton would use a pen for data entry and combined the features of a notepad, calendar, and fax machine. Even more important, it had "intelligence;" the machine could understand and interpret everyday language, like "schedule lunch with Bob next Tuesday." The operational challenges for Apple, however, were significant. For these products to be big hits, research suggested that they must sell for $500 or less. In addition, consumers needed to be educated about the new technology, and Apple would have to sell

PDA through entirely new channels. To solve these problems, Sculley enlisted the help of Japanese consumer electronics giants, particularly Sharp, Toshiba, and Sony. Although the relationship differed with each firm, Apple typically asked its Japanese partner to manufacture the hardware, while the partner got a license for Apple's software with the rights to sell the final product under its own brand name.

Organization

When Sculley described his vision of Apple in the 1990s as a federation, he saw the Mac forming the mature and profitable core while other businesses, such as the IBM and Japanese joint ventures, grew around it. (See **Exhibit 18–2**.) Each business had its own management with profit and loss responsibility. Where in the past, Mac had dominated the entire organization, Sculley hoped that the new structure would give both independence and visibility to the new areas of growth. He envisaged that the Mac core would constitute the bulk of Apple's revenues for at least five years, generating the cash resources needed to invest in the new businesses. Sculley explained, "We will push resources out from the center to the new businesses. At the corporate level, we will only keep the smallest possible staff."

This was a dramatic blueprint for a company characterized by a traditionally amorphous and fluid structure. Indeed, some parts of the company had no organization charts in early 1992. According to one senior executive, "this is still run like a baby company. Decision making is kept simple. A core group of people gets together frequently, and that's what really holds this company together." A senior executive explained that "we have to see Mac as *a* business, not *the* business. When Mac was the center of the business, there was no objective way to consider the other parts on their own terms."

Resource Allocation

Sculley hoped that the new structure would help make resource allocation more explicit. According to Graziano, "the Mac group has to operate now under tighter financial controls in order to free up funding for the new product areas." Sculley emphasized, however, that investment in new product areas would not be entirely at the expense of the Mac. Apple wanted its partners to share the cost. In 1992, roughly 80% of R&D went to the Mac core and 20% to the new businesses. To improve Apple's productivity on R&D, Sculley and Spindler both started giving product development engineers very specific goals with shortened time horizons. The initial results had been very impressive. After numerous slips of the late 1980s, many analysts were once again touting Apple's technology leadership. Particularly in software, Apple brought to market in 1992 several key innovations, like making it easy to give voice commands to a computer. Sculley's dilemma was how to fund the new businesses which would be critical to Apple in the late 1990s. The ongoing price wars in the IBM PC world was leading companies like Compaq to drop prices as much as 50% every six months. While the Mac could command a premium in the marketplace, that premium was shrinking, putting enormous pressure on Apple's margin. Moreover, Sculley continued to feel that future resource decisions would be constrained by the need to keep the Mac business highly profitable. "There's little sympathy," remarked Sculley, "in the investment community if we can't make the core business support itself. If it doesn't, our shareholder value will plunge overnight. And since most of our prized employees are compensated with stock options, I constantly worry that a falling stock price will lead to a large scale exodus."

Apple Management in 1992

Apple headed into 1992 with a strong, cohesive executive team and a small but very active board. According to Sculley, "our team is now very pragmatic, very operational." One longtime board member agreed, "Apple management is a lot better today. Its people now are very good, and there is much less politics." A senior manager explained:

> Before it was Sculley and the warlords—Loren and Gassee—and there was lots of destructive energy internally. Now, for the first time, Sculley has a cohesive executive team that is communicating a clear vision. When Spindler took charge, he made people more accountable. Spindler provides strong leadership; he understands most aspects of the business. Sculley is a great intellect—he's always excited about the next initiative. And Spindler helps make these happen.

JOHN SCULLEY Sculley generally worked 12 to 14 hour days over 7 day weeks and was described by colleagues as "very intense" and "without much of a sense of humor." He typically rose by 4AM to catch the latest economic news from Japan and Europe, before a run, work-out, and 7AM staff meeting (see **Exhibit 18–4** for schedule of a typical Sculley day). Sculley read an enormous amount of material, including a daily customized electronic newspaper that tracked product reviews, and industry trade publications. In addition, either Sculley or his assistant reviewed his electronic mail messages, often numbering over 100, each day. As one board member described:

> John is one of the hardest working and brightest chief executives I know. He grasps things quickly and is very open to new ideas. He may be the least arrogant CEO I've seen. He doesn't put people down. . . . His strength is his ability to see where the industry is going. He has gained a real understanding by immersing himself in the technology in recent years. In the past he was dependent on techies who gave him bad information; in addition, he used to get sold quickly on bad people. . . . He's much better today.

Sculley's new hands-on approach, which evolved from his role as CTO, gave him many more opportunities to impact product development. While he could not write computer code or design a chip, he worked with technical people to define how the system would be presented to the end user. He was instrumental, for instance, in getting engineers to include key features in the Powerbook which greatly enhanced the product's functionality and user-friendliness.[3]

[3]One example mentioned by Sculley of prodding his engineers to find better solutions was Remote Access, user-friendly software which allows the user to connect to his-her desktop in the office and access his-her files from any location.

Exhibit 18-4 John Sculley Representative Calendar, Fall 1991

9:00-9:30	Conference call with Sony executives
10:00-11:00	General Magic Board meeting (an Apple spin-off: Apple holds minority share)
12:00-3:00	EMT meeting, including lunch
4:00-6:00	Meeting and update with Spindler

Tuesday

7:00-7:30	Meeting with staff assistants
7:30-8:00	R&D update meeting
8:00-8:30	Human resources update meeting
8:30-10:00	IBM conference call
10:00-11:00	Meeting with Pacific PR re. conference in Japan
11:00-11:30	Apple International internal meeting
11:30-12:00	Lunch
12:00-1:00	Meeting with outside PR-review upcoming interviews
1:00-1:30	Meeting with Finance staff
2:00-2:30	Update with IS&T
3:30-5:00	Patent Award meeting and gathering
6:00	Dinner with Board member

Wednesday

7:00-7:30	Meeting with staff assistants
7:30-8:00	Advanced technology update meeting
8:00-10:30	Dress rehearsal for Product Introduction speech
10:30-11:30	Meeting with Bank of Boston
11:30-12:00	Conference call with General Magic executives
1:00-3:00	Meeting re. new products
4:00-6:00	Claris Corp. Board of Directors meeting (Apple's wholly-owned software subsidiary)
6:00	Dinner w/Claris BOD members

Thursday

7:00-7:30	Meeting with staff assistants
7:30-8:00	R&D meeting
8:00-10:00	IBM update meetings (internal)
10:30-11:00	Interview/*Fortune* Magazine
11:00-12:00	Review Analysts Meeting speech
12:00-1:00	Lunch
1:00-3:00	Attend COO staff meeting
4:00-5:00	Conference call International Foundation

Friday

7:00-7:30	Meeting with staff assistants
7:30-8:00	R&D update
8:00-10:00	Technology staff meeting
10:00-11:30	Review speeches for Sales meeting and Employee Communications meeting
11:30-12:00	Lunch
12:00-3:00	EMT Strategy meeting
3:00-4:00	CSPP conference call
4:00-4:30	Interview/Editor, *Wall Street Journal*
4:30-6:00	Final review of Product Introduction speech

This attentiveness to details also made him much more responsive to problems. Despite the great success of Apple's new notebook computer in 1992, for example, its low-end model (the Powerbook 100) ran into immediate problems. Literally within a few weeks of inventory starting to build, Sculley was closely monitoring the product. His assistant tracked the products sales and gave Sculley weekly reports on inventory. Within a month, he and Spindler jointly decided to start selling at a discount to avoid a costly write-off. Sculley noted, "We clearly made a mistake with Powerbook 100—it was somewhat underpowered compared to competitive offerings—but we very successfully kept it from becoming a crisis."

Sculley divided his time evenly between the Mac core and the new businesses, developing both internal and external relationships in each area. He sat on no outside boards other than a committee involved in education—a core Apple franchise. He hoped eventually to "get someone to run the entire Mac business" so that he could focus on Apple's new businesses.

Sculley was the ultimate idea-driven manager. He was constantly thinking of new ways to grow the company, reconfigure the product line, and diversify into related technology. In 1990, he focused heavily on building volume in the low end computer market; in early 1991, he was exploring new semiconductor technologies and ways to deepen Apple's presence in large corporations; in late 1991, early 1992, he was aggressively seek-ing partners for PDAs; in mid-1992, he was exploring how to leverage Apple's imaging (printer, scanner, etc.) technology. One member of Sculley's staff noted, "John announces publicly where the company will be, then leaves us to fill in the details." Another observed, "John believes that a good company should constantly be stretching. Just when you think you want to put your feet up and say, 'There, we've done it,' he comes in and provokes change." A third senior manager concurred: "Sculley is like the elder statesman of technology. He absorbs and effectively communicates a vision that comes collectively from outside and inside Apple. He articulates a far-sighted vision very broadly, at a 50,000 foot level. We then have to figure out how to turn that vision into concrete plans."

Managing for the 1990s

Sculley noted with pride that "Apple now has a strong team of managers that can help lead us into the 1990s." At the highest level, the most significant decisions were made by the executive management team (EMT) that included Sculley, Spindler, Graziano, Kevin Sullivan, Albert Eisenstat, and since April 1992, Edward Nagel, (see **Exhibit 18–5** for biographies). Below the EMT, there were several layers of managers, most of whom had been with Apple only two to three years by 1992. Apple had traditionally acquired senior management talent by hiring it from the outside. Hiring and promotion patterns showed that 50% of the EMT and their direct reports were either hired directly into their current job or assumed their position within a year of joining Apple. Apple's senior managers (directors and above) averaged 43 years of age and had been with the company for 5.5 years.[4] Operating in a structure of autonomous divisions, Apple managers were often functionally and geographically specialized with little lateral mobility.

Sculley also noted that the work environment was improving. Apple remained a very pleasant place to work: its offices were bright, modern, high-tech buildings. The atmosphere was still casual, reflecting the California lifestyle of many of the employees—55% of whom were situated in Silicon Valley. And the company's historically strong, individualistic culture was reinforced by Apple's own technology. All employees were connected on a worldwide computer network called *Applelink*, which included *Can We Talk?*, an employee conferencing system. This electronic bulletin board featured many ongoing (and sometimes intense) employee debates of current events, social issues, and corporate issues.

Yet one senior manager observed: "The work environment is leaner and moves faster, but it's not enough. People love the work environment, but they don't like the work." People were being pushed to the limits; long hours and limited resources were leading to more "burnouts." The new financial model also left workers with only average pay and no pension benefits, so it was less attractive for some employees to stay. Another manager commented, "John is reengineering the future. Michael is relentlessly trying to extract value from the Mac at the same time as reducing expenses. That's a tough thing to do. I worry that we haven't dropped anything. People are simply working harder with less resources. We haven't fundamentally reengineered anything. This cannot continue; people are going to run out of gas." A

[4]In contrast to senior management statistics, the average Apple employee was 36 years of age (up from 29 years in 1987) with 3.8 years tenure in the company.

Exhibit 18-5 Biographies of Apple's Executive Management Team

John Sculley, Chairman of the Board, Chief Executive Officer, and Chief Technology Officer (age 52). He joined Apple as president and CEO and a director in May 1983, and was named chairman in January 1986. In November 1991, he was elected to the additonal position of CTO.

Michael H. Spindler, President and Chief Operating Officer (age 49). He joined Apple as European Marketing Manager in September 1980, was promoted to VP, Europe, in January 1984, was named VP, International, in February 1985, and was promoted to Senior VP, International Sales and Marketing in November 1986. Spindler was appointed Senior VP, International in January 1988, Senior VP, Apple Europe Division in April 1988, and was promoted to Senior VP and President, Apple Europe Division in August 1988. In January 1990, Spindler was promoted to COO and Executive VP and in November 1990 he was elected President. In January 1991, he was elected a member of Apple's Board of Directors.

Albert A. Eisenstat, Executive Vice President and Secretary (age 61). Eisenstat joined Apple in July 1980 as VP, General Counsel and Secretary. In November 1985, he was promoted to Senior VP and was appointed a member of the Board of Directors. Eisenstat served as General Counsel until January 1989 and as Acting General Counsel from April 1989 to June 1989. He also served as Acting CFO from January 1989 to June 1989. In November 1990, Eisenstat was elected Executive VP. In 1992, Eisenstat was also a director of Commercial Metals Company and Sungard Data Systems.

Joseph A. Graziano, Executive Vice President and Chief Financial Officer (age 48). Graziano joined Apple in June 1989 as Senior VP and CFO. In November 1990, he was elected Executive VP. Before joining Apple, Graziano was CFO by Sun Microsystems from June 1987 to June 1989. Graziano also served as a director of ShareData and IntelliCorp in 1992.

Kevin J. Sullivan, Senior Vice President, Human Resources (age 50). Sullivan joined Apple in April 1987 as VP, Human Resources and was promoted to Senior VP, Human Resources in October 1988. Before joining Apple, Sullivan was employed by DEC from 1980 to 1987, serving most recently as Corporate Personal Manager.

David C. Nagel, Senior Vice President, Advanced Technology Group (age 46). Dr. Nagel joined Apple in June 1988 as Manager of Applications Technology within the Advanced Technology Group (ATG). Between June 1988 and May 1990, he was promoted to Manager of User Technologies, Director of User Technologies, and VP of ATG in May 1990. In November 1991, Dr. Nagel was promoted to Senior VP, ATG. Previously, Dr. Nagel was employed by NASA Ames Research Center from 1973 to 1988, and most recently served as Chief of the Aerospace Human Factors Research Division.

1992 survey also suggested that the vast majority of employees perceived that the company did not "invest" in its workforce and that executive management was not concerned about career opportunities. Even more disturbing was the 1992 survey which showed no improvement over the previous year, with most employees still believing that the best people were passed over for promotion. Of course, this was nothing new: because of rapid growth, Apple employees had constantly been stretched in their jobs and were often promoted with little time to develop appropriate management skills. However, one industry analyst commented that there continued to be "a lot of entrenched managers at Apple whose employees think (they) are incompetent."

A big question for Sculley and Spindler was whether Apple could retain its relatively informal style as the company grew bigger and more far-flung. Work was still done largely through committees, meetings, and consensus. One em-

ployee observed, "We are low on systems and high on the human side. There are very few formal rules or processes." Another remarked, "There is no consistent process; every time we do something we do it a different way." The informal approach to management meant that influence tended to be the primary way of achieving one's objectives. An HR manager said that, "Apple is highly relationship and network oriented. If you know the right people you can get things done—there are lots of inner circles." The same was true for organization. One manager commented that, "Apple is fluid and volatile. We use reorgs to make changes. Reorganization is inherent in our organizational structure."

Sculley told employees in the spring of 1992, "as we make this transition from a company with lots of technology that wants to turn them into lots of businesses, the only way we will implement it successfully is to get people working together." While Spindler believed that progress had been made in establishing more accountability and fact-based management, he acknowledged that "we're probably still more technology-rich than we are field-effective."

To bring the organization in line with the new strategy, Sculley and Spindler began to spend a significant amount of time simply communicating their vision of the new Apple to the organization. In May of 1992, for example, they held a meeting for 5000 Apple employees at the San Jose Convention Center, which was broadcast live around the world to all Apple locations. At this session, Sculley and Spindler explained their long-term vision for the company, the present operating plans, and took questions from the audience on topics ranging from strategy to ethics. Sculley also communicated to employees through announcements and internal videos of discussions between him and Spindler. In addition, forums were held each quarter during which 12 to 15 employees drawn by lottery spent a day together and a day with Sculley and Spindler. According to Sculley, these videotaped forums indicated a "much greater appreciation that management is not a dirty word."

Beginning in 1991, the EMT also held executive forums with senior management, facilitated by Apple University, to discuss how they could improve the speed and effectiveness throughout Apple. Some senior managers perceived that Apple lacked highly-focused, actionable strategies. According to one executive, strategic priorities were either overly "cosmic" or else highly product-specific. Out of these meetings came several new initiatives, including Executive Readiness, the roll-out of Apple Quality Management, Apple Critical Performance Indicator metrics, and a restructuring of the marketing organization. All of these programs were designed to create better operational systems and clearer organizational structures at Apple.

Executive Readiness

Capable leadership is essential to Apple's immediate and long-term success. Thoughtful planning and execution of executive capabilities will be a strategic edge for Apple as we move forward.[5]

To strengthen management benchstrength and build a more flexible organization, the EMT initiated a company wide planning process for reviewing and developing senior managers (see **Exhibit 18-6**). The Executive Readiness program, launched in early 1992, aimed to develop critical leadership resources through a disciplined organizational review process that assessed Apple's management strength.

The first round of organizational review meetings in April 1992 involved a two-way discussion of the EMT with each general manager or president. In these informal and confidential meetings, the EMT strove to promote a "helpful"

[5]"Executive Readiness" Position Paper, Apple University, April 14, 1992.

Exhibit 18-6 Executive Capabilities Required at Apple in 1980s versus 1990s.

1980s	Capability Needed	1990s	Capability Needed
20-30% Growth	Operational	5-10% Growth	Operational and Strategic
Moderate	Product-focused	Intense	Product-focused and
Competition	Understand U.S.	Competition	Customer-oriented
U.S. dominated	market and		Understand global
	environment	Global market	economic, political, and
	Introduce U.S. and		cultural issues
Gross margin	localize		Manage global time to
Go it alone	Maximize profit	Market share	market
	Recruit and staff		Market creation with less
	Individual		resources
	achievement		Cultivate and manage
			relationships
			Team development and
			collaboration

Source: "Executive Readiness" Position Paper, Apple University, April 1992.

climate conducive to an honest appraisal of leadership talent. Executive Readiness was not conceived as a one-time event, but rather as an important annual management process. By June 1992, the EMT had met with senior managers in Mac Hardware and Worldwide Operations, Advanced Products Group (Newton), Advanced Technology Group, and Apple USA. An EMT review meeting was planned at the end of that month to evaluate the success of the first series of reviews.

There was skepticism within Apple about this process and concern about closed door discussions. People were already stretched. Some questioned whether senior management viewed Executive Readiness as a long-term investment in people or a short-term fix to immediate business needs. Another issue was whether it was reasonable or desirable to develop people across divisional lines, given the way Apple was organized. Others questioned if the company could afford to be unable to move individuals quickly to fill unexpected gaps in leadership. One longtime Apple University manager asserted that "there is no slack in the system and no clear rotation paths."

There were indications that this was changing, however. By May 1992, the Apple University manager in charge of Executive Readiness had sat down with each general manager and created a "list" of the core competencies needed in that division. One surprising result was that all operational divisions identified customer focus as a key capability—"that would never have happened before. What started as a top-down process, is now percolating back up."

Apple Quality Management

Seeking a tool to help them build better products faster and in a more cost effective way, Apple's Worldwide Manufacturing organization began employing total-quality management techniques. In August, Spindler commissioned a cross-functional steering committee to develop a plan for using total-quality management throughout Apple. In February 1991, the EMT approved their proposal for an Apple Quality Management (AQM) program.

Beyond improving production processes and product quality, AQM stressed focusing on customers and using data to make decisions. Spindler, who defined quality as "the organiza-

tional performance of the entire corporation," viewed AQM as a way to "get real focus and discipline into the way each of us works." He argued, "We have to change organizational behavior by focusing on process. We've got to be more systematic now. In a sense it means losing our innocence and working a lot more professionally." The corporate AQM director added, "When we were a high-growth, high-profit company, we could always fix a problem by throwing more money or people at it. Moreover, Apple has had a history of everyone doing their own agendas. Now that the industry has flattened out, the practices of the past that were OK are no longer acceptable." (See **Exhibit 18–7** for AQM process.)

The AQM steering committee developed a plan to implement AQM in four simultaneous phases: (1) Education and leadership (getting the senior management on board); (2) Functional process improvement (training and small PDCA[6] projects); (3) Integrating systems (cross functional process improvement and large PDCA projects); (4) Policy deployment (linking long term corporate objectives with department policy and activity plans). The AQM director explained the decision to do all four phases in parallel instead of serially: "We can't wait three to ten years to get results. We won't be alive if we wait that long. Moreover, if we don't demonstrate quick wins, Apple people won't buy it. This is a really skeptical company with the attitude 'Prove it. I'm the designer; I know best.' So we're trying to demonstrate at various levels in various departments how these tools and techniques make sense." A 16-person steering committee set 90% of the strategy—10% was done with the EMT—as well as the tactical implementation within each division. Most members were part-time and represented their respective divisions. AQM training was accomplished through AQM "101" and "102" courses given by Apple University and was also incorporated into established employee training programs.

AQM began attracting company wide attention—both positive and negative—in 1992. Management commitment to AQM was tested after the EMT announced a reorganization in March of 1992. Employees queried the EMT on whether it

---

[6]AQM was based on the Plan-Do-Check-Act (PDCA) model of process improvement used by many total-quality companies worldwide, such as Komatsu.

Exhibit 18-7 Implementing Apple Critical Performance Measures

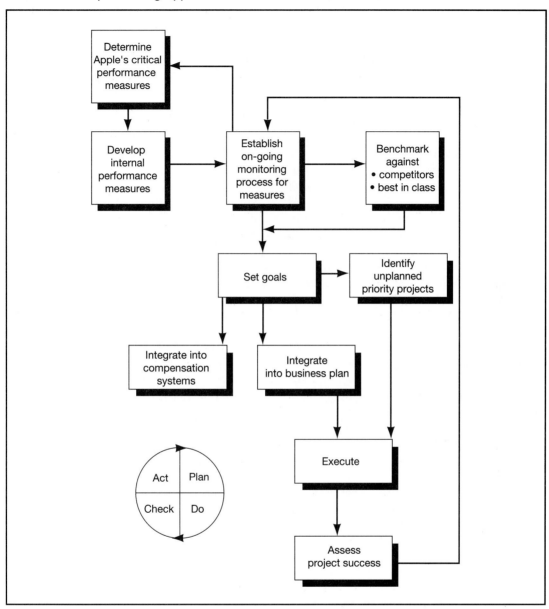

Source: Company documents.

had used the AQM process in making its decision. Sculley admission over AppleLink that the EMT did not formally use AQM made many employees cynical. Nonetheless, by May 32% of the company had completed AQM orientation and 20% of the managers had completed AQM Integration (against goals of 50% for both areas in 1992). Over 100 functional projects were in process in Apple worldwide, including Apple Assistance Center (which reduced written response time from six weeks to one day); Apple France (which cuts the expense statement cycle from four weeks to five days). AQM had also contributed to more complex, phase (3) successes. For example, a cross-functional effort to redesign product packaging using new "brown boxes" addressed environmental, marketing, manufacturing, and distribution issues and saved Apple $3.1 million in 1992.

Reactions to AQM varied. One senior manager noted that the "EMT lost credibility when they espoused AQM for the masses but not for themselves." Another senior executive and long-time employee dubbed AQM "the strategy du jour." One of the biggest debates, however, was whether AQM should be an education process and state-of-mind, or whether it should be a formal system of measurements. According to one senior software manager, "AQM is a great idea as long as its an educational tool. Let's make sure everyone understands what quality means. But it would be a disaster for us to hire directors of quality, appoint a vice president of quality, and then move to a 'six-sigma' like system. Such a formalized system just can't work in a organization that emphasizes creativity." The AQM corporate director acknowledged that "we've met resistance in engineering. We're starting to be successful, but we still have to break through the mindset 'I'm creative; I don't need a process.'" Some employees were irritated by reading materials distributed in AQM classes that detailed TQM applications in other companies, protesting "we don't want to be like 'them.'" Some AQM classes were canceled because of low sign-up rates.

Apple Critical Performance Indicators

The fourth phase in implementing AQM—policy deployment—involved tying all the process improvement activities into the company's long term objectives. In order to make process improvements in areas that truly impacted Apple, the EMT set goals and measurements around five Apple Critical Performance Indicators (ACPIs): employee alignment and commitment, core competencies, shareholder value, market share, and customer satisfaction. The EMT then put together cross-functional teams to establish these metrics in each of the 16 divisions. For example, shareholder value was being integrated into the business plan, put into the compensation system, and measured on how it impacted the bottom line (see **Exhibit 18–8**). An executive noted that "this is radically different from two years ago." Spindler added that "metrics don't take away intuition. ACPIs just add another dimension of managing the company that is more fact-based."

Shareholder value was one of the first ACPIs to be integrated into Apple's operations. The EMT began broad training through Apple University of operating and planning managers in early 1992 to incorporate a shareholder value framework into decision-making processes. Maximizing shareholder value was included as an important goal in the 1993 business plan, and executive compensation was based on shareholder value-creating behavior.

ACPIs were being written into the performance reviews and bonuses of many divisions in 1992, as Spindler strove to have everyone measured against them by 1994. ACPIs were anchored in the performance criteria of Spindler's direct reports, in terms specifically relating to his/her job. Spindler noted that 50% of his compensation in 1993 depended upon the execution of ACPIs. For example, when the company did not meet its shareholder value goal in 1992, Spindler and other senior and middle managers did not receive that portion of their bonus. In Worldwide Operations, quality improvement goals were decided as a team. One engineer explained, "The whole group said, 'This is what our customer needs; this is what we're going to do to get there. Here's our target; that's what we're going to get bonuses against.'"

The debate on ACPIs was how far down should management push this system into the organization. A manager who worked for Spindler noted, "ACPIs are fine for Spindler and they're fine for me, but what about my direct reports? And that person's direct reports? Does it make sense for someone three or four levels down in the organization to be rewarded on shareholder value, even though they have little ability to impact the share price directly? If we are not careful at Apple, we will move from a company that clearly lacked adequate systems to a big bureaucracy that tries to measure everything."

Further reorganization

In order to better align Apple's operational execution, the EMT added a market-based overlay to the way they planned and managed Apple. Agreeing that a generic approach to reaching customers had become outdated, they focused on four key markets: K-12 education; institutional

Exhibit 18-8 Example of Deployment of an Apple Critical Performance Indicator

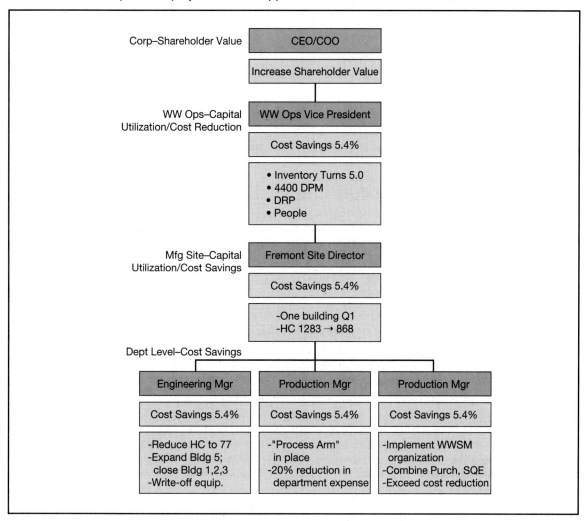

Source: Company documents.

such as the government, large businesses, and higher education; consumers; and small and medium businesses. Spindler explained the intent at an employee communications meeting:

> Most PC companies in the 1970s were organized around territories. That isn't necessarily the right model for the 1990s. We have to get much closer to the customer. . . . Our most important U.S. franchise is K-12, in which we have a 60% market share. We have people in front of the customer, understanding what they want and using a channel which helps us to sell to them. We'd like to do this in other markets. So we're restructuring organizations that deal with the consumer market and crafting chan-

nels that help us get to the user, not the other way around. We can't be held hostage by the channel in place. . . .

When asked at an employee communications meeting in May if he was satisfied with the pace of progress in the Apple USA reorganization, Spindler responded that he was not. Sculley added that they had to develop new market segments faster, and align with the right channels in these markets earlier than the competition. For example, every computer company except Apple offered mail order in May 1992. In addition, Apple was moving into mass merchandiser channels, but it was late. "So," Sculley stressed, "we must get even more aggressive in opening up these markets and channels and realigning peo- ple because the only way our business proposition works is if we can get high growth. So we have to go faster."

Leading the Next Generation

Sculley knew that Apple was venturing into uncharted territories. There was a lot to implement, given scarce resources, perishable technology, lack of management benchstrength, and a culture that resisted greater use of systems. Yet he knew that Apple's success would depend upon how they resolved these issues. It was one thing to run a startup with creative people doing creative things. But Apple was now a $7 billion business exploring multiple markets with multiple technologies.

As Sculley reflected on Apple's situation in the summer of 1992, he commented:

> We have done an extraordinary job in the last two years. Our gains in marketshare, profitability, etc. are more than anyone should have expected. But we are in such a tough industry, I am constantly worried about how to maintain the level of performance. Everyone in the company is feeling pressure that we are cutting their funding. But I think we have to move faster and change faster. We can cut more expenses out of the organization. I also think it is better to get people to work harder rather than cutting out projects. There is deep resistance within

management to cutting resources in the Macintosh division. But if we can rebalance our resources—put more money into the new technologies, we could be one of the dominant technology companies in the world by the end of the decade. I think that as early as the second half of 1993, the results will be clear to the employees and the financial markets. In some ways we have a great dilemma—we have more great technology than we can turn into great products than anyone in the world.

> What I have learned in the last ten years is that I should have been involved in the technology [as CTO] much earlier; we should have moved much faster to gain market share and become a more open systems computer company; and we should have exploited more aggressively our broad technology base in software, networking, imaging, and user-interface. In the coming years, I want to move Apple in the direction of corporations like Pepsi, where you can have an aggressive firm with deep management, flexible systems and a great deal of autonomy across diverse divisions. As we go forward, I would like the EMT to become more of a portfolio manager and create the same kind of depth, breadth, and professionalism at Apple.

Appendix: The Evolving Personal Computer Industry 1976–1992[7]

In some ways, the personal computer was a very simple device. Most PCs were composed of five, widely available components: memory storage, a microprocessor (the brains of the PC), a main circuit board called a mother board, a disc drive and peripherals (e.g., display, keyboard, mouse, printer, etc.). Most manufacturers also bundled their PC hardware with critical software packages, especially an operating system (the software required to run applications). But from the beginning, PCs have been available in almost infinite variety. They could vary in speed, storage, physical size, weight, functionality, and so on.

During the early years of the industry, venture capital in the United States encouraged the entry of new firms, which offered products in every conceivable shape and size. By 1980, new entrants flooded the market, promoting distinct standards and unique technical features. Virtually every firm had a different configuration of hardware and software, making communication or sharing applications between machines virtu-

[7]This Appendix is drawn from "Apple Computer 1992," HBS Case No. 782-081.

ally impossible. The first PCs introduced by Commodore and Apple had relatively little speed or memory. However, even these early computers allowed managers to perform tasks that were either very time consuming or reserved for expensive ($50,000 to >$1 million), multi-user mini and mainframe computers. For under $5,000, anyone could now do spreadsheet analysis and word processing.

Before IBM entered the market in 1981, most products were considered "closed" or proprietary systems. A closed system, like mainframes, minicomputers, and Apple's PCs, could not be copied or cloned because it was protected by patents or copyrights. However, closed systems typically rendered the computer incompatible with competitor's products. IBM's entry in 1981 changed the playing field by offering an "open" system. IBM released the specifications of its PC, allowing independent hardware companies to make compatible machines and independent software vendors (ISVs) to write applications that would run on different brands. Open systems had a big advantage for customers because they were no longer locked into a particular vendor's product, and they could mix and match hardware and software from different competitors to get the lowest system price. And as long as manufacturers could buy the key components, particularly Microsoft's DOS (disk operating system) and Intel's X86 family of microprocessors, they could manufacture a product which could piggy back on IBM's coattails. Between 1982 and 1986, the majority of the industry consolidated around IBM's MS-DOS/Intel X86 microprocessor standard. Among the various proprietary PC systems, which had included names like DEC, Xerox and Wang, only Apple thrived.

Although IBM had created an open system which fostered imitators, few firms were capable of competing head-to-head with IBM. On the strength of its brand name and product quality, IBM captured almost 70% of the Fortune 1000 business market during its first four years. In addition, the personal computer was still a relatively new machine through the mid-1980s, and users were uncertain about quality, compatibility, service, and reliability. Concerns over the bankruptcies of companies, like Osborne and Leading Edge, as well as the occasional incompatible machine, led the majority of corporate buyers to buy brand name computers through respected, high service retail channels, such as ComputerLand. Most retailers, however, only had space on their shelves for four or five major brands. In the mid-1980s, the typical retailer carried three core, premium brands: Apple, which was the leader in user-friendliness and applications like desktop publishing; IBM, which was the premium priced, industry standard; and Compaq, which built IBM compatible machines with a strong reputation for quality and high performance. The multitude of smaller clone companies had to compete for the remaining one or two spaces on the retailer's shelf.

The early growth in PCs was built partly on rapidly changing innovative hardware and partly on exciting software applications. In its first five years, IBM and compatibles went through four major hardware product generations—the PC (based on Intel 8088), PC XT (based on 8086 and a hard drive), PC AT (based on Intel 80286), and 80386 PCs; in the meantime, Apple went from the Apple II to Macintosh—a major breakthrough in user-friendliness and functionality. The PC explosion was also fueled by software applications. Programs like Lotus 1-2-3 and WordPerfect were nicknamed "killer apps" because they were so powerful compared to their predecessors, everyone wanted them. Most of the best programs for business applications were written for the IBM standard, while Apple dominated educational applications and graphics.

The late 1980s saw revolution turn into evolution in both hardware and software. On one front, IBM faltered, losing almost half its market share. A new generation of PC clones manufacturers such as Dell and Gateway stole share, particularly when most customers found they could no longer distinguish between low priced and premium brands. The most significant shift was that the greatest differentiation in the industry had been between standards—IBM versus Apple. However, when Microsoft introduced its "Windows" 3.0 graphical user interface in 1990, the differences in user-friendliness between IBM machines and Macs narrowed significantly.

By 1992, the personal computer was a $50 billion hardware business, with another $30 billion in software and peripherals. The installed base of PCs approached 100 million units. However, the business had changed from a high growth industry to an industry with a few high growth segments. In addition, cutthroat pricing was the rule in the mainstream products. New products, like notebook computers, and traditional products sold through new channels, like direct mail, continued to sell at double digit growth rates. But fierce competition was driving down margins for leaders and followers alike.

19. Bill Gates and the Management of Microsoft

Despite the fact that we've been successful financially, there's an ongoing need to anticipate where this industry is going, and to be at the forefront of changing the products. And this is every bit as challenging as it's ever been—and perhaps more so.

BILL GATES, MICROSOFT CHAIRMAN AND CEO, 1991

On June 30, 1991, Microsoft Corporation closed the books on another year of dazzling growth. Revenues for the Redmond, Washington, software developer surpassed $1.8 billion, up 56% from the previous year, and ten times the level of 1986 (see **Exhibit 19–1**). Profitability remained exceptionally high, with net income reaching $463 million, 25% of revenues (see **Exhibit 19–2**).

The founder and chief executive of this company was 35-year-old William H. (Bill) Gates III, arguably the most influential person in the computer industry. He was also one of the wealthiest Americans, owning 30% of Microsoft stock with a market value of $4 billion. Under Gates' leadership, Microsoft had successfully navigated the transition from a start-up firm to a major corporation. The dominant supplier of personal computer (PC) operating system software during the 1980s, Microsoft had by the end of the decade surpassed such competitors as Lotus Development Corporation in sales of applications software. The release in 1990 of Windows 3.0, which enabled applica-

tions programs to work together in a user-friendly graphics environment, had been a spectacular success, selling over three million copies in its first year. Microsoft's success was reflected in a stock price of 30 times earnings, well above the industry average. Adjusting for splits, the stock price had increased by a factor of 20 since the company went public in 1986 (see **Exhibit 19–3**).

Looking ahead, however, Microsoft confronted a fresh set of challenges. It had expanded into new areas, including networking and consulting, and faced increasingly strong competition from a growing number of firms. Product development was becoming more complex, and demanded an integrated approach that was not part of the company's tradition. In addition, Microsoft's sheer growth imposed a number of organizational and managerial challenges. As Gates and his top management team developed their strategy for the 1990s, they recognized that further transitions would be necessary to ensure continuing success.

Assistant Professor Philip M. Rosenzweig prepared this case as the basis for class discussion rather than to illustrate either effective or ineffective handling of an administrative situation.

Microsoft: The Early Days

Bill Gates was the middle child of a prominent Seattle family. As a boy he attended the Lakeside School, where he was introduced to computers. Along with several other classmates, including Paul Allen, Gates spent many free hours and evenings learning about computing and programming. By the time Gates was 14, he and Allen had developed an expertise as programmers, and had formed their own company.

In 1973, Gates began his college studies at Harvard. The next year, Paul Allen moved to the Boston area and took a job with Honeywell. Both were convinced that huge opportunities lay ahead in the computer industry and they looked for an opportunity to which they could apply their programming talents. The right opportunity soon materialized. Stopping at a newsstand in Harvard Square in the autumn of 1974, Allen spotted the current issue of *Popular Electronics* with a headline trumpeting the "World's First Microcomputer Kit." The machine was the Altair 8080, marketed by a small company called MITS, with a price tag of $397. Built around an Intel 8080 microprocessor, the Altair was little more than a set of boards and switches. It came with neither a screen nor a keyboard, and contained only 256 bytes of memory, expandable to 4K. A further limitation was that the Altair could be programmed only in the complex 8080 machine level language. A first step toward making the Altair usable was to provide it with a programming language.

Excited by the opportunity, Gates and Allen threw their energies into the development of a BASIC language for the Altair, no small challenge given the 4K memory constraint. After long days and nights of programming, they accomplished their goal, and licensed the resulting program to MITS. A few months later, Allen moved to New Mexico to work more closely with MITS, and Gates followed the next year, abandoning his studies at Harvard.

Gates and Allen recognized that the Altair was only the beginning in a computing revolution. Intel's 8080 was a considerable improvement over its predecessor, the 8008, but was only one of many steps in the ongoing improvement of semiconductor technology. Integrated circuits were growing exponentially in power and were simultaneously dropping in price. If that trend continued, Gates and Allen reasoned, at some point in the future computers would be infinitely powerful and would cost nothing. And if computer hardware were available to everyone, then computer software would become the scarce resource. Rather than focus on building hardware, as their

Exhibit 19-1 Employee and Revenue Growth at Microsoft Corporation, 1975-1991

Year	Employees	Revenues ($000)	Net Income ($000)
1975	3	16	N/A
1976	7	22	N/A
1977	9	382	N/A
1978	13	1,356	N/A
1979	28	2,390	N/A
1980	38	8,000*	N/A
1981	130	16,000*	N/A
1982	220	24,486	3,507
1983	476	50,065	6,487
1984	778	97,479	15,880
1985	1,001	140,417	24,101
1986	1,442	197,514	39,254
1987	2,258	345,890	71,878
1988	2,793	590,827	123,908
1989	4,037	803,530	170,538
1990	5,635	1,183,446	279,186
1991	8,226	1,843,432	462,743

*approximate figure.

Source: Microsoft Corporation.

peers at Apple were doing, Gates and Allen decided to devote themselves to developing software. In 1975, Microsoft was created as a partnership, with Gates owning 60% to Allen's 40%, reflecting Gates' greater share of the development of BASIC.

For the next three years, Gates and Allen lived in Albuquerque and developed other languages for the 8080, including FORTRAN and COBOL. Along the way, they hired a few additional programmers. In 1977 Microsoft developed BASIC for Tandy's TRS-80 computer, and also licensed a version of BASIC for the a new personal computer called the Apple II. Two years later, with sales continuing to grow and the company expanding in size, Microsoft moved its operations from New Mexico and set up shop in an office building in Bellevue, Washington, near Seattle. By 1980 the firm had 38 employees and revenues of $8 million. In addition to his duties as a programmer, Gates took responsibility for marketing and negotiations. Sensing a need to bolster the company's management, he contacted a friend from Harvard days, Steve Ballmer, and for a 6% stake in the company brought him aboard as assistant to the president. In time, Ballmer became indispensable to Gates as a sounding board, marketing expert, and co-leader.

In 1980, IBM began to develop its own personal computer and needed an operating system. It contacted a number of software firms and, not wanting to rely on a single operating system, chose three. Among them was Microsoft's entry, called MS-DOS (Microsoft Disk Operating System). Because the success of an operating system depended on the popularity of applications programs that used it, Gates worked feverishly over the next several months with independent software firms, urging, prodding, and cajoling them to develop a family of products that would run on MS-DOS. The effort paid off—MS-DOS became the most popular operating system and eventually the de facto industry standard. "Believe me, it was not IBM who made MS-DOS the standard," Gates asserted. "It was up to us to get people to focus their development on it, and to get other PC manufacturers to license it." Soon every IBM PC and IBM-compatible PC was sold with MS-DOS, bringing a steady flow of royalties to Microsoft. By 1990, there were more than 70 million users of MS-DOS PCs worldwide.

During the early 1980s Microsoft consisted of a small band of bright young software developers. The prevailing credo, according to one longtime employee, was "reverence for the developer." The tone at Microsoft reflected the qualities of its leader: self-assured, energetic, creative, and intense. The atmosphere was informal but harddriving, passionate about software development, and highly competitive. Employees worked long hours, often staying overnight developing key products. Their drive was based on a love of the product, not on projections that Microsoft would one day make them wealthy. Salaries were modest, and as revenues grew, there was a need to let employees earn shares of the company. As a partnership, Microsoft could not easily distribute shares, and in 1981 Microsoft incorporated, with Bill Gates the Chairman and CEO. Paul Allen held the largest number of shares after Gates, and continued to work actively in programming until 1983, when he was diagnosed with Hodgkin's disease and took a leave of absence from the company.

Looking back on those early days, one veteran employee remembered, "When I joined Microsoft in 1981, we used to argue about whether there could ever be a $100 million PC software company. It didn't seem possible at the time." But Gates never doubted the potential market for PC software. He predicted publicly in 1981 that Microsoft would surpass $100 million in revenues by 1985. In fact, 1985 revenues reached $140 million.

Building Management Systems

By 1982, Microsoft had 220 employees and revenues of $24 million. Expanding beyond operating systems software, which controlled the inner working of the computer, the firm introduced its first applications software product: Microsoft Multiplan electronic worksheet. But the firm was reaching the limits of its administrative capacity. Microsoft needed more than brilliant software developers—it also needed management processes to handle the growing administrative, financial, and logistical duties. "When Bill realized we had crossed a certain point," one employee recalled, "he knew he needed professional managers."

In July of 1982, Gates hired James F. Towne, an experienced manager at Tektronix,

Exhibit 19-2A Microsoft Corporation Income Statement, 1986-1991 ($ millions)

	1991		1990		1989		1988		1987		1986	
Net Revenues	$1,843	100%	$1,183	100%	$803	100%	$591	100%	$346	100%	$197	100%
Cost of Revenues	363	20	253	21	204	25	148	25	74	21	41	21
Research and Development	235	13	181	15	110	14	70	12	38	11	21	11
Sales & Marketing	534	29	318	27	219	27	161	27	85	25	58	29
General & Administration	62	3	39	3	28	3	24	4	22	6	18	9
Operating Income	$650	35	$393	33	$242	30	$187	32	$127	37	$61	31
Non-Operating Income	21		23		17		11		9		5	
Stock Option Program Expense			(6)		(8)		(14)		(14)			
Income Before Taxes	671	36	411	35	251	31	184	31	121	35	66	34
Provision for Taxes	208	11	131	11	80	10	60	10	49	14	27	14
Net Income	$463	25%	$279	24%	$171	21%	$124	21%	$72	21%	$39	20%

Source: Microsoft Corporation Annual Report.

Exhibit 19-2B Microsoft Corporation Balance Sheet, 1986-1991 ($ millions)

	1991	1990	1989	1988	1987	1986
ASSETS						
Current Assets						
Cash & Short-term Investments	$ 686.3	$449.2	$300.8	$183.2	$132.5	$102.7
Accounts Receivable	243.3	181.0	111.2	93.6	55.1	34.5
Inventory	47.1	55.6	37.8	53.5	16.6	8.0
Other	51.8	34.1	19.2	15.0	8.8	2.8
Total Current Assets	$1,028.5	$719.9	$468.9	$345.3	$213.0	$148.0
Property, Plant, & Equipment	530.2	325.4	198.8	130.1	70.0	19.5
Other Assets	85.5	60.0	52.8	17.6	4.7	3.2
Total Assets	$1,644.2	$1,105.3	$720.6	$493.0	$287.8	$170.7
LIABILITIES & SHAREHOLDERS' EQUITY						
Current Liabilities						
Accounts Payable	85.9	51.0	42.0	43.1	20.5	9.7
Customer Deposits	25.7	17.2	10.0	6.0	6.3	7.0
Accrued Compensation	41.6	28.8	25.7	15.1	5.1	1.3
Notes Payable	19.5	6.5	25.4	20.3	5.2	--
Income Tax Payable	44.4	42.6	30.3	16.1	2.2	7.5
Other	76.2	40.8	25.4	17.0	9.3	5.9
Total Current Liabilities	$293.4	$186.8	$158.8	$117.5	$48.6	$31.4
Stockholders Equity	394.5	219.5	110.5	90.0	76.8	50.8
Retained Earnings	956.3	688.9	455.6	285.0	161.1	89.2
Translation Adjustment	0.0	10.2	(4.3)	0.3	1.1	(0.7)
Total Stockholders Equity	$1,350.8	$918.6	$561.8	$375.5	$239.1	$139.3
Total Liabilities & Stockholders Equity	$1,644.2	$1,105.3	$720.6	$493.0	$287.8	$170.7

Source: Microsoft Corporation Annual Report.

Inc., as Microsoft's president and chief operating officer (COO). The relationship between Gates and Towne did not work well, in part because Gates was very product-oriented and found it difficult to communicate with an executive from a different industry. Within a year Gates decided that a change had to be made, and Towne resigned. As a replacement, Gates chose Jon Shirley, a 25-year veteran of Tandy and at the time its vice president of Computer Merchandising. Gates had known Shirley for years, as Tandy had been a retail outlet for Microsoft products. Among his peers, Shirley was regarded as "the ultimate businessman": professional in manner and experienced in running a business.

Jeff Raikes, a veteran software developer, recalled:

> Bill always had a high degree of respect for Jon. Jon was someone who loved computer products, but he also had knowledge of marketing, of finance, and of the computer industry. Plus, Jon was a known quantity, and it was extremely important for Bill to hire a known quantity at that time. What if Bill had made a mistake with a second COO? Would he ever have had the confidence to get a third COO?

Hiring Jon Shirley turned out to be an excellent choice. Industry watcher Stewart Alsop noted: "As you watch how Microsoft has developed, what you see is Gates realizing well in ad-

Exhibit 19-3 Growth of Microsoft Corporation Share Price, 1986 - 1991 (Source: Compiled from Interactive Data Corporation.)

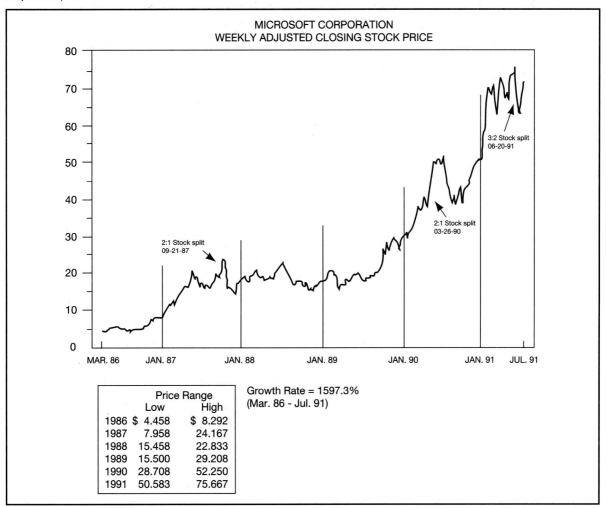

MICROSOFT CORPORATION
WEEKLY ADJUSTED CLOSING STOCK PRICE

2:1 Stock split 09-21-87
2:1 Stock split 03-26-90
3:2 Stock split 06-20-91

	Price Range	
---	Low	High
1986	$ 4.458	$ 8.292
1987	7.958	24.167
1988	15.458	22.833
1989	15.500	29.208
1990	28.708	52.250
1991	50.583	75.667

Growth Rate = 1597.3%
(Mar. 86 - Jul. 91)

vance what he's not good at and finding exactly the right person to do the job. [When Towne left] Gates went out and hired Jon Shirley. And he was absolutely the right guy. . . . The process of identifying the mistake, figuring out the problem, and fixing it, is what makes Bill Gates different. I've seen him do it over and over again."

When Shirley joined Microsoft in 1983, he found little of the infrastructure needed to run a $50 million business. Corporate accounting was handled on an outdated Radio Shack PC. Orders were entered on a time-share system based in San Francisco that was frequently inaccessible. The manufacturing operation was little more than a parts warehouse from which work was subcontracted.

"I was hired to give Bill more time, to take things he worried about off his back," Shirley recalled. Leaving Gates to focus on the technical side of Microsoft, Shirley set about building the financial, manufacturing, and human resources systems. One of his first moves was to hire Frank Gaudette as Microsoft's first chief financial officer (CFO). Gaudette put in place a managerial accounting system that tracked revenues and expenses by each product and each sales channel, providing exceptional visibility for decision making. It also extended profit and loss responsibility to as many managers as possible, and was flexible enough to accommodate a rapidly growing company. "One of the smartest things Bill ever did was bring in business people and let them do their thing," Gaudette remarked.

Microsoft's compensation policy continued to emphasize employee participation in the company's fortunes. In addition to salaries, which were somewhat below industry levels, new employees received a sizable stock grant that vested fully over four and a half years. After three years, employees were considered for an additional stock grant. While some prospective employees were reluctant to accept a lower salary than available elsewhere, others found the principle of participating in the firm's growth to their liking.

By 1985, Microsoft employees numbered over 1,000. Gaudette remembered:

> Shortly after I got here, Bill said to me: "Frank, I don't know everybody's name any more." He acted like that was bad. I said: "Bill, we can make it small again if that's what you really want."

Despite its surging growth, Microsoft tried to retain the feel of a small firm. Once a year, all Microsoft employees came together for a presentation from top management. At Christmas time, employees gathered for a holiday party; in the summer, they held picnics. Many employees cited the extensive use of electronic (e-) mail as an important element of direct and open communication: employees used e-mail to communicate directly to Gates and Shirley on a variety of issues, and typically received answers quickly and personally.

But Microsoft's informal manner belied its intense atmosphere. "The Microsoft style is pretty aggressive," remarked one manager. "People jump on each other all the time—but it's not personal. It's a challenging, aggressive style." Stories abounded of combative meetings and "yelling matches" between groups of software developers, each advocating features for coming products. Critical e-mail messages, often sarcastic or sharp in tone, were known around the company as "flame mail."

Young Developers, Experienced Managers

"We're in the intellectual property business," Gates remarked. "It's the effectiveness of developers that determines our success." Because of the constant need to develop new and better products, hiring top talent and quickly bringing their contributions on-line was a top priority. Gates described Microsoft's approach:

> We've always had the most aggressive approach of any software company in finding people with high IQs and bringing them in. We wanted to be known as *the* software company that knew how to take people right out of college and turn talent and energy into a good development engineer. That was very explicit. We also pushed to the absolute limit the number of smart people that we brought in from overseas. It was also explicit that we design a development methodology that was not dependent on a few prima donnas, but that could make use of many people's talent.

Steve Ballmer took a leadership role in college recruiting, seeking out bright graduates with high aptitude for problem solving under pressure. In contrast to its practice of hiring software developers out of college, Microsoft often sought for key managerial positions people with significant industry experience. In addition to Shirley and Gaudette, key managers in marketing and international positions had substantial experience. "Although the software industry was new, and we were creating the rules," Gates recalled, "we found that the business experience these people had was very valuable."

Software Development

As the company grew, Gates remained in charge of product development, overseeing directly the development of systems software and applications soft ware. He was a demanding manager, with strong ideas about the future of personal computing and about specific features of new products. Product review meetings with Gates, known as "Bill meetings," were legendary, characterized by sharp and relentless questioning, stinging criticism, and ambitious deadlines. But along with a reputation for being abrupt and hard-driving, Gates was also described by a long-time software developer as attentive to individual needs:

> Bill is not a nerd like some people think. He can be very attuned to personal issues. He can go in and pump you up and make you feel that you're handling a really great mission for the company. There's great attention to keeping people happy.

Unlike its early language products, such as BASIC, and its operating system, MS-DOS, several of Microsoft's products were not immediately successful. Its first applications program, Multiplan, was intended to overtake the popular spreadsheet, VisiCalc, but was soon overtaken by an even stronger program, Lotus Development Corporation's popular 1-2-3, and registered disappointing sales. In 1983, Microsoft began to focus on graphics user interface, a system by which users could interact easily with computers. In 1985, after lengthy delays in development, Microsoft introduced Windows, a graphics-based operating environment that ran on MS-DOS and allowed users to run several programs at the same time. Windows used drop-down menus and icons that gave users visually-oriented tools for easy interaction with their computers. The first version of Windows, however, was slow and had poor graphics, and met with only limited success. In subsequent years, new versions of operating systems and applications products were released with improved features and greater efficiency.

During the mid-1980s, Microsoft released updated versions of MS-DOS, along with applications software products including Excel (spreadsheet), Word (word processing), and Works (multi-purpose software). Microsoft products were sold through two channels: original equipment manufacturer (OEMs) and retailers. The OEM channel comprised computer manufacturers who bundled Microsoft operating systems with their products. OEM sales provided Microsoft with a steady flow of royalty income. The retail channel consisted of stores that stocked their shelves with applications programs, such as spread sheets and word processing programs. The mix of revenues among these channels reflected an increasing reliance on applications (see **Exhibits 19–4** and **19–5**), which reached 48% in 1990. In addition, Microsoft had aggressively established subsidiaries abroad in the early 1980s, and by 1989 foreign sales exceeded U.S. sales.

By 1988, Microsoft had overtaken major competitors such as Lotus Development Corp., VisiCorp, MicroPro, and Ashton-Tate to become the market leader in PC applications software as well as operating systems software (see **Exhibit 19–6**). While its spreadsheet program, Excel, remained second to Lotus 1-2-3, and its word processing program, Word, ranked second to WordPerfect, Microsoft was in first place overall. Gates credited Microsoft's success to its commitment to graphics user interface and to its efficient development process.

Management Accounting

Microsoft's philosophy of personal responsibility was reinforced by a management accounting system in which, as CFO Frank Gaudette stressed, "Everyone has a profit and loss statement." Under this system, all revenues and costs, identified by product and by sales channel, were fed into a single, consolidated ledger. This data base was then exploded into many P/L statements, each focusing on a particular business unit, marketing channel, or geographic area. Every Business Unit Manager, Channel Manager, and Foreign Subsidiary Man-

Exhibit 19-4 Microsoft Corporation Software and Hardware Products, 1989 (Partial Listing)

	Operating System	
	MS-DOS	Apple Macintosh
Business application software		
Microsoft Chart	X	X
Microsoft Excel	X	X
Microsoft File		X
Microsoft Learning DOS	X	
Microsoft Mail	X	X
Microsoft Multiplan®	X	X
Microsoft Powerpoint®		X
Microsoft Project	X	
Microsoft Word	X	X
Microsoft Works	X	X
Microsoft Write		X
The Microsoft Office		X
Systems/Languages software		
Microsoft BASIC	X	
Microsoft C	X	
Microsoft COBOL	X	
Microsoft FORTRAN	X	
Microsoft Macro Assembler	X	
Microsoft Pascal	X	
Microsoft QuickBASIC	X	X
Microsoft QuickC Compiler	X	
Microsoft QuickC Compiler with Quick Assembler	X	
Microsoft QuickPascal	X	
Microsoft Windows/286	X	
Microsoft Windows/386	X	
Hardware, Recreation, and CD-ROM products		
Microsoft Mouse	X	
Microsoft Flight Simulator	X	X
Microsoft Bookshelf (CD-ROM)	X	
Microsoft Programmer's Library (CD-ROM)	X	
Microsoft Small Business Consultant (CD-ROM)	X	
Microsoft Stat Pack (CD-ROM)	X	

Source: Microsoft Corporation 1989 Annual Report.

ager had a profit and loss statement which revealed his or her contribution to Microsoft's bottom line. For example, the sale of an Excel spreadsheet through the retail channel would appear as revenue in two places: the Analysis Business Unit and the retail channel. The same held for the OEM sales of MS-DOS in Germany: both the Systems Business Unit and the German subsidiary recorded the sale as revenue, from which each deducted its controllable and allocated costs to determine its contribution to Microsoft profits.

Microsoft's largest discretionary cost was for marketing, and was controlled according to a strict formula: 12% of targeted revenues were budgeted for marketing expenses, with occasional exceptions made for major product introductions, variations across countries, or for opportunities to gain market share. The marketing budget was divided between product marketing (roughly 60%) and channel marketing (roughly 40%). Expenses were monitored closely, with managers responsible not only for meeting profitability targets but also for meeting each line item of expense. Actual sales and expense figures could be reviewed via an on-line system, which displayed results according to product, channel, and geographic region. Frank Gaudette provided a monthly review of financial results for the Board, which also met quarterly to review Microsoft's financial performance. Although Gates left the analysis of week-to-week financial results to others, he examined monthly and quarterly results in detail. "At the quarterly meetings," said Gaudette, "Bill zeroes in on everything."

Exhibit 19-5 Distribution of Revenues by Product, Channel, and Region, 1986-1990

	1990	1989	1988	1987	1986
Revenue by Product Group					
Systems/Languages	39%	44%	47%	49%	53%
Applications	48	42	40	38	37
Hardware, Books, Other	<u>13</u>	<u>14</u>	<u>13</u>	<u>13</u>	<u>10</u>
Total	100%	100%	100%	100%	100%
Revenue by Channel					
Domestic OEM	13%	14%	17%	21%	25%
Domestic Retail	<u>30</u>	<u>29</u>	<u>32</u>	<u>35</u>	<u>32</u>
	43%	43%	49%	56%	57%
International OEM	13%	18%	14%	14%	21%
International Finished Goods	<u>42</u>	<u>37</u>	<u>34</u>	<u>28</u>	<u>19</u>
	55%	55%	48%	42%	40%
Microsoft Press & Other	2	2	2	2	3
Total	100%	100%	100%	100%	100%

General Management in 1991

In 1990, Jon Shirley retired after seven years as Microsoft president and COO. At 52 years of age, and with more than one million shares of Microsoft stock, Shirley decided to trade in the long hours at Microsoft for a less consuming schedule. He expressed his desire to retire in 1989, giving the Microsoft board one year to find a replacement. Following an extensive search, the Microsoft board selected Michael R. Hallman, a 20-year veteran of IBM and president of Boeing Computer at the time. Hallman's experience with Boeing made him especially well-qualified as Microsoft increasingly relied on sales to corporate customers.

Hallman inherited a much different company from the one Shirley had encountered seven years earlier. Whereas Shirley had imposed management controls on the growing business, Hallman found that he had to scale back certain controls:

> When I got here, I found the president had to sign all employment requisitions, even for temporary employees. I was the fourth signature needed to approve a resignation! Once I asked what would happen if I didn't sign? Would we really hold the fellow hostage?
>
> The degree of centralized approval just wasn't sustainable as we got larger. Delegation was needed for two reasons: not only because it was too cumbersome to continue to centralize, but also to make sure that others were trained to take responsibility.

Gates and Hallman divided the responsibilities of general management. "If you look at the organization chart," said Gates, "you see that only the COO reports to me. But if there's a product strategy question, I'll be involved. I work more closely with Steve Ballmer and Mike Maples than Mike Hallman does." Hallman agreed: "Chief Operating Officer is the right title for my job. Bill Gates manages product development directly. I deal with technical projects only on an administrative basis." Hallman described his priorities as sales and marketing, including calling on major customers, and managing the operations. Gates and Hallman divided foreign reviews equally: each visited half the subsidiaries around the world one year, switching the following year to visit the other half.

By the summer of 1991, Microsoft employed more than 8,000 people, almost all of whom were located at the Microsoft "campus" on a large tract of wooded land in Redmond, 10 miles east of Seattle. Software development was concentrated in a series of contiguous buildings on the campus. Manufacturing plants were situated in nearby Bothel, WA, as well as in Puerto Rico and in Dublin, Ireland. Customer service and support were handled from three centers, two in the Seattle area and one, established in 1990, in North Carolina. Microsoft's 21 foreign subsidiaries were spread from Italy to India, from Argentina to Korea.

Microsoft's organization structure was split into two major divisions: product development and product sales (see **Exhibit 19–7**). Product development, in turn, was divided into systems software, run by Steve Ballmer, and applications software, headed by Mike Maples, a 23-year veteran of IBM who joined Microsoft in 1988. Manufacturing, logistics, finance, and human resources all reported to Frank Gaudette, senior vice president of administration and CFO. At the next level, product development was composed of nine Business Units, each responsible for a family of products, and run by a Business Unit Manager (BUM). The Business Units were organized functionally, with managers for Product Development, Testing, User Education, Program Management, and Product Marketing. Domestic sales and channel marketing were handled by the U.S. Sales and Marketing Division (USSMD), while foreign sales were the responsibility of the 21 foreign subsidiaries.

Managing Innovation and Product Development

Bill Gates worked out of a modern but unimposing office in Microsoft's executive suite. Five personal computers—usually switched on and running various programs—occupied desks and tabletops, making Gates' office look more like a software lab than the chairman's office in a $1.8 billion corporation. One large bookshelf was crammed end-to-end with software documentation. Another held biographies of scientists and business people, novels, and a half-dozen atlases. Over Gates' desk was the framed photo and autograph of another American industrial pioneer— Henry Ford.

Gates estimated that he spent half of his time on direct contact with major customers, industry relations, visits to subsidiaries, review meetings, and acting as ambassador for the company. He was known for having a "broad bandwidth"—company terminology for expertise in a

Exhibit 19-6 Microsoft Corporation Share of the PC Software Market (Source: Compiled from Softietter, Watertown, MA.)

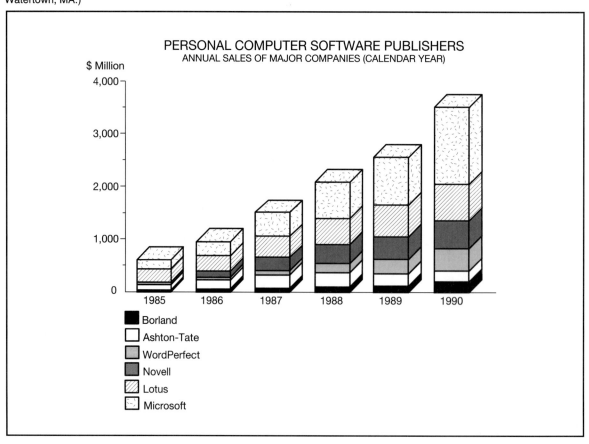

Exhibit 19-7 Microsoft Corporation, Partial Organization Chart, 1991

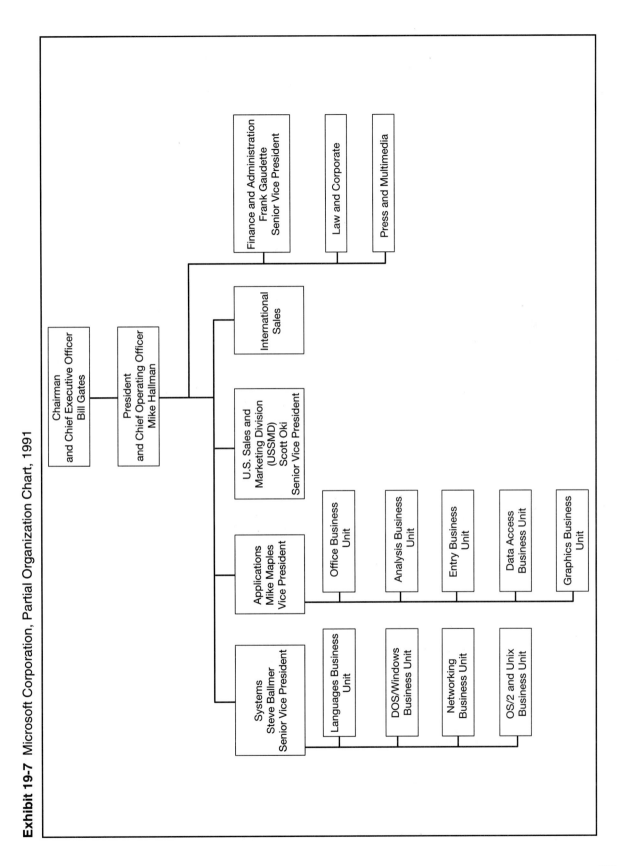

wide variety of issues, including legal, financial, administrative, and industry matters. "I'm very much the CEO," he noted. The other half of his time continued to be devoted to managing new product development.

As Gates described it: "My role is to set the product direction for the company." Starting with an idea for a new product—what it should do and when it should be released—Gates and his top managers worked backwards to determine the level of staffing and other resources required. Several top managers marvelled that major allocations did not require 100-person task forces or lengthy written reports. The key, according to one, was Gates' judgment: "Bill will not study an issue to death. Once Bill is convinced, he'll get his best brains together, and say, 'Let's do it.'"

For example, the development of Multimedia, which enabled personal computers to integrate information from a variety of forms—including text, sound, graphics, and video—was based on a simple conviction, according to one executive: "We decided four years ago that we would invest whatever it takes, irrespective of revenues." Similarly, perseverance in the development of Windows was due to Gates' unwavering confidence in the project.

Once the product direction had been set, Gates remained directly involved in many product development efforts, working with the top technical architects to make sure they shared a common vision. Six top software architects, possessing the highest ranking of "Level 15," reported directly to Gates. "I also make sure I spend time with the developers one notch down from that, the 14s," Gates added. Mike Maples concurred: "Bill knows the developers and he reviews all of their products. He likes to take part in arguments about product features. He challenges developers; he stretches them." Gates estimated that he knew more than 150 developers personally.

As the complexity of Microsoft programs grew, the demands for product development shifted. Mike Maples observed:

> Our applications products used to work on a stand-alone basis. They were like tools: you could make an electric drill, you could make a hammer, and you could make a saw, and put them on the same rack, but they were integrated by the user. What we're headed for is where the products have to work together.

The need for software products to work together required a change in Microsoft's approach toward product development. As one manager noted: "Our culture has been: 'I'm going to get a small band of guys and against all odds I'm going to build this great product.' "But as Microsoft products increasingly had to work together, product development required the simultaneous efforts of multiple teams. Most important was not excellence in individual design, but excellence in overall systems architecture. As a consequence, Gates assumed a central role in coordinating the efforts of development teams. At times, he determined the composition of development teams: "If I see that a group is having unexpected difficulties or is moving slowly, I might assign a 14 to join the group, determine the problem, and help out." At other times, Gates interceded directly in discussions among various development teams whose efforts were interdependent. One development team might point out that their program depended on a certain feature that a second team was developing, and that second team might, in turn, be dependent on a third team. Gates' approach was to say to each: "Don't worry about the others; I'll guarantee that they deliver their product with the right specifications at the right time. You just develop your piece and don't worry about the rest." This way, the various teams could work simultaneously rather than sequentially, speeding up the development process, and avoiding friction of having to negotiate with each other.

Going Forward: Microsoft in the 1990s

As Microsoft moved into the 1990s, several forces were changing the way it did business. Most notable were improvements in microprocessor technology, and the increasing sophistication of computer users. These trends were described in Microsoft's 1989 Annual Report:

> The role of the personal computer is changing.

"One person, one computer" was miracle enough just a few years ago. But as hardware evolves and the market grows, customers are beginning to realize that no computer is an island and that interconnections of business require that the tools of business be interconnected, too.

Microsoft's vision was always ambitious—the idea of "a computer on every desk" suggests that people will want to share information and ideas from one desktop machine to another. So it's no surprise that local area networks (LANs) are among the fastest-growing segments in the computer business.

Advances in the power of microprocessors meant that companies no longer linked "dumb" terminals to mainframe computers or minicomputers, but could place powerful PCs on every desktop. Increasingly they sought to link these PCs into corporate-wide networks. At the same time, improvement in computer power was matched by the growing sophistication of computer users. Corporations relied more and more on their information systems, of which Microsoft products were an increasingly vital part. Microsoft products no longer performed isolated functions for individual users, but were frequently essential to the customer's operations. In industry parlance, Microsoft products were often "mission critical." In response to these trends, Microsoft moved beyond PC operating systems and PC application software, and began to address the integrated computing needs of customers.

The 1990s: Strategic Challenges

In a memo to senior managers in May 1991, Gates reviewed the company's competitive position and outlined its strategic challenges. Some ongoing challenges included an FTC investigation and a pending lawsuit by Apple Computer, which alleged that Microsoft had improperly used the "look and feel" of the Macintosh. More significantly, the company faced growing competition on several fronts. In operating systems software, Microsoft's collaboration with IBM had ended and IBM was seeking to develop its own successor to MS-DOS. Novell, the leader in networking software, enjoyed a substantial headstart over Microsoft. Software firms like Borland, which acquired Ashton-Tate in July 1991, offered high quality applications programs at prices that undercut Microsoft. The combined effect of these competitive threats constituted a

serious challenge. If Microsoft could not maintain strength in these three areas, it risked losing its position of prominence.

Microsoft's response to these challenges rested on Windows. "Our strategy for the 1990s is Windows," Gates declared in his memo to managers. "Everything we do should focus on making Windows more successful." Despite Microsoft's record of growth, Gates recognized that continued success could not be taken for granted. He reflected:

> Growth isn't a given at all. I don't wake up in the morning and think, "Of course we're going to continue to grow, now let's think about how many employee picnics we should have this summer." I wake up and think, "What are we going to do to have better products to sell more software?" Growth isn't a given, it's a variable. And we're not going to continue growing unless we come up with some incredibly good products.

Developing "incredibly good products" depended, as always, on having top software talent. In addition to its ongoing college recruiting of entry-level software developers, Microsoft began to hire several senior software developers from other companies. "We've done real well at bringing strong technical people in," Gates allowed. "If you ask me what I'm most excited about today, it's the two senior developers we hired just recently."

Product Usability and Support

Another emerging challenge was posed by exploding product support costs, stimulated by the combination of hugely increasing numbers of Microsoft users and by the growing complexity of product features. Microsoft's Product Service and Support (PSS) group, which fielded phone calls from users, was finding it increasingly difficult to handle the volume of calls. By 1991, service and support costs had surpassed 5% of total revenues. These costs were allocated to the products according to their share of total revenue.

The size and rate of growth in support costs prompted much discussion in Microsoft's executive suite. Mike Hallman noted:

> Microsoft has been known for its products. We're not well known for our customer support. By 1995, I want Microsoft to be as well known for its customer

service and support as for its products. I want Microsoft to be the "Maytag repairman" of software.

The emphasis on reducing product support costs was one aspect of a larger emphasis on improved quality. As Microsoft dealt directly with customers, built mission critical applications, and grew in size, greater attention to quality in all phases of the operation—from product development to product support—was vital. Bill Gates agreed that software usability and support had received insufficient attention and urged that it become a top priority. Mike Hallman remarked:

> This whole issue of total quality and continuous improvement is critical. But we can't impose a campaign of Total Quality, with banners and everything, like they do at some other companies. Having a "Vice President of Total Quality" wouldn't work here.

Corporate Sales and Consulting

By 1991, Microsoft recognized that it had undergone a fundamental change in its relationship to customers. Hallman explained:

> Five years ago, we built operating systems that we sold through OEMs, and we never talked to end users. Then we developed applications which we sold through retail channels, and still we never talked to end users. It's only in the last two years that we've come to grips with the fact that, at least for large corporations, we are a strategic technology provider. We're on all of their PCs and operating systems, we're a key part of their applications strategy, and they often use our networking products.
>
> More than one company has come to us and said, "We're trying to identify our strategic technology partners and we list AT&T and IBM and Digital, yet we find we may have most dependency on you. How do we deal with you?"

Microsoft's emergence as a "strategic technology provider" made direct contact between Microsoft and its corporate customers very important and led to the creation, in 1990, of Microsoft Consulting Services. It was led by vice president Bob McDowell, who explained: "The customer says, 'If I'm going to bet part of the farm on this product, I'll need dedicated technical assistance. I get that kind of help from IBM—and I'll need it from Microsoft.'"

The growing importance of selling and consulting to corporations was indicative of a broader shift in Microsoft's activities. Many senior managers believed that future success depended on the ability to understand customer needs and to present Microsoft products as an integrated information systems solution. In McDowell's words, the traditional credo of "reverence for the developer" had to be matched by "reverence for the customer." Other managers, however, were concerned by Microsoft's shift away from the traditional emphasis on technical skills. As one software development manager observed:

> We have always been a technically driven company. What if our sales and support staffs keep growing at their present rates? Will we still be a technical company, with a small and elite technical corps, or will the technical people get overwhelmed?

Managing Growth: Organizational Issues

As it grappled with the new challenges of networking, consulting, and usability, Microsoft also faced the challenge of executing its traditional operations on a bigger scale. Top executives estimated that if Microsoft's Windows strategy continued to be successful, the company could reach $5 billion in sales and employ between 14,000 and 16,000 people by 1995. Such growth posed a set of internal challenges, quite apart from strategic and product development issues.

As Microsoft grew, its organizational subunits had become larger. The Office Business Unit, for example, had grown in revenues from $100 million in 1988 to $400 million in 1990. In an effort to retain the benefits of smaller organizations, Jeff Raikes, manager of the Office Business Unit, divided his unit into three subunits, each of which would be responsible for program management, project management, and so forth. Further subdivisions were anticipated, as well. Yet the desire to retain small working units ran headlong into the need to coordinate product development across organizational units. Mike Maples noted the conflict:

> I'm going to keep subdividing Business Units. I think that communication and development work

are so much more efficient—maybe by orders of magnitude—in small teams than in big teams. The question is: how do you make sure that these small teams share technology and experiences so that everything works together?

One solution was to establish linking mechanisms across subunits. Committees were established to agree on consistency in key issues, such as the use of direct marketing, approaches to the educational market, and the use of computer-based training. Furthermore, one employee in each functional area was designated a "director" and coordinated that function across the various Business Units, producing a kind of matrix. Thus, there was a director of Marketing, a director of Development, and a director of Program Management. Employees began serving as directors on a part-time basis, in addition to their regular job; in a few instances, however, where these responsibilities demanded full-time attention, the directorship became a full-time assignment which rotated among employees.

In addition, Gates noted the importance of focusing each Business Unit on the competitive task at hand. He observed:

> It's important to set the image of what competition means to us. It doesn't mean pricing our software very low, and it doesn't mean undermining our competitors. We have to make sure that's well understood. Competition to us means coming out with very innovative products.
>
> Each Business Unit is focused on its competition. We have a Spreadsheet Business Unit: they wake up every morning thinking about Lotus. We have a Word Processing Business Unit, they wake up thinking about WordPerfect. We have a Networking Business Unit and they wake up thinking about Novell. Those are very entrenched competitors, and we're going to have to develop far better products in order to dislodge them. We're not going to back off competing with them. There are other competitors that can write software well, like Borland, that would come along if we weren't pushing ourselves to the max.

Managing Growth: Hiring, Training, and Compensation

The prospect of doubling the number of employees in four years posed severe challenges in management development. By 1991, Microsoft's rapid growth meant that management slots were opening faster than employees could fill them. Existing employees were not gaining experience on the job quickly enough, and in sufficiently large numbers, to fill management openings internally. One executive commented: "We can't wait for the demographics to catch up with demand."

Microsoft responded by hiring more experienced people with specific skills. It also began to place concerted attention on employee development and training programs. Frank Gaudette asserted:

> We've got to keep training employees if they're going to grow. That's the only thing you can do when each person is doing the biggest job they've ever done.
>
> We have to create a part of our corporate culture that wasn't here in the early days. We need to agree that training, too, is part of our culture. When people talk about Microsoft, we want them to say, "Boy, they can train!"

At the same time, the company was considering a change in its compensation policy, moving to a more traditional reliance on salary, with stock grants somewhat less important in the future. Although managers remained optimistic about the growth potential of Microsoft stock, they recognized that it was not likely to continue growing twenty-fold in five years. Gaudette explained:

> The law of diminishing returns applies to us, too. There will have to be a shift in compensation—we'll have to get more traditional in the methodology. But the underlying philosophy in wage and salary administration will remain: we are a meritocracy. Compensation is always related to contribution.

Growth in the company workforce also forced managers to think about physical expansion. Many questioned whether a single site was practical if Microsoft grew to more than 14,000 employees. Some managers argued that a second site would allow Microsoft to tap a new labor market, but others countered that it would inevitably make coordination and integrated product development more difficult, and could further erode Microsoft's traditional small company feel.

Continuing growth also spelled changes for the work environment. E-mail threatened to smother top management; in 1991, Gates and Hallman were receiving up to 100 e-mail messages per day. Change was also evident in growing measures to ensure security. Top managers had been concerned about lax security for a number of years, but had been reluctant to impose stricter measures unilaterally. Frank Gaudette recalled:

When I got here in the mid-1980s, asking employees to wear a badge would have been considered "Big Brother"-ism. But over time, it was the software developers, who had always been against rules, who said, "We've got all this valuable software lying around where anyone can walk in and see it—we better get this stuff locked up!"

After much discussion, a security system was installed, and employees were given picture-badges with magnetic strips that allowed them entry to specific buildings. Wearing a badge remained optional during working hours, but was mandatory after-hours and on weekends. "Where we have become more bureaucratic," Gaudette explained, "it's because employees determined it was the right thing to do, and not because some executive decided it was the right thing to do."

The combined effect of these changes engendered concern among several managers. A human resources manager noted: "Some companies are concerned about cultural change. My biggest mission here is 'culture keep'—how to keep what's good about the company alive and well." A vice president commented:

In a small company you can lead by example. But as the newer hires become farther and farther re-moved from the old-timers, how do they pick up the company's values? How do they see that the extra weekend they work, or the good idea they have, really makes a difference in a $5 billion company? How do they develop that commitment to be successful?

Looking Ahead

In the summer of 1991, Microsoft could look back on a 16-year history of remarkable technical and financial achievement. Its growth and consistently high profits bore witness to a successful transition from start-up company to major corporation. Going forward, Gates had enunciated a clear strategic vision for the company in the 1990s based on Windows. Yet he realized that the company faced many challenges, and that questions remained as to how Microsoft should be managed as it pursued that strategy.

Reflecting on these challenges, Gates remarked:

This is a business where if you don't stay ahead, you can lose market share very quickly. We have to figure out what the opportunities for innovation will be, based on changes in hardware and changes in what users want, and then we have to implement those things very rapidly. For us, that means setting systems standards and shipping innovative applications.

This business is getting more and more complex, yet it has to be fun for people, so that they feel empowered and feel they can do things. At the same time, the products have to fit together. It's a very tough problem.

20. Intel Corporation (C): Strategy for the 1990s

Introduction

Intel's revenues fell during 1985 and 1986 as its top management discontinued several low-margin product lines and reduced its work force of 25,400 by 7,200. Intel's losses for 1986 exceeded $200 million. The entire industry suffered as it adjusted to the new Japanese capacity and slackening demand.

In 1987, Intel began to emerge from the recession. While the company adopted a sole sourcing strategy for its microprocessor products, demand grew dramatically for its 386™ microprocessor[1] product line. In the middle of 1989, the company's expected sales had nearly tripled to $3.1 billion. In 1989, it had the highest return on sales of any major semiconductor company in the world. (See **Exhibits 20–1** and **20–2**.)

As Andy Grove, Intel's chief executive officer since 1987, described the emergence of the "new" Intel late in 1990, he wondered about the implications of the changing structure of the semiconductor industry on his company. He wondered what Intel's technology strategy should be and whether the Intel of the 1990s should plan to be a dominant player in the erasable programmable read-only memory (EPROM) business. He also wondered about the emergence of reduced instruction set computer (RISC) architecture and the implications that held for Intel's core microprocessor business. Finally, the growing importance of Intel's systems business raised some touchy issues about the company's relations with its customers.

DRAM in 1990

After the decision to stop developing the 1-megabit direct random-access memory (DRAM) in late 1984, Andy Grove had traveled to Portland several months later to address the DRAM technology development group. He had started his announcement to the group by saying: "Welcome to the mainstream of Intel."

---

[1]386 is a trademark of Intel Corporation.

This case was prepared by George W. Cogan, under the supervision of Associate Professor Robert A. Burgelman.

Case Copyright © 1989 by The Trustees of Leland Stanford Jr. University. Revised 1991. Reproduced by special permission.

327

While there had been significant resistance to the decision to exit DRAMs on the part of some high-level managers, the DRAM technology development group accepted the decision. Sun Lin Chou, then the leader of the group, said:

> I guess one of the reasons that we didn't feel so bad about the DRAM decision is that we felt we had done our part by regaining a leading technical position with the 1-meg DRAM. We were allowed to continue development for several months, so that by the time we stopped, we had functioning 1-meg DRAM parts.
>
> The company was really caught in a no-win situation. We were trying harder and harder, but it seemed that our efforts would not lead to a big success.

Intel's experience in the DRAM marketplace mirrored that of several other U.S. competitors who also exited during the 1985–1986 recession. In 1985, the entire DRAM market shrank by over 50% to $1.4 billion. However, by late 1987, demand once again began to outpace supply, and DRAM suppliers enjoyed market growth and renewed profitability. By 1987, Japanese companies controlled the overwhelming majority of the DRAM market since only two U.S. manufacturers, Texas Instruments and Micron Technology, remained.[2]

By 1990, Japanese companies commanded 87% of the $8 billion DRAM market, U.S. companies held about 8%, and Korean companies held the remaining 5%.[3] Korean market share was likely to increase as Korean firms announced investment plans of over $4 billion by the early 1990s. In order to address marketing concerns that the company have a full product line, Intel, in 1987, had signed a long-term sourcing agreement with Samsung Semiconductor for DRAM chips under which Intel would market the Korean chips under its own name. *Electronic Buyers News* reported that Intel had sold more than 10 million 256K and 1-megabit DRAMs during 1988 through its commodity operation. Prevailing prices suggested that the DRAM reseller business generated well over $100 million in revenue by 1990.

The dramatic decline in U.S. position led some industry observers to predict the eventual downfall of the entire U.S. semiconductor industry. The concern over U.S. competitiveness and dependence on foreign suppliers led several companies to announce plans to form a joint DRAM venture. A group of semiconductor and computer companies[4] agreed in June 1989 to form U.S. Memories, Inc., investing an initial $50,000 each. The venture required $1 billion in capitalization over several years and intended to use IBM's design for a 4-megabit DRAM as its introductory product offering early in 1991. The unusual arrangement between competitors would require federal antitrust clearance[5] and faced opposition from some vocal critics.

New Technology Drivers

Until 1985, Intel managers thought of DRAMs as the company's technology driver. Historically, DRAMs had always been the first products to employ new technology. Even though it never went into production, the 1-megabit DRAM was Intel's first attempt at a 1-micron geometry. Sun Lin Chou said it was typical for DRAMs to precede logic products in linewidth reduction by at least one year.

In 1990, Sun Lin Chou expressed some skepticism in discussing the cumulative volume model for learning in the semiconductor industry:

> The traditional model of a technology driver says that the more you do, the more high-volume products you run, the more productive you get. That means in order to stay on the leading edge, you need

[4]The group included Hewlett Packard, Intel, IBM Corp., Digital Equipment Corp., LSI Logic Corp., National Semiconductor, and Advanced Micro Devices.

[5]*Wall Street Journal*, June 21, 1989, p. B5, and *San Francisco Chronicle*, June 22, 1989, p. C1. Some companies (notably Apple and Sun Microsystems) were reluctant to invest in U.S. Memories, due to relationships with existing DRAM manufacturers. *San Francisco Chronicle*, September 26, 1989, p. C1.

[2]Although IBM does not sell DRAMs, it is one of the world's largest producers for its own internal uses.

[3]These figures do not include U.S. captive suppliers (IBM and AT&T). If captive suppliers are included, Japan's share of the U.S. market falls to 65%. (Captive estimate from Gilder, *Microcosm*, Simon and Shuster, 1989, p. 152.)

Exhibit 20-1 Selected Intel Corporation Financial Data, December 31, 1979-1990 (in millions of dollars)

	1979	1980	1981	1982	1983	1984	1985	1986	1987	1988	1989	1990
Sales	$663	$854	$788	$900	$1,122	$1,629	$1,364	$1,265	$1,907	$2,875	$3,127	$3,921
Cost of goods sold	313	399	458	542	624	883	943	861	1,043	1,506	1,721	1,930
Gross margin	$350	$455	$330	$358	$498	$746	$421	$404	$864	$1,369	$1,406	$1,991
Research and development	67	96	116	131	142	180	195	228	260	318	365	517
Sales, general, and administrative expenses	131	175	184	198	217	315	287	311	358	456	483	666
Operating profit	$152	$184	$30	$29	$139	$251	$(61)	$(135)	$246	$595	$557	$858
Interest and other	(3)	2	10	2	40	47	55	(76)	42	34	-96	336
Profit before tax	$149	$186	$40	$31	$179	$298	$(6)	$(211)	$288	$629	$583	$486
Income tax	71	89	13	—	63	100	(7)	8	40	176	192	336
Net income	$78	$97	$27	$31	$116	$198	$1	$(203)	$248	$453	$391	$650
Depreciation	$40	$49	$66	$83	$103	$114	$166	$173	$171	$210	$190	$292
Capital investment	97	152	157	138	145	388	236	154	301	477	351	680
Cash and short-term invest	34	127	115	85	389	230	188	74	630	970	1,064	1,785
Working Capital	115	299	287	306	608	568	717	649	506	1,036	1,242	1,806
Fixed Assets	217	321	412	462	504	778	848	779	891	1,122	1,284	1,658
Total Assets	500	767	871	1,056	1,680	2,029	2,152	1,977	2,498	3,549	3,994	5,377
Long-term debt	0	150	150	197	127	146	270	287	298	479	412	345
Equity	303	432	488	552	1,122	1,360	1,421	1,245	1,276	2,080	2,549	3,592
Employees	14,300	15,900	16,800	19,400	21,500	25,400	21,300	18,200	19,200	20,800	22,000	24,600
ROS	11.8%	11.4%	3.4%	3.4%	10.3%	12.2%	0.1%	(16.0%)	13.0%	15.8%	12.5%	16.6%
ROA	21.9%	19.4%	3.5%	3.6%	11.0%	11.8%	.05%	(9.4%)	9.9%	12.8%	9.8%	12.1%
ROE	38.0%	32.0%	6.3%	6.4%	21.0%	17.6%	0.1%	(14.3%)	19.5%	21.8%	15.3%	18.1%

Source: Intel Corporation, annual reports, various years.

Exhibit 20-2 Selected Competitor Data for 1988 (in millions of dollars)

	Intel	Nat'l Semi.	Texas Inst.	Adv. Micro Devices	Motorola	Hitachi	Toshiba	NEC	Fujitsu
Total sales	$2,874	$1,648	$6,294	$1,125	$8,250	$39,800	$28,579	$21,893	$16,374
Cost of goods sold	1,505	1,280	5,778	661	5,040	29,535	20,583	15,120	10,713
Research and development	318	264		208	incl.				
Sales, general, and administrative expenses	456	236		224	1,957	8,259	7,115	5,863	4,704
Other	(36)	55		18	642	(643)	(122)	344	108
Profit	$631	$(187)	$516	$14	$611	$2,649	$1,003	$566	$849
Profit after tax	453	(23)	366	19	445	1,094	485	204	337
Depreciation	211	184	389	153	543	2,351	1,412	1,310	1,094
Capital expenditure	477	277	628	131	873	2,333	1,469	2,016	1,527
Total assets	3,550	1,416	4,427	1,081	6,710	44,969	27,673	23,426	18,532
Long-term debt	479	52	623	130	343	3,462	4,423	3,576	2,413
Total equity 1987	1,276	1,013	1,885	623	3,008	14,607	4,061	3,523	4,660
Total equity 1988	2,080	848	2,243	645	3,375	16,148	5,743	4,784	6,616

Source: Compiled from financial data presented in the various companies' annual reports.

a product you can ramp into high-volume production rapidly. There is some truth to the model, but it can be carried to an extreme.

There are certainly ways of learning that can be carried out at much lower volumes. Our recent experience suggests that you can learn without massive volumes. If so, that takes away the requirement or urgency to have a traditional technology driver. We think it is possible to achieve mature yields by processing only about 10,000 wafers versus the old model's predicted requirement of 1,000,000 wafers. But you have to use intelligence.

You don't learn quickly when you increase volume by brute force. You have to learn by examining wafers. Learning is based on the number of wafers looked at, analyzed, and the number of effective corrective actions taken. Even if you have processed 1,000 wafers, the technical learning probably only came from the 10 wafers you analyzed. Technical learning is time and engineering constrained, not number of wafers constrained.

There are also a great number of things you can do in an open loop system. For example, you can see or guess where particles are coming from and remove them without really knowing for sure whether they are a yield limiter. You don't take the time to get the data to justify the fix; you don't do a detailed study; you just fix what seems broken. You have an intuition about what to do. The Japanese have really led the way on this. You don't undertake an ROI analysis to figure out the cost/benefit for every little improvement. You just fix everything you can think of. Everyone can participate.

Craig Barrett, Executive Vice President and General Manager of the Microcomputer Components Group, believed the importance of DRAMs to technology leadership had been overestimated by most industry observers:

At one time DRAMs really were a technology driver for Intel. DRAMs are still the single biggest product in the industry as a whole. They are about $8–10 billion of a $50 billion market. And they are certainly a learning vehicle for some.

When we got out of DRAMs we were concerned that we might suffer from the lack of volume. We tried to address that concern by selectively staying in the EPROM business. Even though the EPROM volume is not as big, it is a volume product. But I would have to conclude that after two generations post-DRAM we do not miss it as a technology driver.

I think that the industry used the notion of technology driver as a crutch. We were late waking up to the fact that we did not need to run volume in order to learn. There are other ways to be intelligent. You don't have to depend on volume if you depend on good engineering.

We have data to show that our learning as represented by lowering defect density has actually accelerated in the past two generations when plotted as a function of time or as a function of cumulative wafers put through the fab. For each generation since 1985, 1.5 micron, 1 micron, and most recently 0.8 microns, each defect density trend line is downward sloping with the most recent generations having the steepest slopes.

While we have some volume from our EPROM line and we make lots of efforts to transfer learning from one facility to another, we focus on basic techniques to accelerate learning: design of experiments, statistical process control, and just plain good engineering.

While we do have a lot of high-margin wafer starts, we still have a significant mixture of products. We have 256K EPROMs, 1 meg, 2 meg, and just recently, 4 meg in addition to our microcontrollers which are all very cost sensitive. We chose to stay in those commodity businesses partly because it does "keep us honest." Of course, it also represents a significant part of our revenue and it helps to amortize R&D expenditures.

Gerry Parker, Vice President of Technology Development, had a slightly different perspective on the issue of technology drivers:

There is no single technology driver at Intel. We focus our technology development on logic and nonvolatile memory products. More than ever before, we watch what the rest of the industry is doing and try to follow trends. The DRAM is the industry's driver, because it is the highest-volume product and DRAM suppliers are the biggest equipment purchasers. There have been some really fascinating developments in the industry. I think that the entire industry paradigm has shifted in the past several years.

I spend a lot of time now following what the DRAM people are doing and talking with equipment manufacturers. A great deal of the know-how is now generated at the equipment suppliers. We try to stay in the mainstream by purchasing the most advanced equipment, but then we optimize it to maximum advantage for our products.

For example, I know that a certain stepper vendor is developing a new tool that will accommodate a certain maximum chip size. It will not be able to process larger chips. The size is driven by the needs of Toshiba's next generation DRAM. They are building the equipment to satisfy the demands of their largest customer.

You can bet that all of Intel's next generation parts will be designed to capitalize on the DRAM tool. We will put that constraint on our designers. The equipment vendor will be ready to produce those steppers in volume and will be happy to supply us with a few machines. We could ask them to design a special tool for us, but it would be inferior because we wouldn't command the same level of attention that Toshiba gets.

Attitude is important and has led to the changes. The Japanese really have taught us something. They expect excellence from equipment vendors and make *them* develop the expertise to provide the best possible equipment. If a piece of equipment has a problem, the vendor is right there in the fab area fixing it, and he can make appropriate changes on the next generation.

Our approach has traditionally been different. We would modify the equipment ourselves and not even tell the vendor. We sometimes didn't even let the vendors into our fabs. We have changed a lot in our openness, and we are beginning to use sole source suppliers for each category of equipment, but we could still do more.

I was talking to a guy at Applied Materials, one of our equipment suppliers, about the differences between our approach and that of the Japanese. In Japan, all the technicians set the machines to the exact settings that are specified by Applied Materials. If the process doesn't work, Applied Materials gets blamed. In the United States, we tend to be more inventive: each technician sets the machine to an optimum that he has determined. When you operate like that, it becomes more difficult to blame the vendor when the yields are down.

As a result of this fundamental change in the equipment suppliers' role, learning now resides in the industry not just in the company. That is a complete shift. Just to prove it, look at this example. A Japanese ball bearing company, NMB,[6] with no expertise in the semiconductor industry, had $500 million in excess cash and decided to get into the DRAM business. They got vendors to sell them equipment and set it up, and they contracted with consultants to sell them a process and get it running. In a short time they were the most automated semiconductor factory in the world. That could never have happened even five years ago.

I certainly don't want to minimize the importance of process development. NMB now has to go out and buy a new process for the next generation. There is plenty of process development that distinguishes companies from each other. But, the latest equipment is essential to getting the highest yields. Equipment vendors allow Intel and even new start ups to keep up with the latest industry advances.

[6]Casewriter's note: For more on NMB, see *Microcosm*, (Simon and Shuster, 1989, p. 154–159). Takami Takahashi, NMB President, views DRAMs as the ultimate commodity: "a chip is merely a miniature ball bearing—flattened out, with a picture on it." In 1989, NMB was on a yearly sales run rate of $350 MM, having reached sales of $200 MM in 1988 on an estimated investment of $200 MM in plant and equipment. The plant had a total of 160 employees working four shifts.

EPROM and Flash

By the end of 1986, Intel had exited the DRAM and static random-access memory (SRAM) businesses, stopped development of electrically erasable programmable read-only memory (E^2PROM), sold its memory systems division, and sold its bubble memory subsidiary. Intel's only remaining position in memory businesses was in EPROMs. In 1986, Intel commanded a 21% share of the $910 million market versus 17% of an $860 million market two years earlier. In 1989, EPROMs were manufactured in five of Intel's fabrication sites.

Intel's continued dominance in the EPROM business arose partly from a successful legal battle against Hitachi and other Japanese companies accused of selling EPROMs below cost in the United States. Intel successfully fended off the attack through actions taken by the U.S. government.

In September 1986, Intel top management requested a middle-level manager to prepare a study of each memory business and make recommendations for Intel's long-term strategy. The manager recommended that Intel maintain its position in the EPROM business.

Intel top management decided to keep the EPROM operation as a relatively high-volume product to drive learning, but primarily as an enabling technology for the microcontroller business. Intel's microcontrollers integrate EPROM functionality and use an EPROM process technology. In 1989, Intel remained the EPROM market leader, with 21% market share of a billion-dollar market.

Flash

The middle manager also recommended that the company devote resources to a new memory technology called Flash. He said:

People say necessity is the mother of invention, and it sounds trite, but it's true. Those two years at Intel were incredibly stressful for the entire company. But, out of that time emerged several paradigm changes.

One very important one was Flash memory. Flash is very similar to E^2PROM, in functionality, but it is much cheaper to make. Basically, it costs less than EPROM, but you can erase it electrically instead of with light. This is a major cost-functionality discontinuity in EPROM semiconductor technology and has significant implications. One can envision low-end solid-state reprogrammable systems for instance, as well as simpler field service for ROM/EPROM-based systems.

Contrasting Flash to DRAM reveals some interesting perspectives. Flash does not have the flexible write functionality of DRAM, but it is nonvolatile. Additionally, Flash is actually a simpler-to-manufacture read-write technology because it is not constrained by the need for a large capacitor in each memory cell. About 80% of the current DRAM cell is active, whereas only 5% of the Flash cell is. That means that Flash can shrink like mad.

Another paradigm change has resulted in our working on a truly parallel processor, or neural network, that uses a version of Flash technology. By making an analog instead of a digital device, we can develop a low precision but very high performance "trainable analog-memory processor." It remains to be seen what applications will evolve from this capacity but it has exciting possibilities.

If Flash leads to miniaturization of computers from portable to hand-held units, neural nets may solve handwriting recognition. This combined with a notebook computer would result in a very user-friendly tool for a large market.

As you think about it, Flash may ultimately have implications for the microprocessor business. If you look out far enough, you can see a whole new era for semiconductor technology.

By 1990, some industry observers began to recognize the potential for Flash as a replacement for conventional magnetic disk drives in laptop computers.[7] Some industry specialists noted that solid-state disks, when compared to traditional Winchester drives, can consume up to 300 times less power, are 15 times more durable, can withstand much more heat, and are up to 100 times faster. Other industry specialists, however, noted that there has been a 100-fold "shrink" in the size of 20–40 MB drives since the late 1970s (from 2,300 cubic inches for the 14-inch drive to 23 cubic inches for the current 1-inch drive) and that during that time, price has decreased by a factor of 10 and access time improved by a factor

of 2.[8] **Exhibit 20–3** shows projections of prices for various 2.5-inch disk drive capacities.

In the portable PC market, the London based company, Psion PLC, already had plans to introduce two notebook computers in 1990, which would use Flash instead of magnetic storage. While the current installed base of portables is estimated at fewer than 5 million units, the future potential is estimated at more than 20 million.[9]

The market for ultraportables (falling between today's 6-pound notebook and the 1-pound pocket type) was estimated to grow from less than 1 million in 1990 to 12 million in 1994.[10]

Although Flash was still more expensive than traditional magnetics, its learning curve was much steeper. **Exhibit 20– 4** shows price projections for different storage technologies.

In October 1990, Intel announced a credit card size "Flash memory card," which will be available in 1-and 4-megabyte storage units and priced at $298 and $1,198, respectively. Intel said that the new storage system will offer an important alternative to floppy and hard disk drives in portable computers because it uses less power and offers improved performance. The reduced power demands, for instance, will extend battery life between 10 and 100 times for portable computers. The company expected to begin mass production of the Flash memory card in December 1990.

By 1994, Intel predicted it would have a 16-megabit Flash chip. The chip would enable a cost-competitive alternative to the industry standard 50-megabyte hard drive on a credit card size format.

Western Digital was reportedly developing Flash subsystems that could be managed like magnetic media and could be interfaced into a system like a disk drive.[11] Texas Instruments was also developing its own Flash technology, which reportedly used less power than Intel's during data writing.

---

[7]Microsoft has decided to support the technology by releasing file-management software that lets MS-DOS treat Flash like disk drives.

[8]"You Can Take It With You," Forum on Portable Computers and Communications, October 2–3, 1990, Bear Stearns & Co., New York.

[9]Ibid.

[10]"You Can Take It With You," Forum on Portable Computers and Communications, October 2–3, 1990, Bear Stearns & Co., New York.

[11]Ibid.

Exhibit 20-3 Cost per 2.5-Inch Drive, 1988-1994 (20-200 megabyte drives, midyear OEM quantities) (Source: "You Can Take It With You," *Forum on Portable Computers and Communications,* October 2-3, 1990, Bear Stearns & Co., New York.)

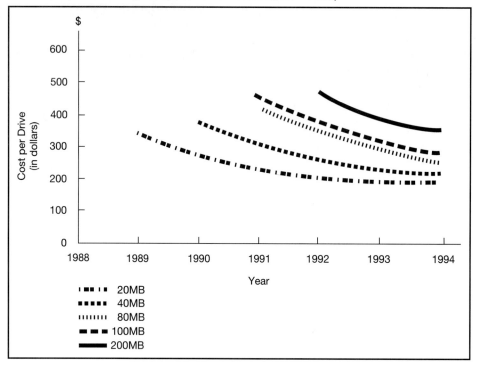

Exhibit 20-4 PC Card Cost Projection, 1990-1993 (Source: "You Can Take It With You," *Forum on Portable Computers and Communications,* October 2-3, 1990, Bear Stearns & Co., New York.)

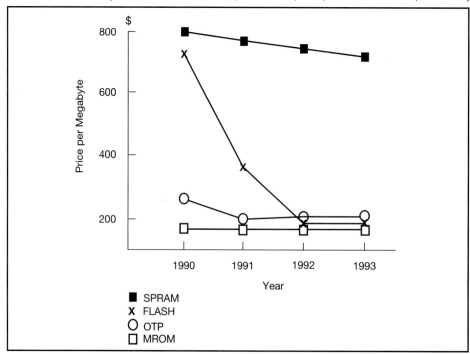

New Microprocessor Strategy

During the same week in October 1985 when Intel made the decision to close Fab 5 in Oregon for DRAM production, it announced shipment of the 32-bit 80386. The electronics industry received the 386™ microprocessor with great enthusiasm. Just one year later, in the third quarter of 1986, customers had completed development of new products, and the first products to contain the 386™ were shipped. By then, the new microprocessor had garnered over 200 design wins by virtue of its upward compatibility with existing personal computer software and its broad applications in other markets.

The power of the 386 to leverage previous software led to the most rapid ramp-up of production for any microprocessor in Intel's history. By the end of 1987, just two years after the 386's introduction, Intel had shipped an estimated 800,000 units as compared to 50,000 for the earlier 8086 at two years after its introduction. By 1989, some analysts believed that Intel was too dependent on the i386™ and its support chips, estimating that they generated nearly $1 billion, or between 30% and 40% of the company's revenues during fiscal 1988.

A new corporate strategy added to Intel's early success with the 80386. During previous generations, Intel supported a cross-licensing agreement with AMD (Advanced Micro Devices) in which AMD acted as a second source and provided development of support chips. Intel's top management made the decision to make AMD perform under the existing agreement or be prepared to act as a sole source for the 386™.[12]

Craig Barrett described some of the factors that figured in the decision:

> Basically, Intel got to the point where it could generate enough customer confidence to pull it off. There were at least several forces at work.
>
> Our quality thrust of the early 1980s began to pay off in improved consistency on the manufacturing line and overall better product quality. In addition, customer-vendor partnerships became more prevalent throughout our business. For example, we had recently started selling Ford a microcontroller product, the 8061. They proclaimed that total cost was more important than purchase price alone and decided to work with us closely and exclusively—sort of on the Japanese model. We learned a great deal from that which carried into our other customers and to our vendors.
>
> We had also decided to pursue a "vendor of choice" strategy in 1984 which led to improved customer satisfaction. Finally, the experience with earlier x86 generations led us to believe that we could accurately forecast demand for the 386™ and put sufficient manufacturing capacity in place.
>
> With improved manufacturing consistency and better forecast accuracy, we realized that it wasn't always necessary to have a second source to keep the customer satisfied. As our second source deal with AMD came unraveled, we put in the capability to never miss a shipment by adding strategic inventory and redundant capacity. Since then we have never missed an 80386 customer commitment.
>
> The pitfalls of our strategy are obvious. You can fall on your sword. And it only takes once to lose the confidence of your customers. Also, the business is sufficiently profitable that everyone is gunning for you. They try to make clones of your product or substitutes.

Bob Reed, Chief Financial Officer, underlined the importance of intellectual property to Intel and to the semiconductor industry:

> Intel has looked around for an edge against competitors. When we look back 10 years from now we may see that intellectual property protection saved the U.S. semiconductor market.[13] The protection will essentially lead to a segmentation of the semiconductor industry into maybe 10 industries, all with leaders. Intel's sole source strategy for the i386™ is a good example of a winning strategy. Now Motorola is also a sole source.
>
> This does not imply much more complicated contractual relationships with customers. For example, Intel has no penalty clauses for nondelivery of parts; however, we never miss a delivery. The stakes have been raised on both sides of the table.
>
> At Intel, the legal department has grown from 5 to 20 internal people in the past 5 years. In addition, we retain outside counsel. We vigorously pursue anyone who infringes on our intellectual property rights.

[12]Intel believed that AMD did not earn rights to the 386™ design under the existing licensing agreements. Intel's decision led to a widely publicized dispute with AMD which was still in the final stages of binding arbitration at the time of this case development.

[13]In a landmark decision in 1986, the U.S. Courts agreed with Intel that computer code embedded in silicon is covered by U.S. copyright laws, thus affording protection for Intel's chip designs.

In order to support the sole sourcing strategy, Intel converted its new Israel facility, originally designed for EPROMs, to make microprocessor products. In addition, the Portland technology development group began developing a 1-micron version of the 386™, a significant reduction in chip size from the original 1.5-micron geometry.

While increased performance and the need for ever-increasing price-performance advancements were the key forces driving microprocessor development, high integration and increased functionality were also important. Increased functionality and integration depend on the ability to "shrink" the microprocessor, allowing more space to integrate new features. Jack Carsten, formerly an Intel senior vice president and currently a venture capitalist in Silicon Valley, said:

> Lots of people talk about the design team that developed Intel's 386™ chip. It's a great product. But, the great unsung heroes at Intel are the people who successfully developed the "shrink" technology for the 386™. That reduction in geometry led to higher-performance parts as well as greatly increased yields.

Exhibit 20–5 shows the evolution of the result of the shrinking CPU technology.

Sun Lin Chou discussed the role of the Portland Technology Development Group:

> In the past 2 years the situation has changed significantly. We don't just do process development in Portland. We have designers in Portland who leverage our ability to make use of leading-edge technology sooner. Some of those designers are old DRAM designers who have been retrained.
>
> In the old days, memory was always the first product to use a new process. First, we would get the yields up on memory, then a couple of years later the logic product would use the process. We stabilized the process on memory, then did logic. Since logic takes longer to design, it is easier to do it that way. Now we have no DRAMs; the concept of technology driver has changed.
>
> Our challenge is to get logic products up on new processes sooner than we ever have before. To do that, we have accelerated and integrated the design process. We use the Portland designers to design standard cells which can then be used by chip designer groups. We also take existing logic parts that have proven designs and use the new standard cells to generate "shrink" designs.

> Instead of using memory to ramp production, we are now using logic products redesigned with smaller geometrics. That is a fundamental change, because demand is not infinite for logic products. We may only have to use a small fraction of one fab's capacity to satisfy the world demand for a particular logic product.
>
> We also have a group of designers that actually work on new chip designs with the design group in Santa Clara. There was a lot of skepticism about having split design teams, but this arrangement allows us to have a set of designers who are much closer to the process. For example, the Portland design group designed the entire cache RAM block that goes into the 80486™ chip.

The 80486™ was introduced in April 1989. With over 1 million transistors, the i486™ microprocessor[14] contained nearly four times the circuit elements in the 386™. The i486 had taken a total of 130 person-years in design effort compared to 80 for the 386. It had benefited from a fourfold increase in proprietary specialized design tools created by Intel. The overall investment in the i486 development had been more than $200 million. In keeping with its strategy of upward compatibility, Intel had designed the new offering to run software developed for its predecessors. The 486™ was expected to be especially important in the growing market for a new class of "servers," which could store information for an entire corporation and send it out as needed to PCs in response to queries from different types of users (engineers, accountants, marketing specialists, senior executives). In 1990, the market for servers was projected to grow from $4 billion to $12 billion by 1994.[15]

RISC versus CISC

By 1990, Intel had established a dominant position in the personal computer microprocessor business based on complex instruction set computer (CISC) design. Every manufacturer of advanced IBM-compatible personal computers had to purchase a 386 or 486 microprocessor from Intel. Similarly, those manufacturers or their customers had to purchase operating system

---

[14]486 is a trademark of the Intel Corporation.
[15]*Business Week*, November 26, 1990, p. 122.

software from Microsoft Corporation[16] in order to maintain backward compatibility with the thousands of programs already developed for the PC market. During 1990, NCR was the first Intel customer to decide to use Intel microprocessors throughout its entire product line. Some analysts believed that Intel's penetration in the CISC microprocessor market would continue throughout the 1990s (see **Exhibit 20–6**).

In the meantime, a new market for microprocessors led to a proliferation of microprocessor designs. The engineering workstation market—characterized by high-performance graphics and computation ability—was pioneered by Sun Microsystems. In some of its earlier systems, Sun used the Intel 386 chip, but instead of MS-DOS chose the UNIX operating system.[17]

Sun Microsystems' president, Scott Mc-

Nealy, believed that Intel was charging too much for its processor, so he initiated the development[18] of a new processor using a computing architecture called RISC (reduced instruction set computer).[19] Following a strategy of "open" standards, McNealy made the Sun RISC chip design (SPARC) available to his competitors.

In addition to the SPARC chip, several other RISC chips had reached the marketplace by 1990, including offerings from MIPS and Motorola. Each of the new RISC chips was capable of supporting some version of the UNIX operating system environment.

[18]While Sun designed the RISC chip, it did not have chip making expertise and farmed out the actual manufacturing of the chip to several silicon foundries.

[19]The RISC (reduced instruction set computer) actually preceded the CISC (complex instruction set computer) architecture. Instructions are the lowest level commands a microprocessor responds to (such as "retrieve from memory" or "compare two RISC numbers"). CISC microprocessors support between 100–150 instructions while RESC chips support 70–80. As a result of supporting fewer instructions, RISC chips have superior performance over a narrow range of tasks and can be optimized for a specific purpose. Through combinations of the reduced instruction set, the RISC architecture can be made to duplicate the more complex instructions of a CISC chip, but at a performance penalty.

[16]Microsoft was the sole source for the IBM-PC operating system, MS-DOS. In conjunction with IBM, Microsoft also developed a new operating system, OS2, which took advantage of the 286 and 386's multitasking features, while maintaining backward compatibility.

[17]Unlike MS-DOS, the UNIX operating system is capable of taking advantage of the multiprocessing feature of the 386. In addition, UNIX is an "open" program and available from multiple sources (although many of the versions are not compatible).

Exhibit 20-5 Silicon Trends and PC Integration

SILICON TRENDS AND PC INTEGRATION

SL SUPERSET SOLUTION

INTEL PC ON-A-CHIP

1984   1987   1990   1993

10 CHIPS + MEMORY

1 CHIP + MEMORY

70 CHIPS + MEMORY

170 CHIPS + MEMORY

◆ Higher Transistor Budgets ──► Higher Integration

◆ Intel's Process Technology and Design Tools Lead the Way

◆ Less Board Space Needed for Standard PC Core

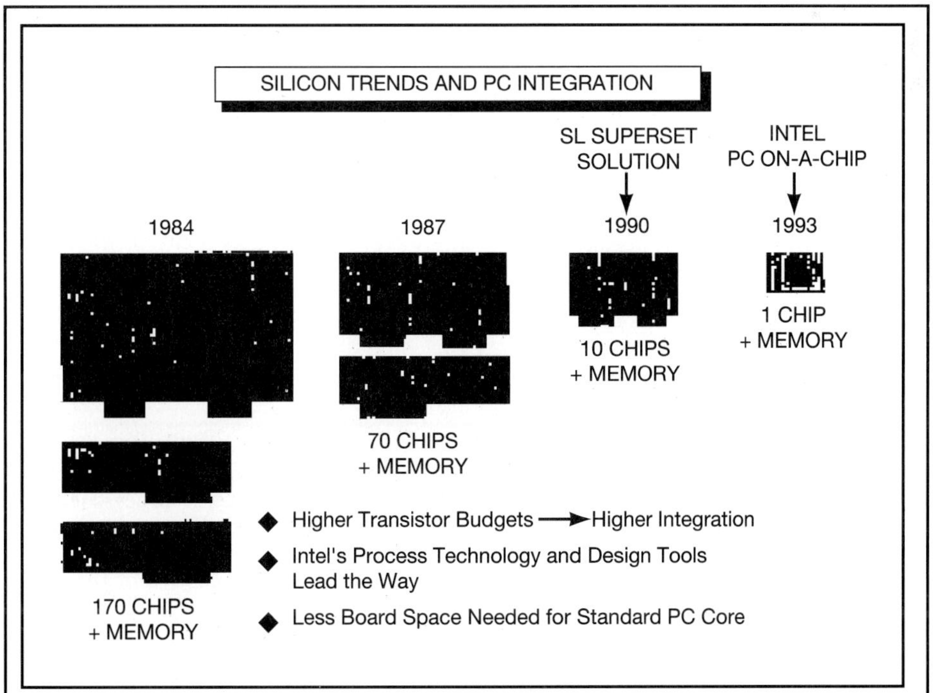

Source: Santa Clara Microcomputer Division, Intel Corporation.

Exhibit 20-6 Intel X86-Compatible Computers Will Dominate PCs, Workstations, Midrange, and Eventually All Computing (Source: Intel company records.)

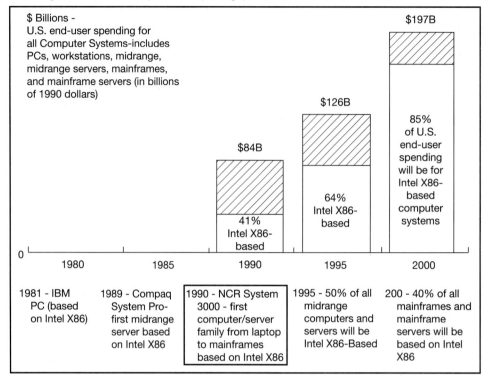

In 1990, various analysts were debating the future of RISC versus CISC. One analyst observed that while RISC microprocessors were simpler than CISCs, the system logic that surrounds the RISC microprocessor is more complex, and all that RISC does is to transfer system complexity from the microprocessor to the system logic. This analyst also noted that RISC is far behind CISC on the learning curve and that, for instance, in 1990, Intel alone shipped over 8 million 32-bit CISC microprocessors, while the 10 RISC suppliers combined shipped no more than 200,000 units.[20]

Another analyst observed that the success of RISC versus CISC is likely to depend on whether a totally seamless software bridge can be created enabling all IBM PC-compatible application software to be run fast enough on UNIX-based machines. The question is who could do that, and what their incentive would be to do so.[21]

The *i*860 Story

In 1988, Intel's official response to RISC architecture was to call it "the technology of the have nots." As several companies announced new RISC chips, Intel developed an internal jargon referring to the competitor chips as YARPs, or "yet another RISC processor."

Yet, within the Intel design organization, a designer named Les Kohn had been trying for several years to initiate a RISC program:

I joined the company in 1982 after working for National on their 32000 processor. At that time, I realized that RISC architecture had some definite technical advantages. That was very difficult to see from Intel's perspective of the x86 architecture. So

[20]"The Future of Microprocessors," Goldman Sachs, April 23, 1990.
[21]"Institutional Research: Intel Corporation," Hambrecht & Quist, Inc., September 12, 1990.

Intel Corporation (C): Strategy for the 1990s

even at a technical level, there was no clear consensus that RISC was the right approach.

Between 1982 and 1986, I made several proposals for RISC projects through the Intel product planning system, but I wasn't successful. RISC was not an existing business and people were not convinced that the market was there. Also, the company had had a bad experience with a new architecture, the 432, which was not commercially successful. Experience makes skeptics. The design would have been way too big to do in a skunkworks.

In 1986 I saw that our next generation processors would have 1 million transistor chips, and I started working on the idea of a RISC-based processor that would take full advantage of that technology. This proposal had more aggressive goals and was more convincing than previous ones. Several people including Sai Wai Fu and Kanwar Chadha got interested in the idea, and we drafted a product requirement document that outlined market size, pricing, and rough development cost. Then we had several breaks that made the project go.

First of all, we positioned it as a coprocessor to the 80486 and made sure that it could be justified on that basis. We designed it as a stand-alone processor, but made it very useful as an accessory to the 486™.

We made sure it was very different from the x86 family so that there would be no question in the customer's mind of which product to use. The really fortuitous part came when presentations to several large customers generated a lot of positive feedback to senior management. Feedback helps because at a technical level, members of senior management are not experts.

There was also a whole group of customers who did not previously talk to Intel because they were more interested in performance than compatibility. 3D graphics, workstation, and minicomputer accounts all got very interested. In the end, it looked like the i860™ would generate a whole new business for Intel.[22]

During the development of the RISC chip, it was code named the N10 and perceived by top management as a coprocessor for the i486™. The N10 had a 64 bit architecture with floating point and integer processing as well as enhanced graphics capability. According to Kohn, the chip utilized design concepts found in supercomputers. The design team of 50 wore tee shirts with a miniaturized CRAY supercomputer icon resting on a chip.

Kohn commented on Intel's unique position to produce a 1 million transistor RISC chip:

Intel has historically led the industry in having the most transistors—at least in terms of widely used, commercial microprocessors. To do it on the schedule we did required a very close working relationship between technology development and the design teams.

In a lot of cases, RISC companies worked with external vendors for the fabrication of parts so they either had to design for the lowest common denominator of those technologies or they wouldn't necessarily get access to the most advanced technology.

Another factor was the design tools. Intel made a strategic decision to invest in advanced CAD tools. Our new data base manager allowed us to manage the several thousand files that go into this chip. It made sure that people didn't make changes that got lost or that two different people weren't making changes to the same file at the same time. We also used a new generation of workstation-based circuit design that was very graphic, allowing the engineers to work directly with schematics and display results graphically.

In February 1989, Intel announced the i860 not as a coprocessor, but rather as a stand-alone RISC processor. Top management decided to join the RISC processor race. Grove said:

We had our own marketing story for the chip, but our customers changed it. They said, "Listen, this isn't just a coprocessor chip. This could be the central processor of a supertechnical workstation." Occasional sarcastic jibes aside, we're in no position now to dump on RISC as a technology. Our chip shows what the real potential of RISC is.[23]

Craig Barrett viewed the i860™ as part of a rational strategy emerging through the championing of a top-flight engineer:

There has been competition between the RISC and CISC architectures for some time. If we assume that the market will split, this gives us a position in both markets.

Intel's bread and butter clearly is still in the x86 family. There is a 586 on the drawing board and a 686 planned to follow that. If there was ever any question of which comes first, it could be answered very quickly. But if there are enough people out there who want to buy YARPs, then we call the i860 a YARP killer. It is the highest-performance RISC processor on the market.

---

[22]860 is a trademark of the Intel Corporation.

[23]*Wall Street Journal*, February 28, 1989, pp. A1 and A8.

Les Vadasz became senior vice president and general manager of the Intel Systems Business in 1985. In 1988, the business had nearly kept pace with the dramatic microprocessor growth so that it accounted for about $750 million of Intel's $2.8 billion in sales. In 1990, it was expected to contribute over $1 billion.

Originally, the Systems Business provided technology to enable the growth of Intel's semiconductor business. For example, development systems, which allowed customers to design their own systems and to write software for microprocessor applications, provided a significant portion of revenue.

In 1985, top management had made the strategic decision to increase the Systems Business's share of total revenue. Vadasz said:

> In 1985, the Systems Business was still devoted to accelerating the deployment of our silicon technology. We were providing customers multiple choices at different levels of integration. If they wanted microprocessors or board-level products, we could provide either.
>
> Now we are more like an independent business. We make a range of products: PC-compatibles for OEMs, mainframes through a joint venture,[24] and even parallel supercomputers based on the i386™ and i860™ processors. We also make PC enhancement boards and sell them through retail channels. Microprocessor-based technology is the future in computers, even in supercomputers.
>
> We have organized around segmented strategies for each market. We must recognize that each of our segments requires a different business structure. For example, supercomputers and PCs require entirely different manufacturing disciplines. The PC enhancement business requires a retail understanding, its own sales force, a different kind of documentation, and, of course, its own product engineering.
>
> As you grow, and stake out new territories, you test and develop new capabilities for the company. Each new capability can then be deployed into other areas. But you must exercise discipline in how you use your capabilities.

Several of the businesses started as ventures in the Intel Development Organization (IDO), which Vadasz also headed. Vadasz continued:

[24]BIIN Computer, a joint venture with Siemens, was founded in the summer of 1988 to develop a fault tolerant computer. The joint venture was dissolved in October 1989.

IDO looks a bit like an internal venture capital fund. It is funded by the corporation and has its own miniboard of Gordon Moore, Bob Reed, and me. It serves to isolate a new idea from the quarterly cycles of Intel's business. We create an isolated investment unit and see how it does. These units are managed with an iron hand, but on their own merits.

The guiding question at Intel is: Where can we add intellectual value? Some semiconductor people used to grow crystal ingots [raw material for semiconductors], but they found they could not add value there. Others, specializing in crystal growth, became more effective suppliers. DRAMs have become like that. Manufacturing DRAMs does not tell you how to make computers. The lowest value added component in the chain always tends to spread, so you get perfect competition in that area.

Some industry observers believed Intel's Systems Business represented a bold strategy which might alienate its customers. Not only did Intel have a sole source position, it could become a potential competitor to some of its customers—companies like Compaq, Tandy, or Olivetti.

Questions in 1990

In reviewing the recent history of the company, Mr. Grove wondered how to top the "awesome new $3 billion Intel." Among the U.S. semiconductor companies, Intel was clearly a leading performer in 1990, but what steps would be necessary to continue that performance?

During the strategic reorientation of 1985, Intel's top management had completely revised the company's strategic long-range planning (SLRP) system and had resolved to emphasize a set of overriding corporate strategies which would guide lower levels in developing specific objectives. The three-point corporate strategy was to:

1. increase architectural and technological leadership,
2. be our customers' preferred supplier, and
3. be a world-class manufacturer.

Five years later, this strategy still seemed right. The company continued to invest large amounts of resources in R&D (some $500 million in 1990), and its track record of innovation continued unabated.

However, some adjustments might be necessary. In particular, Grove wondered about the future role of the relatively low-margin EPROMs in what was now "the microprocessor company." Should Intel get out of EPROMs to free resources for microprocessors, or should they be continued? This was particularly important in light of the potential future of Flash. He also questioned the role of RISC and the implications of Intel's endorsement of that technology. Was RISC a distortion of Intel's microprocessor strategy or part of it? What options could Intel pursue? Finally, he wondered what larger environmental forces might help or inhibit Intel in sustaining its current growth and profitability throughout the 1990s.

21. Acer Incorporated

"This is probably the most agonizing decision that our company, and Stan Shih as a person, has ever faced." A senior manager and long-time employee of Acer Inc. was reflecting on the issues confronting Acer in early January, 1991. "If we go ahead with this lay-off, it may appear (even to many of our own people) that we are abandoning one of the basic principles that have made us such an admired company in Taiwan. In fact, very few large companies in this country have ever laid-off a lot of people at one time. Taiwan is not quite as rigid about this as Japan, but almost. On the other hand, if the market remains as sluggish and competitive as it has been recently, we will severely damage the financial health of our company if we don't do something quickly. Other, even much bigger, computer companies in other parts of the world are laying off people or forcing early retirements to keep their costs in line.

"Another thing that this decision brings into sharp focus," he continued, "is that the kind of commitment our people are willing to make to this company today is different from what it was during Acer's early years. In my opinion, this is largely due to the fact that we are no longer the little company, fighting against the industry giants, that we used to be. Now we are the largest personal computer (PC) company in Taiwan, and that gives people a sense of security that isn't realistic given the competitiveness of this industry. We are also a public company now, so we have to think about the interests of our external shareholders and don't have the same degree of freedom that we once did. We have to find new ways of motivating our people, given our current situation."

Company Background

Acer had grown from nothing in 1976 to sales of about US$1.0 billion in 1990: 70% from computer manufacturing operations, and the remainder from its computer-related trading and publishing

Professor Robert H. Hayes prepared this case as the basis for class discussion rather than to illustrate either effective or ineffective handling of an administrative situation.

activities. It had been founded by Mr. Stan Shih, his wife (who had been Acer's vice president of Finance for several years, and now served as its supervising director[1]), and three others. Before then, Mr. Shih had been the vice president, and effectively the chief operating officer, of Qualitron, the largest Taiwanese manufacturer of hand-held calculators. In trying to turn the company into a mini-conglomerate in the early 1970s, Qualitron's founder diverted the profits from his calculator business into other investments. Deprived of necessary reinvestment, the company eventually failed. Seeing this, Shih invited two of Qualitron's key people to join him in starting a new company.

Originally named Multitech, during its first few years Shih's new company operated as a distributor of electronic products (which increasingly consisted of personal computer hardware and software) within Taiwan. In 1983, as the potential size of the PC market became apparent, Multitech decided to begin manufacturing IBM-compatible PCs, both for other companies and under its own brand name. Originally targeting only the markets in Taiwan and other developing countries in Southeast Asia, the company prospered. During its first 10 years, its sales growth rate averaged 100% per year.

In mid-1989 it shipped its one-millionth PC. Of the 400,000 units shipped that year, about 40% were sold under other labels, including those of some of the largest computer companies in the world. Acer had the largest share, with over 20%, of Taiwan's PC market. It was also either first or second in market share in several other countries, including Thailand and Chile.

In the mid-1980s, Mr. Shih began to encourage his company to expand its goals. He knew that Multitech could not continue to grow and prosper against its big multinational competitors if it continued to be a follower in technology, lacked a well-known brand name, and remained just a regional company—moreover, one whose home market was relatively small. He therefore opened sales offices around the world. By 1989,

32% of the company's total sales came from Europe and 31% from North America. He also increased spending on R&D to about 5% of PC sales (an unusually high percentage in Taiwan), and this investment soon began to pay off.

The company was the first in its industry to offer a Chinese-language processor, which eventually led it into a joint venture with Microsoft to develop a Chinese version of MOS-DOS. It also was one of the early developers of software and hardware input/output packages for Japanese, Korean, Arabic, and Thai. In 1986 it shocked the industry by being one of the first to announce a 32-bit PC based on Intel's new 386 microprocessor. That PC's offspring, the 1100/16 was rated a "Best Buy" by *PC World* magazine. Another, the 1100/33, was widely acknowledged to be "the fastest PC in the world" soon after it was launched in early 1989, and selected as "Editor's Choice" by *PC Magazine*.

By 1987 Acer was designing its own customized integrated circuits (ICs), and the masks used in making them. As evidence of its growing reputation for engineering and manufacturing excellence, in 1989 it entered into a strategic alliance with National Semiconductors to design and build sophisticated customized input/output ICs for personal computers. That same year it was selected by Texas Instruments to join with it in building a new US$326 million plant in Taiwan to produce 4-megabit DRAMS (high density IC memories). Scheduled to start production during the latter half of 1991, this facility's initial capacity was to be 20,000 wafers per month. Acer's US$85 million investment gave it 58% of the joint venture's equity.

In 1991 its product line (**Exhibit 21-1**) included nine models of IBM-compatible PCs, ranging from "notebook" size to low-end workstations, a LAN Server, five video color monitors (one an ultra high resolution model), two laser printers, and a computer keyboard, all designed and produced internally. It supplemented these products with assorted others that it bought for resale.

In the mid-1980s the company learned that the name Multitech was already being used by a small U.S. company. After a careful analysis of alternative names and their connotations in various important languages, it changed its name to Acer, Inc. in 1988. The new name, as well as Acer's growing reputation for quality and techni-

---

[1]Under Taiwanese law, all public companies must designate one of their Directors to be the company's Supervisor. This person is authorized to look into any aspect of the company's activities on behalf of its shareholders, and given access to whatever internal data is required to fulfill that responsibility.

Exhibit 21-1 Representative Acer Products

Acer 1100LX (386 SX Processor)
"Lunchbox" Design with Detachable Keyboard

Acer 1100/25 (386 25 MHz Processor)

Acer 1200 (486 25 MHz Processor)
CAD/CAM Workstation

cal excellence, were the focus of a major new advertising campaign. It also began a rapid expansion of the distribution systems for its products in the United States and Europe.

In the same year, as part of its continuing efforts to raise funds to support its rapid growth and expand its public image, Acer made its first public offering (of 10% of its total shares) and was listed on the Taiwan stock exchange. Over the years, Stan Shih's personal stake in the ownership of the company gradually fell from 60% to 10%, while Acer's employees increased their share to about 70%. This public offering, and a subsequent issuance of new stock, coincided with a spectacular bull market in Taiwan, and Acer stock—whose book value at the time it went public was about NT$25 per share[2]—soon skyrocketed to over NT$150. Acer managers who had invested in buying stock during the company's early years (under an arrangement to be described later) found themselves suddenly wealthy. Much of this wealth disappeared just as quickly, when in 1990 the Taiwan stock market collapsed to under 20% of the value at its high point.

Until 1989, Acer's products were manufactured only in Taiwan. Its biggest factory, in Hsinchu, contained five floors, each the size of two football fields, and had a capacity of about 600,000 PCs per year. Hsinchu's floorspace was being doubled in late 1990. In 1989, Acer built its first factory on foreign soil—in Penang, Malaysia, where by late 1990 it was making most of its color monitors and keyboards. The success of this factory had led it to plan a doubling of capacity

there (to 30,000 color monitors and 40,000 keyboards per month), and consider moving some of its more mature, higher-volume PCs to Malaysia.

In 1990 it bought a small Dutch PC manufacturer, to serve as a base for expanding its penetration of the European market. In early 1991 this plant was assembling about 2000 PCs a month (roughly 15% of European demand) from kits shipped from Taiwan.

In mid-1990 Acer acquired Altos Computer Systems, a $140 million U.S. company that specialized in high-end multiuser UNIX computer networks. A "typical Silicon Valley company," Altos had lost money the two previous years. In early 1991, Acer was combining its North American operations into a single organization, comprising about 600 people (300 of them in manufacturing and R&D). Altos continued to develop and produce computers under its own brand name. The two organizations were producing 3,000–4,000 units a month, or about a third of combined North American demand. Over the long term, plans were being made to integrate the Altos and Acer product lines.

By 1991 Acer had 44 overseas facilities in 13 countries, and over 5300 employees, 1500 of them outside of Taiwan. It was in the process of setting up a small R&D facility in Japan, as a "window into Japanese technology." "With our recent expansion of Hsinchu, we probably now have too much production capacity in Taiwan," commented one manager. "As we expand production in other locations we will need less and less capacity here." Selected financial information is contained in **Exhibit 21–2**.

Corporate Organization

In 1989, as the company's dramatic growth and geographical spread put increasing strains on its managers and systems, Acer decided to divide up its organization into five divisional SBUs (Strategic Business Units), each of which was to operate as a profit center. The new organization is depicted in **Exhibit 21–3**. The two major groups of SBUs were the Personal/System Computer Business Group, which was organized along product lines (e.g., standard PCs, portable computers, peripheral products, and Altos), and the Regional Business Unit (RBU) Group, which was organized around geographic markets.

The largest by far of these RBUs, with 1990 sales of about US$250 million, was its original business, now named Sertek. The sole distributor of Acer's products in Taiwan (accounting for 10% of its total production), it also sold and serviced a variety of other PC-related products, primarily

[2]NT$ stands for New Taiwan Dollars. In early 1991, NT$26 = US$1, approximately.

Exhibit 21-2 Acer Inc. and Subsidiaries Consolidated Income Statement (March 1, 1991)

	1990[a]	%	1989	%	1988	%
Total Revenue	$875,011,739	100	$688,968,032	100	$530,945,864	100
Cost of goods sold	668,765,969	76.4	532,701,804	77.3	389,372,397	73.3
Gross profit	206,245,770	23.6	156,266,228	22.7	141,573,467	26.7
Selling expense	107,322,757	12.3	77,455,755	11.2	65,337,110	12.3
G&A expense	69,850,401	8.0	40,731,887	5.9	22,864,550	4.3
R&D expense	31,137,655	3.6	25,359,690	3.7	17,758,804	3.3
Total operating expense	208,310,814	23.8	143,547,332	20.8	105,960,464	20
Operating gain (loss)	(2,065,044)	-0.2	12,718,896	1.8	35,613,003	6.7
Non-operating gain (loss)	5,231,682	0.6	(6,323,057)	-0.9	(7,986,616)	-1.5
Combined earnings	3,166,638	0.4	6,395,839	0.9	27,626,387	5.2
Income tax	1,024,679	0.1	994,527	0.1	1,262,040	0.2
Earnings before minority interest	2,141,959	0.2	5,401,312	0.8	26,364,347	5
Minority interest	1,390,565	0.2	370,485	0.1	142,944	0
Net earnings	3,532,524	0.4	5,771,797	0.8	26,507,291	5

[a]Unaudited. For reference only.

through its 100 AcerLand retail outlets. The joint venture with TI operated as an autonomous SBU. Each division was asked to manage itself as if it were a self-owned corporation, with its own marketing strategy, product strategy, and profit objectives.

Products were transferred between them at negotiated prices, which had led to some friction. "There has to be a better way, and I wish I knew what it was," observed Dr. Ronald Chwang. Currently Vice President of the new Acer America Corporation, he had received his Ph.D. in electrical engineering in the United States and worked for Intel for several years before joining Acer four years previously. "I'm convinced that direct negotiation between two profit centers can be suboptimal for the company as a whole. On the other hand, this is far better than the old, centralized organization, where we couldn't tell what the cost or the profitability of any individual product was."

In his drive to make Acer a truly multinational company, Stan Shih continually empha-

sized the importance of being a "global citizen" and not imposing a home country orientation, or even a "Chinese mentality" on its foreign subsidiaries. Each was expected to hire local talent, contribute to local communities, respect local customs, and develop long-term relationships with local customers and suppliers. Headquarters delegated great authority to local managers, while trying to maintain a consistent image around the world and avoiding duplication of efforts. English was the company's international language.

To assist him in making Acer a truly multinational company, in early 1989 Shih recruited Dr. Leonard Liu from IBM to be Acer's President. Born in mainland China, Liu received a U.S. doctorate in computer science and had been IBM's highest ranking Chinese-American. Although his responsibilities covered Acer's global operations, Liu was particularly concerned with building its North American business. Shih continued as Chairman and CEO.

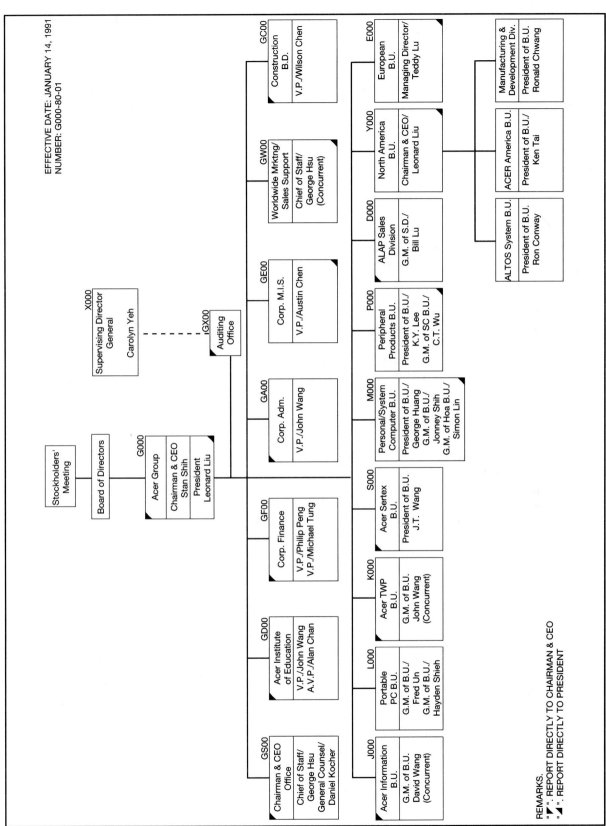

EFFECTIVE DATE: JANUARY 14, 1991
NUMBER: G000-80-01

Exhibit 21-3   Acer Group Organization Chart

REMARKS.
"■": REPORT DIRECTLY TO CHAIRMAN & CEO
"◣": REPORT DIRECTLY TO PRESIDENT

347

By early 1991, 46 year old Stan Shih had become one of the best known and most admired businessmen in Taiwan. He was a resolutely "M.I.T" (Made In Taiwan) product, whose career in many respects paralleled his country's development. The middle class family that he was born into was impoverished when his father died suddenly when Stan was four years old. Stan helped his mother sell groceries in the market, and later credited his skill with numbers to that early experience. "I had to convert between taels [a Chinese measure of weight] and grams, calculate prices to the penny, and make change—all in my head," he recalled.

Although his later scholastic accomplishments entitled him to enter National Taiwan University, the most prestigious institution of higher education in the country, he chose instead to attend National Chiao Tung University because he felt that training in electronics engineering would provide a more rapid road to success. And, whereas the majority of his fellow students went abroad for their graduate training, if their grades permitted, Shih chose to remain in Taiwan for his M.S. in electronics engineering. "I come from a rural area," he once admitted, "and it's not my nature to follow what's fashionable."

After graduation, Shih went to work for Unitron, designing hand-held calculators. Eventually he was invited by Unitron's owner to help him start up a new company, Qualitron. There Shih headed the development of a number of innovative products, including the first digital watch-in-a-pen, and soon was given managerial assignments. He rose rapidly in the organization, becoming in 1973 the vice president for calculator operations, where he managed over 1000 employees. "He ran the main business while the owner was off wasting money on risky diversification projects," recalled one old friend. "That was a good lesson for Stan."

His early poverty, his gratitude to his country for subsidizing his education, and his managerial experience at Qualitron all had a profound influence on Shih. From the hardship came an empathy for common people. This was reflected in Acer's "culture of the common man," which emphasized simplicity, frugality, and an egalitarian approach to dealing with customers, suppliers, and fellow workers. "You should understand," explained one senior manager, "that most of Acer's early employees were engineers. This means they didn't come from the upper social class, whose children tend to go into financial careers." From humble, mostly rural backgrounds and without any social connections, the struggling young company had to look for customers wherever it could find them. Its primary sales tool was the promise of superior service. "'Every customer is important,' was and is our motto," he continued, "and we were fanatical about keeping whatever promises we made to them."

The "culture of the common man" also underlay Acer's emphasis on simple, reliable product designs. And its frugality was apparent in its spartan offices and its admonition to use "both sides of every piece of paper." "If we can spend less than our competitors to do the same things, we will end up being more successful than they are," Shih argued.

Acer also tried to be a model corporate citizen. For example, feeling that Taiwan lacked enough written material about computer-related issues, Shih created the Third Wave Publishing Co., which soon became the country's largest publishing house for the information industry. "Publishing isn't anywhere near as profitable as selling computers," confided one manager, "but Stan feels that Taiwan needs access to this kind of information."

In addition, Acer sponsored the "Acer Table Tennis Team," composed of 22 carefully selected elementary and junior high school students who committed themselves to train with Acer for four or five years and whose goal was to represent Taiwan in the 1996 Olympics. Shih was also instrumental in setting up FORA, an international marketing and distribution company for Taiwan's small and mid-sized companies. "There is no shortcut to building a company's image," he argued. "It takes time, money and a long term commitment, so one should start while one is still small."

Finally, Acer tried to set an example that other Taiwanese companies could emulate—demonstrating that it was possible for them to be large, innovative, and international, and thereby compete successfully against the giant Western and Japanese multinationals. This was not an easy thing to do, given the traditional Chinese approach to business. "The Chinese people historically have preferred small, usually family-oriented, companies," explained a senior official in Taiwan's Ministry of Economic Affairs, and he quoted an old saying to the effect that "it is better to be the head of a chicken than the tail of an ox." He added, "As a result, as his company grows a Chinese manager is increasingly inclined to leave it and start up his own business. Needless to say, that makes it hard to build a big company. It takes a remarkable person to hold a big organization together in this country."

He continued:

> We are also a very pragmatic people. That gives us certain strengths, particularly when we compete against companies that approach business too theoretically or idealistically, and makes us very production-oriented. We have been very successful for many years at competing on the basis of low price, and operating with thin profit margins. But it also makes us reluctant to invest in intangible things. We may be willing to invest in a new machine, but we are not as willing to invest in innovation or infrastructure. At a national level, for example, we always seem to wait until almost too late to build mass transportation systems, highways, and parks. At a company level, to invest in building information and communication systems, or in brand names and worldwide distribution systems.
>
> Very few Taiwanese companies have developed their own brand names; most are satisfied to be OEMs, selling their products to be sold under someone else's brand name, so they don't have to invest in, or be bothered with, R&D, marketing, distribution, and advertising. This also makes it easier for them to avoid dealing with non-Chinese people, something they historically have found difficult be-

cause we are a very homogenous people, like the Japanese. That is reinforced by our "island mentality," and makes it difficult for us to think globally. But, even though restricting yourself to producing products—and not creating and merchandising them—simplifies your life and keeps costs down, it also limits your potential growth. I worry that our companies will become captives of their giant Japanese competitors, who have widely admired brand names, innovate continually, and control the distribution channels for their products. Taiwanese companies need to become more marketing-oriented.

> Finally, as a result of the attributes I have just described, as well as our education system (which emphasizes memorization because of our character-based writing system) and our Confucian respect for the direction of our elders, Chinese companies have tended to be followers in technology. We have many outstanding young engineers in our country—in fact, the technical abilities of our people are one of our great strengths. But I don't feel that there is enough real innovation going on in our companies, and they spend far too little on R&D. As a country, Taiwan only spends a little over 1% of its GNP on R&D—less than half what the United States, Japan, and West Germany spend. Possibly that is why Acer is such an admired company. And most people attribute its success largely to Mr. Shih, who has shown unusual vision and leadership in our business community.

In recognition of his accomplishments, Stan Shih received a number of honors. In 1981, for example, he was chosen as one of Taiwan's Outstanding Young Entrepreneurs, and two years later the International Junior Chamber of Commerce selected him as one of the Ten Most Outstanding Young Men in the World. The people working at Acer, many of them old friends and former schoolmates of Shih, appeared to share this admiration.

Corporate Culture and Values

His experience at Qualitron had convinced Shih that the authoritarian management style traditional in Taiwanese companies could not tap the full potential of a company's human resources. According to Shih,

> Rather than assume automatically that people will not work hard, or will do the wrong thing, unless you continually watch and direct them, I believe that most people are essentially good. Therefore,

one should trust them and allow them to study each situation they encounter and use their own judgment in dealing with it. That way they come to feel that they are their own boss. We don't have any time clocks at Acer, but our employees are continually encouraged to think of ways to cut costs and perform their tasks more effectively. Of course, some of our emphasis on individual initiative is out of necessity; Chinese people are not very systematic, and don't really like to follow procedures. Perhaps a more positive way to express this is to describe them as "self driving."

If you give them such freedom, of course, sometimes they will make mistakes. In the process, however, they learn important lessons and how to avoid future mistakes. I feel that this opportunity to learn, together with the motivation that comes from doing well on their own, more than compensates for any errors. In a sense, its like a tuition payment.

There was one iron rule, however, that no employee could violate: they could not take risks that might endanger the company's future. This rule reflected Shih's innate financial conservatism—another residue of his experience at Qualitron. The riskier projects, like R&D, were never funded with borrowed money.

A part of this trust in people was a deep-seated belief in the importance of continual self-improvement. Acer believed that giving people challenging jobs, moving them around a lot (even to jobs for which they were not trained), and providing them with ample opportunities to develop themselves both professionally and socially, would ultimately improve both them and the company. For example, every Acer employee was required to spend at least one day each month in classroom learning. Another unusual practice was that every employee was assigned to two jobs, so that every job had a back-up available. Despite the longer hours its employees were expected to work, Acer paid about the same wages as did other companies in Taiwan.

It did, however, provide a pension plan, group insurance, certain employee benefits (such as discount tours and a housing plan), and a stock purchase plan that was instituted long before Acer's initial public offering. Under this plan, any worker with at least three years experience (managers were only required to be with the company one year) was eligible to purchase up to US$5000 worth of company stock each year at its Book Value per share. Before the public offering, no ac-

tual stock certificate was conveyed, of course; one's ownership was simply a bookkeeping entry. This implicit stock could be sold back to the company after five years. During most of Acer's history, its book value grew at an average rate of 25% per year. Not only did this program motivate employees to equate the company's well-being with their own, it also provided a substantial portion of Acer's capital needs for several years.

Finally, Acer believed that team efforts were more important than individual contributions. In recognition of this philosophy, Acer's salesmen did not earn sales commissions—since the customer's decision to buy one of Acer's sophisticated products was not based solely on the salesman's efforts, but reflected the contribution of people throughout the company. "Performance Awards are better motivators than commissions," argued one manager. Such awards were based not only on an assessment of one's sales performance, but also on the recommendations of one's colleagues.

Acer's approach to selecting people for management jobs reflected the same philosophy. Although Shih preferred to promote people from among existing employees, Acer's rapid growth had forced him to recruit increasingly from the outside. Anybody who was a candidate for a management position, however, had to be interviewed by his potential subordinates, who were asked to judge whether he met the qualifications they wanted in a boss.

As a result of its economic success, its recognition as a role model for Taiwan business, and its unusual corporate philosophy, Acer was very well known and highly regarded in Taiwan. In 1990, for example, graduating Taiwanese college students selected it as the best company in the country to work for. Moreover, until recently its turnover rate had been under 5% per year—far less than the average in Taiwan. Among those who had worked for the company at least three years, the turnover rate was only 1%.

Approach to Competition

Almost from the beginning, Sta. Shih believed that Acer would eventually have to start designing its own products. "An OEM is not really in control of his destiny," he argued. "My goal was to become an

'OBM'—meaning an Original Brand-Name Manufacturer." This emphasis on internal product development was extremely deep-seated. "Despite his allegiance to Qualitron, Stan decided to leave when its financial problems got so severe that the owner proposed to close down their R&D group," recalled George Huang, one of Acer's co-founders, and now the President of the Personal System Business Unit. The importance Shih placed on technical capabilities was reflected in his first major purchase upon co-founding Multitech: he spent 70% of the US$25,000 that the fledgling company started with on testing equipment for his engineers.

Huang continued:

> The PC industry is intensely competitive. It has very short product life cycles, and profit margins are being squeezed. Competition takes place at three levels. At the top level are IBM, Compaq, Apple, and the big Japanese companies, who get higher margins because of their brand names. At the second level are companies like AST, Everex, Epson, and Acer. The third level is composed of companies who produce "knock-offs" that don't have recognized brand names. They engage in head-on competition, largely on a price basis, and have the lowest margins of all. Stan keeps emphasizing that Acer has to become a "world player." If we are to do that, and break into the top tier, we have to improve our brand image and develop new products faster. We also have to meet the market's fragmenting needs for specialized services."

Although its sales of its own products exceeded US$750 million in 1990, Acer still had not achieved a "critical mass," in the opinion of J. T. Wang, President of Sertek. He stated,

> We still have only about 3% of the world PC market, and are maybe only number 10 in the industry. If we are to survive over the long run, we have to break into the top five.

In order to do that, Leonard Liu believed,

> We have to speed up our decision processes. Chinese aren't quite as deliberate as the Japanese in deciding whether to do something, but we also aren't as fast at implementing a decision once it is made. We have to speed up all our organizational processes, from our production throughput time to our product development cycle.

The Taiwan Economy

Despite a population of only 20 million people, Taiwan's personal computer industry was the largest in Asia, except for Japan's. It had an installed base of over 720,000 machines and about 260,000 were sold in 1990. This represented about 38% of the total Asian market outside of Japan, and half again as many as were sold in Korea, whose population was more than twice as large as Taiwan's. Observers felt that this growth was due both to Taiwan's increasing technical base and to the fact that rapidly rising wages were changing the relative benefits of buying a PC rather than adding more people.

In 1990, after several years of double-digit wage increases, the average hourly earnings for a Taiwanese factory or clerical worker, expressed in U.S. dollars and including fringe benefits, approached half that in the United States. This did not necessarily imply that the average worker enjoyed half the standard of living of a U.S. worker, however. For one thing, with a population density of about 20 times that of the United States, the cost of comparable housing in Taiwan was many times that in North America or Europe.

Taiwan was also one of the world's largest producers of PCs. Hundreds of domestic manufacturers, most of them small, accounted for 25% of all the IBM-compatible PCs sold. In Taiwan, non-branded PCs accounted for about 52% of total sales, as compared with 21% in Korea and 28% in Hong Kong. In Thailand and Malaysia, two fast-growing markets, non-branded PCs accounted for over 65% of sales.

The Situation in Late 1990

In 1990, Taiwan's economic growth slowed dramatically, to about 5%. The manufacturing sector suffered even more, with industrial output actually falling for the first time in 15 years. The PC industry was particularly hard hit, and Acer's sales and profits came under increasing pressure. Its profit margin had shrunk during the previous year, but top management felt that had been largely due to its decision to add people and production capacity in advance of anticipated growth. Toward the end of 1990 it became clear that this growth would not occur as rapidly as had been expected. Moreover, Acer's management became increasingly concerned that its overhead had become bloated. As Stan Shih and his senior managers worked to hammer out a budget for 1991, they saw that Acer would not be able to do any better than break even if it did not reduce costs substantially.

Some were strongly in favor of a substantial lay-off. One long-time manager commented:

We simply have too many people for the amount of work that has to be done. Our policy of assigning a backup person to every job and, in effect, two sets of responsibilities to every person, is basically inefficient. That means that two people have to agree on every decision, no matter how trivial. Letting people operate without close supervision is also a luxury that we can't afford right now. Outside analysts have told us for several years that our overhead costs are higher than those of many of our competitors. Every 100 unnecessary middle managers represents well over a million U.S. dollars in lost profit. We've got to get our Total Operating Expenses back under 20% of sales. We probably also have 10% too many production workers.

A breakdown of Acer's employees by category and region is contained in **Exhibit 21–4**.

Another commented:

Just as important, people are so comfortable, being employed by a big, prestigious company, that they aren't working as hard as they used to. They don't feel the continual pressure that drove us during the early years. We need to reestablish a crisis atmosphere here.

Another reflected on the decline in the work ethic in Taiwan as a country:

We've experienced tremendous growth over the past few years, both our company and the economy as a whole. During the last seven years our economy grew at almost 9% per year. And during the last three years of that boom our stock market took off like a rocket. People forgot what had made them prosperous in the first place; they began speculating wildly, spent all their time watching stock prices and forgot about their jobs.

I think the political liberalism that has taken place here over the past few years has also had an effect. Now people want more freedom, and won't take direction as well. When combined with our tight labor market (our unemployment rate has been only about 1% over the past couple of years), people lost their former allegiance to their companies. They started chasing higher wages. The labor turnover rate among production and clerical workers in Taiwan as a whole was well over 3% a *month* last year.

Another manager expressed the view that it might be good to remove the bottom 5% of the people in an organization periodically.

Others argued, however, that laying-off people and moving to a more traditional work system would violate two of the central tenets of Acer's philosophy. "Our employees didn't decide to add people in advance of growth; we in management did," asserted one manager. "We should let normal attrition take its course, and accept the higher costs until our cost structure is where we want it to be." "Unfortunately, attrition alone may take too long," rejoined another. "The slowdown in the economy's growth rate, and the losses people experienced in the stock market, have made them appreciate their jobs more. Our turnover rate is slowing rapidly, particularly among middle management, where the biggest problem is. It's probably less than 1% a month for them now, whereas the rate for factory and clerical workers is still over 2% a month."

Others debated the merits of moving to a shorter work week and cutting salaries. "I worry that if we cut salaries while the labor market is so tight, people will leave," stated one. "After all, the kind of person we're talking about doesn't earn that much, usually less than US$15,000 per year, including fringe benefits. And the ones who decide to go somewhere else tend to be the best ones. We in management should be the ones deciding who leaves and who stays."

Another summarized, "The issue is not simply *whether* to lay off people, it's also how many, and where in the organization. It would probably be easier, and might be regarded as fairer, if we took the same percentage from each department and region, but I don't think that would be the right thing for us to do. On the other hand, it also

Exhibit 21-4 Acer Incorporated Staffing Distribution

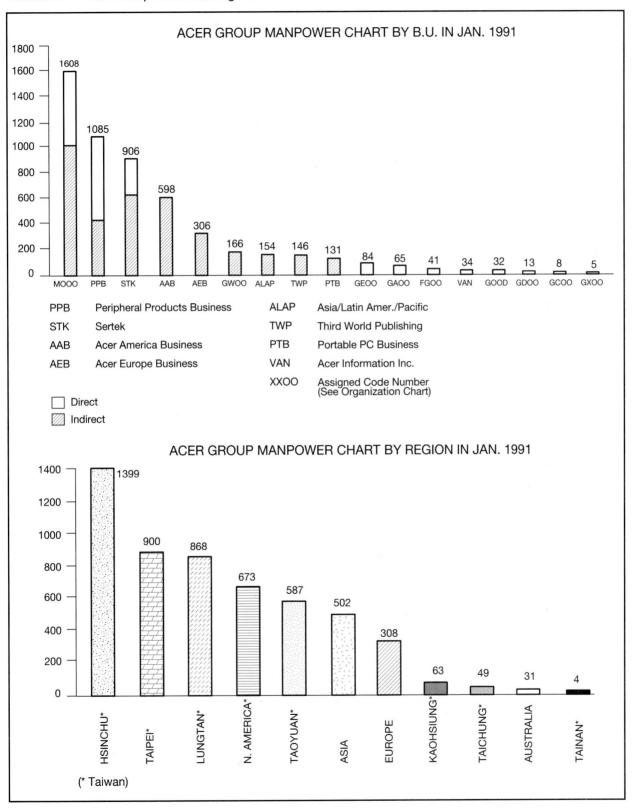

ACER GROUP MANPOWER CHART BY B.U. IN JAN. 1991

PPB	Peripheral Products Business
STK	Sertek
AAB	Acer America Business
AEB	Acer Europe Business

ALAP	Asia/Latin Amer./Pacific
TWP	Third World Publishing
PTB	Portable PC Business
VAN	Acer Information Inc.
XXOO	Assigned Code Number (See Organization Chart)

☐ Direct

▨ Indirect

ACER GROUP MANPOWER CHART BY REGION IN JAN. 1991

(* Taiwan)

Exhibit 21-5 Task Achievement and Job Satisfaction

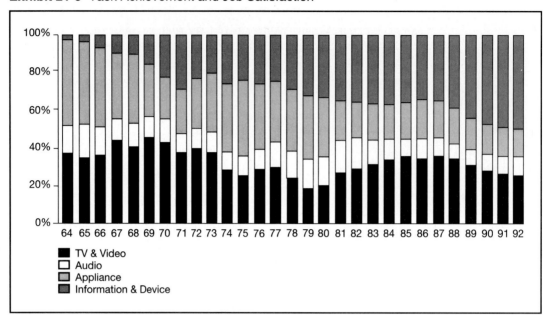

wouldn't be right to confine it to a narrow segment of our workforce."

Stan Shih, as was his custom, was listening to all sides and playing the role of "honest broker":

I've always believed in building up the organization in advance of growth, so we could grow as fast as the market would let us. But I'm not sure how long this current slump is going to last. I'm wondering whether we shouldn't sacrifice some potential growth for a little better profitability during this period. It would probably be easier to make this decision if our company weren't so well known. Now everybody watches us so closely.

The Issue of Motivation

Opinions were just as sharply divided about whether Acer should take new steps to motivate its employees. Some argued that the company ought to adopt some of the approaches used in Western companies, like bonuses and stock options. Others, such as Ronald Chwang, believed that many of the causes of lower worker commitment were correcting themselves as the economy slowed and the stock market hovered near its recent low. "I believe we ought to stick to the approach that got us where we are," he argued. "Provide challenging jobs, the opportunity to be one of the major players in the world, the chance to advance very rapidly if you're good and willing to make the effort."

George Huang agreed. He felt Acer should try harder to get its employees to integrate their private goals with their career. "Before I had my first job, I promised myself that one day I would walk across the Golden Gate Bridge, climb the Statue of Liberty, and walk around the Eiffel Tower. In the course of my career at Acer, I have done all those things. This can be a tremendous source of motivation."

An even bigger problem, most agreed, was getting their Chinese employees to become more open in expressing their feelings and in identifying and confronting problems. Chwang explained:

In the United States it is much easier to surface issues, but Chinese are much more reserved. For one thing, they don't like to say "no." A western company may come to them with a request, saying: "I need this by a certain date. Can you do it?" A Chinese is likely to respond, "That will be very difficult, but I will do my best." A Westerner will think there is a good chance the request will be met, but the correct translation is "no."

Others felt their people needed to learn to "disagree more effectively: listening to other people's views, explaining their position to others, and making decisions that some people may disagree with, all while maintaining respect for one another." As Leonard Liu expressed it, "Our people have to become more mature and professional, and change from a small company mentality to that of a large one.

Another manager disagreed. "This company has simply gotten too big. We ought to split it up into four or five smaller, separate companies."

22. Sharp Corporation: Corporate Strategy

Established in 1912, Sharp Corporation owed its name to the invention of the "Ever-Sharp" mechanical pencil by founder Tokuji Hayakawa. By 1992, with sales of ¥1,518 billion (US$11,497 million) and net income of ¥39 billion (US$296 million)[1], Sharp had grown to include businesses ranging from consumer electronics and information systems to electronic components employing 41,000 people (**Exhibit 22–1**).

Founded on the creed "Sincerity and Creativity," entrepreneurship and technological innovation had always been mainstays of the company. However, Sharp had traditionally been seen as a second-tier assembler of television sets and home appliances which competed mainly on price. Although the company had introduced a number of new products, most of them were quickly imitated by larger competitors, including Matsushita, Hitachi, and Toshiba. A critical turning point therefore came in the 1970s when Sharp began manufacturing integrated circuits (ICs) and won the Japanese "calculator wars" by introducing very thin calculators incorporating the new liquid crystal display (LCD) technology. Sharp then developed expertise in certain electronic devices, such as specialized ICs and LCDs, which it used to develop innovative end products (**Exhibit 22–2**). As a result, the company had consistently improved its performance so that, by 1992, it was regarded as a world leader in optoelectronics and a premier comprehensive electronics company.

[1]Sharp's fiscal year ends March 31.

Doctoral Candidate Tomo Noda prepared this case under the supervision of Professor David J. Collis as the basis for class discussion rather than to illustrate either effective or ineffective handling of an administrative situation.

EXHIBIT 22-1 Sharp Corporation—Financial Summary

	Dollar Millions	Japanese Yen Millions												
	1992	1992	1991	1990	1989	1988	1987	1986	1985	1980	1975*	1970*	1965*	1960*
Consolidated														
Sales	11,497	1,517,538	1,496,111	1,344,799	1,238,401	1,225,186	1,148,881	1,216,048	1,166,651	514,884	190,185	120,822	30,210	19,922
Gross Profit	3,309	436,794	437,232	388,389	315,835	247,253	235,602	283,373	285,511	129,712	27,429	24,130	5,995	5,273
Selling, General, Administration	2,777	366,597	351,185	307,457	262,093	228,584	219,156	239,956	220,067	100,243	22,662	12,501	4,502	2,493
Operating Income	531	70,197	86,047	88,932	53,742	20,669	16,466	43,417	65,444	29,469	4,767	11,628	1,493	2,780
Income Before Tax	629	83,103	99,648	93,511	68,586	43,196	42,831	70,875	78,326	29,596	4,112	8,226	1,070	2,701
Net Income	295	39,057	46,918	41,720	29,103	20,341	20,775	35,935	39,903	16,747	2,617	5,271	805	1,429
Total Assets	16,270	2,147,690	2,077,030	2,032,598	1,764,662	1,618,625	1,400,352	1,232,747	1,110,153	450,205	168,347	99,673	32,506	14,039
Long-Term Debt	1,558	205,652	261,639	247,515	196,075	145,787	125,865	128,446	130,394	27,195	13,512	6,420	1,947	0
Shareholders' Equity	5,724	755,561	726,763	685,351	534,758	477,925	390,107	379,471	357,891	128,263	38,664	30,540	11,669	5,225
Acquisition of Plant and Equipment	995	131,373	122,670	116,675	80,722	55,264	59,328	82,042	91,794	39,192	6,881	12,355	N/A	1,751
Depreciation and Amortization	758	100,107	89,625	75,032	68,449	61,268	58,864	55,451	45,645	15,549	5,936	3,839	805	226
Return on Sales (%)		2.57%	3.14%	3.10%	2.35%	1.66%	1.81%	2.96%	3.42%	3.25%	1.38%	4.36%	2.66%	7.17%
Return on Assets (%)		1.82%	2.26%	2.05%	1.65%	1.26%	1.48%	2.92%	3.59%	3.72%	1.55%	5.29%	2.48%	10.18%
Return on Equity (%)		5.17%	6.46%	6.09%	5.44%	4.26%	5.33%	9.47%	11.15%	13.06%	6.77%	17.26%	6.90%	27.35%
Income per Share (Yen)		36.61	44.13	39.57	30.57	22.40	28.19	49.01	54.57	31.28	11.08	25.10	6.71	35.73
Dividend per Share (Yen)		11.00	11.00	11.00	11.00	11.00	11.00	11.00	11.00	7.50	8.25	9.00	6.00	10.70
Number of Employees	41,029	41,029	36,539	34,017	32,298	29,351	29,346	28,873	28,221	18,743	9,804	15,442	5,591	4,457
Non Consolidated														
Sales	9,106	1,202,014	1,152,678	1,057,282	992,665	872,707	868,587	955,252	909,581	395,246	190,185	120,822	30,210	19,922
Net Income	273	36,063	44,340	37,536	26,232	18,857	20,104	34,735	33,863	12,526	2,617	5,271	805	1,429

*Non-consolidated. (Consolidated data for these years are not available.)

Source: Sharp Corporation.

EXHIBIT 22-2 Sharp's New Products

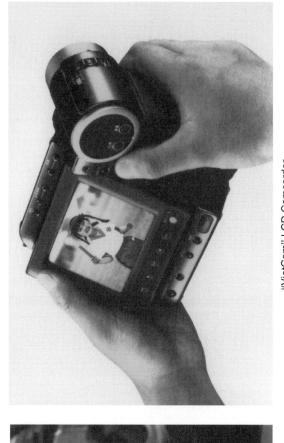

"VietCam" LCD Camcorder

Automotive 4" Color LCD TV

"Wizard" Electronic Organizer

"LCD Museum" Wall-mount Color LCD TV

Source: Sharp Corporation.

The Era of Tokuji Hayakawa (1912–1970)

Tokuji Hayakawa began his career as a live-in apprentice in a metal workshop in Tokyo (**Exhibit 22–3**). Making a snap belt buckle which he had designed himself, he opened his own workshop with two employees in 1912. After three years, Hayakawa invented a mechanical pencil, consisting of a retractable graphite lead in a metal rod, and named it the Ever-Sharp pencil. Expanding sales of mechanical pencils then enabled him to introduce assembly line processes uncommon in Japan at that time. Unfortunately, the Great Kanto Earthquake of 1923 took everything away from Hayakawa: he lost his wife, two infant sons, many employees, and his workshop.

In 1924, Hayakawa reestablished his company in Osaka with three employees. With radio broadcasting scheduled to begin in Japan the following year, he bought one of the first imported, crystal radio sets. Although he and his employees did not have any background in radio, they mastered the technology by disassembling this American model, and the company began to assemble Japan's first domestically-produced crystal radio sets in 1925. When, in 1929, several competitors entered the market seeking to improve the crystal radio, Hayakawa instead developed a radio using vacuum tubes that could amplify signals and receive them from a wider range. The mass production of this radio, called the Sharp Dyne, and the commencement of its export to South Asia established the company as a leading manufacturer of radios. In 1935, the Hayakawa Metal Works Institute Co. was incorporated with the ¥300,000 in capital. The company was renamed Hayakawa Electric Industry Co. (Hayakawa Electric) in 1942.

After WW2, anticipating the approach of the TV era, and having already succeeded in developing its own prototype TV receiver, Hayakawa

EXHIBIT 22-3 Sharp Corporation—Corporate History

1912	Founded by Tokuji Hayakawa in Tokyo. Invented the *snap buckle*.
1915	Invented a *mechanical pencil* [a] named the Ever-Sharp Pencil.
1925	Relocated to Osaka after the 1922 Great Kanto Earthquake. Established as Hayakawa Metal Works. Began production of *crystal radio sets* [b] and components.
1929	Began production of *AC vacuum-tube radio sets.* [b]
1930	Started export of crystal radios.
1935	Incorporated as Hayakawa Metal Works Institute Co.
1942	Renamed Hayakawa Electric Industry Co.
1953	Developed *black-and-white TV sets.* [b]
1962	Developed *microwave ovens.* [b] Established a marketing subsidiary in the United States.
1963	Introduced a multi-divisional organization structure.
1964	Developed and began mass-production of *all transistor-diode electronic desktop calculator-Compet.* [a]
1968	Established a marketing subsidiary in Germany.
1970	Established Advanced Development Planning Center (Central Research Laboratories, ELSI Plant and training center) in Tenri, Nara. Renamed Sharp Corporation.
1971	Established Sharp Digital Information Products Inc. Established production companies in Taiwan and Brazil.
1973	Developed *COS electronic calculator incorporating LCD.* [a] Established a production company in Korea.
1976	Organized New Life Committee.
1979	Established Sharp Manufacturing Company of America. Started local production of color TVs in Memphis.
1985	Established Sharp Manufacturing Company of Europe. Established Creative Lifestyle Focus Center in Osaka.
1988	Developed *14" TFT color liquid crystal.* [a]
1990	Established Sharp Laboratories of Europe, Ltd.
1992	Established the Multimedia Systems Research and Development Center.

[a] World's first.
[b] Japan's first.

Electric negotiated a license from RCA in 1953 to manufacture Japan's first black-and-white TV sets under the Sharp brand name. By 1955, the company was a leading Japanese TV manufacturer with nearly a quarter of the market.[2] This positioned Sharp to grow with the Japanese electrical goods market at more than 30% p.a. as first black-and-white and then color TV sets, refrigerators, washing machines, and air conditioners became household status symbols. The company increased production capacity, developed market channels, and expanded its operations to include home appliances, and Japan's first microwave ovens (using technology learned while working with Litton, the U.S. innovator in microwave ovens). By 1965, TVs and radios accounted for 53% of the company's sales, down from 84% in 1960.

Throughout this period, founder Hayakawa advocated making innovative products that competitors would want to imitate. However, the company remained primarily an assembler because its limited size and capital restricted its ability to vertically integrate and competitors were able to rapidly copy its products. These problems were exacerbated in the mid-1960s when the Japanese economy experienced a severe recession. Prior to this time, most electrical products had been sold to consumers by independent "mom and pop" retailers. Faced with the sharp decline in consumer demand, many of the retailers who had previously carried Sharp brands became exclusive retailers for the large electrical goods producers, such as Matsushita, Toshiba, and Hitachi, which offered broad product lines and favorable terms. Despite its best efforts, Hayakawa Electric was only able to build a distribution network one seventh the size of Matsushita's and one third that of Hitachi's and Toshiba's. Because of its smaller distribution network and the continuing imitation of its products, Hayakawa Electric's market share in radios and TVs began to decline.

At the same time, Hayakawa, like many other large electrical products manufacturers, invested in the emerging computer technology. In 1961, it established a corporate research laboratory to begin research on computers, solar cells, and microwaves. However, the Ministry of International Trade and Industry (MITI) soon restricted the benefits of its industrial policy for the computer industry to six companies, in effect shutting Hayakawa Electric out of the development of mainframe computers. In order to continue their work, Hayakawa Electric's researchers chose desktop electronic calculators as an alternative target. Top management supported this choice partly because calculators matched the company's orientation toward the mass consumer market.

The company's refocusing of its computer research led to its introducing the world's first all transistor-diode electronic desktop calculator, called Compet, in 1964. The Compet weighed 25 kilograms (55 pounds), was 25 centimeters (8.7 inches) thick, and sold for ¥535,000 (about $1,500 at that time), almost as much as a 1300 cc passenger car. Sony, Canon, and Oi Electric introduced their own electronic calculators within several months of Compet's introduction. Casio, a leading producer of mechanical calculators, then followed suit, beginning the so-called electronic calculator wars.

In response, under the direction of Dr. Sasaki, a recently hired outsider who had been a researcher at Bell Laboratories and RCA, Hayakawa Electric introduced the world's first electronic calculators incorporating integrated circuits (ICs) in 1966. These calculators used Bipolar ICs which processed commands faster but consumed more electricity than MOS ICs (metal oxide semiconductors). However, Dr. Sasaki judged that whereas speed was important for mainframe computers, energy efficiency would be critical for consumer electronics. He also thought that MOS ICs would be better for making calculators smaller because their chip density could be easily increased.[3] Although MOS ICs had not been tested widely, Dr. Sasaki convinced Hayakawa Electric to use them and found a supplier, North American Rockwell Company. By employing this new technology, the company quickly assumed a leading position in electronic calculators.

[2]Hideo Hirayama, *Waga Kaisoroku: Sharp (My Memories on Sharp)* (Tokyo: Denpa Shimbunsha, 1991), p. 52.

[3]Masahiko Tonedachi, *Dentaku-to-Shinkansen (Electronic Calculators and Super Express Trains: The Arts of the Japanese Advanced Technologies)* (Tokyo: Shinchosha, 1983), p. 75.

The Era of Akira Saeki
(1970–1986)

On a visit to Rockwell in 1969, Mr. Saeki, then senior executive vice president of Hayakawa Electric, saw a replica of the Apollo moon capsule and was impressed by Rockwell's state-of-the-art semiconductor technology that had made the space mission possible. Although he had spent most of his career in finance and accounting and did not have a technology background, he was convinced of the semiconductor's potential. Worried about his company's position as an assembler, Saeki also recognized the importance of in-house manufacturing of key components in developing unique products.[4] He repeatedly said, "We can hardly contribute to society if we only make the same products that other manufacturers do . . . [We need to develop] products which others cannot imitate even if they want to do so."[5]

With the support of President Hayakawa, Saeki proposed canceling the company's participation in the international exhibition scheduled for the following year in *Senri*, so that the company could build a semiconductor factory in nearby *Tenri*, instead. Despite the puzzlement of other executives, who considered participation in the exhibition to be critical in establishing the image of Hayakawa Electric as a top Japanese company, the company built a C-MOS LSI (Large Scale Integration) plant and a central research laboratory. Investing ¥7,500 million (US$21 million) in the projects (one quarter of the company's equity), the catch-phrase of "Tenri rather than Senri" appeared almost spontaneously in the company as Hayakawa Electric became the thirteenth semiconductor manufacturer in Japan. However, lacking technology and expertise, manufacturing yields in the new semiconductor factory were low, and the operation incurred annual losses of ¥400–¥600 (approximately $1.3–$2 million) in its first five years.[6] Only in the mid-1970s, did the company's production of C-MOS semiconductors turn profitable.

In January 1970, Hayakawa Electric was renamed Sharp Corporation to reflect the company's brand name and herald its transition from an electrical appliance manufacturer to a comprehensive electronics company. Mr. Saeki formally assumed the presidency when Tokuji Hayakawa retired from day-to-day operations to become chairman later that year. At the same time, competition in electronic desktop calculators intensified, particularly in August 1972, when Casio introduced the revolutionary Casio Mini, a six-digit calculator costing only ¥12,800 (about $40 at that time). Challenged by Casio's low-cost strategy, most firms, including Sony, exited the market.

Stunned by the "Casio Shock" and trying to avoid a price war, a project team headed by Atsushi Asada (who was a senior executive vice president in 1992) sought to develop by April, 1973 a thinner calculator which would consume less electricity and, so, would be truly portable. The team's efforts resulted in the world's thinnest calculator, the LC Mate, which cost ¥26,800, but weighed only 200 grams (0.44 pounds) and was only 2.1 centimeters (0.7 inch) thick. This palm-sized model consumed less than 1/100 of the electricity of conventional fluorescent tube models by incorporating an LCD into a calculator for the first time ever, and used chip-on-sheet (COS) process technology which involved assembling the LCD, LSIs, and other circuits onto one glass substrate.

LCDs consume little electricity because the liquid crystals themselves do not emit light; rather their molecules are arranged along an electric field, allowing external rays to pass through when voltage is applied. A Sharp engineer had learned about the application of liquid crystals to displays, which had been pioneered by RCA in the late 1960s, while watching a television program about the United States. RCA had since stopped LCD research and exited the business because Sharp management believed that RCA senior management saw only a small market for the product at that time.

Sharp soon improved upon the LC Mate, developing a 7 mm-thick electronic calculator using in-house CMOS LSIs in 1976, and a 1.6 mm one using better COS and manufacturing technologies in 1979. The incorporation of photovoltaic cells nearly eliminated the need for an electricity source, and the introduction of a fully-automated

---

[4]Sharp Corporation, *Seii-to-Soi: Hachijunen no Ayumi (Sincerity and Creativity: The 80-year History of Sharp Corporation)* (Tokyo: Sharp Corp, 1992), p. 42.

[5]Hirayama, H., p. 79.

[6]Hirayama, H., p. 85.

manufacturing process contributed to a drastic reduction in product price. As a result of these efforts, Sharp won the Japanese calculator wars and held nearly half of the domestic market share by the end of the 1970s.

Using the same distribution channels developed for calculators, Sharp quickly diversified within the information equipment business in the 1970s. It developed a broad range of office automation products, including micro-computers (1971), electronic cash registers (1971), liquid toner copiers (1972), personal computers (1979), Japanese word processors (1979), Japanese word processors (1979), and facsimiles (1980).

During the same period, the domestic market for TVs and other appliances was approaching saturation. In response, Sharp abandoned its previous goal of catching up with its rivals in sales volume and concentrated on "distinguishing between where [it could] win and where [it could not], and winning completely in the former."[7] In 1975, a task force proposed introducing "New Life Products" to meet the demands of more diversified and sophisticated customers. The New Life Committee, composed of directors, general managers of business groups, and top managers of sales subsidiaries, was organized to achieve this in 1976. One of the first New Life Products was a 3-door refrigerator with a freezer at the bottom, which was introduced because customer research had shown that the frequency of use was 80% for coolers and 20% for freezers. With the cooler at the top, users had to bend less frequently. In addition to functionality, the New Life committee emphasized color and design, which most manufacturers considered to be of secondary importance at that time, and it carefully coordinated these elements across several business groups. With the successful promotion of a series of New Life products, Sharp's appliance business attained annual growth of 10% in the late 1970s and early 1980s, despite the sluggish 3% annual growth of the industry as a whole during the period.[8]

Sharp's other achievements during the 1970s, led to a strategic thrust to redefine the company as an opto-electronics company. Sharp had developed the world's largest solar cells for a lighthouse in 1963, and further research led to the development of solar cells for satellites in 1976. The central R&D laboratory also developed electro-luminescent (EL) displays and laser diodes. While the potential of electro-luminescence for displays had been known for a long time, most firms had discontinued research in this area because of technological difficulties. Sharp, however, persevered and developed an EL panel in 1978, which was used in space shuttle displays. A few years later, it mass-produced ultra-thin, high-definition EL displays. As for laser diodes, the "optical needle" for compact disks and video disks, Sharp's development of a durable diode in 1981 gained it the leading position in the world market.

The Era of Haruo Tsuji (1986–present)

Sharp's steady growth was interrupted in 1985 by the drastic appreciation of the Japanese yen against the U.S. dollar because of the Plaza Accord. The company's fiscal 1987 nonconsolidated sales dropped by about 10% and operating profits by more than 60%. In this difficult environment, Haruo Tsuji, a company veteran with extensive experience in the appliance business, assumed the post of president.

Under Tsuji, Sharp continued its New Life Strategy to design products that appealed to modern consumers' lifestyles. The company introduced new products, such as electronic organizers (i.e., the Wizard in the United States), dual-swing door refrigerators, home-use facsimile machines, and the first combination cordless telephone/answering machines, and furthered its reputation among retailers and customers for user-friendliness.

In addition to experiencing continued success in consumer electronics and appliances, Sharp made advances in electronic devices, particularly in LCDs, which it chose to develop in preference to the cathode ray tubes it had always purchased from outside vendors, even for TV sets. Since its first use of LCDs in calculators, Sharp had maintained its leadership in the technology by continuing to develop larger, higher

[7]Comment of Masaki Seki originally cited by Hirayama, H., p. 93.

[8]Takeuchi, H., Sakakibara, K., Kagono, T., Okumura, A. and Nonaka, I *Kigyo no Jiko Kakushin (Self-Renewal of the Japanese Firms)* (Tokyo: Chuokoronsha, 1986), p. 85.

quality LCDs. It introduced an alphabetical LCD for calculators in 1979 and a large monochrome LCD for personal computers and word processors in 1983. Using a new thin-film-transistor (TFT) active-matrix technology, it then developed a 3-inch color LCD with faster response and a higher picture quality in 1986, a 14-inch color TFT LCD in 1988, and a 16.5-inch wide-vision and multimedia compatible color TFT LCD in 1992. Based on these LCDs, the company continuously introduced a number of first-in-the-world products, such as a 110-inch color LCD video projector, a 8.6-inch wall-mount LCD monitor (1991), and the "ViewCam" camcorder with a 4-inch color LCD monitor (1992), even though some of these products were initially unprofitable because they only met a small market need.

As Sharp recorded five years of consecutive growth in sales and operating profits to fiscal 1991, its reputation in Japan grew stronger. One corporate image survey showed Sharp climbing from 63rd. to 21st. in the three years to 1992. Another survey on excellent Japanese companies ranked Sharp in ninth position in 1992. In the United States, Sharp was ranked twenty-fifth among all companies, U.S. and foreign, in patents filed behind such technological giants as IBM, GM, GE, AT&T, Du Pont, and 3M.[9]

Globalization

Sharp's overseas activities began in 1930, with the export of crystal radios to Thailand, and grew rapidly with the introduction of vacuum tube radios throughout South Asia. After World War II, Hayakawa Electric rapidly expanded its exports to the United States under the Sharp brand name, starting with transistor radios and then adding black-and-white TV sets in the 1960s (**Exhibit 22–4**). It established a wholly-owned sales subsidiary in the United States in 1962, and gradually developed a global sales network with subsidiaries in West Germany (1968), the United Kingdom (1969), Australia (1971), and Canada (1974). In 1971, to support overseas sales and respond better to the needs of local customers, Sharp established its first overseas design and development center in the United States.

Also, in the early 1970s, in response to cost pressure because of the yen's appreciation, Sharp transferred labor-intensive activities overseas, establishing production companies in Taiwan (1971), Brazil (1971), Korea (1973), and Malaysia (1974). These overseas production facilities were established as joint ventures based on technology licensing rather than as wholly-owned subsidiaries. This structure reflected Tokuji Hayakawa's philosophy that his company would not exploit developing countries, but rather prosper with them.

To mitigate U.S. trade frictions, particularly concerning TV sets, Sharp established the Sharp Manufacturing Company of America (SMCA) to produce color TVs in 1979. SMCA steadily expanded its operations, adding LCD production by 1992. Similarly, a manufacturing facility was established in the U.K. in 1985 to further localize Sharp's overseas operations. Finally, in order to better exploit rapid changes in technology, the company established a research laboratory in the U.K. in 1990, which conducted basic research in opto-electronics and information processing technologies (e.g., Pan-European translation technology).

[9]*Business Week,* August 3, 1992, pp. 68–69.

Sharp's Businesses in 1992

Sharp products fell into four broad areas: consumer electronics, appliances, information and office automation equipment, and electronic devices (**Exhibits 22–5, 22–6** and **22–7**).

Consumer Electronics and Appliances

The TV and Video Systems Group was the largest single manufacturing group in the company with sales of about ¥400 billion (25.9% of the company's total) in fiscal 1992. The company strove

EXHIBIT 22-4 Sharp Corporation—Exports and Exchange Rates

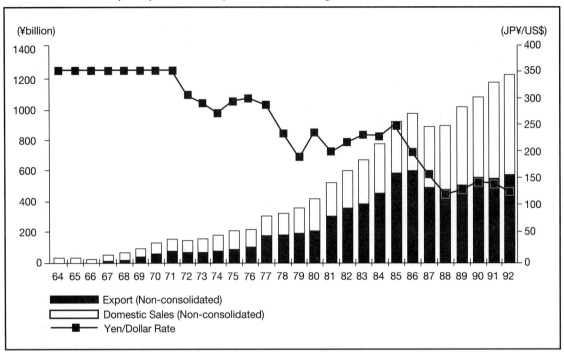

EXHIBIT 22-5 Sharp Corporation—Transition of Business Portfolio (on a nonconsolidated basis)

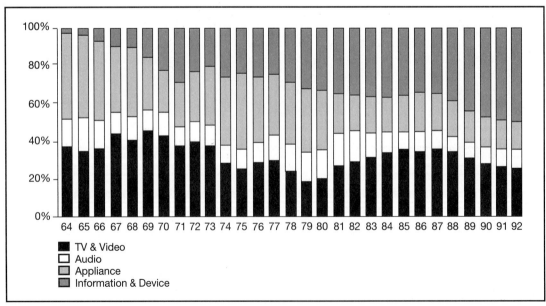

EXHIBIT 22-6 Sharp Corporation—Current Businesses (Overview)

Area	Manufacturing Groups	Consolidated Sales (FY 1992)	Manufacturing Division	Major Products	Major Competitors
Consumer Electronics	TV & Video System Group	¥393.4 billion (US$2,981 million) 25.9%	• TV Systems Division • LCD Visual Systems Division • Video Systems Division	Color TVs, TVs with built-in VCRs, video cameras, video camera recorders, LCD color TVs, LCD projectors, personal workstations, video printers, HDTV converters and decoders, etc.	1. Hitachi, Toshiba, Mitsubishi Electric, Fuji Electric (started as heavy electric machinery manufacturers)
	Audio System Group	¥171.6 billion (US$1,300 million) 11.3%	• Audio Equipment Division • Personal Communications Systems Division • Business Communication Systems Division	Radio cassette tape recorders, headphone stereos, stereo component systems, CD players, laser disc players, DAT tape decks, car stereo systems, cordless telephones, facsimilies, DAT memory storage systems, optical disc storage systems, etc.	2. Sony, JVC, Pioneer, Aiwa, Kenwood, Akai Electric (Specialized in audio-visual products)
Home Appliances	Appliance System Group	¥265.7 billion (US$1,850 million) 17.5%	• Refrigeration Systems Division • Kitchen Appliances Systems Division • Air-Conditioning Systems Division • Laundry Systems Division	Central heating and air conditioning systems, kerosene heaters, electric blankets, refrigerators, microwave ovens, dishwashers, washing machines, vacuum cleaners, tele-control systems, electric kitchen tools, etc.	3. Matsushita Electric, Sanyo Electric, NEC Home Electronics, Fujitsu General (started as appliance manufacturers)
Information Systems & Office Automation Equipment	Information Systems Group	about ¥350 billion* (US$2,640 million) about 23%	• Computer Division • OA Equipment Division • Personal Equipment Division • Calculator Division • Nara Plant	Calculators, electronic organizers, office computers, personal computers, integrated communication systems, word processors, etc.	Casio, Canon, NEC, Fujitsu, Toshiba, Hitachi, Mitsubishi Electric, Matsushita
	Printing & Reprographic Systems Group		• Reprography Division • Printer and Scanner Division	Copiers, scanners, POS systems, electronic medical devices, FA systems, CAD systems, OA peripherals, etc.	NEC, Toshiba, Canon, Ricoh, Matsushita Electric, Fuji Xerox, Seiko-Epson, Konica
Electronics Components/ Devices	Integrated Circuits Group	about ¥350 billion* (US$2,640 million) about 23%	• Tenri Plant • Fukuyama Plant I • Fukuyama Plant 2	LSIs, ICs, gate arrays, LCD drivers, etc. flash memory, masked ROM	NEC, Hitachi, Toshiba, Fujitsu, Matsushita Electronic, Sanyo Mitsubishi Electric, Oki Electric
	Electronic Components Group		• Electronic Components Division • Opto-Electronic Devices Division • Photovoltaics Division	LEDs, semiconductor laser diode units, satellite transmission, components, electronic tuners, printed circuit boards, solar batteries, optomagnetic disks, optoelectric terminals, etc.	Hitachi, Toshiba, Sanyo, Matsushita Electric, Mitsubishi Electric
	Liquid Crystal Display Group		• Nara Plant • Tenri Plant	Passive matrix LCDs, TFT active matrix LCDs, etc.	Seiko-Epson, Optrex (Asahi Glass & Mitsubishi Electric), Hitachi, Hoshiden, Toshiba, Sanyo, Citizen Watch

*Estimates of the case writer. (A breakdown of sales and share between information and electronic devices was not publicly available.)

EXHIBIT 22-7 Sharp Corporation—Market Shares for Major Products

Consumer Electronics and Home Appliances

Color TVs (a)		VCRs (a)		Camcorders (a)		Mini Stereo Sets (a)	
1 Matsushita	22.5%	1 Matsushita	25.0%	1 Sony	43.0%	1 Sony	24.0%
2 Toshiba	14.5%	2 Toshiba	13.0%	2 Matsushita	32.0%	2 Pioneer	18.0%
3 Sharp	14.5%	3 JVC	13.0%	3 JVC	10.0%	3 Kenwood	16.0%
4 Hitachi	10.5%	4 Mitsubishi	12.5%	4 Hitachi	3.0%	4 Matsushita	13.0%
5 Sony	10.5%	5 Sharp	12.0%	5 Canon	2.0%	5 JVC	11.0%

Home Phones (d)		Refrigerators (a)		Air Conditioners (a)		Microwave Ovens (a)	
1 Sharp	22.5%	1 Matsushita	22.5%	1 Matsushita	23.0%	1 Matsushita	27.8%
2 Sanyo	18.9%	2 Toshiba	18.0%	2 Toshiba	18.0%	2 Sharp	20.4%
3 NTT	16.0%	3 Hitachi	16.0%	3 Hitachi	15.0%	3 Hitachi	12.4%
4 Matsushita	11.0%	4 Sanyo	11.0%	4 Mitsubishi	13.0%	4 Toshiba	9.2%
5 Pioneer Comm.	8.2%	5 Sharp	8.2%	5 Sanyo	11.0%	5 Mitsubishi	9.1%

Information & Office Systems and ICs

Facsimiles (e)		Plain Paper Copiers (a)		Electronic Calculators (b)		Japanese Wordprocessors (b)	
1 Matsushita	16.2%	1 Ricoh	30.2%	1 Casio	53.5%	1 Sharp	19.8%
2 Ricoh	16.0%	2 Canon	30.1%	2 Sharp	39.0%	2 Toshiba	15.0%
3 Canon	16.0%	3 Fuji Xerox	22.1%	3 Canon	2.8%	3 NEC	12.4%
4 Sharp	11.0%	4 Sharp	6.8%	4 Sanyo	2.3%	4 Fujitsu	12.3%
5 NEC	10.0%	5 Konica	4.8%	5 Toshiba	2.2%	5 Matsushita	10.2%

Personal Computers (c)		Office Computers (c)		Mainframe Computers (e)		Integrated Circuits (f)	
1 NEC	53.1%	1 NEC	27.3%	1 Fujitsu	25.0%	1 NEC	21.1%
2 Fujitsu	12.7%	2 Fujitsu	27.1%	2 Japan IBM	23.8%	2 Toshiba	17.1%
3 Toshiba	10.8%	3 Toshiba	9.5%	3 Hitachi	18.0%	3 Hitachi	13.4%
4 Seiko-Epson	8.2%	4 Japan IBM	9.0%	4 NEC	17.33%	4 Fujitsu	12.5%
5 Japan IBM	7.0%	5 Mitsubishi	8.5%	5 Japan Unysis	10.1%	5 Mitsubishi	9.5%

- The data is based on the survey by "'Nihon Keizai Shimbun (The Japanese Economic Journal).'"
- The product's market share is calculated based on (a) its domestic unit shipment, (b) its domestic unit production, (c) its total unit production, (d) its domestic sales amount, (e) its domestic production amount, and (f) its total production amount including exports.
- Sharp holds the sixth position or below for those products where its name is not listed.

Source: "Nikkei Sangyo Shimbun," June 11, 1992.

to develop new market niches by applying state-of-the-art LCD technologies to this relatively mature business segment. For example, it introduced 5.6-inch, portable, flat screen, LCD color TVs, only 2 inches deep, which were increasingly installed in cars and used as second or third sets in homes, and LCD projectors, which offered television set picture quality with a 100-inch screen. In preparation for the coming of HDTV, Sharp also developed HDTV projection systems using LCDs and broke a new price point when it introduced a vacuum tube HDTV set in 1992 for ¥1,000,000, a price one-third that of competitors.

The Communication and Audio Systems Group recorded a 40% increase in sales between 1989 and 1991 because of its market leadership in combination cordless phone/answering machines, pioneered by Sharp. In 1992, the ¥40 billion facsimile business, which had the largest share of the U.S. market, was transferred from the Information Equipment Group to this group because top management anticipated the spread of facsimiles to homes and their integration with telephones.

Sales of the Appliance Systems Group amounted to ¥266 billion, or 17.5% of the company's total in fiscal 1992. Sharp's New People Products, such as a refrigerator with bi-directional doors and a microwave oven with a fuzzy-logic control system, were particularly popular with young people because of their unique functions and appealing designs and colors. However, their share of company sales was declining as the industry matured.

Sharp's major competitors in consumer electronics and appliances fell into three groups based on their original business foci (**Exhibit 22–8**). The first group, comprising Hitachi, Toshiba, and Mitsubishi Electric, had started as heavy electric machinery manufacturers and diversified into appliances early in their histories. Hitachi was the largest, with products ranging from atomic power generators, semiconductors, and computers to consumer electronics. When the demand for appliances, such as refrigerators and washing machines, boomed in the 1950s, its reputation for quality electric motors enabled it to consistently increase its market share. Toshiba was the second largest, having introduced several appliances to Japan, including refrigerators and washing ma-

chines (1930), vacuum cleaners (1931), and fluorescent lamps (1940).

The second group of competitors, including Matsushita Electric and Sanyo, had been established as appliance manufacturers. Matsushita was the world leader in consumer electronics, well-known for its National brand in Japan and its Panasonic brand overseas. Founded in 1917, it had long dominated the industry because of its unparalleled nationwide retail network (National Shops). Sanyo was founded by a former senior executive director of Matsushita in 1947 and was regarded primarily as a low-cost player. Sharp was often compared with Sanyo because it was the same size and was located in the same district, but the two firms differed significantly in their corporate cultures and strategies.

The third group of competitors, comprising Sony, JVC, Pioneer, Aiwa, and Kenwood, did not produce white goods and concentrated instead on audio-visual products. Sony was particularly well-known for its innovative products and technologies, such as the world's first transistor radios, portable cassette recorders, CD players, and 8-mm camcorders.

Information Systems and Office Automation Equipment

In fiscal 1992, the area of Information Systems and Office Automation Equipment generated about 23% of Sharp's sales. Major products of the Information Systems Group were calculators, electronic organizers, office and personal computers, and Japanese word processors, all of which used displays of one type or the other. The Printing and Reprographic Systems Group produced copiers, scanners, OA peripherals, and associated products. For these products, Sharp concentrated on its color capability, stressing, for example, 4-color copiers, rather than monochrome ones.

As technology evolved, several firms in areas such as computers, communications equipment, cameras, and appliances, entered the information equipment business. Sharp's competitors and market share therefore differed by product market. In electronic calculators and organizers, Sharp had a leading market share and its main competitors were Casio and Canon. In Japanese word processors, where it also had a

EXHIBIT 22-8 Sharp Corporation—Major Competitors in Consumer Electronics and Appliances (Fiscal 1992)

	Sharp	Hitachi	Toshiba	Mitsubishi	Sony	JVC	Pioneer	Matsushita	Sanyo (FY1991)*
(Million Yens)									
Revenue	1,554,920	7,765,545	4,722,383	3,343,271	3,915,396	838,669	613,009	7,449,933	1,615,887
(previous year)	(1,532,571)	(7,736,961)	(4,695,394)	(3,316,243)	(3,690,776)	(926,256)	(599,693)	(6,599,306)	(1,496,085)
Operating Profit	61,640	352,027	118,460	146,702	166,278	−18,331	57,649	388,957	49,511
	(76,041)	(506,419)	(262,103)	(208,757)	(297,449)	(−13,396)	(72,323)	(472,590)	(48,611)
Net Income	39,057	127,611	39,487	36,074	120,121	1,990	28,469	132,873	16,837
	(46,918)	(230,185)	(120,852)	(79,760)	(116,925)	(16,010)	(34,315)	(225,000)	(17,499)
Total Assets	2,147,690	8,857,910	5,724,439	3,448,673	4,911,129	664,830	519,294	9,019,707	2,062,575
	(2,077,030)	(8,526,121)	(5,530,370)	(3,318,058)	(4,602,495)	(670,698)	(488,152)	(8,761,143)	(1,998,354)
Shareholders' Equity	755,561	2,917,951	1,182,050	810,204	1,536,795	309,121	329,670	3,495,867	742,412
	(726,763)	(2,811,141)	(1,178,753)	(792,243)	(1,476,414)	(308,937)	(310,508)	(3,434,747)	(738,212)
R&D Expenditures**	98,129	411,614	279,200	183,000	240,591	41,000	23,600	418,100	77,237
	(89,351)	(391,898)	(265,300)	(183,000)	(205,787)	(39,288)	(8,080)	(383,912)	(69,531)
(%)									
Return on Sales	2.5%	1.6%	0.8%	1.1%	3.1%	0.2%	4.6%	1.8%	1.0%
	(3.1%)	(3.0%)	(2.6%)	(2.4%)	(3.2%)	(1.7%)	(5.7%)	(3.4%)	(1.2%)
Return on Assets	1.8%	1.4%	0.7%	1.0%	2.4%	0.3%	5.5%	1.5%	0.8%
	(2.3%)	(2.7%)	(2.2%)	(2.4%)	(2.5%)	(2.4%)	(7.0%)	(2.6%)	(0.9%)
Return on Equity	5.2%	4.4%	3.3%	4.5%	7.8%	0.6%	8.6%	3.8%	2.3%
	(6.5%)	(8.2%)	(10.3%)	(10.1%)	(7.9%)	(5.2%)	(11.1%)	(6.6%)	(2.4%)
Equity ratio	35.2%	32.9%	20.6%	23.5%	31.3%	46.5%	63.5%	38.8%	36.0%
(Yen)									
Earning per Share	36.60	36.90	12.00	15.90	293.10	63.00	158.50	60.70	8.60
Dividend per Share	11.00	11.00	10.00	10.00	50.00	7.50	25.00	12.50	7.50
Employees**	21,521	82,221	73,714	49,566	18,130	13,561	8,707	47,634	29,638
(Number of Exclusive Retailers)									
Retailer Network	3,800	11,000	12,000	5,500	1,500	N/A	N/A	27,000	4,500

*Sanyo's fiscal year ends on November 30. Fiscal years for other companies end on March 31.

**Non-consolidated.

Source: "Japan Company Handbook" (Tokyo, Toyo Keizai Inc., 1991 & 1992), and "Kaden Gyokai (Appliance Industry)" (Tokyo: Kyoikusha 1987, p.88) (for retailer network).

leading market share, and in personal computers, where it had only a foothold, its main competitors were NEC, Toshiba, Fujitsu, Japan IBM, and Seiko-Epson. Sharp had a strong market position in facsimiles against Matsushita, Ricoh, and Canon, but a smaller share of the plain paper copier market against Ricoh, Canon, Fuji Xerox, and Konica.

Electronic Components/Devices

In the late 1980s and early 1990s, Electronic Components were the driving force behind Sharp's growth. As a result of aggressive investment, this sector had grown to about 23% of total sales in fiscal 1992, as compared with only about 8.0% in 1975.

The Integrated Circuits Group was in the semiconductor business. In contrast to larger companies, such as NEC, Toshiba, Hitachi, and Fujitsu, which manufactured commodity chips and aggressively competed on price and processing performance by exploiting scale economics and accumulated learning, Sharp generated 80% of its semiconductor sales from customized and semi-customized products. It had applied the CMOS technology first used for electronics calculators to gate-arrays and microprocessors, and held a 35% global market share in masked ROMs (manufacturer-programmed memory chips) used in VCRs, video games such as Nintendo game cassettes, and microwaves.

The Electronics Component Group developed products such as high-frequency satellite transmission components, printed circuits boards, opto-magnetic discs, light-emitting diode (LED) panels, semiconductor laser diode units, electro-luminescent (EL) panels, and solar cells. Among these, opto-electronic devices were the most unique to Sharp. Sharp had been the world leader in this segment for eight consecutive years up to 1992,[10] holding dominant global market shares for a number of products, such as 60% for electro-luminescent displays, 40% for laser diodes, and 65% for remote control beam receiver units for VCRs, TVs, and other audio visual products.[11]

The Liquid Crystal Display Group was spun off from the Electronic Components Group in 1990. The company's LCD business had grown so remarkably that Sharp was increasingly associated with LCDs. Considered the most promising flat panel display technology in the early 1990s after several recent technological breakthroughs, LCDs were used for a wide range of end products and were expected to replace cathode ray tubes in most applications, including TVs, by the beginning of the twenty-first century. Worldwide production for LCDs reached ¥299 billion in fiscal 1992, and were predicted to exceed ¥1 trillion (US$7.1 billion) by fiscal 1995 and ¥2 trillion by the turn of the century. Sharp was the largest supplier of LCDs in the world, and its sales of passive-matrix and TFT active-matrix LCDs represented a dominant 40% world share. The company was particularly well represented in the most advanced TFT color LCDs. Sharp's major competitors in LCDs included Seiko-Epson, OP-TREX (a joint-venture between Asahi Glass and Mitsubishi Electric), Hitachi, Hoshiden, Toshiba, Citizen Watch, and Sanyo. Despite the huge initial investment and accumulated manufacturing experience required to start an LCD business, several other Japanese companies, such as NEC, Matsushita, Canon, and Kyocera were also entering the industry. To further strengthen its leading position and obtain a 50% world market share in active matrix LCDs by fiscal 1996, Sharp planned to make a capital investment of ¥80 billion (US$ 640 million) in LCD plants between fiscal 1993 and 1995.

International Business

In 1992, Sharp had 19 sales subsidiaries and 27 manufacturing bases in 18 countries and 4 R&D laboratories in 3 countries. Exports represented 45% of company sales in 1992, although their importance was decreasing with the increase in local manufacturing (about 25% of total overseas sales in 1992) as Sharp strove to integrate design and manufacturing capabilities in local markets. The geographical composition of exports was 40% for North America, 30% for Europe, and 30% for the rest of the world. Eighty-five percent of exports were final products (92% of which were sold under the Sharp brand name), and the rest were components/devices.

[10]A survey by Data Quest.
[11]*Business Week,* April 29, 1991, pp. 84–85.

Organization Structure

In 1992, Sharp's organization structure shared responsibilities among eight manufacturing groups, five sales and marketing groups, an international business group, a corporate research and development group, and a number of central service groups (**Exhibit 22–9**). All of these groups, except the International Business Group, reported directly to the five top managers—the president and the four senior executive vice presidents. The manufacturing groups, the International Business Group, and the sales and marketing groups were profit centers, while the corporate R&D group and central service groups were cost centers. Reconfiguration of this organization structure occurred frequently in response to market and technological changes. Examples were the consolidation of the phone equipment business, which had previously been handled both by the Appliance System Group and by the Audio System Group, and the transfer of the facsimile business to the Audio System Group. Also, as the company had grown in size and product scope, it had expanded from three to eight manufacturing groups since the early 1980s.

The manufacturing groups were at the core of Sharp's organization structure. The name "manufacturing group" reflected the company's traditional orientation toward production. Each group controlled its domestic production facilities and was responsible for the technical performance of overseas production facilities. It was also in charge of new product development on a worldwide basis. A manufacturing group did not, however, have authority for sales and marketing. Instead, it negotiated sales targets and price levels with domestic sales and marketing groups and overseas sales subsidiaries while assuming overall responsibility for product profitability. Typically, a manufacturing group consisted of its own laboratory, a staff of up to 100 for accounting, purchasing, and other administrative functions, and several product divisions, also called manufacturing divisions. Each of these in turn comprised several departments, including product planning, engineering, and production. Central to each division was the product planning department which coordinated R&D, manufacturing, and marketing for its products. Located in the manufacturing group, managers in this department met weekly to discuss projects and problems, but spent substantial amounts of time with the marketing groups. The head of the product planning department for the Wizard, for example, spent about two and a half months each year in the U.S. sales subsidiary.

Of the five sales and marketing groups, four were in charge of domestic sales and one was in charge of the international sales of ICs and electronic components. The four domestic sales and marketing groups were organized by distribution channel. One sold consumer electronics products through an exclusive network of independent retailers, called Sharp Friend Shops. Offering advisory and repair services and building up long-term personal relationships with their local customers, these shops were the dominant, though declining, distribution channel for consumer electronics and appliances. The second group was responsible for marketing consumer electronic and information equipment to special outlets, including independent large-volume retailers. These retailers appeared in the 1970s, concentrating in such districts as Akiwabara in Tokyo, and quickly gained popularity among price-sensitive consumers. The third domestic sales and marketing group distributed communication and information equipment to specialized retailers, such as stationery stores and office equipment retailers. The fourth domestic sales and marketing group marketed electronic devices directly to other manufacturers.

The International Business Group coordinated the company's exports and international activities, acting, for example, as a liaison between sales subsidiaries in the various countries and the manufacturing groups in their twice-yearly transfer price negotiations. Each country's sales subsidiary negotiated independently with the manufacturing groups in order to foster internal competition and resolve the allocation of scarce products. The International Business Group also supervised the overseas sales subsidiaries, which were each independent profit centers, and was responsible for overseas manufacturing, deciding on the location of new manufacturing sites and coordinating production

EXHIBIT 22-9 Sharp Corporation—Organization Structure

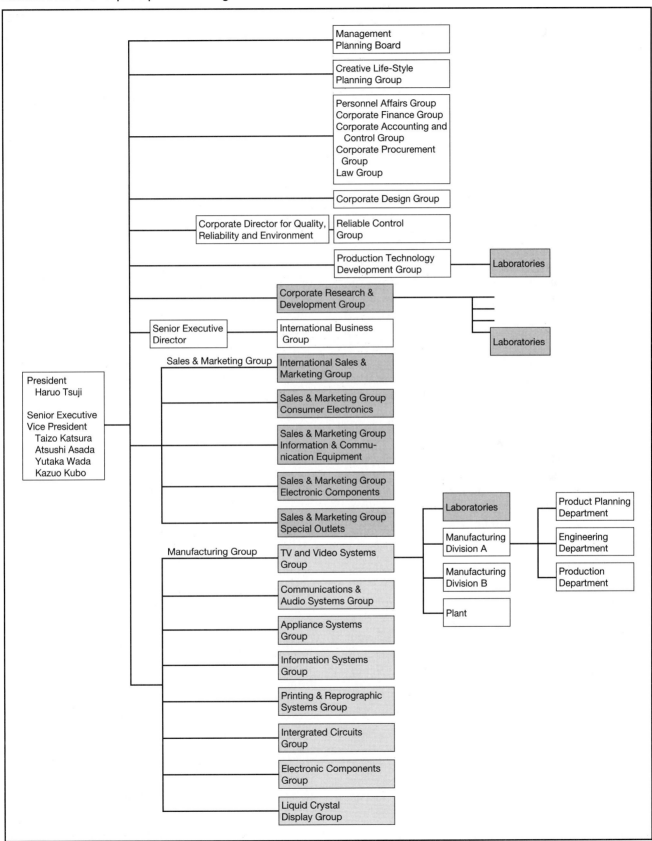

Source: Sharp Corporation.

across the company's international TV and VCR factories.

The corporate Research and Development Group was established in 1976 to more effectively coordinate the activities of the manufacturing group laboratories with those of the central research laboratories. It was restructured with the establishment of the Multimedia Systems Research and Development Center in 1992, which prepared the company for computerized fusion of visual and audio information.

In 1992, about 1,500 people worked at the central service groups, engaged in strategic planning, administrative support, and coordinating activities across business groups and subsidiaries.

The Role of the Corporate Office

Top Management

In 1992, Sharp had about 20 senior directors who, in addition to their individual assignments, coordinated functions across groups. These executives met formally twice a month, attending an executive committee meeting in the morning and a management meeting (called "Keiei Kaigi") in the afternoon to ratify critical decisions and to discuss the company's future.

In contrast to other large Japanese companies with bottom-up, consensus-building decision-making styles, Sharp had a tradition of top-down decision-making with most critical decisions being made by a team of top decision makers who complemented one another in personalities and skills. The technological creativity and entrepreneurship of founder Hayakawa was complemented by the administrative skills of Akira Saeki. During his presidency, Saeki benefited from the marketing expertise of Masaki Seki and the techno logical insights of Dr. Tadashi Sasaki. Haruo Tsuji, well-known for his cosmopolitan marketing sense, was initially assisted by two senior executive vice presidents, Taizo Katsura, who had a background in international, and Dr. Atsushi Asada, who had a background in technology. Tsuji was well-known for frequently walking around business groups and divisions to gather information, and he sometimes provided specific business ideas for new products.

Culture and Business Philosophy

Sharp emphasized its business philosophy and creed (**Exhibit 22–10**) and believed its acceptance by employees worldwide was critical to the company's long-term prosperity. The creed was displayed in each office, and employees were asked to commit themselves to its ideals.

Sharp's culture of innovativeness was also enhanced by a feeling of crisis. Hiroshi Nakanishi, the senior manager of the Information Systems Group, who had headed the electronic organizer development project, explained:

> A strong pressure prevails in our manufacturing divisions. We are always afraid that we might be behind other consumer electronics companies. We also feel threatened by low-cost Asian countries. These pressures continuously force us to expand the range of functions of existing products and think about what will come next.

Human Resources Management

Like most Japanese companies, Sharp had a paternalistic relationship with its employees, and top management reinforced the view that the company was a family, or community, whose members should cooperate. Employee turnover was very low in accordance with the practice of life-time employment. If a research project or a manufacturing plant closed, researchers and workers were not laid off but transferred elsewhere inside the company. Sharp extended these human resource policies outside Japan: for example, Sharp Manufacturing Company of America celebrated its 10-year anniversary in 1988 with nearly half of its original 230 person workforce.

In the early 1990s, Sharp's performance measurement and reward system was undergoing a gradual transition from an egalitarian seniority system to a merit system in an attempt to

EXHIBIT 22-10 Sharp Corporation—Business Philosophy and Creed

Business Philosophy

We do not seek merely to expand our business volume. Rather, we are dedicated to the use of our unique, innovative technology to contribute to the culture, benefits and welfare of people throughout the world.

It is the intention of our corporation to grow hand-in-hand with our employees, encouraging and aiding them to reach their full potential and improve their standing of living.

Our future prosperity is directly linked to the prosperity of our customers, dealers, and shareholders . . . indeed, the entire Sharp family.

Business Creed

Sharp Corporation is dedicated to two principal ideals: "Sincerity and Creativity."

By committing ourselves to these ideals, we can derive genuine satisfaction from our work, while making a meaningful contribution to society.

Sincerity is a virtue fundamental to humanity . . . always be sincere.

Harmony brings strength . . . trust each other and work together.

Politeness is a merit . . . always be courteous and respectful.

Creativity promotes progress . . . remain constantly aware of the need to innovate and improve.

Courage is the basis of a rewarding life . . . accept every challenge with a positive attitude.

Source: Sharp Corporation.

motivate employees, particularly young ones who were becoming more individualistic and less loyal to the organization. There were three parts to an employee's reward—salary, bonus, and promotion. Salary was based on three equal criteria—seniority, job type, and performance (60% on management-by-objectives goals and 40% on quantitative goals), although the assessed variance in performance among individuals was not significant. The semi-annual bonuses, which constituted a major part (about one third) of compensation in Japan, varied on a forced curve within a range of plus and minus 10% among the workers of a job category. Promotion was the most critical element of reward because of the limited variance in salary and bonus and because of the importance of rank in Japanese society. The evaluation for promotion was based 30% on behavior, 20% on results, and 50% on how a worker developed skills and capabilities. In reality, however, most career-track employees were promoted mainly on seniority and subtle skills, such as

teamwork and communication, until they reached a middle management position.

General managers of profit centers were evaluated on their unit's performance, although specific criteria varied by group and by division. For example, in 1992, performance criteria for the general manager of the LCD Group included financials, market share, and product availability. For the general manager of the International Business Group, the criteria were primarily financial, but included balanced product sales, employee training, and the cultivation of new distribution channels.

Career-track employees were regularly transferred across manufacturing groups and between functions (e.g., between R&D and marketing and between domestic and overseas operations). In addition, Sharp employed several other personnel schemes to exploit employees' diversity and creativity. The top 3% of each rank of researchers were compulsorily transferred between laboratories every three years in a process called "chemicalization." As Tadashi Sasaki said, "It is only hydrochloric acid that is produced when hydrochloric acid is added to hydrochloric acid: while, a new material will come out when hydrochloric acid and something else are blended."[12] Chemicalization was further promoted by the company's aggressive head-hunting and mid-career hiring. Out of thirty board members in 1992, ten had been scouted or joined the company after extensive experience at another company. Similarly, four of the seven general managers of the Corporate Research and Development Group's laboratories and centers had been recruited from outside Sharp.

The company's system of in-house job application was also designed to exploit the full potential of its employees (the "right person for the right job") and to promote their creativity and ambition. Every year, the company announced available managerial or staff positions and invited applications from all employees. Those who were interested could apply confidentially—an important condition in Japan where applying for another job could be interpreted by a supervisor as a sign of disloyalty. Once an application was accepted, divisions could not oppose the transfer. Roughly 100 employees, most of them engineers, moved in this way each year.

Strategic Planning

The Management Planning Board, chaired by Senior Executive Vice President Taizo Katsura, prepared Sharp's overall strategic plans. The planning process consisted of a 10-year vision, a 3-year medium-term plan revised every year, and six-month operating plans, which, in the words of Executive Director Yutaka Iuchi, "existed to be altered." Plan targets for each business group were established mainly in terms of sales, overall profit, and market share. The planning staff then disaggregated the targets and allocated them to individual divisions and products. Financial budgets were made twice a year in parallel with operating plans.

The basic rule for capital expenditures was that each profit center could spend its depreciation plus half of its profit after tax. However,

each project exceeding ¥5 million had to be authorized by corporate management. In addition to basic financial criteria, strategic criteria were considered in approving these capital expenditures. For example, Sharp's ¥100 billion investment in LCD factories from 1990 to 1992 was based on top management's faith that LCD technology could be leveraged into several end products in the future. Conversely, Sharp had avoided DRAMs, capacitors, and resistors as commodities readily available from competitive suppliers and instead focused on masked ROMs and microprocessor chips for electronic organizers. As Dr. Asada stated, "Our guiding principle for investment should be quality not quantity."

After plans were set up, they were extensively communicated to all the levels of the organization. The president presented the company's basic management policy in his New Year's address via satellite to middle managers, explaining the company's long-term goals and its annual slogan and strategic objectives. Group general managers then explained the annual goals to their members and outlined detailed strategies for their groups.

In 1992, Sharp's long-term vision was called STAR 21—(Strategic and creative minds, Total customer satisfaction, Advanced technology, and Rapid action for the 21st. century). Its strategic target was to attain ¥5 trillion consolidated sales by the year 2000, one third from each of the three areas, Consumer Electronics and Appliances, Information Systems, and Electronic Components.

Technology Strategy

Sharp's R&D expenditures had increased steadily, reaching ¥98 billion or 8.2% of nonconsolidated sales in fiscal 1992. The company's overall research and development activities were supervised by the Corporate Research and Development Group, which specified research themes and coordinated basic research and product development (**Exhibit 22–11**). The Corporate R&D Group's five laboratories and two R&D centers were engaged in fundamental research looking more than 4–5 years ahead. They accounted for 10% to 15% of total R&D expenditures, and employed 800 out of 7,600 total engineers. The manufacturing groups' six laboratories handled

[12]Takeuchi, H. *et al.,* p. 87.

EXHIBIT 22-11 Sharp Corporation—R&D Organization Structure

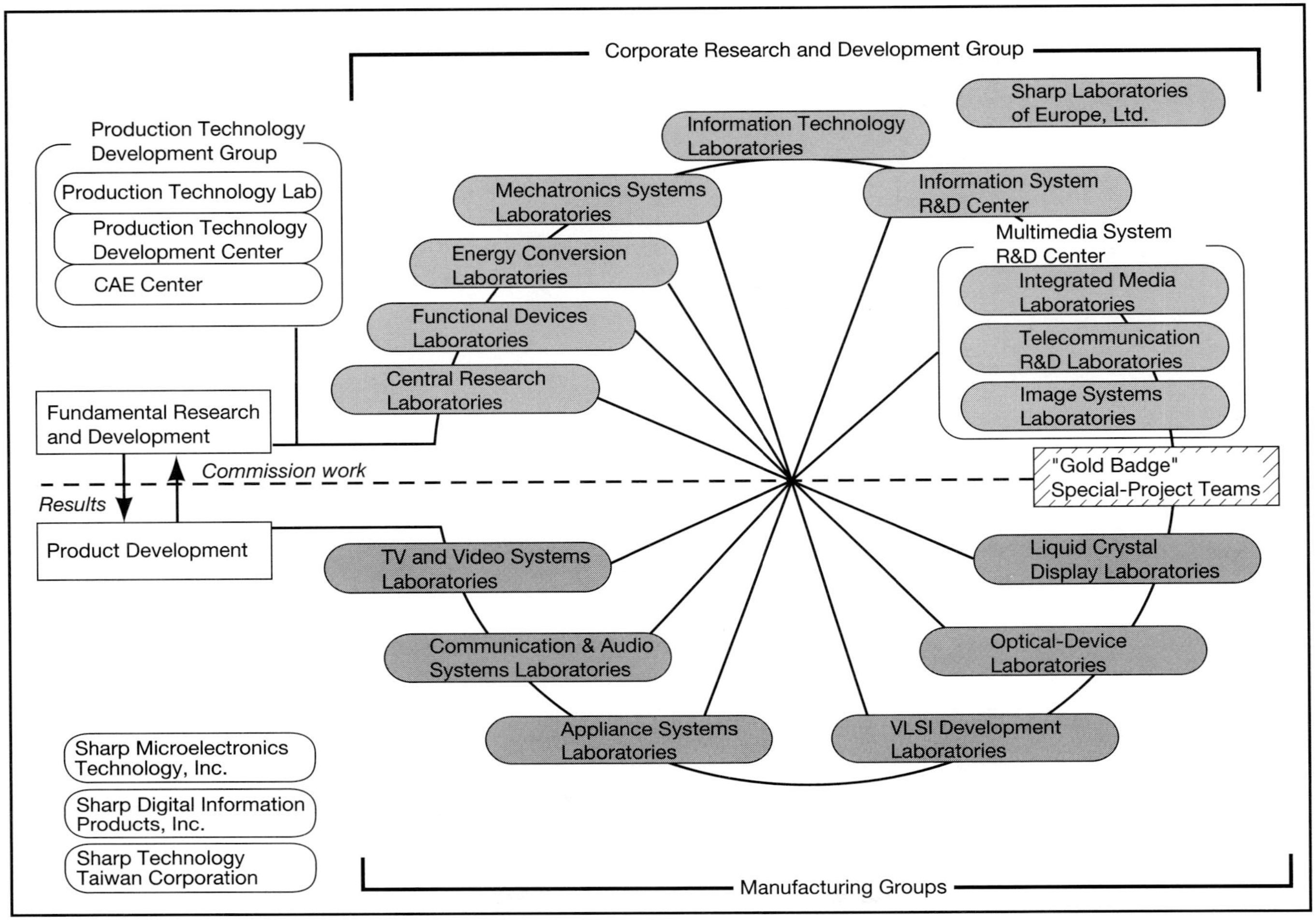

Source: Sharp Corporation.

product development that would pay off in 2–3 years and accounted for about 30% of corporate R&D. The remaining R&D expenditures were concentrated on more immediate product development in the manufacturing divisions. Careful attention was paid to coordinating activities across the three levels and to promoting the effective transfer of technology between R&D and product development. Once a technology or a product was developed in a laboratory, there was a formal program to transfer that learning to manufacturing groups. Indeed, personnel often followed from the R&D laboratory to the manufacturing group as a technology was commercialized.

The company's overall technology strategy was extensively discussed in a monthly Corporate Technical Strategy Meeting at which one division would also present its research plans for approval (**Exhibit 22–12**). This meeting was chaired by the general manager of Corporate Research and Development Group and attended by the president,

the senior executive vice presidents, the general managers of the manufacturing groups, and the directors of the research laboratories. Prior to this meeting, the laboratory directors met monthly to examine technical matters in detail.

After reviewing the technological capabilities of the company ("technological seeds") and the needs of potential customers ("market needs"), technologies for development were identified where needs existed but seeds did not (**Exhibit 22–13**). Dr. Asada's view was that, "We invest in the technologies which will be the 'nucleus' of the company in the future. Like a nucleus, such technologies should have an explosive power to self-multiply across many products." Decision criteria that ultimately determined whether a technology was to be developed in-house included the extent of competition around that technology, the availability of the technology on the outside, the technology's potential to be a source of differentiation to end products, its minimum efficient scale of pro-

EXHIBIT 22-12 Sharp Corporation—Technology Development

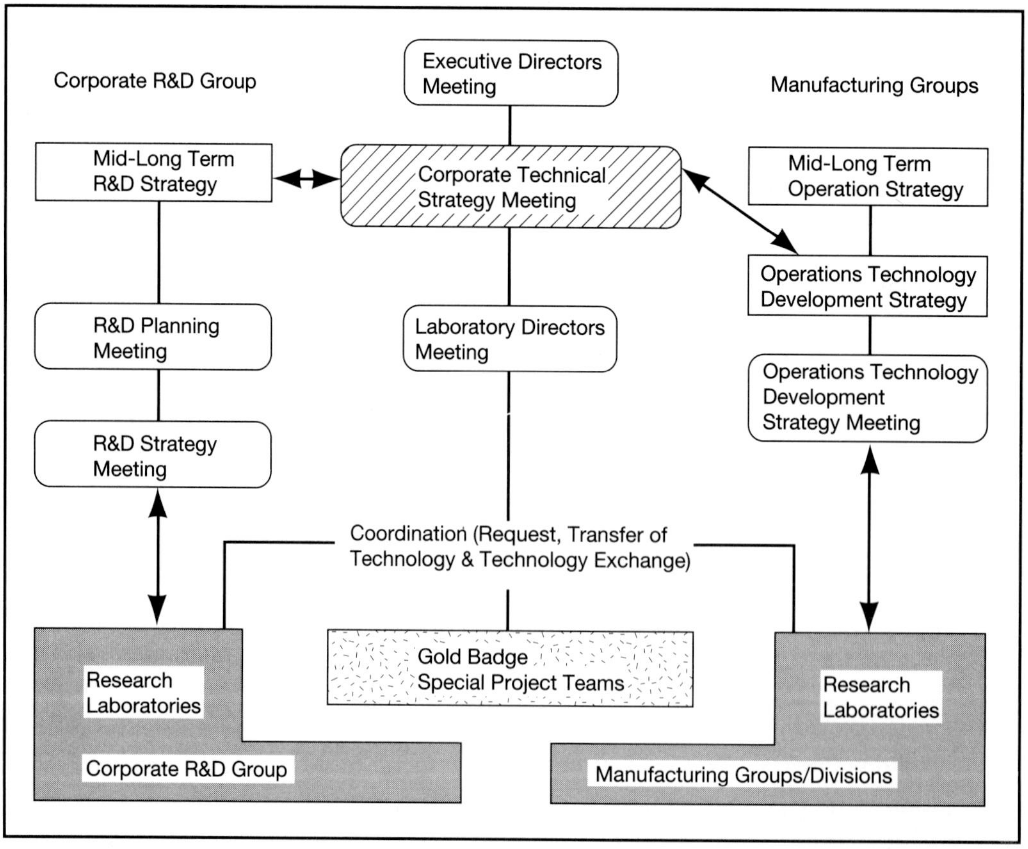

Source: Sharp Corporation.

EXHIBIT 22-13 Sharp Corporation—Seeds & Needs Coupling (Source: JMA Management Center ed. *Sharp no Gijutsu Senryaku (Technology Strategy of Sharp)* (Tokyo: JMA, 1986) p. 47.

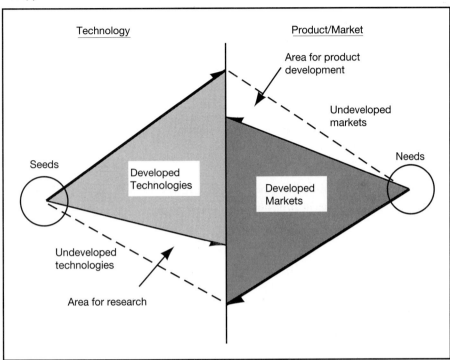

duction, its potential to make Sharp a world leader in an area, the future market size, and its potential to promote valuable learning.

Once it chose to develop a technology, Sharp committed to it for the long term. For example, it pursued LCD research throughout the 1970s, although the market for LCDs did not take off until the 1980s. Similarly, it continued research in gallium arsenide laser diodes long after most competitors had abandoned their research in this area until the first big market for CD players developed in the mid-1980s. Even if a technology seemed to be going nowhere, Sharp continued researching it, though on a very slim budget. For example, it continued its research in solar cells, using the amorphous silica technology it had learned in active-matrix LCDs, although the market for this technology remained tiny. As Dr. Asada noted:

Unlike the purchaser of real estate who decides which land to buy and which not to buy, technology decisions can hardly set a clear boundary for areas to invest. They are essentially the judgment of possibilities. If the potential of one technology is certain, we are going to assign a large number of researchers. However, even though the other technology has a lot of uncertainties, we cannot stay away from it. In such a case, we let, for example, one researcher study it. If it turns out to have more potential, we will allocate more researchers. If not, and the uncertainties have been resolved, we will stop at that time.

Because of such technological uncertainty, Sharp often maintained small R&D projects on alternative technologies. It was currently researching all possible alternatives to the TFT active-matrix LCD technology, including Ferro LCDs, light-emitting diodes (LED), and plasma and electro-luminescent (EL) displays.

Dr. Hiro Kawamoto, general manager of Corporate Staff Planning and Development at the Tokyo Research Laboratories, also mentioned:

We do not spend much on basic research. LCDs, MOS ICs, solar cells, semiconductor laser diodes were originally developed elsewhere. But we are prepared to make bets on what we judge will be key technologies for the future and commit ourselves to make them work. Our approach is incremental, yet consistent. We make a small start on a technology in response to tiny existing market needs. Engineers work to generate a new product. We earn some money, invest it on R&D, gradually expand activities, thus approaching, over time, a long term vision. We do not exit from a technology as RCA did from VCRs. . . . We do not follow the behavior of our rivals, rather purposefully avoiding the "herd behavior." We invest in niches, which might grow up to become grand niches.

New Product Development

After the success of the electronic calculators project, Sharp formalized its task-force-based product development process in order to increase development speed and to enhance the effective transfer and integration of technologies among manufacturing groups. To do so, it established a system of Gold Badge projects in 1977. Nearly one-third of the total corporate R&D budget was spent on the 10–15 Gold Badge projects in progress at any time. These were selected at the Corporate Technical Strategy Meeting according to whether the product was differentiated and based on original technologies, whether it involved many cross-group linkages, and whether it would be a core of the company's competitiveness. Projects often focused on areas where technological seeds existed but where Sharp did not offer products that met existing market needs (**Exhibit 22–13**).

Once selected, Gold Badge projects were financed by corporate because it was believed that since projects cut across manufacturing groups, no one group would be willing to finance a project alone. Manufacturing groups ultimately paid back half of a project's expenditures when they began to market a product that resulted from the project.

A senior manager at the rank of general manager or higher was chosen to be a project's champion, and a middle level researcher was chosen to be its leader. The leader freely chose his or her 20–40 member staff from the company as a whole. During the one-and-a-half or two-year project period, all project members reported directly to the company president, wore the same gold-color badge as did the president, and were vested with his authority. As such they received top priority for the time of specialists in other divisions that they would not normally have access to. Project members were given wide discretion regarding the way they conducted their project, although the project champion and leader were held accountable for the initial schedule set up at the monthly Corporate Technical Strategy Meeting. Once completed, a Gold Badge project was turned over to the relevant manufacturing group.

One successful Gold Badge project was the Wizard electronic organizer. This project was proposed by the Information Systems Group in response to the slowing growth of its core calculator business. Observing that customer needs for data storage and organization, which had been satisfied by stationery such as the Filofax, could be better met electronically, the project aimed to develop a combined calculator and information processing product by integrating several Sharp technologies, such as CMOS chips, LCD displays, solar cells, and software. Other Gold Badge projects had included a Color LCD TV, an HDTV Projector with an LCD screen, a magnet-optical disc memory, and an EL display.

Sharp's regular product development activities were coordinated through several committees that cut across manufacturing groups. The New People Strategy Meeting attended by the president, vice presidents, and the general managers of manufacturing groups and sales and marketing groups discussed both the basic goals of the New People strategy and the details of specific new products using input from the Creative Life-Style Planning Group. This group conducted market research and surveys with extensive input from the manufacturing groups and overseas sales subsidiaries. Additionally, the Corporate Design Group coordinated design and colors across manufacturing group products.

The components groups were also involved in intense discussions with end product groups to understand their needs. The group general manager of the LCD Group, for example, attended a monthly product development meeting with end product groups.

Operations Strategy

Sharp's domestic manufacturing plants were clustered in seven geographical locations. The LCD plant, for example, was onsite with the semiconductor facility in part because they shared similar production processes. Sharp manufactured a product in Japan until its life cycle had matured and innovations no longer occurred. The manufacturing of nearly all calculators, for instance, had been transferred outside of Japan. The company also outsourced components and products, such as CRTs and black and white TVs, whenever it saw poor profitability in their production and no potential for technological breakthroughs.

At the corporate level, the Production Technology Development Group developed and integrated the company's process technology. Its group general manager chaired a monthly meeting—attended by the president, senior executive vice presidents, group managers of manufacturing groups, and laboratory directors—to enhance information sharing and technology transfer across plants and laboratories. The corporate Quality, Reliability and Environmental Reliability Control Group monitored the manufacturing groups' product quality and coordinated company-wide quality circle activities.

Internal Coordination

Despite its strategic emphasis on components/devices in the late 1980s and early 1990s, Sharp viewed it as necessary to compete in both end products and devices because improvement in device technologies required continuous feedback on final customer needs. Indeed, Taizo Katsura suggested, "Real value added comes from the link." However, Sharp's involvement in the components business brought about conflicts between components and end product groups. For components also available from outside suppliers, the company took an internal-market approach to resolve such conflicts. The components groups could choose what and to whom they could sell—to the outside customers or the inside end product groups. Similarly, the end product groups had no obligation to purchase from the components groups. They could freely purchase from outside suppliers if the quality or price was better.

All component sales to end product groups took place at an agreed upon transfer price that was normally close to the market price. These transfer prices were determined through inten-

sive discussions at the same time as the six month operating plans and budgets were set. Prices were, however, renegotiated in response to unexpected changes in the market. According to Yutaka Iuchi, former head of the LCD Group:

> We never sell our LCDs below cost to the other groups. We need profits to fund our vast capital investment expenditures. Even when one of our end products groups and one of our outside customers compete in the same market, for example, in notebook computers, the supply price of our LCDs should be the same for both. If we sell LCDs cheaper and give a cost advantage to our notebook computer division, the division will be spoiled and its long-term competitiveness in the market will decline.

When components were in short supply, as had occurred in LCDs, about 80% of which were sold to outside customers, the components groups faced the difficult decision of allocating its output between inside and outside customers. In general, this was resolved by giving priority to all customers with whom Sharp expected to have a long term relationship. Yutaka Iuchi commented:

> There were several instances in the past where we had to give some priority to satisfying the demand of our internal groups at the time of supply-demand imbalance. Our group, however, has to maintain a reliable relationship with outside customers. My biggest task is therefore to carefully predict the future demand of LCDs, expand production capacity based on those predictions, and avoid a shortage of our supply capacity.

The timing of the introduction of new components could also be a source of tension because the company's end product groups preferred delaying the availability of new components to competitors if those components enabled them to differentiate their products. Such dilemmas were solved on a case-by-case basis through intensive discussions. In most situations, new components were introduced to both inside and outside customers at the same time. However, the external launch of a few components of substantial strategic importance had been deferred after the involvement of the president and senior executive vice presidents.

Transfer prices were also a major issue between the manufacturing groups and sales and marketing groups. Again, Sharp employed an internal market approach. Although it had never happened, the sales and marketing groups could, in principle, refuse to sell a manufacturing group's product if it was of unsatisfactory quality or price. For new products, transfer prices took into account the strategic objective of establishing a competitive position in the market, and both sides were expected to make concessions to reach an agreement.

Transfer prices for exports were determined by direct negotiation between manufacturing groups and overseas sales subsidiaries. Yutaka Wada, Senior Executive Vice President for International Business, commented:

> Competition is our principle. [The International Business Group] sets up basic rules, but in general, lets sales subsidiaries negotiate directly with manufacturing groups. We do not employ a set transfer pricing approach, such as marginal cost plus a certain mark-up. Such a rule is easy to apply and can be energy-saving. We believe, however, that it would weaken management muscles in the long run.

Major Issues Facing Sharp in 1992

In 1992, Sharp was facing several new challenges. The Japanese economy, which had been over-inflated during the late 1980s, entered into recession as the "bubble" burst and stock and land prices declined. As domestic demand for consumer electronics products and information systems fell, Sharp's operating profits declined, though less so than other companies, after five years of growth.

More fundamentally, as Sharp grew in size and scope, it faced increasing technological opportunities and uncertainties. President Tsuji commented:

> Technological innovation is more and more accelerated all over the world. Also, its structure is changing drastically, and keeping up with developments in hardware and software is getting increasingly important. In such an environment, it is difficult for one firm to do everything itself. Companies with similar goals need to cooperate to develop new businesses by complementing each other.

In 1992, Sharp was considering two major strategic alliances—one with Intel for flash memories and the other with Apple for pocket-sized computers. Flash memory was a high-density, nonvolatile technology which retained stored information even when the power was turned off. As its name suggested, it could be rapidly erased and reprogrammed. As a storage alternative to hard and floppy disks, flash memory was better suited to the consumer marketplace due to its cost-effectiveness, reliability, and performance. In 1992, the market for flash memories was approximately $130 million, 85% of which was supplied by Intel, and it was projected to grow to nearly $1.5 billion by 1995. Sharp and Intel planned to jointly design and manufacture flash memories in the future. The partnership would allow Sharp to buy flash memories from Intel for use in its own products or for resale under the Sharp name and to develop new applications for flash memory in its own consumer-oriented markets. In return, Sharp would build a new $500 million plant in Japan that would be the main production base for flash memories for Intel and Sharp in the future.

The Apple and Sharp partnership aimed to jointly develop, manufacture, and market the next generation personal information product, the Newton, by combining Apple's computer and system software know-how with Sharp's display technologies and expertise in consumer electronics. This alliance was expected to allow Sharp to prepare for the approaching multi-media era.

As Sharp set a goal of becoming a premier "creative-intensive" company in the 21st. century, while for the first time relying on external partners for innovation, it faced the challenge of meeting Tsuji's belief that, "As a manufacturing company, Sharp has to contribute to society by developing innovative products that create market demand and fulfill new customer needs."